The ART of Watching FILMS

Eighth Edition

DENNIS W. PETRIE
Trine University

JOSEPH M. BOGGS
Late of Western Kentucky University

The McGraw·Hill Companies

Connect
Learn
Succeed™

Published by McGraw-Hill, an imprint of The McGraw-Hill Companies, Inc., 1221 Avenue of the Americas, New York, NY 10020. Copyright © 2012 by Dennis Petrie. All rights reserved. No part of this publication may be reproduced or distributed in any form or by any means, or stored in a database or retrieval system, without the prior written consent of The McGraw-Hill Companies, Inc., including, but not limited to, in any network or other electronic storage or transmission, or broadcast for distance learning.

This book is printed on acid-free paper.

1 2 3 4 5 6 7 8 9 0 DOC/DOC 1 0 9 8 7 6 5 4 3 2 1

ISBN: 978-0-07-338617-1
MHID: 0-07-338617-0

Vice President and Editor in Chief: *Michael Ryan*
Publisher: *Christopher Freitag*
Associate Sponsoring Editor: *Betty Chen*
Director of Development: *Nancy Crochiere*
Developmental Editor: *Sarah Remington*
Marketing Manager: *Stacy Best Ruel*
Production Editors: *Michelle Gardner and Brett Coker*
Production Service: *Laserwords Private Limited*
Manuscript Editor: *Sheryl Rose*
Design Manager and Cover Designer: *Preston Thomas, Cadence Design*
Interior Designer: *Kay Lieberherr*
Photo Research Coordinator: *Sonia Brown*
Buyer: *Debra Sylvester*
Media Project Managers: *Jennifer Barrick and Bethuel Jabez*
Composition: *10/12 Janson Text by Laserwords Private Limited*
Printing: *45# New Era Matte by R.R. Donnelley & Sons*

Credits: The credits section for this book begins on page C-1 and is considered an extension of the copyright page.

Library of Congress Cataloging-in-Publication Data

Petrie, Dennis W.
  The art of watching films / Dennis W. Petrie, Joseph M. Boggs. —8th ed.
    p. cm.
  ISBN 978-0-07-338617-1 (alk. paper)
  1. Film criticism. I. Boggs, Joseph M. II. Title.
  PN1995.B525 2011
  791.43'015—dc22

                                          2011003434

The Internet addresses listed in the text were accurate at the time of publication. The inclusion of a Web site does not indicate an endorsement by the authors or McGraw-Hill, and McGraw-Hill does not guarantee the accuracy of the information presented at these sites.

www.mhhe.com

For R. D. BRILES

contents

The Diving Bell and the Butterfly

4
Visual Design 74

Avatar

5
Cinematography
and Special Visual Effects 103

Inception

6
Editing 155

Up

7
Color 190

The Hurt Locker

8
Sound Effects and Dialogue 219

Crazy Heart

Across the Universe

Shutter Island

A Serious Man

The Girl With the Dragon Tattoo

The Dark Knight

The Lives of Others

Online Appendixes

www.mhhe.com/petrie8e

Writing a Film Analysis

Selected Bibliography and Study Materials

preface

Making films is an art, but so is watching them. Most students come into an introductory film course having watched plenty of movies, but in the course of the semester they develop ways to engage in the experience on a deeper, more meaningful level.

With an emphasis on the narrative film, *The Art of Watching Films* challenges students to take their film experience further by sharpening their powers of observation, developing the skills and habits of perceptive watching, and discovering complex aspects of film art that they might otherwise overlook. The first chapter offers a rationale for film analysis while providing suggestions for deepening film appreciation from day one of the course. Following Chapter 1, the text presents a foundation for understanding theme and story, key aspects of understanding narrative films (Chapters 2 and 3), before moving on to discussions of dramatic and cinematic elements (Chapters 4 to 11). A framework for integration and application of these elements into an analysis of the whole film is set forth in Chapter 12. Subsequent chapters explore special topics including adaptations, genre films, remakes, and sequels.

The Art of Watching Films introduces the formal elements and production process of films, and helps students analytically view and understand films within their historical, cultural, and social contexts. The text presents an analytical framework that can be applied to all movies as distinctly different as *Avatar, The Girl with the Dragon Tattoo, Vertigo, Iron Man, Man on Wire,* and *The Hurt Locker:*

- **Images and Captions:** More than 450 images with extensive, informative captions illustrate key points in the text to provide context and a critical look at the examples.
- **Balanced Selection of Films:** Quintessential classics such as films by Alfred Hitchcock, *The Great Train Robbery,* and the French New Wave remain as great examples, while the addition of new films, such as *Fantastic Mr. Fox* and *The Kids Are All Right,* illustrate cinematic concepts in relevant and relatable ways. As always, we include a large number of contemporary films that today's students are likely to have seen (*New Moon, Knocked Up, Indiana Jones 4*). We do this with the understanding that students learn better and are more engaged by the subject matter when they start with what they know. However,

we also include numerous examples from American film classics, which are discussed in a way that does not assume prior knowledge. Moreover, throughout the text, we examine a variety of films from different countries and genres.

- **Unique Chapter on Adaptation:** *The Art of Watching Films* features an entire chapter on adaptation (Chapter 13), a major aspect of current filmmaking that is rarely covered in textbooks. Adaptation pertains not only to works of literature, but also to television series, computer games, graphic novels, children's books, and even magazine articles. It's an area from which many feature films today are born.

- **Coverage of Film and Society:** A chapter on film and society (Chapter 15) covers such thought-provoking topics as the treatment of sex, violence, and language; censorship and the MPAA Rating System; the "foreignness" of foreign language and silent films; and social problem films, including documentaries. These topics provide social context for students to become more aware viewers of themes and meanings behind films.

- **Encouragement of Active Viewing:** End-of-chapter "Watching for . . ." exercises offer a hands-on immediacy to the study of film. Assuming that most students have access to a DVD player, we have devised exercises for nine of the chapters in the text. For examination of specific scenes, simply follow the descriptive references in the "chapters" indicator of the main menu.

- **Analysis of Film Themes and Techniques:** Questions at the end of every chapter help students apply chapter concepts to the analysis of any film. They increase students' involvement in the film experience, encouraging them to participate actively in an engaging quest rather than respond passively to the surface details.

- **Mini-Movie Exercises:** Chapters 3 through 15 also provide students with exercises for examining a short film or "cinema sampler" (part of a feature film that is virtually self-contained). These exercises permit scrutiny of "complete," unified works rather than just fragmented bits and pieces of a feature-length film. They should be especially helpful to students and teachers who necessarily work within limited time periods.

- **DVD Filmmaking Extras:** Chapters 3 through 15 contain annotated lists of topic-specific materials about the filmmaking process to be found on DVD versions of many movies. In addition, instructions are given for locating many "Easter eggs" (special hidden features) on DVDs.

- **Films for Study:** Chapters 2 through 15 provide lists of film titles that lead students to further examination of additional movies.

NEW AND UPDATED IN THE EIGHTH EDITION

Refreshed Photo Program With Over 380 New Film Images

We have replaced the vast majority of the images in the book with full-color screenshots captured from the films themselves. Publicity and production stills do not depict actual shots in the films. More than ever before, the image program shows students what the films really look like, indicating accurate framing, color, and aspect ratio.

More Currency and Relevancy With 179 New Films

About 40 percent of the films discussed in the book have been updated to represent more current titles or more effective examples. Of course, classic films and ones that will always serve as good examples have been retained.

New Photographic Technique Illustrations

Fresh images illustrate photographic techniques and effects such as lighting for depth, foreground framing, and direction and character of light. These new images appear in Chapters 4 and 5.

Updated Coverage of Current Technology

The technological coverage has been updated throughout the new edition, with an emphasis on the technologies and resources that students today use most frequently: DVD, Blu-Ray, Netflix, and so on. We also strengthened the coverage of computer-generated graphics (CGI) and the process of directing with digital film.

New Timelines With Revised "Flashback" Features

Six boxed "Flashback" features give students a brief historical overview of such topics as the history of film editing (Chapter 6); the use of color in filmmaking (Chapter 7); acting in silent films (Chapter 10); the role of the screenwriter (Chapter 13); and the art of documentary filmmaking (Chapter 15). A new timeline in each Flashback provides additional context and presents the curious student with more entry points to explore film history. "Flashback" features are illustrated by one or more photos.

Improved Organization for More Straightforward Information

Chapters 1–3 include more headings and key terms to guide students new to the analysis of films.

New Exercises for More Application and Appreciation

Two new Mini-Movie Exercises help students appreciate visual design (*Fantastic Mr. Fox*, Chapter 4) and directors' unique styles (*Paris, Je T'aime*, Chapter 11).

ADDITIONAL TEACHING AND LEARNING RESOURCES

Student CD-ROM With Film Clips and Commentary

This CD-ROM, designed specifically for *The Art of Watching Films,* provides short film clips that reinforce the key concepts and topics in each chapter. Along with each film clip is commentary that relates the film clip to the ideas discussed in the text. A short quiz accompanies each clip and commentary. Film clips are from such movies as *The Graduate*, *Psycho*, *Pleasantville*, *Meet the Parents*, *Do the Right Thing*, *Vertigo*, and *Shakespeare in Love*. The CD-ROM was created by Donna Davidson-Symonds of College of the Canyons, Santa Clarita, CA.

The Art of Watching Films comes with an optional CD-ROM of resources. To purchase the CD-ROM with the textbook, please have your bookstore order this package using ISBN 0-07-748776-1. The CD-ROM is also available as a stand-alone (ISBN 0-07-737973-X).

Writing About Film

Many instructors ask students to write about the films they watch—either informally in a journal or formally in an essay to give structure and logic to their own critical responses. In the text's Online Learning Center (www.mhhe.com/petrie8e), we offer guidelines for writing a film analysis and three sample student essays. The first is a lengthy, complete examination of John Ford's *The Grapes of Wrath*, showing how a student might approach a paper assigned as a major class project. The second is a shorter, simpler paper focusing on important techniques employed in Martin Scorsese's *Taxi Driver*. Both of these essays illustrate the types of analysis that one might expect students to write by using this text and a video source for multiple viewings. So that students using this book can grasp the interrelationship of the text, film, and finished essay, we have noted in the margins of both papers the pages in *The Art of Watching Films* that helped each student writer. The third student essay is a sharply focused analysis of Scorsese's *The Age of Innocence* without textual annotations.

Online Learning Center at www.mhhe.com/petrie8e

An Online Learning Center (OLC) for *The Art of Watching Films* includes tools for both instructors and students.

For instructors, the OLC offers:

An instructor's manual including chapter outlines, chapter summaries, lecture ideas, discussion questions, and lists of recommended films.

A test bank containing, for each chapter, over 30 multiple-choice, matching, and true-false questions.

EZ Test Computerized Test Bank, a flexible and easy-to-use electronic testing program that allows instructors to add their own questions and export tests for use with course management systems such as Blackboard or WebCT. It is available for Windows and Macintosh environments.

PowerPoint presentation includes chapter outlines, discussion questions, and images from the book.

Questions for use with the **Classroom Performance System (CPS),** a revolutionary wireless response system that allows instructors to pose questions to students and have their responses tabulated instantly. Go to www.mhhe.com/cps or ask your McGraw-Hill sales representative for further details.

Instructors also have access to all the assets in the Student edition of the OLC, including:

The special feature "Writing About Film," described above, which provides guidelines for writing a film analysis and three sample student essays.

A selected bibliography and list of resource materials.

Self-testing quizzes for each chapter, including multiple-choice and true-false questions.

Study materials for every chapter, including chapter outline, Internet exercises, and Web links.

CourseSmart

CourseSmart is a new way to find and buy eTextbooks. At CourseSmart you can save up to 50 percent off the cost of a print textbook, reduce your impact on the environment, and gain access to powerful Web tools for learning. CourseSmart has the largest selection of eTextbooks available anywhere, offering thousands of the most commonly adopted textbooks from a wide variety of higher education publishers. CourseSmart eTextbooks are available in one standard online reader with full text search, notes and highlighting, and e-mail tools for sharing notes between classmates. For further details contact your sales representative or go to www.coursesmart.com.

Create

Craft your teaching resources to match the way you teach. With McGraw-Hill Create, www.mcgrawhillcreate.com, you can easily rearrange chapters, combine material from other content sources, and quickly upload content you have written like your course syllabus or teaching notes. Find the content you need in Create by searching through thousands of leading McGraw-Hill textbooks. Arrange your book to fit your teaching style. Create even allows you to personalize your book's appearance by selecting the cover and adding your name, school, and course information. Order a Create book and you'll receive a complimentary print review copy in 3–5 business days or a complimentary electronic review copy (eComp) via e-mail in about one hour. Go to www.mcgrawhillcreate.com today and register. Experience how McGraw-Hill Create empowers you to teach your students your way.

ACKNOWLEDGMENTS

To illustrate the eighth edition of *The Art of Watching Films*, we proudly present hundreds of new photographs, most of which are frame captures. We believe that this revised approach will more readily allow film students to view dynamic images as they actually appear in the films themselves, rather than merely as static publicity stills. With considerable technological and editorial assistance, I have personally chosen each new image in this book both for the visual pleasure it may give readers and, most crucially, for the direct manner in which it supports the text. Our central goal here has been to create a consistently instructive, streamlined volume that may also entertain anyone who loves, or is simply curious about, the eternally magical world of cinema.

To my patient and encouraging family, friends, colleagues, and students, I wish to express enormous gratitude. For constant and wonderfully generous support, I especially offer my heartfelt thanks to Robert Briles, Roberta Tierney, Thomas Tierney, Jane Tubergen, and Sue Van Wagner.

In addition, Marcia Adams, Deborah Blaz, Michael Blaz, Jeanne Braham, Carol Briles, Miriam Briles, Reneé Gill, Ray Hatton, Miles Hession, Tim Hopp, Jacqueline Orsagh, Robert Petersen, Sandy Ridlington, Jeanine Samuelson, and Kathie Wentworth all continue to win my genuine appreciation for their many kindnesses.

As in the past, the talented, engaged professionals at McGraw-Hill Higher Education have provided a happy and productive home for *The Art of Watching Films*. Most noteworthy in their quiet dedication to the project have been publisher Chris Freitag, associate sponsoring editor Betty Chen, photo editor Sonia Brown, cover designer Preston Thomas, production manager Michelle Gardner, copyeditor Sheryl Rose, marketing manager Pam Cooper—and, once again, particularly, the invaluable director of development Nancy Crochiere and senior production editor Brett Coker.

This eighth edition simply could not have existed without the creativity, wise guidance, and calm devotion of developmental editor Sarah Remington. I am very pleased to acknowledge my vast debt to her. Likewise, I wish to thank Ron Nelms, Jr., for his artful, industrious, and lengthy pursuit of all the "just right" images we requested.

I also thank all of my colleagues who served as reviewers for this edition:

Jiwon Ahn, Keene State College

Michael Benton, Bluegrass Community and Tech College

Mitch Brian, University of Missouri–Kansas City

Jackie Byars, Wayne State University

Jim Compton, Muscatine Community College

Corey Ewan, College of Eastern Utah

Molly Floyd, Tarrant County College

Ken Golden, Hartwick College

Jason Genovese, Bloomsburg University of Pennsylvania

Steve Gilliland, West Virginia State University

William J. Hagerty, Xavier University

Jennifer Hopp, Illinois Central College

Tania Kamal-Eldin, American University

J. Paul Johnson, Winona State University

Terrence Meehan, Lorain County Community College

Dennis Maher, University of Texas–Arlington

Michael Minassian, Broward College

Carol Lancaster Mingus, Modesto Junior College

Gary Serlin, Broward College

Frank Tomasulo, Florida State University

Robert West, Cuyahoga Community College

Dex Westrum, University of Wisconsin–Parkside

Finally, I gratefully salute Donna Davidson-Symonds, College of the Canyons, who created the excellent student tutorial CD-ROM that accompanies this text.

Dennis W. Petrie

The **ART** *of Watching* **FILMS**

The ART of WATCHING FILMS

Star Trek (2009)

The cinema is a work of art when motion conforms to a perceptible rhythm with pause and pace and where all aspects of the continuous image relate to the whole.
—JOSEF VON STERNBERG, DIRECTOR

THE UNIQUENESS OF FILM

The tremendous expense involved in producing motion pictures reminds us that film is both an industry and an art form. Each film is the child of a turbulent marriage between businesspeople and artists. Yet despite an ongoing battle between aesthetic and commercial considerations, film is recognized as a unique and powerful art form on a par with painting, sculpture, music, literature, and drama. A. O. Scott, a film reviewer for *The New York Times*, has eloquently identified other tensions within our insatiable appetite for going to the movies: "[I]t is at once collective and radically solitary, an amalgam of the cohesive social ritual of theatergoing and the individualist reverie of novel-reading. . . . [M]oviegoing is perhaps still . . . the exemplary modern cultural activity. It splices together . . . the line at the box office and the solitary dreaming in the dark. . . ."[1]

As a form of expression, the motion picture is similar to other artistic media, for the basic properties of other media are woven into its own rich fabric. Film employs the compositional elements of the visual arts: line, form, mass, volume, and texture. Like painting and photography, film exploits the subtle interplay of light and shadow. Like sculpture, film manipulates three-dimensional space. But, like pantomime, film focuses on *moving* images, and as in dance, the moving images in film have rhythm. The complex rhythms of film resemble those of music and poetry, and like poetry in particular, film communicates through imagery, metaphor, and symbol. Like the drama, film communicates visually *and* verbally: visually, through action and gesture; verbally, through dialogue. Finally, like the novel, film expands or compresses time and space, traveling back and forth freely within their wide borders.

What Makes Film Unique

Despite these similarities, film is unique, set apart from all other media by its quality of free and constant motion. The continuous interplay of sight, sound, and motion allows film to transcend the static limitations of painting and sculpture—in the complexity of its sensual appeal as well as in its ability to communicate simultaneously on several levels. Film even surpasses drama in its unique capacity for revealing various points of view, portraying action, manipulating time, and conveying a boundless sense of space. Unlike the stage play, film can provide a continuous, unbroken flow, which blurs and minimizes transitions without compromising the story's unity. Unlike the novel and the poem, film communicates directly, not through abstract symbols like words on a page but through concrete images and sounds. What's more, film can treat an almost infinite array of subjects—"from the poles to the equator, from the Grand Canyon to the minutest flaw in a piece of steel, . . . from the flicker of thought across an almost impassive face to the frenzied ravings of a madman. . . ."[2]

Film has the capability to represent just about anything we can imagine or perceive. Time can be slowed or speeded up so that the invisible is revealed. As if by magic, a bullet's trajectory through the air or the many stages of a flower's bloom can be made visible and comprehensible. Film can afford us experiences not normally available to mortals. Until movies like *Harry Potter* and *Avatar* came out, how else—other than in our dreams—have human beings been able to feel the motion of swooping through a canyon on the wings of a wild bird? What better way to understand the depth, pathos, and genius of Mozart's life than through his own music (*Amadeus*)? Even the universe itself feels palpable when Han Solo shifts his ship into warp speed and stars collapse outside his window in *Star Wars: A New Hope*.

The medium is unlimited not only in its choice of subject but also in its approach to that material. A film's mood and treatment can range from the lyric to the epic. In point of view, a film can cover the full spectrum from the purely objective to the intensely subjective; in depth, it can focus on the surface realities and the purely sensual, or it can delve into the intellectual and philosophical. A film can look to the remote past or probe the distant future; it can make a few seconds seem like hours or compress a century into minutes. Film can run the gamut of feeling from the most fragile, tender, and beautiful to the most brutal, violent, and repulsive.

Increasing Realism as Technology Evolves

Of even greater importance than film's unlimited range in subject matter and treatment, however, is the overwhelming sense of reality it can convey. The continuous stream of sight, sound, and motion creates a here-and-now excitement that immerses the viewer in the cinematic experience. Thus, through film, fantasy assumes the shape and emotional impact of reality (Figure 1.1). The technological history of film can in fact be viewed as a continual evolution toward greater realism, toward erasing the border between art and nature. The motion picture has progressed step by step from drawings, to photographs, to projected images, to sound, to color, to wide screen, to 3-D and beyond. Attempts have been made to add the sense of smell to the film experience by releasing fragrances in the theater. Aldous Huxley's classic novel *Brave New World* depicts a theater of the future in which a complex electrical apparatus at each seat provides tactile images to match the visuals: "Going to the Feelies this evening, Henry? . . . I hear the new one at the Alhambra is first-rate. There's a love scene on a bearskin rug; they say it's marvelous. Every hair of the bear reproduced. The most amazing tactual effects."[3]

Although Huxley's "Feelies" have not yet become reality, the motion picture has succeeded—through Cinerama, IMAX, and other wide-screen, curved-screen, large-screen projection or computerized virtual reality techniques—in intensifying our experience to a remarkable degree. In fact, by creating images that are larger than life, films have sometimes been made to seem more real than reality. A cartoon published shortly after the release of the first Cinerama film (*This Is Cinerama*, 1952) illustrates the effectiveness of this device. The drawing pictures a man groping for a seat during the famous roller-coaster sequence. As he moves across a row of theater seats, another spectator, in a panic, grabs his arm and screams hysterically, "Sit down, you fool! You'll have us all killed!" This comic exclamation echoed similar ones from early silent film patrons who reacted nervously to the first train that swiftly entered a cinema's "station." What awesome delights must await us consumers of movie **CGI (computer-generated imaging)** in future decades.

FIGURE 1.1 **Making Fantasy Become Reality**   The film medium gives such fantasy movies as Guillermo del Toro's *Pan's Labyrinth* the texture and emotional impact of reality.

THE CHALLENGES OF FILM ANALYSIS

The properties that make film the most powerful and realistic of the arts also make analysis challenging. A motion picture moves continuously in time and space. Once frozen, a film is no longer a "motion" picture, and the unique property of the medium is gone. Therefore, film analysis requires us to respond sensitively to the simultaneous and continuous interplay of image, sound, and movement on the screen. This necessity creates the most challenging part of the task: We must somehow remain almost totally immersed in the experience of a film while we maintain a high degree of objectivity and critical detachment. Difficult though it may seem, this skill can be developed, and we must consciously cultivate it if we desire to become truly "cineliterate." Innovations in digital videodisc (DVD) and Blu-Ray players and recorders can help, initially at least, by simply making screenings (as well as multiple viewings) of a film easier than in the past.

The technical nature of the medium also creates challenges. It would be ideal if we all had some experience in cinematography and film editing. In the absence of such experience, we should become familiar with the basic techniques of film production so that we can recognize them and evaluate their effectiveness. Because a certain amount of technical language or jargon is necessary for the analysis and intelligent discussion of any art form, we must also add a number of important technical terms to our vocabularies.

The most challenging part of our task has already been stated: We must become almost totally immersed in the experience of a film and at the same time maintain a high degree of objectivity and critical detachment. The complex nature of the medium makes it difficult to consider all the elements of a film in a single viewing; too many things happen too quickly on too many levels to allow for a complete analysis. Therefore, if we wish to develop the proper habits of analytical viewing, we should see a film at least twice whenever possible. In the first viewing we can watch the film in the usual manner, concerning ourselves primarily with plot elements, the total emotional effect, and the central idea or theme. Then, in subsequent viewings, because we are no longer caught up in the suspense of what happens, we can focus our full attention on the hows and whys of the filmmaker's art. Constant practice of the double- or multiple-viewing technique should make it possible for us gradually to combine the functions of two or more viewings into one.

We must also remember that film analysis does not end when the film is over. In a sense, this is when it really begins. Most of the questions posed in this book require the reader to reflect on the film after viewing it, and a mental replay of some parts of the film will be necessary for any complete analysis.

Finally, as we move through the chapters that follow toward the analysis of individual films, we must always remind ourselves that if the medium can truly be called an "art," then it is definitely a *collaborative* one. Scores, if not hundreds, of commercial professionals are involved in the production of the average "picture" (to use the term that many filmmakers themselves prefer). When we analyze a literary work such as a novel or poem, we judge the toil of a single creative individual. By contrast, our close examination of a film requires an awareness of the talents of many different artists, including producers, directors, production/ costume/makeup designers, and, of course, actors. Usually, though, in the beginning is still the word, and the screenwriter—who has historically been viewed as the least respected major team player in Hollywood—remains the primary *originating* force within cinematic art.

THE VALUE OF FILM ANALYSIS

Before we turn to the actual process of film analysis, it may be worthwhile to look into certain fundamental questions that have been raised about the value of analysis in general.

Either/Or Positions About Analysis

Perhaps the most vocal reactions against analysis come from those who see it as a destroyer of beauty, claiming that it kills our love for the object under study. According to this view, it is better to accept all art intuitively, emotionally, and subjectively, so that our response is full, warm, and vibrant, uncluttered by the intellect. However, an either/or, black-and-white polarization of intuition and analysis is flawed. It denies the possibility of some middle ground—a synthesis that retains the best qualities of both approaches and embraces as equally valid both the emotional/ intuitive and the intellectual/analytical avenues.

The Two Sides Can Coexist: This Book's Position

This book rests on that middle ground. It assumes that the soul of the poet and the intellect of the scientist can coexist within all of us, enriching and enhancing the film experience. Analysis need not murder our love of the movies. We can experience beauty, joy, and mystery intellectually as well as intuitively. With the tools of analysis, we can discover the deepest reaches of understanding that only the poet within us can fully appreciate (Figure 1.2). By creating new avenues of awareness, analysis can make

FIGURE 1.2 **Learning to Dive** Watching classic film dramas like Ingmar Bergman's
The Seventh Seal helps us to understand our human selves with a depth that might elude
us otherwise.

our love for movies stronger, more real, more enduring. The analytical approach is
essential to the art of watching films, for it enables us to see and understand how each
part functions to contribute its vital energy to the pulsing, dynamic whole.

Analysis, generally, means breaking up the whole to discover the nature, proportion, function, and interrelationships of the parts. Film analysis, then, presup-
poses the existence of a unified and rationally structured artistic whole. Therefore,
the usefulness of this book is restricted to structured or narrative films—films developed with a definite underlying purpose and unified around a central theme. Limiting our approach to structured films does not necessarily deny the artistic value of
unstructured films. Many of the movies that experimental and underground filmmakers produce do communicate effectively on a purely subjective, intuitive, or
sensual plane and are meaningful to some degree as experiences. But because these
films are not structured or unified around a central purpose or theme, they cannot
be successfully approached through analysis.

It would be foolish to suggest that a structured film cannot be appreciated
or understood at all without analysis. If a film is effective, we should possess an
intuitive grasp of its overall meaning. The problem is that this intuitive grasp is
generally weak and vague; it limits our critical response to hazy generalizations and
half-formed opinions. The analytical approach allows us to raise this intuitive grasp
to a conscious level, bring it into sharp focus, and thereby make more valid and
definite conclusions about the film's meaning and value. The analytical approach,
however, does not reduce film art to rational and manageable proportions. Analysis
neither claims nor attempts to explain everything about film. The elusive, flowing
stream of images will always escape complete analysis and complete understanding.

In fact, no final answers exist about any work of art. A film, like anything else of true aesthetic value, can never be entirely captured by analysis.

But the fact that there are no final answers should not prevent us from pursuing some important questions. Our hope is that, through analysis, we can reach a higher level of understanding about films, a level where we are reflecting on the most significant aspects of the film art as opposed to the merely mundane, the practical, and the technical. Film analysis enables us to understand some elements habitually, thus freeing our minds to concentrate on the most significant questions.

Analysis Enhances Our Love of Films

Analysis helps us to lock an experience in our minds so that we may savor it in memory. By looking at a film analytically, we engage ourselves with it intellectually and creatively and thus make it more truly our own. Furthermore, because our critical judgments enter into the process, analysis should fine-tune our tastes. A mediocre film can impress us more than it should at first, but we might like it less after analyzing it. A great film or a very good one will stand up under analysis; our admiration for it will increase the more deeply we look into it.

Film analysis, then, offers several clear benefits. It allows us to reach valid conclusions on a movie's meaning and value; it helps us to capture the experience of a film in our minds; and it sharpens our critical judgments overall. But the ultimate purpose of analysis, and its greatest benefit, is that it opens up new channels of awareness and new depths of understanding. It seems logical to assume that the more understanding we have, the more completely we will appreciate art. If the love we have for an art form rests on rational understanding, it will be more solid, more enduring, and of greater value than love based solely on irrational and totally subjective reactions. This is not to claim that analysis will create a love of films where no such love exists. Love of movies does not emerge from a book or from any special critical approach. It comes only from that secret, personal union between film and viewer in a darkened room. If that love does not already exist for the viewer, this book and its analytical approach can do little to create it.

But if we truly love films, we will find that analysis is worth the effort, for the understanding it brings will deepen our appreciation. Instead of canceling out the emotional experience of watching the movie, analysis will enhance and enrich that experience. As we become more perceptive and look more deeply into the film, new levels of emotional experience will emerge.

BECOMING A RECEPTIVE VIEWER

Before we begin our analysis, we need to consider obstacles to objectivity and maximum enjoyment that we create through our prejudices and misconceptions and by the particular circumstances in which we watch the film. Each of us reacts in a unique and complex way to internal and external forces that are beyond the filmmaker's control. Although these forces lie outside the film itself, they can have an effect on how we experience a film. Awareness of these forces should help us overcome them or at least minimize their effect.

FIGURE 1.3 **Suspending Our Disbelief**   To enjoy movies such as *Lord of the Rings: The Return of the King*, we must undergo the memorable experience of challenging our preconceived notions of reality—or, as the Romantic poet Samuel Taylor Coleridge suggested, "suspend our sense of disbelief" in narratives that break the natural, logical rules of everyday existence.

Be Aware of Personal Biases

One of the most difficult prejudices to overcome is that which leads us to dismiss certain categories of films. Although it is natural to prefer some types to others, most of us can appreciate or enjoy aspects of almost any film. We should keep in mind that not all films will fit our preconceived notions. For example, a person who dislikes gangster movies might stay away from *Bonnie and Clyde*; another, who dislikes musicals, might shun *Chicago*, and a third, who dislikes fantasy movies, might ignore *The Lord of the Rings: The Return of the King* (Figure 1.3). All would lose a memorable film experience, for those three films are more than simple formula pieces.

Others may reject worthwhile movies because of their unwillingness to venture beyond the norm. Some may stay away from black-and-white films, always preferring color. Others may shun foreign-language films because they dislike reading subtitles or because they are bothered by dubbing that is not perfectly synchronized with mouth movement.

Also narrow in their outlook are filmgoers who have inflexible preconceptions about what movies are supposed to be. This type of categorical rejection may be illustrated by two extreme examples. At one end of the spectrum are filmgoers who say, "I just want to be entertained," and are offended by a film that is grim and depressing. At the other end are viewers, equally limited in their outlook, who expect every film to make a profound artistic statement about the human condition and who are disappointed if a film is *not* grim and depressing. Closely related are those who set up their own criteria for what makes a good film and reject movies that operate under different rules. Viewers who demand to comprehend all the plot details by the film's end would reject, for example, Christopher Nolan's *Memento*, which deliberately requires multiple viewings. Moviegoers who insist that a film hold them in a tight grip may dismiss Stanley Kubrick's *2001: A Space Odyssey* for its slow-moving segments. Excellent films may be discounted because the characters are not sympathetic or the action is not realistic. We must avoid these kinds of misconceptions and instead try to be open to the film's goals and meanings.

Watch the Whole Film

Almost as detrimental as categorical rejection is the blindness caused by over-responding to individual elements rather than to the film as a whole. An example of this prejudice is offered by viewers who are infected with a near-fatal case of actor worship or antipathy: "I just love all Johnny Depp pictures!" or "I can't stand Julia Roberts movies!" Such extreme reactions are certainly common among viewers who refuse to see the actor as subordinate to the film.

Less radical illustrations of this blindness include over-response to certain film elements. The two ingredients most likely to cause this kind of reaction are sex and violence. Certainly, some filmmakers exploit these ingredients and emphasize them to the point of the ridiculous, but this is not always the case. Films sometimes demand the use of nudity or violence to present honestly the story they have to tell. Thus, a perceptive filmgoer does not condemn the use of sex or violence per se, without considering the film as a whole, and neither does he or she reject or praise a movie simply because of its treatment of sex or violence. For example, many would argue that the violent ending of *Bonnie and Clyde* does not, by itself, determine the overall quality of that film. And works as diverse as *The Girl With the Dragon Tatto* and *The Twilight Saga: Eclipse* actually require some emphasis on sexuality to tell their stories. The popular film reviewer Roger Ebert, in responding to an objection by one of his readers about the sexual scenes in Paul Schrader's *Auto Focus*, repeated what Ebert has often identified as one of his favorite and most telling critical observations: "a crucial rule for anyone seriously interested in movies: It's not *what* the movie is about that makes it good or bad, but *how* it is about it" (see rogerebert.suntimes.com). Even if viewers reject this suggestion about the supremacy of style or "form," they also must surely not insist that subject matter or "content" is always most significant.

Consider Your Expectations

Another subjective factor that influences film evaluation is expecting too much from a movie, whether it has won awards, critical acclaim, or great reviews from our friends. Expectations may also run too high if we are particularly fond of a novel that is later adapted to film. When our expectations are too high, a film can't possibly measure up, and our disappointment clouds a work that we would otherwise have liked immensely.

THE FILM-VIEWING ENVIRONMENT

Many movie lovers argue that ideally we should view any film in what they call its "proper" environment: a comfortable and attractive theater, preferably one with modern stadium seating and the highest quality projection and audio equipment. There, these advocates further claim, we may not only consume films in their state-of-the-art glory, but we can also participate in one of the primary social rituals of

FIGURE 1.4 **Sharing Happiness With Others in the Dark**   Here, in a scene from one of Woody Allen's most popular films, *Annie Hall,* the title character (Diane Keaton) and her boyfriend (Woody Allen) wait in a cinema queue. While impatiently discussing their own relationship, they interact with other offbeat moviegoers, who provide laughs and groans in equal measure for this film's "mirror" audience.

modern life: watching movies with others in a public setting (Figure 1.4). In fact, our theater-going experiences are often much less than perfect. Noisy patrons chat and argue over and about the film's dialogue, rattling their popcorn bags and candy wrappers; often, they not only allow cell phones to ring repeatedly, but then talk loudly into them. Certainly, in a well-equipped theater, sound and image wash over you, immerse you, massage you. You need not direct your attention. Seeing a movie in a good theater is like diving into heavy surf with the tide coming in; seeing a movie on a standard television screen is like taking a sponge bath out of a gallon pail. As the actor Richard Dreyfuss describes it, "[F]ilm has a power over us. When we sit in a darkened room and symbolically hold hands with one another . . . we will be swept up with it. . . . But if it's on TV, who cares? . . . It has no impact on a primal level."[4]

Still, even as attendance at movie theaters continues to grow (although probably never again to the numbers during the glory days of American film in the late 1940s), more and more of us most frequently view films in our own homes via the domestic magic of modern technologies. Increasingly, we have larger and sharper television screens—some of them wondrously flat and lightweight, constructed of LCD, LED, and plasma panels. The wealthiest movie watchers, of course, may also be able to afford spacious, elaborate, and elegantly appointed home theaters. But even those viewers must be aware that the home film-watching experience still differs radically from that in the multiplexes—in both negative and positive ways.

Most of the negative aspects of home viewing center upon the quality of the sight and sound delivery systems. First, consider the simple factor of size. An image approximately twenty feet high on the average movie screen is reduced to a maximum height of about three feet on the typical home TV. Becoming physically involved in the action of a narrative as we would in a theater is nearly impossible at home. For example, a theater viewer who is susceptible to motion sickness may

FIGURE 1.5 Reducing Viewers' Involvement Watching such larger-than-life films as *2012* on a small television screen may decrease the intensity of our involvement and, hence, the quality of our total movie experience.

get a little queasy during the chase scenes in *The Dark Knight* or the Quidditch matches in the Harry Potter movies. But the same visceral sensation is nearly always lacking when we're watching at home. The events occurring on television seem remote, locked in the safety of a 27-inch (or even a 65-inch) screen. The change in size reduces the intensity of our experience and decreases our involvement (Figure 1.5).

Not only is the size of the image changed, but in many cases, the basic shape of the composition is altered as well. For instance, when a film shot in a **wide-screen** (rectangular) **format** (see Figures 4.1 and 4.2 in Chapter 4, pp. 77–78) is squeezed onto an essentially square traditional TV screen, crucial visual information is often lost. Wide-screen formats were initially adapted to the standard television shape by a special editing process called **panning and scanning.** A scanning device determined when the most significant information in each frame was so far to the left or right of center as to be outside the perimeter of the narrower television picture. TV (and also videocassette and DVD) producers then adjusted accordingly by centering this peripheral information in the transmitted or re-recorded image. Of course, the cinematographer's art suffered from this process, because the visual composition was compromised when a large portion of the original image was sliced off each side. The process frequently introduced camera movement not intended by the film's creators, and thereby could alter significantly the visual rhythms of the film. The alternative to this cinematic mutilation—at least when the "square" TV shape is involved (vs. the newer high-definition television's [HDTV] 16 [wide] × 9 [high] aspect ratio)—is the use of black bands at the top and bottom of the screen (termed **letterboxing**). This feature irritates many viewers and, ironically, makes some believe that they are being cheated of the whole original image.

Throughout its brief history, the videocassette (whose use now continues in rapid decline) seldom presented wide-screen films in their original format, and, even now, among television cable channels, few except Turner Classic Movies adamantly present films in what is called their "theatrical release aspect ratio." Initially, the advent of the DVD format brought great hopefulness to enthusiasts of watching wide-screen films at home. Often, in fact, the enormous storage space on DVDs allowed producers to satisfy everyone by offering both the wide-screen and the pan and scan version on opposite sides of the same disc. For a few years, however, large-volume video rental and sales companies such as Blockbuster reportedly convinced producers to release more of their films exclusively in the "standard," "full-screen" version, fearing that their customers would be too naïve to understand the beauty *and* practicality of wide-screen films. Happily, though, the expanding sales of wide-screen televisions has generally stopped this practice.

Television viewing of films has traditionally compromised sound even more than image. A modern movie theater equipped with multiple speakers can surround viewers with sound, immersing them in an encompassing aural environment. In the *Jurassic Park* movies, for instance, the rumble of a dinosaur passing back and forth in a landscape moves all over the theater as the sound dramatically increases and decreases in volume and shifts from place to place. Historically, most common television sets, even the largest ones, have had inadequate speakers by comparison, and many didn't even have tone controls. However, electronics manufacturers have been vastly improving sound quality, and so-called "home theater sound systems" have become commercially commonplace during the past few years.

Thus, seeing (and hearing) movies at home, though still not "ideal" for many of us, may rapidly be gaining desirability. The sales momentum of the DVD player since the device's first wide availability in the fall of 2001 has greatly outperformed even that of the audio compact disc. And Blu-Ray's sharp potential for swiftly increasing our "cineliteracy" surpasses even that of the so-called "video revolution" with the advent of the videocassette in the late 1970s. DVDs are beginning to re-educate film viewers about the art form's possibilities. Director David Cronenberg (*Eastern Promises*, *A History of Violence*, *Spider* [2003], *Crash* [1996], *The Fly* [1986]) has expressed well what many filmmakers and fans now feel: "I love, love, love DVDs. . . . You have to understand, when I was a kid, you had to see the movie when it came to the theater, and that was it. . . . So the idea that you could possess a movie like a book on your bookshelf . . . is fantastic."[5]

The editors at *IFCRant* (a publication of the Independent Film Channel) have also observed that DVDs "allow film aficionados a chance to get better insight into the people who brought the film to life" by "encourag[ing] other forms of expression beyond just the release title. . . . [W]ho knows what crazy things people might start making in the form of supplementary material. . . ."[6] And critics and reviewers have begun to answer, in summary form, this implied question: "As the DVD audience broadens, so does appreciation of the disc's extra features. . . . Extra scenes, outtakes, . . . behind-the-scenes looks at movies being made, [and] the movie-length director's commentary [are] proving popular enough to encourage reams of filmmakers' reflection in special editions. . . ."[7]

This book attempts to encourage the reader to explore the frequently rich elements of data contained in DVDs beyond these entertainments and routine audio commentaries. At the ends of Chapters 3 through 15 in this edition of *The Art of Watching Films*, we have provided a feature called "DVD Filmmaking Extras," which is a kind of road map for digitally augmenting the various topics discussed.

FIGURE 1.6 **Reading Movie Reviews** When we consult movie reviews before watching a film new to us, we are almost always vulnerable to the kinds of value judgments they offer, whether negative or positive. Such critical opinions of Nora Ephron's film *Julie and Julia* (starring Mery Streep), for example, influenced many viewers about the overall quality of the fact-based work.

PREPARING TO SEE A FILM

How much should we know about a film before we see it? There is no simple answer to this question. Often we have little control over how much we know about a movie before we see it. Sometimes it is pleasurable (if now almost impossible) to enter a theater without one bit of information about what we are going to watch. Then we can see it free from others' opinions and judge it purely on its own merits. But given the increased price of movies, few of us can afford this freedom. We find other ways to gauge our interest in seeing the newest films. In any case, a few general guidelines on how to prepare for watching a film might be helpful.

1. Reviews An easy way to gain some knowledge about a film before seeing it is to read reviews. Whether found online or in traditional print sources such as newspapers or magazines, worthwhile reviews include many of the same basic components. They usually provide factual information: film credits, running time, MPAA (Motion Picture Association of America) rating (G, PG, PG-13, R, or NC-17), a summary of the subject matter and plot. Most reviews also mention the elements in the film that are significant and worthy of attention. They may help us place the film in context by relating it to similar films by other directors or to other films by the same director or production team. A review may analyze the film, breaking it into its parts and examining the nature, proportions, function, and interrelationship of these parts. Although most "journalistic" reviews are written quickly against deadlines, they almost always include some kind of value judgment, some negative or positive opinions of the film's overall worth (Figure 1.6).

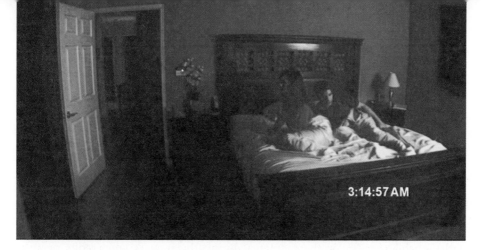

FIGURE 1.7 **Succeeding by Word of Mouth** Sometimes, filmmakers with very modest expectations for their movie's commercial success discover an enormous audience for their work via the grapevine: oral recommendations by friends and relatives who have seen and enjoyed the movie. In this manner, *Paranormal Activity,* an independent film produced on a miniscule budget, became an enormous box-office success.

In those cases where we do consult the opinions of reviewers before we head out to the multiplex, we should remember not to place too much faith in any one notice, unless we are already familiar with the tastes and biases of its author. Better, we might choose to read several reviewers' work, preferably published in sources that we know represent a variety of philosophical bents.

Indeed, when reading reviews, we must remember that criticism—journalistic, academic, or otherwise—is a highly subjective process. If we take any single review or even a series of reviews too seriously before seeing a film, we will restrict our ability to judge the work independently. Also, if we rely too much on the reviews, we may completely lose faith in our own judgment and end up in a tug-of-war between critical opinions.

2. Publicity   Reviews, of course, are not the only source of information and attitudes about films. The enormous amount of publicity generated for almost every movie (both by producers and studios and also, frequently, the media outlets owned by conglomerates that also own the studios) can influence our reactions. Ubiquitous television talk shows continuously feature interviews with actors and directors of recently released films. Viewers can access interviews online at any time of day or night. Expensively produced trailers (often *not* made by a film's creators), once available only in movie theaters, are likewise just a mouse click (or iPhone or iPad touch) away.

3. Word of Mouth   A great deal of important information can also be picked up from the grapevine, the word-of-mouth reviews by friends who have seen the movie (Figure 1.7). Online blogs and chat rooms now enable unlimited numbers of people to convey their opinions and communicate in real time about current movies.

4. Dedicated Web Sites   Two indispensable sites are the Internet Movie Database (www.imdb.com) and Rotten Tomatoes (www.rottentomatoes.com). The latter's idiosyncratic name and the gossipy tone of the former's very visible daily news entries may at first repel some readers. Nevertheless, film students should perhaps begin their "cineliteracy"

journey with *The Art of Watching Films* by visiting each site at length, becoming familiar with the multipaged insights and delight available there, including everything from movie facts and still photos to preview clips that we can download and view.

DEEPENING OUR RESPONSES TO FILMS

As students of film, once we have gathered facts, decided what movies to see, and attempted to clear our minds of preconceptions, then what? We should begin to deepen our perceptions.

After watching a film, we naturally start to think about our reactions to it. Sometimes, though, we hesitate to speak with others about our experience. Typically, we want to deal with our personal, emotional responses first, perhaps silently, perhaps while we "savor the moment" during the movie's end credits or even throughout the ride home. At other times, we are compelled immediately to speak out loudly with friends or family members who have accompanied us on our cinematic journey, sharing their joy or misery, or arguing not only about the work's emotional landscape, but also about its logical sharpness or stupidity. If the film has indeed encouraged any cerebral responses, we may especially desire to record our reactions in written form, all the better to understand our experience.

Now, as we turn directly to the analytical approach to film viewing, consider keeping a movie journal. Record what movies you see and, quite literally, what you see in them. Take note of both the emotional and the intellectual levels of your watching. Ask yourself questions about every aspect of the film, and let these questions lead you to other, more complex ones in your continuing to read this book. As you progress, stop to consider the questions for analysis that accompany each of the following chapters.

ANALYZING YOUR RESPONSES TO A FILM

1. Do you have any strong prejudices against this particular type of film? If so, how did these prejudices affect your responses to the film? Does this film have any special qualities that set it apart from other films of the same type?
2. How much do your personal subjective responses to the following aspects of the film affect your judgment: actors, treatment of sexual material, and scenes involving violence? Can you justify the sex and violence in the film aesthetically, or are these scenes included strictly to increase box-office appeal?
3. What were your expectations before seeing the film? How did these expectations influence your reaction to the film?
4. Was your mood, mental attitude, or physical condition while seeing the movie less than ideal? If so, how was your reaction to the film affected?
5. If the physical environment in which you watched the film was less than ideal, how did this fact influence your perception?
6. If you watched the movie on a TV or computer screen, in which scenes do you feel you lacked the intensity of involvement needed to enjoy the film most completely? In which scenes does the small-screen format work?
7. If you read reviews or scholarly essays before your viewing, what observations or opinions caught your interest? What is your own opinion after having seen the movie?

THEMATIC ELEMENTS

Precious

Movies are about things—even bad movies are about things. Rambo III
is about something. It has a theme, even if it doesn't want to have a
theme. . . . You have to know in some way what you are about to do.
Even if that theme gets rerouted or ends up in subtext, somehow there
has to be some sense of why you are doing this.

—PAUL SCHRADER, DIRECTOR AND SCREENWRITER

THEME AND FOCUS

In the context of novels, plays, and poetry, the word *theme* connotes an idea—the central idea, the point, the message, or the statement made by the work as a whole. For film analysis, however, that definition of theme is too narrow. The theme of a film is not necessarily an idea at all.

In the context of film analysis, **theme** refers to the unifying central concern of the film, the special focus that unifies the work. As the director Sidney Lumet has observed, "What the movie is about will determine how it will be cast, how it will look, how it will be edited, how it will be musically scored, how it will be mixed, how the titles will look, and, with a good studio, how it will be released. What it's about will determine how it is to be made."[1]

A filmmaker may choose to focus on ideas but is just as likely to emphasize one of the four other major elements: (1) plot, (2) emotional effect or mood, (3) character, and (4) style or texture. All five elements are present in *all* films; but in any given film, one is predominant. Keeping in mind this broader concept of theme will help us to analyze films ranging from *Inception* to *Joan Rivers: A Piece of Work* or from *The Girl Who Played With Fire* to *Summer Hours*.

Focus on Plot

In adventure stories and detective stories, the filmmaker focuses on plot—on what happens. The aim of such films is generally to provide escape from the boredom and drabness of everyday life, so the action is exciting and fast paced. Characters, ideas, and emotional effects are subordinate to events, and the final outcome is all-important. Events and the final outcome, however, are important only within the context of the specific story being told; they have little real significance otherwise. The theme of such a film can best be captured in a concise summary of the plot (Figure 2.1).

Focus on Emotional Effect or Mood

In a relatively large number of films, the director creates a highly specialized mood or emotional effect. In such films, it is possible to identify a single mood or emotion that prevails throughout the film or to view each segment of the film as a step leading to a single powerful emotional effect. Although plot may be very important in such a movie, events are subordinate to the emotional response they produce. Most horror films, the Alfred Hitchcock suspense thrillers, and romantic tone poems such as *A Man and a Woman* can be interpreted as having a mood or emotional effect as their primary focus and unifying element.

The theme of such films can best be stated by identifying the prevailing mood or emotional effect that the filmmaker has created (Figure 2.2).

In some films, a balanced combination of two emotions may make it difficult to tell which emotion is dominant. Ang Lee's *Taking Woodstock*, for example, might be classified as a comedy/drama, *The Twilight Saga: Eclipse* as a romantic/horror film.

FIGURE 2.1 **Focus on Plot** *Quantum of Solace, 300,* and *Spider-Man 2* are fast-paced action films that focus on what happens.

FIGURE 2.2 **Focus on Emotional Effect or Mood** A wide variety of emotional effects or moods can serve as a thematic concern in modern films. There are movies to scare us, like *The Shining* (top left), movies to make us cry, like *Once* (top right), movies to make us feel romantic, like *Away We Go* (bottom right), and movies to make us laugh, like *The Hangover* (bottom left).

FIGURE 2.3 **Mixed Emotions**   Some films do not focus on building a single emotional effect but instead blend two different emotions in the same story, as does *Little Miss Sunshine,* with its idiosyncratic blend of comedy and pathos.

An analysis of such films needs to consider the elements that contribute to each effect and the way the two prevalent emotions play off each other (Figure 2.3).

Focus on Character

Some films, through both action and dialogue, focus on the clear delineation of a single unique character. Although plot is important in such films, what happens is significant primarily because it helps us understand the character being developed. The major appeal of these characters lies in the qualities that set them apart from ordinary people. The theme of such films can best be expressed in a brief description of the central character, with emphasis on the unusual aspects of the individual's personality (Figure 2.4).

Focus on Style or Texture or Structure

In a relatively small number of films, the director tells the story in such a different way that the film's style or texture or structure becomes its dominant and most memorable aspect, making a stronger impact on our minds and senses than any of the other thematic elements. Such films have a quality that sets them apart—a unique look, feel, rhythm, atmosphere, tone, or organization that echoes in our minds and senses long after we leave the theater. The unique style, texture, or shape permeates the film (not just isolated segments), and all the cinematic elements are woven together into one rich tapestry. Such films are often not commercially successful because the mass audience may not be prepared for or comfortable with the unique viewing experience that they provide (Figure 2.5).

FIGURE 2.4 **Focus on Character**   Some films, such as *The Soloist* (Jamie Foxx) (top left), *The Reader* (Kate Winslet) (right), and *Milk* (Sean Penn) (bottom left), focus on the unusual aspects of unique people.

FIGURE 2.5 **Focus on Style, Texture, and/or Structure**   Both *Memento* (top) and *Where the Wild Things Are* (bottom) leave us feeling we have experienced a one-of-a-kind movie.

Focus on Ideas

In most serious films, the action and characters have a significance beyond the context of the film itself—a significance that helps to clarify some aspect of life, experience, or the human condition. The idea may be communicated directly through a specific incident or stated by a particular character. Most often, however, the idea is presented more subtly, and we are challenged to find an interpretation that we feel best fits the film as a whole. This indirect approach increases the likelihood of varying interpretations, but ones that are not necessarily contradictory. They may be equally valid, complementary statements saying essentially the same things in different terms or approaching the same idea from different angles.

Perhaps the first step in identifying the central idea is accurately identifying the abstract subject of the film in a single word or phrase—for example, *jealousy, injustice, prejudice*. If this is as specific as we can get in determining the theme, we should not despair; some concepts can be stated explicitly but others cannot. At any rate, the identification of the true subject is a valuable first step in film analysis. If possible, however, we should attempt to carry the determination of central idea beyond the mere identification of the subject and see if we can formulate a statement that accurately summarizes the subject that is dramatized in the film and conveyed by all its elements. If such a specific statement of the film's primary concern is possible, the film's central idea might fall into one of the following categories.

1. **Moral Implications.** Films that make moral statements are intended primarily to convince us of the wisdom or practicality of a moral principle and thereby persuade us to apply the principle in our own lives. Such principles often take the form of a maxim or proverb such as "The love of money is the root of all evil." Although many modern films have important moral implications, very few are structured around a single moral statement, and we must be careful not to mistake a moral implication for a moral statement or judgment (Figure 2.6).

2. **The Truth of Human Nature.** Quite different from films that focus on unique characters are those that present universal or representative characters. The characters in such films take on significance beyond themselves and the context of the particular film in which they appear. These characters are representative of humanity in general, and they serve as cinematic vehicles to illustrate some widely or universally acceptable truth about human nature (Figure 2.7).

3. **Social Problems.** Modern filmmakers are frequently obsessed with social problems and show their concern in movies that expose social vices and follies or criticize social institutions. Although the underlying purpose of such films is social reform, they rarely spell out specific methods of reform; usually they concentrate instead on defining the problem and emphasizing its importance. A social problem film may treat its subject in a light, satirical, or comic manner, or it may attack the subject in a savage, harsh, and brutal manner. The social problem film, unlike the human nature film, concerns

FIGURE 2.6 **Moral Implications**   Such films as *Atonement* (left) and *The Visitor* (right) lead us to think carefully about the consequences of the moral decisions we make in our lives.

FIGURE 2.7 **The Truth of Human Nature**   Films like *No Country for Old Men* (Javier Bardem) and *Synecdoche, New York* (Philip Seymour Hoffman) take a penetrating look at the nature of humankind when the thin veneers of civilization or "everyday reality" have been removed.

itself not with criticism of the human race in general or with the universal aspects of human nature but with the special functions of human beings as social animals and with the social institutions and traditions they have created (Figure 2.8).

4. **The Struggle for Human Dignity.** Many serious films portray a basic conflict or tension between two opposing sides of human nature. One is the desire to surrender to animal instincts and wallow in the slime of human weakness, cowardice, brutality, stupidity, and sensuality. The other is the struggle to stand erect, to display courage, sensitivity, intelligence, a spiritual and moral sense, and strong individualism. This conflict is best shown when the central characters are placed in a position of disadvantage, having been dealt a bad hand in some way, so that they must play against tremendous odds. The conflict may be external, with the character struggling against some dehumanizing force, system, institution, or attitude. Or the conflict may be internal, with the character struggling for dignity against the human weaknesses present in his or her own personality (Figure 2.9).

FIGURE 2.8 Social Problem Films
Films like *Away From Her* (domestic upheaval arising from Alzheimer's disease), *The Secret Life of Bees* (spousal and child abuse), and *Gran Torino* (prejudice against immigrants) force us to examine current social problems.

FIGURE 2.9 The Struggle for Human Dignity   In *The Messenger*, we follow two military men (Woody Harrelson and Ben Foster) as they dispatch their tasks of notifying next-of-kin survivors of Iraqi War casualties. Almost heroically, they struggle through grief, hurt, anger, and violence to maintain a nonjudgmental sense of human dignity.

FIGURE 2.10 The Complexity of Human Relationships In the documentary *Man on Wire*, tightrope walker Philippe Petit maintains his balance on a wire stretched between the Twin Towers of the World Trade Center in 1974, but then he "stumbles" upon losing his female partner. Heath Ledger and Jake Gyllenhaal play illicit lovers who lose all for love in *Brokeback Mountain* (top right). *An Education* creates a low-key epiphany for a smart-but-naive young English woman (Carey Mulligan) who is elatedly pursued by a much older man (Peter Sarsgaard).

A triumphant victory is sometimes, but certainly not always, achieved. However, the struggle itself gives us some respect for the character, win or lose. Boxers are often treated in films with the dignity theme. In *On the Waterfront*, Terry Malloy (Marlon Brando) achieves his dignity by leading the dock workers to rebel against a corrupt union, but Malloy's summary of his boxing career echoes clearly his personal struggle: "I could'a had class . . . I could'a been a contender . . . I could'a been *somebody!* . . . Instead of just a bum, which is what I am." Sylvester Stallone takes the character of Terry Malloy and gives him the chance to be "somebody" in each film of the *Rocky* series. In *Requiem for a Heavyweight*, over-the-hill fighter Mountain Rivera (Anthony Quinn) fails to achieve dignity but wins respect for his effort. Recently, protagonists in two popular boxing narratives—Hilary Swank in *Million Dollar Baby* and Russell Crowe in *Cinderella Man*—have constituted studies in this theme. And Mickey Rourke's protagonist in *The Wrestler* also strives for a simple dignity.

5. **The Complexity of Human Relationships.** Some films focus on the problems, frustrations, pleasures, and joys of human relationships: love, friendship, marriage, divorce, family interactions, sexuality, and so on (Figure 2.10). Some show the gradual working out of a problem; others help us gain insight into a problem without providing any clear resolution. Although a great many films of this sort deal with universal problems in the relationships between men and women, we must also be on the lookout for unusual treatments such as *Midnight Cowboy* (a "love" story about two men).

FIGURE 2.11 **Coming of Age** In movies like *Is Anybody There?* (left) and *My One and Only* (right), young people go through experiences that cause them to become more aware or more mature.

FIGURE 2.12 **Compounding the Problems** Coming of age is always difficult, but it is almost overwhelming when, like the title character (Jamie Bell) in *Billy Elliot,* you love ballet but your father hates it—or when, like the adolescent hero of *Harry Potter and the Half-Blood Prince* (Daniel Radcliffe), you are caught between the demands of growing up and being a wizard in training.

6. **Coming of Age/Loss of Innocence/Growing Awareness.** The major character or characters in such films are usually, but not always, young people going through experiences that force them to become more mature or to gain some new awareness of themselves in relation to the world around them. Such concepts can be treated comically, seriously, tragically, or satirically. The central character of these films is always **dynamic**—that is, different in some way at the end of the film from what he or she was at the beginning. The changes that occur may be subtle internal changes or drastic changes that significantly alter the character's outward behavior or lifestyle (Figures 2.11, 2.12).

7. **A Moral or Philosophical Riddle.** Sometimes a filmmaker may purposely strive to evoke a variety of subjective interpretations by developing a film around a riddle or puzzling quality. The filmmaker attempts to suggest or mystify instead of communicating clearly and attempts to pose moral or philosophical questions rather than provide answers. The typical reaction to such films is "What's it all about?" This type of film communicates primarily through symbols or images, so a thorough analysis of these elements will be required for interpretation. After even the most perceptive analysis, a degree

FIGURE 2.13 A Moral or Philosophical Riddle In *Persona* (top left), *Fight Club* (top right), and *Broken Embraces* (bottom), directors Ingmar Bergman, David Fincher, and Pedro Almodovar suggest multiple meanings that mystify us.

of uncertainty will remain. Such films are wide open to subjective interpretation. But the fact that such activity is required does not mean that the analysis of all film elements can be ignored. Individual interpretation should be supported by an examination of all elements (Figure 2.13).

IDENTIFYING THE THEME

Identifying the theme of a film is often difficult. The theme is not likely to reveal itself in a flash of light midway through the screening. Although simply watching a film may give us a vague, intuitive grasp of its basic meaning, accurately stating the theme is quite another matter. Sometimes we cannot do so until we leave the theater and begin thinking about or discussing the film. Frequently, just describing the movie to someone who has not seen it will provide an important clue to the theme, because we tend to describe first the things that make the strongest impression on us.

Identifying the theme can be considered both the beginning and the end of film analysis. After seeing a film, we should make a tentative identification of its theme to provide a starting point for close examination. The analysis itself should clarify our vision of the film and show all its elements functioning together as a unique whole. However, if our analysis of the individual thematic elements does not support our original view of the film's theme, we should be prepared to reconsider our opinion in light of the new direction that our investigation indicates.

Plot, emotional effect or mood, character, style or texture or structure, and ideas are the central concerns of most films. There are exceptions, however—films that do not focus exclusively on any one element and films that focus on more than one. In our efforts to identify theme, we must also be aware that certain films may possess, in addition to the single unifying central concern that we define as *theme*,

FIGURE 2.14 **Themes Universal or Limited in Time and Place**   *Easy Rider* (right) dealt with problems and issues that seemed very relevant in the late 1960s and early 1970s, but many of its concerns may seem old-fashioned today. Although the characters (such as Ma Joad, here) in John Ford's film (left) adapted from John Steinbeck's famous novel *The Grapes of Wrath* are specifically trying to survive the Great Depression in America, their struggles can often seem truly universal.

other, less important, areas of emphasis called **motifs.** These are images, patterns, or ideas that are repeated throughout the film and are variations or aspects of the major theme. Above all, we should remember that the statement of the theme cannot convey the full impact of the film itself. It merely clarifies our vision of the film as a unified work and enhances our appreciation of its thematic elements as they function together in a unique artistic whole.

EVALUATING THE THEME

Once we have identified the theme, it is important to make some kind of evaluation of it, especially in a serious film that attempts to do more than simply entertain. For the most part, theme evaluation is a subjective process, and any attempt to provide systematic guidelines for making this kind of value judgment would be prejudicial. A few generalizations, however, are permissible.

One standard commonly applied in theme evaluation is universality. A universal theme is one of lasting interest, one that is meaningful not just to people here and now but to all human beings in all ages. Therefore, a theme with universal appeal may be considered superior to one with an appeal strictly limited in time and place. Four social problem films illustrate this point. Those strictly limited in time and place like *Wild in the Streets* (the generation gap of the 1960s) and *Easy Rider* (a grab bag of 1960s problems) had a powerful impact on young film audiences when they were released but may seem dated today. However, *On the Waterfront* (union corruption in the 1950s) and *The Grapes of Wrath* (the plight of migrant farm workers in the 1930s) speak to us in loud, clear voices today, despite their age. Migrant farm workers still have problems, and corrupt unions still exist; but those films have universal appeal because of the real and powerful characters portrayed, the heroic struggles waged for human dignity, and the artistry with which both films were made (Figure 2.14).

FIGURE 2.15 **Universal Romance** Although the specific problems forced upon Rick (Humphrey Bogart) and Ilsa (Ingrid Bergman) by World War II have long since disappeared, *Casablanca* lives on because of strong universal themes that reach beyond the specific romantic love story at its core.

There is, of course, no real formula for the classic film, the kind we never grow tired of seeing. The classic film has a sense of rightness to it time and time again. Its power does not fade or diminish with the passing years but actually grows because of its universal themes and motifs. *The Grapes of Wrath* is not simply about migrant workers forced to leave the Oklahoma Dust Bowl in the 1930s. It is about the common man, the downtrodden, the underdog, about courageous men and women, about people who endure and constantly struggle to preserve their dignity. In the same way, *Casablanca* is more than just a story about two people losing and then finding each other in a world too chaotic for romantic dreams. It is a story about a beautiful woman and a mysterious man, about war, responsibility, courage, duty, and most of all, about doing the right thing. Such classics endure because of their strong, universal themes (Figure 2.15).

This does not mean that we place no value on themes that lack universality. Even if a theme's appeal is limited to a specific time and place, it may have some relevance to our own experience. Still, we will naturally consider a theme that says something significant to us superior to one that does not.

We also have the right to expect that a thematic idea be intellectually or philosophically appealing. In other words, if a film attempts to make a significant statement, that statement should be neither boring nor self-evident but should interest or challenge us.

On Theme and Focus

What is the film's primary focus: plot, emotional effect or mood, character, style or texture or structure, or ideas? On the basis of your decision, answer one of these questions:

1. If the film's primary concern is plot, summarize the action abstractly in a single sentence or a short paragraph.
2. If the film is structured around a mood or emotional effect, describe the mood or feeling that it attempts to convey.
3. If the film's focus is on a single unique character, describe the unusual aspects of his or her personality.
4. If the film seems to be built upon a unique style or texture or structure, describe the qualities that contribute to the special look or feel of the film.
5. If the film's primary focus is an idea, answer these questions:
   a. What is the true subject of the film? What is it really about in abstract terms? Identify the abstract subject in a single word or phrase.
   b. What statement does the film make about the subject? Formulate a sentence that accurately summarizes the idea dramatized by the film.

On Identifying the Theme

1. Although a director may attempt to do several things with a film, one goal usually stands out as most important. Decide which of the following was the director's *primary* aim, and give reasons for your choice.
   a. providing pure entertainment—that is, temporary escape from the real world
   b. developing a pervasive mood or creating a single, specialized emotional effect
   c. providing a character sketch of a unique, fascinating personality
   d. creating a consistent, unique feel or texture by weaving all of the complex elements of film together into a one-of-a-kind film experience
   e. criticizing society and social institutions and increasing the viewer's awareness of a social problem and the need for reform
   f. providing insights into human nature (demonstrating what human beings in general are like)
   g. creating a moral or philosophical riddle for the viewer to ponder
   h. making a moral implication to influence the viewer's values or behavior
   i. dramatizing one or more characters' struggle for human dignity against tremendous odds
   j. exploring the complex problems and pleasures of human relationships
   k. providing insight into a growth experience, the special kinds of situations or conflicts that cause important changes in the character or characters involved
2. Which of the items listed in the previous question seem important enough to qualify as secondary aims?

On Evaluating the Theme

1. Is the film's basic appeal to the intellect, to the funny bone, to the moral sense, or to the aesthetic sense? Is it aimed primarily at the groin (the erotic sense), the viscera (blood and guts), the heart, the yellow streak down the back, or simply the eyes? Support your choice with specific examples from the film.
2. How well does your statement of the film's theme and focus stand up after you have thoroughly analyzed all elements of the film?
3. To what degree is the film's theme universal? Is the theme relevant to your own experience? How?
4. If you think the film makes a significant statement, why is it significant?
5. Decide whether the film's theme is intellectually or philosophically interesting, or self-evident and boring, and defend your decision.
6. Does the film have the potential to become a classic? Will people still be watching it twenty years from today? Why?

WATCHING FOR THEME

Watch the first 5 minutes of any two of the following films: *Billy Elliot, (500) Days of Summer, Winter's Bone, Raiders of the Lost Ark, Eat Pray Love, Shane, To Kill a Mockingbird,* and *Persepolis.* Then answer these questions.

1. From the 5-minute segments you have just seen, can you make intelligent guesses about each film's primary concern?
2. What does the music suggest about the emotional quality of each film? Will the film be happy, sad, or bittersweet? Funny, serious, or a mixture of the two?
3. What do you learn about the characters introduced in the beginning? Which of the characters are point of view characters (characters with whom we identify and through whose eyes we experience the film)? Which of the characters will we end up viewing more objectively, from a distance?

FILMS FOR STUDY

Focus on Plot

Black Hawk Down (2001)
Gladiator (2000)
Independence Day (1996)
Raiders of the Lost Ark (1981)
The Road Warrior (1981)
Salt (2010)
Spider-Man 3 (2007)
Titanic (1997)

Focus on Emotional Effect or Mood

Bang the Drum Slowly (1973)
De-Lovely (2004)
The Piano (1993)
Psycho (1960)
The Silence of the Lambs (1991)
Somewhere in Time (1980)

Focus on Character

A Beautiful Mind (2001)
Capote (2005)
Cinderella Man (2005)
Coal Miner's Daughter (1980)
Crumb (1994)
Elizabeth (1998)
The Great Santini (1979)
Grizzly Man (2005)

The King's Speech (2010)
Patton (1970)
Raging Bull (1980)
The Social Network (2010)
The Soloist (2009)
Zorba the Greek (1964)

Focus on Style, Texture, or Structure

The Age of Innocence (1993)
Brazil (1985)
Bright Star (2009)
Days of Heaven (1978)
Fargo (1996)
McCabe & Mrs. Miller (1971)
Memento (2000)
The New World (2005)
Pulp Fiction (1994)
Raising Arizona (1987)
The Saddest Music in the World (2003)
3 Women (1977)

Focus on Human Nature

Babies (2010)
Deliverance (1972)
Groundhog Day (1993)
A History of Violence (2005)
House of Sand and Fog (2003)
Lord of the Flies (1963)
Requiem for a Dream (2000)
Shane (1953)

Struggle for Human Dignity

The Grapes of Wrath (1940)

The Insider (1999)
Invictus (2009)
On the Waterfront (1954)
One Flew Over the Cuckoo's Nest (1975)
Precious: Based on the Novel "Push" by Sapphire (2009)
Schindler's List (1993)
The Tillman Story (2010)

Complexity of Human Relationships

The Hours (2002)
The Hurt Locker (2008)
Inside Job (2010)
Junebug (2005)
The Kids Are All Right (2010)
Magnolia (1999)
Midnight Cowboy (1969)
Terms of Endearment (1983)
Three Colors: Blue (1993), *White* (2004), *Red* (1994)
The War of the Roses (1989)
When Harry Met Sally . . . (1989)
The World According to Garp (1982)

Coming of Age/ Growing Awareness

About a Boy (2002)
Almost Famous (2000)
Billy Elliot (2000)
Empire of the Sun (1987)
Finding Nemo (2003)
The Karate Kid (2010)
Hearts in Atlantis (2001)

A Little Princess (1995)
Sixteen Candles (1984)
Summer of '42 (1971)
To Kill a Mockingbird (1962)
Where the Wild Things Are (2009)
Winter Solstice (2004)
Y Tu Mamá También (2001)

Moral or Philosophical Riddle

Being John Malkovich (1999)
Blue Velvet (1986)
Fight Club (1999)
Knowing (2009)
Northfork (2003)
Run, Lola, Run (1998)
2001: A Space Odyssey (1968)
Waking Life (2001)

Focus on Social Problems

Bully (2001)
Dead Man Walking (1995)
Do the Right Thing (1989)
Far From Heaven (2002)
Mississippi Burning (1988)
Natural Born Killers (1994)
Norma Rae (1979)
The Rainmaker (1997)
Vera Drake (2004)
Welcome to the Dollhouse (1995)

FICTIONAL *and* DRAMATIC ELEMENTS

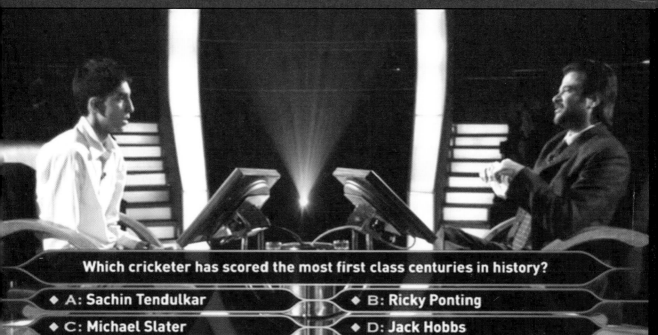

Which cricketer has scored the most first class centuries in history?

◆ A: Sachin Tendulkar   ◆ B: Ricky Ponting

◆ C: Michael Slater   ◆ D: Jack Hobbs

Slumdog Millionaire

I don't want to film a "slice of life" because people can get that at home, in the street, or even in front of the movie theater. . . . Making a film means, first of all, to tell a story. That story can be an improbable one, but it should never be banal. It must be dramatic and human. What is drama, after all, but life with the dull bits cut out?
—ALFRED HITCHCOCK, DIRECTOR

FILM ANALYSIS AND LITERARY ANALYSIS

Film has properties that set it apart from painting, sculpture, novels, and plays. It is also, in its most popular and powerful form, a storytelling medium that shares many elements with the short story and the novel. And because film presents its stories in dramatic form, it has even more in common with the stage play: Both plays and movies act out or dramatize, show rather than tell, what happens.

Unlike the novel, short story, or play, however, film is not handy to study; it cannot be effectively frozen on the printed page. The novel and short story are relatively easy to study because they are written to be read. The stage play is slightly more difficult to study because it is written to be performed. But plays are printed, and because they rely heavily on the spoken word, imaginative readers can conjure up at least a pale imitation of the experience they might have watching a performance on stage. This cannot be said of the screenplay, for a film depends greatly on visual and other nonverbal elements that are not easily expressed in writing. The screenplay requires so much filling in by our imagination that we cannot really approximate the experience of a film by reading a screenplay, and reading a screenplay is worthwhile only if we have already seen the film. Thus, most screenplays are published not to be read but rather to be remembered.

Still, film should not be ignored because studying it requires extra effort. And the fact that we do not generally read films does not mean we should ignore the principles of literary or dramatic analysis when we see a film. Literature and films do share and communicate many elements in similar ways. Perceptive film analysis rests on the principles used in literary analysis. Therefore, before we turn to the unique elements of film, we need to look into the elements that film shares with any good story.

Dividing film into its various elements for analysis is a somewhat artificial process, for the elements of any art form never exist in isolation. It is impossible, for example, to isolate plot from character: Events influence people, and people influence events; the two are always closely interwoven in any fictional, dramatic, or cinematic work. Nevertheless, the analytical method uses such a fragmenting technique for ease and convenience. But it does so with the assumption that we can study these elements in isolation without losing sight of their interdependence or their relationship to the whole.

THE ELEMENTS OF A GOOD STORY

What makes a good story? Any answer to this question is bound to be subjective; however, some general observations might be made that will apply to a large variety of film narratives.

A Good Story Is Unified in Plot

The structured film is one that has some broad underlying purpose or is unified around a central theme. Regardless of the nature of its theme—whether its focus is on plot, emotional effect, character, style or texture or structure, or idea—the fictional film generally has a plot or storyline that contributes to the development of that theme. Therefore, the plot and the events, conflicts, and characters that constitute it must be carefully selected and arranged so that their relationship to the theme is clear.

A unified plot focuses on a single thread of continuous action, where one event leads to another naturally and logically. Usually a strong cause-and-effect relationship exists between these events, and the outcome is made to seem, if not inevitable, at least probable. In a tightly unified plot, nothing can be transposed or removed without significantly affecting or altering the whole. Thus, every event grows naturally out of the plot, and the conflict must be resolved by elements or agents present in the plot itself. A unified plot does not introduce out of thin air some kind of chance, coincidental, or miraculous happening, or some powerful superhuman force that swoops down out of nowhere to save the day.

Although plot unity is a general requirement, exceptions do exist. In a film whose focus is the clear delineation of a unique character, unity of action and cause-and-effect relationships between events are not so important. In fact, such plots may be episodic (that is, composed of events that bear no direct relationship to each other), for the unity in such films emerges from the contribution each event makes to our understanding of the character being developed, rather than from the interrelationships of the events.

A Good Story Is Credible

To become fully involved in a story, we must usually be convinced that it could be true. A filmmaker can create the illusion of truth in a variety of ways.

1. **Externally Observable Truths: The way things really are.** The most obvious and common kind of truth in a film story is the approximation of life as it is. To borrow Aristotle's phrase, these are stories that "might occur and have the capability of occurring in accordance with the laws of probability or necessity." This kind of truth is based on overwhelming evidence in the world around us, so it may not always be a pleasant truth. Human beings are flawed creatures. Married couples don't always live happily ever after, and tragic accidents, serious illnesses, and great misfortunes often befall people who don't seem to deserve them. But we accept such truths because they conform to our own experience of the way life is (Figure 3.1).

2. **Internal Truths of Human Nature: The way things are supposed to be.** Another set of truths seems true because we want or need to believe in them. Some of the greatest film classics do not even pretend to represent the actualities of real life; instead, they offer a fairy-tale or happily-ever-after ending. The good guy always wins, and true love conquers all. But in a very special way, these stories are also believable, or at least can be made to seem so, because they contain what might be called internal truths—beliefs in things that are not really observable but that seem true to us because we want or need them to be. Indeed, the concept of poetic justice (the idea that virtue will be rewarded and evil punished) serves as an example of such an internal truth. We seldom question poetic justice in a story simply because it is the way things are supposed to be. Thus many film stories are convincing because they conform

FIGURE 3.1 The Way Things Really Are
Greenberg (top left), *Sunshine Cleaning* (top right), and *The Wrestler* (bottom) are credible because they conform to what we perceive as real-life experiences.

FIGURE 3.2 The Way Things Are Supposed to Be Movies such as *Mr. Smith Goes to Washington* (left) and *The Great Debaters* (right) present credible images of the world as we might like it to be.

to an inner truth and satisfy a human need to believe. Of course, such truths can ring false to those who do not want or need to believe them (Figure 3.2).

3. **Artistic Semblance of Truth: The way things never were and never will be.** Filmmakers are also capable of creating a special kind of truth. With their artistry, technical skills, and special effects, they can create an imaginary world on the screen that, for the duration of the film, seems totally believable. In such films, truth depends on the early and thoroughly convincing establishment of a strange or fantastic environment, sense of another time, or unusual characters, so that we are caught up in the film's overall spirit, mood, and atmosphere. If the filmmaker is skillful at creating this semblance of truth, we willingly agree to suspend our disbelief (as Samuel Taylor Coleridge observed), and we leave our skepticism and our rational faculties behind as we enter the film's imaginary world. If the fictional reality is successfully established, we may think to ourselves, "Yes, in such a situation almost anything can happen." By communicating this pervasive and real sense of an unusual

FIGURE 3.3 **The Way Things Never Were and Never Will Be** By using their special brand of artistry, film-makers can create on the screen an imaginary world that makes us willingly accept incredible settings, characters, and events in such films as *Edward Scissorhands* (top left), *Be Kind Rewind* (top right), *Ratatouille* (bottom right), and *In the Loop* (bottom left).

situation or environment, filmmakers in effect create a new set of ground rules by which we judge reality (Figure 3.3). And for the brief period of two hours or so, we can believe thoroughly in the truth of *Rosemary's Baby, The Day the Earth Stood Still, Inception, The Lord of the Rings, The Wizard of Oz, E.T. The Extra-Terrestrial*, or *Avatar*.

Thus the plausibility of a story depends on at least three separate factors: (1) the objective, external, and observable laws of probability and necessity; (2) the subjective, irrational, and emotional inner truths of human nature; and (3) the semblance of truth created by the filmmaker's convincing art. Although all these kinds of truths may be present in the same film, usually one kind of truth is central to the film's overall structure. The other truths may contribute but play supporting roles.

A Good Story Is Interesting

An important requirement of a good story is that it capture and hold our interest. A story can be interesting in many ways, and few if any stories have equal appeal to all filmgoers, for whether a story is interesting or boring is, to a great extent, a subjective matter. Some of us may be interested only in fast-paced action/adventure films. Others may be bored by anything without a romantic love interest at its center. Still others may be indifferent to any story that lacks deep philosophical significance.

But regardless of what we expect from a motion picture—whether it be the relaxation gained from being entertained or a clue to understanding the universe—we never go to the movies to be bored. Our tolerance for boredom seems very

FIGURE 3.4 **Suspense**   Beginning with its opening, brilliantly formulated scenes, Quentin Tarantino's *Inglourious Basterds* (2009) (featuring Oscar Winner Christoph Waltz) locks the viewer into multiple modes of intense suspense.

limited: A film may shock us, frustrate us, puzzle us, or even offend us, but it must *never* bore us. Thus, we fully expect the filmmaker to heighten the film's reality by doing away with irrelevant and distracting details. Why should we pay to watch the dull, the monotonous, or the routine when life provides them absolutely free of charge?

Even the Italian neorealist directors, who stress everyday reality in their films and deny the validity of invented stories, argue that their particular brand of everyday reality is not boring because of its complex echoes and implications. As Cesare Zavattini puts it, "Give us whatever 'fact' you like, and we will disembowel it, make it something worth watching."[1] To most of us, the expressions "worth watching" and "interesting" are synonymous.

Suspense   To capture and maintain our interest, the filmmaker employs a multitude of devices and techniques, most of which are in some way related to suspense. These elements heighten our interest by exciting our curiosity, usually by foreshadowing or hinting at the outcome. By withholding bits of information that would answer the dramatic questions raised by the story, and by floating some unanswered question just beyond our reach, the filmmaker provides a motive to keep us constantly moving with the story's flow (Figure 3.4).

Action   If a story is to be interesting, it must contain some elements of action. Stories are never static; some sort of action or change is essential if a story is to be worth telling. Action, of course, is not limited to physical activities such as fights, chases, duels, and great battles. It may be internal, psychological, or emotional. In films such as *Star Wars*, *The Last of the Mohicans*, and the *Indiana Jones* series, the action is external and physical (Figure 3.5); in *In the Mood for Love* and *Bright Star*, the action occurs within the minds and the emotions of the characters (Figure 3.6).

FIGURE 3.5 **External Action**   The exciting action in *Indiana Jones and the Kingdom of the Crystal Skull* gives us little time for reflection. We are kept on the edge of our chairs throughout and, by film's end, are totally exhausted by the constant, fast-paced tension.

FIGURE 3.6 **Internal Action**   Although director Jane Campion's elegant *Bright Star* contains little physical action, what is happening in the minds and hearts of the characters played by Ben Whishaw and Abbie Cornish is extremely vibrant and exciting.

Both sorts of films have movement and change. The interest created by the exciting action in *The Road Warrior* is obvious and needs no explanation. But the action within a human being is not so obvious. Nothing very extraordinary happens externally in *The Remains of the Day*, but what takes place in the hearts and minds of its characters is extremely interesting and exciting.

Internal action stories require more concentration from the viewer, and they are more difficult to treat cinematically. But they are worthwhile subjects for film and can be as interesting and exciting as films that stress external and physical action.

A Good Story Is Both Simple and Complex

A good film story must be simple enough so that it can be expressed and unified cinematically. Edgar Allan Poe's idea that a short story should be capable of being read in a single sitting applies to film. Experiencing a film is less tiring than reading a book, and the single sitting for a film may be a maximum of, say, two hours. Beyond that time limit, only the greatest films keep us from becoming restless or inattentive. Thus the story's action or theme must usually be compressed into a unified dramatic structure that requires about two hours to unfold. In most cases, a limited, simple theme, such as that in *8 Mile*, which focuses on a small part of one person's life, is better suited for the cinema than is a story that spans the ages in search of a timeless theme, as D. W. Griffith attempted in *Intolerance*. Generally, a story should be simple enough to be told in the time period allotted for its telling.

However, within these limits, a good story must also have some complexity, at least enough to sustain our interest. And although a good story may hint at the eventual outcome, it must also provide some surprises or at least be subtle enough to prevent the viewer from predicting the outcome after the first hour. Thus, a good story usually withholds something about its conclusion or significance until the very end.

But new elements introduced into the plot at the very end may make us question the legitimacy of the surprise ending, especially if such elements bring about an almost miraculous conclusion or make too much use of coincidence or chance. A surprise ending can be powerful and legitimate when the plot prepares us for it, even when the plot elements and the chain of cause and effect leading up to the ending escape our conscious attention (as in *The Sixth Sense*). The important thing is that the viewer never feel hoodwinked, fooled, or cheated by a surprise ending. The viewer should gain insight by means of the ending. Such insight occurs only when the surprise ending carries out tendencies established earlier in the story (often called "foreshadowing"). A good plot is complex enough to keep us in doubt but simple enough so that the seeds of the outcome can all be found.

A filmmaker's communication techniques must also be a satisfying blend of simplicity and complexity. Most often, the filmmaker must communicate simply, directly, and clearly to all viewers. But to challenge the minds and eyes of especially perceptive viewers, he or she must also communicate through implication and suggestion, leaving some elements open to interpretation. Many viewers are bored by films that are too complex, that make too much use of such subtlety. Other viewers—those who prefer an intellectual challenge—are not interested in films that are too direct and simple. Thus, a filmmaker must please both those who do not appreciate films they cannot easily understand and those who reject films they understand all too easily.

Filmgoers' views of life also influence their attitudes toward a film's complexity or simplicity. Those who see life itself as complex and ambiguous are likely to demand that kind of complexity and ambiguity in the films they see (Figure 3.7). Such viewers may also reject an escapist film because it falsifies the nature of existence by making it seem too easy, too neat, too pat. Other viewers may reject the complex view of life presented in realistic or naturalistic films for the opposite reason—because the film is too full of ambiguities, too complex, or because it

FIGURE 3.7 **Complexity**   The levels of confusion created by the constant jumping back and forth between illusion and reality, and present and past, in *Duplicity* may stimulate some viewers but may be too complex to provide the relaxing entertainment expected by others.

FIGURE 3.8 **Simplicity**   The exuberant musical sequences in *Mama Mia!* may entertain viewers looking for escapist entertainment but bore others who demand more depth and complexity.

does not conform to the inner subjective truth of life—life as they would like it to be (Figure 3.8).

A Good Story Handles Emotional Material With Restraint

A strong emotional element or effect is present in almost any story, and film is capable of manipulating our emotions. But this manipulation must be honest and appropriate to the story. Usually we reject as sentimental films that overuse emotional material. Such films might even make us laugh when we're supposed to cry. So a filmmaker must exercise restraint.

Reactions to emotional material depend on the individual viewer. One viewer may consider Clint Eastwood's film *The Bridges of Madison County* a beautifully touching

FIGURE 3.9 Emotional Restraint   Simple dialogue creates eloquent understatement during crucial dramatic scenes in *To Kill a Mockingbird*.

and poignant experience, whereas another scoffs and calls it "sentimental trash." The difference often lies in the viewers themselves. The first viewer probably responded fully to the film, allowing himself to be manipulated by its emotional effects without considering the filmmaker dishonest. The second viewer probably felt that the film unfairly attempted to manipulate her emotions, and she responded by rejecting it.

When the emotional material in a film is understated, there is little danger of offending. In understatement the filmmaker downplays the emotional material, giving it less emphasis than the situation would seem to call for. In *To Kill a Mockingbird* (Figure 3.9), Atticus Finch (Gregory Peck) uses a simple phrase to thank the boogeyman, Arthur "Boo" Radley (Robert Duvall), for saving the lives of Scout and Jem: "Thank you, Arthur . . . for my children." The effect of understatement is demonstrated by the tremendous emotional weight carried by the simple phrase "thank you," which we often use for the most trivial favors. The normally insignificant phrase takes on great significance, and we are moved by what is *not* said. The voice-over narration from the same film offers another example of understatement: "Neighbors bring food with death and flowers with sickness and little things in between. Boo was our neighbor. He gave us two soap dolls, a broken watch and chain, a pair of good luck pennies, and our lives."

A wide variety of elements and techniques influence our emotional response to a film. Both understatement and the overuse of emotional material are reflected in the way the plot is structured, in the dialogue and the acting, and in the visual effects. Elements of a film's visual environment or setting (discussed at length in Chapter 4), and its creation of atmosphere, can also appeal to the viewer's senses and affect his or her emotional reaction. But a filmmaker's approach to presenting emotional material is perhaps most evident in the musical score, which can communicate on a purely emotional level and thus reflects the peaks and valleys of emotional emphasis and understatement (see Chapter 9).

FIGURE 3.10 **Significant Titles** Students of film should try to make themselves aware of both the sources and significance of movie titles. In the case of *All the King's Men*, Robert Penn Warren, on whose novel two films have been based, appropriated the phrasing and theme of a famous nursery rhyme.

THE SIGNIFICANCE OF THE TITLE

The importance of a suitable title is not overlooked by writers like Neil Simon, who says, "When looking for a fun title, you're looking for something that's going to grab them. . . . When I don't have it, I'll work very hard because it's as important to me as writing the first scene, getting the title. I feel comfortable if it sounds right."[2]

In most films, we can understand the full significance of the title only after seeing the film. In many cases, the title has one meaning to a viewer before seeing the film and a completely different, richer, and deeper meaning afterward. Titles are often ironic, expressing an idea exactly the opposite of the meaning intended, and many titles allude to mythology, biblical passages, or other literary works. For example, the title *All the King's Men* (Figure 3.10) is taken from "Humpty Dumpty" and reminds us of the nursery rhyme, which provides a nutshell summary of the plot. *All the King's Men* concerns a southern dictator (king) who rises to a position of high power (sat on a wall) but is assassinated (had a great fall). As in the case of Humpty Dumpty, "all the king's men" are unable to put the king together again. On another level, the title literally tells us what the story is about. Willie Stark, the politician, is the primary energy force. However, Jack Burden, Stark's press secretary and right-hand man, is actually the focal character, and the story is very much concerned with the lives of others who work for Stark in one capacity or another. Thus, the story is in a sense about "all the king's men." On yet another plane the title links the fictional character Willie Stark to the real-life politician Huey Long, on whose career the story is loosely based. Long's favorite nickname for himself was "The Kingfisher," from a character on the old *Amos 'n' Andy* radio show, and

Long once wrote a song around his campaign slogan, "Every man a king, but no one wears a crown."

Some titles may call attention to a key scene that becomes worthy of careful study when we realize that the title of the film has been taken from it. Although the title seldom names the theme (as it does in *Sense and Sensibility* and *Good Will Hunting*), it is usually an extremely important clue in identifying it. Thus, it is essential to think carefully about the possible meanings of the title after seeing any film.

DRAMATIC STRUCTURE

The art of storytelling as practiced in the short story, novel, play, or film has always depended on a strong dramatic structure—that is, the aesthetic and logical arrangement of parts to achieve the maximum emotional, intellectual, or dramatic impact. Dramatic structure can be linear or nonlinear, depending upon the author's needs and wishes. Both patterns contain the same elements: exposition, complication, climax, and dénouement. They differ only in the arrangement of these elements.

Linear, or Chronological, Structure

Legendary screenwriter Ernest Lehman (*North by Northwest*) described films having the linear, or chronological, structure in terms of acts: "In the first act, who are the people, what is the situation of this whole story? Second act is the progression of that situation to a point of high conflict and great problems. And the third act is how the problems and the conflicts are resolved."[3]

The first part of the story, called the **exposition,** introduces the characters, shows some of their interrelationships, and places them within a believable time and place. In the next section, the **complication,** a conflict begins and grows in clarity, intensity, and importance. Because dramatic tension and suspense are created and maintained during the complication, this is usually the longest section. When the complication has reached its point of maximum tension, the two forces in opposition confront each other at a high point of physical or emotional action called the **climax.** At the climax, the conflict is resolved and there follows a brief period of calm, the **dénouement,** in which a state of relative equilibrium returns (Figure 3.11).

Nonlinear Structures

There are many variations of nonlinear structure, including *in medias res* beginnings and episodic structures, in which the elements are not arranged chronologically. A story that begins *in medias res* (a Latin phrase meaning "in the middle of things") opens with an exciting incident that actually happens *after* the complication has developed. This technique, used by Homer to begin his epic narratives the *Iliad* and the *Odyssey*, captures the audience's interest at the outset and creates a state of dramatic tension. The necessary expository information is filled in later as the situation permits, through such means as dialogue (characters talking about the situation or events that led to the complication) or **flashbacks** (sequences that go back in time to provide expository material). In this manner exposition can be built

FIGURE 3.11 **Linear Structure** In the teen-pregnancy comedy/drama *Juno*, director Jason Reitman and screenwriter Diablo Cody chose to tell their story using strict chronological order.

up gradually and spread throughout the story instead of being established at the beginning, before dramatic interest starts to build.

Providing exposition is not the only function of flashback. The use of visual flashback gives a filmmaker great flexibility. By using flashback, the filmmaker can present information as he or she desires, when it is most dramatically appropriate and powerful or when it most effectively illuminates the theme. (**Flash-forward,** a filmed sequence that jumps from the present into the future, has been tried in such films as *Easy Rider, They Shoot Horses, Don't They?* and *Love! Valour! Compassion!*, and at the end of the HBO series *Six Feet Under.* It is doubtful whether this device will ever gain widespread acceptance.) As long as coherence is maintained so that the relationship between one scene and another is clear, the director can violate strict chronological order at will.

Sometimes, however, a director may purposely try to confuse the time sequence. In the haunting and mystifying *Last Year at Marienbad,* Alain Resnais seems determined to keep us wondering whether the scene we are watching is taking place in the present (this year) or in the past (last year) or, in fact, whether it really takes place at all. Writer-director Quentin Tarantino has used some unusual scrambled chronology in his films, including *Reservoir Dogs, Pulp Fiction,* and the *Kill Bill* movies (Figure 3.12), establishing a stylistic trademark.

Endings: Fine-Tuning the Dénouement

Movies and plays, unlike short stories and novels, are often field-tested before an audience. Just as plays have often had tryouts on the road before they open on Broadway, yet-to-be-released films are given sneak previews in carefully

FIGURE 3.12 **Nonlinear Structure**   Director Quentin Tarantino's *Pulp Fiction* (starring John Travolta and Uma Thurman) has become a modern film favorite in part because it manipulates so skillfully its nonlinear structure containing multiple, suspenseful flashbacks.

selected locations to see how audiences like them. Highly sophisticated test-marketing techniques are employed to determine the final version of many films. Such diverse filmmakers as Woody Allen, Frank Capra, and Danny DeVito have all been strong believers in using sneak previews to test audience response. As DeVito puts it: "It's like asking the audience to be your barometer. It's a very, very informative process. As far as I'm concerned, the audience has the final cut."[4]

Filmmakers are especially interested in the audience's response to the ending, or dénouement, of their films. An unsatisfactory ending often results in poor word-of-mouth (WOM), and poor WOM means poor results at the box office. According to Griffin Dunne, star and coproducer of *After Hours*, "If the last five minutes are disturbing, it has an overriding effect on the first ninety."[5] *After Hours* originally ended with Dunne's character (encased in a plaster cast) being mistaken for a sculpture and "carted away toward an unknown, but surely ugly future." Audience response was negative, and a new ending that was "less stifling" and "more positive" was shot. Both endings were then previewed, and audiences expressed a clear preference for the happier ending.

In the original ending of *Fatal Attraction*, Michael Douglas's fingerprints were found on the knife that Glenn Close used to commit suicide, evidence that sent Douglas to jail for murder. The preview audience, however, had so strongly identified with Douglas and his family that that ending proved totally unsatisfactory and a different ending was shot. Another change that pleased viewers was altering the original conclusion of *My Best Friend's Wedding*. The preview audiences insisted that the Julia Roberts character end up dancing with her gay friend (played by Rupert Everett) rather than marry the less interesting romantic lead (played by Dermot Mulroney) (Figure 3.13).

FIGURE 3.13 **Ending Up Changed**   Recently, after test audiences seemed to reject the original unhappy ending of Lasse Hallstrom's *Dear John,* the director decided to reshoot and use a possibly more upbeat conclusion for his romantic drama starring Amanda Seyfried and Channing Tatum.

CONFLICT

In his essay "Why Do We Read Fiction?" Robert Penn Warren observes,

> A story is not merely an image of life, but of life in motion . . . individual characters moving through their particular experiences to some end that we may accept as meaningful. And the experience that is characteristically presented in a story is that of facing a problem, a conflict. To put it bluntly: No conflict, no story.[6]

Conflict is the mainspring of every story, whether it be told on the printed page, on the stage, or on the screen. It is the element that really captures our interest, heightens the intensity of our experience, quickens our pulses, and challenges our minds (Figure 3.14).

Although there may be several conflicts within a story, some kind of major conflict at its core ultimately has the greatest importance to the story as a whole. The major conflict is of great importance to the characters involved, and there is some worthwhile and perhaps lasting goal to be gained by the resolution of that conflict. Because it is highly significant to the characters, and because significant conflicts have important effects on people and events, the major conflict and its resolution almost always bring about an important change, either in the people involved or in their situation.

The major conflict has a high degree of complexity; it is not the sort of problem that can be quickly and easily resolved by an obvious or simple solution. Thus, its outcome remains in doubt throughout the greater part of the film. The complexity of the struggle is also influenced by the fact that the forces in conflict are nearly equal in strength, a fact that adds greatly to the dramatic tension and power of the work. In some films, the major conflict and its resolution may contribute greatly to the viewer's experience, for it is the conflict and its resolution (or sometimes its lack of resolution) that clarify or illuminate the nature of human experience.

FIGURE 3.14 **Conflict** The mainspring of practically any film is the dramatic tension created by human conflict. In *One Flew Over the Cuckoo's Nest*, mental patient Randall McMurphy (Jack Nicholson) and Nurse Ratched (Louise Fletcher) battle constantly throughout the narrative.

Some major conflicts are primarily physical, such as a fistfight or a shootout in a western. Others are almost completely psychological, as is often the case in the films of Federico Fellini or Ingmar Bergman. In most films, however, the conflict has both physical and psychological dimensions, and determining where one stops and the other begins is often difficult. It is perhaps simpler and more meaningful to classify major conflicts under the broad headings of external and internal.

In its simplest form, an **external conflict** may consist of a personal and individual struggle between the central character and another character. On this level the conflict is nothing more than a contest of human wills in opposition, as might be illustrated by a prizefight, a duel, or two suitors seeking to win the affections of the same woman. Yet these basic and simple human conflicts have a tendency to be more complex than they first appear. Conflicts can seldom be isolated completely from other individuals, society as a whole, or the value systems of the individuals involved. Thus, they often grow into representative struggles between groups of people, different segments of society or social institutions, or different value systems.

Another type of external conflict pits the central character or characters against some nonhuman force or agency, such as fate, the gods, the forces of nature, or the social system. Here the forces the characters face are essentially nonhuman and impersonal. Jefferson Smith's (James Stewart) struggle against the political corruption and graft of the "Taylor machine" in *Mr. Smith Goes to Washington* is an example of an external conflict that pits a single individual against "the system." A more physical type of external conflict occurs in *Cast Away*, in which Tom Hanks struggles to prove his worth against the dehumanizing forces of nature.

An **internal conflict** centers on an interior, psychological conflict within the central character (Figure 3.15). The forces in opposition are simply different

FIGURE 3.15 **Internal Conflict** James Ivory's *The Remains of the Day* presents life at an English manor house (including servants portrayed by Emma Thompson and Anthony Hopkins) over a period of decades. Although numerous external class and political conflicts help to propel the narrative, the tension within individual lives lies at the heart of the film.

aspects of the same personality. For example, in James Thurber's celebrated short story "The Secret Life of Walter Mitty," we have a conflict between what a man actually is (a small, timid, incompetent creature, henpecked by an overbearing wife) and what he wants to be (a brave and competent hero). By escaping constantly into the world of his daydreams, Mitty reveals himself to be living in a permanent state of conflict between his heroic dreams and the drab reality of his existence. In all such internal conflicts, we see a character squeezed between the two sides of his or her personality, torn between equally strong but conflicting desires, goals, or value systems. In some cases, this inner conflict is resolved and the character grows or develops as a result, but in many cases, like that of Walter Mitty, there is no resolution.

The standard Woody Allen character in films such as *Annie Hall*, *Manhattan*, and *Play It Again, Sam*, is torn by internal conflicts and insecurities. In *Play It Again, Sam*, the central character tries to overcome his self-doubts and insecurities by emulating his screen hero, Humphrey Bogart.

CHARACTERIZATION

The celebrated, "name-above-the title" American director Frank Capra (*It Happened One Night*, *It's a Wonderful Life*) once observed, "You can only involve an audience with people. You can't involve them with gimmicks, with sunsets, with hand-held cameras, zoom shots, or anything else. They couldn't care less about those things."[7] And then Capra suggested that if we are not interested in a film's most human elements—its characters—there is little chance that we will be interested in the film as a whole. To be interesting, characters must seem real, understandable, and worth caring about. For the most part, the characters in a story are believable in the same way that the story is believable. In other words, they conform to the laws of probability and necessity (by reflecting externally observable truths about human

FIGURE 3.16 **Characterization Through Appearance**   In *Fargo*, police chief Marge (Frances McDormand), pregnant and wearing a floppy-earmuffed cap, makes an early impression on the viewer that belies the officer's shrewd and swift intelligence (left). Likewise, in *The Devil Wears Prada*, the unfashionable clothes worn by the job candidate Andrea (Anne Hathaway) initially mislead movie watchers about her smart persistence (right).

nature), they conform to some inner truth (humans as we want them to be), or they are made to seem real by the convincing art of the actor.

If characters are truly credible, it is almost impossible to remain completely neutral toward them. We must respond to them in some way: We may admire them for their heroic deeds and their nobility or pity them for their failures. We may love them or identify with them for their ordinary human qualities. We may laugh at them for their ignorance or laugh with them because theirs is a human ignorance that we all share. If our reaction to them is negative, we may detest them for their greed, their cruelty, their selfishness, and their underhanded methods. Or we may scorn them for their cowardice.

Characterization Through Appearance

Because most film actors project certain qualities of character the minute they appear on the screen, characterization in film has a great deal to do with casting. A major aspect of film characterization is revealed visually and instantaneously. Although some actors may be versatile enough to project completely different qualities in different roles, most actors are not. The minute we see most actors on the screen, we make certain assumptions about them because of their facial features, dress, physical build, and mannerisms and the way they move. Our first visual impression may be proven erroneous as the story progresses, but it is certainly an important means of establishing character. Consider the immediate reactions we have to Julia Roberts when she appears for the first time in *Erin Brockovich* or Anne Hathaway in *The Devil Wears Prada*, or to Frances McDormand in *Fargo* (Figure 3.16).

Characterization Through Dialogue

Characters in a fictional film naturally reveal a great deal about themselves by what they say. But much is also revealed by how they say it. Their true thoughts, attitudes, and emotions can be suggested in subtle ways through word choice and through the stress, pitch, and pause patterns of their speech. Actors' use of grammar, sentence structure, vocabulary, and particular dialects (if any) reveals a great deal about their characters' social and economic level, educational background, and mental processes. Therefore, we must develop a keen ear, attuned to the faintest

FIGURE 3.17 **Characterization Through Dialogue**   Neil LaBute's *Possession* tells dual, interrelated stories about two couples who live in different centuries. Various methods, including obvious contrasts in costuming, help viewers to differentiate between the two separate narratives and their time levels. Most significantly, the formal diction of the Victorian lovers (Jennifer Ehle and Jeremy Northam) clashes with the casual vernacular spoken by the modern lovers (Gwyneth Paltrow and Aaron Eckhart).

and most subtle nuances of meaning revealed through the human voice—listening carefully not only to what is said but also to how it is said (Figure 3.17).

Characterization Through External Action

Although appearance is an important measure of a character's personality, appearances are often misleading. Perhaps the best reflections of character are a person's actions. It must be assumed, of course, that real characters are more than mere instruments of the plot, that they do what they do for a purpose, out of motives that are consistent with their overall personality. Thus, there should be a clear relationship between a character and his or her actions; the actions should grow naturally out of the character's personality. If the motivation for a character's action is clearly established, the character and the plot become so closely interwoven that they are impossible to separate, and every action that the character takes in some way reflects the quality of his or her particular personality.

Of course, some actions are more important in revealing character than others. Even the most ordinary choice can be revealing, for some kind of choice is involved in almost everything we do. Sometimes the most effective characterization is achieved not by the large actions in the film but by the small, seemingly insignificant ones. For example, a firefighter may demonstrate his courage by saving a child from a burning building, yet such an act may be only a performance of duty rather than a reflection of a choice. His essential character might be more clearly defined by risking his life to save a little girl's doll, because such an action would be imposed on him not by his duty as a firefighter but by his personal judgment about the value of a doll to a little girl.

Characterization Through Internal Action

There is an inner world of action that normally remains unseen and unheard by even the most careful observer/listener. Yet the dimension of human nature that this world embraces is often essential to a real understanding of a character. Inner action occurs within characters' minds and emotions and consists of secret, unspoken thoughts, daydreams, aspirations, memories, fears, and fantasies. People's hopes, dreams, and aspirations can be as important to an understanding of their character as any real achievement, and their fears and insecurities can be more terrible to them than any real catastrophic failure. Thus, although the Benicio Del Toro character in *Traffic* is a drab, insignificant creature, scarcely worth caring about when judged purely by his initial external behavior, he becomes an exciting and interesting personality as we gain insight into his character.

The most obvious way in which the filmmaker reveals inner reality is by taking us visually or aurally into the character's mind so that we see or hear the things that the character imagines, remembers, or thinks about. This may be achieved through a sustained interior view or through fleeting glimpses revealed by means of metaphors. In addition to providing glimpses into the inner action by revealing the sounds and sights the character imagines he sees and hears, the filmmaker may employ tight close-ups on an unusually sensitive and expressive face (reaction shots) or may utilize the musical score for essentially the same purpose, as Brian De Palma does repeatedly in *Dressed to Kill* (1980).

Characterization Through Reactions of Other Characters

The way other characters view a person often serves as an excellent means of characterization. Sometimes, a great deal of information about a character is already provided through such means before the character first appears on the screen. This is the case in the opening scene of *Hud*. In this sequence Lonnie (Brandon DeWilde) is walking along the main street of the little Texas town at around 6:30 in the morning, looking for his uncle, Hud (Paul Newman). As Lonnie passes a beer joint along the

FIGURE 3.18 Dramatic Foils In Peter Ustinov's 1962 film version of *Billy Budd,* Herman Melville's allegory of good and evil, the sweet, naive, and innocent Billy (Terence Stamp) contrasts sharply with the grim, satanic Master of Arms Claggart (Robert Ryan). The striking opposites in their characters are emphasized by their features, facial expressions, clothing, and voice qualities. Stamp is baby-faced; his features are soft and smooth, his expressions sweet, almost effeminate; his eyes are light blue, wide open, innocent. Ryan's face is mature and lined, the jaw and mouth strong and hard set; his expressions are sour and cynical; his eyes are dark, narrow, piercing, malevolent. Billy's fair complexion, blond (almost white) hair, and white shirt contrast with Claggart's dark hair and clothing. Billy's voice is soft, sometimes melodious; Claggart's is deep, unctuous, cold.

way, the owner is out front, sweeping up the pieces of glass that used to be his large front window. Lonnie notices the broken window and observes, "You must have had quite a brawl in here last night." The owner replies, "I had *Hud* in here last night, that's what I had." The man's emphasis on the name "Hud" and his tone of voice clearly reveal that "Hud" is a synonym for "trouble." A complex and intriguing characterization is provided through the conversations of other characters about Rick (Humphrey Bogart) in *Casablanca* before the character is ever seen on the screen. An effective bit of reactive characterization is also seen in *Shane,* as the gunfighter Wilson (Jack Palance), a personification of pure evil, walks into a saloon, empty except for a mangy dog curled up under a table. As Wilson enters, the dog puts his ears back and his tail between his legs and slinks fearfully out of the room.

Characterization Through Contrast: Dramatic Foils

One of the most effective techniques of characterization is the use of **foils**— contrasting characters whose behavior, attitudes, opinions, lifestyle, physical appearance, and so on are the opposite of those of the main characters (Figure 3.18). The effect is similar to that achieved by putting black and white together—the black appears blacker and the white appears whiter. The tallest giant and the tiniest person might be placed side by side at the carnival sideshow, and the filmmaker sometimes uses characters in much the same way. Consider, for example, the effective contrasts in the television characters played by Andy Griffith and Don Knotts on the old *Andy Griffith Show*. Griffith, as Sheriff Taylor, was tall and a little heavy, and he projected a calm, self-confident, easygoing personality. Knotts, as Deputy Fife, was the exact opposite—short, skinny, insecure, and a bundle of nerves. The strange love story of the main characters in *Harold and Maude* also turns on characterization through contrast.

As the movie poster reads: "Harold's 20 and in love with death . . . Maude's 80 and in love with life."

Characterization Through Caricature and Leitmotif

In order to etch a character quickly and deeply in our minds and memories, actors often exaggerate or distort one or more dominant features or personality traits. This device is called **caricature** (from the technique used in cartooning). In television's *M*A*S*H*, the perpetual womanizing of Hawkeye Pierce (Alan Alda) and the eternal naiveté, innocence, and keen hearing of Radar O'Reilly (Gary Burghoff) are examples of caricature, as, in film, are Felix Unger's (Jack Lemmon) obsession with neatness and Oscar Madison's (Walter Matthau) messiness in *The Odd Couple*. A physical feature, such as the way a person moves, may also be caricatured, as seen in John Mahoney's exaggerated, stiff-legged limp in his portayal of the Crane father on *Frasier*, or in Michael Richards's manic entrances through Jerry Seinfeld's apartment door as neighbor Cosmo Kramer. Voice qualities and accents may also function in this way, as illustrated by the unmistakable voices employed by Dan Castellaneta and Julie Kavner as Homer and Marge Simpson, and Megan Mullally as Karen Walker on "Will and Grace."

A similar means of characterization, **leitmotif,** is the repetition of a single action, phrase, or idea by a character until it becomes almost a trademark or theme song for that character. Because it essentially exaggerates and emphasizes (through repetition), such a device acts very much like caricature. Examples of leitmotif might be seen in the repeated Fred Astaire dance routines performed by the prosecuting attorney (Ted Danson) in *Body Heat* or in the repetition of the phrase "sports fans" by Colonel Bull Meechum (Robert Duvall) in *The Great Santini*. One of the union henchmen in *On the Waterfront* adds dignity to his yes-man role by constantly using the word *definitely*. Perhaps Charles Dickens rates as the all-time master of both techniques. Recall Uriah Heep from *David Copperfield*, who continually wrings his hands (caricature) and says, "I'm so 'umble" (leitmotif). Modern films still employ such techniques effectively, although not quite as extensively (Figure 3.19). In Quentin Tarantino's *Kill Bill, Vol. 2*, the title character's playing of his flute creates a leitmotif.

Characterization Through Choice of Name

One important method of characterization is the use of names possessing appropriate qualities of sound, meaning, or connotation. This technique is known as **name typing.** A screenwriter usually thinks out his characters' names very carefully, as Paul Schrader's choice of name for the Robert De Niro character in *Taxi Driver* illustrates:

> It has to be euphonious, because you want people to repeat the name. . . . And Travis Bickle was successful in that way. . . . Beyond that, you want to have at least one component which is evocative and/or symbolic. Travis is evocative rather than symbolic, Travis/travel. . . . Then Bickle. Travis is romantic, evocative, and soft—and Bickle is hard, an unpleasant name. And it fits the character.[8]

FIGURE 3.19 Leitmotif   In this scene from *Blood Work*, retired FBI profiler Terry McCaleb is examined by the cardiologist (Angelica Huston) who performed his recent heart transplant. Throughout the film, director-actor Clint Eastwood, who plays McCaleb, frequently touches his chest—a gesture that works as a suspenseful leitmotif that reminds the viewer of this tough-but-aging hero's vulnerability.

Because a great deal of thought goes into the choice of names, they should not be taken for granted but should be carefully examined for the connotations they communicate. The connotations of some names, such as Dick Tracy, are rather obvious and clear: Dick is slang for *detective;* Tracy derives from the fact that detectives trace criminals. Other names may have only generalized connotations. Gomer Pyle has a small-town or country-hick ring to it; Cornelius Witherspoon III has an opposite kind of sound. Certain sounds in names have unpleasant connotations. The "sn" sound, for example, evokes unpleasant associations, because a large majority of the words beginning with that sound are unpleasant—*snide, sneer, sneak, snake, snail, sneeze, snatch, snout,* and *snort* are a few examples. Thus, a name like Snerd or Snavely has an unpleasant ring automatically (Figure 3.20). Sometimes a name draws its effect from both its meaning and its sound, such as William Faulkner's Flem (read "phlegm") Snopes. In this vein, because of the connotative power of names, film actors' names are often changed to fit the image they project. John Wayne's real name was Marion Morrison; Cary Grant's was Archibald Leach.

Varieties of Characters

Another method for analyzing film characterization utilizes three different types of pairings: stock characters and stereotypes, static versus dynamic characters, and flat versus round characters.

Stock Characters and Stereotypes   It is not essential or even desirable for every character in a film to have a unique or memorable personality. **Stock characters** are minor characters whose actions are completely predictable or typical of their job or profession (such as a bartender in a western). They are in the film simply because the situation demands their presence. They serve as a natural part of the setting, much as stage properties like a lamp or a chair might function in a play.

FIGURE 3.20 **Name Typing**   In *Shadow of the Vampire,* director E. Elias Merhige "recreated" the life of a real silent film actor with the singular name Max Schreck. In this fanciful horror film, Schreck's ironically apt name evokes the mystery and danger within a fictional character played by actor Willem Dafoe.

Stereotypes, however, are characters of somewhat greater importance to the film. They fit into preconceived patterns of behavior common to or representative of a large number of people, at least a large number of fictional people. Examples of stereotypes are the rich playboy, the western hero's sidekick, the pompous banker, and the unmarried aunt. Our preconceived notions of such characters allow the director to economize greatly in treating them.

Static Versus Dynamic or Developing Characters   It is often useful to determine whether the most important characters in a film are static or dynamic characters. **Developing characters** are deeply affected by the action of the plot (internal, external, or both) and undergo some important change in personality, attitude, or outlook on life as a result of the action of the story (Figure 3.21). The change they undergo is an important, permanent one, not just a whimsical shift in attitude that will change back again tomorrow. The character will never be the same person he or she was when the action of the film began.

The change can be of any type but is significant to the total makeup of the individual undergoing the change. Dynamic characters become sadder or wiser, or happier and more self-confident. They might gain some new awareness of life, become more mature or more responsible, or become more moral or less so. They may become simply more aware and knowing and less innocent or naive. Examples of developing characters include T. S. Garp (Robin Williams) in *The World According to Garp,* Tom Joad (Henry Fonda) in *The Grapes of Wrath,* and Michael Corleone (Al Pacino) in *The Godfather.*

Static characters remain essentially the same throughout the film (Figure 3.22). The action does not have an important effect on their lives (as might generally be the case with the hero of an action/adventure film). Or they are insensitive

FIGURE 3.21 Developing or Dynamic Characters Some film characters undergo important personality change or growth in the course of a film—change that permanently alters their attitudes about life. Such is the case with the title character in *Michael Clayton* (top left, with George Clooney), the Jim Carrey character in *The Truman Show* (top right), and Helen Mirren's Elizabeth II in *The Queen* (bottom).

FIGURE 3.22 Static Characters Some film characters are not capable of growth or have such strong personalities that they remain unaffected by the important action of the film. This is comically true with Sally Hawkins's character in *Happy Go Lucky* (left) and pathetically so with the Judi Dench character in *Notes on a Scandal* (right).

to the meaning of the action and thus are not capable of growth or change, as is the case with the title character in *Hud* (Paul Newman) and, perhaps, with Charles Foster Kane (Orson Welles) in *Citizen Kane*.

Screenwriter Robert Towne (*Chinatown*) feels that static characters are essential to comedy and dynamic characters are necessary for serious drama: "[A]lmost implicit in comedy is something that is repetitious, static. . . . Repetitive or even compulsive behavior is what *makes* comedy. . . . In dramatic writing the very *essence* is character change."[9]

Flat Versus Round Characters Another important distinction exists between flat characters and round characters. **Flat characters** are two-dimensional, predictable characters who lack the complexity and unique qualities associated with psychological depth. They often tend to be representative character types rather than real flesh-and-blood human beings. Unique, individualistic characters who have some

FIGURE 3.23 **Allegory** In *Hiroshima, Mon Amour* (right), director Alain Resnais creates a haunting allegory about love and war, focusing on the need for remembering profound and traumatic experiences. In *High Noon* (left), Gary Cooper plays a duty-bound lawman who must single-handedly face down revenge-bent desperadoes because the cowardly townspeople have deserted him. The film is generally considered to be an allegory of the McCarthy purge in Hollywood.

degree of complexity and ambiguity and who cannot easily be categorized are called **round characters** or **three-dimensional characters.**

Round characters are not inherently superior to flat characters. The terms merely imply how different characters function within the framework of a story. In fact, flat characters may function *better* than round characters when attention needs to be directed away from personalities and toward the meaning of the action—for example, in an allegory.

ALLEGORY

A story in which every object, event, and person has an abstract (as opposed to merely concrete) meaning is known as an **allegory.** In allegory, each element is part of an interdependent system that tells a clear, separate, complete, didactic story on a purely figurative level (Figure 3.23).

A major problem with allegory is the difficulty of making both levels of meaning (the concrete and the figurative) equally interesting. Often, so much importance is placed on the figurative story that we lose interest in the concrete story. Unfortunately, allegorical characters, to be effective as emblems, cannot have many unique characteristics, for the more specific the characters are, the less representative they may be. But these difficulties do not necessarily prevent allegory from being effective in cinematic form, as is evidenced by such excellent films as *Woman in the Dunes, Swept Away . . . by an unusual destiny in the blue sea of August* (1975), *Lord of the Flies* (1963), and *The Seventh Seal.* In both film and literature, however, the most frequently used (and more subtle) method of conveying meaning beyond the literal involves symbolism.

SYMBOLISM

In the most general terms, whether in a work of art or in everyday communications, a **symbol** is something that stands for something else. It communicates that something else by triggering, stimulating, or arousing previously associated ideas in the mind of the person perceiving the symbol.

All forms of human communication involve the use of symbols. We understand the meaning of a symbol if we already possess the ideas or concepts associated with or built into the symbol. A traffic light, for example, communicates its message symbolically. When the light turns green or red, we do more than observe with interest the change from one color to another; we respond to the symbolic message it gives. To a person who has never seen a traffic light, however, the change in color has no symbolic meaning. Therefore, it would be very dangerous for that person to walk around in the heart of a busy city at rush hour.

Approaching a work of art requires some understanding of the nature, function, and importance of its symbols. Almost anything can take on symbolic meaning in a film. In many stories, the setting has strong symbolic overtones. Characters are often used symbolically, and once characters become symbolic, the conflicts in which they take part become symbolic also. Therefore, it is essential to become aware of the special nature of symbolic communication in film.

In any story form, a symbol is something (a particular object, image, person, sound, event, or place) that stands for, suggests, or triggers a complex set of ideas, attitudes, or feelings and thus acquires significance beyond itself. A symbol is a special kind of energized communication unit that functions somewhat like a storage battery (or better, in this digital age, a "nonvolatile" USB flash memory device). Once a symbol is charged with a set of associations (ideas, attitudes, or feelings), it is capable of storing those associations and communicating them any time it is used.

Universal and Natural Symbols

Filmmakers can use universal symbols, or they can create symbols for a particular film. Universal symbols are precharged—ready-made symbols infused with values and associations that most of the people in a given culture understand. By using objects, images, or persons that automatically evoke complex associations, filmmakers save themselves the job of creating each of the associated attitudes and feelings within the context of each film. They need only use symbols appropriately to make full use of their communication potential. Thus, the American flag (triggering the complex set of feelings and values that we associate with America) and the cross (evoking a variety of values and feelings associated with Christianity) can be used effectively as symbols for a broad audience. Viewers' reactions will vary according to their attitudes toward the ideas represented, but all people from the same culture will understand the general symbolic message.

Many universal symbols are charged with their meanings externally—through past associations with people, events, places, or ideas—rather than through their own inherent characteristics. For example, there is nothing inherent in the shape of a cross to suggest Christianity; rather, the religious values and ideas attached over the ages to the crucifixion of Christ have given the cross its symbolic meaning.

Some objects, however, have natural or inherent qualities that make them particularly well suited to be symbols. A buzzard is an easily recognized symbol of death. Buzzards are black, a color associated with death, and the habits of the buzzard also make it an effective symbol. A buzzard is a scavenger, a creature that feeds only on dead flesh and will not even come near a living creature. Also important is the buzzard's visibility: By soaring in long, lazy circles over an area where something is dead or dying, the buzzard signals the presence of death. Thus, buzzards communicate the idea of death indirectly but clearly, so an observer need not see the dead object itself to know that death is present. The habits or lifestyles of hawks and doves are equally significant in determining their symbolic meaning.

Creating Symbolic Meanings

In many cases, filmmakers cannot depend on precharged symbols but must create symbols by charging them with meaning derived from the context of the film itself. They do this by loading a concrete object or image with a charge of associations, feelings, and attitudes and then employing it to evoke those associations. In charging an object with symbolic value, storytellers have a dual purpose. First, they want to expand the meaning of the symbolic object in order to communicate meanings, feelings, and ideas. Second, they want to make clear that the object is being treated symbolically. Thus, many of the methods used to charge an object symbolically also serve as clues that the object is taking on symbolic value.

There are four principal methods of charging symbols:

1. **Repetition.** Perhaps the most obvious way of charging an object is by drawing attention to it more often than a simple surface object might seem to deserve. Repetition increases the significance and symbolic power of the object at each appearance (Figure 3.24).

2. **Value Placed on an Object by a Character.** An object is charged symbolically when a particular character places value and importance on it. By showing extraordinary concern for an object (as in the father's obsession with his Windex bottle in *My Big Fat Greek Wedding*), or by repeatedly mentioning an object or idea in the dialogue, the character indicates that an object or idea has more than ordinary significance. Symbols charged in this way may be of relatively minor importance, functioning only to offer insight into the character. Or they may have major significance to the overall dramatic structure, as illustrated by the famous "Rosebud" symbol in *Citizen Kane*—or, more significantly, the glass snow globe used in the Welles film (Figure 3.25).

3. **Context.** Sometimes an object or image takes on symbolic power simply through its placement in the film, and its symbolic charge is built up through associations created (1) by its relationship to other visual objects in the same frame, (2) by the editorial juxtaposition of one shot with another, or (3) by the object's importance in the film's structure.

   A symbolic image in the film version of Tennessee Williams's play *Suddenly, Last Summer*—the Venus flytrap—illustrates all three methods of charging an image through context. The Venus flytrap is a large,

FIGURE 3.24 Repeated Images of Symbolic Separation In this scene from *Shane*, the farmer's wife, Marian (Jean Arthur), stands inside the house while Shane (Alan Ladd), the ex-gunfighter who is now the farmer's hired hand, stands outside looking in the window. This symbolic separation is repeated visually throughout the film. Shane is always an outsider, present with but not part of the warm family circle or the close-knit group of farmers. On several occasions, Shane is framed through an open doorway, looking in on a warm family scene or sitting off to the side by himself in a meeting of the farmers. The scene shown here has additional levels of meaning: Shane and Marian have a strong but unspoken mutual attraction but keep a wall between themselves out of basic human decency and their mutual love and respect for the farmer (Van Heflin).

white-flowered plant whose leaves have two hinged blades. When an insect enters the space between them, the blades close like a mouth, trapping the insect inside. The plant then feeds on the insect. In *Suddenly, Last Summer*, once the nature of the plant and its feeding habits are made clear, the Venus flytrap is used to suggest or represent a major idea—the carnivorousness or cannibalism of the characters.

The plant's nature is explained by Mrs. Venable (Katharine Hepburn), and the plant occupies a position near her chair so they share the same visual frame. As Mrs. Venable talks about her dead son, Sebastian, we begin to see the relationship between the woman and the plant, for her conversation reveals her to be a cannibal, savagely feeding on and deriving her nourishment from the memory of her son. The same effect could be achieved through

FIGURE 3.25 **Symbolic Details**   One critic, Robert Carringer, has convincingly argued that the most potently charged symbol in *Citizen Kane* is a simple glass paperweight—a snow globe that is broken in the film's famous opening scene.

editorial juxtaposition—by cutting immediately from a close-up of Mrs. Venable's mouth as she drones on about her son to a close-up of the jaws of her Venus flytrap snapping shut on an unsuspecting insect.

Even if it were not repeatedly charged within the context of the film, the Venus flytrap could still function as a symbol. Consider, for example, how the image might be used only at the beginning and the end of the film: As the film begins, a close-up of the Venus flytrap serves as a background to the titles. Then, as the titles draw to a close, an insect lands on the flower and is trapped as the jaws close suddenly around it. The plant is not seen again until the film's closing shot, where it appears, seducing another insect into its folds. In this case its position in the film's structure would force us to consider its symbolic function and its meaning to the film as a whole. The film *Cabaret* uses distorted images of Nazi armbands in this same manner.

4. **Special Visual, Aural, or Musical Emphasis.** Film has unique ways of charging and underscoring symbols and providing clues that an object is to be seen as a symbol. Visual emphasis may be achieved through dominant colors, lingering close-ups, unusual camera angles, changes from sharp to soft focus, freeze frames, or lighting effects. Similar emphasis can also be achieved

through sound effects or use of the musical score. Individual natural sounds or musical refrains can become symbolic in their own right if complex associations are built into them by any of the three methods discussed above.

Although filmmakers want to express their ideas clearly, they may not always want to express them too simply. Thus, some symbols may be very clear, and others may be complex and ambiguous. Symbols of the latter type can seldom be interpreted with one obvious and certain meaning; there may be no single right answer to what a given symbol means, but several equally valid but different interpretations. This is not to say that a filmmaker using ambiguous symbols is deliberately trying to confuse us. The intention is usually to use complexity to enrich or enhance the work.

Symbolic Patterns and Progressions

Although symbols may function singly without a clear relationship to other symbols, they often interact in what might be called *symbolic patterns*. In such a case, the filmmaker expresses the same idea through several symbols instead of relying on just one. The resulting symbolic pattern may have a certain progression, so that the symbols grow in value or power as the film develops.

An excellent example is the complex pattern of symbols that gradually builds up to the climax of *Suddenly, Last Summer*. The idea of a savage universe inhabited by creatures who devour each other is established by the Venus flytrap and Mrs. Venable. Other symbolic images with the same meaning are used to achieve a pattern of ever increasing dramatic power. The third symbolic image in this pattern appears in Mrs. Venable's description of a sight she and her son Sebastian had witnessed on the Encantadas:[10] "... the just-hatched seaturtles ... started their race to the sea.... To escape the flesh-eating birds that made the sky almost as black as the beach! ... And the sand was all alive, all alive, as the hatched seaturtles made their dash for the sea, while the birds hovered and swooped to attack and hovered and—swooped to attack!"

Having set up three symbols for the same idea (the Venus flytrap, Mrs. Venable, and the birds), the playwright gives us a suggestion of their significance as Mrs. Venable continues her story by relating how Sebastian had been horrified, exclaiming, " 'Well, now I've seen Him,' and he meant God.... He meant that God shows a savage face to people and shouts some fierce things at them, it's all we see or hear of Him...."

The next shocking image in the pattern occurs when Sebastian's friend Catherine (Elizabeth Taylor) remembers, "Cousin Sebastian said he was famished for blonds, ... that's how he talked about people, as if they were—items on a menu—... I think because he was nearly half-starved from living on pills and salads...." The pattern continues to develop through an effort to link the children that constitute this image with the earlier vision of the carnivorous birds: "a band of frightfully thin and dark naked children that looked like a flock of plucked birds ... would come darting up to the barbed wire fence ... crying out 'Pan, pan, pan!' ... The word for bread, and they made gobbling voices with their little black mouths ... with frightful grins!"

At the film's climax, the image of the carnivorous birds is repeated, but this time on a completely human level, which makes it even more shocking:

> Sebastian started to run and they all screamed at once and seemed to fly in the air. . . . I screamed. I heard Sebastian scream . . . just once. . . . I ran down . . . screaming out "Help" all the way. . . . Cousin Sebastian had disappeared in the flock of featherless little black sparrows, he—he was lying naked as they had been naked against a white wall, and this you won't believe, nobody has believed it, nobody would believe it, nobody, nobody on earth could possibly believe it, and I don't blame them!—they had devoured parts of him.

This incident takes place in a village whose name is also symbolic: Cabeza de Lobo, which means "Head of the Wolf," another savage and carnivorous image.

Thus, by means of a complex pattern of symbols, the film makes a statement about the human condition. The idea of Earth as a savage jungle where creatures devour each other is made clear by a series of symbols: the Venus flytrap, the turtle-devouring birds, Sebastian's own hungers, and the little human cannibals of Cabeza de Lobo. Williams has arranged these symbols so that they become increasingly vivid, powerful, and shocking as the story unfolds.

Symbolic Values in Conflict

Some conflicts in films are self-contained and have no meaning beyond themselves. Most conflicts, however, tend to take on symbolic qualities so that the individuals or the forces involved represent something beyond themselves. It seems natural for the forces in opposition to align themselves with different generalized concepts or value systems, and even the most ordinary whodunit and typical western at least vaguely imply a conflict between law and order and lawlessness and chaos, or simply between good and evil. Other symbolic ideas that might be represented by a film's conflict are civilization versus barbarism, sensual versus spiritual values, change versus tradition, idealism versus pragmatism, and the individual versus society. Almost any conflict can be stated in symbolic or generalized terms. Because comprehension of such symbolic interpretations is often essential to identifying and understanding a film's theme, the major conflict should be analyzed on both the literal and the symbolic levels.

Metaphors

Closely related to symbolism is the filmmaker's use of **visual metaphors.** Whereas a symbol stands for or represents something else, a visual metaphor is a comparison that helps us better understand an image because of its similarity to another image. This comparison is usually achieved through the editorial juxtaposition of two images in two successive shots. An example is a metaphor in Sergei Eisenstein's *Strike:* Shots of workers being pursued and killed are alternated with shots of a butcher slaughtering a bull.

In this example, the secondary image (the butchering) is extrinsic—that is, it has no place within the context of the scene itself but is imposed artificially into the scene by the filmmaker. In a realistic or naturalistic film, **extrinsic metaphors** may seem forced, heavy-handed, or even ludicrous, destroying a sense of reality that may be very important to the film. In contrast, comedy or fantasy films can use such

FIGURE 3.26 **Visual Metaphors**   In Jean-Pierre Jeunet's *Amélie*, a young waitress (Audrey Tatou) experiences great conflicts about the direction her life will take. Whether she is merely enjoying a movie or trying to assist her father and her neighbors in amusing ways, the director manages to translate the tensions of Amélie's inner reality into delightful images. A world-travelling garden gnome plays a significant role, for example, and at one point, the protagonist is literally reduced to a puddle of love.

images freely, as can serious films that stress an interior or subjective viewpoint. The French film *Amélie* relishes its judicious use of such metaphors, which sometimes also serve as visual puns (Figure 3.26).

Intrinsic metaphors emerge directly from the context of the scene itself and are more natural and usually more subtle than extrinsic metaphors. *Apocalypse Now* contains an intrinsic metaphor very similar to the extrinsic butchering metaphor in Eisenstein's *Strike*. While Captain Willard (Martin Sheen) is in the temple carrying out his assignment—"terminating Kurtz (Marlon Brando) with extreme prejudice"—the camera cuts to the courtyard, where a giant bull is axed in a gruesome ritual sacrifice.

The dramatic power and communicative effectiveness of any symbol or metaphor depend also on originality and freshness. A tired and worn-out symbol can no longer convey profound meanings, and a metaphor that has become a cliché becomes a hindrance rather than a help. This is problematic in watching older films, for metaphors and symbols that are clichés today might actually have been fresh and original when the film was made.

Overreading Symbolism

However, symbolic interpretation can be carried to ridiculous extremes, as an Alfred Hitchcock collaborator, screenwriter Ernest Lehman, reveals:

> Hitch and I used to laugh sometimes when we read about the symbolism in his pictures, particularly in *Family Plot*. . . . [S]ome French journalist had the license plate in the picture all worked out: 885 DJU. . . . When he got through explaining it, I said, "I hate to tell you this, but the reason I used that license plate was that it used to be my own. . . ." So much for symbolism.[11]

We should always keep in mind that although decoding a film's symbols may lead to rich and profound insights, it can also be carried to the point of absurdity. As Sigmund Freud, the granddaddy of symbolism, once put it: "Sometimes a cigar is just a cigar."

IRONY

Irony, in the most general sense, is a literary, dramatic, and cinematic technique involving the juxtaposition or linking of opposites. By emphasizing sharp and startling contrasts, reversals, and paradoxes, irony adds an intellectual dimension and achieves both comic and tragic effects at the same time. To be clearly understood, irony must be broken down into its various types and explained in terms of the contexts in which it appears.

Dramatic Irony

Dramatic irony derives its effect primarily from a contrast between ignorance and knowledge. The filmmaker provides the audience with information that a character lacks. When the character speaks or acts in ignorance of the true state of affairs, the dramatic irony functions to create two separate meanings for each line of dialogue: (1) the meaning of the line as it is understood by the unenlightened character (a literal or face-value meaning), and (2) the meaning of the line to the enlightened audience (an ironic meaning, opposite to the literal meaning).

By knowing something that the character does not know, we gain pleasure from being in on the joke or secret (Figure 3.27). In Sophocles' drama *Oedipus Rex*, for example, Oedipus does not realize that he has already killed his father and married his mother when he refers to himself as "the child of Good Luck" and "the most fortunate of men." Because *we* are aware of the truth, we hear the line as a painful joke. On a less serious plane is an example from *Superman*. Although *we* know that Clark Kent is really Superman, Lois Lane does not. Therefore, every time Lois accuses Clark of cowardice because he disappears whenever trouble starts, we have to chuckle because of our inside knowledge.

Dramatic irony may function in a purely visual way, either for comic effect or to build suspense, when the camera shows us something that the character on the screen cannot see. For example, a character trying to elude a pursuer in a comic chase may be crawling toward the same corner as his pursuer, but only *we* see and anticipate the coming shock of sudden confrontation. Horror films employ similar scenes to both intensify and prolong suspense. Because of its effectiveness in enriching the emotional and intellectual impact of a story, dramatic irony has been a popular technique in literary and dramatic art since Homer employed it in the *Odyssey;* and it remains popular and effective to this day.

Irony of Situation

Irony of situation is essentially an irony of plot. It involves a sudden reversal or backfiring of events, so that the end result of a character's actions is exactly the opposite of his or her intentions. Almost the entire plot structure of *Oedipus Rex*

FIGURE 3.27 Dramatic Irony In this scene from *Fatal Attraction*, Anne Archer, as Michael Douglas's wife, does not have an inkling that her husband has had a torrid affair with Glenn Close, who has appeared at their apartment pretending to be interested in leasing it. Because we not only know about the affair but also know that Close is capable of extremely bizarre behavior, this relatively ordinary scene is loaded with suspense and intensifies our sympathy for the unsuspecting Archer.

involves irony of situation: Every move that Oedipus and Jocasta make to avoid the prophecies actually helps to bring them about. This particular type of irony is often associated with the American short story writer O. Henry. An excellent example is his story "The Ransom of Red Chief," where two hoodlums kidnap a child who is such a demon that they end up having to pay his parents to take the boy back.

Irony of Character

Irony of character occurs when characters embody strong opposites or contradictions or when their actions involve sharp reversals in expected patterns of behavior. Oedipus, for example, is probably the most ironic character ever created, for the opposites built into his character constitute an almost endless list: He is both the detective and the murderer he is seeking; he sees, yet he is blind (in direct contrast to his foil, the blind "seer" Tiresias); he is the great riddle-solver, but he does not know his own identity; he is his mother's husband and his children's brother; and in the end, when he finally "sees," he blinds himself.

Irony of character may be present when a character violates our stereotyped view of him, as illustrated by this imaginary scene. Two soldiers, played by Woody Allen and John Wayne, are trapped in a foxhole by enemy gunfire. When mortar shells start falling around the foxhole, the John Wayne character panics, buries his head under his arm, and begins sobbing uncontrollably. The Woody Allen character puts his bayonet between his teeth, grabs a grenade in each hand, and charges the enemy position alone.

FIGURE 3.28 Irony of Setting   This idyllic lakeside scene (complete with blooming flowers) seems the perfect setting for a tender moment in *Frankenstein*, when the childlike monster finds a young friend who does not fear him. For a few brief moments, they share flowers and happily toss them into the water. Then the monster realizes he has no more flowers to toss and reaches out toward the girl. . . . In *Doubt*, the movie's title immediately strikes almost any viewer as ironic when the drama's setting is revealed to be a church/school where priests and nuns attempt to teach "true" knowledge and belief.

Irony of Setting

Irony of setting occurs when an event takes place in a setting that is exactly the opposite of the setting we usually expect for such an event—for example, a birth in a graveyard, or a murder in an idyllic setting (Figure 3.28).

Irony of Tone

Because film communicates simultaneously on several different levels, it is well suited for many types of irony, but irony of tone can be especially effective. In essence, irony of tone involves the juxtaposition of opposites in attitudes or feelings. In literature it is exemplified by Erasmus's *The Praise of Folly*. The reader must read between the lines to discover that the work is actually a condemnation of folly. Swift's classic essay "A Modest Proposal" is another example. The author's proposal—put forth in rational, calm, and modest style—is outrageous: The Irish people ought to sell their year-old children to be eaten like suckling pigs by the wealthy English landlords. In film, such irony may be effectively provided through contrasting emotional attitudes communicated simultaneously by the soundtrack and the visual image. Consider, for example, the juxtaposition of an optimistic "What a Wonderful World" that accompanies the bombing sequence in *Good Morning, Vietnam*.

Many different kinds of irony are possible in film because of film's ability to communicate on more than one level at a time. In fact, the multilayered nature can become so complex that its effect is difficult to describe. This is the case in the final scene of *Dr. Strangelove*, which combines three separate contrasting elements: (1) the visuals, composed of multiple shots of atomic mushroom clouds filmed in slow motion; (2) the soundtrack, where Vera Lynn's voice, sticky and sweet, sings "We'll Meet Again Some Sunny Day"; and (3) the action, which, significantly, is the end of all life as we know it. The irony is provided by the ingenious touch of the Vera Lynn song's adding a haunting quality to the pictorial element, so that we become aware of the almost breathtaking beauty of the mushroom clouds. This ironic combination of beauty and horror creates a powerful effect. Such moments are rare in film, but the filmgoer must be constantly aware of the potential for ironic expression in the musical score, in the juxtaposition of sight and sound, and in transitions of almost any kind.

Cosmic Irony

Although irony is basically a means of expression, the continuous use of ironic techniques might indicate that the filmmaker holds a certain philosophical attitude, or ironic worldview. Because irony pictures every situation as possessing two equal sides, or truths, that cancel each other out or at least work against each other, the overall effect of ironic expression is to show the ridiculous complexity and uncertainty of human experience. Life is seen as a continuous series of paradoxes and contradictions, characterized by ambiguities and discrepancies, and no truth is ever absolute. Such irony implies that life is a game in which the players are aware of the impossibility of winning and the absurdity of the game even while they continue to play. On the positive side, however, irony's ability to make life seem both tragic and comic at the same moment keeps us from taking things too seriously or too literally.

Looked at on a cosmic scale, an ironic worldview implies the existence of some kind of supreme being or creator. Whether this supreme entity be called God, Fate, Destiny, or the Force makes little difference. The implication is that the supreme being manipulates events deliberately to frustrate and mock humankind and is entertained by what is essentially a perpetual cruel joke on the human race.

Although irony usually has a humorous effect, the humor of cosmic irony bites deep. It can bring a laugh but not of the usual kind. It will be not a belly laugh but a sudden outward gasp of air, almost a cough, that catches in the throat between the heart and mind. We laugh perhaps because it hurts too much to cry.

ANALYZING FICTIONAL AND DRAMATIC ELEMENTS

On Story

How does the film stack up against the five characteristics of a good story?

1. How well is it unified in plot or storyline?
2. What makes the story credible? Pick out specific scenes to illustrate the kinds of truth that are stressed by the film:
   a. objective truth, which follows the observable laws of probability and necessity
   b. subjective, irrational, and emotional inner truths of human nature
   c. the semblance of truth created by the filmmaker
3. What makes the film interesting? Where are its high points and its dead spots? What makes you bored by the film as a whole or by certain parts?

4. Is the film a satisfying blend of simplicity and complexity?
   a. How well is the length of the story suited to the limits of the medium?
   b. Is the film a simple formula that allows you to predict the outcome at the halfway point, or does it effectively maintain suspense until the very end? If the ending is shocking or surprising, how does it carry out the tendencies of the earlier parts of the story?
   c. Where in the film are implication and suggestion effectively employed? Where is the film simple and direct?
   d. Is the view of life reflected by the story simple or complex? What factors influenced your answer?
5. How honest and sincere is the film in its handling of emotional material? Where are the emotional effects overdone? Where is understatement used?

On the Significance of the Title

1. Why is the title appropriate? What does it mean in terms of the whole film?
2. How many different levels of meaning are expressed in the title? How does each level apply to the film as a whole?
3. If the title is ironic, what opposite meanings or contrasts does it suggest?
4. If you recognize the title as being an allusion, why is the work or passage alluded to an appropriate one?
5. If the title calls your attention to a key scene, why is that scene important?
6. How is the title related to the theme?

On Dramatic Structure

1. Does the film use linear (chronological) or nonlinear structure? If it begins with expository material, does it capture your interest quickly enough, or would a beginning "in the middle of things" be better? At what point in the story could an *in medias res* beginning start?
2. If flashbacks are used, what is their purpose and how effective are they?

On Conflict

1. Identify the major conflict.
2. Is the conflict internal (individual against self), external, or a combination of the two? Is it primarily a physical or a psychological conflict?
3. Express the major conflict in general or abstract terms (for example, brains versus brawn, human being[s] against nature).
4. How is the major conflict related to the theme?

On Characterization

1. Identify the central (most important) character or characters. Which characters are static and which are developing? Which characters are flat and which are round?
2. What methods of characterization are employed and how effective are they?
3. Which of the characters are realistic and which are exaggerated for effect?
4. What about each character's motivation? Which actions grow naturally out of the characters themselves? Where does the filmmaker seem to be manipulating the characters to fit the film's purpose?

5. What facets of the central character's personality are revealed by what he or she chooses or rejects?
6. Which minor characters function to bring out personality traits of the major characters, and what do these minor characters reveal?
7. Pick out bits of dialogue, images, or scenes that you consider especially effective in revealing character, and tell why they are effective.
8. Which characters function as stock characters and stereotypes? How can their presence in the film be justified?

On Symbolism

1. What symbols appear in the film, and what do they represent?
2. What universal or natural symbols are employed? How effective are they?
3. Which symbols derive their meaning solely from their context in the film? How are they charged with symbolic value? (In other words, how do you know they are symbols and how do you arrive at their meaning?)
4. How are the special capabilities of film (the image, the soundtrack, and the musical score) employed to charge symbols with their meaning?
5. Which symbols fit into a larger pattern or progression with other symbols in the film?
6. How are the major symbols related to the theme?
7. Is the story structured around its symbolic meanings to the extent that it can be called an allegory?
8. Which symbols' meanings are clear and simple? Which symbols are complex and ambiguous? What gives them this quality?
9. Are visual metaphors employed effectively? Are they primarily extrinsic (imposed artificially on the scene by editing) or intrinsic (a natural part of the setting)?
10. How fresh and original are the film's symbols and metaphors? If they seem clichéd or timeworn, where have you encountered them before?

On Irony

1. What examples of irony can you find in the film?
2. Is irony employed to such a significant degree that the whole film takes on an ironic tone? Is an ironic worldview implied?
3. Do any particular examples of irony achieve comic and tragic effects at the same time?
4. Where in the film is suspense or humor achieved through dramatic irony?
5. How do the ironies contribute to the theme?

WATCHING FOR FICTIONAL AND DRAMATIC ELEMENTS

To locate the sequences for these video exercises using DVDs, simply identify and choose the appropriate chapters in the lists provided on most discs.

1. **Treatment of Emotional Material.** Watch the final segments of *Love Story* [1:28:03 to end] and *Terms of Endearment* [1:52:42 to end]. Describe the treatment of the emotional materials in each of the stories. Where is

understatement used? Which of the two films better mixes its emotions of sorrow with humor? How are special film techniques like music and visual elements employed? Which ending is the more powerful and why?

2. **Title Information.** In addition to the words of the title, the visual design of the title (the way it appears on the screen) also has significance. Look at the main titles and opening credits of *Bonnie and Clyde*, *Se7en*, *Fahrenheit 451*, *Splice*, *Vertigo*, and *To Kill a Mockingbird*. What is revealed in or suggested by the design of the titles and the way that information is put on the screen? How does the soundtrack or title music reinforce that information?

3. **Dramatic Structure.** Directors often structure scenes in unusual ways to achieve dramatic effects. Watch the "Tom Joad's Homecoming" scene from *The Grapes of Wrath* [0:23:04 to 0:28:42], and then answer these questions:
   a. Why do Tom and Casey hang around outside the house when they arrive, instead of going right in?
   b. What happens to Casey during this sequence? Why?
   c. Why do Connie and Rose of Sharon ride in the back of the truck instead of in the cab with Al?
   d. How are all these things important to the effectiveness of this sequence?

4. **Characterization.** Watch the first 20 minutes of *Casablanca*, paying special attention to every bit of information, both visual and verbal, that relates to the character Rick (Humphrey Bogart). What do we know about Rick at the end of this short segment?

5. **Symbolism**
   a. Watch the first 5 minutes of *Summer of '42*. During the opening voice-over, the camera very clearly charges an object with symbolic value. What is the symbolic object, how is its importance identified, and how does it relate to the film as a whole?
   b. Watch the last sequence in *Patton* [Part II: 1:06:00 to end]. While a voice-over tells us of the practice of honoring conquering Roman generals, a visual image suggests a symbolic facet of Patton's personality that has been repeated throughout the film. What is the image and what does it suggest?

6. **Irony.** Watch the final sequences of *Dr. Strangelove* [1:30:00 to end] and the baptismal sequence in *The Godfather*, and explain how the contrasting elements function together to create an extremely powerful effect. In your discussion, consider the role played by all the various film elements (visual details, dialogue, music, sound effects, editing, and so on).

MINI-MOVIE EXERCISE

[Some movies have virtually self-contained scenes or sections that can be lifted from their feature-film contexts and examined as if they were mini-movies themselves. The following suggestion is the first of many similar ones in this book. In

each case, follow the instructions for "isolating" these passages on readily available DVDs and study such "cinema samplers" as complete, unified works, rather than as mere fragments.]

Examine the fictional and dramatic elements in one of the most celebrated scenes in modern cinema: Chapter 10 ("The Conversation") of the "Special Edition" DVD version of Mike Nichols's 1967 film *The Graduate*. The location is a Taft Hotel guest room; the scene begins with Benjamin Braddock (Dustin Hoffman) begging Mrs. Robinson (Anne Bancroft) to talk, "this time," and ends with a directly contradictory request ("Let's not talk at all").

DVD FILMMAKING EXTRAS

The Art of Screenwriting

Taxi Driver (Collector's Edition):
An interactive feature makes it easy for the viewer to move back and forth between completed scenes and corresponding pages in Paul Schrader's shooting script. (*Note:* Many other DVDs advertise this kind of feature, but most of them work only through the DVD-ROM function.)

Across the Universe (Two-Disc Deluxe Edition):
In *Creating the Universe,* a thirty-minute documentary featurette, the controlling hand and imagination of director Julie Taymor appear to be the major narrative forces in this film—not the credited screenwriters.

For interviews and perspectives from other screenwriters, refer to the bonus features on the latest DVD releases of *A Beautiful Mind* (Akiva Goldsman), *Chinatown* (Robert Towne), *The Sound of Music* (Ernest Lehman), and *Gosford Park* (Julian Fellowes).

FILMS FOR STUDY

Affliction (1997)
All the King's Men (1949)
Amélie (2001)
Bad Education (2004)
Batman Begins (2005)
Billy Budd (1962)
Catch-22 (1970)
Citizen Kane (1941)
Collateral (2004)
The Contender (2000)
Cyrus (2010)
Dinner for Schmucks (2010)
Downfall (2004)
Frida (2002)
The Good Girl (2002)

Hustle & Flow (2005)
Identity (2003)
Last Year at Marienbad (1961)
Lord of the Flies (1963)
Million Dollar Baby (2004)
Napoleon Dynamite (2004)
The Passion of the Christ (2004)
Punch Drunk Love (2002)
Reservoir Dogs (1992)
Spirited Away (2001)
The Squid and the Whale (2005)

The Sweet Hereafter (1997)
Syriana (2005)
The Stunt Man (1980)
Taking Woodstock (2009)
Three Kings (1999)
Traffic (2000)
2046 (2004)
The Upside of Anger (2005)
A Very Long Engagement (2004)
The Village (2004)
Walk the Line (2005)
Woman in the Dunes (1964)

4 VISUAL DESIGN

The Diving Bell and the Butterfly

Production designers function as architects, interior designers, . . . historians, . . . diplomats, and, ultimately, observers of human behaviors—and all of the fragilities of the human heart. . . .

—WYNN THOMAS, PRODUCTION DESIGNER

The story, incorporating many of the fictional and dramatic elements discussed in Chapter 3 and shaped into a screenplay format, is the basis and the starting point for any film production. But even a beautifully structured and written screenplay is little more than a bare skeleton for a motion picture. The key members of the production team who together will plan the visual design or look of the film—the director, the cinematographer, the production designer, and the costumer—must analyze that skeleton. Each member of this team focuses on a single goal: creating a master plan for a consistent visual texture or style that is artistically suited to the film story to be told.

To accomplish this goal, the production team needs to answer a number of extremely important questions: Does the story to be filmed demand color, or would black and white be more effective? Do the story and its setting require a wide-screen format, or would the standard screen frame work better? What kind of lighting will best convey the mood or tone of the story? What aspects of the story's setting should be emphasized, and can this emphasis best be accomplished in a studio or on location? What kind of costumes and makeup will best fit the personalities and lifestyles of the characters? Answering these questions requires weighing a variety of complex factors.

COLOR VERSUS BLACK AND WHITE

Planning the look of a film begins with considering a question about the most basic element of a movie's style: Should the story be photographed in color or in black and white? Sixty years ago, this decision was a critical part of design planning for most movies. Color photography had become more than a novelty, and new film stocks and processing techniques were offering filmmakers opportunities for greater creativity and flexibility. But although color photography was quickly becoming the preference of movie audiences, many directors, cinematographers, and production designers maintained their loyalty to black and white. They felt that black-and-white images kept audiences focused on the characters and the story being told, helping them avoid distraction from gaudy, cluttered backgrounds. Some filmmakers believed that shooting in color was less artistic, because color photography did not require the subtle lighting they used when shooting in black and white. Director John Ford explains his preference for black and white: "[Color is] much easier than black-and-white for the cameraman. It's a cinch to work in. . . . For a good dramatic story, though, I much prefer to work in black-and-white; you'll probably say I'm old-fashioned, but black-and-white is real photography."[1]

Even as late as 1971, director Peter Bogdanovich consciously chose to film *The Last Picture Show* in black and white. He remembers, "I didn't want the film to look pretty. I didn't want it to be a nostalgia piece. . . . Color always had tendency to prettify, and I didn't want that."[2]

Eventually, the audience demand to see color images—both in the movie theater and on television screens—forced filmmakers to adapt and to develop new techniques that incorporated the subtleties of black-and-white filmmaking with the added richness and depth made possible by the use of color. Most modern filmmakers feel that color cinematography allows them to create more powerful, realistic images and to communicate better with audiences. As members of the design team plan the look of a film, they are likely to consider establishing a **color palette**—a limited number of specific colors used or emphasized throughout the film to subtly communicate various aspects of character and story to the viewer. Color used in this way becomes more than mere decoration for the film; it enhances the movie's dramatic elements. Cinematographer Nestor Almendros says, "I prefer color. The image carries more information. . . . As it reached its apogee, black-and-white cinematography ended its cycle and exhausted its practical possibilities. In color photography there is still room for experimentation."[3]

Although the role of black-and-white cinematography in modern film is greatly diminished, black and white is making a small comeback. It is sometimes contrasted with color images for various special effects. Since the late 1970s, however, more than 95 percent of all American feature films have been made in color. Thus, filmmakers need to stay current with developments in color photography and keep its impact on viewers in mind as they plan a movie's visual design. (For a detailed examination of the use of color, see Chapter 7.)

SCREEN FORMAT (ASPECT RATIO)

Another important element for the design team to consider is screen format—the size and shape of the projected image. The visual boundaries established for the image dictate the photographic composition of the frame and, according to cinematographer Almendros, help the audience know how to read beyond the obvious information provided on the screen: "I need the frame with its four sides. I need its limits. . . . By means of the camera's viewfinder, the outside world goes through a process of selection and organization. Things become pertinent; thanks to the parameters of the frame, they take shape in relation to vertical and horizontal limits."[4]

Essentially, there are two basic shapes (**aspect ratios**) for the projected image: standard screen and wide screen. The width of the **standard screen** (often called "Academy ratio") is approximately 1.33 times its height. The width of the **wide screen** (known by trade names such as **Cinemascope, Panavision,** and Vistavision) varies from 1.85 to 2.55 times its height. The different dimensions and shapes of these screens create different types of compositional problems (Figures 4.1, 4.2).

The wide screen lends itself to a panoramic view of a vast landscape or large numbers of people, as well as to the rapid motion characteristic of westerns, war dramas, historical pageants, and fast-paced action/adventure dramas. The standard screen is more suitable for an intimate love story set in a small apartment, requiring the frequent use of tight close-ups and very little movement of subjects in space. A wide screen can actually distort an image and detract from the film's visual effectiveness if the physical set is too narrow for its field of view. The wide-screen formats such as Cinemascope and Panavision, however, can contribute significantly to the effectiveness of horror or suspense films. A kind of visual tension is created by

STANDARD SCREEN–1.33:1

The *standard screen* was the dominant screen shape until 1953. The traditional television frame has these (or slightly wider) dimensions, as do *most* 16mm prints. Thus Cinemascope and other wide-screen films have visual information cut off on both sides in 16mm or older TV formats.

WIDE SCREEN–1.85:1

The wide screen is also called the *standard American wide screen* to distinguish it from its European counterpart, a slightly narrower format with a 1.66:1 aspect ratio. A popular compromise shape (between the standard screen and the ultrawide formats), the wide-screen image is achieved by masking off the top and bottom of the standard frame.

PANAVISION–2.2:1

Panavision is probably the most popular ultrawide system in use today, perhaps because its slightly narrower format is more flexible from a compositional standpoint than its predecessor, Cinemascope. Both Panavision and Cinemascope employ anamorphic lenses, which "squeeze" a wide image onto standard-frame 35mm film in the camera and then "stretch" the image into a wide-screen format when projected.

CINEMASCOPE–2.55:1

FIGURE 4.1 Popular Aspect Ratios Cinemascope can be said to have two aspect ratios. In the 1950s its dimensions were 2.55:1; it has since been narrowed slightly, to 2.35:1, to accommodate an optical soundtrack. When theaters began installing special screens for Cinemascope in the 1950s, many of the screens were curved slightly to enhance the three-dimensional effect. Although popular with the public, the system had many critics, among them director George Stevens, who claimed, "the wide screen is better suited to a boa constrictor than a man." The lines drawn on this shot from the wide-screen extravaganza *Ben-Hur* (1959) show the amount of side information lost when wide-screen films are reduced to the 16mm or traditional TV format.

a slow **panning** (horizontal moving) or dollying camera that heightens suspense by bringing new visual information into view at the outer edges of the screen, increasing our feeling of vulnerability. Most current films (and many TV projects) use a wide-screen ratio of 1:1.78 or larger.

FIGURE 4.2 **The Projected Image** The four different screen sizes and shapes are illustrated here by four different croppings of the same scene from *The Three Burials of Melquiades Estrada.*

a. Standard screen 1.33:1

b. Wide screen 1.85:1

c. Panavision 2.2:1

d. Cinemascope 2.35:1

FIGURE 4.3 Smooth-Grain Film Stock   Director Michael Patrick King appears to have used smooth-grain color film stock in *Sex and the City* to give his film the luscious, silky sheen we see in this scene that features his mostly female central cast.

FILM STOCK AND HIGH-DEFINITION VIDEOGRAPHY

Film stock may have an important effect on the visual image. **Smooth-grain film stock** produces an image that is extremely smooth, or slick. Such film also registers a wide range of subtle differences between light and dark, enabling the director to create fine tones, artistic shadows, and contrasts. Because of the clarity and artistic perfection of these images, they often have a more powerful visual impact than does reality.

Rough-grain film stock produces a rough, grainy-textured image with harsh contrasts between blacks and whites and almost no subtle contrasts. Because newspaper pictures and newsreels traditionally have had a coarse, rough-grain look, this type of film has become associated with a documentary here-and-now quality, as though reality had to be captured quickly, with little concern for clarity and artistic perfection.

A cinematographer may employ both types of stock for different effects. A romantic love scene would probably be shot with smooth-grain film (Figure 4.3), a riot or a furious battle scene with rough-grain film (Figure 4.4). Now, however, more and more frequently, even major Hollywood filmmakers are choosing to shoot in a digital, high-definition format instead of using film stock. Still, some high-profile players (including, most notably, Steven Spielberg and Christopher Nolan) have expressed a continuing devotion to exposing and editing real celluloid rather than manipulating pixels.

FIGURE 4.4 Rough-Grain Film Stock   The look of rough-grain film stock is simulated in many parts of first-time writer-director Courtney Hunt's crusty *Frozen River*. Here, for example, as the protagonist, played by Melissa Leo, transports a new partner (Misty Upham) to an illegal-immigrant deal, the camera peers through a dirt-spattered windshield that yearns to be a filmic metaphor for the pickup itself.

PRODUCTION DESIGN/ART DIRECTION*

Once decisions about color versus black and white, screen format, and film stock are made, the awesome task of production design gets under way, and "a true aptitude for movie magic is needed to . . . make moviegoers feel at home far, far away in another galaxy, turn New York City into a maximum security prison, or show how Los Angeles might look . . . in the year 2020."[5]

Modern production designers meet those sorts of challenges and finally are being recognized for their critical contributions to the look of modern films (Figure 4.5). The production designer first makes elaborate and detailed sketches and plans for the set and then supervises, down to the last detail, the construction, painting, furnishings, and decoration until he or she achieves the exact look intended. In every stage of filmmaking the production designer consults with three other people directly responsible for the visual texture of the film: the director, the cinematographer, and the costumer. All three work together closely, seeking each other's opinion, conferring, and coordinating their efforts to achieve a unified visual effect.

In the modern film, this collaboration is often so integrated that art directors are asked to suggest camera angles and lighting in their design—decisions that in

---

*There is some confusion about the difference between an art director and a production designer. The titles are synonymous when only one or the other is listed in the credits for a film. When both titles are listed, the production designer has conceived the look or visual texture of the film, and the art director has been responsible for supervising the work required to execute that plan.

FIGURE 4.5 **Award-Winning Design** The elaborate sets created for David Fincher's *The Curious Case of Benjamin Button*, including this one featuring backward-aging Brad Pitt won Academy Awards for production design (Donald Graham Burt and Victor J. Zolfo) and makeup (Greg Cannom).

the past were left completely to the director and cinematographer. Such requests make very good sense because production design has such a tremendous influence on the look of a film. It affects the cinematographer's choice of lighting, angles, and focus. Many overhead and low-angle shots in Tim Burton's *Batman*, for example, are literally dictated by Anton Furst's Oscar-winning sets of Gotham City, where they not only enhance the sense of vertical space but also make painted backdrops and miniature models more convincing. Likewise, the director's decisions about many other factors may be subtly altered by the mood created by a finely wrought set, as in *Metropolis, Blade Runner, Dark City, Moulin Rouge! (2001)*, and *Inception*.

The Script: The Starting Point

As is true at every step in the filmmaking process, the basic blueprint is the script. It is the script that provides the unity of vision for a film. As production designer Paul Sylbert puts it, "You cannot impose a style on a film. . . . Style in film results from every part of it, and those parts must cohere. . . . Design is not self-expression. It is an expressive use of objects, forms, and colors in the service of the script.[6]

Sometimes the script suggests visual metaphors and reinforces the need for a specific color palette, so that a few carefully chosen colors are emphasized to suggest a mood or atmosphere. For example, production designer Patrizia Von Brandenstein saw Mozart and Salieri, the two major characters in Milos Forman's *Amadeus*, as being polar opposites, and she incorporated that interpretation into her visual design: "everything about Salieri was . . . Italianate, full of passion, but from an older time, dark and turgid, heavy like the music—like the fabrics he wore, velvet and wool. . . . Mozart's world was reflective, bright, silvery, pastel, . . . faceted like his music. It was the music that drove the design."[7]

Paul Sylbert made similar use of visual metaphor in the design of Paul Schrader's *Hardcore*. He created two totally different environments through the use of two different color palettes:

> The first is the Calvinism of Grand Rapids, Michigan, and the second is the world of pornography. . . . The contrast . . . was between Calvinism and hell. . . . The narrowness of the palette of the Grand Rapids scenes—the brown tones and the blue delft and the wood—was a reflection of the spirit of Calvinism. . . . [O]nce I got into this new [porn] world, I was suddenly free to do anything. . . . I was allowed to go red, white, pink, orange, black, powder blue in the motel rooms and whorehouses. The wildness was a color version of the anarchy that went on in that other world.[8]

The production designer can also help to enhance concepts from the script by controlling the sense of space in a given scene (Figure 4.6). To emphasize the fearful power of Cardinal Wolsey in *A Man for All Seasons*, designer John Box created a strong sense of claustrophobia to portray Sir Thomas More's meeting with Wolsey:

> [Director] Fred Zinneman's intention was to present Wolsey as power and authority. That, to me, meant a feeling of claustrophobia which would accentuate the character and power of Wolsey, and would involve the audience with Thomas More as he was confronted by the great man of the time. So we put Wolsey in a small room to emphasize his largeness. He wears red robes, so we don't want any other colors to lead your eye away from the central figure, so the walls become a darker shade of the same red. There are no corners in the room. The table at which he sits is smaller than it would have been in reality, to accentuate Wolsey's size.[9]

Sometimes a production designer wants to do just the opposite—to create within a limited space the illusion of a large space. Using the technique known as **forced perspective,** the designer physically distorts certain aspects of the set and diminishes the size of objects and people in the background to create the illusion of greater foreground-to-background distance. Charles Rosher, cinematographer of F. W. Murnau's classic silent film *Sunrise*, describes the technique:

> I worked with a wide-focus lens of 35 to 55mm, for the scenes in the big cafe. All the sets had floors that sloped slightly upwards as they receded, and the ceilings had artificial perspectives: the bulbs hanging from them were bigger in the foreground than in the background. We even had dwarfs, men and women, on the terrace. Of course all this produced an amazing sense of depth.[10]

Setting and Its Effects

The **setting** is the time and place in which the film's story occurs. Although the setting may often seem unobtrusive or be taken for granted, it is an essential ingredient in any story and makes an important contribution to the theme or total effect of a film. Because of the complex interrelationships of setting with other story elements—plot, character, theme, conflict, symbolism—the effects of setting on the story being told should be analyzed carefully. And because of its important visual function, setting must also be considered a powerful cinematic element in its own right.

FIGURE 4.6 **The Claustrophobic Set**   In *Downfall (Der Untergang)*, a documentary-like account of the last days in the Third Reich, virtually all of the action occurs in the narrow confines of a fortified underground bunker, where, among other solemn (and some-times macabre) activities, Adolph Hitler (Bruno Ganz) says goodbye to his mistress, Eva Braun (Juliane Köhler), before his suicide (top). Bob Fosse, in directing *Cabaret* (bottom), demanded that most of the film be shot in a smoky, restricted space to create a feeling of constraint in both his actors (including Liza Minnelli) and his audience.

   In examining the setting as it relates to the story, it is necessary to consider the effect of four factors on the story as a whole:

1. **Temporal factors:** The time period in which the story takes place

2. **Geographic factors:** The physical location and its characteristics, including the type of terrain, climate, population density (its visual and psychological

impact), and any other physical factors of the locale that may have an effect on the story's characters and their actions

3. **Social structures and economic factors**

4. **Customs, moral attitudes, and codes of behavior**

Each factor has an important effect on the problems, conflicts, and character of human beings and must be considered as an integral part of any story's plot or theme.

Setting as Determiner of Character   The four aspects of setting listed above are important to understanding the naturalistic interpretation of the role of setting. This interpretation is based on the belief that our character, destiny, and fate are all determined by forces outside ourselves, that we may be nothing more than products of our heredity and environment, and that freedom of choice is only an illusion. Thus, by considering the environment a significant shaping force or even a dominant controlling one, this interpretation forces us to consider how environment has made characters what they are—in other words, how characters' nature has been dictated by factors such as their time in history, the particular place on Earth they inhabit, their position in the social and economic structure, and the customs, moral attitudes, and codes of behavior imposed on them by society. These environmental factors may be so pervasive that they serve as something much more important than a backdrop for the film's plot.

In some cases the environment may function as an antagonist in the plot. Protagonists may struggle against environmental forces pressing upon them, seeking to express some freedom of choice or escape from a trap. Thus, the serious consideration of the cruel, indifferent, or at least powerful forces of the environment is often a key to understanding a character and his or her dilemma. Director Sean Penn's *Into the Wild*, an adaptation of Jon Krakauer's nonfiction book, introduces a young protagonist who is quite literally trapped in a demanding natural landscape that he has naively chosen to inhabit.

Setting as Reflection of Character   The environment in which a person lives may provide the viewer with clues to understanding his or her character. This is especially true for the aspects of their environment over which individuals exercise some control. Houses, for example, may be excellent indicators of character. Their usefulness is illustrated by the following examples of exterior views that might appear in a film's opening shot.

Picture a small, neat, white, green-shuttered cottage with red roses around the doorstep and bright and cheerful curtains at the windows. It is surrounded by a newly whitewashed picket fence. Such a setting has been traditionally used in films to suggest the happy honeymoon couple, full of youth, vigor, and optimism for a bright future.

At the other extreme, consider the image evoked by Edgar Allan Poe's description of the Usher house in his classic short story "The Fall of the House of Usher": bleak gray walls, vacant eyelike windows, crumbling stones, rotten woodwork, and a barely perceptible zigzag crack in the masonry from roof to foundation. This

FIGURE 4.7 **Setting as a Reflection of Character** The vicious dark side of Mrs. Venable (Katharine Hepburn, seen here with Montgomery Clift) in *Suddenly, Last Summer* is reflected by her taste in art—this grotesque sculpture in her courtyard.

opening picture, a reflection of the Usher family's decadence, becomes even more significant as the story progresses, for Roderick Usher and the house in which he lives are so closely interwoven symbolically and metaphorically that they become one: The house's vacant eyelike windows portray the eyes of Roderick Usher, and the zigzag crack in the masonry is equated with the crack in Usher's mind.

The filmgoer must be aware of interactions between environment and character, whether the setting is serving as a molder of character or merely as its reflection (Figure 4.7).

Setting for Verisimilitude One of the most obvious and natural functions of the setting is to create a semblance of reality that gives the viewer a sense of a real time and a real place and a feeling of being there. Filmmakers recognize the great importance that an authentic setting plays in making a film believable. Thus, they may search for months to find a proper setting and then move crew, actors, and equipment thousands of miles to capture an appropriate backdrop for the story they are attempting to film.

To be convincing, the setting chosen should be authentic in even the most minute detail. In a film set in the past, even the slightest anachronism may be jarring. A filmmaker shooting a story about the Civil War must be careful that the skies do not show jet vapor trails or the landscapes do not include high-tension power lines.

Some films capture the unique qualities of the time and place in which they are set so effectively that these factors may become the most important elements of the film—more powerful and memorable than the characters or the storyline. *McCabe & Mrs. Miller, The Fifth Element, Blade Runner, The Last Picture Show, Northfork, Under the Tuscan Sun, Synecdoche, New York,* and (perhaps) *A Serious Man* are good examples of such films.

Setting for Sheer Visual Impact   When doing so is permissible within the limits of a film's theme and purpose, filmmakers choose a setting with a high degree of visual impact. For example, the plot and structure of westerns such as *Shane* and *True Grit* do not demand great scenery, but the filmmakers realized that the beauty of the wide western landscape, with its snowcapped mountains and rainbow-colored rock formations, would be effective as long as it did not violate the overall tone or atmosphere of the films. David Lean is especially successful in choosing settings with a powerful visual impact, as demonstrated in *Dr. Zhivago, Ryan's Daughter*, and *Lawrence of Arabia*. The barren Australian desert provides an otherworldly backdrop for the action of *The Road Warrior. Legends of the Fall*, filmed in western Canada, and *Out of Africa* owe much to the images of the landscapes behind their stories, as do both versions of *Insomnia* (1997, set in arctic Norway, and Christopher Nolan's 2002 remake, shot in Alaska).

Setting to Create Emotional Atmosphere   In certain specialized films, setting is important in creating a pervasive mood or emotional atmosphere. This is especially true in horror films and to some extent in the science fiction or fantasy film (such as the *Alien* films, Stanley Kubrick's *The Shining*, and James Cameron's *Avatar*), in which the unusually charged emotional atmosphere created and maintained by the setting becomes an important factor in achieving a suspension of disbelief by the viewer. Setting may also create a mood of tension and suspense in keeping with the overall tone of the film, in addition to adding credibility to plot and character elements (Figure 4.8).

Setting as Symbol   The setting of a film story may take on strong symbolic overtones when it is used to stand for or represent not just a location but some idea associated with the location, as in Agnieszka Holland's version of *The Secret Garden* (1993) and Steven Soderbergh's *Bubble*, which was shot entirely in a small Ohio–West Virginia border town. Another example of a symbolic environment is the garden setting for *Suddenly, Last Summer*. The "fantastic" garden becomes a symbol for the worldview reflected by the other symbols: Men are carnivorous creatures living in what is essentially a savage jungle in which they devour one another in a constant struggle of fang and claw, obeying only the law of the survival of the fittest. This worldview is delineated in Tennessee Williams's own description of his play's set, which is "like . . . the prehistoric age of giant fern-forests. . . . The colors . . . are violent . . . [and] massive tree-flowers . . . suggest organs of the body, torn out, still glistening with undried blood; . . . harsh cries and sibilant hissings [insinuate] beasts, serpents and birds, all of a savage nature. . . ."[11]

Setting as Microcosm   A special type of symbolic setting is the type known as a **microcosm,** meaning "the world in little," in which the human activity in a small and limited area is representative of human behavior or the human condition in the world as a whole. In such a setting special care is taken to isolate the characters from all external influences so that the "little world" seems self-contained. The limited group of people, which contains representative human types from various walks of life or levels of society, might be isolated on a desert island, in an

FIGURE 4.8 Setting for Emotional Atmosphere, Characterization, and Visual Impact   In sharp contrast to the drab, ordinary, run-down Bates Motel in *Psycho* (1960) is the Bates home, located on a hill behind the motel. Its strange, foreboding, haunted quality contributes immensely to the emotional atmosphere of the film. The house also contributes to the characterization of Norman Bates (Tony Perkins), as both reflection and determiner of his character. The starkness of the house, silhouetted against the sky, makes a strong visual impact.

airplane, on a stagecoach, or in a western town. The implication of the microcosm often comes very close to being allegorical: The viewer should see strong similarities between what happens in the microcosm and in the world at large, and the film's theme should have universal implications. Screenwriter Paddy Chayefsky has described his *Hospital* as a microcosm-of-society picture. The hospital represents an advanced, highly technical, and affluent society that is incapable of running itself. Films such as *Lord of the Flies*, *Ship of Fools*, and *High Noon* can all be seen as microcosms; television's *Gilligan's Island*, however, lacks the universal implications of a microcosm, though it possesses many microcosmic qualities.

Studio Versus Location Shooting

In recent years, production designers have been doing much of their work in studios because many directors are returning to the sound stages, preferring to stylize a realistic background rather than to go on location. There are three reasons for this preference. One is that many directors were raised on the studio-made products of the 1930s, 1940s, and 1950s and admired their look and feel so much that they are now trying to create similar styles in their own films. Another reason is the need to compete with made-for-television movies, which are usually filmed on location, have relatively small budgets, and pay less attention to visual texture and production design than do movies made for the big screen. A more impressive look is created for the big screen, where the attention, care, and expenditures necessary for obtaining the desired look can be better appreciated.

Perhaps the single most important reason why directors prefer to shoot a film in a studio is the completely controlled environment. Lighting can be easily manipulated in a studio; on location the primary light source, the sun, is constantly moving from east to west. In cities, traffic must usually be controlled in some way, and natural environmental sounds can be bothersome. Prolonged shooting in cities or residential areas can be very disruptive to everyday life, and residents often come to view movie crews with the hostility usually reserved for an army of occupation. (A major exception to this axiom, of course, involves director Cameron Crowe, who was able to shoot a dream sequence for *Vanilla Sky* with Tom Cruise for several hours in a completely deserted Times Square.)

The decision to go on location, however, is usually dictated by the script, and the work of the production designer is just as important on location as in the studio. He or she works closely with the director to choose the places where the film will be shot and then designs and oversees the construction of any sets needed on location. For *Days of Heaven* production designer Jack Fisk worked closely with director Terrence Malick to scout locations. When they finally found the perfect place in Canada (for a story set in Texas), the beauty of the rolling fields of wheat blowing in the wind reminded Fisk of the ocean, so he designed an unusual farmhouse with features that vaguely resembled a ship. To build this set required a battle with the producers, who wanted an ordinary-looking ranch house. Like most other designers, Fisk believes that audiences are disappointed with a truly realistic setting and expect to see a kind of heightened reality, which he attempts to provide.

A more realistic, contemporary story calls for a subdued form of heightened reality. Working on *The River* (1984), production designer Chuck Rosen was thrilled when a local man told him: "My Lord, Lord almighty, this farm here looks exactly like my granddaddy's farm." To achieve this look on location near Kingsport, Tennessee, had been no easy matter, however. Universal purchased 440 acres of mountain forest specifically for the movie. Sixty of those acres were leveled to create a river-bottom farm, and Rosen designed and constructed a two-story farmhouse, a main barn, an equipment building, and a double corncrib. A dam was built below the farm on the Holsten River, raising the water level by four feet, and a levee was built to keep the farm from flooding. Because filming continued into late November, bright autumn foliage had to be sprayed with green paint for summer scenes. In contrast, a huge cornfield by the river was planted late and was so well watered that four rows of corn had to be sprayed brown or replaced with dead stalks for the autumn flood scene. Although this was the first "60-acre set" Rosen had ever done, he achieved the main thing he had hoped for: "It looks like it belongs."[12]

Sometimes a script will force production designers to jump back and forth between a controlled studio set and a distant exterior location, creating the illusion that both sets are part of the same neighborhood. In *Raiders of the Lost Ark*, for example, Harrison Ford escapes from a huge rolling boulder in an interior cave set filmed in England and emerges from the cave in Hawaii (Figure 4.9).

FIGURE 4.9 **Composite Settings** Production designers are often required to create the illusion that two completely different sets in different locations are different parts of a single location. In this scene from *Raiders of the Lost Ark*, Harrison Ford is running to escape the huge rolling boulder in a cave interior set in England. A few seconds later in the film, he emerges from the cave into a sunlit exterior in Hawaii.

Period Pieces

A **period piece** is a film that takes place not in the present but in some earlier period of history. To recreate the look of a period, the production designer must do extensive architectural research. To get a feel for life in the period, the production designer reads books, letters, newspapers, and diaries. Martin Scorsese's *GoodFellas*, which begins in the 1950s and ends in the 1980s, provides an excellent example of all the factors that the production designer has to consider. Kristi Zea, *GoodFellas* production designer, recalls the project:

> The film presented a challenge for both the costumes and the sets, because there was a need for us to quickly reflect certain trends within each of the time periods. Overall, the make-up, hair, and clothing were more sensitive to time passage than the actual locations were. Of course, cars immediately give you a period. The fifties had a sepia-like, subtle color scheme. The cinematographer, Michael Ballhaus, actually changed the film stock to maximize the chromatic look of the sixties. The early seventies was pretty garish, too. Then the eighties were more somber, more kinetic, more drugged out. . . . The interior of the cab stand, the house, and everything from the fifties actually had a late forties look to it. They were poor; they wouldn't have brand-new furniture. . . . For the sixties scenes we wanted to say sixties. All of these guys had new cars. No one would drive around in a ten-year-old car, so that kept us in a very specific period.[13]

Living Spaces and Offices

To construct sets showing living quarters or offices, designers refer to the script to make decisions that support the story and the characters. Settings are consciously designed as personalized environments that reflect a character and underscore or

FIGURE 4.10 Settings as Personalized Environments   The book-stuffed space inhabited by Donald Sutherland and Keira Knightley (playing father and daughter) in Jane Austen's *Pride and Prejudice* (2005) and this starkly
furnished retail area (staffed by Claire Danes) in Steve Martin's *Shopgirl* are meant to speak volumes about the
films' personalities.

enhance the mood of each scene (Figure 4.10). Production designer Robert Boyle
(*North By Northwest*) describes the challenge:

> If the script says this is about a homeless person, you better do it within the parameters
> of the logic of the homeless. The first thing I ask is how much do these people make,
> what can they afford, because economics are the basis of our lives. Then I want to know
> who their friends are. I want to know what their educational background is: Did they
> go to college, did they drop out of high school, are they from the streets, or are they
> more earthy, country people? Then there's that whole range of sexual choice: Are
> they heterosexual or homosexual? You have to know all this before you can sit down
> with a pencil and start to draw.[14]

If the film is based on a novel, the designer may choose to go to the novel for
descriptive details about the setting and the character. A design with this kind of
research behind it can help the actor settle into the role and deliver a fuller, more
accurate performance.

When designing interior sets that have windows, the production designer
will also create a world outside, often using scenic backings that have been photographed. They provide an extra dimension to the film's world in the same way that
off-screen environmental sounds do.

Fantasy Worlds

Perhaps the most serious challenge that a production designer faces is building a
complete fantasy world. For *Blade Runner*, production designer Lawrence G. Paull
created a complete futurescape for the year 2020 by using additive architecture—
that is, by building protrusions onto existing structures. The structures used were
located on the New York street set in the back lot of Burbank Studios. *Blade Runner*
also required twenty-five interior sets, including one created inside an industrial
refrigerator locker. Through inventive production design and the use of practically
every technical trick in the book, Paull created a set that enabled director Ridley
Scott to "build layers of texture, so that visual information is imparted in every
square inch of screen" and to convince viewers that they have been transported to
another time and another place—in this case a time and place that no one has yet
experienced in reality (Figure 4.11).[15]

FIGURE 4.11 Inventive Production Design Lawrence G. Paull built multiple layers of texture into his set for *Blade Runner* so that director Ridley Scott could pack every square inch of the screen with visual information. The result was a set so powerful that it nearly overwhelms the characters and the story, even in action scenes featuring Harrison Ford.

COSTUME AND MAKEUP DESIGN

By the time the costume designer is called in, the production designer has already made many decisions about the look of the costumes. An integrated or coherent design synchronizes the colors of the set with the patterns and colors of the costumes. After the color palette is determined, many people, with widely differing degrees of control over decisions, enter into the total process of costume design: the director, the production designer, the costumer, and the actor, as well as the hairstylist and the makeup artist (Figure 4.12). Like production design, costume design begins with the script. Edith Head, the dean of American costume designers, describes the interaction of design team members and performers: "What we do is create an illusion of changing an actor or actress into someone else. It is a cross between magic and camouflage. . . . We have three magicians—hairstylist, makeup artist, and clothes designer—and through them we're supposed to kid the public that it really isn't Paul Newman, it's Butch Cassidy."[16]

To successfully transform an actor into his or her character requires that the actor feel a comfortable sense of rightness with the clothing. Charlton Heston, for example, made a point of wearing a costume as much as he could. He wanted the costume to feel like clothing, not like a costume. For many actors, the process of internalizing the character to be played really begins when they see themselves in costume.

A skilled costume designer can improve an actor's figure. The use of a little extra fabric can slim the appearance of a woman with a boxy, high-waisted build and create the illusion of a wonderful figure. In each *Die Hard* movie and in *Hudson Hawk*, the on-screen appearance of Bruce Willis, who is short in the leg and long in the body, was improved by costume designer Marilyn Vance. She gave him a

FIGURE 4.12 Costuming, Hairdressing, and Makeup The important contributions of the costume designer, hairdresser, and makeup artist are evident in these pictures from *Sunset Boulevard* and *King Kong*. Gloria Swanson's glittering, metallic top, heavy necklace and bracelet, dark lipstick, and perfectly sculpted coiffure literally shout out glamour and confidence, even boldness, even in this high-contrast frame. Fay Wray's look, however—her flowing, diaphanous gown, her long, loosely curled hair, and her understated makeup—is a soft whisper of old-fashioned feminine vulnerability (every big ape's dream).

longer-legged look by increasing the rise of his trousers (the distance between the crotch and the waist) to reduce the apparent length of his torso.

> The degree of a director's involvement with costume design varies. Edith Head recalls working with Alfred Hitchcock, George Roy Hill, and Joseph L. Mankiewicz: "Hitch is the only person who writes a script to such detail that you could go ahead and make the clothes without discussing them. . . . A Hitchcock script is so completely lucid. . . . A lot of scripts give no clues at all."
>
> When we did *The Sting* and *Butch Cassidy and the Sundance Kid*, George Roy Hill had done as much research as I had. In fact, he did more on some of it. He is a perfectionist. When you work with him day by day, it's as though he were another designer.
>
> Mankiewicz I never met, because they borrowed me just to do clothes for Bette Davis. He called me and said, "I love your work. Just do what you think is right."[17]

Period films create a tremendous challenge for a costume designer. Extensive research is required to determine the total costume—not just the right clothes but the hats, the hairstyles, the jewelry, and the gloves. Edith Head explains why films in contemporary settings don't make the same kind of demands: "Today's pictures are mostly men. There are very few women's pictures, and the women's pictures are mostly character pictures. In the past we made all men handsome and all women sexy and glamorous. Now we just buy them both a pair of blue jeans!"[18]

Actors often provide valuable input to costuming, especially when they have clear and definite ideas about the characters they are to play. Mary Astor, a star of the 1930s and 1940s, took an active role in designing her character's attire in *Act of Violence:*

I worked out the way this poor alley cat should look, and insisted firmly (with [director Fred] Zinneman's help) that the one dress in the picture would not be made at the MGM wardrobe, but be found on a rack at the cheapest department store. We made the hem uneven, put a few cigarette burns and some stains on the front. I wore bracelets that rattled and jangled and stiletto-heeled slippers. I had the heels sanded off at the edges to make walking uncomfortable. I wore a fall, a long unbecoming hairpiece that came to my shoulder. And I put on very dark nail polish and chipped it. I used no foundation makeup, just too much lipstick and too much mascara—both "bled," that is, smeared, just a little. Zinney said, "You look just right!" And camera helped with "bad" lighting.[19]

Makeup decisions also help to create the desired look. Makeup can enhance the natural look of an actor or transform an actor into a different version of himself or herself or into a totally different person. The transition may be accomplished through gradual and subtle changes throughout the film, or it may be abrupt. Orson Welles, as Charles Foster Kane, undergoes an effective aging transition in *Citizen Kane*, as does young Kirsten Dunst in *Interview With the Vampire* and *Little Women*. Jack Nicholson takes on a very different face for the role of Jimmy Hoffa in *Hoffa*. Extreme examples of the makeup artist's skill are roles that call for the actor's look to be totally transformed—for example, the role that Roddy McDowell plays in *Planet of the Apes* and John Hurt in the title role in *The Elephant Man*—and the reverse-aging feat that Brad Pitt performs in *The Curious Case of Benjamin Button*, of course.

Although some actors begin to internalize their roles with costuming, makeup can also be an important step. Sir Laurence Olivier, whose stage experience taught him the skills of makeup, claimed that he couldn't "get" a character until he found the right nose. He typically experimented with several putty noses until satisfied. Indeed, sometimes the true test of a makeup person's artistry arises when an actor or actress well known for movie-star beauty takes on the challenge of becoming a serious and believable character who is somewhat less than stellar in appearance. When Tony Curtis convinced a director to award him the role of the Boston Strangler, and when, more recently, Nicole Kidman was called upon to portray British novelist Virginia Woolf in *The Hours*, convincing nose prosthetics saved the day—and also enhanced the dramatic casting possibilities for two glamorous careers (Figures 4.13, 4.14).

FIGURE 4.13 **Winning By a Nose, Part I:** After almost two decades as a famous, handsome, romantic "matinee idol" (left, with Jack Lemmon), Tony Curtis attained "serious actor" status in 1968 by donning a false nose for his role as the title character in *The Boston Strangler* (right).

FIGURE 4.14 **Winning By a Nose, Part II:** Likewise, Nicole Kidman successfully abandoned (at least temporarily) her glamorous movie-star career, and won a Best Actress Oscar for *The Hours*, by putting on the alleged olfactory apparatus of famous English novelist Virginia Woolf.

Orson Welles, as director of *Citizen Kane*, used makeup for a unique purpose. He knew that his Mercury Theatre actors were totally unknown to movie audiences, so, to make them seem more familiar, he asked his makeup man to create the look of character stereotypes common in popular genre films.

LIGHTING

Does the action of the film take place in the daytime or at night, indoors or outdoors? Is the film set in Transylvania or Las Vegas? The nature of the story and the shooting location have a significant effect on the contribution of lighting to the look of a film.

Ingmar Bergman's films are usually set in Sweden. There, the sun never rises high in the sky, so strong side lighting is dominant. The quality of light in the dry air of the California desert is very different from the quality of light in a tropical rain forest. Such geographic factors must be accepted as givens. Certain aspects of lighting, however, can be artistically controlled, and some of the most critical decisions affecting the film's look concern lighting. In the hands of skilled directors and cinematographers lighting becomes a powerful, almost magical tool. As Todd Rainsberger puts it in his excellent work on James Wong Howe:

> Just as no two artists use the same brush strokes, no two cameramen control light in exactly the same manner. The angle, quality, and intensity of the light can vary in an infinite number of ways. Recording a scene on film is thus not a copy of a single unchanging reality, but the selective recording of a filmic reality which is the unique result of a particular choice of light sources.[20]

By controlling the intensity, direction, and diffusion of the light, a director is able to create the impression of spatial depth, delineate and mold the contours and planes of the subject, convey emotional mood and atmosphere, and create special dramatic effects. The way a scene is lit is an important factor in determining the scene's dramatic effectiveness. Subtle variations in lighting create mood and atmosphere for the action that is to take place. Because lighting should reinforce the

FIGURE 4.15 **Low-Key and High-Key Lighting** Low-key lighting puts most of the set in shadow and shows the subjects with just a few highlights, increasing the intimacy and dramatic intensity of the scene. High-key lighting opens up the frame with light in background areas and balances the lighting throughout the set. Although high-key lighting diminishes the intimacy and dramatic intensity that the scene has with low-key lighting, it provides more complete visual information about the two women and the setting.

mood of each scene, close observation of the lighting throughout a film should reveal the film's overall mood or tone.

Two terms designate different intensities of lighting. **Low-key lighting** puts most of the set in shadow; just a few highlights define the subject. This type of lighting heightens suspense and creates a somber mood; thus, it is used in mystery and horror films. **High-key lighting,** in contrast, results in more light areas than shadows, and subjects are seen in middle grays and highlights, with far less contrast. High-key lighting is suitable for comic and light moods, such as in a musical. Generally speaking, high-contrast scenes, with a wide range of difference between light and dark areas, create more powerful and dramatic images than do scenes that are evenly lit (Figure 4.15).

The direction of the light also plays an important role in creating an effective visual image. The effect created by flat overhead lighting, for example, is entirely different from the effect created by strong side lighting from floor level. Back lighting and front lighting also create strikingly different effects (Figure 4.16).

Whether light is artificial or natural, the director has the means to control what is commonly referred to as the character of the light, which can generally be classified as direct, harsh, or hard; medium and balanced; or soft and diffused (Figure 4.17).

Because the character of light on actors' faces can suggest certain inner qualities, cinematographer James Wong Howe individualized the major characters in *Hud* with lighting designed to fit the personalities the actors were portraying. The lighting for Patricia Neal was strong and undiffused. Paul Newman was generally seen in dark contrasts; Melvyn Douglas was shadow lit; and Brandon DeWilde was brightly lit.

The intensity, direction, and character of light affect the dramatic effectiveness of an image. The director and cinematographer together plan the look they want for the lighting. Then the cinematographer assumes the primary responsibility for the lighting.

FIGURE 4.16 Directions of Lighting These pictures illustrate the different effects achieved by overhead lighting (above left), side lighting (above middle), front lighting (above right), and back lighting (right).

FIGURE 4.17 Character of Light These pictures illustrate the different effects of changing the character of the light: direct, harsh, or hard lighting (left); medium and balanced lighting (center); and soft and diffused lighting (right).

FIGURE 4.18 **Natural Lighting**   Some cinematographers, like Nestor Almendros (*Days of Heaven*), insist upon using natural lighting sources as much as possible in their films. For directors who subscribed to a cinema movement called "Dogma 95," this requirement was in fact "law"—just one of many rules they agreed to follow (including using only hand-held cameras) that were meant to simplify and "purify" modern filmmaking. This scene, which includes actresses Björk and Catherine Deneuve photographed in available light that does not flatter or idealize their appearance, is from *Dancer in the Dark,* a controversial Dogma 95-esque musical created by the Danish director Lars von Trier.

Today's filmmakers generally strive for a very natural effect in their lighting (Figure 4.18). Scenes often look as though the cinematographer used no supplemental light at all. Vilmos Zsigmond (*McCabe & Mrs. Miller, Close Encounters of the Third Kind, The Deer Hunter*), one of the great modern cinematographers, describes his philosophy in this way:

> . . . I like to have windows in my shots—windows, or candles or lamps. Those are my true light sources. Studying the Old Masters, Rembrandt, Vermeer, de la Tour, I found that they painted their best works relying on light effects coming from realistic sources. . . . They simplified and eliminated multiple shadows to concentrate on the dramatic. That is what a cinematographer does: improves on nature.[21]

Master cinematographer Nestor Almendros also stresses the importance of naturalness: "I use a minimum of artificial light. . . . *Days of Heaven* was shot with very little light. Rather than create an artificial moment, I'd wait for the real one to happen. One great moment is worth waiting for all day."[22] Even when he is working on interiors in a studio for a film like *Kramer vs. Kramer,* Almendros stresses a natural light technique by imagining the sun outside Kramer's apartment, justifying a subject lit from behind by a window or lamp, and making sure that all lighting seems to come from windows and table or floor lamps.

Vilmos Zsigmond was not the first person to seek inspiration from paintings. As early as the 1920s, Cecil B. DeMille and other directors were attempting to use lighting to imitate the effects achieved by painters like Rembrandt.

Some forty years later, Franco Zeffirelli achieved painterly effects successfully in his *Taming of the Shrew.* He created the soft, muted color of faded paintings by placing a nylon stocking over the camera lens and lighting his interior scenes in the Rembrandt manner.

John Ford and Gregg Toland, his cinematographer, designed *The Grapes of Wrath* to suggest the look of Dorothea Lange's stark black-and-white photographs of the Dust Bowl. Howard Hawks used lighting in *Rio Bravo* to suggest the hard lighting in the western paintings of Frederick Remington. In preparing to shoot *The Verdict*, Sidney Lumet and his cinematographer, Andrzej Bartkowiak, spent an entire day studying a collection of prints of Caravaggio's paintings. They analyzed his treatment of backgrounds, foregrounds, and textured surfaces, paying particular attention to the sources of light. Then they applied what they had learned to *The Verdict*, with what Lumet called "extraordinary" results. (See Chapter 7—"Color"—for further discusssion and illustration of this concept.)

THE BUDGET'S EFFECT ON THE FILM'S LOOK

The visual design elements discussed in this chapter can play important roles in the overall effectiveness of a movie. Many filmmakers, however, do not have a budget that allows them to develop a unified look for their projects. Inventive camera angles, subtle lighting effects, authentic costuming, and detailed settings take time and money to create, and many low-budget films must be made without a distinctive visual style.

Sometimes, a lack of polished or expensive artistic flourish can work to a film's advantage. And sometimes, high-quality screenwriting and powerful acting performances can be presented more effectively to an audience that is undistracted by flashy visual effects or complicated editing styles. Low-budget films like *Breaking Away, Return of the Secaucus Seven, Sex, Lies, and Videotape, Clerks, My Big Fat Greek Wedding,* and *Napoleon Dynamite* have been executed with great success despite the absence of a distinct visual style.

ANALYZING VISUAL DESIGN

On Color Versus Black and White

1. Was the filmmaker's choice of color or black and white correct for this story? What factors do you think influenced this decision? Try to imagine the film as it would appear in the other film type. What would the differences in total effect be?
2. Are any special color effects used to achieve a unique overall look? If so, what was the director trying to achieve with the unusual effect? How successfully is the overall effect carried out?

On Screen Format (Aspect Ratio)

1. Was the film originally shot for a standard screen or a wide screen? Does the choice of screen format suit the story being filmed?
2. Try imagining the film in the opposite format: What would be gained or lost?

On Production Design/Art Direction

1. How important is the set or location to the overall look of the film? Is it essentially a realistic or authentic set, or is it stylized to suggest a heightened reality?
2. Was the movie filmed primarily on location or in the studio? What effect does the place of filming have on the style or look of the film?
3. How do the settings serve as personalized environments to enhance or reinforce the actors' performances? To what degree do the settings underscore or enhance the mood or quality of each scene?
4. Is the setting so powerful and dominant that it upstages the actors?
5. If the film is a period piece, a fantasy, or a science fiction story taking place in a future time or on a strange planet, is the set convincing enough to make us believe (during the film) that we are really in another time and place? If so, what factors or details present in the set contribute to its convincing effect? If the set is not completely convincing, why does it fail?
6. Which of the four environmental factors (temporal factors; geographic factors; social structures and economic factors; and customs, moral attitudes, and codes of behavior) play significant roles in the film? Could the same story take place in any environment?
7. Which environmental factors are most important? What effect do these factors have on the plot or the characters?
8. Why did the filmmaker choose this particular location for filming this story?
9. How does the film's setting contribute to the overall emotional atmosphere?
10. What important interrelationships exist between the setting and the characters or between setting and plot?
11. Is the setting symbolic in any way? Does it function as a microcosm?

On Costume and Makeup Design

1. What details of costuming and makeup help the actors be "in character"? Do these factors also play a role in creating a sense of time and place?
2. Does the makeup for the film's major characters simply enhance the natural look of the actors or significantly transform their appearances? If significant or sometimes subtle changes (such as aging) are required by the script, how effectively are these changes achieved?

On Lighting

1. Is the lighting of the film as a whole (a) direct, harsh, and hard; (b) medium and balanced; or (c) soft and diffused? Does high-key or low-key lighting predominate? How do the lighting decisions fit the film's story?
2. Does the lighting throughout seem artificial, coming from places where there are no visible light sources, or does it seem to emanate naturally from sources visible or suggested on-screen?
3. How does the lighting contribute to the overall emotional attitude or tone of the film?

1. Watch *Psycho* (1960), *The Taming of the Shrew*, *I Am Love*, or *Get Low* and describe the unique visual details built into the interior sets for each film. How do the interior sets contribute to a sense of the characters who live there or function as an appropriate backdrop for the action that takes place?
2. Watch the first 10 minutes of any of the following films; then list and describe the important visual details that help establish a sense of time and place in this short time frame: *Casablanca*, *Shane*, *The Grapes of Wrath*, *Summer of '42*, *To Kill a Mockingbird*, *Manhattan*, *Blade Runner*, *Brazil*, *Rent*, *The Hurt Locker*, and *Shutter Island*. How do basic film elements other than the visual image (music, sound, dialect, and so forth) help contribute to a sense of time and place in these short segments?

MINI-MOVIE EXERCISE I

Dressed to Kill (1980), one of director Brian De Palma's most celebrated works, stars Angie Dickinson as a sexually frustrated wife and mother and Michael Caine as her psychiatrist. Early in this movie, the filmmaker utilizes an almost-wordless eleven-minute "film-within-a-film" to build his characters, to promote his plot, and to shock his viewers in the tradition of his cinematic master, Alfred Hitchcock. A multitude of elements in this sequence are worthy of close attention, but a good place to begin is with the film's production design. Watch Chapter 3 ("Scenes From a Museum") on the "Special Edition" DVD and consider the thematic significance of settings, costumes, and "stage properties."

MINI-MOVIE EXERCISE II

In Wes Anderson's first animated feature film, *Fantastic Mr. Fox* (based on a children's book by Roald Dahl), the experienced director chose an older, more time-consuming, and currently less popular method than computer rendering. To bring his talking woodland creatures to life, he embraced stop-motion crafts-manship. Obtain this film in one of its video formats (including a "Blu-Ray + DVD + Digital Copy" three-disc set) and watch the brief opening sequence [0:54 to 04:30] that may be perceived as a "mini-movie." Then consider not only its rudimentary-yet-"realistic" plot and character development, but also—especially—the hyperintricacy of its production design. Finally, among the special features available, check out the eight-minute documentary called "The Look of *Fantastic Mr. Fox*." (A crucial creative decision, we learn there, involved the filmmakers' banishing green from the work's color palette.)

DVD FILMMAKING EXTRAS

Production Design

The Diving Bell and the Butterfly:
   The celebrated American painter Julian Schnabel directed this remarkable drama. For discussions of visual aspects of the film, see, on this disc, both the feature "Submerged: The Making of . . ." and the substantial interview by Charlie Rose. (Note also the expressive final images presented during the credit sequence at the end of the film itself: icebergs, not falling but *rising*. . . .)

The Royal Tenenbaums (The Criterion Collection):
   David Wasco is credited with the design of this production, but various elements of the two-disc DVD make it abundantly clear that the obsessions of director Wes Anderson are largely responsible for the film's visual details in 300 different sets. Note especially the segment "With the Filmmaker: A Portrait by Albert Maysles" and the collection of murals by Eric Anderson.

For interviews and perspectives from other production designers, refer to the bonus features on the latest DVD releases of *Chocolat* (David Gropman), *Forrest Gump* (Rick Carter), *Men in Black II* (Bo Welch), *Pulp Fiction* (David Wasco), and *The Salton Sea* (Tom Southwell).

Makeup and Costumes

Rick Baker is a modern legend for both the high quality and fecundity of his movie makeup designs. Three DVDs that well display his work:

Planet of the Apes (Two-Disc Special Edition):
   In director Tim Burton's 2001 remake, Baker and his crew transform such actors as Michael Clarke Duncan, Helena Bonham Carter, Tim Roth, and Paul Giamatti into believable simians. Watch the segments called "Face Like a Monkey" and "Ape Couture" for interviews about Baker's makeup and Colleen Atwood's costume design.

Nutty Professor II: The Klumps (Collector's Edition):
   Here, time-lapse photography demonstrates Baker's metamorphosis of Eddie Murphy into two of the five "makeup enhanced" family members he inhabits ("Papa" and "Ernie").

Dr. Seuss' How the Grinch Stole Christmas (Collector's Edition):
   Director Ron Howard engaged Baker to create the strange creatures in this film because he knew that the "Make-up and Application Designer" would be able to cover Jim Carrey's countenance (via sophisticated prosthetics) without obstructing the actor's elastic facial expressions.

A Single Man:
> Tom Ford was a world-famous clothing designer before he directed his first motion picture. He talks extensively in this DVD's "Making of . . ." extra (and also in his audio commentary) about the connections between character and costumes, plot and place, as well as about the strong visual inspiration in his source work, Christopher Isherwood's novel.

Some films feature stories and characters that require extraordinary costuming and makeup design. For interviews with the people who make these transformations possible, refer to the bonus features on the latest DVD releases of *Sunset Boulevard* (Edith Head), *A Beautiful Mind* (Greg Cannom), and *Shallow Hal* (Tony Gardner).

FILMS FOR STUDY

Avatar (2009)
Barry Lyndon (1975)
Batman Begins (2005)
Beloved (1998)
Black Swan (2010)
Blade Runner (1982)
Brokeback Mountain (2005)
Cabaret (1972)
Capote (2005)
Casablanca (1942)
Citizen Kane (1941)
A Clockwork Orange (1971)
Dead Man (1995)
The Diving Bell and the Butterfly (2007)
Down with Love (2003)
Fanny and Alexander (1982)

The Fighter (2010)
Gangs of New York (2002)
The Ghost Writer (2010)
Good Night, and Good Luck (2005)
The Grapes of Wrath (1940)
Harry Potter and the Goblet of Fire (2005)
The Hours (2002)
Inception (2010)
The Kids Are All Right (2010)
The King's Speech (2010)
L.A. Confidential (1997)
Manhattan (1979)
The Messenger (2009)
Moulin Rouge! (2001)

Nine (2009)
127 Hours (2010)
The Others (2001)
The Portrait of a Lady (1996)
Psycho (1960)
The Road (2009)
The Social Network (2010)
The Terminal (2004)
3-Iron (2004)
Traffic (2000)
TRON Legacy (2010)
True Grit (2010)
Tsotsi (2005)
The White Countess (2005)
The Widow of St. Pierre (2000)
Young Frankenstein (1974)

CINEMATOGRAPHY *and* SPECIAL VISUAL EFFECTS

5

Avatar

The camera is the "eye" of the motion picture. It is not merely a mechanical thing of cogs and wheels and optical glass that records an image on a strip of film. Rather, it is an artistic tool—like a painter's brush, or a sculptor's chisel. In the hands of a craftsman it becomes the instrument through which a dramatic story can be placed on film—so that later on, in darkened theaters all over the world, vast audiences can see the film, react to it, and be entertained.

—HERBERT A. LIGHTMAN, EDITOR OF *AMERICAN CINEMATOGRAPHER*

THE IMPORTANCE OF THE VISUAL IMAGE

Film speaks in a language of the senses. Its flowing and sparkling stream of images, its compelling pace and natural rhythms, and its pictorial style are all part of this nonverbal language. So it follows naturally that the aesthetic quality and dramatic power of the image are extremely important to the overall quality of a film. Although the nature and quality of the story, editing, musical score, sound effects, dialogue, and acting can do much to enhance a film's power, even these important elements cannot save a film whose images are mediocre or poorly edited.

As important as the quality of the image may be, however, it must not be considered so important that the purpose of the film as an artistic, unified whole is ignored. A film's photographic effects should not be created for their own sake as independent, beautiful, or powerful images. In the final analysis, they must be justified psychologically and dramatically, as well as aesthetically, as important means to an end, not as ends in themselves. Creating beautiful images for the sake of creating beautiful images violates a film's aesthetic unity and may actually work against the film.

The same principle applies to overly clever or self-conscious camerawork. Technique must not become an end in itself; any special technique must have some underlying purpose related to the purpose of the film as a whole. Every time a director or cinematographer employs an unusual camera angle or a new photographic technique, he or she should do so for the purpose of communicating (either sensually or intellectually) in the most effective way possible, not simply to show off or try a new trick. A sense of naturalness, a feeling that something had to be done in a certain way, is more praiseworthy than clever camerawork.

Because the visual element is the motion picture's primary and most powerful means of communication, cinematography can completely dominate a film, taking it over by sheer force. But when this occurs, the artistic structure of the film is weakened, the dramatic power of the film fades, and watching the film becomes simply an orgy of the eyeballs. As cinematographer Vilmos Zsigmond (*The Deer Hunter*) puts it, "I believe photography should never be dominating . . . . The performances, the directing, the music, the camerawork are all on the same level. That's what I like about it, and that's what I think photography should be."[1]

THE CINEMATIC FILM

A cinematic film takes advantage of all the special properties and qualities that make the film medium unique. The first and most essential of these is the quality of continuous motion. A cinematic film is truly a *motion* picture—a flowing, ever-changing stream of images and sounds sparkling with a freshness and vitality all its own, a fluid blend of image, sound, and motion possessed by a restless compulsion to be vibrantly alive, to avoid the quiet, the still, and the static.

The second quality of a cinematic film evolves naturally out of the first. The continuous and simultaneous interplay of image, sound, and motion on the screen sets up varied, complex, and subtle rhythms. Clear, crisp visual and aural rhythms are created by the physical movements or sound of objects on the screen, by the pace of the dialogue, by the natural rhythms of human speech, by the frequency of editorial cuts, by the varying length of shots between cuts, and by the musical score.

The pace of the plot also has distinct rhythms. All these serve to intensify the film's unique sense of pulsing life.

A cinematic film also makes maximum use of the great flexibility and freedom of the medium: its freedom from the spoken word and its ability to communicate directly, physically, and concretely through images and sounds; its freedom to show us action from any vantage point, and to vary our point of view at will; its capability to manipulate time and space, expanding or compressing them at will; and its freedom to make quick and clear transitions in time and space.

Although film is essentially a two-dimensional medium (the current popular taste for "3-D" movies notwithstanding), a cinematic film overcomes this limitation by creating an illusion of depth. It creates the impression that the screen is not a flat surface but a window through which we observe a three-dimensional world.

All these qualities are present in a truly cinematic film. If they are not present in the subject matter, it is up to the director, the cinematographer, and the editor to build them in. Otherwise, the film's dramatic scenes are not communicated in all the fullness of the medium's potential.

CINEMATIC POINTS OF VIEW

To appreciate fully the workings of the cinematic film, we must be willing to watch in a little different way, focusing not just on *what* we are seeing but also on *how* it is being shown and *why* it is being shown that way. To increase our perception effectively, we must become familiar with the different ways the movie camera sees the action taking place before it—that is, with different **cinematic points of view.*** This first stage in sharpening our watching skills requires constantly considering the following questions for every segment of the film we intend to analyze:

- From what position and through what kind of eyes does the camera see the action?
- What effect do the position of the camera and its particular ways of seeing the action have on our response to the action?
- How is our response affected by changes in the point of view?

This last question is extremely important, for it shows us that cinematic point of view need not be consistent (unlike literary point of view, for example). In fact, consistency of viewpoint would be boring in a film and would impede effective communication. Thus, we expect a filmmaker to spirit us about from one vantage point to another, but we assume that visual continuity and coherence will be maintained so that we can follow intuitively.

Four points of view are employed in motion pictures:

- objective (camera as sideline observer)
- subjective (camera as participant in the action)
- indirect-subjective
- director's interpretive

*Because cinematic point of view is largely a matter of camera placement, it is introduced here as part of the discussion of cinematography. To understand the effects of shifting from one point of view to another, see Chapter 6 on editing.

FIGURE 5.1 **Objective Viewpoint**   In this objective shot of a baseball game in progress, we are clearly sideline observers, not really involved in the action.

Generally, all four can be used in every film to varying degrees, depending on the demands of the dramatic situation and the creative vision and style of the director.

Objective Point of View

The **objective point of view** is illustrated by the great director John Ford's "philosophy of camera." Ford considered the camera to be a window and the audience to be outside the window viewing the people and events within. We are asked to watch the actions as if they were taking place at a distance, and we are not asked to participate. The objective point of view employs a static camera as much as possible in order to produce this window effect, and it concentrates on the actors and the action without drawing attention to the camera. The objective camera suggests an emotional distance between camera and subject; the camera seems simply to be recording, as straightforwardly as possible, the characters and actions of the story. For the most part, the director uses natural, normal, straightforward types of camera positioning and camera angles. The objective camera does not comment on or interpret the action but merely records it, letting it unfold. We see the action from the viewpoint of an impersonal observer. If the camera moves, it does so unobtrusively, calling as little attention to itself as possible.

In most films, continuity and clear communication of the dramatic scene demand that some use be made of the objective point of view. The objective viewpoint forces us to pinpoint subtle but perhaps significant visual details by ourselves (Figure 5.1). Overuse, however, may cause us to lose interest.

FIGURE 5.2 Subjective Viewpoint In this subjective shot, the camera puts us in the game, giving us the catcher's view of the action.

Subjective Point of View

The **subjective point of view** provides us with the visual viewpoint and emotional intensity felt by a character participating in the action. Alfred Hitchcock, whose philosophy of camera was opposite to that of John Ford, specialized in creating a strong sense of direct involvement by the audience. He employed elaborate camera movement to create visual sequences that bring us into the suspense, literally forcing us to become the characters and experience their emotions. According to Hitchcock, an important tool in creating this kind of subjective involvement is skillful editing and a viewpoint close to the action, as this passage from his essay "Direction" indicates:

> So you gradually build up the psychological situation, piece by piece, using the camera to emphasize first one detail, then another. The point is to draw the audience right into the situation—instead of leaving them to watch it from outside, from a distance. . . . If you played the whole scene straight through, and simply made a photographic record of it with the camera always in one position, you would lose your power over the audience. . . . and you would have no means of concentrating their attention on those particular visual details which make them feel what the characters are feeling.[2]

When the cinematic point of view is subjective, our experience becomes more intense and more immediate as we become intimately involved in the action. Generally, this viewpoint is maintained by a moving camera, which forces us to see exactly what the character is seeing and in a sense to become the character (Figure 5.2).

It is almost impossible to sustain a purely subjective point of view throughout a film, as was attempted in *Lady in the Lake*. The story of this 1946 film by Robert Montgomery was told entirely through the eyes of its detective hero, and the only time the hero's face was seen was in a mirror. His hands and arms occasionally appeared below eye level, as they would normally be seen from his viewpoint. The difficulty of sustaining such a viewpoint over an entire film is obvious, for clarity of communication and continuity usually demand that a film switch back and forth between the objective and subjective points of view.

The change from objective to subjective point of view is often accomplished in the following manner. An objective shot that shows a character looking at something off-screen (called a **look of outward regard**) cues us to wonder what the character is looking at. The following shot, called an **eye-line shot,** shows us subjectively what the character is seeing. Because the simple logical relationship between the two shots provides a smooth and natural movement from an objective to a subjective point of view, this pattern is common in film.

The alternation of objective and subjective viewpoints, and the tight link between sight and sound, are further illustrated by the following scene:

Establishing shot: Objective camera view from street corner, focusing on a workman using an air hammer in center of street (apparent distance: 50 to 75 feet). *Sound:* Loud chatter of air hammer mingled with other street noises.

Cut to subjective view: Close-ups of air hammer and violently shaking lower arms and hands of workman, from workman's point of view. *Sound:* Hammer is almost deafening—no other sounds heard.

Cut back to objective camera: Heavy truck turns corner beyond workman, bears down on him at top speed. *Sound:* Loud chatter of air hammer, other street noises, rising sound of approaching truck.

Cut to subjective view: Close-up of air hammer and workman's hands as seen from his viewpoint. *Sound:* First, only deafening sounds of air hammer, then a rising squeal of brakes mixed with hammer noise.

Quick cut to a new subjective view: Front of truck closing quickly on camera from 10 feet away. *Sound:* Squeal of brakes louder, hammer stops, woman's voice screaming, cut short by sickening thud, followed by darkness and momentary silence.

Cut back to objective viewpoint (from street corner): Unconscious figure of workman in front of stopped truck. Curious crowd gathering into circle. *Sound:* Mixed jumble of panicked voices, street noises, ambulance siren in distance.

The alternation between the objective and the subjective view provides both a clear understanding of the dramatic flow of events and a strong sense of audience involvement.

Indirect-Subjective Point of View

The **indirect-subjective point of view** does not provide a participant's point of view, but it does bring us close to the action so that we feel intimately involved and our visual experience is intense. Consider a close-up that conveys the emotional

FIGURE 5.3 Indirect-Subjective Viewpoint Although we do not have any character's point of view, this indirect-subjective shot brings us close to the action and involves us in it as we focus on the tension in the batter's hands as he awaits the pitch. Because we are so close to the batter, we identify with him and feel his tension.

reaction of a character. We recognize that we are not the character, yet we are drawn into the feeling that is being conveyed in a subjective way. A close-up of a face contorted in pain makes us feel that pain more vividly than would an objective shot from a greater distance. Another example is the kind of shot that was common in the old westerns. With the stagecoach under attack by outlaws, the director inserts close-ups of pounding hoofs to capture the furious rhythm and pulsing excitement of the chase, bringing us close to the action and increasing the intensity of our experience. The indirect-subjective point of view gives us the feeling of participating in the action without showing the action through a participant's eyes (Figure 5.3).

The key to the effectiveness of the indirect-subjective viewpoint is this closeness to the action, as Alfred Hitchcock explains:

> So what you are doing is . . . taking the audience right close up into the scene, and . . . the various effects get . . . the audience involved. . . . Say you are at a boxing match and you are eight to ten rows back; well, you get a very different effect if you are in the first row, looking up under those ropes. When these two fellows are slugging each other, you get splashed almost.
>
> In *Psycho* once that figure comes in and starts to stab, you're in it. Oh, you're absolutely in it. The distance of the figures, you see.[3]

This "distance of the figures" makes the viewer's response to the shower scene in *Psycho* so very different from the response to the equally violent ending of

FIGURE 5.4 **Director's Interpretive Viewpoint** By choosing an extremely low-angle view of the batter, the director makes us see him in a special or unusual way, perhaps to give us the pitcher's emotional perspective as he prepares to pitch to a powerful slugger in a close game.

Bonnie and Clyde. Indirect-subjective close-up shots of Bonnie and Clyde are used sparingly in the slow-motion dance of death, but the primary viewpoint is objective, and the viewer, like the camera, stands off to the side, out of harm's way. In *Psycho*, the rapid editing between occasional subjective viewpoints and close-up indirect-subjective shots puts the viewer in the shower with Janet Leigh and creates a real sense of *personal* danger.

Director's Interpretive Point of View

The director is always manipulating our viewpoint in subtle ways. The filmmaker chooses not only what to show us but also how we will see it. By photographing a scene from special angles or with special lenses, or in slow or fast motion, and so on, he or she imposes on the image a certain tone, emotional attitude, or style. We are thus forced to react in a certain way to what we see, thereby experiencing the **director's interpretive point of view.** We are *consciously* aware that the director wants us to see the action in some *unusual* way (Figure 5.4).

There are examples of all four points of view in the following typical western sequence showing a stagecoach being attacked by bandits:

Objective point of view: Stagecoach and horses as seen from the side (from a distance of 50 to 75 feet) being pursued by bandits. Shot here could be either from a panning camera (i.e., one moving from left to right, or vice versa) in fixed position or from a mobile camera tracking alongside or parallel to the path of the stagecoach.

Subjective point of view: Camera shot from stage driver's point of view, looking out over horses' backs, with arms and hands holding and slapping reins seen below eye level.

Indirect-subjective point of view: Close-up of stage driver's face from side as he turns his head to look back over his shoulder (a look of outward regard). His face registers fear, determination.

Subjective point of view: Camera shot of bandits in hot pursuit of stage-coach, from the point of view of driver looking back over top of stage.

Indirect-subjective point of view: Close-up of face of driver, now turned frontward again, registering strain, jaw set in determination, sweat streaming down face, screaming at horses.

Director's interpretive point of view: Slow-motion close-up of horses' heads in profile, their eyes wild with strain, mouths in agony straining at their bits, flecks of foamy sweat shaking from their necks. (By filming this shot in slow motion, the director in effect comments on the action, telling us how to see it. The slow-motion photography conveys the horses' exhaustion, intensifies the tremendous effort they are putting out, and gives us a sense of the futility of the stage's attempt to escape.)

Although some practice may be required to spot the cinematic viewpoints in a segment of film, it is basically a very simple process. The next stage in the art of watching films, analyzing the different aspects of cinematic composition and fully appreciating the skills of the cinematographer, is a bit more complex.

ELEMENTS OF CINEMATIC COMPOSITION

Principles of visual composition have been well established since antiquity. Evidenced in painting and still photography, these so-called natural laws focus on three fairly simple visual concepts:

1. Vertical lines suggest strength, authority, and dignity.

2. Diagonal lines crossing the frame suggest action and dynamic movement—the power to overcome obstacles (Figure 5.5).

3. Curved lines denote fluidity and sensuality; compositions that suggest a circular movement evoke feelings of exaltation, euphoria, and joy.

According to Nestor Almendros, a cinematographer must know these principles but must "then forget them, or at least not consciously think about them all the time."[4]

Because a cinematic film is a unique medium, the problems in composition that it poses for the director and cinematographer are also unique. Both must keep in mind that every **shot** (a strip of film produced by a single uninterrupted running of the camera) is but a segment, a brief element in a continuous flow of images. And they must create each shot with a view to its contribution to the whole. The difficulty of creating a shot is compounded by the movement of the image itself. The image is in a constant state of flux, and the camera records those movements

FIGURE 5.5 **Powerful Composition**   The strong diagonal lines of the hallway parallel the crisp lines of the soldiers' uniforms to create a dynamic composition in this striking scene from *The Band's Visit*.

at a rate of twenty-four frames per second. Every frame in a shot cannot be set up according to the aesthetic principles of composition used in still photography. The cinematographer's choices in each shot are dictated by the nature of the film medium. Every shot must be designed with the goals of *cinematic* composition in mind. These goals are (1) directing attention to the object of greatest significance, (2) keeping the image in constant motion, and (3) creating an illusion of depth.

Focusing Attention on the Most Significant Object

Above all, a shot must be so composed that it draws attention into the scene and toward the object of greatest dramatic significance. Only when this is achieved are the film's dramatic ideas conveyed effectively. Several methods of directing attention are open to the filmmaker.

- **Size and Closeness of the Object.** Normally, the eye is directed toward larger, closer objects rather than toward smaller, more distant objects. For example, the image of an actor's face appearing in the foreground (closer to the camera and therefore larger) is more likely to serve as a focal point for our attention than is a face in the background. In a normal situation, then, the size and relative distance of the object from the camera are important factors in determining the greatest area of interest (Figure 5.6).
- **Sharpness of Focus.** The eye is also drawn almost automatically to what it can see best. If a face in the foreground is slightly blurred and a face in the background, though smaller and more distant, is sharp and clear, our eyes are

FIGURE 5.6 Size and Closeness of the Object
In most cases, our attention is naturally drawn to larger, closer objects or faces, such as the woman's face in this picture, rather than to smaller, more distant objects or faces.

FIGURE 5.7 Sharpness of Focus When a larger, closer face in the foreground is in soft focus or blurred, our attention is drawn to a smaller and more distant face in sharp focus. The eye is drawn almost automatically to what it can see best.

drawn to the background face because it can be seen best. An object in sharp focus can divert our attention from a closer, larger object in soft focus, even if the larger object fills half the screen (Figure 5.7).

- **Extreme Close-Ups.** A **close-up** is a shot of a person or object taken at close range. A tight or extreme close-up brings us so close to the object of interest (an actor's face, for example) that we cannot look elsewhere. The face so fills the screen that there is nothing else to see (Figure 5.8).
- **Movement.** The eye is also drawn to an object in motion, and a moving object can divert our attention from a static one. Thus, a single moving object in an otherwise static scene draws our attention. Conversely, if movement and flow are a general part of the background, moving objects do not divert our attention from static but more dramatically important objects (Figure 5.9).
- **Arrangement of People and Objects.** The director focuses our attention by his or her arrangement of people and objects in relation to each other. Because each arrangement is determined by the nature of the dramatic moment being enacted and the complex interrelationships involved, the director must depend more on an intuitive sense of rightness than on any positioning formulas (Figure 5.10).
- **Foreground Framing.** The director might decide to frame the object of greatest significance with objects or people in the near foreground. To make sure that our attention is not distracted by the framing objects or people, the director generally emphasizes the most important subject with the brightest lighting and sharpest focus (Figures 5.11, 5.12).

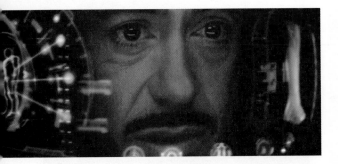

FIGURE 5.8 Extreme Close-Up There's no doubt about where our attention is directed in this dramatic close-up of Robert Downey Jr.'s face in *Iron Man*.

FIGURE 5.9 Background in Motion Although the warriors in the background of this scene from *House of Flying Daggers* are moving, they are part of a generalized traffic movement across the woods, so our attention remains on the relatively static but dramatically more important maneuvers in the foreground by Ziyi Zhang.

FIGURE 5.10 Dramatic Arrangement of People and Objects There are no set formulas for positioning characters and objects within the frame. The director must rely on an intuitive sense of rightness in composing each shot to communicate the nature of the dramatic moment and in positioning actors to reveal subtle and complex interrelationships. In this scene from Lina Wertmüller's *Seven Beauties*, we focus our attention on Giancarlo Giannini because of the physical locations of the other characters and because Giannini's position in the center of the architectural frame created by the grand foyer in the background and his standing posture make him dominant.

FIGURE 5.11 **Foreground Framing** In *E.T. The Extra-Terrestrial* Peter Coyote and Dee Wallace talking in the foreground set up a frame that calls our attention to the listener, Henry Thomas. Subtle differences in lighting and Thomas's position in the center of the plastic tunnel also direct our attention to him.

FIGURE 5.12 **The Menacing Frame** While unfamiliar New Yorkers move around her, a frightened, newly immigrated bride (Tabu) uneasily remains the center of the viewer's attention in this frame from Mira Nair's *The Namesake*.

FIGURE 5.13 **High Contrast** These pictures from *Gandhi* and *Two Lovers* use high contrast in very different ways to focus our attention. In the scene from *Gandhi*, the figure of Gandhi (Ben Kingsley) stands out against the bright sunlight on the parched Indian landscape beyond. In *Two Lovers*, the darkness of Joaquin Phoenix's room in his parents' apartment draws our attention to his face, which is highlighted only by an outside lamp—from the direction of his lover's (Gwyneth Paltrow) window.

- **Lighting and Color.** Special uses of light and color also help draw the eye to the object of greatest significance. High-contrast areas of light and dark create natural centers of focal interest, as do bright colors in a subdued or drab background (Figure 5.13).

In composing each shot, the filmmaker continually employs these techniques, either separately or in conjunction with each other, to focus our attention on the object of greatest dramatic significance. The filmmaker guides our thoughts and emotions where he or she wants them to go. Focusing our attention is certainly the most fundamental concern of cinematic composition, but, as we shall see, it is not the only one.

Keeping the Image in Motion

Because the essential characteristic of the cinematic film is continuous motion—a flowing, ever-changing stream of images—the director or cinematographer must build this quality of movement and flux into every shot. To create the stream of constantly changing images, the cinematographer employs several techniques.

Fixed-Frame Movement   The fixed camera frame approximates the effect of looking through a window. In **fixed-frame movement,** the camera remains in one position, pointing at one spot, as we might look at something with a frozen stare. The director works movement and variety into the shot by moving the subject. This movement can be rapid and frantic (like the physical action of a barroom brawl) or calm and subtle (like the changing facial expression of an actor speaking and gesturing normally).

Several types of movement are possible within the fixed frame. Movement can be *lateral* (from the left to right of the frame), *in depth* (toward or away from the camera), or *diagonal* (a combination of lateral and in-depth movements). Purely lateral movement creates the impression of movement on a flat surface (which the screen is) and therefore calls attention to one of the medium's limitations: its two-dimensionality. So, to create the illusion of three dimensions, the cinematographer favors in-depth movement (toward or away from the camera) and diagonal movement over purely lateral movement.

Panning and Tilting   Usually when the camera remains in a fixed physical location, it captures movement by approximating the head and eye movements of a human spectator. The camera's movements incorporate what is essentially a human field of view. With the body stationary, if we turn the head and neck from left to right and add a corresponding sideward glance of the eyes, our field of view takes in an arc slightly wider than 180 degrees. And if we simply move the head and eyes up and down, our eyes span an arc of at least 90 degrees. Most movements of the camera fall within these natural human limitations. A closer look at these camera movements will clarify these limitations.

Panning   Moving the camera's line of sight in a horizontal plane, to the left and right, is called **panning.** The most common use of the camera pan is to follow the lateral movement of the subject. In a western, for example, the panning camera may function in this way. The wagon train has been attacked by bandits and has moved into a defensive circle. The camera for this shot is set up in a fixed location looking over the shoulder of one of the settlers as she attempts to pick off circling bandits with a rifle. The circling bandits move from right to left. The camera (and the rifle) move to the right and pick up a subject (target bandit). Then, both camera and rifle swing laterally to left as the subject bandit rides by; when he reaches a center position, the rifle fires and we watch him fall off the horse and roll to the left of the center. Then either the camera pans back to the right to pick up a new target or an editorial cut starts the next shot with the camera picking up a new target bandit (far right), and the pattern is repeated.

Another type of pan is used to change from one subject to another. This might be illustrated by a shootout scene in the middle of the street of a western town. The camera occupies a fixed position on the side of the street, halfway between the dueling gunfighters. After establishing the tense, poised image of the gunman on the right, the camera leaves him and slowly pans left until it focuses on the other man, also tense and poised.

Because the eye normally jumps instantaneously from one object of interest to another, a pan must have a dramatic purpose; otherwise, it will seem unnatural and conspicuous. There are several possible reasons for using a pan. In the gunfight scene, the slow fluid movement of the camera from one man to the other may help expand time, intensifying the suspense and the viewer's anticipation of the first draw. Also, it may reflect the tension in the environment as a whole by registering the fear and suspense on the faces of the onlookers across the street, who become secondary subjects as we see their facial expressions in passing or catch glimpses of them frantically diving for cover. Finally, the pan may simply help to establish the relative distance between the two men. Although this type of pan can be effective, it must be used with restraint, particularly if there is a great deal of **dead screen** (screen area with no dramatically or aesthetically interesting visual information) between the two subjects.

On rare occasions, a complete 360-degree pan may be dramatically effective, especially when the situation calls for a sweeping panoramic view of the entire landscape. A full 360-degree pan, as in Sidney Lumet's *A Long Day's Journey Into Night*, clearly indicates the impossibility of escape and the hopelessness of the situation. Also, a 360-degree pan might be useful in dramatizing the situation of a character waking up in an unfamiliar and unexpected environment. A person waking up in a jail cell, for instance, would turn his or her body enough to survey the surroundings completely.

Tilting Moving the camera's line of sight in a vertical plane, up and down, is called **tilting.** Tilting approximates the vertical movement of our head and eyes. The following hypothetical sequence illustrates how the tilt is used. The camera occupies a fixed position at the end of an airport runway, focused on a jet airliner taxiing toward the camera. As the plane lifts off, the camera tilts upward to follow the plane's trajectory to a point directly overhead. At this point, although it would be technically possible to create an axis to follow the plane in one continuous shot, the shot stops and a new shot begins with the camera facing in the opposite direction. The second shot picks up the plane still overhead and tilts downward to follow its flight away from the camera. This movement approximates the way we would normally observe the incident if we were standing in the camera's position. As the plane turns right and begins to climb, the camera follows it in a diagonal movement that combines the elements of both panning and tilting. Thus, though the camera is in a fixed location, it is flexible enough to follow the movement of the plane as represented by the following arrows: takeoff to directly overhead ↑, crossover to turn ↘, turn and climb ↗.

In most panning and tilting shots, the movement of the camera approximates the normal *human* way of looking at things. Many shots in every film are photographed in this manner, showing the story unfolding as a person watching the scene might view it.

The Zoom Lens In the techniques described so far, the camera remains in a fixed position. The fixed camera, however—even though it can pan and tilt—lacks the fluidity necessary to create a truly cinematic film. The zoom lens offers a solution

FIGURE 5.14 **Zooming in on the Action** These three pictures represent different stages in a continuous shot of a single action using a zoom lens. At the start of the zoom, the cameraman picks up the center fielder as he starts after a fly ball. At this stage, the player's image fills a very small portion of the screen. At the midway point in the zoom, the player's image is magnified—he appears about three times larger. By the time he catches the ball, the zoom lens has continued to increase magnification until his figure almost fills the whole screen.

to this problem. The **zoom lens**—a series of lenses that keep an image in constant focus—allows the camera to appear to glide toward or away from the subject, but without any movement of the camera. Zoom lenses can magnify the subject ten times or more, so that we seem to move closer to the subject although our actual distance from the camera does not change.

To a camera stationed behind home plate in a baseball stadium, the center fielder, some four hundred feet away, appears extremely small, the same size that he would appear to the naked eye. By zooming in on him, the cinematographer is able to keep him in constant focus, and in effect we glide smoothly toward the center fielder until his figure almost fills the screen, as if we were seeing him from a distance of forty feet or less (Figure 5.14). The camera simply magnifies the image, but the effect is one of moving toward the subject. By reversing the process, the cinematographer can achieve the effect of moving away from the subject.

The use of the zoom lens not only allows us to see things more clearly but also gives us a sense of fluid motion in and out of the frame, thereby increasing our interest and involvement. And all of these variations are possible without ever moving the camera.

The Mobile Camera   When the camera itself becomes mobile, the possibilities of movement increase tremendously. By freeing the camera from a fixed position, the cinematographer can create a constantly shifting viewpoint, giving us a moving image of a static subject. By mounting the camera on a boom or a crane (itself mounted on a truck or dolly), the cinematographer can move it fluidly alongside, above, in front of, behind, or even under a running horse. The mobile camera can thus fulfill almost any demand for movement created by a story situation.

Film stories are often framed effectively by slow camera movement for beginnings and endings. By moving the camera slowly and fluidly forward to enter a scene, the cinematographer creates a sense of mystery, discovery, and anticipation while bringing us into the heart of the narrative and involving us in the action. The opposite—fluid camera movement away from the scene—is often used to give a powerful sense of ending to a film. It can be especially effective when it pulls away from continuing action, as in the final helicopter camera shot in *Zorba the Greek*, picturing Zorba (Anthony Quinn) and his friend (Alan Bates) dancing on the beach. Our slow exit while the action is in progress gives us the feeling that the dance continues indefinitely.

The mobile camera can also provide the tremendous sense of immediacy and dynamism that French director Abel Gance strove for in his 1927 *Napoleon*. Film historian Kevin Brownlow describes Gance and his film in the *Napoleon* program brochure for its 1981 reissue:

> To him, a tripod was a set of crutches supporting a lame imagination. His aim was to free the camera, to hurl it into the middle of the action, to force the audience from mere spectators into active participants.
>
> Technicians in the German studios were putting the camera on wheels. Gance put it on wings. He strapped it to the back of a horse, for rapid inserts in the chase across Corsica; he suspended it from overhead wires, like a miniature cable-car; he mounted it on a huge pendulum, to achieve the vertigo-inducing storm in the convention.[5]

In some films, the dynamism of the camera evokes the drama of a scene. During a crucial moment in a scene of *North Country*, director Niki Caro somewhat abruptly moves her camera around the corner post of a front porch on which a mother (Charlize Theron) talks to her teenage son about the secret of his paternity: This cinemagraphic motion seems to emulate the affective evolution that the scene records.

Two modern developments have greatly increased the potential of the mobile camera. The first of these, the **Steadicam,** is a portable, one-person camera with a built-in gyroscopic device that prevents any sudden jerkiness and provides a smooth, rock-steady image even when the person carrying it is running up a flight of steps or down a rocky mountain path. The second development, the **Skycam,** is a small, computerized, remote-controlled camera that can be mounted on the top of a lightweight magnesium pole or can "fly" on wires at speeds of up to twenty miles an hour and can go practically anywhere that cables can be strung. Helicopter mounts with gyroscopic stabilizers also create spectacular gyrosphere shots.

FIGURE 5.15 **The Packed Screen** The most obvious way to keep the screen alive is to pack almost every square inch of its surface with visual information, as in this scene from *The Last King of Scotland* (starring Forest Whitaker and James McAvoy).

Editing and Movement The editing process also contributes greatly to the cinematic film's stream of images. The editing, in fact, often creates the most vibrant visual rhythms in a film, as the editorial cuts and transitions propel us instantaneously from a **long shot** (a shot, taken from some distance, that shows the subject as well as its surroundings) to a close-up, from one camera angle to another, and from one setting to another.

The cinematographer thus uses a wide variety of techniques, either separately or in various combinations, to keep the visual image in constant motion:

- the movement of the subject within the fixed frame
- vertical or horizontal movement of the camera (tilting and panning)
- apparent movement of the viewer toward or away from the objects in the frame (zoom lens)
- completely free movement of the camera and constantly changing viewpoint (mobile camera and editorial cuts)

Dead Screen and Live Screen The director must be concerned with keeping the image alive in another sense. In almost every shot, the director attempts to communicate a significant amount of information in each frame (Figure 5.15). To achieve this **live screen,** each shot must be composed so that the visual frame is loaded with cinematic information, and large blank areas (dead screen) are avoided—unless, as in some cases, there is a dramatic purpose for dead screen.

Creating an Illusion of Depth

Cinematic composition must be concerned with creating an illusion of depth on what is essentially a two-dimensional screen (Figures 5.16, 5.17). To achieve this, the cinematographer employs several different techniques.

FIGURE 5.16 Moving Background, Vibrant Foreground A director attempts to incorporate some kind of motion into almost every shot and often uses natural background movement to keep the screen alive. This kind of background motion, a very subordinate type, does not divert our attention from the primary subjects. In this scene from *The Bourne Ultimatum,* a running shot of Matt Damon is further enlivened by filming him in front of other people on the moving escalators.

FIGURE 5.17 Strong Visual Impact in a Static Background The figures of Diane Keaton and Woody Allen occupy a very small portion of the frame in this scene from *Manhattan.* The imposing architecture of the Queensborough Bridge in the background provides an aesthetically pleasing composition and a strong sense of three-dimensionality and underscores the sense of place that is an integral part of the film.

1. **Movement of Subject (Fixed Frame).** When using a fixed frame, the director creates the illusion of depth by filming the subject moving toward or away from the camera, either head-on or diagonally. Purely lateral movement, perpendicular to the direction in which the camera is aimed, creates a two-dimensional effect and, to avoid a flat image, should be minimized.

2. **Movement of Camera.** A camera mounted on a truck or dolly may create the illusion of depth by moving toward or away from a relatively static object. As it passes by or goes around objects, we become more aware of the depth of the image. Because the camera eye actually moves, the objects on both sides of its path constantly change their position relative to one another. The change varies according to the changing angles from which the moving camera views them. Director Allan Dwan describes this illusion: "To get the real effect of a dolly at any time, you have to pass something. . . . If you dolly past a tree, it seems to revolve. It turns around. It isn't flat anymore. But stand still and photograph a tree and it's just a flat tree."[6]

3. **Apparent Camera Movement (Zoom Lens).** By magnifying the image, the zoom lens gives us the sensation of moving closer to or farther from the camera. Not surprisingly, the zoom lens may also be used to create the illusion of depth. But because camera position does not change during zooming, there is no real change in perspective. The objects to the sides do not change their position in relation to one another as they do when the camera moves. For this reason, a zoom lens does not create the illusion of depth quite as effectively as a mobile camera.

4. **Change of Focal Planes (Rack Focus).** Most cameras, including still cameras, are designed to focus on objects at different distances from the lens.

FIGURE 5.18 Rack Focus—Moving Deeper Into the Frame   Because our attention is naturally drawn to what we can see best, the illusion of depth can be created by changing the focus during a continuous shot. These three pictures represent different stages in a single running shot. In the first picture, our attention is drawn to the sharply focused image of the batter. As the shot continues, the camera focuses on the pitcher and then on the shortstop, giving us the feeling that we are being drawn deeper into a three-dimensional frame. (The order could also be reversed, beginning the shot with the shortstop in focus and ending with the batter in focus.)

Because the eye is ordinarily drawn to what it can see best—that is, to the object in sharpest focus—the cinematographer can create a kind of three-dimensionality by using **rack focus**—in one continuous shot focusing the camera lens, in turn, on objects in different planes of depth (different distances from the camera). If the frame includes three faces, all at different distances from the camera, the cinematographer may first focus on the nearest face and then, while the shot continues, focus on the second face and then on the third, thus, in effect, creating the illusion of depth within the frame (Figure 5.18).

5. **Deep Focus.** In direct contrast to the change in focal planes is **deep focus**—the use of special lenses that allow the camera to focus simultaneously and usually with equal clarity on objects anywhere from two feet to several hundred feet away. This depth of focus approximates most clearly the ability of the human eye to see a deep range of objects in clear focus (Figure 5.19). The sustained use of this technique has a profound effect on the way the audience views the dramatic action. Writing about cinematographer Gregg Toland's use of deep focus in *Citizen Kane*, Frank Brady explains:

> [Deep focus] permitted the camera to record objects at varying distances in the same shot, in sharp, clear focus, rather than deemphasizing background. By allowing several points of view or interest to occur simultaneously, this deep-focus

FIGURE 5.19 **Deep Focus** In this frame from Adrienne Shelly's *Waitress,* the actors (including Nathan Fillion and Keri Russell) are essentially all in focus despite their clearly different distances from the camera.

photography encompassed the same range of vision as the human eye. It permitted the spectator, not the camera, to decide which character or piece of action to concentrate upon. Essentially, this form of cinematography provided the same kind of freedom that a playgoer has while watching a stage play, where the audience is not forced to look at a close-up or a single character, for example, as he must in a film, but can allow his eyes to take in anything—or everything—that is happening on stage. . . . It was an innovative and daring technique, and [director Orson] Welles had Toland shoot as many scenes as possible using the vitality of deep focus.[7]

Because each shot is loaded with rich visual and dramatic information in several planes of depth, the pace of editing needs to be slow when deep focus is used.

6. **Three-Dimensional Arrangement of People and Objects.** Perhaps the most important consideration in creating a three-dimensional image is how to arrange the people and objects to be filmed. If they are placed in separate focal planes, the cinematographer has a truly three-dimensional scene to photograph. Without such an arrangement, there is no real purpose for the various effects and techniques described above (Figure 5.20).

7. **Foreground Framing.** A three-dimensional effect is also achieved when a shot is set up so that the subject is framed by an object or objects in the near foreground. When the object that forms the frame is in focus, a strong sense of three-dimensionality is achieved. When the foreground frame is thrown out of focus, or seen in very soft focus, the three-dimensional effect is weakened somewhat but not lost, and the entire mood or atmosphere of the scene changes (Figure 5.21).

FIGURE 5.20 **Three-Dimensional Arrangement of People and Objects** The characters around Humphrey Bogart are carefully positioned for a three-dimensional effect in this scene from *Casablanca*.

FIGURE 5.21 **Foreground Framing** In one shot, the mug and bottle in the foreground framing the woman's face are in focus. In the other, they are completely out of focus.

FIGURE 5.22 **Lighting for Depth**   In the left photo, the flat lighting serves to minimize the sense of depth. When the direction, intensity, and quality of the light are changed, the same scene has greater depth and more dramatic punch.

8. **Special Lighting Effects.** By carefully controlling the angle, direction, intensity, and quality of the lighting, the director can further add to the illusion of depth (Figure 5.22). Occasionally, the director may even control the source and direction of the lighting for the purpose of expanding the limits of the frame. By positioning the light source out of camera range—to either side of, or behind, the camera—the filmmaker can cause the shadows of objects outside the frame to fall inside the frame, thus suggesting the presence of those objects. When these shadows come from objects behind the camera, they can add greatly to the three-dimensionality of the shot (Figure 5.23).

9. **Use of Reflections.** Directors also make imaginative use of reflections to create a sense of depth and pack additional information into a frame. In *The Grapes of Wrath*, for example, as the Joad truck travels across the Mohave Desert at night, the camera looks out through the windshield at the strange world it is driving through. At the same time, the pale, ghostly reflections of Tom, Al, and Pa are seen on the glass as they talk about what they are seeing. In this way, information that would usually require two shots is compressed into one. The same technique is used in *Hardcore*, where the garish neon lights of a big-city porn district are reflected on the windshield of (and, thus, superimposed upon) the worried face of a father (George C. Scott) as he tries to track his runaway daughter (Figure 5.24). In *Citizen Kane*, just after the protagonist's second wife has left him, a whole bank of mirrors lining both sides of a grand hallway in Xanadu reflect not one but multiple Charles Foster Kanes. As it is used, late in the film, the effect intensifies the essential mystery of personality developed throughout. The film reveals to its journalistic investigators that, externally, the extraordinary Kane is many men in one. The viewer understands that, internally, too, like most humans, Kane is vastly

FIGURE 5.23 **Three-Dimensional Shadows** In this scene from Charles Laughton's *The Night of the Hunter,* the orphaned boy, John, stands guard over his sleeping sister, Pearl, and looks out the window at the villainous "preacher," Harry Powers (Robert Mitchum). Mitchum sits on a bench in the yard, a gas lamp behind him casting his shadow through the window and onto the room's back wall. If the scene were evenly lit, with no shadows, it would have only two important planes of depth: Pearl, sleeping in the foreground, and John, standing in the background. Although the shadows add only one *real* plane of depth (the wall), our mind's eye is aware of objects or shapes in five different planes: Mitchum seated in the yard, the window frame, Pearl sleeping on the bed, John, and the back wall. Even more important to the scene's dramatic power is the very real sense of Mitchum's presence in the room as his shadow looms over and threatens the shadow of John on the wall.

fragmented. The celebrated hall of mirrors sequence at the end of *The Lady From Shanghai* finds Orson Welles using this technique again—this time for sustaining psychological suspense.

The nine effects described in this section have nothing to do with specialized three-dimensional projection systems such as 3-D and Cinerama. But most of them do provide a fairly effective illusion of depth. Despite a revival of studio and popular interest in 3-D films, and some new projection techniques, the effect has not been much improved—except in the case of super-expensive, meticulously engineered productions like *Avatar.* And the troublesome 3-D glasses are usually still required. The sometimes-low "literary" quality of films released in 3-D also hasn't

FIGURE 5.24 **Special Use of Reflection**   A worried father (George C. Scott) searches for his runaway daughter through a big-city porn district in this scene from *Hardcore*. By showing a reflected image on the car's windshield, director Paul Schrader has not only provided an additional plane of depth but has in effect doubled the information in the frame. We see not only what the father sees but also his reaction to it.

done much to help sell the product. Lily Tomlin perhaps sums up the problem best when it involves "live action" features:

> *Bwana Devil* in 3-D was modestly billed as "The Miracle of the Age." On the poster it promised, "A Lion in Your Lap! A Lover in Your Arms!". . . What more could one ask for? Well, a better script, perhaps. Is there a rule somewhere that says that for every giant techno-step we take forward we must take one step back and touch base with banality? So often, what we expect to be techno-leaps turn out to be techno-trash.[8]

(See further references to 3-D–enhanced movies below in the "F/X of Animated Films" section of this chapter.)

SPECIALIZED CINEMATIC TECHNIQUES

Directors and cinematographers also employ a variety of specialized visual techniques that enhance certain qualities of the action or dramatic situation being filmed.

Handheld Camera

Related to the concept of cinematic point of view is the specialized dramatic effect achieved through use of a handheld camera. The jerky, uneven movement of the camera heightens the sense of reality provided by the subjective viewpoint. In *Alambrista!* Robert Young employed a handheld camera, making the perspective jump madly to reflect the disassociation his Hispanic hero feels in a foreign country. If the viewpoint is not intended to be subjective, the same technique can give a sequence the feel of a documentary or newsreel. The handheld camera, jerkiness and all, is especially effective in filming violent action scenes because the random, chaotic camera movement fits in with the spirit of the action. During the past several decades, however, the handheld camera has been overused in so-called slasher horror films in an attempt to create suspense.

Camera Angles

Cinematographers do more with the camera than simply position it for one of the four basic viewpoints. The angle from which an event or object is photographed is an important factor in cinematic composition. Sometimes cinematographers employ different camera angles to add variety or to create a sense of visual balance between one shot and another. Camera angles also communicate special kinds of dramatic information or emotional attitudes. Because the objective point of view stresses or employs a normal, straightforward view of the action, unusual camera angles are used primarily to present other points of view, such as the subjective viewpoint of a participant in the action or the interpretive viewpoint of the director.

When the camera is placed below eye level, creating a **low-angle shot,** the size and importance of the subject are exaggerated. If a child is the principal figure in a film, low-angle shots of adults may be very much in evidence, as the director attempts to show us the scene from a child's perspective. For example, in *Night of the Hunter* (see, again, Figure 5.23) two children are attempting to escape from the clutches of a Satanic itinerant preacher (Robert Mitchum) who has already murdered their mother. As the children attempt to launch a boat from the bank, Mitchum's figure is seen from a low angle as he crashes through the brush lining the bank and plunges into the water. The terror of the narrow escape is intensified by the low camera angle, which clearly communicates the helplessness of the children and their view of the monstrous Mitchum.

A different effect is achieved in *Lord of the Flies* (1963), where Ralph, pursued to the point of exhaustion by the savage boys on the beach, falls headlong in the sand at the feet of a British naval officer. The low-angle shot of the officer, exaggerating his size and solidity, conveys a sense of dominance, strength, and protectiveness to Ralph. This kind of shot is used repeatedly throughout Richard Rush's *The Stunt Man* to establish and maintain the image of the film director, Eli Cross (Peter O'Toole), as a kind of all-powerful, godlike figure.

An effect opposite to that of the low-angle shot is generally achieved by placing the camera *above* eye level, creating a **high-angle shot,** which seems to dwarf the subject and diminish its importance. When an extremely high camera angle is combined with slow, fluid camera movement, as though the camera were slowly floating over the scene, the impression is that of a remote, external, detached spectator carefully examining a situation in an objective, almost scientific, manner (Figure 5.25). Consider, for example, a high-angle shot that would show Gulliver's view of the Lilliputians. Writer-director Francis Ford Coppola and cinematographer Bill Butler open *The Conversation* with a high-angle shot of Union Square in San Francisco. The tantalizing, persistent memory of this camera angle continues to color viewers' perception throughout the film—on levels of plot, character, and theme.

FIGURE 5.25 **Extremely High Camera Angle** When the mobile camera seems to float slowly high above the action, as in both the opening and closing scenes of director Sean Penn's *The Pledge* (starring Jack Nicholson as a man who may have gone mad from the weight of his promises), we become very remote and detached, and our objectivity (like our viewpoint) becomes almost godlike.

The director may employ certain camera angles to suggest the feeling he or she wants to convey about a character at a given moment (Figure 5.26). In *Touch of Evil*, Orson Welles employs a high camera angle to look down on Janet Leigh as she enters a prison cell. The shot emphasizes her despair and her helplessness. By making us see the character as he sees her, Welles interprets the emotional tenor and atmosphere of the scene for us. In one of the most famous shots in *Citizen Kane*, Gregg Toland utilizes an extremely high camera angle as Kane makes a political speech; the protagonist is shown as a tiny, insignificant figure in the film frame. Most shrewdly, though, Welles places this image in front of a gigantic poster of Kane that creates the opposite effect simultaneously: The politician looms power-fully above the world. Thus, the interior conflicts within Kane's life are presented cinematically.

Color, Diffusion, and Soft Focus

Directors use filters to create a wide range of specialized effects. They may use special filters to darken the blue of the sky, thereby sharpening by contrast the whiteness of the clouds, or they may add a light-colored tone to the whole scene by filming it through a colored filter. For example, in *A Man and a Woman* a love scene was filmed with a red filter, which imparted a romantic warmth.

On rare occasions, a special filter may be used to add a certain quality to a whole film. An example is Franco Zeffirelli's film version of *The Taming of the Shrew*, where a subtle light-diffusing filter (a nylon stocking over the camera lens) was used to soften the focus slightly and subdue the colors in a way that gave the whole film the quality

FIGURE 5.26 The Effect of Changing Camera Angles   In these three pictures, we see the effects created by three different camera angles on the same subject in the same position. The first picture is taken from what might be called a normal angle: The camera is looking directly at the pitcher at about eye level. The second picture is taken with the camera slightly in front of the mound but located five or six feet above the pitcher's head, looking down on him in a high-angle shot. For the third picture, the camera is located on the ground in front of the pitcher, looking up at him in a low-angle shot.

of an old master's painting (for more examples of this phenomenon, see Chapter 7, "Color"). This technique was designed to give the film a mellow, aged quality, intensifying the sense that the action was taking place in another time period. A similar effect was employed in *McCabe & Mrs. Miller* and *Summer of '42*, but in the latter the quality suggested was not of a historical era but of the hazy images of the narrator's memory. In a crucial family reunion scene in *Bonnie and Clyde*, director Arthur Penn and cinematographer Burnet Guffey deliberately overexposed their film footage to create similar effects. For *Excalibur*, director John Boorman used green gel filters over his arc lamps to give the forest exteriors a lyric vernal glow, emphasizing the green of the moss and the leaves and creating a sense of otherworldliness.

Soft (slightly blurred) focus can also help to convey certain subjective states. In *Mr. Smith Goes to Washington*, soft focus is used to reflect a warm, romantic glow (falling in love) that comes over Saunders (Jean Arthur) as Jeff Smith (Jimmy Stewart) describes the natural beauties of the Willet Creek country where he plans to build his boys' camp.

In Mike Nichols's *The Graduate*, Elaine Robinson (Katharine Ross) is seen out of focus as she learns that the older woman with whom Benjamin had an affair

FIGURE 5.27 **The Effects of Wide-Angle and Telephoto Lenses** These two pictures illustrate the different effects achieved by photographing the same scene with a wide-angle lens and a telephoto lens. The wide-angle shot (left) makes the distance between the man and woman seem much greater, and the frame covers a much wider area in the background. The telephoto shot (right) seems to bring the man and woman closer together and narrows the area of background in the frame.

wasn't "just another older woman." The blurred face expresses her state of shock and confusion, and her face comes slowly back into focus only when she fully takes in what Benjamin (Dustin Hoffman) is trying to tell her. A similar technique is used earlier in the film to convey Benjamin's panic. After hearing Mr. Robinson's car pull up, Benjamin races hurriedly from Elaine's bedroom to return to the bar downstairs. As he reaches the foot of the stairs, Benjamin is shown in blurred focus as he dashes down the hall to the bar. He comes back into focus only as he reaches the relative safety of the barstool, just as Mr. Robinson enters the front door.

Special Lenses

Special lenses are often employed to provide subjective distortions of normal reality. Both wide-angle and telephoto lenses distort the depth perspective of an image, but in opposite ways. A **wide-angle lens** exaggerates the perspective, so that the distance between an object in the foreground and one in the background seems much greater than it actually is. A **telephoto lens** compresses depth so that the distance between foreground and background objects seems less than it actually is (Figure 5.27).

The effect of this distortion becomes most apparent when background-to-foreground movement is introduced. In *The Graduate*, for example, near the end, the track-star hero is filmed running toward the camera in a frantic race to interrupt the wedding ceremony, and a telephoto distortion makes him appear to gain very little headway despite his efforts, thus emphasizing his frustration and his desperation. Had a wide-angle lens been used in the same way, his speed would have been greatly exaggerated.

FIGURE 5.28 Fish-Eye Lens The distortion of a fish-eye lens conveys the fear and frustration felt by Ellen Burstyn's character in Darren Aronofsky's *Requiem for a Dream* as she endures the effects of diet drugs she is taking.

A special type of extreme wide-angle lens, called a **fish-eye lens,** bends both horizontal and vertical planes and distorts depth relationships. It is often used to create unusual subjective states such as dreams, fantasies, or intoxication (Figure 5.28).

Fast Motion

If a scene is filmed at less-than-normal speed and then projected at normal speed, the result is **fast motion.** Fast motion resembles the frantic, jerky movements of improperly projected old silent comedies and is usually employed for comic effect or to compress the time of an event. Stanley Kubrick used fast motion for comic effect in a scene from *A Clockwork Orange.* Alex (Malcolm McDowell) picks up two young girls and takes both to his room for a frantic sex romp, which is filmed in fast motion and accompanied musically by the *William Tell* Overture. (For a discussion of **slow motion,** see Chapter 6.)

An extreme form of fast motion is **time-lapse photography,** which has the effect of greatly compressing time. In time-lapse filming, one frame is exposed at regular intervals that may be thirty minutes or more apart. This technique compresses into a few seconds something that normally takes hours or weeks, such as the blossoming of a flower or the construction of a house. Supported by a kinetic, mesmerizing score by Philip Glass, this camera technique is used to great emotional and thematic effect in the nonnarrative 1983 film *Koyaanisqatsi* and its two sequels, *Powaqqatsi* (1988) and *Naqoyqatsi* (2002).

Special Lighting Effects

In *The Grapes of Wrath*, Gregg Toland employs a light reflected in the pupils of Tom Joad's (Henry Fonda) eyes at his first emotional meeting with Ma Joad (Jane Darwell) after four years in prison. Although the special lighting is done with such subtlety that it is not obvious to the casual viewer, it gives the moment a unique quality. Tom's eyes literally light up as he greets her.

Another special moment of reunion is created by lighting on the eyes of Lara (Julie Christie) in *Doctor Zhivago* when she sees Zhivago (Omar Sharif) in a remote village library after a year of separation. By highlighting her eyes, the cinematographer intensifies the emotional impact of the scene. Either Christie's eyes did not express the emotion fully enough or the change was so subtle that it needed to be pulled out from background details to create the desired effect.

Subtle changes in lighting are also employed in another touching scene from *The Grapes of Wrath*. As Ma Joad burns her souvenirs while preparing to leave for California, she discovers a pair of earrings she wore as a young woman. As she puts them up to her ears, subtle changes in the direction of light, accompanied by some gradual diffusion, make her seem to grow younger before our eyes. Then, as she takes them down again and the memory fades, we see the wrinkling and hard lines reappear as the original lighting returns (see Figure 2.14 again).

At the conclusion of the superb documentary film *Visions of Light: The Art of Cinematography* (available on DVD), several master cinematographers offer observations about the power and future of cinematic storytelling. Ernest Dickerson, who was the director of photography (DP) on Spike Lee's *Do the Right Thing* and *Malcolm X*, says that "if the director is . . . the author of the performances [and] . . . story of the film, the cinematographer is the author of the use of light in the film and how it contributes to the story." John Bailey, who shot Robert Redford's *Ordinary People* and Paul Schrader's *Mishima*, believes that "today in motion picture technology, we are really at a precipice, a jumping off point into an . . . unknown but possibly very exciting future, in the same way that, in the '50s, when Cinemascope and . . . Cinerama, all these new formats, really shook up the whole way we were looking at films. We have that opportunity now." Finally, Allen Daviau, the cinematographer for Steven Spielberg's *E.T.* and Barry Levinson's *Avalon*, begins to capture the subtlety and mystery of the form: "Someone once said that the lighting, the look of a film, makes the pauses speak as eloquently as the words—that you have moments in films that happen because of what is there visually, how someone is lit or not lit. You put something in the audience's mind visually and they will carry away images as well as the words."[9]

MOVIE MAGIC: SPECIAL VISUAL EFFECTS IN THE MODERN FILM

As admission prices escalated and the lure of television kept more and more people at home for their entertainment, motion pictures began to incorporate elements that television could not provide. One was the special effect, which created visual spectacle on a grand scale and showed audiences things they had never seen before.

Recent advances in technology have made elaborate special effects (F/X) an important part of the modern film. Given proper time and money, there are few things modern special-effects technicians cannot realize on-screen—though truly top-quality visuals can be prohibitively expensive. This capability has opened a new frontier to the filmmakers; it allows them to use the medium to its fullest extent and enables them to really show viewers what they wish to show, instead of just telling them about it. This increased flexibility is also a great asset to the industry. Too often, however, elaborate visual effects do not just serve to enhance the story but become the focus of the film. Certainly, F/X masters Rick Baker and Richard Edlund provide the most striking aspects of *The Nutty Professor* (1996; and its sequel, *The Klumps*) and *Multiplicity*, respectively. In the former, special makeup effects enable Eddie Murphy to play not only a very fat Sherman Klump but also most of the members of his hilarious family; in the latter, miraculous visual effects permit Michael Keaton to portray three cloned versions of his overworked protagonist. In David Fincher's *The Social Network*, magical cinematic technology allows actor Armie Hammer convincingly to portray *both* of the film's real-life, six-foot-five-inch Winklevoss twins, Olympic athletes from Harvard. Robert Zemeckis explains in his commentary on the DVD version of his film *Contact* that nearly every shot utilized some form of visual effect, either obvious or unobtrusive. James Cameron spent more than a decade perfecting the astounding special visual effects for *Avatar*.

Special effects have been an integral part of film throughout its history. Such cinema pioneers as Georges Mèliés (*A Trip to the Moon*, 1902), D. W. Griffith (*Intolerance*, 1916), Fritz Lang (*Metropolis*, 1926), and Willis O'Brien (special effects coordinator for Merian C. Cooper's *King Kong*, 1933) originated the most basic techniques such as the now-standard **matte** and **glass shots.** But only recently has technology produced effects so sophisticated that the audience often cannot distinguish between footage of a real object and a special-effect miniature. Not all effects are of the flashy laser-blast variety. They range from ones that simply recreate in dramatic form a familiar, historic, or real event to those that create totally fantastic people, creatures, places, or occurrences that stretch the viewer's imagination. Modern masters such as Douglas Trumbull of the Future General Company and John Dykstra of George Lucas's Industrial Light and Magic wield the tools of technological "motion control"—the **blue-screen** (or, more currently, green-screen) **process,** optical printers, and **computer-generated imaging (CGI)**—to weave their magic spells (Figure 5.29).

Miniaturization was used to recreate the sinking of the American naval fleet at Pearl Harbor on December 7, 1941, in *Tora! Tora! Tora!* Special effects, often the backbone of disaster films, simulate the destruction of Los Angeles in *Earthquake!*, the loss by aging of the Genesis planet in *Star Trek III: The Search for Spock*, the exploding of the White House in *Independence Day*, and even the burning of Atlanta in *Gone With the Wind*.

Other effects extend human powers: *Time Bandits'* Evil Wizard casts lightning bolts from his fingertips, *Excalibur's* Merlin weaves his magic, Clark Kent defies gravity as Superman, Spider-Man springs aloft, and Harry Potter commands his broom (Figure 5.30).

Flying-vehicle effects, a staple of many science fiction films, range from the frenetic outer-space dogfights in *Star Wars*, to the majestic liftoff of the Mothership

FIGURE 5.29 **Special-Effects Miniatures**   Creating the illusion (with the complex assistance of advanced CGI technology) that miniature models are full-sized is essential to making us believe the incredible size, speed, and radical capabilities of the title performers in *Transformers: Revenge of the Fallen.*

FIGURE 5.30 **Flying Special Effectively**   The green-screen and computer-driven special effects that allow the exciting flight scenes in *Harry Potter and the Goblet of Fire* constitute quantum leaps beyond the techniques used in levitating such earlier flying creatures as Superman (in his various incarnations).

from *Close Encounters of the Third Kind,* to the spectacular shift to warp speed by *Star Trek*'s Starship *Enterprise.* This optical effect is created in the printing process. The primary image (such as a spaceship) is superimposed on another image (such as a starfield background), and the two are composited onto one strip of film by an optical printer. Modern optical printers are guided by computer, affording precise matching of a tremendous number of different images.

Movie audiences are so fascinated with strange creatures that the unnatural monsters can be as crude as the early Godzilla (a man in a rubber suit) or as convincing as Alien (likewise, a man in a rubber suit). They may be remote controlled (like the title creature in *E.T. The Extra-Terrestrial*), a sophisticated puppet (like the Jedi master Yoda from *The Empire Strikes Back* and *Return of the Jedi*, and computer-generated (Yoda in *Attack of the Clones* and *Revenge of the Sith*), or **stop-motion animated** (like the ape in the original *King Kong*); or they may combine several techniques (like the dragon Vermithrax Pejorative in *Dragonslayer*). They may be subtly inhuman, like certain forms of Count Dracula in *Bram Stoker's Dracula*, or unmistakably monstrous, like the giant snake in *Conan the Barbarian* or *Anaconda* (Figure 5.31). The master of this technique is Ray Harryhausen. Perhaps the most appealing use of such technology so far has been in George Miller and Christopher Noonan's *Babe*, the 1995 film for children of all ages that combined puppets and computer-generated effects with real animals to create a seamless and believable entertainment.

The mythical concept that some human beings can magically transform themselves into other life forms has enjoyed tremendous popularity over the years. This effect has come far since 1941, when Lon Chaney Jr., became the Wolfman (Figure 5.32). Subsequent transformations have turned men and women into snakes (*Conan the Barbarian*), black panthers (*Cat People*), reptilian monsters (*The Sword and the Sorcerer*), primates and amorphous superconscious beings (*Altered States*), enormous insects (*The Fly*), and, of course, werewolves (*The Howling, An American Werewolf in London,* and *Wolf*)—all on-screen. Curiously, many of these makeup effects were not makeup in the traditional sense at all but rather were sculpted remote-controlled models (such as the transforming head from *American Werewolf*). So unorthodox were the transformation effects for *The Thing* (1982) that an effort was made to have artist Rob Bottin's work classified as visual effects instead of makeup. The title character in *Bram Stoker's Dracula* becomes a study in the transformation process, taking not just one but several physical forms: bats, wolves, rats, and even an evil, fast-creeping mist.

Gore effects—the simulation of many different kinds of deaths, decapitations, and eviscerations—are at least partly responsible for the upsurge of murder movies in the "hack 'n' slash" horror vein.

Creative production designers work with special-effects teams to create diverse locales such as the glittering crystalline world of Krypton in *Superman*, the drug-induced, hallucinogenic reality of *Altered States*, the interior of the human body in *Fantastic Voyage*, the sparkling high-tech starship bridge of *Star Trek: The Wrath of Khan*, the oppressive, smog-shrouded futurescape of *Blade Runner,* and, of course, the "real" world of the *Matrix* films. In 2010, Christopher Nolan accented the intersection of architecture and dreamscape in his challenging, provocative film *Inception*.

The effects that are currently available provide filmmakers with a seemingly endless variety of tricks to use, yet many of the effects that seem so amazing and fascinating today will probably seem tame and outdated when they are compared with those in next season's releases. The primary factor in this rapid increase in technology is **CGI**—computer-generated imaging. In June 1990, when active discussions began about making Michael Crichton's novel *Jurassic Park* into a film, the computer programs that would be needed to animate the dinosaurs didn't exist.

FIGURE 5.31 Evolving Life Forms
Creature effects are becoming more and more sophisticated in modern films, progressing from the rather primitive but effective single-frame animation of the original *King Kong* (top) to the combination of animation and remote-controlled movement in the multiple F/X magic of *Babe* (middle). And now the puppet face of the Jedi master Yoda from *The Empire Strikes Back* has evolved to the remarkably expressive CGI (computer-generated imaging) face and mobile form of that character in *Star Wars, Episode II: Attack of the Clones* and *Episode III: Revenge of the Sith* (bottom).

FIGURE 5.32 **Transformation** In *The Wolf Man* (left), Lon Chaney Jr., became the Wolfman at the full moon by having his makeup applied in six or seven stages while the camera was turned off, creating the illusion of a slow, miraculous transformation when the film was run continuously. The man-becomes-beast techniques used in such films as *The Howling, An American Werewolf in London, Altered States,* and *Wolf* are much more complex and employ sculpted, remote-controlled latex models of the actors' heads. And the visual effects team must have worked overtime in constructing convincing talons for Hugh Jackman in *X-Men Origins: Wolverine.*

They not only exist today, but *Jurassic Park* and its sequels, including *The Lost World,* have established a new benchmark for measuring the effectiveness of realistic computer animation in film. The prehistoric creatures move seamlessly through the frame, their motions just as believable and lifelike as those of their human costars. Actually, computer animation is only part of the story, for the special effects often combine several different technologies, as Peter Biskind describes the first Tyrannosaurus rex attack in the first film.

> The scene itself plays like a blur of motion, but in reality, only the top half of the dinosaur was built [as a full-scale puppet], and it was set on top of a flight simulator, which was bolted to the soundstage floor. "It was like a giant shark up on legs," says [Rick] Carter [production designer], "and perfectly designed to be as threatening as you could ever imagine." The motion was achieved by moving the sets around the dinosaur, and the live action footage was enhanced by a computer. Anytime the entire dinosaur is visible in the frame, computer animation is responsible.[10]

Computer animation was also used to fill the skies over Germany with B-17 bombers in *Memphis Belle.* The unusual and powerful images in *The Abyss* and *Terminator 2: Judgment Day* utilized reflection mapping, a technique that simulates reflections of real-world images on three-dimensional objects that are modeled and rendered on a computer. The results are especially convincing in *Terminator 2* and *Terminator 3: Rise of the Machines,* featuring superhuman villains with powers of regeneration that previously could be realized only by Looney Tunes animators. A similar technique was used in *The Matrix Reloaded* to realize hundreds of identical Agent Smiths (Hugo Weaving) whom Neo (Keanu Reeves) fights.

The real measure of an effect's success has become how well the effect is integrated into the storyline of the film. No longer is it a challenge to make the effect

itself believable. In the modern film, the integration of special effects, not the domination of special effects, is the proper measure of success.

The best films use their special effects as little—or as much—as necessary, and no more. *Star Wars* incorporated some 365 individual visual effects, all of which serve to propel the story forward. In contrast, *Time After Time* (1979) uses only a few simple optical effects to send H. G. Wells into the future, but they effectively establish that film's whimsical nature. Tremendous time and money were devoted to the flying sequences of *Superman* (1978) because it was crucial to the film's credibility that the audience believe a man could fly.

In the best films, the visuals create the atmosphere for the story and impel the story forward; they become simply one of many properly integrated elements of the film. *E.T. The Extra-Terrestrial* is filled with dazzling effects from beginning to end; E.T. itself is on-screen for a great portion of the picture. Yet all these dazzling effects do not impair the warm, friendly ambience of the film because they are well integrated.

The potential power of such visuals, however, often tempts filmmakers to overuse them, to let them overwhelm the story. *The Thing* (1982) featured so many transformation sequences that the internal suspense the director was striving for was destroyed, and so much focus was placed on *Blade Runner*'s grimly detailed futurescape that its characters sometimes seem lost in it. Francis Ford Coppola's *Bram Stoker's Dracula* provides us with many special effects from the entire sweep of cinema history, causing one critic to complain that "the film throws so much fancy technique at its story that the usually foolproof drama at its core gets drowned in a tide of images."[11]

At the other extreme is Mike Nichols's *Wolf.* Jack Nicholson transforms gradually, first by subtle changes in his personality after being bitten by a wolf, then finally into the animal, with little emphasis on the special effects required.

There is a final role that special effects can play, achieving the novel or nontraditional effect, or gimmick, called for by certain films. Noteworthy novelty effects include the use of clips from classic films to allow Steve Martin to interact with stars like Humphrey Bogart in *Dead Men Don't Wear Plaid* and Woody Allen to interact with Calvin Coolidge and Herbert Hoover in *Zelig* (Figure 5.33). Advances in computer-generated imagery took this interaction effect one step farther in *Forrest Gump.* The film's chocoholic hero interacts directly with historical figures such

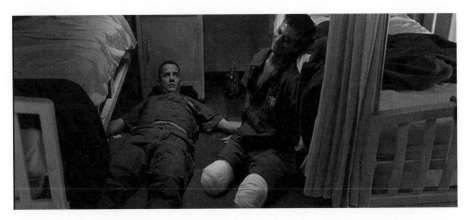

FIGURE 5.34 Credible F/X In *Forrest Gump*, the protagonist (Tom Hanks) admires and assists his former military boss, Lieutenant Dan (Gary Sinise), who has lost his legs in the Vietnam War. Through the magic of computer imaging, the effect is so convincing that many viewers cannot believe that the actor has not shared his character's medical fate. Successful special visual effects help to ensure that narratives will be credible.

as Presidents Kennedy, Johnson, and Nixon, shaking hands with them and engaging in what seem to be two-way conversations.

Special visual effects are also used in a serious, thematically integrated fashion in *Forrest Gump*. During the Vietnam conflict, Gump's buddy Lieutenant Dan loses his legs in combat. Through the magic of digital manipulation, special-effects wizards used computers to "erase" the lower limbs of the fully ambulatory actor Gary Sinise; the effect was so realistic that many viewers were amazed. Upon seeing the film, for example, the actress Anne Bancroft said she "was so shocked. I thought [Sinise] had lost his legs. I turned to Mel [Brooks, her husband] and I said, 'Mel, did he lose his legs?' And Mel said, 'I don't know.' I felt so sorry for that poor man."[12] (More recently, for serious dramatic purposes, the filmmakers digitally erased one of actor Clifton Collins, Jr.'s arms in *Sunshine Cleaning* with a similar effect.) Such magical movie moments, of course, gladden the hearts of special-effects creators (Figure 5.34).

James Cameron (also the director of *The Abyss*, *Terminator 2*, *True Lies*, and *Titanic*) once observed that in the future actors would be able to perform without boundary, through images stored in computers. Such a performance has already been effected in *Sky Captain and the World of Tomorrow*. In this film, Laurence Olivier, though long deceased, made a major appearance via the magic of computer manipulation of images and sound. Likewise, Marlon Brando performs posthumously in *Superman Returns*.

As Joe Dante, director of the *Gremlins* movies, points out, however, a special effect now is "only as good as an actor's reaction to it. So if you have a really great effect and you cut to an actor who doesn't look like he's believing what he's seeing, then your effect is no good." The magic still has plenty of reasons to endure, though. Richard Edlund thinks that "visual effects will continue to expand, and, as long as they continue to satisfy the audience's desire to be put in a place they couldn't otherwise possibly be put, they will continue to be successful."[13]

FIGURE 5.35 **Grown-Up Money for Animated Films** Among Pixar's consistently commercial and critical successes has been *The Incredibles,* an expensively made animated film which grandly entertains children with its clever superhero action characters and also makes their parents (and other adults) laugh at its satire of contemporary life.

THE F/X OF ANIMATED FEATURE FILMS . . . ESPECIALLY FOR ADULTS

In the United States, the stereotypic audience for animated cartoons was once a theater full of screaming kids. This perception has changed radically in the last decade, and in recent years animated films (including the *Shrek* series, *Finding Nemo, The Incredibles* [Figure 5.35], and *Up*) have been among the nation's top-grossing movies, indicating their broad appeal. In recognition of the popularity and artistic merit of animated films, a new Oscar category has been added to the Academy Awards—Best Animated Feature Film. Now, in all three of the primary types of animation (drawing, stop motion, and computer generated), the central aim of artists is to engage a decidedly adult audience. It should be noted, however, that the very best feature-length animated films have seldom been created exclusively for children, even in the golden age of Walt Disney's prime productions.

Almost from its earliest use, drawn animation encouraged the mixing of live action and artwork. Thus, the intricacies of this technique have, over the years, enabled Gene Kelly to dance on-screen with the jaunty cartoon creature Jerry the mouse (*Anchors Aweigh,* 1945) and, in one of the most complex utilizations, Bob Hoskins to interact with a whole universe of toon stars (*Who Framed Roger Rabbit,* 1988). Computers have now facilitated such activity far beyond the imaginations of animation pioneers. However, the Japanese animation master Hayao Miyazaki has continued to push the art of hand drawing to its exquisite limits in *Princess Mononoke, Spirited Away, Howl's Moving Castle,* and *Ponyo* (Figure 5.36). And in France, Sylvain Chomet has demonstrated enormous skill and wit in *The Triplets of Belleville* and *The Illusionist* (Figure 5.37).

Along with drawn animation, a second type of animated film developed on a parallel track: stop-motion animation. During this process, small objects or puppetlike figures are moved repeatedly in increments of 24-per-second while being

FLASHBACK

ANIMATION: ONCE AN OPENING ACT, NOW A MAIN EVENT

Like the puppet shows from which they evolved, animated films have long been seriously embraced by the world of international art. The first moving pictures were actually animations, not live action. A Victorian parlor amusement called the Zoetrope produced the illusion of movement when one spun a cylinder and, through slots on the cylinder's side, viewed drawings that depicted succeeding actions.[14]

Later in the nineteenth century, the illusions produced through these simple drawings of early animation developed into those of still photographs being manipulated swiftly, either mechanically or via projection. As the cinema progressed along more or less realistic lines, though, such animation pioneers as Winsor McCay, a New York newspaper cartoonist best known for his *Gertie the Dinosaur* (1914), began to explore possibilities within the fantasy worlds of animated film. By 1928, when Walt Disney created *Steamboat Willie* (and first introduced the world to a talking Mickey Mouse), animated shorts, shown before feature films, were already being produced in abundance by such artists as Max Fleischer (creator of Betty Boop) and Walter Lantz (Woody Woodpecker). Later the Warner Brothers luminaries Chuck Jones, Tex Avery, and Fritz Freleng (among many others) gave audiences the energetic antics of a whole stable of animated personalities,

1830s
Victorian toys like the Zoetrope feature moving pictures that constitute the earliest form of animation.

1914
Gertie the Dinosaur, an early narrative animated film, is released to popular acclaim.

1890s
Cinema progresses along more or less realistic lines when inventions like the Kinetoscope, which features still photographs instead of drawings, reach a public audience.

1928
Walt Disney introduces a talking Mickey Mouse.

including Bugs Bunny and Porky Pig. But it was not until the mid-1930s that Walt Disney became obsessed with the idea of entertaining viewers with animated films that were themselves the main show.

Premiering in late 1937, Disney's *Snow White and the Seven Dwarfs* set rigorously high standards that today still guide animation artists. In the Disney studio's watershed year of 1940, both *Pinocchio* and *Fantasia* appeared. These now-classic works were followed during the next two decades by a series of popular animated entertainments (including *Dumbo, Cinderella, Alice in Wonderland, Peter Pan,* and *Lady and the Tramp*), whose stories frequently originated in well-known literary narratives. The least-accomplished of these movies appeared to be targeted more progressively at younger audiences.

After Disney's death in 1966, his studio continued to make drawn animated films, but the creative energy lessened, and the company's focus shifted to producing live-action films. Then, in 1989, *The Little Mermaid* gave Disney animation new life *and* led an astonishing string of new musical animated features. Two years later, *Beauty and the Beast* emerged from an artistic process that utilized computers to assist in the conventional drawing techniques, and the film won an Academy Award nomination for Best Picture, the first such accolade for an animated feature. Like these two films, the best ones that followed—including *The Lion King, Aladdin,* and *Mulan*—continued the classic Disney conventions: bold visuals, shrewd scripts, and both thematic universality and surprise that we find in all great films, animated or otherwise.

1937
Snow White and the Seven Dwarfs released, popularizing feature-length animations.

1989
The success of *The Little Mermaid* renews interest in musical animated features.

2003
Spirited Away (Hayao Miyazaki) wins an Oscar for Best Animated Feature.

1966
Walt Disney dies; feature-length animations begin to lose popularity.

1998
DreamWorks releases its first feature-length animated film, *Antz*.

2010
Disney campaigns for *Toy Story III*'s nomination for an Oscar for Best Picture.

FIGURE 5.36 **Japanese Animation Master**   Even after Hayao Miyazaki created the beautiful, hand-drawn *Princess Mononoke* and "retired" from his exhausting art, he returned to give the world three more masterpieces: *Spirited Away*, *Howl's Moving Castle*, and *Ponyo* (shown here).

FIGURE 5.37 **Witty French Artist**   One of the most strangely endearing of recent animated films, *The Triplets of Belleville*, directed by Sylvain Chomet, features not only the eponymous three sisters, but also a determined young bicycle racer, his amazing grandmother, and a dog that possesses a very un-Hollywood-like charm.

FIGURE 5.38 **British Magician** A modern master of stop-motion animation is Nick Park, whose films such as *The Wrong Trousers* and *The Curse of the Were-Rabbit*, starring Wallace and his dog Gromit, provide dry, unsentimental, but affecting humor.

photographed. Past masters of the technique have included such legendary special-effects animators (working in live-action fantasy films) as George Pal (*When Worlds Collide*), Willis O'Brien (*King Kong* and the original *Mighty Joe Young*), and Ray Harryhausen (*Mighty Joe Young* and *Clash of the Titans*). Contemporary artists of stop-motion animation who best command our imaginations are the British animator Nick Park and the American Henry Selick—with detail-obsessed Wes Anderson making an impressive entry into the field with his *Fantastic Mr. Fox*.

Park, most celebrated for his Best-Animated Oscar-winning films featuring the character Wallace and his dog Gromit—including *A Grand Day Out*, *The Wrong Trousers*, *A Close Shave*, and *The Curse of the Were-Rabbit* (Figure 5.38)—has said that he personally gets "turned off" by certain characteristic elements in the newer Disney animated musical films: "the sanitized stories and the sickly-sweet characters."[15] And Park himself projects a droll, unsentimental sense of humor through his figures, as we can see in *Chicken Run*, his first longer feature.

Henry Selick directed both Tim Burton's *The Nightmare Before Christmas* and *James and the Giant Peach*—the former a stop-action film that is wholly original and sometimes immensely frightening in its images, the latter an adaptation of Roald Dahl's popular children's book that begins in live action and segues impressively into stop-action animation before returning to live action at its end. *James and the Giant Peach* pulls no punches with its presentation of violence and its treatment of monumental fears (abandonment, for example) that are no less vividly real for adults than for children, and just the title of Tim Burton's *Corpse Bride* (directed by Mike Johnson and Burton) suggests the principally "adult" nature of its subject matter and humor (Figure 5.39).

FIGURE 5.39 Scary American Magicians The stop-motion animator Henry Selick, working with multi-talented director Tim Burton, amazed and frightened audiences of all ages with *The Nightmare Before Christmas* and *James and the Giant Peach*. Later, Burton collaborated with animator Mike Johnson to intensify those films' delights in the Best–Animated Oscar-nominated *Corpse Bride*. And Selick created *Coraline* (shown here), which showcases the sophistication of both its graphic technology and its story.

Noonan and Miller's charming *Babe* (1995), nominated for a Best Picture Oscar, and its critically acclaimed, poorly released, and little-seen sequel, *Babe: Pig in the City* (1998), both combine live action, puppets (in the form of intricate animatronic devices), and computer animation. Public reaction to the comic violence involving animals in *Pig in the City* ensured that its small and primary audience would most likely be adults, not children.

Throughout many modern animation features, a certain dark, sometimes even macabre, humor abides. A similar "adult" amusement has also become a staple in the third and latest type of animated feature film, which is generated solely by art filtered through computer technology. This process often appears almost to synthesize the smooth movement of drawn images and the plastic surfaces of stop-motion puppets. The first such film, 1995's *Toy Story* (Figure 5.40), directed by John Lasseter for his Pixar studio, contains the sort of gentle satire that we have come to expect in children's films. But it also presents a sequence in which a child plays with dolls that have been mutilated and reassembled in monstrous new shapes. And the excellent sequel, *Toy Story 2* (1999), provided further evidence of its creators' interest in the darker side of all life. Pixar (now owned by Disney) has also produced *Monsters, Inc.*, whose lovable monsters appealed to children while its satiric humor was clearly aimed at adults, and other large commercial and critical successes, including *Finding Nemo* (Figure 5.41), *The Incredibles*, *Cars*, *Ratatouille*, *WALL-E*, *Up*, and, in 3-D, *Toy Story 3* (Figure 5.42).

FIGURE 5.40 Contemporary Animation Pioneers The first wholly computer-generated animated feature, Pixar's *Toy Story* (1995), was directed by John Lasseter and starred the cowboy Woody (voiced by Tom Hanks) and his comic adversary, Buzz Lightyear (Tim Allen), an astronaut. Its almost universal acceptance by audiences and critics alike led to *Toy Story 2* four years later—and *Toy Story 3*, in 3-D, in 2010; between *2* and *3*, the saga's human characters aged in real time.

FIGURE 5.41 Lost Children Despite their being "movies for children," classic Disney animated films often included wrenching themes of violence and loss. Pixar's immensely popular *Finding Nemo* carried on this tradition with an opening scene in which literally hundreds of fish babies lose their mother in a shark attack. Ultimately, Nemo, the sole survivor, is also separated from his father during a frightening yet splendidly adventurous journey. Here the little clownfish (Alexander Gould) attempts to talk with a helpful—if comically memory-deficient—fellow traveler named Dory (Ellen DeGeneres).

Finally, if we try to seek proof that contemporary animated feature films invite adults to be a major part of their audience, we need to turn back to *The Prince of Egypt*. Here is a movie that takes as its subject one of the most archetypal narratives of world myth (not to mention Judeo-Christian scripture) and, in addition, envisions its Moses-led characters through immensely stylized and sophisticated visual modes (including elongated El Greco faces). And we immediately recognized that the animated feature had begun to grow up when its makers, the Dreamworks team

FIGURE 5.42 **Animation Yearns to Transcend the Past—By Embracing an "Old" Technology**   In competition with Disney and Pixar, Dreamworks and other studios contributed to the plethora of animated features released in the first decade of the twenty-first century. One older "niche" technology regained some of its original, 1950s vigor: improved 3-D techniques helped also to popularize such diverse movies as Tim Burton's *Alice in Wonderland (2010)* and *A Christmas Carol* and *Beowulf* (both directed by Robert Zemeckis).

of Steven Spielberg, Jeffrey Katzenberg, and David Geffen, initially flatly refused to authorize any miniature toy or product advertising tie-ins with fast-food chains. Katzenberg summarized their attitude: "We tried to be uncompromising here—there's nothing cute and adorable in the film. In other words, we didn't make a camel funny."[16]

At its release in 1998, film reviewer Richard Corliss described *The Prince of Egypt* as "a grand experiment, a crusade to expand the frustratingly narrow boundaries of feature animation."[17] And Roger Ebert welcomed the film as revolutionary in its aim, scope, and artistic achievements, saying that

> "The Prince of Egypt" is one of the best looking animated films ever made. It employs computer-generated animation as an aid to traditional techniques, rather than as a substitute for them, and we sense the touch of human artists in the vision. . . . This is a film that shows animation growing up and embracing more complex themes, instead of chaining itself in the category of children's entertainment.[18]

More than a decade later, however, American commercial film animation—as proudly elemental, evolutionary, and "complex" as it remains—is still seeking a solid maturity in the worlds of both children's storytelling and adult, *global* cinematic art.

On the Cinematic Film

1. To what degree is the film cinematic? Cite specific examples from the film to prove that the director succeeds or fails in (a) keeping the image constantly alive and in motion; (b) setting up clear, crisp visual and aural rhythms; (c) creating the illusion of depth; and (d) using the other special properties of the medium.
2. Does the cinematography create clear, powerful, and effective images in a natural way, or does it self-consciously show off the skills and techniques of the cinematographer?

On Cinematic Points of View

Although the director probably employs all four cinematic viewpoints in making the film, one point of view may predominate to such a degree that the film leaves the impression of a single point of view. With this in mind, answer these questions:

1. Do you feel that you were primarily an objective, impersonal observer of the action, or did you have the sense of being a participant in the action? What specific scenes used the objective point of view? In what scenes did you feel like a participant in the action? How were you made to feel like a participant?
2. In what scenes were you aware that the director was employing visual techniques to comment on or interpret the action, forcing you to see the action in a special way? What techniques were used to achieve this? How effective were they?

On Elements of Cinematic Composition

1. Which methods does the director use to draw attention to the object of greatest significance?
2. Does the director succeed in keeping the screen alive by avoiding large areas of dead screen?
3. What are the primary or most memorable techniques used to create the illusion of three-dimensionality?

On Specialized Cinematic Techniques

1. Although a thorough analysis of each visual element is impossible, make a mental note of the pictorial effects that struck you as especially effective, ineffective, or unique, and consider them in light of these questions:
   a. What was the director's aim in creating these images, and what camera tools or techniques were employed in the filming of them?
   b. What made these memorable visual images effective, ineffective, or unique?
   c. Justify each of these impressive visual effects aesthetically in terms of its relationship to the whole film.
2. Are special lighting effects used for brief moments in the film? If so, what are the effects intended, and how successful are they?

1. How effective are the special effects employed in the film? Do they dominate the film to the point that it is just a showcase for the effects, or are they an integrated part of the film?
2. To what degree does the credibility of the entire film depend on the audience believing in its special effects? Do special effects overshadow the major characters so much that they seem secondary to the effects?

WATCHING FOR CINEMATOGRAPHY AND SPECIAL VISUAL EFFECTS

1. **Cinematic Qualities.** Watch the first 10 minutes of the following films: *The Grapes of Wrath, Citizen Kane, The Taming of the Shrew, Terms of Endearment,* and *2001: A Space Odyssey.* Evaluate each brief segment in terms of the two questions under "On the Cinematic Film" (above). Which film is the most cinematic? Which is the least cinematic? Explain your choices in as much detail as possible.
2. **Deep Focus.** Watch the brief sequence from *Citizen Kane* in which Mr. Thatcher comes to pick up young Charles (Chapter 6). How is deep focus employed in this sequence, and what is its effect? How does the use of deep focus affect the editing of this sequence? What role does sound play in reinforcing the illusion of a three-dimensional image here?
3. **Lighting.** Watch all of the sequences in *The Grapes of Wrath* in which a character called Muley Graves appears [0:12:15 to 0:23:07] and describe the different kinds of lighting employed in those sequences. What effect is created by each type of lighting used? In which scenes is the lighting most effective?
4. **Cinematic Viewpoints.** Watch the first 5 minutes of *The Grapes of Wrath, Casablanca,* and *Citizen Kane.* Try to identify the cinematic viewpoint of each shot in all three segments, and then answer question 1 under "On Cinematic Points of View." How does the editing differ in each of these three films?

MINI-MOVIE EXERCISE: CINEMATOGRAPHY

Strange Days (1995), produced and co-written by James Cameron (director of *Titanic* and *Avatar*) and starring Ralph Fiennes, Angela Bassett, and Juliette Lewis, is stylish, violent, and suspenseful. Its director, Kathryn Bigelow (who later won two Oscars for

The Hurt Locker), immediately signals all three of these qualities in the first five minutes of her film by commencing with a completely discrete (and yet integrated) sequence that, in its cinematography alone, is virtuosic. Look closely at this opening

"mini-movie" and then, to learn how it was made, listen to the only commentary provided on the DVD: Bigelow's fascinating, detailed account of its creation. (See also Chapter 6 in this book.)

MINI-MOVIE EXERCISE: ANIMATED F/X

Many parts of the animated film *Waking Life* might be viewed as "mini-movies." The work, though, is clearly a treat meant for adults, not children—in both content and form; in fact, it is R-rated (mostly for a bit of rough language). As

described in summary, it may sound boring: Throughout long passages, what might be termed talking heads have philosophical discussions. But discerning viewers surmise quickly that these talks will range from superbly serious to absolutely loony, and they also discover that the look of the whole film is mesmerizing. Its images, composed of constantly moving lines, textures, and hues, may even invoke a kind of seasickness in some watchers, but most others will gladly be pulled overboard into its loosely drawn narrative.

Chapter 10 on the DVD of this movie is a six-and-one-half minute, virtually self-contained dissertation called "Dreams." Seek it out, study its poetic observations, and pay close attention to how the filmmakers' choice of animated form ultimately elevates its story elements.

If the technical aspects of this film interest you, consult the last item in "DVD Filmmaking Extras" below.

DVD FILMMAKING EXTRAS

The Art of Cinematography

Three Kings:
  Director of photography Newton Thomas Sigel explains in a conversation here that he desaturated images of the Iraqi desert to provide the "not colorless, but drained of color" look desired by director David O. Russell in the early sections of their film. Later, he says, he "warmed up" his palette to reflect a thematic awakening in the narrative.

Insomnia (2002):
  The documentary "In the Fog" on this DVD shows how Christopher Nolan's third film (after *Following* and *Memento* and before *The Prestige*, *Batman Begins*, *The Dark Knight*, and *Inception*) benefited greatly from the combined talents of production designer Nathan Crowley and director of photography Wally Pfister.

For interviews and commentaries by other masterful directors of photography, refer to the bonus features on the latest DVD releases of *Who's Afraid of Virginia Woolf?* (Haskell Wexler), *The Man Who Wasn't There* (Roger Deakins), and *American Beauty* (Conrad L. Hall).

The creators of DVDs sometimes offer their viewers the opportunity to examine the storyboarding techniques used by directors and cinematographers, and then to make comparisons between those preplanning activities and the completed film scenes. Four discs that use split-screen demonstrations to show such movement are *Fiddler on the Roof (Special Edition)*, *Men in Black (Collector's Series)*, *Toy Story*, and *Toy Story 2 (Three-Disc Set Collector's Edition)*.

The Art of Special Visual Effects

The Lord of the Rings: The Fellowship of the Ring (Special Extended DVD Edition):
This four-disc set contains thirty minutes of "new and extended scenes" (an alternative edit, a director's cut . . .)—and literally hours of information about every aspect of this first part of the J. R. R. Tolkien trilogy, including multitudinous data and demonstrations concerning its various visual and sound effects.

The Matrix:
Most interesting on this DVD is the feature in which the film's creators introduce and explicate what they call "bullet time."

A.I. Artificial Intelligence:
Included here is "a visit to Stan Winston Studios with early 'Teddy' footage" and interviews with the Academy Award–Winning team at George Lucas's Industrial Light and Magic.

Spider-Man:
This DVD not only includes considerable information about its special effects, it also has an interactive feature that gives access to its F/X materials *while* you watch the feature.

Once Upon a Time in Mexico:
Here, in both "The Good, The Bad and The Bloody" and "Ten-Minute Flick School," the energetic director gives the viewer entertaining explanations of individual scenes in the movie. In addition, in "Film Is Dead: An Evening With Robert Rodriguez," director Rodriguez lectures passionately (following his mentor, George Lucas) about his love for shooting in the digital video (HD) format, instead of using film.

John Carpenter's The Thing (Collector's Edition):
"Terror Takes Shape" offers 80 minutes of interviews with (and demonstrations by) the director, special effects makeup designer Rob Bottin, matte artist Albert Whitlock, and others who helped to create this landmark F/X movie.

The Art of Special Effects Animation

Animation Legend Winsor McCay:
The history of both early film generally and the art of animation specifically is encompassed by this DVD, which examines the life and work of the creator of Little Nemo and Gertie the Dinosaur. The great cartoon genius Chuck Jones

(who often gave life to such creatures as Bugs Bunny and the Road Runner) has favorably compared McCay with Walt Disney in his influence on the art of animation.

A Bug's Life:

If "To act is to blow your lines" is a true thespian axiom, check out, for validation, the two sets of hilarious bug/actor "outtakes" on this disc.

The Incredible Adventures of Wallace and Gromit (A Grand Day Out, The Wrong Trousers, and A Close Shave):

What more could an animation junkie need? Herein is a full half-hour tour of Aardman Studios, overseen by creator Nick Parks. (This tour is more satisfying than the rushed one included on *The Curse of the Were-Rabbit* DVD.)

Princess Mononoke:

The great anime master Hayao Miyazaki (*Spirited Away*) released this film in the United States in 1997, after it had become the highest-grossing movie in Japanese history. The featurette on the disc circles through brief interviews with several of the actors who provided voices for the newly engineered English-dubbed version.

Waking Life:

Among the elements on this disc is an extended section called "The Waking Life Studio" that appears to act as a trash-bin collection of very loosely related odds and ends. But well worth the visit to this attic is a treasure called "Bob Sabiston's Animation Tutorial," a twenty-minute feature in which the movie's art director explains in great detail how the unique motion picture was created via a "rotoscoping" process. As Sabiston tells viewers, the entire film was first shot on video with live actors and completely edited; then more than twenty-five different artists, using their very separate styles and the same special multi-layered computer animation software, "hand drew" each frame from the video template. See also director Richard Linklater's later work *A Scanner Darkly*, which uses this same animation process.

FILMS FOR STUDY

Cinematography

Blood Simple (1984)
Boogie Nights (1997)
Casablanca (1942)
Citizen Kane (1941)
A Clockwork Orange (1971)
The Dark Knight (2008)
Good Night, and Good Luck (2005)
The Graduate (1967)
The Grapes of Wrath (1940)
Jaws (1975)
The Kids Are All Right (2010)
Kill Bill, Volume 1 (2003) and *Volume 2* (2004)
Mao's Last Dancer (2009)
March of the Penguins (2005)
Metropolis (1927)
Napoleon (1927)
Raging Bull (1980)
Sunrise (1927)
The Third Man (1949)
Who's Afraid of Virginia Woolf? (1966)
Winter's Bone (2010)

Special Visual Effects

The Abyss (1989)
Adaptation (2002)
Avatar (2009)
Beetlejuice (1988)
Dark City (1998)

The Fifth Element (1997)
Harry Potter and the Half-Blood Prince (2009)
House of Flying Daggers (2004)
Inception (2010)
Lord of the Rings: The Return of the King (2003)
Pan's Labyrinth (2006)
Spider-Man 2 (2004)
Star Trek (2009)
2001: A Space Odyssey (1968)

Animated Feature Films F/X

Alice in Wonderland (1951)
Beauty and the Beast (1991)
Coraline (2009)
Dumbo (1941)
The Emperor's Nightingale (1949—Czechoslovakia)
Fantasia (1940)
The Illusionist (2010)
Monsters, Inc. (2001)
The Nightmare Before Christmas (1993)
Persepolis (2007)
Pinocchio (1940)
The Princess and the Frog (2009)
Shrek (2001)
Snow White and the Seven Dwarfs (1937)
Spirited Away (2001—Japan)
Toy Story (1995), *Toy Story 2* (1999), *Toy Story 3* (2010)
UP (2009)
WALL-E (2008)
Who Framed Roger Rabbit (1988)

EDITING

Inception

A feature-length film generates anywhere from twenty to forty hours of raw footage. When the shooting stops, that unrefined film becomes the movie's raw material, just as the script had been the raw material before. It now must be selected, tightened, paced, embellished, and in some scenes given artificial respiration, until the author's and the director's vision becomes completely translated from the language of the script to the idiom of the movies.
—RALPH ROSENBLUM, FILM EDITOR

Of utmost importance to any film is the contribution made by the editor, whose function is to assemble the complete film, as if it were a gigantic and complex jigsaw puzzle, from its various component visual parts and soundtracks. The great Russian director V. I. Pudovkin believed that editing is "the foundation of the film art" and observed that "the expression that the film is 'shot' is entirely false, and should disappear from the language. The film is not *shot*, but built, built up from separate strips of celluloid that are its raw material."[1] Alfred Hitchcock reinforces this viewpoint: "The screen ought to speak its own language, freshly coined, and it can't do that unless it treats an acted scene as a piece of raw material which must be broken up, taken to bits, before it can be woven into an expressive visual pattern."[2]

Because of the significance of the editing process, the editor's role may nearly equal that of the director. Regardless of its quality, the raw material that the director provides may be worthless unless careful judgment is exercised in deciding when each segment will appear and how long it will remain on the screen. This assembly of parts must be done with artistic sensitivity, perception, and aesthetic judgment as well as a true involvement in the subject and a clear understanding of the director's intentions. Therefore, for the most part, the director and the editor must be considered almost equal partners in the construction of a film. In some cases, the editor may be the true structuring genius, the master builder or architect. In fact, the editor may have the clearest vision of the film's unity, and he or she may even make up for a lack of clear vision on the director's part.

Such would seem to be the case with many of Woody Allen's films. According to Ralph Rosenblum, who edited six of them, Allen is obsessed with keeping a strain of seriousness running through practically any film he makes. Much of this seriousness Rosenblum eliminates in the cutting room. *Annie Hall*, for example, was shot as a philosophical film (working title—*Anhedonia*). The focal character was Alvy Singer, Annie was a secondary character, and the mood fell somewhere between those later used in *Interiors* and *Manhattan*. In the editing process, Rosenblum refocused the film on the Alvy/Annie relationship by eliminating whole sequences and plot lines, and he helped Allen develop and shoot a new ending to match the new focus. The end result was a film that won Academy Awards for best picture, director, actress, and original screenplay. However, the editor, who changed the whole emphasis and tone of the film from what was originally conceived and shot by the director, was not even nominated. Evan Lottman, editor of *Sophie's Choice*, explains the problem. Editing, he says, is "invisible. Seeing the finished product cannot tell you the value of the editing. . . . You don't know whether moments in the movie were created in the editing room or whether they were part of the director's original conception. But if the picture works, the editing works, and nobody's going to call special attention to it."[3]

In this chapter's "Flashback," we explore the history of this invisible work. (See "Flashback: Film Editors: A History Behind the Scenes," pp. 158–159.)

To appreciate the role that editing plays, we must look at the basic responsibility of the editor: to assemble a complete film that is a unified whole in which each separate shot or sound contributes to the development of the theme and the total effect. To understand the editor's function, it is also important to comprehend the nature of the jigsaw puzzle. The basic unit with which the editor works is the **shot** (a strip of film produced by a single continuous run of the camera). By joining or splicing a series of shots so that they communicate a unified action taking place at one time and place, the editor assembles a **scene.** The editor then links a series of scenes to form a **sequence,** which constitutes a significant part of the film's dramatic structure much in the same way that an act functions in a play. To assemble these parts effectively, the editor must successfully carry out his or her responsibilities in each of the following areas.

SELECTIVITY

The most basic editing function is selecting the best shots from several **takes** (variations of the same shot). The editor chooses the segments that provide the most powerful, effective, or significant visual and sound effects and eliminates inferior, irrelevant, or insignificant material. Of course, we cannot fully appreciate the editor's selectivity because we do not see the footage that ends up on the cutting-room floor (or, as with most film projects now, in storage). *Black Rain* editor Tom Rolf describes the editing process: "It's imposing my choice over yours, having the arrogance to say this is better than that. It's being a critic. . . . It's like having an enormous picture puzzle—1,000 pieces will make it look perfect but they give you 100,000."[4]

When deciding what to eliminate, the editor considers several different takes of the same piece of action. While the film is being shot, the director begins the selection process by telling the continuity supervisor which takes are good enough to be printed. Soon after each day's shooting, **dailies** (also called *rushes*) are viewed by the director, the cinematographer, and others. After screening the dailies, which are unedited, the director may decide to throw out more shots—shots that contain flaws not spotted during the shooting. By the time the editor finally gets the film, obviously bad footage has been discarded. But there are still many difficult and subtle decisions to be made.

For a given five seconds' worth of action, the editor may be working with ten takes of that segment of action and dialogue, filmed with three different cameras from three different angles. If the sound quality is adequate in each shot, the editor chooses a shot to fill that five-second slot in the finished film after considering these factors: the camera technique (clear focus, smooth camera movement, and so on), composition, lighting, acting performance, and best angle to match the previous shot.

If each shot were equal in quality, the decision would be simple: The editor would go with the best angle to match the previous shot. But usually it's not that easy, and some of the editor's decisions amount to difficult compromises. According to *Ben-Hur* editor Ralph Winters:

> A good editor will choose the path which gives him the most amount of material. It depends on the way it was shot. I've had sequences that had three, four, or five angles and we played it all in one angle, because when we looked at the film everyone felt that the scene sustained itself. . . . I can have my eye shift back and forth where it wants instead of being directed by close-ups. If you are playing a two-shot and you can make it better by intercutting close-ups because those performances are better, then you should do it. If you're given a mediocre scene and you have no coverage, that's the way it's going to play.[5]

FLASHBACK

FILM EDITORS:
A HISTORY BEHIND
THE SCENES

In the 2004 film *The Final Cut*, Robin Williams plays a very serious character, Alan Hakman, a special kind of filmmaker who edits real people's lives. In the futuristic world of the movie, one out of every twenty humans has been given, at birth, a "Zoe implant," which records every moment of existence through his or her eyes. At a crucial point in the drama, Hakman explains that "cutters" like him are sometimes called "sin eaters," because they erase weaknesses and errors in lives before family and friends can hold a viewing of the deceased's memories. Thus, they "edit" lives that have been fragmented, feeble, and wrong so that the lives appear to have been whole, strong, and worthy.

Although this clever concept is hardly given its due in the film's melodramatic plot, it might nevertheless serve as an apt metaphor for the magic that real film editors have created throughout a century of cinema history. "What makes a movie a movie is the editing," says Zach Staenberg, the Oscar-winning editor of the *Matrix* trilogy. Without skillful editors to obscure the professional foibles of writers and directors, modern movies would hardly exist, and wise actors have long known that editors can make or break their performances on film.

Late in the nineteenth century, cinematic pioneers like Thomas Edison and brothers Louis and Auguste Lumière did not truly envision the narrative possibilities that editing could bring to their new medium. Only with Edwin S. Porter's creation of *The Life of an American Fireman* (1902) and, especially, *The Great Train Robbery* (1903) did editors first manipulate technology for skillful, extended storytelling. Later, director D. W. Griffith, in his films *The Birth of a Nation* (1915) and *Intolerance* (1916), began to establish the strict "rules" of so-called

classical editing, a "masked" manipulation of film clips that endeavored to make the film seem fluid in its movement. Wide (or "master") shots usually came first, followed most often by "two shots," and finally, "single shots," establishing a smooth and predictable progression of images for the viewer. Even the first uses of close-up and flashback shots were incorporated seamlessly into his films. As film editor Sally Menke (*Pulp Fiction*) observed, cutting was "the Invisible Art."

Unfortunately, the editors who did the work also remained invisible to the movie-going public, who were unaware of these artisans' essential power over the films they watched. Editors' invisibility, a natural result of classical editing techniques, became even more profound during the "movie factory" atmosphere of 1930s, 1940s, and 1950s America, when large and powerful Hollywood studios marginalized the roles of such technicians. In contrast, with the advent of the French New Wave in 1959,

1890s
Early movies incorporate little editing.

1902, 1903
The Life of an American Fireman and *The Great Train Robbery* feature innovative editing and effects, including long shots and close-ups.

1915
In *The Birth of a Nation* D. W. Griffith establishes formal editing conventions and techniques, resulting in increasingly fluid films.

1930s–1950s
Editors' work is de-emphasized during "movie factory" era of big production studios.

films like Jean-Luc Godard's *Breathless* had begun a frontal assault upon the traditional editing style, using such techniques as frequent jump cuts (defined on p. 172) to create deliberately erratic rhythms.

Such rule-breaking in the art of editing began gradually in America, but became particularly evident in *Bonnie and Clyde* (1967), with wonderfully kinetic cutting by the estimable Dede Allen (*Dog Day Afternoon, Reds, The Breakfast Club, The Wonder Boys*, and *The Final Cut*). The ultimate result of this movement was "free-form" editing, which probably reached a commercial peak in Joe Hutshing's work on the Oliver Stone film *JFK* (1991)—a film that involved much "fragmenting of time and space." However, even within popular movies of the 1980s, cuts happened faster and faster. By the late 1990s and early 2000s, many action directors had come to feature films from the frenetic world of MTV music videos and television commercials. Consider the quick-cutting styles, for example, of Michael Bay (*The Rock*) or Rob Cohen (*XXX*). Interestingly, director Martin Scorsese (*Raging Bull, The Aviator*), who began his film career as an editor (*Woodstock*), has expressed concern about what effect this assumption may have on our culture's sense of real time, not merely movie time.

Not all contemporary directors demand speed from their editors. For example, *New Yorker* critic Anthony Lane notes that Gus Van Sant (*Drugstore Cowboy, My Own Private Idaho, Good Will Hunting*), in such recent films as *Milk, Elephant*, and *Last Days*, "refuses to go in fear of the long take. This sets him apart from many of his contemporaries, for whom every movie is a kind of slasher flick, sliced and diced within an inch of its life. By contrast, Van Sant is prepared to hang around and see how a scene unfolds." Likewise, writer/director Rodrigo Garcia takes his time in the drama *Nine Lives*, which consists exclusively of nine singular, unbroken takes. Surely the champion of this "slower" technique remains Alexander Sokurov's *Russian Ark*, whose ninety-five-minute running time is a single take, with all the film's "editing" done inside the camera's frame (that is, by manipulating the elements of mis-en-scène rather than by [see page 184]).

Currently, more and more financially strapped independent directors are choosing to shoot in a high-definition digital video format, and some commercially successful directors, like George Lucas, Robert Rodriguez, and Steven Soderbergh, are famously embracing and promoting the technology. *Time* reviewer Richard Corliss even notes, "If moviemakers won't shoot digitally, they'll edit digitally, citing ease and efficiency." However, there are still major holdouts: Corliss spotlights the accomplished editor Michael Kahn and Kahn's creative collaborator, director Steven Spielberg, who says, "I still love cutting on film. I just love going into an editing room and smelling the photochemistry and seeing my editor with mini-strands of film around his neck. The greatest films ever made were cut on film, and I'm tenaciously hanging on to the process."

Although directors' and actors' careers may often hang in the balance of the film editor's art, no one is more dependent on good editing than the screenwriter. For, as writer/director Quentin Tarantino proclaims, "The last draft of the screenplay is the first cut of the movie, and the final cut of the movie is the last draft of the script." Ultimately, then, all filmmakers are "saved" by the art of these invisible editors.

Sources: The Cutting Edge: The Magic of Movie Editing (Warner Bros., 2004), directed by Wendy Apple, written by Mark Jonathan Harris; Anthony Lane, "Opting Out," *The New Yorker*, 1 August 2005, 90–91; Richard Corliss, "Can This Man Save the Movies? (Again?)," *Time*, 12 March 2006, 66–72.

1959
French New Wave emerges in films like *Breathless*, featuring frenetic jump cuts and a faster film-editing style.

2000s
Quick-cutting style reaches its pinnacle; feature films employ fast cuts similar to those in music videos and commercials.

1967
American film *Bonnie and Clyde* features the fast cutting embraced by the French nearly a decade earlier.

2002
Russian Ark is shot in single long take with no editing in postproduction.

The best shot in terms of lighting and composition may be the weakest in acting performance and dramatic impact. Or the best acting performance may be poorly composed or have lighting problems or be slightly out of focus.

COHERENCE, CONTINUITY, AND RHYTHM

The film editor is responsible for putting the pieces together into a coherent whole. He or she must guide our thoughts, associations, and emotional responses effectively from one image to another, or from one sound to another, so that the interrelationships of separate images and sounds are clear and the transitions between scenes and sequences are smooth. To achieve this goal, the editor must consider the aesthetic, dramatic, and psychological effect of the juxtaposition of image to image, sound to sound, or image to sound, and place each piece of film and soundtrack together accordingly (Figure 6.1).

TRANSITIONS

In the past, filmmakers made routine use of several **opticals**—effects created in the lab during the printing of the film—to create smooth and clear transitions between a film's most important divisions, such as between two sequences that take place at a different time or place. These traditional transitional devices include the following:

- **Wipe.** A new image is separated from the previous image by means of a horizontal, vertical, or diagonal line that moves across the screen to wipe the previous image away.
- **Flip Frame.** The entire frame appears to flip over to reveal a new scene, creating a visual effect very similar to turning a page.
- **Fade-Out/Fade-In.** The last image of one sequence fades momentarily to black, and the first image of the next sequence is gradually illuminated.
- **Dissolve.** The end of one shot gradually merges into the beginning of the next. The effect is produced by superimposing a fade-out onto a fade-in of equal length or imposing one scene over another.

Each of them is most effective in a specific situation or context. Generally speaking, dissolves signal relatively great transitions and are used to make the viewer aware of major scene changes or the passage of time. Flips and wipes are faster and are employed when the time lapse or place change is more logical or natural.

Modern filmmakers have used these devices in films such as *The Sting* and *Pennies From Heaven* to suggest the film style that was typical of the period when the story takes place. But most modern filmmakers do not make extensive use of them and instead rely on a simple cut from one sequence to another without giving any clear transitional signal. This change can be attributed to audiences' visual conditioning by TV commercials to follow quick cuts without confusion. The soundtrack has also taken on some of the transitional functions formerly handled optically.

FIGURE 6.1 Editing Sequence—Action and Reaction Part of the editor's job is to weave a coherent tapestry of action and reaction, rendering the sequence of events crystal clear while building dramatic effect, tension, and suspense by cutting back and forth between the characters involved in the action and the action itself. Sometimes the editor achieves this effect by cutting the action into minute bits and showing significant character reaction to each bit of action. The complex relationship between action and reaction is clearly illustrated by the final ambush sequence from *Bonnie and Clyde*.

Spooked by the appearance of a number of lawmen in a small Louisiana town, Bonnie and Clyde (Faye Dunaway and Warren Beatty) drive off, much to the relief of their accomplice C. W. Moss (Michael J. Pollard), who watches from a window. Meanwhile, down the road, a trap is being set by C. W.'s father, Malcolm (Dub Taylor). The editor, Dede Allen, establishes a relationship between Malcolm's "flat tire" and Bonnie and Clyde's trip with a few quick cuts between them. Sighting Malcolm, Clyde pulls over and gets out to help with the tire. Several quick events (an approaching car, a covey of quail suddenly flushed from a nearby bush, and Malcolm's quick dive under his truck) evoke dramatic reactions from Bonnie and Clyde before the shooting from the nearby bushes begins.

▲ 1.   ▼ 3.

▲ 2.   ▼ 4.

▲ 5.   ▼ 7.

▲ 6.   ▼ 8.

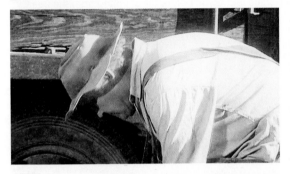

▼ 9.

▼ 10.

▼ 11.

▼ 12.

▲ 13.   ▼ 15.   ▲ 14.   ▼ 16.

▼ 17.   ▼ 18.

▼ 19.   ▼ 20.

▲ 21.   ▼ 23.   ▲ 22.   ▼ 24.

▼ 25.   ▼ 26.

▼ 27.   ▼ 28.

▼ 33.   ▼ 34.

▼ 35.   ▼ 36.

▲ 37.   ▼ 39.

▲ 38.   ▼ 40.

▼ 41.

▼ 42.

▼ 43.

▼ 44.

Regardless of the nature of transitions, whether they are long and obvious (as in a slow dissolve) or short and quick (as in a simple instantaneous cut), the editor is the person who must put them together so that they maintain continuity—so that the flow from one sequence to another or merely from one image to another is logical.

When possible, the editor uses a **form cut** to smooth the visual flow from one shot, scene, or sequence to another. In this type of cut, the shape of an object in one shot is matched to a similarly shaped object in the next shot. Because both objects appear in the same area of the frame, the first image flows smoothly into the second. In Stanley Kubrick's *2001*, a piece of bone flung into the air dissolves into a similarly shaped orbiting object in the following sequence. In Sergei Eisenstein's *Potemkin*, the handle of a sword or dagger in one shot becomes the similarly shaped cross around a priest's neck in the following shot. Although form cuts provide smooth visual transitions, they may also create ironic collisions of sharply contrasting ideas.

Similar to the form cut are cuts that use color or texture to link shots. For example, a glowing sun at the end of one shot may dissolve into a campfire at the beginning of the next. Of course, there are limitations to this type of transition; and when they are overdone, they lose the sense of naturalness that makes them effective.

The editor must also assemble shots to achieve coherence *within* a sequence. For example, many sequences require an **establishing shot** at the beginning to provide a broad picture of the setting so that we get a feel for the environment in which the scene occurs. The editor must decide if an establishing shot is necessary for a clear understanding of the closer and more detailed shots that follow.

Two different editing patterns have become more or less standard in making transitions in time and space. The more traditional pattern, **outside/in editing**, follows a logical sequence and concentrates on orienting us to the new setting. It allows us to move into a new setting from the outside and gradually work our way inside to the details. The logical context of each step is clearly shown so that we always know exactly where we are. We get our bearings with an establishing shot of the whole setting, move into the setting itself, and then focus our attention on the details of that setting.

Inside/out editing does the exact opposite. We are jolted suddenly from a line of action that we completely understand to a close-up detail in a new and unfamiliar place. We don't know where we are or what is happening. Then, in a sequence of related shots, we back off from the detail of the first close-up and gradually find out where we are and what is happening. Thus, we move from a disorienting shot to distant, more general shots that help us fully understand the action in the context of the new scene (Figure 6.2).

The disaster epic *Airport '77* begins with a couple of burglars breaking into an airport office at night and stealing information from a file cabinet. While that burglary is in progress, we jump immediately to a close-up of a hand pushing throttle levers forward. In the next shot, we back up to establish that the hand belongs to Jack Lemmon, who is in the pilot's seat of a jetliner, and a view through the cockpit glass shows the runway in front of the plane. The next shot takes us one step farther back, and we see that Lemmon is not in a real cockpit at all but in a simulator training cockpit. Thus, the viewer is jolted with a transition first, and the overall location

FIGURE 6.2 Editing Sequence in *Saturday Night Fever*—Outside/In and Inside/Out This sequence combines two common patterns of editing. In the first, the outside/in pattern, we get our bearings with an establishing shot of the new setting and then move closer in to focus on the main characters and details of the new environment. This can be accomplished in a variety of ways: The editor may begin with a static distant shot and take us closer and closer by cutting to shots taken from a static camera positioned in progressive stages closer to an object of interest. The same basic effect can also be accomplished with a slow zoom that gradually magnifies the object of interest or by a continuous shot from a mobile camera that physically moves closer to the subject.

In **the outside/in portion** of this editing sequence, two methods are used. The first three photos represent excerpts from a continuous shot taken from a helicopter. The shot begins with an establishing shot of the Manhattan skyline with the Brooklyn Bridge in the foreground. The camera then swings around the bridge and heads toward the heart of Brooklyn. The sound through this part of the sequence has been subdued: soft, muffled traffic noises. The editor then cuts to a close-up of an elevated train moving diagonally toward the camera. The sound suddenly overwhelms us as the fast-moving train approaches, and we suddenly feel ourselves in the city. The next shot is taken from a camera rotated 180 degrees to pick up the train as it speeds away. The following shot focuses on a detail that has no logical connection to the train: a close-up of a shoe display in a store window. At this point, the outside/in portion of the sequence ends and **the inside/out portion** begins.

As the strong beat of the *Saturday Night Fever* theme ("Stayin' Alive") starts up, a foot outside the window is placed alongside the displayed shoe. The next shot picks up that foot and its mate walking to the beat down a city sidewalk. Succeeding shots move upward from the feet to show a swinging paint can and the torso and face of the character Tony (John Travolta). Shots in the sequence continue to show Tony's interaction with his environment (turning to look after a pretty girl and finally stopping at a cellar-level pizza joint). To connect our location with the opening outside/in sequence, the editor also includes a quick shot of an elevated train passing during Tony's strut.

▲ 1.　　▼ 3.

▲ 2.　　▼ 4.

▲ 5.   ▼ 7.

▲ 6.   ▼ 8.

▼ 9.

▼ 10.

▼ 11.

▼ 12.

of the scene is established later. The inside/out pattern creates a dynamic, explosive, exciting edit, which adds oomph and suspense to the transition. Kathryn Bigelow, in the virtuoso opening of *Strange Days*, uses a similar editing pattern. The scene introduces the audience to a kinetic and thrilling robbery (photographed using constant subjective point-of-view shots) that seems to end with the camera's—and the viewers'—falling off the top of a tall building. Suddenly, though, it is revealed that this heart-thumping excitement is in fact recorded on a futuristic experiential device worn by the film's protagonist, played by Ralph Fiennes. (See again the first Mini-Movie Exercise in Chapter 5, page 150.)

RHYTHMS, TEMPO, AND TIME CONTROL

Many factors work together and separately to create rhythms in a motion picture: the physical objects moving on the screen, the real or apparent movement of the camera, the musical score, and the pace of the dialogue and the natural rhythms of human speech, as well as the pace of the plot itself. These factors set up unique rhythms that blend into the whole. But these rhythms are natural, imposed on the film by the nature of its raw material. Perhaps the most dominant tempo of the film, its most compelling rhythm, results from the frequency of editorial cuts and the varying duration of shots between cuts. The rhythm established by cuts is unique because cuts divide a film into a number of separate parts without interrupting its continuity and flow. Editorial cuts impart to a film an externally controllable and unique rhythmic quality.

The rhythm established by editorial cutting is such a natural part of the film medium that we are often unaware of cuts within a scene, yet we respond unconsciously to the tempo they create. One reason we remain unaware is that the cuts often duplicate the manner in which we look at things in real life, glancing quickly from one point of attention to another. Our emotional state is often revealed by how quickly our attention shifts. Thus, slow cutting simulates the impressions of a tranquil observer, and quick cutting simulates the impressions of an excited observer. Our responsiveness to this convention of **glancing rhythms** allows the editor to manipulate us, exciting or calming us almost at will.

Although the editor generally alternates one tempo with another throughout the film, the cutting speed of each scene is determined by the content of that scene, so that its rhythm corresponds to the pace of the action, the speed of the dialogue, and the overall emotional tone. Editor Richard Marks describes the difference between action cutting and dramatic cutting:

> [W]ith an action sequence you're cutting on movement. It always gives you justification to cut and create its own rhythms. There's an internal rhythm to a movement. The axiom of action cutting is, never complete an action. Always leave it incomplete so it keeps the forward momentum of the sequence. In dramatic cutting you have to create your own rhythms. . . . Yet you must try and remain faithful to the internal rhythms of an actor's performance.[6]

The fact that the story, the action, the dialogue, and the visuals all set up different natural rhythms makes editors often think of their jobs in terms of being sensitive to the "music" already playing in the scene. But sometimes that music is unnatural and totally preplanned in story-boarding before the scene is ever shot, as evidenced by Alfred Hitchcock's use of musical imagery to describe yet another editing rhythm: the carefully thought-out juxtaposition of long shot with close-up, creating a dramatic change in image size:

> It is very, very essential that you know ahead of time something of the orchestration: in other words, image size. . . . Sometimes you see film cut such that the close-up comes in early, and by the time you really need it, it has lost its effect because you've used it already.
>
> Now I'll give you an example of where a juxtaposition of the image size is also very important. For example, one of the biggest effects in *Psycho* was where the detective went up the stairs. The picture was designed to create fear in an audience, and in the anticipation of it, it is all there. Here is the shot of the detective, simple shot going up the stairs, he reaches the top stair, the next cut is the camera as high as it can go, it was on the ceiling, you see the figure run out, raised knife, it comes down, bang, the biggest head you can put on the screen. But that big head has no impact unless the previous shot had been so far away.[7]

EXPANSION AND COMPRESSION OF TIME

Director Elia Kazan, making the transition from stage to film, was enthusiastic about cinematic techniques for manipulating time:

> [F]ilm time is different from stage time. One of the most important techniques a film director has is the ability to stretch a moment for emphasis. On a theatre stage, true time goes its normal course; it's the same on stage as it is in the audience. But in a film we have movie time, a false time. Climaxes in life go clickety-click and they're over. When a film director comes to a crucially important moment, he can stretch it, go from one close-up to another, then to people who are dramatically involved or concerned watching the action, so back and forth to everyone connected with what is happening. In this way time is stretched for dramatic emphasis. Other parts of the film can be slipped over swiftly so that they are given no more time on the screen than their dramatic value justifies. Film time then becomes faster than real time. A film director can choose to leap into the "meat" of a scene or from high moment to high moment, leaving out what, in his opinion, is not worth the attention of the audience. Entrances and exits—unless they're freighted with dramatic substance—mean nothing. It doesn't matter how the character got there. He's there! So cut to the heart of the scene.[8]

Skillful editing can greatly expand our normal sense of time through intercutting a normal action sequence with a series of related details. Take, for example, the brief action of a man walking up a flight of stairs. By simply alternating a full shot of the man walking up the stairs with detailed shots of the man's feet, the editor expands the scene and sense of time of the action. If close-ups of the man's face and his hand gripping the rail are added, our feeling of the time the action takes is expanded even more.

By using **flash cuts,** short machine-gun bursts of images sandwiched together, the editor can compress an hour's action into a few seconds. For example, by choosing representative actions out of the daily routine of a factory worker, the editor can, in a minute or two, suggest an entire eight-hour shift. By overlapping so that the first part of each shot is superimposed over the last part of the preceding shot, the editor can achieve a fluid compression of time.

Another editorial technique used to compress time is the **jump cut,** which eliminates a strip of insignificant or unnecessary action from a continuous shot. For example, a continuous shot in a western follows the movement of the sheriff as he walks slowly across the street, from left to right, from his office to the saloon. To pick up the pace, the editor may cut out the section of film that shows the sheriff crossing the street and jump-cut from the point at which he steps into the street to his arrival at the sidewalk on the other side. A jump cut speeds up the action by not showing a portion of the action.

The term *jump cut* also refers to a disconcerting joining of two shots that do not match in action and continuity. As Ephraim Katz observes in *The Film Encyclopedia,* "Traditionally, such breaks in continuity and smooth transition have been considered intolerable, but some modern filmmakers employ jump cuts freely and deliberately."[9] Indeed, a film's wit can be sharpened considerably by its concerted use of the device. In *Cabaret,* for instance, director Bob Fosse and editor David Bretherton frequently utilize the jump cut for startling effects that are both humorous and affecting. Near the end of the film, Fritz (Fritz Wepper), the young gigolo, confesses to Brian (Michael York) that he is, in fact, a Jew, although he has lied about this element of his identity to the Jewish woman he loves, Natalia Landauer (Marisa Berenson). At the moment of this revelation, he despairs of her ever consenting to marry him. But soon we see Fritz standing at Natalia's front door, exclaiming loudly, "I am a Jew!" And a jump cut takes us immediately to the wedding ceremony.

One of the most effective techniques of editorial cutting is the use of **parallel cuts** (or *intercutting*), quickly alternating back and forth between two actions taking place at separate locations. Parallel cutting creates the impression that the two actions are occurring simultaneously. It can be a powerful suspense-building device. Such films as *Cabaret, The Godfather* (Figure 6.3), and *Mrs. Dalloway* use parallel cutting in a brilliant fashion, ironically uniting darkness and jollity, violence and piety, colorful chaos and authoritarian order. And the recent film *Inception* presents multiple narratives simultaneously—dreams within dreams within dreams—by way of extended sequences that utilize **crosscutting** (as the movie's director, Christopher Nolan, calls the editing technique).

An entirely different kind of time compression is achieved by cutting to brief flashbacks or memory images. This technique merges past and present into the same stream and often helps us understand a character. The motivation of Peter Fonda's beekeeper/grandfather character in Victor Nunez's *Ulee's Gold,* for example, is slowly revealed through such flashbacks.

Filmmakers also use four other key editing techniques to expand or compress time: slow motion, the freeze frame, the thawed frame, and stills.

SLOW MOTION

If the action on the screen is to seem normal and realistic, film must move through the camera at the same rate at which it will be projected, generally twenty-four frames per second. However, if a scene is filmed at greater-than-normal speed and then projected at normal speed (or altered digitally), the action is slowed. This

FIGURE 6.3 Editing Sequence—The Ironic Montage (see page 183) In this powerful segment from *The Godfather*, Francis Ford Coppola intercuts a sequence depicting Michael Corleone (Al Pacino) serving as godfather to the infant son of his sister Connie (Talia Shire) with a montage showing the brutal murders of rival mob leaders ordered by Michael. The soft, golden, spiritual light of the church casts a warm glow over the baptism. The priest intones the ceremony in Latin accompanied by organ music, his voice and the organ droning on as scenes of murder are interspersed with shots from the baptism. The irony of the sequence is intensified by Michael's affirmation (in English) of his belief in God and his pledge, during the most violent moments of the montage, "to renounce Satan and all his works." When the ceremony is completed, Michael immediately orders the murder of Carlo, the father of the just-baptized infant. By juxtaposing these very opposite actions, Coppola ironically underscores Michael's heartlessness as he steps into his new role as the true godfather of the Corleone family.

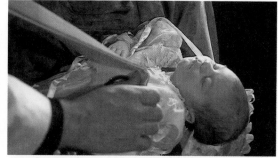

▲ 1.   ▼ 3.   ▲ 2.   ▼ 4.

 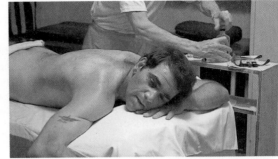

▲ 5.   ▼ 7.   ▲ 6.   ▼ 8.

▼ 9.   ▼ 10.

▼ 11.   ▼ 12.

 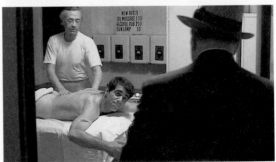

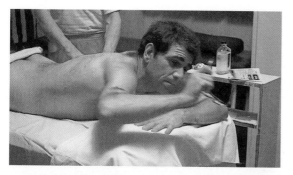 

▲ 13.   ▼ 15.   ▲ 14.   ▼ 16.

▼ 17.   ▼ 18.

▼ 19.   ▼ 20.

▲ 21.   ▼ 23.   ▲ 22.   ▼ 24.

▼ 25.   ▼ 26.

▼ 27.   ▼ 28.

▲ 29.   ▼ 31.

▲ 30.   ▼ 32.

▼ 33.

▼ 34.

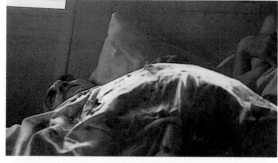

▼ 35.

▼ 36.

▲ 37.   ▼ 39.

▲ 38.   ▼ 40.

▼ 41.

▼ 42.

▼ 43.

▼ 44.

FIGURE 6.4 **Slow-Motion Showcase** Late in Sam Mendes's *Road to Perdition*, the urbane gangster played by Paul Newman walks in heavy rain with his henchmen to a crucial shoot-out scene that is memorably photographed in extensive slow motion. The effect here paradoxically emphasizes both the violence itself and the wrenching emotions felt by some of the participants.

technique is called **slow motion.** (For a discussion of **fast motion,** see Chapter 5.) The use of slow-motion footage creates a variety of effects (Figure 6.4):

1. **To Stretch the Moment to Intensify Its Emotional Quality.** A common goal of slow-motion photography is to concentrate our attention on a relatively brief period of action and intensify whatever emotion we associate with it by stretching out that fragment of time. Ironically, the same footage could be used to make us savor the thrill of victory or suffer the agony of defeat. With the camera located just beyond the finish line, two runners could be photographed in slow motion as they run toward the camera, well ahead of the pack. The winner breaks the tape only a stride ahead of the second-place finisher. If the music swells into a joyous victory theme as the winner breaks the tape and is congratulated at the finish line (still in slow motion), we tend to identify with the winner; we share his joy and savor each handshake and embrace. However, if the same footage is accompanied by slow, discordant music, we tend to identify with the runner-up and share his disappointment as he congratulates the winner and turns to walk away. In *Chariots of Fire* both kinds of moments are stretched by slow motion, and both victories and defeats are further intensified by slow-motion replays of parts of each race.

    In the suicide scene in *Dead Poets Society*, director Peter Weir uses ethereal images, a ghostly slow motion, and an absence of sound as Neil (Robert Sean Leonard) ritualistically prepares himself for death. We do not see him shoot himself or hear the shot. But slow motion has intensified the moment so that we know something horrible is going to happen. Then, as we see the father running in slow motion to find the body, we hope against hope that it hasn't happened, but we know that it has.

    Another almost unbearable stretching of the moment occurs in Daniel Petrie's film *The Dollmaker*, as Gertie Nevels (Jane Fonda) desperately tries to save her daughter from being run over by a slowly moving train. The slow motion intensifies Gertie's anguish and her helplessness as she runs toward the child but fails to reach her in time.

2. **To Exaggerate Effort, Fatigue, and Frustration.** Slow motion effectively conveys a subjective state by exaggerating a character's physical effort, fatigue, or frustration. Many of us have experienced slow-motion dreams in which our feet become leaden when we're trying to escape danger or catch some fleeting object of desire. So we identify with characters who are putting forth tremendous physical effort or experiencing fatigue or even general physical frustration. The action, music, and sound all help to trigger the proper feeling; slow-motion sound is particularly effective (see "Slow-Motion Sound" in Chapter 8).

   In *Chariots of Fire*, Eric Liddell (the Scotsman) is bumped off the track and falls into the grass infield. His fall and the time-consuming effort of getting to his feet to begin running again are exaggerated by slow motion. A similar effect is created in *Bang the Drum Slowly* as the terminally ill catcher Bruce (Robert De Niro) circles under a high pop-up. Slow-motion photography combined with blurred sound makes a relatively simple act seem tremendously difficult, awkward, and tiring.

3. **To Suggest Superhuman Speed and Power.** The most ironic use of slow motion is to suggest superhuman speed and power. Fast motion (see Chapter 5) would seem the more likely technique to suggest speed; however, the herky-jerky movements created by fast motion are comical and even grotesque. Humans moving in fast motion look like insects. Human beings photographed in slow motion look serious, poetic, larger than life. Slow motion suggesting superhuman capabilities is used effectively in films like *Chariots of Fire*, *Superman*, and *Spider-Man*.

4. **To Emphasize the Grace of Physical Action.** Even when the illusion of superhuman speed and power is not called for, slow motion can be used to impart grace and beauty to almost any human or animal movement, especially rapid movement. In *Bang the Drum Slowly* this poetry-in-motion technique is used to enhance Arthur's (Michael Moriarty) pitching, creating the smooth, graceful, seemingly effortless motion of a Major League pitcher.

5. **To Suggest the Passage of Time.** When a series of slow-motion shots are combined in such a way that each shot slowly dissolves into the next, we get the impression that a relatively long period of time is passing. In *Bang the Drum Slowly*, slow-motion shots of unrelated baseball action are joined, compressing into a few choice seconds on the screen the feeling of a long, slow baseball season.

6. **To Create a Sharp Contrast With Normal Motion.** Slow motion can be used to stretch time and build tension before the start of filming at a normal speed. In *Chariots of Fire*, the Olympic runners are pictured in slow motion as they walk into the stadium to prepare for their event. The anticipation of the race is increased as the runners remove outer garments, go through warm-up

exercises, dig their starting holes in the dirt track, and settle into their starting positions. Then the tension and nervousness of preparing for the event are released suddenly as the starting gun sounds and the runners explode off their marks in regular film speed. A sharp contrast is created between the tension of waiting and preparing for a big event and the event itself.

THE FREEZE FRAME, THE THAWED FRAME, AND STILLS

The freeze frame, the thawed frame, and stills provide a sharp contrast to a film's dynamic motion and give the filmmaker powerful ways to convey a sense of ending, a sense of beginning, and transitions. Each technique creates a special emphasis that forces us to think about the significance of what we are seeing. Of course, these techniques, if not used sparingly—for special moments only—quickly lose their impact.

The Freeze Frame

For **freeze-frame** effect, a single frame is reprinted so many times on the film strip that when the film is shown, the motion seems to stop and the image on the screen remains still, as though the projector had stopped or the image had been frozen. The sudden appearance of a freeze frame can be stunning. The frozen image draws our attention because it is so shockingly still.

The most common use of the freeze frame is to mark the end of a powerful dramatic sequence (and serve as a transition to the next) or to serve as the ending of the entire film. At the end of a powerful sequence, a freeze frame jolts us, as though life itself has stopped. Frozen, the image on the screen burns itself into our brain and is locked into our memory in a way that moving images seldom are. At the end of a sequence, a freeze frame is similar to the old tableau effect used on the stage, where the actors freeze in their positions for a brief moment before the curtain falls, creating a powerful image to be remembered during the time that elapses between scenes or acts.

When used as the movie's final image, the freeze frame can be especially strong. With the ending of the movement on the screen comes a sense of finality. As the motion stops, the freeze frame becomes like a snapshot. We can hold it in our minds and savor its beauty or impact for several seconds before it fades from the screen. It also gives us time to resonate and reflect, to catch up with our emotions, our senses, and our thoughts.

The freeze frame can also be used to convey difficult information with taste, delicacy, and subtlety, either at the film's end or at the end of a scene. In the final scene of *Butch Cassidy and the Sundance Kid*, the images of Butch and the Kid are frozen in their last full moment of vitality as a deafening roar on the soundtrack suggests the fusillade of bullets that takes their lives. As the camera slowly pulls back from their frozen images, we remember them in their last moment of life (Figure 6.5). A similar use occurs in *The World According to Garp*. As Garp's car careens up the dark asphalt toward the driveway accident, the camera zooms quickly in on his son Walt, then freezes him in a close-up that is accompanied by a moment of silence. As the next scene opens, Walt is missing and the other members of the family are seen recuperating.

FIGURE 6.5 The Freeze-Frame Ending   Hopelessly outnumbered and totally surrounded by Bolivian soldiers, Butch (Paul Newman) and the Kid (Robert Redford) leave the safety of their barricade and come out shooting. *Butch Cassidy and the Sundance Kid* ends at this point on a freeze frame of the image shown above, as a deafening roar on the soundtrack suggests a fusillade of bullets.

Freeze frames can also signal a transition. In *Chariots of Fire*, a hurdler is caught and frozen in mid-hurdle. The colored freeze frame fades to black and white, and the camera pulls away to reveal the image to be a picture in a newspaper being read the next day, thus providing a quick time/place transition.

In *Match Point*, director-screenwriter Woody Allen twice uses a very brief sequence that begins with slow motion. First, early in the film, he shows us a tennis ball smoothly sailing into the top of a net, and then he freezes the image as the voice-over narrator poses a philosophical question about the role of luck in life. Much later in the movie, Allen echoes this scene by giving us a very similar one involving another, smaller object crucial to his plot, one that he "freezes" briefly in close-up. Our persistent memory of the first instance helps him to create enormous suspense in the second.

The Thawed Frame

A **thawed frame** begins with a frozen image that thaws and comes to life. This technique can be used at the beginning of a scene or of the whole film, or it can serve a transitional function.

At the film's beginning, the frozen image is often a painting or drawing that slowly changes to a photograph and then thaws into life. In *Citizen Kane*, the thawed frame is a transitional device. Kane and one of his friends are seen looking through the front window of a rival newspaper at a group picture of the paper's staff. The camera moves in for a close-up, so we see only the picture. Then there is a flash of light and the group members start to move, revealing that the flash of light was made by a photographer taking a new group picture of the same people, who now work for Kane.

Stills

Stills are photographs in which the image itself does not move. A sense of motion occurs as the camera pulls in or backs off from them or moves over them. When several stills are used in sequence, each still usually dissolves slowly into the next, creating the impression of information slowly unfolding or being remembered. In *Summer of '42*, a grouping of stills under the credits opens the film, creating the impression of snapshots from the narrator's memory. In *Butch Cassidy and the Sundance Kid*, sepia-tone stills are combined in a "Happy Times in New York City" montage. Another striking example of the use of still photography is in Chris Marker's celebrated short film *La Jetée*, which served as an inspiration for *Twelve Monkeys*.

CREATIVE JUXTAPOSITION: MONTAGE

Often the editor is called on to communicate creatively within the film. Through unique juxtapositions of images and sounds, editors can convey a specific tone or attitude. Or they may be required to create a **montage**—a series of images and sounds that, without any clear, logical, or sequential pattern, form a visual poem in miniature. The unity of a montage derives from complex internal relationships that we understand instantly and intuitively (see, again, Figure 6.3 on p. 173).

In creating a montage, the editor uses visual and aural images as impressionistic shorthand to create a mood, atmosphere, transition in time or place, or a physical or emotional impact. The great Russian filmmaker Sergei Eisenstein (*Battleship Potemkin*, 1925; *Alexander Nevsky*, 1938) advanced influential theories of montage—"inspired," perhaps, by the work of pioneer American director D. W. Griffith (*The Birth of a Nation*, 1915; *Intolerance*, 1916). As defined by Eisenstein, a montage is assembled from separate images that provide a "partial representation which in their combination and juxtaposition, shall evoke in the consciousness and feelings of the spectator . . . that same initial general image which originally hovered before the creative artist."[10]

A cinematic montage might be created around images that have universal associations with death and old age. The visual and aural images could be edited as follows:

Shot 1: Close-up of wrinkled faces of aged couple, both in rocking chairs. Their eyes are dim and stare into the distance as the chairs rock slowly back and forth. *Sound:* Creaking of rocking chairs, loud ticking of old grandfather clock.

Shot 2: Slow dissolve to close-up of withered leaves, barely clinging to bare branches, light snow falling, thin layer of snow on the black bare branches. *Sound:* Low moaning wind; grandfather clock continues to tick.

Shot 3: Slow dissolve to seacoast scene. The sun's edge is barely visible on the horizon of the water; then it slips away, leaving a red glow and gradually darkening sky, light visibly fading. *Sound:* Soft rhythm of waves washing up on shore; grandfather clock continues ticking in the background.

Shot 4: Slow dissolve from red glow in sky to a glowing bed of coals in a fireplace. A few feeble fingers of flame flicker and then sputter and die. The glowing coals, as if fanned by a slight breeze, glow brighter and then grow dimmer and dimmer. *Sound:* Continued sound link of ticking grandfather clock.

Shot 5: Return to same scene as shot 1, close-up of wrinkled faces of aged couple rocking in their rocking chairs. *Sound:* Creaking chairs and the continuous tick of grandfather clock; gradual fade to black.

Montage is an especially effective technique when the director desires to compress a great deal of meaning into a very brief informative sequence. In *The Grapes of Wrath*, John Ford uses a montage that might be titled "The Joads' Journey Through Oklahoma" and another that might be called "Invasion of the Big Cats" (tractors) (Figure 6.6). Effective montages appear in Franklin Schaffner's *Patton* (the "Winter Night Battle" montage), in John Avildsen's *Rocky* (the "Training for the Big Fight" montage), in Frank Capra's *Mr. Smith Goes to Washington* (the "Patriotic Washington Tour" montage), in Kirk Jones's *Waking Ned Devine* (the "Informing the Villagers" montage), and in Ron Howard's *EDtv* (the various "Watching Ed on TV Throughout America" montages).

Additionally, discussions of filmmaking generally and editing specifically often use the term "montage" to represent one of two central approaches to both technique and theory. Montage describes the manner by which filmmakers connect and manipulate pieces of exposed film *outside* the camera for narrative purposes. By contrast, the other major approach, traditionally called **mise-en-scène**, focuses upon the creative process that occurs essentially *within* the camera's lens. Loosely adapted from the language of theater, the phrase refers to the visual elements appearing before the camera—all aspects of how the actors and the settings look, what movement occurs within the space, and so on. Referencing the cinema critic and theorist Andre Bazin, Ephraim Katz, in his *Encyclopedia of Film*, attempts to clarify what appear to be sharply defined differences between the two basic maneuvers: "Whereas montage derives its meaning from the relationship between one frame to the next through editing, *mise-en-scène* emphasizes the content of the individual frame. Its proponents see montage as disruptive to the psychological unity of man with his environment and cite such films as Orson Welles's *Citizen Kane* with its deep-focus compositions . . . as examples to support their argument." However, Katz concludes that "the schism between *mise-en-scène* and montage is deeper in theory than in practice; most filmmakers employ both in directing their films."[11]

ANALYZING EDITING

1. How does the editing effectively guide our thoughts, associations, and emotional responses from one image to another so that smooth continuity and coherence are achieved?
2. Is the editing smooth, natural, and unobtrusive, or is it tricky and self-conscious? How much does the editor communicate through creative juxtapositions—ironic transitions, montages, and the like—and how effective is this communication?

FIGURE 6.6 Editing Sequence—Invasion of the Big Cats From *The Grapes of Wrath*

To dramatize the helplessness of the Okies in this sequence from *The Grapes of Wrath*, John Ford employs a dynamic flashback montage suggesting overwhelming power. To introduce the montage, Tom Joad (Henry Fonda) asks Muley Graves to explain why he is hiding out in the Joad house:

"What happened?"

"They come. . . . They come and pushed me off. They come with the cats."

"The what?"

"The cats. . . . The Caterpillar tractors."

The montage that follows consists of a series of nine quick shots of earth-moving equipment, mostly heavy Caterpillar tractors. Each shot in the montage quickly dissolves into the next, and, as indicated by the arrows on the photos, the lines of force or movement are constantly varied, creating the impression that we are under attack from every direction. Throughout the montage, a constant close-up moving image of a heavy metal tractor tread is superimposed over the tractor images, giving us the feeling that we are being run over by something. The montage ends with a Caterpillar tractor actually rolling over the camera.

As the montage ends, Muley sums up the result of this invasion:

"And for every one of 'em, there was ten . . . fifteen families thrown right out of their homes. A hundred folks. . . . And no place to live but on the road."

▲ 1.   ▼ 3.

▲ 2.   ▼ 4.

▲ 5.   ▼ 7.   ▲ 6.   ▼ 8.

▼ 9.   ▼ 10.

▼ 11.   ▼ 12.

3. What is the effect of editorial cutting and transitions on the pace of the film as a whole?
4. How does the cutting speed (which determines the average duration of each shot) correspond to the emotional tone of the scene involved?
5. What segments of the film seem overly long or boring? Which parts of these segments could be cut without altering the total effect? Where are additional shots necessary to make the film completely coherent?

WATCHING FOR EDITING

1. **Editing.** Watch the famous shower sequence from *Psycho* (1960) and the "final ambush" sequence from *Bonnie and Clyde*. In which sequence is your involvement or concern greatest? Why? In which sequence do you feel real physical danger? What causes the difference?

   After Clyde gets out of the car, he and Bonnie do not exchange words, but they do communicate their thoughts and feelings, both to each other and to the audience. What do they say with their faces and body language? (Try to "caption" as many shots as possible.) How does the editing make the meaning of their expressions clear?

   Turn the sound off and watch both sequences again. Which sequence do you think the sound contributes the most to? Why?

   In *Bonnie and Clyde*, what is the purpose of the camera's moving behind the car for the final seconds? Why doesn't the camera remain between the bodies of Bonnie and Clyde so we can view them with Malcolm (Dub Taylor) and the ambush party?

2. **Montage.** Examine each of these examples of montage:
   a. From *The Grapes of Wrath:* "Invasion of the Big Cats" [0:15:28 to 0:16:45] and "The Joads' Journey Through Oklahoma" [0:36:16 to 0:37:53]
   b. From *Patton:* "Winter Night Battle" [Part II: 0:48:38 to 0:50:54]
   c. From *Rocky:* "Training for the Big Fight" [1:30:00 to 1:33:05]
   d. From *Mr. Smith Goes to Washington:* "Patriotic Washington Tour" [0:19:50 to 0:23:07]

   What is the purpose of each montage? How are sound, dialogue, voice-over narration, superimposed images, and music used to help tie the images together?

MINI-MOVIE EXERCISE I

The movie *New York Stories* (1989) consists of three separate (and, overall, critically underrated) short films by three of America's premier directors: Martin Scorsese, Francis Ford Coppola, and Woody Allen. The first and longest (:45) of the sections is Scorsese's "Life Lessons," which focuses on a passionate artist played by Nick Nolte, with Rosanna Arquette as his former assistant and erstwhile lover. The film was edited by Scorsese's creative collaborator Thelma Schoonmaker, with whom he had worked as an editor himself on *Woodstock* (1970). In fact, she has gained

celebrity and enormous respect in the movie industry while acting as primary editor for most of his features, including *Raging Bull* (1980), *GoodFellas* (1990), *Gangs of New York* (2002), *The Aviator* (2004). *The Departed* (2006), *Shutter Island* (2010), and *Hugo Cabret* (2011).

Acquire a DVD of this film and watch how these two long-time colleagues and friends have orchestrated the movement in "Life Lessons." Notice how Schoonmaker, as always, has taken full, subtle advantage of Scorsese's famous constantly moving camera techniques—and how editor and director have also skillfully incorporated into this film some of the oldest and simplest editing devices discussed in this chapter.

MINI-MOVIE EXERCISE II

The title sequence of Andrew Niccol's *Lord of War* is in fact a brilliantly constructed 5-minute discrete film. Its ending includes an act of singular violence that horrifies the viewer—but the mini-movie itself is nevertheless fascinating for its craft, and it works skillfully to foreshadow sharp, dark themes in the movie. As a student of film, examine this sequence carefully, repeatedly. Try to identify the methods that film editor Zach Staenberg has used to sustain the cinematic illusion of continuity or "smoothness" in what is clearly a progression of visual clips.

DVD FILMMAKING EXTRAS

The Art of Editing

Made:

One feature on this DVD—the "Scene Edit Workshop"—offers a student the opportunity to select among various takes of four shots, integrate these choices, and then watch the resulting scene. The exercise gives a good sense of the infinite patience and attention to detail necessary to edit film competently. (A similar feature appears on the *Men in Black [Deluxe Edition]* DVD.)

Requiem for a Dream:

The disc includes a Sundance Channel "Anatomy of a Scene" in which director Darren Aronofsky describes how he and his filmmaking team created what he calls "hip-hop montages." These assemblages, which manipulate both visual images and meticulously captured sounds (see Chapter 8), describe the obsessive nature of various types of addiction.

The Deep End:

An "Anatomy of a Scene," from the Sundance Channel, also appears on this disc, giving its audience a feel for how the film's directors achieved a degree of Hitchcockian suspense through editing skill.

Moulin Rouge! (2001):

Baz Luhrmann, the director (whose partner, Catherine Martin, won Oscars for both production design and costumes), regretted having to cut in and out of the extravagant dance sequences in this film's theatrical edit. So, when he put together the DVD, he took advantage of the storage capacity of its technology and included, separately, not only the full, uncut dance scenes, but also a multiangle feature that allows the viewer to switch perspectives on the tango, cancan, and coup d'etat.

The Big Sleep (1946):

The legendary Humphrey Bogart–Lauren Bacall romance continued on the set of this movie. By the time a "final" edit of the work had already been finished, director Howard Hawks and his studio decided to reshoot some scenes to accentuate Bacall's character—and recut the film to underscore the pair's by-then celebrated chemistry. This DVD says that it "doubles your pleasure" by offering both edits. Notice how, on Side B, in "the less-familiar 1945 prerelease version," the "plot and resolution are more linear in fashion."

FILMS FOR STUDY

Annie Hall (1977)
Avatar (2009)
Black Swan (2010)
Cabaret (1972)
Chicago (2002)
Citizen Kane (1941)
Cold Mountain (2003)
Dressed to Kill (1980)
The Godfather Part II (1974)

Grizzly Man (2005)
The Hurt Locker (2008)
Inception (2010)
Jaws (1975)
JFK (1991)
The King's Speech (2010)
Little Miss Sunshine (2006)
My Architect (2003)
127 Hours (2010)

Prospero's Books (1991)
Raging Bull (1980)
Russian Ark (2002)
The Social Network (2010)
Talk to Her (2002)
Tarnation (2003)
This Is It (2009)
3-Iron (2004)
Traffic (2000)
United 93 (2006)

Up

Color is an integral element of a picture. Its use means much more than the mechanical recording of colors which the camera has heretofore blotted out. Just as music flows from movement to movement, color on the screen . . . , flowing from sequence to sequence, is really a kind of music.

—ROBERT EDMOND JONES, STAGE DESIGNER/COLOR CONSULTANT

The added richness and depth that color provides make awareness of color and its effects on the audience essential to perceptive film watching. Although color probably gives us more immediate pleasure than any of the other visual elements, it is also probably more difficult to understand. Human responses to color are not purely visual responses; they are also psychological or even physiological. Some of color's effects on the human mind and body border on the miraculous: Premature babies born with a potentially fatal jaundice do not require a blood transfusion if they are bathed in blue light. Decorating restaurants in red apparently stimulates the appetite and results in increased food consumption. Blue surroundings can significantly lower human blood pressure, pulse, and respiration rates. And violent children relax, become calm, and often fall asleep within minutes when placed in a small room painted bubble-gum pink.

Color attracts and holds our attention; our eyes are more quickly attracted by color than by shape or form. Any reader skimming through a book with color pictures looks at those pictures first and looks at them more often than at pictures in black and white. As film critic Lewis Jacobs observes, "Color holds a powerful position among the elements of film structure. A kind of universal language, it appeals equally to the illiterate and the sophisticated, to the child and the adult. Its function on the screen is both utilitarian and aesthetic."[1] Advertisers who have run identical ads in full color and in black and white have gotten fifteen times better results from the color ads. Practically every package on the supermarket shelves has at least a touch of red, for red seems to attract attention better than any other color.

Individual responses to color vary, for color is a purely human perception of a visual quality that is distinct from light and shade. Color is simply radiant energy. **Color**—the special quality of light reflected from a given surface—is greatly influenced by subjective factors in the brain. Color not only is seen but is felt emotionally by each viewer and is therefore subject to his or her personal interpretation. The word **hue** is a synonym for *color*.

Value refers to the proportion of light or dark in a color. White is the lightest value perceptible to the human eye, and black is the darkest perceptible value. *Value* is a comparative concept, for we generally compare a colored surface with the normal value of a color—that is, the value at which we expect to find the color represented on a **color wheel** (Figure 7.1). Anything lighter than the normal value is a **tint;** anything darker is a **shade.** Therefore, pink is a tint of red, and maroon is a shade of red.

Saturation and *intensity* are other important concepts. In a discussion of color, these terms are interchangeable. A **saturated color** is a hue so unadulterated and strong that it is as pure as it can be. White and black are both saturated colors of maximum intensity. Pure white cannot be made any whiter; pure black cannot be made any blacker. A saturated or high-intensity red is a pure red—what we might call fire-engine red. It can't be made any redder. If a saturated red were made darker (or grayer), it would become a *shade* of red and would be lower in intensity. If a saturated red were made lighter (or whiter), it would become a *tint* of red and would be lower in intensity. When a color is lowered in intensity, it is said to be a **desaturated** or **muted color.** The term *muted* is perhaps easier to understand because of its clear association with music: A mute on a trumpet, for

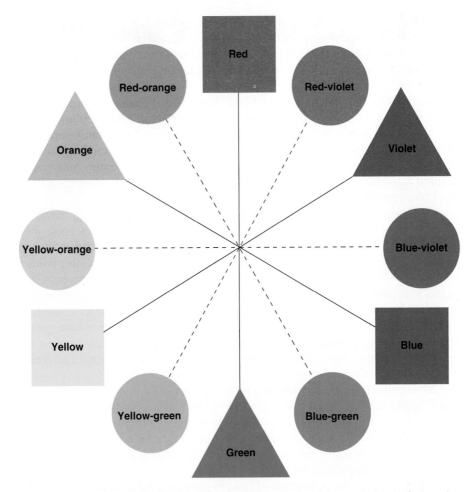

FIGURE 7.1 An Integrated Color Wheel Artists use this device to help clarify the relationships between the primary and secondary hues. The squares show the three primary colors (red, blue, and yellow), and the triangles show the three secondary colors (violet, green, and orange). These colors are separated by six intermediate colors, appearing in the circles.

example, makes the sound of the instrument less pure and clear, less bright, and less loud.

The difficulty in analyzing color is compounded by the fact that objects are seldom viewed in an atmosphere totally removed from all external optical influences. There is a clear distinction between **local color** and **atmospheric color** (Figure 7.2). A green leaf pulled off a tree, placed on a white tabletop in a room with white walls and a white floor, and illuminated by a perfectly white light radiates *local* color. A leaf radiates *atmospheric* color when it is viewed on the tree on which it is growing: The leaf appears translucent and yellowish when the sun shines through it; it turns dark green and opaque when a cloud passes over the sun. As the sun sets, the leaf may first appear ruddy and then look almost blue as the sun drops

FIGURE 7.2 Atmospheric Colors A wide range of color influences come into play in the four pictures shown here. Muted hues and high-contrast lighting direct the viewer's gaze to Nicolas Cage's scared protagonist in this scene from Alex Proyas's *Knowing;* sequences of numbers hand-circled in red on his display board portend ill for the whole planet (top left). The rosy flesh colors on the huge, theater-front poster in Pedro Almodovar's *All About My Mother* both embolden and engulf the red-coated woman (Cecilia Roth) standing bewildered before it, and the double black doors with bars on top are forbidding

(top right). In Guillaume Canet's *Tell No One,* bright red perennial blossoms (seen here behind the boy and girl) act as a visual cue that helps moviegoers to connect present and past within a romantic, suspenseful narrative (bottom right). This shot from Stanley Kubrick's *2001: A Space Odyssey* (below) places the computer HAL at its center, but the spacecraft's instrumentation-panel lights in the foreground cast an ominous, aptly unsettling pinkish glow over the faces of Keir Dullea and Gary Lockwood.

FLASHBACK

DISCOVERING COLOR AT THE MOVIES

Since the beginning of motion picture history, filmmakers have experimented with the use of color. Magic-lantern slide shows, a precursor to moving pictures, featured hand-painted slides that were projected in color. When projected pictures became possible, it was only natural that filmmakers attempted to color the image as well.

It soon became obvious that hand-coloring each frame for even a ten-minute film was tedious and expensive. In *The Battleship Potemkin* (1925), a black-and-white film, the revolutionary battleship flag was photographed as white so that director Sergei Eisenstein could hand-color the white flag red in each frame. This limited use of color in an otherwise black-and-white film focused the audience's attention on the symbol of the entire revolution, the color red.

During the era of silent films, the practice of **tinting** emerged. This process involved coloring the film stock before the image was printed on it, creating a two-color effect: black and the color in which the film had been tinted. Codes or formulas for the use of tinting quickly developed, such as the use of blue-tinted stock for night scenes. The film stock of the time was too slow to allow the filmmaker to shoot scenes at night or to get a clear image by underexposing daylight footage (later called **day-for-night shooting**). Thus, the blue tinting allowed the filmmaker to shoot a nighttime scene in natural daylight. Because modern copies of the old silent films most often have not reproduced the tinting, we sometimes fail to catch the difference between day and night scenes.

We get a clear idea of the effectiveness of tinted stock from Kevin Brownlow's restoration of Abel Gance's *Napoleon* (1927), which did not stick to a rigid formula. Although Gance consistently used amber yellow for interiors and blue for night exteriors, he used both sepia

and black and white for day exteriors. For separate battle scenes, he employed both amber yellow and red.

By the 1920s, more than 80 percent of all American features were tinted in some fashion by means of chemical

1890s
Colorful hand-painted magic-lantern slide shows anticipate filmmakers' and audiences' preoccupation with color in moving images.

1916
D.W. Griffith uses elaborate tinting techniques in *Intolerance,* but most of the original print has been lost.

1925
Hand-colored frames are featured in Russian film *Battleship Potemkin.*

1920s
Two-color Technicolor film allows for color sequences in films such as *Ben-Hur* and *Phantom of the Opera.*

baths. Perhaps the most sophisticated and artistic use of color in the silent era was in the film often called the high point of pioneering director D. W. Griffith's career, *Broken Blossoms* (1919). It is possibly the first case of a director attempting to capture a painterly effect on film. Inspired by a series of watercolors of London's Chinatown by English artist George Baker, Griffith wanted a dreamlike ambiance to match those paintings. Hendrik Sartov, Griffith's assistant cameraman, used his special skills in mood lighting and soft focus to create a highly impressionistic film. A watercolor effect was achieved by tinting the entire film in soft pastels.

Another technique of applying color to film was **toning,** adding dyes to the film emulsion itself so that the lines and tones of the image were colored. Combining the toning process with tinted film stock yielded a two-color image. For example, by using purple toning on a pink stock, the filmmaker could create a purple sea against a pink sunset. Green toning on yellow stock could suggest a green meadow or a forest against a sunny yellow sky.

Tinting and toning produced a more expressive silent cinema than we are able to experience today, but only a few films remain to represent a whole era of experimentation. Look for copies of Edwin S. Porter's *The Great Train Robbery* (1903) with hand-colored costumes, explosions, and gunfire; D.W. Griffith's *Intolerance* (1916); and Henry King's *Tol'able David* (1921) with sequences tinted in orange, green, or blue. Of films that were both tinted and toned, only random stills survive, and no copies exist of Eisenstein's red flag in *Battleship Potemkin* or of the apt "golden touch" applied by Erich von Stroheim in *Greed* (1925).

The technology needed to capture photographic images in color with the camera was not available until the 1920s. Dr. Herbert Kalmus's two-color Technicolor film was employed for color sequences in blockbusters like *Ben-Hur* (1926) and *Phantom of the Opera* (1925). The process was expensive, costing 30 percent more than a similar black-and-white production, and audiences grew bored or irritated by the poor registry of the colors. Caucasian flesh tones, for example, varied from pink to orange. In 1932, the Technicolor Corporation perfected three-color film. Color, though still expensive and difficult to work with, gradually came into its own. Although *Becky Sharp* (1935), Rouben Mamoulian's adaptation of William Makepeace Thackeray's novel *Vanity Fair*, was the first feature film to use color film, it was a commercial failure. The most celebrated early successes of Technicolor appeared in *Gone With the Wind* and in parts of *The Wizard of Oz* (both 1939). After its use in a series of striking Hollywood musicals, the color technique (and also that genre) perhaps reached its apex with *Singin' in the Rain* (1952) (above, top).

For decades, the Technicolor Corporation maintained tight controls over the use of its film, requiring that each production employ Technicolor's cameramen, consultants, and equipment. Although the Technicolor dyes tended to create pure or saturated colors more strikingly brilliant than real-world colors, Technicolor's domination of color cinematography continued only until 1952, when the introduction of Eastman Color film made color production simpler and more economical. Since the mid-1970s, Eastman Color has been the preeminent film type. The late 1990s saw a growing concern for film preservation and a revival of interest in Technicolor in the United States. Such movies as *Far From Heaven* (2002) (above, bottom) and the most recent *Vanity Fair*, Mira Nair's 2004 adaptation, contain Technicolor-like rainbow homages to this indelible color process. Meanwhile, Technicolor technology has survived and flourished exclusively in China, where, for example, the filmmaker Yimou Zhang (*Hero*, *The House of Flying Daggers*) produced such richly hued films as *Ju Dou* and *Raise the Red Lantern*.

1932
Technicolor perfects three-tone Technicolor film.

1952
Eastman Color film, simpler and more economical, comes to the scene.

2002
Far From Heaven released, signaling homages to Technicolor in American films.

1935
The first feature color film, *Becky Sharp*, is a commercial failure.

1990
Ju Dou, by filmmaker Yimou Zhang, features Technicolor technology, which enjoys a resurgence in China around this time.

below the horizon. Thus, under normal conditions, we usually see a complex and constantly changing atmospheric color:

> Local color is always submerged in a sea of light and air—in an atmosphere which combines a wide range of color influences. Not only does the sunlight change constantly through the day, but colored objects influence one another. Neighboring colors enhance or subdue one another; colored lights literally pick up reflections from one another; and even the dust particles in the air lend their own color to the objects.[2]

In planning and shooting a modern color film, the director, the cinematographer, the production designer, and the costumer must be constantly aware of such factors if they are to control and manipulate the color to conform to their aesthetic vision.

COLOR IN THE MODERN FILM

With the technology under control and readily available, and with a theater and television audience not only accustomed to but demanding movies in color, it is important to understand how color functions in the modern film: how it affects our experience of a film, how it affects us generally, and what, if any, advantages color has over black and white. Since the 1950s, the color film has increased greatly in subtlety and sophistication, and its potential seems almost unlimited.

Effects of Color on the Viewer

To begin, let's consider certain basic assumptions about the effects of color and the way it communicates—things that profoundly affect the creative choices of the director, the cinematographer, the production designer, and the costumer.

1. **Color Attracts Attention.** The director has several methods of keeping attention focused on the center of interest. Our eye is drawn to large objects, to the object closest to the camera, to the object in the sharpest focus, to movement, and to close-ups. Dramatic arrangement of people and objects and highlighting the object of greatest interest also attract our attention. Color is another option. By using bright or saturated colors on the object of greatest interest and placing that object against a contrasting background, the director can easily capture the viewer's eye (Figures 7.3, 7.4).

2. **Colors Contribute to Three-Dimensionality.** The director can capitalize on another characteristic of color to ensure that attention is attracted to the proper object: Some colors seem to advance toward the foreground, and others seem to recede into the background. Colors such as red, orange, yellow, and lavender are **advancing colors.** When given high intensity and dark value, they seem to advance, making objects appear larger and closer to the camera than they are. Interior decorators and others know that a chair covered in red will seem larger and closer to an observer than the same chair covered in **receding colors** such as beige, green, or pale blue. Taking advantage of the advancing and receding characteristics of color fosters the illusion that the image on the screen is three-dimensional.

    Several other techniques may be used in a color film to create the illusion of different planes of depth. By controlling the lighting and color choices, the

FIGURE 7.3 **Seeing Red** A saturated red is a great attention-getter, as shown in these striking photographs from *Gone With the Wind* (Ona Munson as Belle Watling) (top left), *Rocky IV* (Sylvester Stallone) (top right), *This Is It* (Michael Jackson, with guitarist Orianthi Panagaris) (bottom right), and *American Beauty* (Kevin Spacey and Mena Suvari) (bottom left).

director can dramatize or accent the illusion of solidity and form by contrasting darkness against lightness, contrasting pure color against grayed color, contrasting warm color against cool color, and contrasting detail, texture, and microstructure against plain or translucent objects.

The problems of creating the illusion of three-dimensionality in black and white are simplified in color, according to production designer Robert Boyle: "Black and white is a little harder to do than color. The difference is you can separate the planes with color, but with black and white you have to separate the planes with values . . . , particularly when you are trying to indicate depth."[3]

3. **Colors Create an Impression or Feeling of Temperature.** Colors convey or at least seem to convey a sense of temperature. The **warm colors** are the colors that advance: red, orange, yellow, and lavender. The **cool colors** are the colors that recede: blues, greens, and beiges. It is likely that warm colors are so designated because of their associations with fire, the sun, and sunsets, and blues and greens are deemed cool because of their associations with water and the shade of trees (Figure 7.5).

FIGURE 7.4 **A Richly Colored Tableau** Director Terence Davies commanded a remark-able color palette in his film adaptation of Edith Wharton's *The House of Mirth* (including the deep purple of plush Edwardian velvet in the photograph used on the movie's poster). Here, the work's protagonist, played by Gillian Anderson, participates in an evening's enter-tainment for wealthy guests: a series of frozen moments of Beauty, briefly revealed, one by one. She seems to represent Ceres, goddess of the harvest, with her sickle and grain; the rich browns, greens, and golds are set in sharp contrast to the deep red of her headdress and lip color—and the delicate pink of her gown.

FIGURE 7.5 **Mixing Warm and Cool Colors** In David Lynch's *Mulholland Dr.*, light and dark, hot and cold are in constant visual opposition, as in this shot of the film's two central characters. Naomi Watts (right) has blond hair and is wearing "cool" colored clothing, white pearls, and a muted shade of lipstick; Laura Elena Harring (left) has black hair, wears a deep red blouse, and possesses even deeper-red lips.

These generalizations, however, are not without certain complications. There are various degrees of color temperature. Red with a touch of blue is cooler than a saturated red. Yellow with a hint of green becomes a cool yellow. A reddish violet seems warm, but a bluish violet is comparatively cool. A blue with a faint purplish tinge suggests warmth, and some greens have enough yellow to seem warm. Filmmakers are aware of these connotations and use them to good effect, as Mark Rydell did in creating the effects of the warm, loving relationship between two women in the house and the bitter cold outside in his film of D. H. Lawrence's *The Fox:* "[E]very object in the house, every color, was chosen in warm tones to support the erotic tension in the house and everything in the exterior was in the blue tones to emphasize the cold. . . . The choice of colors is seemingly inadvertent—but it's not. Every garment is selected for a particular kind of emotional tone."[4]

4. **Colors Function Together in Different Ways.** Certain combinations of color, or color schemes, produce predictable and consistent visual effects. **Monochromatic harmony** results from a scheme based on variations in the value and intensity of one color. **Complementary harmony** results from the use of colors directly opposite each other on the color wheel, such as red and green. Complementary colors react with each other more vividly than do other colors. **Analogous harmony** results from the use of colors adjacent to one another on the color wheel, such as red, red-orange, and orange. Such colors create a soft image with little harsh contrast. **Triad harmony** results from the use of three colors equidistant from one another on the color wheel, such as the primary colors: red, yellow, and blue.

Color-conscious directors generally have a clear vision of the color tone or types of color harmony they want to incorporate into their film, and they convey that vision to the cinematographer, production designer, and costumer during an extensive period of preproduction planning. If special color effects need to be provided by the film laboratory during the printing process, laboratory technicians may also be consulted. Because different types of film stock respond to color in different ways, experts from Eastman Kodak or Technicolor may even be brought into the process.

Color as a Transitional Device

Color has probably been used most often to signal important changes. This can be accomplished by using color in conjunction with black and white or by switching to an obviously different color emphasis or style at the point of transition. Director David Lynch used the latter strategy in *Blue Velvet* (Figure 7.6). The most obvious kind of color transition is the technique used in *The Wizard of Oz*, where the dull, drab Kansas of Dorothy's real world suddenly becomes the glowing Technicolor Oz of her dream (Figure 7.7).

Color also provides a transition between two separate worlds in a unique time-travel film, *The Navigator: A Medieval Odyssey.* Produced in New Zealand and directed by Vincent Ward, the film concerns a journey from the Middle Ages to the present through the center of the Earth. The title character, a young visionary from a primitive medieval Christian clan, lives in a gloomy, stark, black-and-white world

FIGURE 7.6 **Oz in Reverse** In *Blue Velvet,* David Lynch begins his story with an idealized small-town atmosphere portrayed in glowing colors, with brilliant flowers, white picket fences, playing children, and cute dogs. Then the director mutes the color, darkens the image, and takes us on an unforgettable journey into the dark underbelly of vice, evil, and corruption beneath the surface. Shown here is the overly curious Kyle MacLachlan being threatened by Isabella Rossellini.

but dreams or has visions of the modern world in muted color. Through his dreams, he "knows the way" and leads members of his clan through the center of the Earth to deliver a cross to "the other side" (the modern world). As they enter the great vertical cavern that leads to the other world, limited color enters the image transitionally as torches dropping through the pit or carried by the clansmen glow orange without coloring the cavern walls or the faces of the men. Then, as they emerge into the modern world on the outskirts of a large city, we see a night scene with full but very muted color. *Pleasantville,* a seriocomic examination of evolving American life during the past fifty years, also utilizes color as a transitional device. Magically transported to the black-and-white fantasy world of a 1950s television sitcom, two '90s teenaged siblings gradually become the catalysts for blossoming color in characters who manage to attain a strong personal and social awareness (Figure 7.8).

A transition from present to past is keyed through color in *D.O.A.* (1988), which opens in a *film noir* black and white as Dennis Quaid, dying from a slow-acting but fatal poison, staggers into a police station to tell his story. As the detectives begin taping his testimony, we watch him briefly on a black-and-white TV monitor until the film goes into a dramatic flashback, changing to color as it shows the word *color* printed on a blackboard, with Quaid as a college English professor discussing the use of color as metaphor in literature. The film returns to the *film noir* black and white in the midst of the final, violent climax of the flashback.

A more sophisticated use of color for transition occurs in *Sophie's Choice.* During the concentration camp scenes, the color is muted so much that it almost disappears, thus conveying the grimness of those scenes and setting them apart from the bright and cheerful colors of the present-time sequences.

Martin Scorsese's *Raging Bull* uses color for another unusual transitional effect. The opening credits in color are superimposed over a black-and-white slow-motion image of Robert De Niro (as Jake La Motta) shadowboxing alone in the corner of the

FIGURE 7.7 **Still in Kansas** (top) Dorothy (Judy Garland) and Toto sit beneath gathering storm clouds in a dull, drab, black-and-white Kansas during the opening segment of *The Wizard of Oz*. **Not in Kansas Anymore** (bottom) Dorothy and the Scarecrow (Ray Bolger) get acquainted on the yellow-brick road in *The Wizard of Oz*.

FIGURE 7.8 **Lively/Scary Color** In the early sections of *Pleasantville*, the television town exists only in gradations of gray. The inhabitants of *Pleasantville* find the gradual experience of becoming colorful both frightening and exhilarating.

ring. With the color titles, Scorsese seems to be saying, "This is a modern film." With the black-and-white image behind the titles, he seems to be saying, "This is a realistic film. I'm not going to idealize or glorify the subject." Then, suddenly, near the middle of the film, Scorsese integrates La Motta home movies, in color, complete with shaky camera movement, fuzzy focus, and all the other standard ills of home movies. There's a wedding scene and a "kids by the pool" scene. The color provides a realistic, compressed interlude of happier days before La Motta returns to his grim career in the ring.

Expressionistic Use of Color

Expressionism is a dramatic or cinematic technique that attempts to present the inner reality of a character. In film, there is usually a distortion or exaggeration of normal perception to let the audience know that it is experiencing a character's innermost feelings (Figure 7.9).

In Michelangelo Antonioni's *Red Desert*, a variety of interesting color effects are achieved. Whereas traditional films express characters' emotions through acting, editing, composition, and sound, Antonioni uses color expressionistically to make us experience the world of the film through the mind and feelings of the central character, Giuliana, the neurotic wife of an engineer. The garish colors of factory vats, pipelines, slag heaps, poisonous yellow smoke, and a huge black ship passing through the gray mist of the harbor (along with an almost deafening roar and clatter of industrial machinery) make us aware that Giuliana is overwhelmed and threatened by industrialization. In her dull, everyday life, the color is desaturated or muted, taking on a gray, nightmarish cast. But when Giuliana tells her young son a story reflecting her own fantasies, the colors suddenly change from dull browns and grays to the brilliant sea greens, the blue skies, and the golden sand and rocks of a fairy-tale island, calling attention to the vast difference between the real world she lives in and her fantasies.

FIGURE 7.9 Expressionistic Color Color can be used expressionistically to make us experience the world of the film through the mind and feelings of the central characters. In this scene from Neill Blomkamp's horror/sci-fi film *District 9*, a central, hapless creature, lifting a pale flower, almost blends into the washed-out colors of the wasted landscape—as he possibly elicits extreme emotions from his movie-theater or living room audience.

One of the dangers of trying to create internalized or expressionistic effects in color is made clear by two vastly different interpretations of one scene from *Red Desert*, the scene in which Giuliana and Corrado make love in Corrado's hotel room. One critic describes the scene like this:

> Corrado's room is dark brown paneled wood, the color of earth, when Giuliana comes in. After they make love . . . the room appears pink (flesh-colored), almost like a baby's room. Where she had seen Corrado as a strong, masculine figure, he seems to her like a child after her disillusion with him—the color, when Antonioni wants it that way, a correlative of his heroine's sense of things.[5]

Another critic interprets the scene in this manner:

> In a later sequence in the engineer's hotel room, the walls change color from their original hard gray to warm pink because Giuliana feels them pink, with her body next to a warm strong man. He, ironically, neither cares how she feels or how she feels the walls.[6]

Both critics are right about the walls. One wall is dark, paneled wood; the other three are hard gray. The gray walls are the ones that appear pink. But the difference in interpretation here indicates a major difficulty with the expressionistic use of color. We must remember that color is not just seen but is also felt by the individual viewer and is subject to his or her personal interpretation. At least two critics did not experience the pink room of *Red Desert* in the same way.

Color as Symbol

In Ingmar Bergman's *Cries and Whispers*, we see evidence of another problem with communicating clearly with color. In that film, the bedroom of the dying Agnes is literally drowning in saturated reds: red bedspread, red carpet, red walls, red drapes, and even a red dressing screen. Bergman has said that the deep-red sets symbolize his vision of the soul as a red membrane, but individual viewers may be unaware of this symbolism. The red actually is so appealing to the eye that it distracts attention away from the subtle drama that the faces and the dialogue are struggling to convey. Similarly, Peter Greenaway plays with color in his controversial *The Cook, The Thief, His Wife, & Her Lover*. In graphically presenting the erotic passions, jealousies, and angers of its characters, this film first creates brilliantly individuated color schemes for its interior settings (including the various rooms of a large restaurant). Then it changes the colors of the characters' clothing as they walk from room to room. What may be extremely subtle color symbolism for some viewers may be merely confusing for others.

Surrealistic Use of Color

Surrealism is a dramatic or cinematic technique that uses fantastic imagery in an attempt to portray the workings of the subconscious. Surrealistic images have an oddly dreamlike or unreal quality.

The prolonged slaughter at the end of *Taxi Driver* is separated from the rest of the film with slow-motion visuals and surrealistic color (Figure 7.10). As screenwriter Paul Schrader describes it, "The movie goes out of whack at that point. The color goes crazy. You no longer hear the sounds of the street. You get into that weird slow motion. *Intentionally* out of whack."[7]

As Travis Bickle (Robert De Niro) shoots the pimp on the doorstep and enters the building, the dominant color becomes a gritty, sleazy yellow in hallways and rooms dimly lit by naked tungsten bulbs. In this surreal dim yellow glow, the film takes on a nightmarish quality: Even the blood, which is literally everywhere, seems

FIGURE 7.10 **Surrealistic Color**   Robert De Niro appears here as the deranged and suicidal Travis Bickle in the violent climax of *Taxi Driver*. The yellow used in this scene altered the blood's red to appear additionally nightmarish.

gritty and dirty, more real than real. The creative genius behind this extremely powerful effect was neither director Martin Scorsese nor his cinematographer, Michael Chapman, but the Motion Picture Rating Board:

> [A]bsurdly, it made Scorsese overlay the final bloodbath with a chemical tint so that it would look less realistic. The black-red gore turns out to be almost more powerful than the splattering ketchup of the original. Scorsese thinks it is worse.[8]

Leitmotifs in Color

Directors may employ colors associated with given characters for a kind of trademark effect. Robert Altman used this technique in his hauntingly beautiful *3 Women*. In practically every scene, Millie Lammoreaux (Shelley Duvall) is dressed in yellow or yellow in combination with another color. Pinky Rose (Sissy Spacek) dresses, as her name implies, in pink. Willy Hart (Janice Rule) wears muted colors, mostly purples, blues, and grays, throughout. As the film progresses and Millie and Pinky undergo a Bergmanesque role reversal, Pinky's pinks go to reds as her personality becomes dominant, and Millie's bright yellows are subdued. All retain something close to their basic colors until the film's puzzling end, when all three characters merge together into a monochromatic harmony. Millie has taken over the role of Willy as mother figure and adopted her style of dress and manner; Pinky has reverted to childhood and acts like a ten-year-old girl. But all the colors are now muted tints of gray and blue, as if to suggest that all three characters have lost what little individuality or sense of self they ever had.

The clashing, garish colors of the Joker's makeup and costume in *The Dark Knight* help to reinforce his personality (Figure 7.11). As if his evil deeds and twisted mind aren't villainous enough, he also offends us with his green hair, bright orange shirt, purple jacket, and bright red lips. The colors of his outfit also set him apart from the very conservative Batman costume: a rich, dark, formal blue accented by a touch of yellow. In his Euro-gore classics such as *Suspiria*, Dario Argento also uses color intensely.

Color to Enhance Mood

In his romantic tone poem *A Man and a Woman*, French director Claude Lelouche experimented with a variety of film stocks, switching from full realistic color to monochromatic scenes in sepia and blue gray, created by printing black and white

FIGURE 7.12 **The Golden Hour** Cinematographers love to shoot during "the golden hour," the period just before sunset, when the light has a golden glow and strong side lighting can create a romantic mood, as in these scenes from *A Room With a View* (left) and *Lagaan* (right).

on colored stock. Although the scenes depicting the woman's idealized memories of her dead husband (a movie stuntman) are consistently filmed in Hollywood color, the transitions from color to black and white throughout the rest of the film follow no logical formula. Nevertheless, these color transitions blend in perfect harmony with the musical score to enhance the overall delicate mood of the film. Likewise, John Woo utilizes subtle colors to build empathy for his protagonists in such films as *Windtalkers*. And some cinematographers choose to shoot just before sunset to give their actors a "golden" glow (Figure 7.12).

Comic Book Color

For comic book–based *Batman* (directed by Tim Burton), production designer Anton Furst constructed a Gotham that became the single most powerful character in the movie, a personification of contemporary corruption and decay. Vertical towers, domes, and spires reach high into a polluted sky above a base of sewers and claustrophobic alleys, creating a unique architectural style that might best be labeled Deco-Gothic. Sets are angled and lighted for a *film noir* effect and are further distorted by high and low camera angles and harsh side lighting from unseen sources. Deep blue black shadows prevail, and the browns and grays of brick and concrete are muted, totally without warmth. Gray smoke and white steam complete the image of pollution and total corruption. Even the occasional bright spot signals corruption, like the brilliant splash of red in a sleazy street girl's outfit or the sickly pulsing pinkish glow of a dirty neon sign. So pervasive is the atmosphere created by the set that one cannot help but agree with sniggering mobster Jack Napier (Jack Nicholson) when he says: "Decent people shouldn't live here. They would be happier someplace else." Often, in scary sci-fi movies such as *War of the Worlds* (2005), an equivalent sentiment is echoed during under-lighted scenes that suggest the presence of aliens. Dark colors reside in the shadows of the film *In Bruges*, which tells a primal tale of gangster reality—and tortured illusion (Figure 7.13).

FIGURE 7.13 Prevailing Shadows In Martin McDonagh's *In Bruges*, dark blue, green, and black shadows, like those behind Ralph Fiennes's character here, help to create the frightening feeling of the end of this film.

Comic Strip Color

Whereas *Batman* was based on a comic book with relatively sophisticated and subtle color treatment, Warren Beatty's *Dick Tracy* was based on a Sunday-paper comic strip in which bold, primary colors prevail. To achieve this look, Beatty and cinematographer Vittorio Storaro decided to shoot the picture in seven primary and secondary colors, controlling the color by using painted backdrops (called *mattes*) behind the live action. The overall effect is unique (Figure 7.14). The primary colors—red, blue, and yellow—almost explode from the screen; wet city streets glow crimson, blue, and purple. As Storaro tells it, each color choice was carefully thought out, especially in developing what he calls a "dramaturgy of color" for the characters:

> Tracy, with his yellow raincoat and yellow hat, represents one side of the color spectrum: light, day, sun. Tess is mainly represented by orange, a warm color. Red is the Kid. They face the opposite side—Big Boy, Breathless, Pruneface—who belong on the inside of our subconscious, which is blue, indigo, violet. So the story of Dick Tracy and Breathless is really an impossible communion between the sun and moon, day and night, good and evil.[9]

Painterly Effects in Color

More and more directors and cinematographers are beginning to think of filming as being similar to painting. In addition to their attempts to achieve **painterly effects** with lighting, a great deal of experimentation is being done to create a kind of palette in color film, so that the actual nature of the color can be mixed to achieve the same kinds of effects that artists achieve with subtle blendings of the colors on the palette. In *What Dreams May Come*, Vincent Ward takes this kind of effect one step further: When the protagonist, Robin Williams, walks through a beautiful Monet-like landscape, he discovers that its colors literally become oil paints (Figure 7.15).

In *Moulin Rouge* (1952) John Huston attempted what he called "a wedding of black and white and color" in an attempt to give the entire film the look of a Toulouse-Lautrec painting. To achieve this look, it was necessary to flatten the color (rendering it in planes of solid hues) and eliminate highlights and the illusion of three-dimensionality created by the lighting of rounded, three-dimensional

FIGURE 7.14 Comic Strip Colors To achieve a Sunday funnies look for *Dick Tracy*, cinematographer Vittorio Storaro limited himself to seven primary and secondary colors and gave a special color emphasis to each character. Blue, indigo, and violet—colors that Storaro says "belong on the inside of our subconscious"—suggest the dark side of the assembled gangsters in this shot, which focuses, at the head of a saturated red conference table, upon Al Pacino as Big Boy Caprice.

forms. He accomplished this by using a filter that was designed to simulate fog in exterior scenes and by adding smoke to the set so that a flat, monochromatic quality prevailed. As Huston puts it: "It was the first picture that succeeded in dominating the color instead of being dominated by it."[10] Huston further experimented with color in the Elizabeth Taylor/Marlon Brando film *Reflections in a Golden Eye*, where an amber golden look was given to the whole picture through a laboratory process. Studio heads at Warner Brothers/Seven Arts, however, did not like the golden look, fearing that its "artistry" would not please filmgoers generally, so they released the film without the effect.

Because painters are often associated with certain periods, filmmakers have sometimes attempted to achieve a sense of time past by using the look of a well-known painter of the period. Franco Zeffirelli created a fairly effective sense of time past by filtering *The Taming of the Shrew* through a nylon stocking, muting colors and softening sharp edges so that the whole film resembles a faded Rembrandt painting. Some scenes in Barry Levinson's *The Natural* had the look of Edward Hopper paintings, and both *Biloxi Blues* and *Radio Days* were bathed with a warm, yellow-brown, nostalgic glow, approximating a Norman Rockwell look.

For some cinematographers, the perfect period look would be achieved by capturing on film the sepia-tone look of faded photographs. But as Laszlo Kovacs, cinematographer of *F.I.S.T.*, tells it, the sepia-tone look is difficult to achieve: ". . . it's easy to go to amber or to yellowish and reddish tones, but sepia is a brown which is not a color. It's a dirt. It's a combination of everything. Somehow it's almost impossible to create that sepia tone, all that faded quality. . . ."[11]

FIGURE 7.15 **Painterly Effects**   Some filmmakers actively seek to adapt to the motion picture form color techniques most famously used by painters. John Madden mixes rich colors and movement in his *Shakespeare in Love*, with Gwyneth Paltrow and Joseph Fiennes (top). In Peter Webber's *The Girl With a Pearl Earring*, one of Johannes Vermeer's most famous paintings is brought to vibrant life via images of Scarlett Johansson as a young peasant maid working in the artist's household (bottom left). Director Vincent Ward offers a remarkable French Impressionist–inspired landscape for Robin Williams in *What Dreams May Come* (bottom right).

Ironic Use of Color

Directors usually plan to use colors to match the mood of their film, but sometimes they choose color effects that go against the emotional tone of the film. John Schlesinger, who has achieved effective results with both approaches, remembers, "In *Midnight Cowboy*, we wanted a garish street look, with the neon signs resonating—it was grittier, grainier. But with *[Day of the] Locust*, Conrad [cinematographer Conrad Hall] and I wanted a much more golden glow over a fairly dark story."[12]

Color patterns are also used ironically in Woody Allen's *Annie Hall*. When Allen occasionally switches cinematic gears from an exasperating (but funny) love story to a nostalgic re-examination of Alvy Singer's neurotic childhood (funny too), he also changes visual styles. His flashback travels into the past are given the warm glow of fond and colorful tales filtered through the consciousness of the present. And, indeed, the adult Alvy actually appears in that light with his younger self and his elementary school classmates.

FIGURE 7.16 Another Time, Another Place   To be believable, fantasy films often require a special look to convince us that such events really happened in another time, another place. To achieve this look in *The Road*, director John Hillcoat desaturated all of his colors in distressed landscapes filled with ruined nature, rusted metal, and muted fires.

Special Color Effects

A great many of the uses of color are so subtle that they create the desired effect but escape our conscious notice unless we are looking for them (Figure 7.16). In *Deliverance*, for example, director John Boorman and cinematographer Vilmos Zsigmond found that the colors of the bright green leaves as naturally recorded on the film were too cheerful looking. To remedy this, they combined a black-and-white print with a color print to create a sufficiently dark and foreboding woods.

In Kathryn Bigelow's *Near Dark*, the vampire clan must avoid the sun, which literally roasts them alive, so much of the action of the film takes place at night. Cold colors, especially a muted blue, predominate. In one scene, however, when the vampires are attempting to escape from the sunrise, the unhealthiness of the sun (to them) is shown by coloring it a poisonous yellow-green (Figure 7.17).

COLOR VERSUS BLACK AND WHITE

In most movies . . . I have restricted myself to a color or two only. Black and white is like a tuxedo, always elegant. Color, if you're not careful with it, can be vulgar.[13]

—NESTOR ALMENDROS, CINEMATOGRAPHER

Black and white certainly has a "tuxedo elegance," its own aesthetic. It is not simply a poor cousin of color but an entirely separate medium with its own strengths, idiosyncrasies, and the unique power to communicate. Whereas a color film can rely on the relationship of colors for effect (with very little need for

FIGURE 7.17 Special Uses of "Vampire" Color Although director Kathryn Bigelow (*The Hurt Locker*) set her first solo feature film, *Near Dark,* during hot weather in Oklahoma, she actually shot it in very cold temperatures in Arizona. While filming outdoor scenes, then, to avoid having her camera visually record the freezing breath of the actors, she required them to hold ice cubes in their mouths before saying any dialogue (see the DVD's extras). This old moviemaking trick worked well—but it also apparently inspired the filmmakers to realize they could tint these natural emissions a sickly yellow-green color when deathly sunlight assaults the film's vampire characters. And during scenes occurring in open daylight (such as this one featuring Joshua Miller as an ages-old man trapped in a child's body), the red and yellow flames of spontaneous combustion objectify lethal doses of sunlight for vampires.

shadows), black and white must rely on tonal relationships and contrasts produced by controlling light and shade. Black and white produces its strongest impact by emphasizing highlights and shadows.

Perhaps the most important element in the aesthetic of the black-and-white film is that the cinematographer is freed from the reality of color. In black and white, each scene must be reduced to shades of gray, to basic elements of shape, tone, line, and texture, producing an image that is less representational than the same scene in color:

> In contrast to the familiar look of a conventional color photograph, a black-and-white picture carries the viewer immediately into the realm of abstraction. Because it renders colors as light or dark shades of grey, giving its subject new visual identities, black-and-white film is at its best when used to interpret rather than merely record. It is superb at capturing patterns and contrasts, textures and forms, and all manner of tonal relationships, from the most powerful to the most subtle.[14]

Although the theoretical argument about the relative merits of color versus black and white is continuous, on a practical level there is no longer a real struggle. Because a vast television audience awaits almost any worthy movie, the great majority of films today are made in color to improve their chances for eventual sale to television. Stunningly beautiful black-and-white films such as *The Man Who Wasn't There* (2001), by the Coen Brothers, and George Clooney's *Good Night, and Good Luck*, have become modern anomalies. When, in 2009, Francis Ford Coppola presented *Tetro* in black and white, though, he nevertheless utilized color sequences. Two other recent films remarkable for their now-brave embrace of black and white (fully or primarily) are Michael Haneke's stark period drama *The White Ribbon* and Guy Maddin's "docu-fantasia" meditation *My Winnipeg*.

Television has become so saturated with color that advertisers are using black-and-white commercials to catch the viewer's attention, however. These commercials either are completely in black and white or begin in black and white and then go to color. The most subtle effect is highlighting a single object in one color and muting everything else to black and white, such as in ads for Lemon-Fresh Clorox (bright yellow, with lots of bouncing lemons), Nuprin (a tiny yellow tablet), Cherry 7Up (a red liquid), and Gatorade (a green liquid). Steven Spielberg employs a single muted color technique with chilling effect in *Schindler's List* in two brief scenes that emphasize Schindler's humanity. Schindler sits on horseback on a hillside watching Jews being driven from their homes in the Kraków ghetto. A beautiful little girl of five or six (a character not otherwise developed in the film) appears walking alone in the crowd, accented by a pale orange red coat, the only spot of color in the black-and-white action. The camera follows her as she slips into a vacant building, climbs the stairs, and hides under a bed as the sound of marching storm troopers grows louder. We see no more color until about an hour later in the film. With Schindler looking on again, the spot of color reappears briefly as the little girl's body, piled on top of other exhumed bodies, is wheeled by on a pushcart to be incinerated (Figure 7.18).

The apparently insatiable desire of the TV audience to see absolutely everything in color has drastically reduced the number of black-and-white films being produced. In fact, so few black-and-white films are now produced that when one does come out (like Woody Allen's *Celebrity*, or David Lynch's *The Elephant Man*), it is praised for its daring. More than just daring is involved, however. Martin Scorsese presented some convincing arguments in his battle to film *Raging Bull* in black and white:

> Well, they [financial backers] came into my apartment, and I mentioned that I wanted to do the film in black and white. They said, "Black and white?" And I said yes. The reason was that five boxing films were opening. . . . They were all in color. I said, "This has got to be different." And besides that, I told them that . . . I was very upset about the Eastman color stocks fading, the prints fading in five years, the negatives fading in twelve years—things like that. I said, "On top of that, though, it would also help us with the period look of the film." We had an idea of making the film look like a tabloid, like the *Daily News*, like Weegee photographs. That was the concept, so they talked about that, and said, "Okay, all right." They were listening.[15]

Obviously for some films black and white is simply a more powerful and effective medium than color. Of course, the director's decision to use black and white or color should be determined by the overall spirit or mood of the film. A clear demonstration of the correct use of color and black and white can be seen by comparing

FIGURE 7.18 A Poignant Touch of Color
Steven Spielberg's *Schindler's List* creates one of cinema's most touching moments through a tiny splotch of red in what is otherwise an entirely black-and-white film. Like Oscar Schindler (Liam Neeson), an opportunistic German businessman who nevertheless manages to save many Jews from certain death, viewers suddenly spot the color momentarily in the coat of a small girl. Our visual registration of the image seems almost subliminal. Later, along with Schindler, we see the same nameless child again; this time her dead body is atop a heap of corpses. This delicate use of color is filled with terror, poignancy, and, finally, enormous grief for all humanity.

Sir Laurence Olivier's productions of *Henry V* (1945) and *Hamlet. Henry V* is a heroic, or epic, drama, much of which is set outdoors. It has battlefield action, colorful costuming, and pageantry and is ideally suited for color. The mood of the film is positive; it emphasizes the glorious, heroic character of King Henry V, who emerges victorious. *Hamlet*, in contrast, which Olivier chose to make in black and white, is a tragedy, a somber, serious play of the mind. Most of the settings are interior ones, and some scenes take place at night. The brooding, serious, intellectual quality of the hero himself has a starkness to it, a pensive gloom that, in 1947, could not have been captured nearly as well in color as it was in black and white.

By 1990, however, new technology enabled director Franco Zeffirelli to capture the mood of *Hamlet* and the coldness and starkness of medieval Denmark in color. Throughout Zeffirelli's film, starring Mel Gibson, the colors are desaturated (muted). Browns and grays predominate; often the brightest colors are natural flesh tones. Rich and elaborate regal garments are in pastel blues or heavily muted reds. Even an occasional glint of sunlight showing through narrow castle windows provides no cheer or warmth of color and approximates the effect of low-key lighting in a black-and-white film. Glimpses of green vegetation, blue sky, and the sea are so brief that they do nothing to relieve the gloom.

The overall effect of black and white can be paradoxical, for somehow it often seems more true to life, more realistic, than color—despite the fact that we obviously do not see the world around us in black and white. For example, it is difficult to imagine that Stanley Kubrick's *Dr. Strangelove* in color would have been quite as real as it is in black and white. Perhaps Mike Nichols's *Catch-22* would have been much more powerful in black and white for the same reason. The warmth of the color images in *Catch-22*—a warmth that is difficult to avoid when working with color—fights the cold, bitterly ironic tone that underlies the story. Perhaps its sense of starkness is what makes the black-and-white treatment suitable for such film subjects.

The essentially opposite effects of color and black and white might also be explained in terms of another pair of films, *Shane* and *Hud*, both of which are set in

FIGURE 7.19 **Intense Color Synthesis** *Sin City*, based on a violent graphic novel by Frank Miller and directed by the author and Robert Rodriguez, was shot in black and white, but at crucial moments in the narrative, splashes of judiciously-chosen color add dramatic intensity. In this scene, for example, a character played by Bruce Willis (shown here with Jessica Alba) has been wounded and the blood he's shed appears as a decadent gold.

the west. Color is perfectly suited to *Shane*, a romantic western in the epic tradition set in a magnificently huge and beautiful landscape with snowcapped mountains ever present in the background. *Hud*, on the other hand, is a contemporary character study of a heel, set in a drab, barren, and sterile landscape. The film emphasizes the harsh realities and glorifies nothing; this story could find adequate expression only in black and white.

The difference in seriousness and overall tone in Woody Allen's *Annie Hall* (color) and *Manhattan* (black and white) also justifies the choices of different film types. Generally, films that seem to demand color treatment are those with a romantic, idealized, or light, playful, and humorous quality, such as musicals, fantasies, historical pageants, and comedies. Also, films with exceptionally beautiful settings might be better shot in color. Naturalistic, serious, somber stories stressing the harsh realities of life and set in drab, dull, or sordid settings cry out for black and white. There are some that fall into a middle ground and can be treated equally well either way. *Sin City*, based on a dark graphic novel, utilizes a remarkable synthesis of monochrome and color that perfectly fits its subject matter (Figure 7.19).

Experimentation continues, and film technology has advanced rapidly in recent years. By using all the technological know-how available, modern filmmakers are able to create practically any color effect they want to achieve, whether it's done by special lighting, diffusion filters, or special film in the camera or by processing the film in a certain way in the laboratory. This special color effect must of course be consistent in the film from beginning to end, unless it is used only for a special segment set off from the rest of the film—like a flashback, a dream, or a fantasy.

Regardless of what has been accomplished to this point in developing the potential of the color film, there always seems to be more territory to be explored and new worlds to be discovered. A statement by Robert Edmond Jones in his vintage essay "The Problem of Color" could well apply to the situation today:

> Color on the screen is unlike any other kind of color we have ever seen before. It does not belong to the categories of color in Nature or in painting and it does not obey the rules of black-and-white picture making.
>
> We are dealing not with color that is motionless, static, but with color that moves and changes before our eyes. Color on the screen interests us, not by its harmony but by its progression from harmony to harmony. This movement, this progression of color on the screen is an utterly new visual experience, full of wonder. The color flows from sequence to sequence like a kind of visual music and it affects our emotions precisely as music affects them.[16]

Today, filmmakers and audiences alike are becoming more sensitive to the power of color in film. Various organizations, such as the American Film Institute and the television cable channel American Movie Classics, are making extraordinary efforts to preserve the great films of the past—and especially to recapture their fading colors. For example, in preparation for yet another re-release of *Gone With the Wind*, this most popular film's Technicolor values were restored primarily through "dye transfer." Martin Scorsese has observed,

> "Color in the film is important because it reflects the drama . . . and a certain style." Scorsese says that *Gone With the Wind*'s improved look even affects the audience on an emotional and psychological level, evoking the spirit of the Old South. [He believes] "it's as important as the production design or the costuming or the direction of the film, to see it in the proper color."[17]

ANALYZING COLOR

1. If possible, watch the most powerful or memorable moments in the film on a DVD player with the color on the TV turned off. What is altered in each of the segments viewed in black and white?
2. If the film uses bright, saturated colors, turn the color down on the TV so that the colors are muted. What effect does this have on the film?
3. Is color used expressionistically anywhere in the film so that we experience the world of the film through the mind and feelings of a central character?
4. Are trademark colors used in costuming or set decoration to help us understand the personalities of any of the characters? If so, what do these colors convey about the characters?
5. Are obvious changes in color used as transitional devices in the film? If so, how effective are these transitions?
6. How important is atmospheric color in the film? Do the uses of atmospheric color reflect some purpose on the director's part? If so, what is that purpose?

1. **Color 1.** Watch the final segment of *Taxi Driver*, paying close attention to the color. Describe the quality of the color as it changes.
2. **Color 2.** For each of these movies, *Days of Heaven, 2001: A Space Odyssey, Summer of '42, The Conversation, Taxi Driver, Moulin Rouge!* (2001), and *Avatar*, first adjust the color and tint controls on your TV so that the image shows only black and white, and then watch the first 10 minutes. Then readjust the TV image to full, balanced color, watch the same 10-minute segment again, and answer the following questions:
   a. How is the overall effect of each segment altered by the addition of color?
   b. What colors seem to be predominant in the film? Are they generally warm or cool colors?
   c. Are the colors bright and pure (saturated) or toned down and muted (desaturated)? How is this choice related to the nature of the film and the story being told?
   d. Describe specific moments in each segment where color is used to focus attention on the object of greatest interest, enhance three-dimensionality, or suggest something about a character or his or her environment.
   e. Describe specific moments in each segment where atmospheric color is emphasized. What purpose can you attribute to this emphasis?

MINI-MOVIE EXERCISE

The title of *Akira Kurosawa's Dreams* (1990) must first be taken literally. For the film is supposedly a cinematic sleep journal of the famous Japanese director's, who has greatly influenced modern American filmmakers, including, especially, George Lucas in his *Star Wars* series. This film, somewhat like James Joyce's early literary  masterpiece *Dubliners*, consists of sections that cohere thematically, even as each part is a discrete whole. Kurosawa's late anthology is made up of short (:10–:15) narratives whose techniques constitute a veritable encyclopedia of formal possibilities.

Here are the titles of the seven brief works: "Sunshine Through the Rain," "The Peach Orchard," "The Blizzard . . . ," "The Tunnel," "Crows" (in which the film director Martin Scorsese portrays Vincent van Gogh), "Mount Fuji in Red," and "Village of the Watermills." From a DVD print of this movie select one of these tracks and then closely examine its utilization of color. Within the variety of hues in each film, you can expect to find both boldness and subtlety. Attempt to connect the director's choices in colors not only with his visual image-making skill, but also with the themes you discern in his work here.

The Art of Color in Films

O Brother, Where Art Thou?:

In a segment titled "Painting With Pixels," director of photography Roger Deakins explains how "for the first time, the look of an entire live action film was manipulated digitally," with help from Kodak's Cinesite facilities. Although the final edited prints of all films require a process called color balancing, in the case of this Coen Brothers movie, as this DVD extra demonstrates, the photographically captured colors of the entire work were radically changed in post-production. For example, bright greens were transformed to muted golds and browns throughout, and, thus, according to Deakins, "the color in the movie became a character."

What Dreams May Come:

A substantive feature on this DVD called "The Painted Word" presents an interview with visual effects supervisor Joel Hynek and art director Josh Rosen. The two describe the innovative process by which the film is able to create the illusion that Old Master–like oil paintings are set in motion.

Pleasantville:

An extended set of featurettes deconstruct "The Art of Pleasantville." Color effects designer Michael Southard, producer Bob Degus, and director of photography John Lindley examine key scenes that were "technically the most challenging." Declaring that "1,700 digital effects shots" were used in the film (a record number at the time of its release), these artist/technicians are especially revealing in their discussion of how "subliminal" color has been used in black-and-white sequences. Degus announces that "color in this movie is a character."

The General (1998):

Side A of the disc allows the viewer to watch the film in the black and white of director John Boorman's theatrical release; side B permits one to view it in an alternative desaturated color version reportedly demanded (for financial reasons) by the studio that produced the work.

FILMS FOR STUDY

Avatar (2009)
Babe: Pig in the City (1998)
Barry Lyndon (1975)
Black Swan (2010)
Blue Valentine (2010)
Brokeback Mountain (2005)
Burlesque (2010)

A Clockwork Orange (1971)
The Conversation (1974)
The Cook, the Thief, His Wife & Her Lover (1989)
Cries and Whispers (1972)
The Dark Knight (2008)

Days of Heaven (1978)
Do the Right Thing (1989)
Dr. Strangelove (1964)
Elizabeth (1998)
Elvira Madigan (1967)
Eternal Sunshine of the Spotless Mind (2004)

Exit Through the Gift Shop (2010)
The Fighter (2010)
Frida (2002)
The Girl Who Kicked the Hornet's Nest (2009)
The Godfather (1972)
The Godfather Part II (1974)
Gone With the Wind (1939)
Good Night, and Good Luck (2005)
Harry Potter and the Deathly Hallows—Part I (2010)
Hereafter (2010)
Howl (2010)
Howards End (1992)
I Am Love (2009)
Insomnia (2002)
Ju Dou (1990)

Juliet of the Spirits (1965)
The Kids Are All Right (2010)
The King's Speech (2010)
The Lost Boys (1987)
Lost in Translation (2003)
Midnight Cowboy (1969)
Moulin Rouge (1952)
Moulin Rouge (2001)
Napoleon (1927)
The Natural (1984)
The Navigator: A Medieval Odyssey (1988)
Near Dark (1987)
Never Let Me Go (2010)
The New World (2005)
New York Stories: Life Lessons (1989)
O Brother, Where Art Thou? (2000)

One Hour Photo (2002)
Pulp Fiction (1994)
Rabbit Hole (2010)
Radio Days (1987)
Raise the Red Lantern (1991)
Red Desert (1964)
The Red Shoes (1948)
Sky Captain and the World of Tomorrow (2004)
3 Women (1977)
Tron: Legacy (2010)
True Grit (2010)
The Umbrellas of Cherbourg (1964)
Up (2009)
Vera Drake (2004)
Y Tu Mamá También (2001)

SOUND EFFECTS *and* DIALOGUE

The Hurt Locker

In motion pictures both image and sound must be treated with special care. In my view, a motion picture stands or falls on the effective combination of these two factors. Truly cinematic sound is neither merely accompanying sound (easy and explanatory) nor the natural sounds captured at the time of the simultaneous recording. In other words, cinematic sound is that which does not simply add to, but multiplies, two or three times, the effect of the image.

—AKIRA KUROSAWA, DIRECTOR

SOUND AND THE MODERN FILM

Sound plays an increasingly important role in the modern film because its here-and-now reality relies heavily on the three elements that make up the soundtrack: sound effects, dialogue, and the musical score (see Chapter 9 for a discussion of this third part). These elements add levels of meaning and provide sensual and emotional stimuli that increase the range, depth, and intensity of our experience far beyond what can be achieved through visual means alone.

Because we are more *consciously* aware of what we see than of what we hear, we generally accept the soundtrack without much thought, responding intuitively to the information it provides while ignoring the complex techniques employed to create those responses. The intricacy of a finished soundtrack is illustrated by composer-conductor Leonard Bernstein's description of the sound mixer's difficult task in a single scene from *On the Waterfront*:

> For instance, he may be told to keep the audience unconsciously aware of the traffic noises of a great city, yet they must also be aware of the sounds of wind and waves coming into a large, almost empty church over those traffic noises. And meantime, the pedaling of a child's bicycle going around the church must punctuate the dialogue of two stray characters who have wandered in. Not a word of that dialogue, of course, can be lost, and the voices, at the same time, must arouse the dim echoes they would have in so cavernous a setting. And at this particular point no one (except the composer) has even begun to think how the background can fit in.[1]

Five different layers of sound are at work simultaneously in the brief scene that Bernstein describes, and each one contributes significantly to the total mix. But compared to many scenes in the modern film, the sounds in *On the Waterfront* are simple and traditional. They are not nearly as complex as the soundtrack for *Raging Bull*, considered a landmark in film sound.

The fight scenes in *Raging Bull* were extremely powerful, requiring the layering of as many as fifty sounds to create the final effect. As sound man Frank Warner (working in part as a **Foley artist**—i.e., one who adds sound effects during postproduction) tells it:

> It was done in combining sounds. A very basic part of the punch is hitting a side of beef—that's always been used from Day One. That could be your basic beat, but then you can go from there. When a guy is hit and you see it just ripping, tearing the flesh, you can take a knife and stab and you get a real sharp, cutting sound. As the flesh gave away, water would have been added to the punch. The splatter was all done separately.[2]

Unrecognizable animal sounds and abstract bits and pieces of music were also part of the mix. For the high-velocity delivery of punches, Warner blended jet airplane sounds and the "wwwwhhhoooosssh" of arrows slowed down (Figure 8.1).

Filmmakers can also take advantage of digital recording technology to combine and process sounds, creating aural environments that heighten the viewer's emotional response to a scene. For example, sound editor Cecilia Hall combined as many as fifteen different layers of sound—including animal screams and trumpets—to create the fighter jet sounds in *Top Gun*. Recently, the Oscar-winning

FIGURE 8.1 Mixing Marvelous Noises Oscar-winning sound designer/editor Ben Burtt collected and combined as many as 2,600 different sounds to create the effects of *Wall-E*, which features the charming trash-compactor title character and his girlfriend, Eve.

mixers and editors who helped to create Kathryn Bigelow's *The Hurt Locker* continued to expand the complex outer limits of "layering" sound in reproduction technology.

The modern soundtrack demands so much of our conscious attention that if we want fully to appreciate a modern film, we should perhaps be prepared as much to hear the film as to see it.

DIALOGUE

A major part of our attention to sound in the modern film is naturally directed toward understanding the dialogue, for in most films dialogue gives us great deal of important information. Film dialogue is different from stage dialogue, and we need to be aware of the unique characteristics of film dialogue.

Dialogue in a typical stage play is an extremely important element, and it is essential that the audience hear almost every word. Thus stage actors use a certain measured rhythm, carefully speaking their lines in turn and incorporating brief pauses in the question–response pattern so that the person occupying the worst seat in the house can hear each line clearly. This limitation does not apply to film, however, and dialogue can be treated much more realistically in the movies than onstage.

In *Citizen Kane*, for example, Orson Welles employed the overlapping dialogue, fragmented sentences, and interruptions common to everyday conversation without loss of essential information or dramatic power. This was achieved, as it is now in most films, through careful microphone positioning and recording, skillful editing and mixing of the recorded sound, and subtle variations in sound quality (volume, clarity, reverberation, and tonal elements). Through such means, the modern filmmaker creates the impression of a highly selective ear tuned to what it wants or needs to hear. The most important sounds are singled out, emphasized, and made clear; those of less importance are blurred or muted.

Film dialogue can also be delivered at a much more rapid pace than can stage dialogue. Director Frank Capra put this capability to good use in *Mr. Smith Goes to Washington* and *Mr. Deeds Goes to Town*. He utilized compressed, machine-gun-paced dialogue in phone conversations that shove necessary but nondramatic exposition out of the way so he could get down to the serious business of telling his stories.

The old adage that a picture is worth a thousand words is especially true in film. Filmmakers must, first of all, use dialogue with great restraint to avoid repeating what has already been made clear visually. Furthermore, film's dramatic power and cinematic qualities are both diminished if dialogue is used to communicate what could be expressed more powerfully through visual means. In some cases, the most dramatically effective results are achieved through sparse or monosyllabic dialogue, and in a few modern films, dialogue is dispensed with entirely. This is not to say that dialogue should never dominate the screen. But it should do so only when the dramatic situation demands it. As a general rule, dialogue in film should be subordinate to the visual image and should seldom assume the dominant role of dialogue on the stage.

THREE-DIMENSIONALITY IN SOUND

In *Citizen Kane* (1941), which is generally conceded to be the first great modern sound film, Orson Welles created a strong impression of three-dimensional sound without the benefit of the multiple soundtracks and speakers required for true stereo. Perhaps more conscious of the importance of sound and its potential for subtleties because of his radio experience, Welles achieved this effect by varying the sound quality (volume, clarity, reverberation, and tone) of voices and sound effects to reflect their relative distance from the camera. A sense of aural three-dimensionality was achieved to match the three-dimensional image of Gregg Toland's deep-focus cinematography. This three-dimensionality was achieved on one track (monaural sound) by making voices and sounds sound close up or far away—without the left and right separation of stereo (which is achieved by recording on two separate tracks and then using two or more speakers to play back what was recorded).

In 1952, true three-dimensionality of sound was achieved by combining the techniques pioneered by Welles with a six-track stereophonic system in the triple wide-screen *This Is Cinerama*. A four-track system was introduced to match the Cinemascope image of *The Robe* in 1953. But as the number of wide-screen films being produced declined and the studios and independent producers returned to the standard screen format, the interest in stereophonic sound declined also.

In the mid-1970s, a different attempt was made to achieve spectacular sound effects in theaters with Sensurround. The Sensurround system derived its sound from two closet-size speaker cabinets located at the rear corners of the theater. These powerful speakers were designed to literally shake the entire theater, but the system was used for relatively few films, such as *Earthquake* (1974) and *Midway* (1976). In *Midway*, the rear speakers effectively provided a realistic 360-degree sound environment by using techniques such as the following: The camera, positioned on one side of an aircraft carrier, looks up toward a kamikaze plane diving toward the carrier. The soundtrack in front grows louder until the plane roars right overhead. Then the huge speaker boxes in the rear take over to complete the roar and give us the sounds and shock waves of the explosion on the deck behind us.

At about the same period (1974), the Dolby system was introduced. An audio recording system that reduces background noise and increases frequency range, it was combined with a system called "surround sound" from Tate Audio Ltd. to produce a multitrack stereophonic system for theaters. **Dolby-Surround Sound** employs an encoding process that achieves a 360-degree sound field and creates the effect of a greater number of separate speakers than are actually required. It has been used with great power and effectiveness, achieving the effect of hissing snakes all around us in *Raiders of the Lost Ark* and the cheering fight crowd, managers, and trainers in *Raging Bull* and in more recent films, such as *Gladiator* and *Cinderella Man*. In 2010, *Toy Story 3* pioneered the theater use of 7.1 Surround Sound.

In Wolfgang Petersen's *Das Boot*, an incredible sense of a 360-degree sound environment is created both inside the confined quarters of the German U-boat and in the sea around and above it. The quality of each sound is unique: a strumming guitar, a radio, a phonograph, men talking and laughing, clanging horns, engine noises—all seem to come from different sources and give us a sense of being there. *Das Boot* is a film full of listening. The crew first strains to hear the creaking of collapsing bulkheads on a ship they sink; then later, with the sub nestled on the bottom in hiding from a destroyer on the surface, the crew grows deathly quiet so as not to give away the sub's position. Their silence emphasizes every noise, which the Dolby stereo locates with pinpoint accuracy. We hear the destroyer's pinging sonar and every turn of its screw as it passes overhead, growing louder and then softer. As the sub sits on the bottom, at a great depth, we hear the rivets straining, then popping, and the sound of water spraying in as parts of the boat fail to withstand the tremendous pressure (Figure 8.2).

Ironically, despite the care lavished on crafting soundtracks these days, many filmgoers never fully experience them. Too many of the theaters in the United States (most of which are older and small suburban ones) simply do not have the capability to reproduce the quality or the dimensions of the sound recorded in the films they show. Still, according to *Newsweek*, this situation has been steadily "improving": Not so long ago, "only a few hundred theaters were equipped to play ear-blasting digital sound. . . . Today [most multiplex theaters] . . . can handle state-of-the-art digital. The result has been a kind of free market of noise, with filmmakers competing for sounds grabby enough to match their eye-popping visuals. . . ."[3]

FIGURE 8.2 Three-Dimensional Sound
Thanks to the three-dimensional sound effects in Dolby stereo, destroyers rumble menacingly overhead as we are "trapped" in the submarine of *Das Boot,* and even newer, more advanced sound technology enables us to feel, not just hear, the flying dragons over the ruins of London in *Reign of Fire.*

VISIBLE AND INVISIBLE SOUND

In the early days of the sound film, the emphasis was placed on recorded sound that was synchronized with the visual image. As the popular term *talking pictures* indicates, the audience of that time was fascinated by the reproduction of the human voice. Although sound effects were employed, they were generally limited to sounds that would naturally and realistically emanate from the images on the screen—that is, to **visible sounds.**

Although the dramatic power of the human voice and the sense of reality conveyed through sound effects certainly contributed new dimensions to the film art, the tight link between sound and image proved very confining, and filmmakers began to experiment with other uses of sound. They soon discovered that **invisible sound,** or sound emanating from sources *not* on the screen, could be used to extend the dimensions of film beyond what is seen and to achieve more powerful dramatic effects as well. Once they realized the unique and dynamic potential of invisible sound, they were able to free sound from its restricted role of simply accompanying the image. Invisible sounds now function in a highly expressive or even symbolic

FIGURE 8.3 **Off-Screen (Invisible) Sound** In *M*, an early sound film, an inventive use of off-screen sound builds mystery and suspense as the child killer (Peter Lorre) announces his presence by whistling bits of a classical theme before he appears on the screen.

way as independent images, sometimes carrying as much significance as the visual image, and occasionally even more.

This creative use of invisible sound is important to the modern film for a variety of reasons. First of all, many of the sounds around us in real life are invisible, simply because we find it unnecessary or impossible to look at their sources. Realizing this, filmmakers now employ sound as a separate storytelling element capable of providing information by itself. Sound used in this way complements the image instead of merely duplicating its effects. For example, if we hear the sound of a closing door, we can tell that someone has left the room even if we do not see an accompanying image. Thus, the camera is freed from what might be considered routine chores and can focus on the subject of the greatest significance. This is especially important when the emphasis is on reaction instead of action, when the camera leaves the face of the speaker to focus on the face of the listener.

In some cases invisible sound can have a more powerful effect alone than would be possible with an accompanying image. The human mind is equipped with an eye much more powerful than that of the camera. An effective sound image can trigger a response in our imagination much stronger than any visual image. In the horror film, for example, invisible sounds can create a total, terror-charged atmosphere. Story elements that heighten and intensify our emotional response—the clank of chains, muffled footsteps on a creaking stair, a stifled scream, the opening of a creaking door, the howl of a wolf, or even unidentifiable sounds—are much more effective when the sources are *not* seen (Figure 8.3).

As demonstrated by the description of the scene from *On the Waterfront* given at the beginning of this chapter, invisible sounds (such as the sounds of city traffic, wind and waves, and the child's bicycle) are routinely used to intensify the film-goer's sense of really being there. And by encircling the viewer with the natural sounds of the scene's immediate environment, the soundtrack suggests a reality beyond the limits of the visual frame. In some films, however, realistic sounds that naturally occur in the story's environment may be distracting for the audience and must be eliminated to maintain the film's focus. Sound editor Skip Lievsay has used this approach in his work on several films for director Spike Lee:

> Quite often with Spike's movies we don't really have nominal city sounds. We don't [hear] . . . traffic, . . . sirens, . . . crying babies, . . . screaming, . . . shouting matches, because as much as they are a part of ordinary life in the city, they're too dramatic. . . . The relationship in Spike's movies is more between the people than between the people and their environment.[4]

In comedy, sound can effectively substitute for the visual image and is usually used to depict comic catastrophes set up and made completely predictable through visual means. For example, in a scene picturing a crazy inventor trying out a homemade flying machine, the picture may show the launching and then let the soundtrack illustrate the predictable crash. A dual purpose is achieved here: Our imaginations intensify the humorous effect of the crash by forming their own picture of it, while the camera focuses on the reactions registered on the faces of the onlookers, which become the focal point of comic interest. Such use of sound also has clear practical benefits, considering the danger to the stuntman and the destruction of expensive properties that go along with showing the crash visually. If sound is used for the crash, the would-be pilot needs only to stagger on-screen, battered and dirty, draped in a few recognizable fragments of the plane.

Thus, sound effects achieve their most original and effective results not through simultaneous use with the visual image but as independent images, enhancing and enriching the picture rather than merely duplicating it.

POINTS OF VIEW IN SOUND

In a film shot from the **objective point of view** the characters and the action of a scene are perceived as if by a somewhat remote observer who looks calmly on the events without becoming emotionally or physically involved. Camera and microphone perceive the characters externally, from the sidelines, without stepping in to assume the role of participants. The **subjective point of view,** in contrast, is that of one who is intensely involved, either emotionally or physically, in the happenings on the screen. In the completely subjective view, camera and microphone become the eyes and ears of a character in the film; they see and hear exactly what that character sees and hears.

Because maintaining the subjective point of view consistently is difficult if not impossible in film, most directors choose to alternate between the two viewpoints, first establishing each situation clearly from an objective viewpoint, then cutting to a relatively brief subjective shot, and then repeating the same pattern. In each shot, the camera and the microphone *together* create the unified impression of a single viewpoint, so the volume and quality of the sound vary in direct relationship to camera positioning. For example, sounds audible in a subjective close-up may not be audible in an objective long shot, and vice versa. This alternation between the objective and subjective viewpoints, and the tight link between camera and microphone, is further illustrated by the workman-with-air-hammer scene described in Chapter 5:

Establishing shot: Objective camera view from street corner, focusing on a workman using an air hammer in center of street (apparent distance: 50 to 75 feet). *Sound:* Loud chatter of air hammer, mingled with other street noises.

Cut to subjective view: Close-ups of air hammer and violently shaking lower arms and hands of workman, from workman's point of view. *Sound:* Hammer is almost deafening—no other sounds heard.

Cut back to objective camera: Heavy truck turns corner beyond workman, bears down on him at top speed. *Sound:* Loud clatter of air hammer, other street noises, rising sound of approaching truck.

Cut to subjective view: Close-up of air hammer and workman's hands as seen from his viewpoint. *Sound:* First only deafening sounds of air hammer, then a rising squeal of brakes mixed with hammer noise.

Quick cut to new subjective view: Front of truck closing quickly on camera from 10 feet away. *Sound:* Squeal of brakes louder, hammer stops, woman's voice screaming, cut short by sickening thud, followed by darkness and momentary silence.

Cut back to objective viewpoint (from street corner): Unconscious figure of workman in front of stopped truck. Curious crowd gathering into circle. *Sound:* Mixed jumble of panicked voices, street noises, ambulance siren in distance.

Sometimes the soundtrack is used to communicate what goes on in a character's mind. When that is the case, the link between camera and microphone is slightly different. The camera usually only suggests the subjective view by picturing the character's face in tight close-up and relies on the soundtrack to make the subjectivity of the viewpoint clear. Just as the image is in close-up, the sound is in close-up, too. In most cases the sound quality is distorted slightly to signal that the sounds being heard are not part of the natural scene but come from inside the character's mind. The camera also makes this distinction clear by focusing tightly on the character's eyes. The eyes loom large enough to fill the entire screen and thus become a window of the mind through which we read the character's inner state. The camera in such a sequence can remain in tight close-up while the soundtrack communicates the character's thoughts or sounds and voices from his or her memory—or merely silence (Figure 8.4). Or the sequence may merely act as a transition to a *visual* flashback. These sequences are frequently filmed in **soft focus** (a slight blurring of focus for effect), another clue to their subjective nature. These techniques are especially useful to filmmakers in presenting dreams. In *The Conversation*, when Francis Ford Coppola needs to indicate that the uptight Harry

FIGURE 8.4 Silent Eyes as a Window of the Mind In *The Dying Gaul*, writer/director Craig Lucas scrutinizes a suspense-filled love/hate triangle involving a wealthy, influential Hollywood couple (Campbell Scott and Patricia Clarkson) and an aspiring screenwriter (Peter Sarsgaard). At a crucial point in the narrative, while the wife is sitting at her laptop communicating electronically with her new friend, the writer, she experiences a shocking epiphany about her husband. Repeatedly, Lucas's camera snakes up and over the top of the computer, zooming in close on her revealing eyes. Silence intensifies the moment. Simultaneously, as the writer himself experiences a moving series of flashbacks including his recently deceased lover, his eyes are also explored in extreme close-up.

Caul (Gene Hackman) is having a feverish nightmare, the director begins with a tight shot of the character's sleeping face and then returns repeatedly to it as the dream progresses.

Unusual inner emotional states are also represented by the soundtrack through use of variations in volume, reverberation, or other distortions in the voices or natural sounds that the character hears. Physical reactions such as extreme shock, excitement, or even illness are sometimes suggested by drum-beats, which supposedly represent a high pulse rate or a pounding heart. Extreme amplification and distortion of natural sounds are also used to suggest a hysterical state of mind.

SPECIAL USES OF SOUND EFFECTS AND DIALOGUE

The sound formulas described above have been used over and over again. Innovative filmmakers have used sound effects and dialogue creatively for a variety of specialized purposes.

Sound Effects to Tell an Inner Story

Directors manipulate and distort sound for artistic ends—to put us inside a character so that we can understand what he or she is feeling. In a powerful scene from *On the Waterfront*, Elia Kazan employs the sounds of the waterfront to dramatize

FIGURE 8.5 **Telling an Inner Story Via Heightened Natural Sounds** Marlon Brando, playing a supremely conflicted character named Terry Malloy, speaks earnestly and loudly in this scene from Elia Kazan's *On the Waterfront*, but the movie-goer can hardly hear his voice. For, as Malloy attempts to explain to his girlfriend Edie that he bears guilt for her brother's death, the exaggerated ambient sounds of dockworker machinery at once obliterate dialogue and help to clarify the pain of both his confession and Edie's sudden understanding.

the emotions of Terry Malloy (Marlon Brando) and Edie Doyle (Eva Marie Saint). The priest (Karl Malden) has just convinced Terry to confess to Edie (whom he now loves) that he was involved in setting up the murder of her brother by corrupt union officials. The priest and Terry stand on a hill overlooking the waterfront, and when Edie appears walking toward them on the flats below, Terry hurries down the steep hill to meet her. Almost imperceptibly at first, the rhythmic hammering of a pile driver, which has been a part of the natural sound environment, grows increasingly louder as Terry approaches Edie, thus making us aware of the fear he feels about leveling with her. As he reaches the crucial part of his confession, the steam whistle on a nearby ship shrieks loudly, obscuring his words as we watch his anguished face trying to tell the story we already know. With the deafening shriek of the whistle, we are suddenly inside Edie—feeling the shock, the horror, and the disbelief of what she has just heard, as she covers her ears with her hands to protest a truth she cannot accept. The steam whistle stops just before Terry finishes his story, and as he finishes, Edie stares at him for a moment in disbelief, then turns and runs away from him in panic, her action accompanied by high, wailing violins. The scene's dramatic intensity is literally beyond words—the faces and the internalized sounds alone tell the entire story (Figure 8.5).

In *All That Jazz*, Bob Fosse takes a totally different approach in his directing of Joe Gideon's "heart-attack warning" scene. At the opening of the scene, everything is normal. Cast members for a new musical are sitting around reading dialogue from a very funny script. The entire cast periodically breaks into laughter. Suddenly, without warning, we no longer hear the laughter—we still see the faces laughing, but the sound is gone. The soundtrack carries only the close-up sounds of stage-musical director Joe Gideon (Roy Scheider). We hear him striking a match, his finger drumming on the table, a labored breathing, his wristwatch ticking, and his shoe grinding out a cigarette on the floor. With all sound external to Gideon cut off (despite constant visual reminders that we should be hearing it) and every close-up sound of Gideon magnified, Fosse has literally grabbed us by the ears, pulled us inside Joe Gideon's circulatory system, and sent a clear message that something's terribly wrong here. After Gideon holds a pencil in both hands behind the chair, snaps it in two, and drops the pieces, the sound returns to normal, the reading ends, and the room is vacated. The next scene shows three of the producers in the back of the cab discussing his symptoms and the fact that he is now in the hospital undergoing tests.

Distortion of Sound to Suggest Subjective States

In *When a Stranger Calls*, Carol Kane, as a teenage babysitter, receives threatening phone calls from a psychopathic killer, who repeatedly asks her, "Why haven't you checked the children?" The police finally trace the call to another phone *within* the house. Before the police can get there, the children are brutally murdered. The killer is captured and imprisoned. Seven years later, Kane is married and has two children of her own. On the evening that the killer escapes from prison, Kane's husband takes her out for a special dinner celebrating a job promotion, and they leave their children in the care of a babysitter. As they settle down to their meal in the restaurant, a waiter tells Kane that she has a telephone call at the cashier's desk. She unsuspectingly answers the phone, assuming the babysitter has called with a question. We do hear a question in the receiver—but it's the killer's voice, cold and metallic: "Have you checked the children . . . ildren . . . dren . . . ren?" The familiar but distorted voice echoes louder and louder, blending into her hysterical scream as we are suddenly yanked inside her fear and horror. Thus, through sound exaggeration the viewer becomes intensely involved in the emotional state of the character.

An analogous technique is used late in Lisa Cholodenko's *The Kids Are All Right*. A mother played by Annette Bening makes a startling, hurtful discovery while alone. When she soon rejoins her family at dinner, the film's sound editors garble and distort the conversation around the table as it is filtered through this character's newly fragmented consciousness.

The "Personality" of Mechanical Sounds

Mechanical sounds can be integrated into the overall tone of a specific scene by giving them personalities. In *The Grapes of Wrath*, John Ford uses the different personalities of two auto horns to underscore the emotions in a scene. As the Joad family stands around the yard welcoming Tom back from prison, Tom's brother Al drives up in the old Joad truck and joins in the happy scene with a bright cheerful *uugga!* from the truck's horn. The celebration continues for a minute or so until it is suddenly interrupted by an ominous, low-pitched, and insultingly loud horn as the convertible driven by the land and cattle company representative pulls up. The horn freezes the Joads as it sounds, and they wait meekly for the reminder they know is coming: They must be off the land by the next day.

Slow-Motion Sound

Walter Hill matches slow-motion sound to slow-motion action in the final shootout scene of *The Long Riders*. After robbing a bank in Northfield, Minnesota, the James gang finds itself trapped. As gang members attempt their getaway, gunmen on top

FIGURE 8.6 **Slow-Motion Sound**   Unusual effects are achieved by the use of slow-motion sound as members of the James gang are shot up by townspeople as they try to make their escape after a bank robbery in *The Long Riders*.

of buildings and behind barricades throw up a wall of bullets. At first, the action is a mixture of normal and slow motion. As outlaws and townsmen are wounded, the action goes into slow motion as they reel or fall, and the sound slows down. These brief, slow scenes are alternated with scenes shown at normal speed. But as the action intensifies and focuses on the outlaws as they are riddled with bullets, the *whole sequence* goes into slow-motion picture and sound. The surreal slowness of the image draws us closer to the gang members, and the slow-motion sound makes us feel their pain as the bullets tear into their flesh. The total effect is eerie, with low whistling sounds, muffled roars, grotesquely slowed horse whinnies, and low-pitch human grunts and groans (Figure 8.6).

Martin Scorsese similarly uses slow-motion sound in *Raging Bull* to portray Jake La Motta's (Robert De Niro) fatigue in a difficult fight and to isolate the effect of a single, crucial blow.

Ironic Juxtaposition of Sound and Image

Usually picture and sound work together to carry a single set of impressions. It is occasionally effective, however, to create ironic contrasts between them. In *The Grapes of Wrath*, the Joads have just stopped along the road to look down on a lush green valley of California orchards, their first glimpse at the land of milk and honey they expected. There are cries of glee, excitement, and amazement, accompanied by birds chirping. The camera cuts to Ma Joad as she appears around the back of the truck. We know that Grandma is dead and that Ma Joad has concealed this from the others until they could reach the promised land of California. The cheerful noises that continue provide an ironic counterpoint to Ma's tired, grief-stricken face, serving to strengthen its impact.

Placing Unusual Emphasis on Sound

A director who wishes to place some unusual emphasis on sound has several options. Two obvious methods involve de-emphasizing the visual image: (1) dropping the image altogether by fading to black or (2) purposely making the image uninteresting or dull by holding a meaningless shot for a long period or by prolonging the use of **dead screen** (screen area in which there is little or no interesting visual information).

In *Reds*, to catch our attention and introduce us to the unusual device of the witnesses (old people who actually knew John Reed and Louise Bryant), director Warren Beatty starts the witnesses' testimony before the images begin. The voices start about halfway through the opening, as we watch white credits unfold over a black screen. At the end of the film, the witnesses continue their interesting and significant comments as the visual image fades and is followed by the ending credits, shown again in white against black.

In *Citizen Kane*, Orson Welles employs the dead-screen technique during one of Susan Alexander Kane's (Dorothy Comingore) opera performances. The camera cuts from the performance and begins a long, slow tilt upward, following a pair of cables up the bare gray walls behind the scenery. Faced with looking at this incredibly boring dead screen, we are forced to listen to the painfully off-key voice. The slow tilt is stretched out by the use of an optical printer just the right amount of time so that we properly appreciate our reward at the end, when the camera finally stops at the two technicians on the catwalk. We gain relief from our pain (and our suspense at where this long journey upward over the dead gray background is leading) as one of the technicians holds his nose to indicate his response to the music we have all been suffering through.

The simplest and most obvious way to emphasize a sound is to increase its volume. In *Bonnie and Clyde*, Arthur Penn underscores the violence by amplifying the roar of the gunfire and the constant shrieking of Blanche Barrow (Estelle Parsons) (Figure 8.7). A similar amplification of sound to underscore violence occurs in *Shane*, where gunshots and the sounds of a fistfight are exaggerated. An especially effective use of amplified sound occurs in the fight between Shane (Alan Ladd) and Joe Starret (Van Heflin) to see which of them will go to town for a showdown with the Ryker clan. The fight is filmed from an extremely low angle: The combatants are framed under the belly of a panicked horse. As the fighters struggle, the horse prances, and the pounding of each hoof is amplified to match its closeness to the camera. The violence panics other animals, who join in the chorus: A barking dog and a bawling cow trying to break out of her stall join in to accompany the snorts, the whinnies, and the pounding hoofs of the panicked horse. Although the sounds of the fistfight in the background are audible, they are somewhat de-emphasized by the loudness of the closer horse hoofs, but the violence of that fight is actually intensified by the exaggerated sound environment.

Moments of stark terror can also be enhanced through amplified sound. Steven Spielberg had composer John Williams use a sudden loud chord as part of one of the major scare scenes in *Jaws*, as a face suddenly appears through a hole in the bottom of the boat Richard Dreyfuss is examining. As Spielberg describes it, "First you react to the face, then the chord comes a fraction of a second later. It's very

FIGURE 8.7 **Exaggerated Sound Effects** The amplified sounds of gunfire add greatly to the intensity of several action scenes in *Bonnie and Clyde,* including this one in which Blanche Barrow (Estelle Parsons) attempts to outrun "the laws" while wielding a spatula and screaming.

easy to scare people with noise, to lift you from your chair with a loud sound. John Carpenter does it with his films all the time. Billy Friedkin did it in *The Exorcist . . .* in Dolby Stereo."[5]

Using Sound for Texture, Time, and Temperature

In *McCabe & Mrs. Miller,* Robert Altman experimented with a new approach to dialogue and sound recording. In this and such later films as *Nashville, The Player, Short Cuts, Gosford Park,* and *A Prairie Home Companion,* he seems to be moving away from the dramatic enhancement of dialogue and sound and toward a thick, realistic sound texture in which dialogue can become a series of fragmented, blurred, and unseparated utterances, equal to but not dramatically more important than the **ambient sounds** (sounds natural to the scene's environment). By blurring the sharp edges of dialogue and thereby de-emphasizing the words, Altman increases our consciousness of the visual elements and weaves visual and aural elements into a more nearly equal blend, creating a unique texture in the film. The ambient sound is thick, rich, and detailed but not dramatically enhanced. In *McCabe & Mrs. Miller,* the stomping and shuffling of boots against a rough wooden floor are there right along with the mumbled, naturalistic dialogue. Typical of the difference in Altman's approach is a scene in which McCabe (Warren Beatty) and another man pass through a crowded saloon on their way upstairs. Someone is telling a joke at the bar, and we hear fragments of it as they pass through, but as they start up the stairs, their loud footsteps obscure the punch line.

Everything in *McCabe & Mrs. Miller* sounds real: the rain, a chair scraped across a floor, mumbled poker-game dialogue, moaning wind, a jug skidding across the ice, gunshots and their reverberation. Sound is often stacked on sound, voice on voice, but stacked in a new way so that we get a strong sense of being there—in a different place and a different time. The texture is so real that we feel the rain and the cold wind and even smell the smoke. Our experiential faculties demand attention. Altman's films thus insist that audiences watch them repeatedly to be able to see and hear more of the multiple, complex elements he so carefully orchestrates in each movie frame.

Sound can be an important element in **period pieces** (films that take place not in the present but in some earlier period of history). By recording the sounds made by authentic objects from the era, filmmakers can enhance the story's credibility for the audience. Mark Mangini used this technique to add realism to Steven Soderbergh's film *Kafka:* "I spent two months in Prague recording . . . everything that moved so that I would have good, clean recordings of . . . old typewriters, telephones, horse-and-buggies, etc. . . . I recorded . . . them in the acoustically appropriate environment as used in the film. I think this kind of recording adds a verisimilitude to the sound track that cannot be gotten in postproduction."[6]

Sound-effects editors can even influence the audience's perception of temperature. Lawrence Kasdan's film *Body Heat* is set in Florida, and the heat generated by both the weather and the passion of the main characters is central to the story. When the film was shot, however, Florida's temperatures were low, and a cold wind blew constantly. Sound-effects editors added the sounds of crickets, flapping palm fronds, and wind chimes to create the illusion that the film's action occurred in the intense, humid heat of summer.

Skip Lievsay also used sound to raise the temperature of Spike Lee's *Do the Right Thing*, set in New York on the hottest day of summer:

> Certain backgrounds like a breeze in the park, nice birds, and happy things just seemed to us to be too cooling. We went with a dry trafficky sound. We did find if we used a little more top end, it would seem just a little bit hotter. For the sequence where people take showers, I recorded some sound effects, and the hottest one by far was the one that seemed the most like steam; it was a very sizzly sound. The tubby, gurgling sound was much more cooling, so we used the sizzling one instead. The dull traffic we used in the picture made that block seem more remote, almost like it was out in the desert.[7]

SOUND AS A PLOT DEVICE

With innovations in sound-recording technology have come two films that build suspense and important plot elements around recorded sound. Much in the same way that Michelangelo Antonioni used photographic techniques to intensify suspense in *Blow-Up*, Brian De Palma used sound-recording technology to answer a basic dramatic question in *Blow Out* (starring John Travolta): Was the sound just before a fatal car crash caused by a tire blowing out, or were there really two sounds—a rifle shot immediately followed by the blowout? A similar but more intriguing use of recorded sound occurs in Francis Ford Coppola's *The Conversation*. Gene Hackman plays a private investigator specializing in electronic listening devices. While testing some new equipment, he records a young couple's

FIGURE 8.8 Sound as a Plot Device   A professional electronic eavesdropper (Gene Hackman) is troubled by what he has heard in a recorded conversation between a young couple in Francis Ford Coppola's *The Conversation*. The entire plot of the film hinges on interpreting subtle differences in emphasis during their brief exchange. Here, we find Harry Caul literally "in the toilet" as he closes in on the mystery's secret.

conversation, the full import of which he learns only after playing and replaying the tape and reevaluating certain assumptions in light of discovering that the true meaning depends on the subtle emphasis on a single word (Figure 8.8).

SOUND AS A TRANSITIONAL ELEMENT

Sound is also an extremely important transitional device in films. It can be used to show the relationship between shots, scenes, or sequences, or it can make a change in image from one shot or sequence to another seem more fluid or natural.

A fluid and graceful transition between sequences is achieved through the slight overlapping of sound from one shot into the next. The sound from a shot continues even after the image fades or dissolves into an entirely new image. This overlapping usually represents a passage of time, a change of setting, or both. A similar effect is created by the converse—the sound of an *upcoming* sequence slightly precedes its corresponding image. Both versions of this device are used frequently in Mike Nichols's *The Graduate*. In many cases, sound may overlap sound; the sound from one image fades under the rising sound of the succeeding image (watch, for example, the first swimming pool scene in this film). This device provides a smooth flow of sound from one sequence to another when abrupt changes in sound are not desirable.

Sound links, aural bridges between scenes or sequences (changes in place or time), are created through the use of similar or identical sounds in both sequences. For example, a buzzing alarm clock at the end of one sequence becomes a buzzing telephone switchboard at the start of the next. Sound is thus used as a somewhat artificial link between the two sequences to create a sense of fluid continuity. Sometimes even dialogue links provide transition between two sequences. A question asked by a character at the close of one sequence may be answered by another character at the start of the following sequence, even though the two scenes may be set in different times and places.

Sometimes dialogue transitions are ironic, resulting in a sharp or startling contrast between the scenes being joined. Consider, for example, the effect if one scene's last line of dialogue had a character say: "I don't care what happens! Nothing on the face of the Earth could entice me to go to Paris!" and the next scene opened with the same character walking by the Eiffel Tower. Often, as in *The Graduate* and *Cabaret*, this device is used effectively along with the jump cut.

Dozens of examples of dynamic and unusual uses of sound can be found in *Citizen Kane*. Orson Welles—supervising his editor, Robert Wise—employs a variety of sound links to blend scenes and explosive changes in volume to propel us from one scene to another.

VOICE-OVER NARRATION

The filmmaker can also employ sound that has no *direct* relationship to the natural sounds and dialogue involved in the story. A human voice off-screen, called **voice-over narration,** has a variety of functions. It is perhaps most commonly used as an expository device to convey necessary background information or fill in gaps for continuity that cannot be presented dramatically. Some films use voice-over narration only at the beginning to give necessary background, place the action in historical perspective, or provide a sense of authenticity. Others may employ voice-over at the beginning, occasionally in the body of the film for transition or continuity, and at the end.

The flavor of a novelistic first-person point of view is often provided through the use of voice-over. This can be accomplished by setting the story in a frame. A visually introduced narrator tells the story through a series of **flashbacks** (as in *Little Big Man, The Glass Menagerie, Chaplin,* and *De-Lovely*), or the narrator is never introduced visually but is only the voice of a participant recalling past events. In *To Kill a Mockingbird*, for example, the voice-over narration (by an uncredited Kim Stanley) is obviously by an adult relating childhood recollections, but the narrator is never pictured. The adult narrator of that film, in a soft, Southern voice, provides a sense of time and place, describing the pace and style of life in the town of Macomb. Then, by ending the introductory voice-over with "that summer I was six years old" just as Scout Finch appears on the screen, the narrator slips easily from the adult remembering the past into young Scout's viewpoint and the present tense of the film.

The narrator for *Summer of '42* performs a similar function (establishing place, time, and point of view) but comments more philosophically on the significance of the events to Hermie, the point-of-view character. Both *To Kill a Mockingbird* and *Summer of '42* employ great restraint in their use of voice-over narration, as does *The Age of Innocence* (1993) in its utilization of the voice of Joanne Woodward (Figure 8.9).

FIGURE 8.9 **Voice-Over Narration as Remembering**   Formal and restrained use of voice-over narration provides a framework for meditation in Tom Ford's *A Single Man* (starring Colin Firth, seen here in a flashback with Matthew Goode, left).

FIGURE 8.10 **Voice-Over Narration Rejection**   Although director Roman Polanski co-wrote the screenplay for his 2010 suspense drama *The Ghost Writer* with novelist Robert Harris, the two men decided to jettison the first-person voice-over narration of Harris's *The Ghost*. Perhaps for shrewd (if overly cautious?) plot reasons, they instead chose to externalize the unlucky protagonist, portrayed by Ewan McGregor.

The film versions of some novels must depend on voice-over to tell a story that cannot be told effectively through cinematic means. Such is the case with *The Old Man and the Sea*, where the most important part of the story takes place in the old man's mind, in his reactions to what happens rather than in the events themselves. The voice-over becomes a noncinematic compromise. Spencer Tracy, who plays the old man Santiago, simply reads passages from the novel that communicate the character's thoughts and feelings about the action, but the narration is forced to carry far too much of the burden. The literary style of the narration and its excessive use combine to make us feel that we're reading a movie (Figure 8.10).

In Francis Ford Coppola's *Apocalypse Now*, Martin Sheen's narration, necessary to plug holes in the script, flattens the dramatic impact of the visuals by overinterpreting and overexplaining, by telling us too many things we can see for ourselves. Here the voice-over gets in the way. By telling us too much about "the horror," the film prevents us from discovering it for ourselves. As a result, we never really feel that horror. In a similar way, the added voice-over narration in the theatrical version (vs. the director's cut) of *Blade Runner* weakens its drama.

The voice-over technique is sometimes employed as an ironic counterpoint, providing a level of meaning that is in direct contrast to the image on the screen. In *Raising Arizona*, Hi (Nicolas Cage) provides a formal and stilted but touchingly

FIGURE 8.11 Voice-Over Narration as Ironic Counterpoint In the Coen brothers' *Raising Arizona*, the marvelous, idiosyncratic voice of Hi (played by Nicolas Cage) guides us through the action, providing both gently ironic instructions for following the intricate plot and constant entertainment.

FIGURE 8.12 Postmodern Film Narration Christina Ricci, as DeDee in *The Opposite of Sex* (left), narrates the film in voice-over and at the same time comically deconstructs the work, furnishing a wickedly delightful running commentary on its dialogue, plot, symbolism, and characterization as the movie progresses. Similarly, as a toupeé-wearing corporate whistleblower in *The Informant!*, Matt Damon provides almost incessant voice-over chatter, thus injecting into the real-life, "serious" narrative the level of loopy humor that seems to be promised by the exclamation point at the end of Steven Soderbergh's title for his film.

unperceptive interpretation of the zany events unfolding before our eyes. As a result, we get a level of rich humor and some absurd glimpses into a totally lovable and good-intentioned criminal mind (Figure 8.11).

In *The Opposite of Sex*, the narrator, DeDee Truitt, wonderfully played by Christina Ricci, is a "trash-talking teenager from Arkansas . . . [who] chats on the soundtrack during and between many of the scenes, pointing out the clichés, warning us about approaching plot conventions and debunking our desire to see the story unfold in traditional ways." DeDee's unique voice is so strong, in fact, that Roger Ebert concludes his review of the film by observing, "I hate people who talk during movies, but if she were sitting behind me in the theater, saying all of this stuff, I'd want her to keep right on talking"[8] (Figure 8.12).

One of the most powerful voice-over narrations in film to date is that provided by Linda Manz for *Days of Heaven*. There is a distinctive style to her narration, a

FIGURE 8.13 Narration as an Integral Part of Texture   Linda Manz's poetic, ironic narration for Terrence Malick's *Days of Heaven* (1978) functions almost as a part of the musical score (top right). The personality of her voice becomes a dominant factor in the film's unique style and texture. Earlier, in *Badlands* (1973) (top left), Malick had used the same technique. In *The Thin Red Line* (1998), the director continued to utilize the voice-over, but this time with multiple speakers (bottom left), as he did in 2005's *The New World* (bottom right).

poetic rhythm, a texture that permeates the entire film. The unique vocal quality and verbal essence provide more than just the narrative glue to hold the story's structure together; combined with the strange woman-child philosophical reflections and childish utterings, they are integrated so beautifully that they become a major element of the film's uniqueness (Figure 8.13).

Forrest Gump also provides a clear verbal essence in its voice-over. To emphasize Gump's slowness, Gump-as-character often repeats what Gump-as-narrator has just said as new scenes are introduced, contributing to the unusual blend of humor and pathos that runs through the film (Figure 8.14).

Generally, voice-over narration may be very effective if used with restraint. It is not, however, a truly cinematic technique, and overusing it can be seriously detrimental to the quality of the film. In the American (vs. original French) version of the documentary *March of the Penguins* (Academy Award, 2006), Morgan Freeman's pervasive voice-over narration is either very irritating because it is unnecessary or quite endearing because of the warmth that the popular actor brings to the monologue—depending upon a viewer's bias.

FIGURE 8.14 Vocal Repetition for Humor   Like the title character in *Forrest Gump*, Karl (Billy Bob Thornton) in *Sling Blade* (bottom right) engenders both dark humor and riveting character via his "slow" speech patterns. In the film comedy *Heartbreakers*, a wealthy, constantly smoking, lovelorn tobacco company owner (Gene Hackman, basing his performance, surely, upon W. C. Fields) merely, outrageously, coughs repeatedly to grab the viewer's attention (bottom left). James McAvoy (shown at top, with Christopher Plummer as Leo Tolstoy), in *The Last Station*, plays a personal secretary who sneezes comically when he meets an attractive young woman.

SILENCE AS A SOUND EFFECT

In certain situations, a short **dead track,** the complete absence of sound, may be as effective as the most powerful sound effect. The ghostly, unnatural quality of film without sound forces us to look intently at the image. The natural rhythms of sound effects, dialogue, and music become as natural to the film as the rhythms of breathing; and when these rhythms stop, we immediately develop a feeling of almost physical tension and suspense, as though we are holding our breath and can't wait to start breathing again. This effect is used to great advantage in conjunction with the freeze frame. The sudden change from vibrant, noisy movement to silent, frozen stillness can stun us for a moment.

The most common use of dead track is simply to increase, by contrast, the impact and shock effect of sudden or unexpected sounds that follow these moments of silence. In Robert Benton's *Still of the Night*, psychiatrist Sam Rice (Roy Scheider) is following a woman he believes to be Brooke Reynolds (Meryl Streep) through Central Park. The soundtrack is alive with environmental noises: wind, muffled music, and traffic, all blended into a kind of "big-city-alive-in-the-distance" hum. As Rice walks into an underpass and stops, the soundtrack goes dead, providing a few moments of silence to set up the aural shock of a mugger's switchblade springing from its handle a few inches from his face. This dead-track effect is also used momentarily, but in an immensely skillful manner, during what is probably the most suspenseful scene in Steven Spielberg's *Munich*, when a young girl seems about to be blown to bits as she answers a telephone. The opposite effect, the shock of silence after violent sound, is experienced during the moments of almost dead track that immediately follow the final fusillade in *Bonnie and Clyde*.

RHYTHMIC QUALITIES OF DIALOGUE AND SOUND EFFECTS

Both dialogue and sound effects are important for the rhythmic patterns, or cadences, they create. These rhythmic elements often match the visual rhythms and reflect the mood, emotion, or pace of the action. Thus, the pace of the dialogue and the rhythmic qualities of the sound effects influence the pace of the film as a whole.

THE "SOUNDS" OF FOREIGN LANGUAGE OR INTERNATIONAL FILMS

The language barrier obviously poses a challenge to viewing foreign language or international films. Although the image carries the major burden of communication in film, the spoken word still plays an important role. There are traditionally two basic methods of translating dialogue in foreign language films: voice dubbing and the use of subtitles.

Voice Dubbing

In the case of a French film, for example, that also plays in America, the **voice dubbing** works as follows: The actors speak the lines of dialogue in their native language (French), and this dialogue is recorded and becomes a part of the soundtrack for the French version. For the American market, the dialogue soundtrack in French is replaced by an English soundtrack. Voices in English are recorded to correspond to the mouth and lip movements of the French actors. To match image with soundtrack, the translator carefully selects English words that phonetically approximate the French words being spoken, so that the image of the French actor and the words spoken in English seem synchronized. The precision of voice-dubbing technology enables us to watch the film in the usual way, and, because the actors seem to be speaking English, the film does not seem so foreign. Nevertheless, the disadvantages and limitations of voice dubbing are numerous, and few foreign language films are now dubbed into English exclusively (although some DVDs include optional dubbed versions in several languages).

Perhaps the primary flaw is the effect that results from separating actors from their voices: The acting often seems stiff and wooden. Another problem is that perfectly accurate lip synchronization is never possible. For example, although the

French phrase *mon amour* might closely approximate the lip movements of a translation such as *my dearest*, the French word *oui* does not come close to the lip movements of the English word *yes*. Even if perfect lip synchronization were possible, another formidable obstacle would remain: Each language has its own emotional character, rhythmic patterns, and accompanying facial expressions and gestures, all of which seem unnatural when another language is dubbed in. French facial expressions simply do not correspond to English words. Thus, because of the impossibility of perfect synchronization and the differences in national emotional temperaments reflected in expressions and gestures, dubbing can never really capture the illusion of reality. A certain artificial quality often permeates the film and becomes a gnawing irritation to the viewer.

Furthermore, the process of voice dubbing eliminates the natural power, character, and unique emotional quality of the original language, the very sound of which, understandable or not, may be essential to the spirit of the film. When the dubbed voices are not carefully chosen to fit the actors and the general tone of the film, the illusion of reality suffers even more. For example, in the Russian film *War and Peace*, the dubbing, according to Renata Adler (a former reviewer for the *New York Times*), makes the inhabitants of Moscow sound as if they came from Texas. In such situations, a certain degree of authenticity might be saved by having the dubbed voices speak English with a Russian accent.

All too often the artificial quality of dubbed international films is due not to the change of language or the casting of voices but to the poor quality of the dubbing techniques. Sometimes there seems to be a general lack of concern with the dramatic performance of the dubbed voices. The dubbed lines usually have little dramatic emphasis, or are delivered in a melodramatic manner. They often possess either too few or too many natural variations in pitch and stress and the rhythms are all wrong. With all these problems, dubbed lines often provide little more than basic information without vocal subtleties.

Wifemistress (a 1977 Italian film directed by Marco Vicario, starring Marcello Mastroianni and Laura Antonelli) is a classic study in how a reasonably good film can be ruined by poor dubbing. On the positive side, the actors are clearly mouthing English words, for the lip synchronization is extremely well matched. But any sense of credibility ends there. The dubbed dialogue is obviously close-miked in a studio, and the English-speaking actors are so close to a microphone that they have to speak softly to keep from distorting their voices as they are recorded. As a result, each speech gives the impression of being whispered. There is no attempt to achieve any sense of depth. Each voice is recorded at the same volume level regardless of the actor's distance from the camera. And there is no ambient sound during conversations, even when the actors talking are in a room almost full of other people. In some scenes, the music is overdone in an attempt to kill off part of this ghostly silence. Although the dubbed voices are well cast (Mastroianni speaks for himself), the acting sounds like reading; the dialogue is flat, listless, and completely lacking in dramatic punch (Figure 8.15).

In contrast to the problems of *Wifemistress* is the excellent dubbing of *Das Boot* (and the much longer director's cut is now also widely available with subtitles). The natural rhythms, cadence, and pitch of human voices really talking to each other give the dialogue dynamic life even without completely accurate synchronization

FIGURE 8.15 **Dubious Dialogue Dubbing** While many viewers of Giuseppe Tornatore's *Cinema Paradiso* enjoy listening to the Italian rhythms in the delightful relationship between young Toto (Salvatore Cascio, on the right in the photo) and Alfredo (Philippe Noiret, left), these same viewers will immediately recoil from the available dubbed version, which sounds recording-booth flat and melodramatic, completely lacking in nuance.

with lip movement, and three-dimensional ambient sound conveys enough exciting information to make us forget that the film is dubbed.

From an American perspective, at least, poor dubbing would probably be an improvement over the recent practice in the Polish film industry. There, in a method very popular with audiences, predominantly male readers—for all voices— merely narrate movies in a flat, dispassionate manner.

Subtitles

Because of these problems with voice dubbing, most contemporary foreign language films use subtitles for the U.S. market. A concise English translation of the dialogue appears in printed form at the bottom of the screen while the dialogue is being spoken. Reading this translation gives us a fairly clear idea of what is being said by the actors as they speak in their native language.

The use of subtitles has several advantages over the use of voice dubbing. Perhaps most importantly, it does not interfere with the illusion of reality to the same degree as dubbing, even though the appearance of writing at the bottom of the screen is not completely natural to the film medium. But because the actors are not separated from their voices, their performances seem more real and human, as well as more powerful. Furthermore, by retaining the voices of the actors speaking in their native language, the subtitled film keeps the power, character, and unique emotional quality of the culture that produced it. The importance of this last point cannot be overestimated. Renata Adler has observed:

> One of the essential powers and beauties of the cinema is that it is truly international, that it makes language accessible in a highly special way. Only in movies can one hear foreign languages spoken and—by the written word in subtitles— participate as closely as one ever will in a culture that is otherwise closed to one.[9]

Subtitles interfere less with the viewer's overall aesthetic experience of the film, less with the film's cultural integrity, and therefore less with its essential reality. Because much of the film's reality comes through to us intuitively even in a language we cannot understand, it is more important that the voice–image link remain intact than that we clearly understand every word of dialogue.

This is not to say that the use of subtitles does not have its disadvantages. One of the most obvious is that our attention is divided between watching the image and reading the subtitles. Furthermore, most subtitles are so concise that they are oversimplified and incomplete. They are designed to convey only the most basic level of meaning and do not even attempt to capture the full flavor and quality of the dialogue in the original language. Another problem arises if the image behind the subtitles is white or light in color and the subtitles are also white. This was the case in parts of *Tora! Tora! Tora!*, where the white subtitles often appeared against the white uniforms of the Japanese naval officers, and in Jean Renoir's great French film *The Rules of the Game*, where white subtitles were obliterated against light-colored costumes and landscapes. However, more and more international films are released in America (especially in their DVD versions) with easy-to-read yellow-highlighted subtitles.

Despite the disadvantages, the use of subtitles is still perhaps the best solution to the language barrier, especially in a slow-paced film that is edited in such a way that the dialogue can be read before the image changes. In a fast-paced film, where editorial cuts occurring at a very high frequency demand full attention to the image, voice dubbing may be the only answer. Luckily, our new video technology has now made it possible for us to choose either or both of these alternatives: Many DVDs offer menus from which viewers may choose to experience an international film in its own language, or via dubbing (often, into more than one language), or through subtitles (also into multiple languages).

Watching Mel Gibson's greatly popular *The Passion of the Christ*, few viewers, either in theaters or at home, were able to understand all three of the languages used in the film: Aramaic, Latin, and Hebrew. As a result, Gibson offered subtitles to facilitate mass consumption of the word. This conciliatory effort stands in stark contrast to Gibson's use of ultraviolent visual elements in the film, which were clearly meant to stun everyone.

ANALYZING SOUND EFFECTS AND DIALOGUE

1. Where in the film are off-screen or invisible sounds effectively employed to enlarge the boundaries of the visual frame or to create mood and atmosphere?
2. What sound effects in particular contribute to a sense of reality and a feeling of being there?
3. Does the film attempt to provide a sense of three-dimensionality or depth in sound? If a stereophonic soundtrack is used, what does it contribute to the overall effect of the film?
4. Where is sound employed to represent subjective states of mind, and how effective is this use of sound?
5. Where is unusual emphasis placed on sound in the film, and what is the purpose of such emphasis?
6. Is sound used to provide important transitions in the film? Why is sound needed to provide these transitions?
7. If voice-over soundtracks are used for narration or internal monologues (thoughts of a character spoken aloud), can you justify their use, or could the same information have been conveyed through purely cinematic means?

1. **Sound Effects.** Watch the indicated sequences from *On the Waterfront* [1:00:00 to 1:03:22] and *All That Jazz* [1:03:30 to 1:06:33]. Each sequence takes us into the mind and feelings of the characters through clever uses of sound. Describe in detail how each sequence accomplishes its goal, and explain how the two methods differ.

2. **Slow-Motion Sound.** Watch the Northfield, Minnesota, raid sequence from *The Long Riders* [1:15:58 to 1:20:36], and describe the interaction of slow-motion cinematography and slow-motion sound. Some of the slow-motion sounds might be difficult to identify. How is this challenge overcome?

3. **Sound Links.** *Citizen Kane* is known for its innovative use of sound for transitional purposes. Watch the following segments, and describe the methods by which sound links scenes that take place in different locations and at different points in time: [0:22:48 to 0:24:35] and [0:59:34 to 1:00:52].

4. **Voice-Over Narration.** Watch the first 5 minutes of each of the following films, and describe the essential differences in the narrators and the effects of their voice-over narrations in each film: *Days of Heaven, Taxi Driver, Raising Arizona, Stand by Me, The Good Girl, My Architect,* and *A Christmas Story.*

The American writer Ambrose Bierce (1842–1914?) is celebrated for the bitter cynicism of his worldview and for his ironic wit. Both of these qualities are displayed well in one of his best short stories, a Civil War yarn called "An Occurrence  at Owl Creek Bridge." Almost fifty years after Bierce just disappeared (apparently) from the face of the earth, writer and director Robert Enrico interpreted "Occurrence" on film, and the work was a winner at the Cannes Film Festival and also at the Academy Awards (Best Short Film, 1963).

As a type, the short film is not generally popular, in part because it is not commercially profitable, so its longevity is constantly at risk. Luckily for film lovers, though, Enrico's piece caught the attention of Rod Serling, creator of television's "The Twilight Zone." For this immensely popular series, Serling later chose the film as the first to be aired that his own company had not made. "An Occurrence at Owl Creek Bridge" was first shown on

American television on February 28, 1964, and we owe its currently easy availability to that fact. The film now appears on the DVD *Treasures of "The Twilight Zone."*

Although "Occurrence" was shot by artists whose first language was not English, there is no need for subtitles; throughout its twenty-four-minute running time almost no dialogue is spoken. Further, the film's music is chiefly minimalist: one guitar at crucial moments, a vocalist, a solitary drummer. Still, photographed in black and white, Enrico's film depends enormously upon sound editing for its effectiveness. Watch this work casually first, letting its pathos and dark humor spill over you. Then view it again, this time noting how ambient sounds, both natural and exaggerated, significantly help to dictate our acceptance and appreciation of Bierce's narrative.

DVD FILMMAKING EXTRAS

The Art of Sound Effects and Dialogue

The Count of Monte Cristo (2002):
Immensely instructive on this DVD is a feature, "Layer-by-Layer Interactive Sound Design," that allows a watcher to switch easily among four different sound versions of the same scene. One may opt to hear only the dialogue, only the music added to the scene, or only its sound effects—or experience all three of these on the composite track.

Monster:
An interactive feature here allows the viewer-listener to experiment with various combinations of "audio stems" from dialogue, sound effects, and music.

WALL-E (Three-Disc Special Edition):
Ben Burtt, often called "the father of modern film sound design," leads viewers of disc one on a superb 19-minute tour of the history and techniques of his art. See "Animation Sound Design: Building Worlds From the Sound up."

The Sixth Sense:
In a "Music and Sound Design" feature here, director M. Night Shyamalan and composer James Newton Howard discuss the editing subtleties of such questions as "What does the sixth sense . . . sound like?" Their illustrative clips omit all dialogue from the scenes, making it possible to focus intently on the sound effects used, many of which are, in fact, "musically" generated. Shyamalan notes that "all background sounds in the movie are human or animal breaths." Producer Frank Marshall observes that "the music and sound effects in the movie are also characters."

Shrek (Two-Disc Special Edition):
Disc one contains a "Revoice Studio" that permits a viewer to "Record Your Voice Over Your Favorite Characters' Lines and Star in 1 of 12 Entire Scenes!"

Timecode:
In the theatrical version of this film, the screen was divided into four separate images. There, sound volume levels shifted watchers' attention from one

quadrant to another as particular elements of the plot progressed. The default setting on this DVD version uses the same procedure. In addition, an interactive feature allows one to create new sound edit patterns, thereby also conjuring up fresh narrative maps.

For interviews with other notable sound designers, refer to the bonus features on the latest DVD releases of *Star Wars, Episode II: Attack of the Clones* (Ben Burtt), *A. I. Artificial Intelligence* (Gary Rydstrom), *Men in Black II* (Steve Visscher), and *Forrest Gump* (Randy Thom).

FILMS FOR STUDY

Sound Effects and Dialogue

All That Jazz (1979)
Body Heat (1981)
The Bourne Ultimatum (2007)
Citizen Kane (1941)
The Dark Knight (2008)
Do the Right Thing (1989)
The Hurt Locker (2009)
Jurassic Park (1993)
King Kong (2005)
Letters From Iwo Jima (2006)
The Long Riders (1980)
The Lord of the Rings: The Return of the King (2003)
M (1931)
McCabe & Mrs. Miller (1971)
Nashville (1975)
On the Waterfront (1954)
Raging Bull (1980)
Raiders of the Lost Ark (1981)
Shane (1953)
Short Cuts (1993)
Wall-E (2008)
The Way Back (2011)

Voice-Over Narration

About a Boy (2002)
Apocalypse Now (1979)

A Clockwork Orange (1971)
Days of Heaven (1978)
Ferris Bueller's Day off (1986)
Forrest Gump (1994)
The Good Girl (2002)
Life Is Beautiful (1997)
Mrs. Dalloway (1997)
The New World (2005)
The Opposite of Sex (1998)
The Prestige (2006)
Radio Days (1987)
Raising Arizona (1987)
A River Runs Through It (1992)
The Shawshank Redemption (1994)
Stand by Me (1986)
Sunset Boulevard (1950)
Taxi Driver (1976)
The Thin Red Line (1998)
To Kill a Mockingbird (1962)

Foreign Language or International Films
(The original language is noted after the film date.)

All About My Mother (1999); Spanish
Amélie (2001); French
Amores Perros (2000); Spanish

Belle de Jour (1967); French
The Bicycle Thief (1948); Italian
Breathless (1960); French
Burnt by the Sun (1994); Russian
Cinema Paradiso (1988); Italian
City of God (2002); Portuguese
The Conformist (1970); Italian
Das Boot (1981); German
Downfall (2004); German
8½ (1963); Italian
The Girl With the Dragon Tattoo (2009); Swedish
Grand Illusion (1937); French
Hiroshima, Mon Amour (1959); French and Japanese
In the Mood for Love (2000); Cantonese and Shanghainese
La Dolce Vita (1960); Italian
Look at Me (2004); French
Maria Full of Grace (2004); Spanish
The Marriage of Maria Braun (1979); German

Monsoon Wedding (2001); Hindi, Punjabi, and English

Persona (1966); Swedish

Raise the Red Lantern (1991); Mandarin

Rashomon (1950); Japanese

Red (1994); French

The Rules of the Game (1939); French

Run Lola Run (1998); German

The Secret in their Eyes (2009); Spanish

The Seventh Seal (1957); Swedish

Summer Hours (2008); French

Swept Away . . . (1974); Italian

Talk to Her (2002); Spanish

Tokyo Story (1953); Japanese

Tsotsi (2005); Zulu, Xhosa, Afrikaans

2046 (2004); Cantonese

A Very Long Engagement (2004); French

The White Ribbon (2009); German

Y Tu Mamá También (2001); Spanish

The MUSICAL SCORE

9

Across the Universe

> The film composer should have the confidence to use exactly what he needs and no more. He shouldn't use his theatrical license to blow the believability of the picture, and I think that believability is closely connected with understatement. The composer wants to pull the moviegoer's mind into that room that's up on the screen, into that feeling that's up there, and it can take very little to achieve that involvement.
> —QUINCY JONES, COMPOSER

THE REMARKABLE AFFINITY OF MUSIC AND FILM

Music has such a remarkable affinity to film that the addition of the musical score was almost an inevitability. Even in the earliest films, the audience would have felt a very real vacuum of silence because the pulsing vitality provided by the moving image seemed unnatural, almost ghostly, without some form of corresponding sound. In fact, so-called silent films were almost always projected with accompanying live piano, organ, ensemble, or orchestra music. So by the time it became possible to use recorded dialogue and sound effects, music had already proved itself as a highly effective accompaniment for the emotions and rhythms built into the images.

Music has made possible an artistic blending of sight and sound, a fusing of music and movement so effective that composer Dimitri Tiomkin was moved to remark that a good film is "really just ballet with dialogue." Muir Mathieson, in *The Technique of Film Music*, put it this way: "Music . . . judged as a part of the whole film. . . . must be accepted not as a decoration or a filler of gaps in the plaster, but a part of the architecture."[1]

Both film and music divide time into rather clearly defined rhythmic patterns; perhaps that provides the most important common bond. There are certain natural rhythms inherent in the physical movements of many objects on the screen. Trees swaying in the breeze, a walking man, a galloping horse, a speeding motorcycle, and a machine capping bottles on an assembly line—all establish natural rhythms that create an almost instinctive need for corresponding rhythmic sounds. Another rhythmic pattern is provided by the pace of the plot, by how quickly or slowly it unfolds. Still another is created by the pace of the dialogue and the natural rhythms of human speech. Tempo is also established by the frequency of editorial cuts and the varying duration of shots between cuts, which gives each sequence a unique rhythmic character. Although editing divides the film into a number of separate parts, the continuity and the fluid form of the medium remain, because the cuts create clear rhythmic patterns but do not break the flow of images and sound.

Because music possesses these same qualities of rhythm and fluid continuity, it can be easily adapted to the film's basic rhythms, to its liquid contours, or shapes. This affinity between music and film has led us to accept them almost as unity, as part of the same package, as though music somehow exists magically alongside every film.

THE IMPORTANCE OF THE MUSICAL SCORE

Although we often accept film music without question and sometimes even without noticing it, this does not mean that its contribution to the film experience is insignificant. Music has a tremendous effect on our response, greatly enriching and enhancing our overall reaction to almost any film. It accomplishes this in several ways: by reinforcing or strengthening the emotional content of the image, by stimulating the imagination and the kinetic sense, and by suggesting and expressing emotions that cannot be conveyed by pictorial means alone.

Because it has a direct and very significant effect on our reaction to film, the term *background music*, which is so often applied to the musical score, is a misnomer.

Music actually functions as an integral or complementary element. Despite its direct effect on us, however, there is general critical agreement on one point: The role of music in film should be a subordinate one.

Two schools of thought exist on the proper degree of this subordination. The older, traditional view is that the best film music performs its various functions without making us consciously aware of its presence. In other words, if we don't notice the music, it's a good score. Therefore, the music for a good score shouldn't be *too* good, for really good music draws attention to itself and away from the film.

The modern view, by contrast, allows the music, on appropriate occasions, not only to demand our conscious attention but even to dominate the picture, as long as it remains essentially integrated with the visual, dramatic, and rhythmic elements of the film as a whole. At such moments, we may become conscious of how intrinsically beautiful the music is, though we should not be so moved that we lose sight of its appropriateness to the image on the screen.

Both modern and traditional views are therefore in agreement on one essential point: Music that calls too much attention to itself at the expense of the film as a whole is not effective. Regardless of the degree of subordination, a good score will always be a significant structural element, performing its proper functions in a perfectly integrated way, serving as a means to an end rather than an end itself. Composer Quincy Jones captures this idea: "For me, some of the best moments in pictures come when the music is tied in so organically with the image, is so much a part of it, that you can't imagine it any other way. The themes in *The Bridge on the River Kwai* and *The Third Man* seem to come out of the tapestry of the films."[2]

GENERAL FUNCTIONS OF THE MUSICAL SCORE

The two most general and basic functions of the musical score are to create structural rhythms and to stimulate emotional responses, both of which greatly enhance and reinforce the effect of the image.

The musical score creates a sense of structural rhythm both in the film as a whole and in its individual shots by developing a sense of pace corresponding to the pace of the movement within each shot and to the pace of the editing. In this way, the composer articulates and underscores the basic rhythms of the film.

The film score also serves to complement and enhance the narrative and dramatic structure by stimulating emotional responses that parallel each individual sequence and the film as a whole. Because even the most subtle moods are established, intensified, maintained, and changed through the effective use of film music, the musical score becomes an accurate reflection of the emotional patterns and shapes of the film as a whole (Figure 9.1). This does not mean that a film's structured visual rhythms can be separated from its emotional patterns, for both are closely interwoven into the same fabric. Effective film music therefore usually parallels one and complements the other.

The simplest and oldest method of adding music to film is simply selecting a piece of familiar music (classical, pop, folk, jazz, blues, rock, and so on) that fits the rhythmic, emotional, or dramatic demands of the sequence at hand. An excellent example of the use of familiar music was the choice of the *William Tell* Overture for the old "Lone Ranger" radio show. The classical overture not only provided a

FIGURE 9.1 "A Sigh Is Just a Sigh" From its opening credits accompanied by Jimmy Durante's recording of "As Time Goes By," Nora Ephron's *Sleepless in Seattle* leans heavily on familiar ballads to intensify the romantic mood of individual sequences and the film as a whole.

perfect rhythmic counterpart to the galloping hoofbeats and served as a stimulus to the visual imagination, but also gave the program a seriousness of tone that it would not have possessed otherwise. In similar manner, director Stanley Kubrick employed such diverse types of music as *Thus Spake Zarathustra*, *The Blue Danube Waltz*, and "When Johnny Comes Marching Home" to very effective ends in *2001* and *Dr. Strangelove*.

A perfect match of song with dramatic situation—such as Steven Spielberg's choice of "Smoke Gets in Your Eyes" for the romantic dance in the firefighters' Quonset hut in *Always* (selected in part because composer Irving Berlin had denied the director's request to use his first choice, the popular song "Always")—can do much to create a magic moment on film. Many directors, however, prefer to use music specially created and designed for the film—music composed either after the film and its accompanying sound-effects track are completed or while the film is being made—so that composer and director can work together in the same creative atmosphere. Many films, of course, use a combination of familiar and original music.

Film music especially composed for a film can be divided into two types.

1. **Mickey Mousing.** So named because it grew out of animation techniques, **Mickey Mousing** is the exact, calculated dovetailing of music and action. The rhythm of the music precisely matches the natural rhythms of the objects moving on the screen. This synchronization requires a meticulous analysis of the filmed sequence by the composer. Although some sense of emotional tone, mood, or atmosphere can be included in Mickey Mouse scoring, the primary

emphasis is on the kinetic (the sense of movement and action) and rhythmic elements of the sequences in which the music is used. Composers of "serious" modern films tend to avoid this technique, assuming that it lacks subtlety or has been overused in the past.

2. **Generalized Score.** A **generalized score** (also known as an *implicit score*) makes no attempt to precisely match music and movement; instead the emphasis is on capturing the overall emotional atmosphere or mood of a sequence or of the film as a whole. Often, this is achieved through recurring rhythmic and emotive variations of a few main motifs or themes. Although basic rhythms in such scores are varied to suggest the rhythmic structure of individual action sequences, their primary function is to convey an emotion that parallels the story.

SPECIAL FUNCTIONS OF THE MUSICAL SCORE

In the modern film, music is used to perform many varied and complex functions, some of which are rather specialized. Although it is impossible to list or describe all these functions, some of the most basic ones are worthy of our attention.

Heightening the Dramatic Effect of Dialogue

Music is often employed as a kind of emotional punctuation for the dialogue, expressing the feeling underlying what is said. Generally, the musical accompaniment of dialogue must be extremely subtle and unobtrusive, stealing in and out so quietly that we respond to its effects without conscious awareness of its presence. In Neil Jordan's fascinating *The Butcher Boy*, the opposite is too often true. The film, a darkly comic domestic horror story, utilizes Irish accents so thick that subtitles sometimes seem warranted. Elliott Rosenthal's score for it, though aptly indigenous, is frequently performed so loudly that the listener can barely hear the dialogue, much less understand it easily.

The same objection arises, for some first viewers, to Hans Zimmer's score for Christopher Nolan's *Inception*. Initially the music manifests itself as too loud for the dialogue and (worse) overapplied. According to the composer (and a few sharp-eared early interpreters of the film), though, the music contains secrets that can help careful listeners to differentiate among multiple spatial and temporal levels in the work's challenging dream narratives. Conceivably, too, Zimmer may have discovered a clever way to interconnect dialogue and plot rhythms with the beat of his music, using a brief percussive "quotation" from a piece of the Edith Piaf song "Non, Je Ne Regrette Rien."

Telling an Inner Story

Music often moves beyond a merely subordinate or complementary role to assume a primary storytelling function, enabling the director to express things that cannot be expressed through verbal or pictorial means (Figure 9.2). This is especially true when a character's state of mind undergoes extreme and rapid changes that neither words nor action can adequately express.

FIGURE 9.2 Music to Tell an Inner Story   The superb documentary *My Architect* allows an illegitimate son, filmmaker Nathaniel Kahn, a professional space in which to discover and re-create his long-dead father, internationally celebrated architect Louis I. Kahn. While making all the necessary, obvious, and deliberate investigations expected of any good historian, Nathaniel Kahn at one point seems to have taken a little personal break from his labors with some recreational rollerblading. However, he filmed the scene, and then he shrewdly used it in his movie: Here, around the concourse "canal" at the artist-father's majestic Salk Institute campus overlooking the Pacific, the artist-son literally skates upon the face of one of his dad's greatest works. As he moves, with spontaneous, restorative energy, the soundtrack plays Neil Young's "Long May You Run."

A good example of the use of music to tell an inner story occurs in Stanley Kramer's *On the Beach*. An American submarine captain (Gregory Peck) takes an Australian woman (Ava Gardner) to a mountain resort for a final fling at trout fishing before the lethal radioactive clouds reach Australia. The American, whose family was killed in the nuclear war, has failed to adapt to the reality of the situation and continues to think and talk of his family as though they were alive, making it impossible for him to accept the love of the Australian. The two are in their room in the lodge, listening to the dissonant, off-key voices of the drunken fishermen downstairs singing "Waltzing Matilda." In an underplayed dramatic scene, Peck finally realizes the futility of his ties with the past and accepts Gardner's love. As they embrace, the loud and drunken voices become soft, sober, and melodious and blend into perfect harmony, reflecting not any actual change in the voices downstairs but the inner story of the change in Peck's state of mind. The use of massed voices of choirs to express an inner mystical or spiritual transformation (as in Rachel Portman's score for *Beloved*, Howard Shore's music for *The Lord of the Rings: The Two Towers*, or John Williams's sound-effects heightening in *War of the Worlds* [2005]) is a more obvious example of the same function.

Providing a Sense of Time and Place

Certain pieces of music or even musical styles are associated with specific time periods and locations, and composers can utilize such music to provide the emotional atmosphere that a given setting normally connotes. A sense of scenic spaciousness is conveyed by standard western songs such as "The Call of the Faraway Hills" from *Shane*. Completely different qualities, such as the hustle and bustle of people having a good time and a merry, communal feeling, are conveyed by "town" or "saloon" music. Therefore, when the locale in a western changes from the range to the town or saloon, the visual transition is often preceded slightly by a switch to standard saloon music (player piano accompanied by shouting, laughter, general crowd noises, and an occasional gunshot or two). The music not only tells us that a change of scene is coming but also prepares us mentally for the visual scene before it appears, thereby serving a transitional function.

Music associated with different countries or even different ethnic groups can be used in a similar way. Certain instruments are associated with definite settings or groups of people: the zither, the mandolin, the banjo, the Spanish guitar, and the Hawaiian guitar all have fairly concrete geographical connotations, and these connotations can be varied or even changed completely by the style in which the instruments are played.

The time period of the film is also made realistic through appropriate music and instrumentation, as illustrated by the use of the quaint, old sound of a harpsichord for a period piece and otherworldly or futuristic electronic music for a science fiction film.

When the time frame of a story is within most viewers' memories, recent American films have loaded the soundtrack with popular recordings from the era, thus evoking a strong "remembered flavor" of the time. Such music underscores the past-tense quality of the story for the viewer and, by triggering built-in associations, intensifies and personalizes the viewer's involvement with the story itself.

Nostalgic music is used effectively in such films as *Good Night, and Good Luck, Pleasantville, The Last Days of Disco, Taking Woodstock, Forrest Gump, The Big Chill, Coming Home, The Last Picture Show,* and *American Graffiti,* which is literally built around such music. In many cases this music is heard coming from some on-screen source such as a radio or record player, but it usually is used as part of the off-screen musical score as well (Figure 9.3). Such film scores are called "compilation" works.

Foreshadowing Events or Building Dramatic Tension

When a surprising change of mood or an unexpected action is about to occur on the screen, we are almost always prepared for that change by the musical score. By preparing us emotionally for a shocking turn of events, the score does not soften the effect of the shock but actually intensifies it by signaling its approach. In its own way, the music says, "Watch carefully now. Something shocking or unexpected is going to happen," and we respond to the musical signal by becoming more attentive. Even the fact that we know what is going to happen does not relieve the tension thus created, for suspense is as much a matter of when as of what. Music used in this way does not coincide exactly with what is happening on the screen but precedes it, introducing a feeling of tension while the images on the screen retain their calm.

Foreshadowing or tension-building music deliberately plays on our nerves in a variety of ways: by gradually increasing in volume or pitch, switching from a major to

FIGURE 9.3 **A Serious *Good Night* of Nostalgia** Director George Clooney's politics-and-broadcasting drama *Good Night, and Good Luck* spins a tale of hubris and greed in black and white. But the movie's somber tone is balanced somewhat by a surprising and very pleasurable use of music. While the powerful adversaries Senator Joe McCarthy and TV newsman Edward R. Murrow are grimly vying, metaphorically, for center stage, the audience is invited periodically, quite literally, into a CBS sound studio where Dianne Reeves is singing pop and jazz classics of the 1950s period.

a minor key, or introducing percussion instruments and dissonance. The introduction of dissonance into a musical score that has been harmonious to that point automatically creates a sense of nervousness and anxiety. Dissonance in such a situation expresses disorder, chaos, and a breakdown of the normal patterned order of harmony, causing us to become nervous and insecure, exactly the state of mind desired for effective foreshadowing or the building of dramatic tension. For example, composer Bernard Herrmann begins the famous breakfast montage from *Citizen Kane*, showing the increasing alienation between Emily and Charles Foster Kane over a period of years, with a gentle lilting waltz and ends with a dissonant and harsh variation of the same waltz theme. A radical sweet-melody-to-dissonant-noise progression in the musical score is also used frequently with significant effect in the recent revenge drama *Harry Brown*, which stars Michael Caine as an elderly vigilante.

Adding Levels of Meaning to the Visual Image

Sometimes music makes us see the visual scene in a fresh, unusual way by combining with the image to create additional levels of meaning. Take, for example, the opening scene in *Dr. Strangelove*, which shows a B-52 bomber refueling in flight. Extremely delicate maneuvering is required to place the refueling boom correctly, trailing like a giant winged hose from the tail of the tanker plane into the fuel-tank opening in the nose of the giant B-52 bomber, which is flying slightly behind and below the tanker. The music accompanying this sequence is the familiar love song

FIGURE 9.4 **Exquisite Peter-and-the-Wolfing** In Rob Marshall's film version of the popular novel *Memoirs of a Geisha*, composer John Williams created an elegant correspondence between key characters and the musical instruments and themes that symbolize them on screen. Thus, a cello melody played by Yo-Yo Ma represents the central female character (Ziyi Zhang), and a different one performed on violin by Itzhak Perlman identifies the main male figure (Ken Watanabe).

"Try a Little Tenderness," played on romantic violins. If we are alert enough to recognize the song and think of its title, the music not only seems very appropriate to the delicate maneuvering required for the refueling operation but could also lead us to see the whole thing as a gentle love scene, a tender sexual coupling of two giant birds. Because this is the opening sequence of the film, the music also helps to establish the satiric tone that runs throughout the film as a whole.

Highly ironic levels of meaning can be achieved by using music that suggests a mood exactly opposite to the mood normally suggested by what is occurring on the screen. This technique is illustrated at the conclusion of *Dr. Strangelove*, in which the sticky-sweet voice of Vera Lynn singing the World War II–era standard "We'll Meet Again Some Sunny Day" accompanies the image of a nuclear holocaust as it destroys the world.

Characterization Through Music

Music can play a role in characterization. Mickey Mouse scoring may be used to emphasize a peculiar or rhythmic pattern set up by a certain character's physical movement. The score for *Of Human Bondage* (1934), for example, utilizes a "disabled" theme, which rhythmically parallels the main character's limp, thus reinforcing that aspect of his character. Some actors and actresses, such as John Wayne, Marilyn Monroe, and Al Pacino, have distinctive walks that exhibit definite rhythmic patterns and can therefore be reinforced musically.

Instrumentation can also be used to aid in characterization in an effect that might be called **Peter-and-the-Wolfing,** scoring in which certain musical instruments and types of music represent and signal the presence of certain characters (Figure 9.4). Many films of the 1930s and 1940s used this technique, causing the audience to associate the villain with sinister-sounding music in a minor key, the heroine with soft, ethereal violins, and the hero with strong, "honest" music. Although such heavy-handed treatment is not common today, **leitmotifs** (the repetition of a single musical theme or phrase to announce the reappearance of a certain character) were staples of silent-film scores and are still employed to some extent.

Sometimes a character is complex enough to require multiple themes, as composer Jerry Goldsmith discovered while scoring *Patton:*

> [I]t was a challenge to keep the audience aware of the complexity of Patton's personality. We were dealing with three different facets of Patton's imagination. He was a warrior, a man who believed in reincarnation, and a man with stern religious beliefs. . . . At the beginning of the picture I set up the reincarnation theme with the trumpet fanfare, the very first notes of music you hear. . . . The second and most obvious piece of music was the military march, and when he was commanding, this was the predominant theme—the warrior theme. The third was a chorale, which was used in counterpoint to underline his religious character, his discipline, and his determination. When he was the whole man, commanding his troops in victory, the idea was to combine all these musical elements, because he was all of these facets together.[3]

In *Citizen Kane*, composer Bernard Herrmann used two separate leitmotifs for Charles Foster Kane. One, "a vigorous piece of ragtime, sometimes transformed into a hornpipe polka," was used to symbolize the mature Kane's power. The other, "a featherlight and harmonic" theme, symbolized the simpler days of Kane's youth and the more positive aspects of his personality.[4]

A good composer may also use the musical score to add qualities to an actor or actress that that person does not normally have. In the filming of *Cyrano de Bergerac*, for example, Dimitri Tiomkin felt that Mala Powers did not really look French enough for the part of Roxanne. Therefore he Frenchified her by using French-style thematic music whenever she appeared on the screen, thus building up associations in the viewer's mind to achieve the desired effect.

Director Jonathan Demme (*The Silence of the Lambs, Philadelphia*) has said that, in choosing music for his films, he tries "to talk about what kind of music the characters might be hearing in their daily life. It's just more true, more subtle, and more fun, too." Like most directors, he prefers to make the choice of a film's composer as early as possible in the process and observes that "editors love to find a piece of music that works with a scene before the scene is cut."[5] For the scoring of *The Truman Show*, Peter Weir (*The Year of Living Dangerously, Witness*) ultimately selected German-Australian composer Burkhard Dallwitz, but Weir also decided even earlier, through experimenting with a "temp" track, that certain existing pieces by Philip Glass would be included. Weir writes,

> When making a film, I play music constantly during "dailies"—the nightly screenings of the previous day's shooting. I test all kinds of music against the image, searching for the elusive "sound" of the picture.
>
> In the case of *The Truman Show*, since it is the story of a live television program, I was also determining the music that the show's creator, Christof [Ed Harris], would have chosen.
>
> The tracks that seemed to be drawing the most out of the images for me (and presumably Christof) were those of Philip Glass. . . . Complementing these tracks is a score by Burkhard Dallwitz . . . and from the moment he played back his first cue, I knew Christof would have been as delighted with the result as I was.[6]

FIGURE 9.5 **Composing Character** Among the actors who not only performed but wrote songs in character for *Nashville* was Ronee Blakley.

Already-published music by Philip Glass was used so extensively by director Stephen Daldry as a temp score when he was editing his film *The Hours* that he finally just decided to convince Glass himself to compose the movie's music.

One of the great mavericks of modern cinema, Robert Altman (*M*A*S*H*, *Vincent & Theo*, *The Player*, *Short Cuts*), is celebrated for his willingness to work improvisationally with actors. In *Nashville*, his 1975 epic vision of America, this director carried over his playfulness into the creation of the film's musical score. Altman asked several of the actors playing the film's twenty-four central figures (including Karen Black, Ronee Blakley, and Keith Carradine, who won an Oscar for his song "I'm Easy") to compose, *in character*, songs for performance during the narrative's unfolding (Figure 9.5). Although this film-music experiment had an origin very different from that of the 1972 musical film *Cabaret* and the 2002 musical *Chicago*, the three works are similar in their strategy: In each case, all songs are somehow restricted to being performed on a "stage." By the early 1970s, the tradition of the great American movie musicals—in which fictional characters suddenly burst into song in reel life—had died. By most accounts, the tradition's apex had been reached, ironically, in *Singin' in the Rain*, the 1952 comic requiem for the silent-film era.

Triggering Conditioned Responses

The composer takes advantage of the fact that viewers have been conditioned to associate some musical stereotypes or musical codes with particular situations. Such codes can be used with great economy and effectiveness. In old Western movies, the sudden introduction of a steady tom-tom beat accompanied by a high, wailing, wind instrument ranging through a simple four- or five-tone scale effectively signals the presence of Indians even before they appear. The "cavalry to the rescue" bugle call is equally familiar. Such musical codes cannot be treated in a highly creative way, for to do so would cause them to lose some of their effectiveness as code devices. Composers do, however, try to make them seem as fresh and original as possible.

Even stereotyped musical codes can create unusual reactions when they are used ironically. In *Little Big Man*, for example, a lively fife and drum "good guys

FIGURE 9.6 **Traveling Music** In *Breaking Away*, an excerpt from *The Barber of Seville*, a stirring opera by the Italian composer Rossini, provides traveling music for Dave (Dennis Christopher) as he prepares for the big race, and it reinforces the character's obsession with things Italian as well as underscoring the heroic effort involved in his training.

victorious" score accompanies scenes of General Custer's troops as they brutally massacre an Indian tribe. The ironic effect catches us in a tug-of-war between the music and the image. So compelling is the rhythm of the heroic music that we can scarcely resist tapping our toes and swelling with heroic pride while our visual sensibilities are appalled by the unheroic action taking place on the screen.

Traveling Music

Film music is at its best when used to characterize rapid movement. Such music, sometimes called **traveling music,** is often employed almost as a formula or a shorthand code to give the impression of various means of transportation (Figure 9.6). The formulas are varied to fit the unique quality of the movement being portrayed. Thus, stagecoach music is different from horse-and-buggy music, and both differ essentially from lone-rider music. The old steam engine requires a different type of railroad music than the diesel locomotive. On rare occasions, traveling music performs a wide variety of functions, as is illustrated by the use of Flatt and Scruggs's "Foggy Mountain Breakdown" to accompany the famous chase scenes in *Bonnie and Clyde.* The strong, almost frantic sounds of the fast-fingered five-string banjo create a desperate yet happy rhythm that captures precisely the derring-do and spirit of the Barrow gang, the slapstick comedy, desperation, and blind excitement of the chases themselves, and the nostalgic, good-old-days flavor of the film as a whole.

Providing Important Transitions

Music functions in an important way by providing transitions or bridges between scenes—marking the passage of time, signaling a change of locale, foreshadowing a shift in mood or pace, or transporting us backward in time into a flashback. *Citizen Kane* director Orson Welles and composer Bernard Herrmann both had experience in radio, where musical bridges were virtually mandatory. In *Citizen Welles,* Welles's biographer Frank Brady describes the effect of this experience on the use of music in *Citizen Kane:*

> The most frequent use of music in radio is to provide the transition from scene to scene or situation to situation. Even a single note becomes important in telling the ear that the scene is shifting. In film, the eye usually supplies the transition as the scene is cut or dissolves into the next. Welles and Herrmann both believed that an opportunity

to include transitional music, whether it be symbolic or illustrative, to weave parts of the film together or to set it in context, should not be overlooked.

... [A]s Thompson reads Thatcher's diary and his eye travels over the parchment with old-fashioned handwriting, "I first encountered Mr. Kane in 1871 . . . ," Welles asked Herrmann for a fully melodic transition that would evoke all at once the frivolity and innocence of childhood in the snowbound winter of the Victorian era, and Herrmann responded with a piece of lyrical music that used delicate flutes leading to a blizzard of strings and harps that perfectly captured the guiltlessness and simplicity of a former age. The "snow picture" sequence as it grew to be called, became one of the most charmingly innovative transitions to a flashback ever seen or heard on film.[7]

Setting an Initial Tone

The music that accompanies the main titles of a film usually serves at least two functions. First, it often articulates rhythmically the title information itself, making it somehow more interesting than it is. If the music consciously captures our attention anywhere in the film, it is during the showing of the titles and credits. Second, music is especially important here, for at this initial stage it usually establishes the general mood or tone of the film. At the opening of *Bonnie and Clyde*, we start to hear a soft, sweet, lyrical Rudy Vallee pop song of the early 1930s, "Deep Night." As the volume rises from a whisper, while still photographs of both real and cinematic characters are projected, the song's melancholy at once soothes us and subtly foreshadows the uncommon violence of the film that follows. This musical element seems to echo a visual one: The tranquil white titles slowly bleed to dark red in a foreshadowing of the movie's later, surprising carnage.

Title music may even introduce story elements through the use of lyrics, as was done in *High Noon* and *Cat Ballou*. Because the opening or establishing scene is generally under way before the credits are completed, it can also dramatically or rhythmically match the visual image behind the credits.

Musical Sounds as Part of the Score

Certain sound effects or noises from nature can be used in subtle ways for their own sake, to create atmosphere in the same way that music does. Crashing waves, rippling streams, bird calls, and moaning winds all possess clear musical qualities, as do many manmade sounds, such as foghorns, auto horns, industrial noises of various kinds, steam whistles, clanging doors, chains, squealing auto brakes, and engine noises. Such sounds can be built up and artistically mixed into an exciting rhythmical sequence that, because of its naturalness, may be even more effective than music in conveying a mood.

Music as Interior Monologue

In the modern film, songs with lyrics that have no clear or direct relationship to the scenes they accompany are increasingly used as part of the soundtrack. In many cases, such songs are used to reveal the private moods, emotions, or thoughts of a central character. This was the case with the lyrics of "The Sounds of Silence" in *The Graduate* and "Everybody's Talkin' at Me" in *Midnight Cowboy*. Such lyrics function on a more or less independent level as a highly subjective and poetic means of

FIGURE 9.7 **Choreographed Action Music** In *Shrek*, the title character (shown with his comic-irritant buddy, the talking Donkey) conspires to keep his domain private. At one point in the animated film, Shrek rhythmically battles a menacing army to the tune of "Bad Reputation."

communication, capable of expanding the meaning and emotional content of the scenes they accompany.

Music as a Base for Choreographed Action

Usually the director composes, photographs, and edits the images first and adds music later, after the visual elements are already assembled. In some films, however, music is used to provide a clear rhythmic framework for the action, which essentially becomes a highly stylized dance performed to the music (Figure 9.7).

Director John Badham remembers his use of the technique in *Saturday Night Fever*:

> [I]n the opening we took a tape recorder out with us in the street—we already had a demo made by the Bee Gees of "Stayin' Alive," which was their initial version. But they had promised us they'd always stick to the same tempo in any future versions they did. . . . Of course, Travolta's feet are going right on the beat. And that makes a big difference for unifying and getting a synergistic action between the sound and the music.[8]

A similar technique is used when the music originates from some on-screen source, such as a radio or a CD player, and the actor coordinates the rhythms of his

FIGURE 9.8 Music First—and Later One scene in *O Brother, Where Art Thou?* actually "creates" the music that accompanies some of the later action in the film. Here, three prison escapees (Tim Blake Nelson, George Clooney, and John Turturro) become the Soggy Bottom Boys when they record "A Man of Constant Sorrow" in a makeshift country studio.

movements to it. In *Hopscotch*, Walter Matthau, playing a former CIA agent writing his memoirs, comically structures his typing and related tasks to match the rhythms of a Mozart symphony on the record player.

In *Punchline*, Sally Field and her two daughters redefine the phrase "fast food" as they frantically clean house and throw together a formal dinner for husband John Goodman and two Catholic priests he is bringing home on short notice. The frantic action is choreographed to the accompaniment of "The Sabre Dance" on the stereo. With the meal finally ready, the house cleaned, the table set, and the guests seated, they sit down to begin a quiet dinner soothed by *Pachelbel's Canon* until one of the daughters breaks the mood by telling a shockingly filthy joke.

An extreme example of the technique of "music first" is heard in *O Brother, Where Art Thou?* (Figure 9.8). This Coen Brothers film uses "roots" music throughout to help provide a narrative framework, and these sounds combine with Roger Deakins's arresting images to create an indelible movie experience. Some parts of the film, such as the "O Death" segment, are intricately choreographed to the music. In other sections, the dynamic rhythms of the action and the editing are somewhat more subtly designed to complement or contrast with the words and music of melodic songs. Such "traditional" tunes as "You Are My Sunshine," "I'll Fly Away," and "Keep on the Sunny Side" appear from a soundtrack album that was already available and immensely popular well before the film itself was released.

Action that has no essential rhythmic qualities can be edited to music to create an effect very similar to that of choreographed action. The Little League baseball action in *The Bad News Bears* was apparently edited to match the heroic rhythms of

FIGURE 9.9 "Anachronistic" Film Music Strong emotions and multiple levels of meaning are supplemented in *A Knight's Tale*, very loosely based on a Chaucer fable from the Middle Ages, through the use of modern rock music. In scenes such as this one (featuring Paul Bettany and Heath Ledger), Queen's "We Will Rock You" and David Bowie's "Golden Years" add both tension and ballast to the narrative.

orchestral music from the opera *Carmen*, creating the impression of a comic/heroic dance.

Covering Possible Weaknesses in the Film

A nonstorytelling function of the musical score is to disguise or cover up weaknesses in acting and dialogue. When such defects are evident, the director or composer can use heavy musical backing to make weak acting or banal dialogue appear more dramatically significant than it otherwise would. Television soap operas traditionally used organ music for this purpose with great frequency (and little sense of shame). Modern action films are frequently criticized for their disregard of narrative credibility, but, as producer Jerry Bruckheimer (*Con Air*, *Armageddon*) observes, a film can divert the audience's attention from such weaknesses. "Sound," he says, "carries you through moments when the action doesn't. Take away the sound and it's dead."[9] Director Martin Scorsese, in characterizing the score that Elmer Bernstein wrote for *The Age of Innocence*, sees greater complexity in the process generally:

> Film music's kind of a slippery thing. It can take hold of your ear when the rest of the movie eludes your imagination, or just doesn't have the strength to challenge it. It can overwhelm you in a great wash of sound, so dramatic inadequacies don't seem quite so treacherous. It can add punch where the story or the filmmaking craft have abandoned the drama. Or—and this is best—it can give the film another dimension, a separate signature.[10]

And Bernstein's delicate score assisted director Todd Haynes in reaching that other dimension in *Far From Heaven*.

The examples just described represent only the most common and obvious uses of music in the modern film. The point to keep in mind is that we must be aware of the various emotions and levels of meaning that music communicates (Figure 9.9).

SYNTHESIZER SCORING

One trend in film scoring involves the use of electronic synthesizers for instrumentation. A synthesizer is essentially a musical computer played on a piano-like keyboard and equipped with various knobs and buttons that permit all sorts of variation in pitch, tone, and decay. It can imitate the sounds of a large variety of other instruments while still retaining its own distinct quality. Because of its tremendous flexibility, it is the fastest, most efficient way to score a film. A two-person team—one playing the keyboard, the other controlling the sound qualities—can create a full sound comparable to that provided by a complete orchestra. Currently, versions of such sophisticated musical technology are available to cash-strapped independent filmmakers even through apps downloaded very inexpensively to Apple iPads.

Synthesizers have played a part in film scores for some time, at least since *A Clockwork Orange* in 1971, but they have become much more prevalent since *Midnight Express* (1978), which has a complete "synth" score by Giorgio Moroder. Films with synthesizer scores include *Sorcerer, Thief, American Gigolo, Foxes, Blade Runner, Cat People,* and *Beverly Hills Cop.* The great versatility of synth scoring was most evident in *Chariots of Fire* (1981), a period piece that seemed an unlikely choice for an electronic score. *Chariots* composer Vangelis's challenge was to compose a "score which was contemporary, but still compatible with the time of the film." He met the challenge successfully by mixing synthesizer and a grand piano.[11]

Sometimes it is difficult to know whether to classify electronic scores as music or sound effects. In *Cat People* (1982), for example, the synthesizer often functions as an almost subliminal animal presence behind the image, creating the effect of "listening in on the vital processes of other organisms—of other places, other worlds."[12] Horror movies have been less subtle in their overuse of the tension-building, nervous-pulse sounds, which are repeated over and over without musical development.

Electronic scores are still relatively rare in major films because most top composers still prefer to use an orchestra. Even in the case of *The X-Files*, a 1998 film version of the popular television program, the composer, Mark Snow, chose to "enlarge" with orchestral adaptations his celebrated synthesizer themes from the series. Some writers of film music (James Newton Howard in *King Kong* [2005], for example) utilize "synthesized mock-ups" to share ideas with directors and prepare for later full orchestrations.

BALANCING THE SCORE

Generally speaking, economy is a great virtue in film music, both in duration and in instrumentation. The musical score should do no more than is necessary to perform its proper function clearly and simply. However, because of some irresistible temptations to dress up scenes with music whether they need it or not, the normal dramatic film usually ends up with too much music rather than not enough. The Hollywood tendency seems to be toward large orchestras, even though smaller combinations can be more interesting and colorful or even more powerful in their effect on the film as a whole. Typically, European films tend to use less music than do American works—or, in some cases, none at all (Figure 9.10).

FIGURE 9.10 **Movies With No Music Score**   Many cinephiles have long complained about the superabundant and intrusive musical cues in films made by American studios (case in point: check out the myriad, forceful grumblings of reviewers about James Horner's score for the 2006 version of *All the King's Men*). In Europe, however, the expectations of both filmmakers and audiences seem, generally, to be very different. There, less music is considered more appropriate. And in some films, such as Michael Haneke's *Caché* (starring Daniel Auteuil and Juliette Binoche, above), provide no music at all; dialogue, ambient sounds, and silence alone must even carry the weight of building and sustaining suspense.

The proper amount of music depends on the nature of the picture itself. Some films require a lot of music. Others are so realistic that music would interfere with the desired effect. In many cases, the most dramatically effective musical score is that which is used most sparingly. For *All the President's Men*, in 1976, composer David Shire had to be convinced by the director, Alan J. Pakula, that his film needed *any* music written for it. As Shire puts it, "This was a case where a director had a better grasp of what music could do for a film than a composer. That doesn't happen very often." Two years earlier, near the beginning of his career, Shire had shown a similar disinclination for overwriting when he composed the haunting solo piano score for Francis Ford Coppola's *The Conversation*. About that experience, Shire says: "The most economical score is often the best one. . . . But it always depends on the picture. . . . *The Conversation* required very little. In that film, . . . I used a synthesizer to modulate the texture of the piano cues to give a weird, unsettling effect to underscore the [protagonist's] dilemma."[13]

Oscar-winning composer Randy Newman, who wrote the scores for *Ragtime*, *The Natural*, *Meet the Fockers*, and all of the *Toy Story* films, is critical of Woody Allen's *Manhattan* score, which he feels is too big for the film. Although he does not object to the full-orchestra treatment during panoramic scenes of the Manhattan skyline, Newman claims that the music often overwhelms the characters and the action with "great genius music by Gershwin and Wagner—and little Woody Allen and other little guys talking on the phone at the same time. It dwarfed them."[14]

The director Sidney Lumet (*Twelve Angry Men, The Pawnbroker, Murder on the Orient Express, Dog Day Afternoon, Network, Find Me Guilty, Before the Devil Knows You're Dead*) has observed, "When I haven't been able to find a musical concept that adds to the movie, I haven't used a score. Studios hate the idea of a picture without music. It scares them." Besides, he notes, "talking about music is like talking about colors: the same color can mean different things to different people."[15] Usually, though, an attempt at creating film music is definitely worth the resulting colorful dialogue.

Finally, in *Knowing the Score: Film Composers Talk About the Art, Craft, Blood, Sweat, and Tears of Writing for Cinema,* David Morgan has observed:

> Cinema has offered some of the most vibrant and sophisticated music available to mass audiences, yet film music remains an underappreciated art form. . . . Good film music can rise above its material and live on outside of the film, long after the drama for which it was written has been forgotten. And it is a testament to . . . composers . . . that Hollywood has given them opportunities to write their music and have it performed in a wide variety of styles and genres that would be almost impossible to match on stage or in the concert halls.[16]

ANALYZING THE MUSICAL SCORE

On General Functions of the Musical Score

1. Where in the film is music used to exactly match the natural rhythms of the moving objects on the screen? At what points in the film does the music simply try to capture the overall emotional mood of a scene?
2. Where does the film employ rhythmic and emotive variations on a single musical theme or motif?
3. Does the musical score remain inconspicuous in the background, or does it occasionally break through to assert itself?
4. If the music does demand our conscious attention, does it still perform a subordinate function in the film as a whole? How?
5. Where in the film is the main purpose of the music to match structural or visual rhythms? Where is the music used to create more generalized emotional patterns?
6. How would the total effect of the film differ if the musical score were removed from the soundtrack?

On Special Functions of the Musical Score

1. Which of the following functions of film music are used in the film, and where are they used?
   a. to heighten the dramatic effect of dialogue
   b. to tell an inner story by expressing a state of mind
   c. to provide a sense of time or place
   d. to foreshadow events or build dramatic tension
   e. to add levels of meaning to the image
   f. to aid characterization

g. to trigger conditioned responses

h. to characterize rapid movement (traveling music)

i. to provide important transitions

j. to cover weaknesses and defects

2. Does the music accompanying the titles serve basically to underscore the rhythmic qualities of the title information or to establish the general mood of the film? If lyrics are sung at this point, how do these lyrics relate to the film as a whole?

3. Where are sound effects or natural noises employed for a kind of rhythmic or musical effect?

4. If lyrics sung within the film provide a kind of interior monologue, what feeling or attitude do they convey?

5. If music is used as a base for choreographed action, how appropriate is the piece selected? How appropriate are its rhythms to the mood and the visual content? How effectively is the choreographed sequence integrated into the film as a whole?

6. Does the score use a full orchestra throughout, a small number of well-chosen instruments, or a synthesizer? How well suited is the instrumentation to the film as a whole? If it is not well chosen, what kind of instrumentation should have been used? How would a different choice of instrumentation change the quality of the film, and why would it be an improvement?

7. Does the amount of music used fit the requirements of the film, or is the musical score overdone or used too economically?

8. How effectively does the score perform its various functions?

WATCHING FOR THE MUSICAL SCORE

1. **Music 1.** Watch the indicated sequence from *The World According to Garp* [1:15:12 to 1:18:33], paying special attention to the music. What important story elements does the music in this segment convey? What roles do lyrics, vocal styles, and instrumentation play in this sequence?

2. **Music 2.** With the TV sound off, watch the beginning of *The Shining* (1980) through the opening credits with the following musical selections playing on your CD or MP3 player:
   a. "On the Road Again" by Willie Nelson or any instrumental version of "The Orange Blossom Special"
   b. "Greensleeves" by Mantovani, "Scarborough Fair" by Simon and Garfunkel, or any familiar Strauss waltz
   How does the change in music change the way you respond emotionally and visually to this brief sequence? Now turn the sound up on the TV and watch the sequence again—listening this time to the existing music that director Stanley Kubrick chose to use there. What is different about the way you see and experience the sequence now? Describe your responses to each viewing in as much detail as possible.

3. **Music 3.** Watch the "Birth of Humanoid Intelligence" sequence from *2001: A Space Odyssey* [0:08:48 to 0:13:58]. Then turn the TV sound off and replay

the sequence with six or seven different and greatly varied musical selections from your own CD or MP3 collection. Which of your musical scores were most effective and why? How do your most effective scores change the meaning or significance of the original music selected by Stanley Kubrick?

4. **Music 4.** Watch *Sleepless in Seattle* in its entirety, paying special attention to scenes accompanied by music. What thematic strains are repeated frequently during the film? What is their function? How do the popular recorded songs that are used reinforce mood and story elements?

MINI-MOVIE EXERCISE

Although director Jean-Jacques Beineix's elegant, delightful 1982 film *Diva* was shot in French, no subtitles are really needed to understand its almost "self-contained" opening sequence. In fact, its action and, especially, its music make it

function as a kind of "silent" movie, foreshadowing the film's romance, adventure, humor, and suspense. (This 6½-minute passage features only classical—or "lyric," as one character insists—music, but the film later uses punk rock effectively, also.)

Watch *Diva* closely from its beginning (including the credits) through the standing ovation for the gorgeous-looking and -sounding opera singer played by Wilhelmenia Wiggins Fernandez. Be well aware of the vivid impact that the visual elements of this scene have on your expectations: the young man with his motorbike and hidden tape recorder; the "distressed" walls and stage of the Paris Opera House; the beautiful, still, dignified diva; the varied faces of the other characters briefly glimpsed. But, for this exercise, try harder to identify the precise uses of the soundtrack—its musical score and its foil, silence—in this mini-movie that works on multiple levels of both style and substance.

DVD FILMMAKING EXTRAS

E.T. The Extra-Terrestrial (Two-Disc Limited Collector's Edition):
   "The Music of John Williams" offers an introduction to this popular composer for films, using "interviews and footage of the long-standing relationship between John Williams and Steven Spielberg."

War of the Worlds (2005) (Two-Disc Limited Edition):
   In a 12-minute section of disc two called "Scoring 'War of the Worlds,'" documentation of the ongoing symbiotic Williams-Spielberg collaboration continues. Here, the two artists speak about how this film marks the first

time the composer was required to begin work when the director had only finished a few reels of his shooting. Spielberg says that, during the making of his movies, he constantly "hovers between" his editor, Michael Kahn, and his composer, John Williams, giving and taking creative suggestions freely. Williams himself provides many details of his work process. Sound design technicians spent months collecting strange sounds that Williams later joined with synthesizer music to "cover" Morgan Freeman's opening and closing narration.

Memoirs of a Geisha (Two-Disc Wide-Screen Special Edition):
In "The Music of 'Memoirs,'" on this set's second DVD, John Williams announces he was so eager to compose the music for the film version of Arthur Golden's novel that, for the first time ever, he actively sought a movie job. Of course, because Spielberg produced the film, his request was hardly ignored. Director Rob Marshall clearly jumped at the chance to work with Williams, too—along with the virtuoso soloists the composer brought to the project, Yo-Yo Ma on cello and Itzhak Perlman on violin.

The Godfather DVD Collection (five discs):
Included among the wealth of materials here are "Behind the Scenes" featurettes about the films' two composers: Nino Rota, Fellini's frequent collaborator, whom we meet via an audio discussion recorded in Rome by Francis Ford Coppola, shares part of an early piano score for the original film. Carmine Coppola, who scored the third film alone, talks about his professional relationship with the director (his son).

A Knight's Tale (Special Edition):
On one of the DVD's featurettes, "The Rock Music Scene in 1370," director/producer/writer Brian Helgeland comments on his reasons for choosing to use music by the groups Queen, War, and Bachman-Turner Overdrive, in addition to the work of composer Carter Burwell.

In the Mood for Love (The Criterion Collection):
In an interactive essay, writer Joanna Lee discusses the varieties of elegant and haunting music used in this film, and the text is "augmented by links to take the viewer directly to the musical cues within the movie." The DVD also contains separate printed statements by director Wong Kar-wai and composer Michael Galasso.

Planet of the Apes (2001) *(Two-Disc Special Edition)* and *Men in Black II (Wide-Screen Special Edition):*
Both of these DVDs provide extensive and fascinating interviews with Danny Elfman. The first presents the prolific composer during the recording of his "Chimp Symphony, Opus 37," and the other gives the viewer a strong sense of how Elfman has matched his music to the general strangeness in the *Men in Black* films. (A profile of Elfman also appears on the *Spider-Man* DVD.)

Psycho (Collector's Edition):
Alfred Hitchcock's 1960 horror classic is justly celebrated for the shrewdness of its editing. But any film student needs to be acutely aware of how aural, as well as visual, images make the movie work so well. An element of this DVD

allows one to view the famous shower scene montage either with or without its accompanying music by legendary composer Bernard Herrmann.

Fahrenheit 451:

After Bernard Herrmann's illustrious association with Orson Welles (*Citizen Kane*, for example) and a long, fruitful collaboration with the master of suspense (including *Vertigo*), Hitchcock fired the composer during the scoring of *Torn Curtain* in 1966. Herrmann thus reached a nadir in both his personal and professional lives. But the French director François Truffaut admired Herrmann and came to his rescue by hiring him to score a film version of Ray Bradbury's novel *Fahrenheit 451*. In a substantial feature (16½ minutes long) on this disc, Herrmann's biographer, Stephen C. Smith, expertly examines the history, basic nature, and intricacies of this romantic's career, observing how his apt passion for books was especially helpful in creating the wonderfully effective music for *Fahrenheit 451*.

Singin' in the Rain (Two-Disc Special Edition):

The special features on disc two (including a new documentary hosted by star Debbie Reynolds) are delicious treats for any viewer. Most entertaining and instructive, though, for students of the movie musical is a twelve-work collection of excerpts from films that included Arthur Freed/Nacio Herb Brown songs later chosen for reuse in this 1952 film. A spectacular original rendition of "You Are My Lucky Star" (from *Broadway Melody of 1936*) stars Eleanor Powell. Ukelele Ike (Cliff Edwards), who sings the earliest "Singin' in the Rain" (from *The Hollywood Revue of 1929*), later became the voice of Jiminy Cricket.

A Hard Day's Night (Miramax Collector's Series):

In "Listen to the Music Playing in Your Head," Sir George Martin, the Beatles' producer, talks about each of the songs used on the soundtrack, often revealing the songs' origins and discussing their relative effectiveness in relation to the film's visual elements.

Koyaanisqatsi (Life Out of Balance), Powaqqatsi (Life in Transformation), and *Naqoyqatsi (Life as War):*

Although this textbook has otherwise bypassed non-narrative films such as these three, the DVDs are well worth studying because of their focus on the marriage of visuals and music. In the first, for the 1983 work, director Godfrey Reggio and composer Philip Glass (who worked together in what they call "a hand-in-glove operation") discuss "The Essence of Life"; in the second, for the 1988 film, they talk of "The Impact of Progress." On the third disc (2002), Glass conducts a conversation with Yo-Yo Ma and participates in a panel discussion with Reggio and editor/visual designer Jon Kane.

The Usual Suspects (Special Edition):

Along with many other materials, an interview with composer John Ottman, who also edited this film, appears on the DVD. But one must look very carefully to find it, because the feature, a so-called "Easter egg," is hidden (i.e., not announced on the disc's packaging). [For more information on this instance and many similar ones, consult Marc Saltzman's *DVD Confidential: Hundreds of Hidden Easter Eggs Revealed!* (McGraw-Hill/Osborne, 2002) and its sequel.]

King Kong (2005) *(Two-Disc Special Edition):*
On disc two, "Post Production Diaries" include on-camera interviews with composer James Newton Howard and several members of the extensive music team on Peter Jackson's version of this potent American story. The discussion acutely illustrates how film scores are often composed and recorded in an "adrenaline rush" to the opening date, leaving little time for much creative contemplation or even sleep. We also learn that the recording itself was finally done mostly during two-day, provisionally scheduled shifts in three different L.A. sound studios (Todd-AO, Fox, and Warners) that were large enough to accommodate the necessary 108-piece orchestra.

FILMS FOR STUDY

Across the Universe (2007)
Amadeus (1984)
American Graffiti (1973)
Apollo 13 (1995)
Avatar (2009)
The Big Chill (1983)
Body Heat (1981)
Bonnie and Clyde (1967)
Brokeback Mountain (2005)
Burlesque (2010)
Butch Cassidy and the Sundance Kid (1969)
Cabaret (1972)
Chariots of Fire (1981)
Chicago (2002)
A Clockwork Orange (1971)
The Conversation (1974)
Crazy Heart (2009)
Dancer in the Dark (2000)
De-Lovely (2004)
Dr. Strangelove (1964)

Easy A (2010)
8 Mile (2002)
The Graduate (1967)
Hustle & Flow (2005)
The Informant! (2009)
Inception (2010)
Last Tango in Paris (1972)
Living Out Loud (1998)
Mad Hot Ballroom (2005)
A Man and a Woman (1966)
A Mighty Wind (2003)
My Architect (2003)
Nashville (1975)
Nine (2009)
O Brother, Where Art Thou? (2000)
Once (2006)
Out of Africa (1985)
The Piano (1993)
Pink Floyd: The Wall (1982)
Ray (2004)

Rent (2005)
The Saddest Music in the World (2003)
Saturday Night Fever (1977)
The School of Rock (2003)
Schultze Gets the Blues (2003)
Singin' in the Rain (1952)
Slumdog Millionaire (2008)
The Social Network (2010)
The Soloist (2009)
Star Wars (1977)
The Stunt Man (1980)
Sweet and Lowdown (1999)
Tamara Drewe (2010)
Top Hat (1935)
2001: A Space Odyssey (1968)
Up (2009)
Walk the Line (2005)

ACTING

Crazy Heart

An audience identifies with the actors of flesh and blood and heartbeat, as no reader or beholder can identify with even the most artful paragraphs in books or the most inspiring paintings. There, says the watcher, but for some small difference in time or costume or inflections or gait, go I. . . . And so, the actor becomes a catalyst; he brings to bright ignition that spark in every human being that longs for the miracle of transformation.
—EDWARD G. ROBINSON, ACTOR

THE IMPORTANCE OF ACTING

When we consider going to a movie, the first question we usually ask has to do not with the director or the cinematographer but with the actors: Who's in it? This is a natural question, because the art of the actor is so clearly visible. The actor's work commands most of our attention, overshadowing the considerable contributions of the writer, director, cinematographer, editor, and composer of the score. As George Kernodle puts it,

> it is the star that draws the crowds. The audience may be amused, thrilled, or deeply moved by the story, fascinated by new plot devices, property gadgets, and camera angles, charmed by backgrounds that are exotic, or captivated by those that are familiar and real, but it is the people on the screen, and especially the faces, that command the center of attention.[1]

Because we naturally respond to film's most human ingredient, the actor's contribution is extremely important.

Yet despite our tendency to focus attention on the actor, there is general agreement among critics and directors that the actor's role in film should be a subordinate one, one of many important elements contributing to a greater aesthetic whole, the film itself. As Alfred Hitchcock states it, "Film work hasn't much need for the virtuoso actor who gets his effects and climaxes himself, who plays directly to the audience with the force of his talent and personality. The screen actor has got to be much more plastic; he has to submit himself to be used by the director and the camera."[2]

THE GOAL OF THE ACTOR

The ultimate goal of any actor should be to make us believe completely in the reality of the character. If this goal is to be achieved, actors must either develop or be blessed with several talents. First of all, they must be able to project sincerity, truthfulness, and naturalness in such a way that we are never aware that they are acting a part. In a sense, good film acting must seem not to be acting at all.

Sometimes actors achieve a certain naturalness through tricks and gimmicks. Knowing that Ratso Rizzo, the character that Dustin Hoffman plays in *Midnight Cowboy*, had a distinct limp, a fellow actor advised Hoffman on how to make the limp consistent: "Once you get the limp right, why don't you put rocks in your shoe? You'll never have to think about limping. It will be there; you won't have to worry about it." Actors use similar tricks to create a trademark for their characters and to keep the characters consistent. But good acting demands much more than gimmicks. To project the sincerity that a really deep, complex, and demanding role requires, actors must be willing to draw on the deepest and most personal qualities of their inner being. As director Mark Rydell (a former actor himself) says, "I find that acting is one of the bravest professions of all. An actor has to remain vulnerable. . . . I suspect that any time you see a great performance, it's because some actor has been courageous enough to allow you to peek at a very personal, private secret of his."[3]

Actors must also possess the intelligence, imagination, sensitivity, and insight into human nature necessary to fully understand the characters they play—their inner thoughts, motivations, and emotions. Furthermore, actors must have the ability to express these things convincingly through voice, body movements, gestures, or facial expressions, so the qualities seem true to the characters portrayed and to the situation in which the characters find themselves. And actors must maintain the illusion of reality in their characters with complete consistency from beginning to end. It is also important for actors to keep their egos under control, so that they can see their roles in proper perspective to the dramatic work as a whole. Veteran actor and Oscar winner Michael Caine offers this definition of the actor's ultimate goal in playing a movie role: "If I'm really doing my job correctly you should sit there and say, "I'm *involved* with this person, and have no idea there's an actor there." So, really, I'm trying to defeat myself the entire time. You should never see the *actor*, never see the wheels going."[4]

BECOMING THE CHARACTER

If an actor's goal is to obscure his or her own personality and to become another person on the screen, the actor must learn to behave reflexively and naturally as this new character. Although there are many subtle variations in the way actors prepare for roles, they generally choose one of two techniques to develop well-rounded, believable characterizations: the inside approach or the outside approach. Actor Edward James Olmos describes the most basic elements of the two approaches:

> The English form of study teaches you to go from the outside in. You do the behavior and it starts to seep inside. The Stanislavski method teaches you to go from the inside out. You begin with the feeling and memory, and those feelings begin to affect your behavior.
>
> In other words, some people will turn around and get a limp and then figure out where the limp came from. Other people have to figure out why they have to limp before they can do the limp.[5]

Cliff Robertson, an Academy Award winner, believes that he must understand all facets of his character's personality and thought processes. This inside method of preparation allows him to think and respond naturally in the role. For his performance in *Charly*, however, he used no immediate rehearsal; instead, he just tried "going with the instrument," in a process of "osmosis," because he had studied his character for seven years.[6]

Joanne Woodward, honored for her work in *The Three Faces of Eve*, *Rachel, Rachel*, and *The Effect of Gamma Rays on Man-in-the-Moon Marigolds*, describes her outside approach to character development: "Mine is an odd way to work. . . . I always have to know what a character looks like because to me, having studied with Martha Graham, so much that goes on inside is reflected outside. . . . I took Rachel's movements from my child, Nell. She's very pigeon-toed. . . . And somehow, when you move like that—all sorts of things happen to you inside."[7]

In his book about acting for film, Michael Caine advises that: "When becoming a character, you have to steal. . . . You can even steal from other actors' characterizations; but if you do, only steal from the best. . . . Because what you're seeing them do, they stole."[8]

No matter what their methods of preparation, actors who attempt to submerge their own personalities and become a character deserve respect for their efforts, according to director Elia Kazan:

> The beautiful and the terrible thing about actors is that when they work they are completely exposed; you have to appreciate that if you direct them. They are being critically observed not only for their emotions, their technique, and their intelligence, but for their legs, their breasts, their carriage, their double chins, and so on. Their whole being is opened to scrutiny. . . . How can you feel anything but gratitude for creatures so vulnerable and so naked?[9]

DIFFERENCES BETWEEN FILM ACTING AND STAGE ACTING

Acting for motion pictures and acting for the stage have in common the goals, traits, and skills described above, yet there are important differences in the acting techniques required for the two media (Figure 10.1). The primary difference results from the relative distance between the performer and the spectator. When acting in the theater, actors must always be sure that every member of the audience can see and hear them distinctly. Thus, stage actors must constantly project the voice, make gestures that are obvious and clear, and generally move and speak so they can be clearly heard and seen by the most remote observer. This is no problem in a small, intimate theater, but the larger the theater and the more distant the spectator in the last row, the farther the actor's voice must be projected and the broader the gestures must be. As actors make these adjustments, the depth and reality of the performance suffer, because louder tones and wider gestures lead to generalized form and stylization. The finer, subtler shades of intonation are lost as the distance between actor and audience increases.

The problem of reaching a remote spectator does not exist in films, for the viewer is in the best possible location for hearing and seeing the actor. Because of the mobility of the recording microphone, a film actor may speak softly, or even whisper, with full confidence that the audience will hear every word and perceive every subtle tone of voice. The same holds true for facial expression, gesture, and body movement, for in close-ups even the subtlest facial expressions are clearly visible to the most remote spectator. The mobility of the camera further assures the actor that the audience will view the scene from the most effective angle. Thus film acting can be, and in fact must be, more subtle and restrained than stage acting.

Henry Fonda learned this lesson when director Victor Fleming accused him of "mugging" while filming a scene for Fonda's first movie, *The Farmer Takes a Wife*. Fonda had played the role on Broadway, and Fleming explained the problem to him in terms he clearly understood: "You're playing the farmer the way you did in the theater. You're playing to the back row of the orchestra and the rear row of the balcony. That's stage technique." The understated Fonda style, using as little facial mobility as possible, began at that moment and served the actor well in almost a hundred films: "I just pulled it right back to reality because that lens and that microphone are

FIGURE 10.1 **Stage vs. Film Acting** Many performers seem equally adept at satisfying the separate demands of acting for the theater and working in movies. For example, Patrick Stewart can broadly command the stage as Puck in a production of *A Midsummer Night's Dream*, left, and also offer the cinematic nuances of Jean-Luc Picard in the *Star Trek* franchise, right.

doing all the projection you need. No sense in using too much voice, and you don't need any more expression on your face than you'd use in everyday life."[10]

Actor Robert Shaw put it this way: "Here's the difference: On stage, you have to dominate the audience. You don't have to *think* the way you do when you're in the movies. Stage acting is the art of *domination*. Movie acting is the art of *seduction*."[11]

This is not to say that film acting is less difficult than stage acting. The film actor must be extremely careful in every gesture and word, for the camera and microphone are unforgiving and cruelly revealing, especially in close-ups. Because complete sincerity, naturalness, and restraint are all-important, a single false move or phony gesture or a line delivered without conviction, with too much conviction, or out of character will shatter the illusion of reality. Thus, the most successful film actors either possess or can project, with seeming ease and naturalness, a truly genuine personality, and they somehow appear to be completely themselves without self-consciousness or a sense of strain. This rare quality generally seems to depend as much on natural talent as on disciplined study and training.

Another difficulty faces film actors because they perform their roles in discontinuous bits and pieces, rather than in a continuous flow with one scene following the next, as in theater. Only later, in the cutting room, are the fragments assembled in proper sequence. For this reason, assuming the proper frame of mind, mood, and acting style for each segment of the film becomes a problem. For example, actors required to speak in a dialect far removed from their own natural speech patterns may have difficulty capturing the dialect exactly as they did in a scene filmed two weeks earlier, a problem they would not have in a continuous stage performance. But a clear

FIGURE 10.2 **Corporeal Stances** Body language speaks volumes about the characters and their relationships in these scenes picturing Humphrey Bogart and Katharine Hepburn in *The African Queen* (left) and Zekeria Ebrahimi and Ahmad Khan Mahmoodzada in *The Kite Runner* (right).

advantage also arises from this difference. The performance of the film actor can be made more nearly perfect than can that of the stage actor, for the film editor and director can choose the best and most convincing performance from several takes of the same sequence. That way, the film becomes a continuous series of best performances.

Another disadvantage in film acting is that the actors have no direct link with the audience as stage actors do and therefore must act for an imagined audience. Film actors cannot draw on audience reaction for inspiration. Whatever inspiration they receive must come from the director, the crew, and the fact that their work will have more permanence than that of the stage actor.

Film is also for the most part a more physical medium than theater—that is, film actors must use more nonverbal communication than stage actors have to use. Julian Fast discusses this aspect of film acting in his book *Body Language:* "Good actors must all be experts in the use of body language. A process of elimination guarantees that only those with an excellent command of the grammar and vocabulary get to be successful."[12] According to critic Jack Kroll, "Actors who have a genius for this sleight of body are surrogates for the rest of us who are trapped in our own selves. To create a new human being is to recreate the very idea of humanity, to refresh that idea for us who grow stale in our mortality" (Figure 10.2).[13]

The grammar and vocabulary of body language include a vast array of nonverbal communication techniques, but the motion picture is perhaps unique in its emphasis on the eloquence of the human face. Although the face and facial expressions play a part in other storytelling media, such as novels and plays, in film the face becomes a medium of communication in its own right. Magnified on the screen, the human face with its infinite variety of expressions can convey depth and subtlety of emotion that cannot be approached through purely rational or verbal means (Figure 10.3). As Hungarian film critic and theorist Béla Balázs so aptly states, "What happens on the face and in facial expressions is a spiritual experience which is rendered immediately visible without the intermediary of words"[14] (Figure 10.4).

FIGURE 10.3 **The Actor's Face** The immensely popular movie *The Blind Side* allows its stars, Sandra Bullock and Quinton Aaron, clearly to reveal in their faces the inner thoughts and feelings of their characters.

FIGURE 10.4 **Sustained Expression** In *I Am Sam,* Sean Penn convincingly portrays a mentally challenged character by maintaining a "simple" look throughout the film, as in this touching scene with his film daughter (Dakota Fanning).

The human face is a marvelously complex structure, capable of transmitting a wide range of emotions through slight changes in mouth, eyes, eyelids, eyebrows, and forehead. This expressiveness helps to explain another important difference between film acting and stage acting: the film's emphasis on reacting rather than acting. The **reaction shot** achieves its considerable dramatic impact through a

FLASHBACK

SILENT ACTING EVOLVES: THE SUBTLETIES OF EXAGGERATION

The broad and over-the-top gesticulations and grimacing of the silent-film acting style (illustrated in the frame below by the great actress Lillian Gish, in D. W. Griffith's celebrated 1919 drama *Broken Blossoms*) might be difficult to appreciate at first. But once we become accustomed to it, the strangeness recedes into the background, revealing recognizable elements of a distinctive acting technique. Early silent-film actors used theatrical gestures and unnatural expressions that were carry-overs from the melodramatic stage-acting techniques of that day. However, in the last years of the silent-film era, the art of film acting evolved, and actors realized the necessity for restraint in gesture and subtlety of expression. It is a polished art form whose greatest power is that it speaks a universal language.

Audience members in the silent era were fluent in the art of reading actors' faces, gestures, and body movements. However, now that we are used to continuous dialogue in our films, we must work hard to understand the subtlety

1909
Florence Lawrence stars in D. W. Griffith's *Lady Helen's Escapade*. She is perhaps the earliest movie star and is known as the "Biograph girl" because she worked for Biograph Studios.

1917
Mary Pickford stars in *The Poor Little Rich Girl* and *Rebecca of Sunnybrook Farm*. The actress is credited for introducing a subtler style of acting in the silent era.

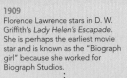

1914
The Perils of Pauline stars Pearl White, whose acting style features the dramatic flourishes of the early melodramatic silent era.

and power of the unique "language" of silent-film acting—a language capable of both silent soliloquy (a single face "speaking" the subtlest shades of meaning) and mute dialogue (a conversation that takes place through facial expressions and gestures). The silent-film language can, through close-up, reveal not only what is visibly written on the face, but also something existing beyond the surface, and it is sometimes even capable of capturing contradictory expressions simultaneously on the same face.

The artistry of silent-film actors is not restricted to the face. The hands, the arms, the legs, and the torso of the actor are also powerful instruments of expression, and speak in a language that is perhaps more individual and personal than the language of words. As each actor in the sound film has vocal qualities that are unique to his or her means of verbal expression, each accomplished actor in the silent film had a personal style of facial and physical expression of emotion.

One of the most powerful means of expression involving the whole body is the actor's walk, which, in the silent film, is usually a natural and unconscious expression of emotion; it became an important aspect of each actor's unique screen personality or style. When used consciously for expression, it could convey such varying emotions as dignity, strong resolution, self-consciousness, modesty, and shame.

Later silent-film actors were able to speak clearly and distinctly to their audience through a pantomime of eyes, mouth, hands, and body movement. The slightest body movement, gesture, or facial expression could express the deepest passion or proclaim the tragedy of a human soul. This highly developed art of pantomime gave the silent film a means of expression that was self-sufficient and capable of conveying narrative visually, with a minimum of subtitles. Especially adept at this art were the three most celebrated film comedians of the silent period: Harold Lloyd (*Safety Last!*, 1923), Buster Keaton (*Sherlock, Jr.*, 1924; *The General*, 1927; *Steamboat Bill, Jr.*, 1928), and Charlie Chaplin (*The Gold Rush*, 1925; *City Lights*, 1931). In the top photo, Lloyd strikes his most famous comic pose in *Safety Last!*. (See also Chapter 11, page 312.)

Anyone who thinks the silent film was a primitive and crude art form compared to the modern sound film needs only to study two of the masterpieces of the late silent era: *Sunrise*, F. W. Murnau's hauntingly beautiful melodrama, and *Napoleon*, French director Abel Gance's great epic. Released in 1927, the next-to-last great year of silent pictures, both films are extremely sophisticated, not just in terms of acting styles, but also in terms of editing, composition, lighting, use of montages, creating the illusion of three-dimensionality, camera movement, superimposed images, and special effects. And both have dynamic, polished acting styles capable of communicating nuances of meaning without titles. In fact, watching silent films of this caliber makes some cinephiles wonder if the movies should ever have learned to talk.

1929
American actress Louise Brooks, known as a "vamp," stars in German filmmaker G. W. Pabst's *Pandora's Box* and *Diary of a Lost Girl*.

1921
Rudolph Valentino stars in *The Four Horsemen of the Apocalypse*, which launches him to stardom and earns him the nickname "Latin Lover."

FIGURE 10.5 **The Reaction Shot** Actor Kevin Zegers, playing the son of Bree, Felicity Huffman's preoperative transsexual character in *Transamerica*, spends much of his time during a road trip with his newly discovered parent registering silent facial reactions to her many questions and instructions.

close-up of the character most affected by the dialogue or action. The actor's face, within the brief moment that it is on the screen, must register clearly yet subtly and without the aid of dialogue the appropriate emotional reaction (Figure 10.5). Some of the most powerful moments in film are built around such "facial acting." Michael Caine elaborates: "[I]n a movie, you cannot get away with just doing a star performance—moving and talking all the time. People become bored with you. . . . [Y]ou have to play according to the reactions of someone else to what you're doing. One of the things I'm known for in movies is not acting but *reacting*."[15]

The stage actor's facial reactions, in contrast, are seldom if ever quite so important to a play's dramatic power.

But even in reaction shots the film actor is often assisted by the nature of the medium, for in film much of the powerful and expressive quality of the human face is created by the context in which it appears, and the meanings of many expressions are determined by skillful editing. Thus, the actor's face may not be so beautifully expressive as the visual context makes it appear. This phenomenon was demonstrated in an experiment conducted in the early 1920s by the young Russian painter Lev Kuleshov and film director V. I. Pudovkin:

> We took from some film or other several close-ups of the well-known Russian actor Mosjukhin. We chose close-ups which were static and which did not express any feeling at all—quiet close-ups. We joined these close-ups, which were all similar, with other bits of film in three different combinations. In the first combination the close-up of Mosjukhin was immediately followed by a shot of soup standing on a table. It was obvious and certain that Mosjukhin was looking at this soup. In the second combination the face of Mosjukhin was joined to shots showing a coffin in which lay

a dead woman. In the third the close-up was followed by a shot of a little girl playing with a funny toy bear. When we showed the three combinations to an audience which had not been let into the secret, the result was terrific. The public raved about the acting of the artist. They pointed out the heavy pensiveness of the mood over the forgotten soup, were touched and moved by the deep sorrow with which he looked on the dead woman, and admired the light, happy smile with which he surveyed the girl at play. But we knew in all three cases the face was exactly the same.[16]

This experiment is not cited to prove that film acting is only an illusion created by editing. But it does show that we are eager to respond to faces, whether or not those faces are really projecting what we think we see.

Film actors must also be able to communicate more with bodily movements and gestures than stage actors. Because the stage actor's chief instrument of expression is the voice, his or her movements are mainly an accompaniment to or an extension of what is said. In film, however, physical movement and gesture may communicate effectively without dialogue (see Flashback: "Silent Acting Evolves: The Subtleties of Exaggeration" in this chapter). The magnification of the human image on the screen enables the actor to communicate with extremely subtle movements. A slight shrug of the shoulders, the nervous trembling of a hand viewed in close-up, or the visible tensing of the muscles and tendons in the neck may be much more important than anything said.

A classic example of the power of body language in film acting is Jack Palance's portrayal of the gunfighter Wilson in *Shane*, a role he parodies in both *City Slickers* movies. Palance plays Wilson as the personification of evil. Every movement, every gesture is slow, deliberate, yet tense, so we get the feeling that Wilson is a rattlesnake, moving slowly and sensuously but always ready to strike in a split second. When Wilson slowly performs the ritual of putting on his black leather gloves in order to practice his profession, Palance makes us sense with horror Wilson's cold, cruel indifference to human life.

Film acting also differs from stage acting in that it requires two kinds of acting. One is the kind required for the action/adventure film. We can refer to it as **action acting.** This type of acting requires a great deal in the way of reactions, body language, physical exertion, and special skills, but it does not draw on the deepest resources of the actor's intelligence and feelings. In contrast, **dramatic acting** calls for sustained, intense dialogue with another person and requires an emotional and psychological depth seldom called for in action acting. Action acting is the art of doing. Dramatic acting involves feeling, thinking, and communicating emotions and thoughts. Action acting is on the surface, with little nuance. Dramatic acting is beneath the surface and full of subtlety. Each type of acting requires its own particular gift or talent.

Some actors can do both, but most are better suited for one or the other and are usually cast accordingly. Clint Eastwood, for example, is essentially an action actor, and Robert De Niro is a dramatic actor (Figure 10.6). Director Sergio Leone, who has directed both, describes them: "Robert De Niro throws himself into this or that role, putting on a personality the way someone else might put on his coat, naturally and with elegance, while Clint Eastwood throws himself into a suit of armor and lowers the visor with a rusty clang. . . . Bobby first of all, is an actor. Clint first of all, is a star. Bobby suffers, Clint yawns."[17]

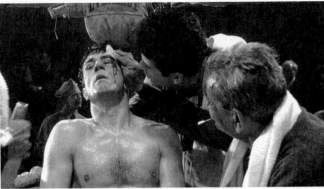

FIGURE 10.6 **Action and Dramatic Acting** Although, like Clint Eastwood Will Smith has sometimes ventured into drama (*Six Degrees of Separation, Seven Pounds*) with success, he has become best known as an action actor (pictured above in *I Am Legend*). Robert De Niro (shown in *Raging Bull*) (right) has consistently been one of our finest dramatic actors. With uneven results, both critically and commercially, all three actors have also starred in comedies.

Although Eastwood, as he has aged, has carved some deeper lines into his "block of granite" with work like *Unforgiven, Million Dollar Baby, Gran Torino*, and *Hereafter*, Leone's description of Eastwood as an actor remains valid today.

Although film acting and stage acting have the same basic goals, film acting utilizes fundamentally different techniques to achieve them.

TYPES OF ACTORS

Besides classifying actors as action and dramatic actors, we can consider how the roles they play relate to their own personalities. In *A Primer for Playgoers*, Edward A. Wright and Lenthiel H. Downs identify three types of actors: impersonators, interpreters and commentators, and personality actors.[18]

Impersonators

Impersonators are actors who have the talent to leave their real personality behind and to assume the personality of a character with whom they may have few characteristics in common. Such actors can completely submerge themselves in a role, altering their personal, physical, and vocal characteristics to such a degree that they seem to become the character. We lose sight of the impersonator's real identity. The roles such actors can perform are almost unlimited.

Interpreters and Commentators

Interpreters and commentators play characters closely resembling themselves in personality and physical appearance, and they interpret these parts dramatically without wholly losing their own identity. Although they may slightly alter themselves to fit the role, they do not attempt to radically change their individual personality traits, physical characteristics, or voice qualities. They choose instead to color or interpret the role by filtering it through their own best qualities, modifying it to fit their own inherent abilities. The end result is an effective compromise between actor and role, between the real and the assumed identity. The compromise adds a unique creative dimension to the character being portrayed, for in their delivery of the lines these actors reveal something of their own thoughts and feelings about the character, but they do so without ever falling out of character. Thus, these actors may simultaneously comment on and interpret the role. Although the range of roles such actors can play is not as wide as that open to impersonators, it is still relatively broad. If they are cast wisely within this range, they can bring something new and fresh to each role they play, in addition to their own best and most attractive qualities.

Personality Actors

Actors whose primary talent is to be themselves and nothing more are **personality actors.** They project the essential qualities of sincerity, truthfulness, and naturalness, and they generally possess some dynamic and magnetic mass appeal because of a striking appearance, a physical or vocal idiosyncrasy, or some other special quality strongly communicated to us on film. These actors, however popular, are incapable of assuming any variety in the roles they play, for they cannot project sincerity and naturalness when they attempt to move outside their own basic personality. Thus, either they must fit exactly the roles in which they are cast, or the roles must be tailored to fit their personality.

THE STAR SYSTEM

In the past, many personality actors and some interpreter and commentator actors were exploited in what became known as the **star system,** an approach to filmmaking based on the assumption that the average movie-goer is interested more in personalities than in great stories or, for that matter, in film art. The stars were, of course, actors with great mass appeal. The big studios did everything in their power to preserve the qualities of the stars that appealed to the public, and they created films around the image of the star personality. Often a star's presence in a film was the main guarantee of financial success, and such films became nothing more than a suitable package in which to display and market the attractive wares of the actors, who had only to project the charm of their personalities (Figure 10.7).

For some directors, the star system offered certain clear advantages. John Ford and Frank Capra, for example, used the star system as a myth-making apparatus, building their films around such stars as John Wayne, Barbara Stanwyck, Jean Arthur, Henry Fonda, James Stewart, and Gary Cooper. These actors projected fairly consistent personalities and embraced a constant set of values in each film they did. They came into each new Ford or Capra film trailing clouds of associations and reverberating strong echoes of earlier parts. By surrounding these stars with their stock company of top-notch secondary actors—also in predictable roles echoing earlier parts—Ford and Capra were, in a sense, using pre-established symbols for the values they wanted their characters to represent, and the mythic worlds of their films could rest on the shoulders of actors who already had mythic dimensions.

FIGURE 10.7 **The Studio Star System**   Although the 1944 *film noir* classic *Double Indemnity* became another triumph for director Billy Wilder, the movie was also clearly a star-system vehicle for the immensely popular Barbara Stanwyck and Fred MacMurray.

The fact that so many stars trailed these clouds of associations influenced Steven Spielberg's 1975 casting of *Jaws:*

> I didn't pursue that idea of getting stars, because I think it's really important when you're watching a movie that you don't sit there and say, "Oh, look who's in this picture. What was his last picture, wasn't that a good one? Didn't you just love her in such and such . . . ?" . . . . I had two producers who . . . agreed that we should not go after the half-million-dollar players, but should get good people who would be good actors in the right part and would be semianonymous.[19]

There was some general agreement with Spielberg's thinking throughout the industry. During the 1960s and 1970s producers began to turn to lesser-known actors who had the range and flexibility to play a variety of roles and who, of course, demanded less money than established stars. Blockbuster hits such as *2001, The Graduate, Taxi Driver,* and *Jaws* were successful without the presence of top box-office stars. A new era began with a small galaxy of gifted actors who promised not the repetition of tested and tried personalities but the guarantee of high-level performances in fresh and exciting roles (people like Dustin Hoffman, Robert De Niro, Jodie Foster, Meryl Streep, Robert Duvall, and Glenn Close).

Much of the success of this new galaxy depends on the actors' skill in choosing the films in which they appear. No longer under studio contract and forced to accept roles assigned by studio moguls, the modern star is often part of a deal package that may include a director and screenwriter who are all clients of the same agent. In many respects, the talent agency has usurped some of the power of the big studios in determining what films are made and who stars in them—and enormous salaries are once again in vogue.

Although the star system has changed greatly over the last half century, it is certainly not dead. The personality cults that spring up periodically around charismatic actors provide ample evidence to the contrary. We will always be attracted to familiar faces and personalities, for we seem to have a psychological need for the familiar, the predictable, and the comfortable. In addition, as Sidney Lumet suggests,

There's a mysterious alchemy between star and audience. Sometimes it's based on the physical beauty or sex appeal of the star. But I don't believe that it's ever just one thing. Surely there were other women as attractive as Marilyn Monroe or men as handsome as Cary Grant (though not many). Al Pacino tries to suit his look to the characters—a beard here, long hair there—but somehow it's the way his eyes express an enormous rage, even in tender moments, that enthralls me and everyone else. I think that every star evokes a sense of danger, something unmanageable. Perhaps each person in the audience feels that he or she is the one who can manage, tame, satisfy the bigger-than-life quality that a star has. Clint Eastwood isn't really the same as you or me, is he? Or Michelle Pfeiffer, or Sean Connery, or you name them. I don't really know what makes a star. But the persona that jumps out at you is certainly a most important element.[20]

CASTING

Steven Spielberg has observed, "Sometimes the best thing I can do is cast the movie well. If you cast well then half the battle is already won. . . ."[21]

Indeed, acting skills aside, the casting of actors in roles that are right for them is an extremely important consideration. If their physical characteristics, facial features, voice qualities, or the total personality they naturally project is not suited to the character, their performance will probably not be convincing. Alec Guinness or Peter Sellers, despite their great ability as impersonators, could not have effectively played the roles assigned to John Wayne, for example, nor could Burt Lancaster have been very effective in roles played by Woody Allen.

Less extreme problems in casting can be solved by sheer genius or camera tricks. For example, in the film *Boy on a Dolphin*, Alan Ladd, who measured 5 feet 6 inches, was cast opposite Sophia Loren, who towered over him at 5 feet 9 inches. But in a scene that showed them walking side by side, Ladd seemed at least as tall as or slightly taller than Loren. What the camera didn't show was that Loren was actually walking in a shallow trench especially dug for the purpose (Figure 10.8). When the male lead is to be something other than the traditional macho hero, relative size does not seem so important. No effort was made to conceal that Dudley Moore was shorter than Mary Tyler Moore in *Six Weeks*. Traditionally, when the story has been a comedy, the romantic male lead could be shorter than his leading lady, as was apparent in the pairing of Gwyneth Paltrow and Jack Black in *Shallow Hal*. And in Mike Nichols's film version of *Who's Afraid of Virginia Woolf?* the character named Honey (Sandy Dennis) is repeatedly referred to as "slim-hipped" despite visual evidence to the contrary. The discrepancy is obscured by Dennis's acting; she projects a psychological type of slim-hippedness that is more convincing than the physical semblance of it.

It is also extremely important that the cast of any film be viewed as a team, not as a hodgepodge of separate individuals, for each actor appears on the screen not alone but in interaction with the other actors. Therefore some thought has to be given to the way they will look on the screen with each other. When casting two male leads such as Robert Redford and Paul Newman, for example, the casting director makes sure that they have certain contrasting features so that they stand out clearly from each other. Actors of the same sex are cast with the idea of contrasting their coloring, builds, heights, and voice qualities. If these differences are not apparent, they can be created through such artificial means as costuming, hairstyle, and facial hair (clean-shaven, mustaches, or beards).

FIGURE 10.8 The Height of Casting Challenges   Because Sophia Loren was three inches taller than Alan Ladd, she was photographed standing a step below him in this scene from the romantic drama *Boy on a Dolphin* (top left). In *The Station Agent* (below), Patricia Clarkson actually towered over her diminutive, but quietly forceful, co-star Peter Dinklage (left, seen with the more conventionally tall and handsome Bobby Cannavale)—but audiences were nevertheless convinced of the genuine attraction between their two complex characters in this drama. Director Stanley Kubrick cast the (then) real-life, tall/not-so-tall couple Nicole Kidman and Tom Cruise in *Eyes Wide Shut* (top right).

FIGURE 10.9 Ensemble Acting In some films, four or more well-known actors may be cast in roles of almost equal importance, and none of them actually dominates the movie. In director Nicole Holofcener's *Please Give*, the large cast includes Catherine Keener and Oliver Platt (right).

The actors must also project, either naturally or through their skill as actors, significantly different personality traits so that they can effectively play off each other as separate and distinct personalities. This is especially important in **ensemble acting,** a performance by a group of actors whose roles are of equal importance; no member of the group has a starring role or dominates the others. Many modern films, such as *The Big Chill, The Right Stuff, Reality Bites, Friends With Money,* and *Please Give,* feature ensemble acting (Figure 10.9).

One of the most difficult jobs in casting is finding combinations of actors with chemistry between them—preferably a chemistry so powerful that the audience wants to see them together again in another film. Most important in Hollywood productions is what is known as the he/she chemistry. Spencer Tracy was paired with a bevy of actresses (Lana Turner, Hedy Lamarr, Jean Harlow, and Deborah Kerr) before he was cast with Katharine Hepburn to form a winning team that could be repeated for success after success (Figure 10.10). The James Stewart/June Allyson combination also proved very successful. The Woody Allen/Diane Keaton team worked well (perhaps better than the Woody Allen/Mia Farrow combination). The simple truth, however, is that real he/she chemistry is very rare, and few combinations in recent years have been strong enough to endure very long.

Physical characteristics and natural personality traits are especially important when members of the audience are likely to have clear mental images of the character before they see the movie, as in films about familiar historical figures or films based on popular novels. We often have a difficult time believing in actors who violate our preconceived notions of such characters, and even outstanding performances seldom overcome this handicap.

FIGURE 10.10 **He/She Chemistry** Studios are constantly searching for the perfect couple, so that they can be played opposite each other in film after film. So far, few modern teams have enjoyed the success experienced by Katharine Hepburn and Spencer Tracy (top left, in *Adam's Rib*), or Richard Burton and Elizabeth Taylor (top right, in *Taming of the Shrew*). One possibility: Penelope Cruz and Javier Bardem (bottom right, in *Vicky Cristina Barcelona*).

Financial considerations also play an important part in casting. A well-known actor may be the perfect choice for a starring role but may be too high priced for a film with a limited budget. Or an actor may have commitments that prevent her or him from taking the part. Thus, casting becomes a matter of selecting the best available talent within the limits of the film's budget and shooting schedule.

For actors who have an established and loyal following, producers may take a chance and cast them in a role at odds with their established image, hoping that they will automatically draw their special fans. Thus, Mary Tyler Moore was cast as the cold mother in *Ordinary People*, Robin Williams in *The World According to Garp*, *Dead Poets Society*, and *Insomnia*, Steve Martin in *Pennies From Heaven* and *Parenthood*, Jim Carrey in *The Truman Show*, and Charlize Theron in *Monster*.

Billy Wilder's methods of casting were perhaps unique because Wilder wrote many of the stories he directed, but he does provide an excellent example of the importance of casting. Instead of selecting a cast to fit an existing story, Wilder often started with a story idea alone and then proceeded to select and sign up his cast. Only after the actors he wanted agreed to do the film did the actual writing of the script begin. As Wilder put it, "What good is it to have a magnificent dramatic concept for which you must have Sir Laurence Olivier and Audrey Hepburn if they're not available?"[22]

Casting Problems

Casting a feature film is often a more difficult matter than just visualizing the right actor for the part and signing him or her to a contract. German director Werner Herzog's experiences with casting *Fitzcarraldo* are certainly not typical, but they do illustrate a variety of problems that can occur on almost any production. Jack Nicholson had originally expressed interest in playing the lead, but then lost interest. Later, Warren Oates agreed to play the title role. However, Oates, who had never signed a contract, backed out four weeks before shooting was to begin because he didn't relish spending three months in a remote jungle location. After a two-month delay, with Jason Robards replacing Oates, and Mick Jagger in a supporting role, shooting finally got under way. Six weeks later Robards came down with amoebic dysentery and flew home. Shortly after that, Mick Jagger had to drop out to honor other commitments. Unable to find a suitable replacement for Jagger, Herzog wrote his character out of the script. Production was then suspended for two months while the director searched for a new leading man. Although Klaus Kinski (subsequently the subject of Herzog's documentary *My Best Fiend*) was not an ideal choice because he could not project the warmth and charm of the obsessed Irishman, Herzog hired him for the part because further delay would certainly have killed the project.

Fate seems to play a hand in casting, for actors often become stars in roles that were turned down by others. Robert Redford got the part of the Sundance Kid only after Marlon Brando, Steve McQueen, and Warren Beatty had turned it down. During a very brief period, Montgomery Clift turned down four roles that virtually made stars of the actors who finally played the parts: the William Holden role in *Sunset Boulevard*, the James Dean role in *East of Eden*, the Paul Newman role in *Somebody Up There Likes Me*, and the Marlon Brando role in *On the Waterfront*. Gene Hackman was offered the part of the father in *Ordinary People* and wanted to do it, but he could not work out the kind of financial deal he wanted. Richard Dreyfuss was originally set to play Joe Gideon in *All That Jazz*, but he was afraid of the dancing the role would require and was used to working with directors who allowed the actor more freedom than Bob Fosse allowed. So the role went to Roy Scheider.

Although the names on the marquee are usually important factors in the success of a film, there are exceptions. *Midnight Express* is one. The film did not have any name stars, and the director, Alan Parker, had made only one film, so his name was not a household word either. Yet the film succeeded because its great intensity and excellent performances from relatively unknown actors stimulated audience interest. Likewise, Steven Soderbergh directed *sex, lies, & videotape* with a starless cast long before he became famous himself with *Erin Brockovich* and *Traffic*—and then returned to a completely starless cast in such independent, shot-on-digital-video features as *Bubble* (Figure 10.11).

The Typecasting Trap

Typecasting consigns an actor to a narrow range of almost identical roles. It is a natural result of two situations. First, the studios have a great deal of money invested in every film they do. Thus, they naturally want to cast an actor in the same kind of role that was successful before, in the hope of repeating the earlier success. Second, if an actor repeats a similar role two or three times, the qualities that the actor projected in the role may take on mythic proportions, and the actor may become a figure on whom movie-goers hang their fantasies (Figure 10.12). If this happens, the movie-going audience not only expects, but demands, that the

FIGURE 10.11 **The Starless Cast**   Occasionally, a movie can attract considerable attention even when all of the actors are completely unknown. An extreme example of this phenomenon involves *Bubble,* an independent film that director Steven Soderbergh created as part of his experimentation with conventional motion picture distribution patterns. The film, shot inexpensively on digital video, was released almost simultaneously on the screens of Mark Cuban's Landmark Theatre chain, on pay-per-view cable, and on sale in the DVD format. Its "stars," real-life citizens of the small town that served as the location for the movie's shooting (Debbie Doebereiner, Misty Wilkins, and Dustin James Ashley), had never acted in films before.

FIGURE 10.12 **Typecasting**   In choosing actors for the four lead "senior" roles in *Space Cowboys,* director Clint Eastwood and casting director Phyllis Huffman obviously took full advantage of the personality types that Eastwood, Donald Sutherland, James Garner, and Tommy Lee Jones, had respectively projected steadily in their roles as younger, popular actors.

role be repeated again and again, with only slight variations. To the fans, anything else is a betrayal, a personal affront to those who have developed what to them is a very personal relationship with a fictional character on the silver screen.

There is a real danger that an actor who is too convincing in an early role will be typecast for the rest of his or her career. For example, Sissy Spacek, early in her career, projected a fairly consistent screen image: a young, innocent, intelligent, sensitive, but somewhat unsophisticated small-town or country girl. She played Loretta Lynn so convincingly in *Coal Miner's Daughter* that people actually believe that Sissy Spacek *is* that character, "just plain folks," in real life. But the fact is that Sissy Spacek is an extremely versatile actress capable of playing practically any part. Her Oscar-nominated mature performance in *In the Bedroom* shows her versatility.

Robert De Niro created such a strong impression with his Georgia farm-boy Bruce in *Bang the Drum Slowly* that people were saying how sad it was that he had such a strong Georgia accent, for he'd be limited to roles that called for that kind of a character. De Niro, now well known for his meticulous research, had taken a tape recorder to Georgia to study the speech patterns of the residents so he could capture the dialect of the character he was cast to play. By carefully choosing his roles, De Niro has completely broken the typecasting trap. He has shown not only that he can play a variety of roles but that he can alter himself both mentally and physically to project entirely different qualities in each part he plays. In *Bang the Drum Slowly*, playing the second-rate big-league catcher with Hodgkin's disease, he projects a kind of fragile quality, a small man among giants. In *The Deer Hunter*, he stands tall and strong, a quiet, confident leader among men. In *Raging Bull*, he changes his image within the film itself, playing a young, trim, perfectly conditioned fighter (Jake La Motta) in the beginning and then ballooning his weight sixty pounds to play the middle-aged La Motta at the film's end. His transformations are so perfectly executed and his character is so completely transformed that we lose sight of the fact that we're seeing the same actor in all three roles. Dustin Hoffman too has this rare ability, as seen in his portrayal of extremely different characters in *The Graduate*, *Midnight Cowboy*, *Tootsie*, *Rain Man*, *Billy Bathgate*, *I ♥ Huckabees*, and *Meet the Fockers*, as does Ralph Fiennes in *Schindler's List*, *Quiz Show*, *The English Patient*, *Spider*, *The Constant Gardener*, and *The White Countess*. (Figure 10.13).

Many actors are wary of falling into the typecasting trap and plan their careers accordingly, doing everything possible to avoid the dangers. Gary Busey, who like De Niro has altered his weight and his appearance greatly in some of the roles he's played, expresses his philosophy this way: "My idea is to look for roles that make right-angle turns from one film to the next. I try to bring a freshness and spontaneity to each part and scene I play."[23]

As far as casting is concerned, there are often disadvantages for the male actor who is too handsome or the female actor who is exceptionally beautiful, because the strength of their attractiveness cuts down somewhat on the number of roles they can play. Actor Paul Newman, in midcareer, said that his ability to choose roles was limited by the expectations of the audience: "When I first started working in films, I think the audience allowed me greater leeway to experiment. . . . It's too bad . . . if you know that by your very presence . . . the image that audiences have created for you will work against whatever you bring to the film."[24]

A limited group of fine leading actors might be called "the ordinary people," actors who have everyday kinds of faces. Such actors seldom have the star quality to become fantasy objects or matinee idols, but their special gift of blandness frees them to become actors of great range and flexibility. Chameleonlike, they can blend into any surroundings, and they seem convincing and natural in almost any part they choose to play. Actors such as Gene Hackman, Robert Duvall, Jane Alexander,

FIGURE 10.13 **The Actor as Chameleon**   Without even the aid of special makeup, Ralph Fiennes transforms himself from the brutal SS officer Amon Goeth in *Schindler's List* (top left) into the gentle blind American diplomat and (later) club owner Todd Jackson in *The White Countess* (shown, top right, with Natasha Richardson). Similarly, Oscar-winner Angelina Jolie moves convincingly from her sexy, dangerous spy-wife character in *Mr. and Mrs. Smith* (bottom left, with Brad Pitt) to the austere, distraught mother in *Changeling* (bottom right).

Ben Kingsley, Laura Linney, and Ed Harris have perhaps a wider range of roles open to them simply because they are not stereotypically glamorous Hollywood stars (Figure 10.14). Although they are very attractive in their own ways, an everyman or everywoman quality to their appearance prevents them from becoming typecast. Gene Hackman, who never worries about the fact that he is seldom recognized in public, doesn't really want to be a star: "I like to be thought of as an actor. It could be conceived as some kind of a cop-out, I guess. But I'm afraid that if I start to become a star, I'll lose contact with the normal guys I play best."[25]

Supporting Players

The casting process does not begin and end with the selection of stars for the leading roles. Almost as important as the leading players in any production are the supporting players. Although they may not provide the box-office draw of the big names, the supporting players may be even less interchangeable from movie to movie than the major stars. For example, George Raft was originally chosen to play Sam Spade, the "hero" in *The Maltese Falcon*, and it is fairly easy to imagine him in the role. But could anyone other than Peter Lorre play the idiosyncratic secondary role of Joel Cairo?

FIGURE 10.14 **Ordinary People** The extraordinary talent concealed behind these rather ordinary faces helps give such performers as Laura Linney (right, in *The Savages*) and Ed Harris (left, in *Pollock*) greater acting flexibility than more glamorous stars would have in the same roles.

Supporting players do exactly that—*support* the major roles. The major stars play off them, as friends, adversaries, employers, employees, leaders, or even **foils** (contrasting characters that serve to clearly define the personality of the main character). Supporting players make the stars shine brighter, sharper, and more clearly, providing a sounding board that both helps to bring out all the dimensions of the star's character and makes the most important facets stand out in bold relief.

But supporting players often do much more. Sometimes they create characters that are brilliant in their own right. Although their glow may be less radiant than that of the star players they support, the supporting players often create, usually with (but often without) the star, some of the most memorable moments in film. Consider the contributions of Gene Hackman, Estelle Parsons, Dub Taylor, Gene Wilder, and Michael J. Pollard to *Bonnie and Clyde*; Hattie McDaniel and Butterfly McQueen to *Gone With the Wind*; Thomas Mitchell to *Mr. Smith Goes to Washington* and *Stagecoach*; Sterling Hayden and Slim Pickens to *Dr. Strangelove*; Ben Johnson to *The Last Picture Show*; Strother Martin to *True Grit, Butch Cassidy and the Sundance Kid*, and *Cool Hand Luke*; Thelma Ritter to practically anything; Lucille Benson to *Slaughterhouse Five* and *Silver Streak*; Paul Dooley to *Popeye* (as Wimpy) and to *Breaking Away* (as the father); Scatman Crothers to *Silver Streak, The Shining*, and *One Flew Over the Cuckoo's Nest*; John Goodman to *Everybody's All-American, Sea of Love, Always, Raising Arizona*, and *The Big Lebowski*; Martin Landau to *Tucker, Crimes and Misdemeanors*, and *Ed Wood*; and Steve Buscemi to *Fargo* and many other independent films. These great performances highlight how important a contribution supporting actors make to the overall quality of any film (Figure 10.15).

With the possible exception of Macaulay Culkin, Haley Joel Osment, Dakota Fanning, and Saoirse Ronan, the modern film has not had child stars of the magnitude of Shirley Temple, Judy Garland, Mickey Rooney, or later, Tatum O'Neal and Jodie Foster. Children still make important contributions in supporting roles and often steal the show from the starring actors. Most of these young actors seem to have a gift for projecting the naturalness and sincerity so essential for film acting. Remarkable performances by child actors in films like *Alice Doesn't Live Here*

FIGURE 10.15 **Supporting Players**   By interacting with the stars playing leading roles and each other, supporting players help define the most important aspects of the stars' characters and in the process may create some of the most memorable moments in film. Pictured here are Amy Ryan (as the irresponsible mother in *Gone Baby Gone*) (right) and Hal Holbrook (as a grandfather-figure for Emile Hirsch in *Into the Wild*). (Both of these note-worthy films, incidentally, were directed by famous *actors*—Ben Affleck and Sean Penn, respectively.)

Anymore, Paper Moon, E.T. The Extra-Terrestrial, Sleepless in Seattle, The Black Stallion, Witness, Cinema Paradiso, Forrest Gump, The Piano, Jerry Maguire, The Sixth Sense, Ponette, The Butcher Boy, War of the Worlds (2005), and *Finding Neverland* indicate the quality that can be achieved with careful casting (Figure 10.16).

Special Casting Challenges

An unusual kind of casting problem exists when a film must follow a character throughout many years of his or her life. If only two periods are featured—in youth and in maturity, for example—casting directors can easily hire two different actors. In *Titanic*, the major young character played by Kate Winslet thus becomes the elderly one portrayed by Gloria Stuart. A number of superb illustrations of how well this ploy can work appear in *Once Upon a Time in America*, in which Scott Schutzman seamlessly becomes Robert De Niro, Jennifer Connelly believably transforms into Elizabeth McGovern, and Rusty Jacobs ages smoothly into James Woods. Not quite so credible, for most viewers, is the metamorphosis of the character Toto in *Cinema Paradiso*. From mischievous tot (Salvatore Cascio), Toto becomes a handsome teenager and young man (Mario Leonardi), and finally a suave middle-aged filmmaker (the real-life filmmaker Jacques Perrin). In the film, such characteristics as facial and cranial structure, teeth, hair, and skin tones do not match especially well. In one remarkable case, though, Steven Soderbergh's *The Limey* (1999), the match was perfect: The older actor Terence Stamp actually played himself as a young man via brief scenes from his 1967 film *Poor Cow* that were intercut with those shot in the late '90s. (Ironically, Soderbergh, in his DVD commentary about the film, observes that this was the only "young" performance by Stamp that he could use, for all of the actor's other early characters were "strange" looking or acting, in one way or another.)

Usually, when such movement within a character occurs after maturity, directors elect to use makeup techniques for the job, as Ron Howard did in *A Beautiful Mind*, in which John and Alicia Nash (Russell Crowe and Jennifer Connelly) age from young lovers to old ones. In *Iris*, director Richard Eyre needed to follow the celebrated British novelist Iris Murdoch from her early professional years down

FIGURE 10.16 **The Tender Years** The enormous success of M. Night Shyamalan's *The Sixth Sense* owed much to the convincing performance by the young actor Haley Joel Osment (shown in the top photo with his co-star Bruce Willis). Mark Herman's Nazi-era drama *The Boy in the Striped Pajamas* established an unusual, but convincing, friendship between the young son of a concentration camp commander (Asa Butterfield) and a boy who is a prisoner (Jack Scanlon).

to her death from Alzheimer's disease, so he chose two different accomplished actresses, Kate Winslet (again, in one part of a dual role) and Judi Dench. Although the women never shot scenes at the same time, somehow they nevertheless managed to create, through a little research by each and much intuition, a magnificent symbiosis of character (Figure 10.17). Director Stephen Daldry, in *The Hours*, tried to use this same approach with the character Laura, played by Julianne Moore, who

FIGURE 10.17 **Growing Up**   Great care is usually taken in casting younger versions of characters who will mature during a film's story. This illustration suggests the superb choices of Kate Winslet (left) and Judi Dench (right) to become the early and later incarnations of the English novelist Iris Murdoch in Richard Eyre's *Iris*.

develops from a young wife and mother to an elderly woman. At first, after he had used Moore in all of the earlier, longer scenes, he hired a much older actress for the continuation of the role and photographed her in one later, very dramatic scene. Ultimately, though, after his film had essentially been completed, Daldry watched the results and concluded that only Moore, aged through makeup and prosthetics, could capture the quality and texture of personality that was needed consistently throughout the role. He reshot the later scene to accommodate this casting.

Extras and Small Parts

The casting of extras is another important consideration, for extras are often called on to perform some very important scenes. If they are not reacting properly, if their faces do not show what is being called for by the scene they are in, the scene may be ruined. Extras are, in a sense, actors in their own right, not just background for the story. For that reason studios hire casting directors to hire extras to fit the film's requirements. Often this job is done on the actual shooting location. The extras casting director goes to the location in advance of the crew and spends a great deal of time finding the right faces, backgrounds, and personalities to fit the story.

Jody Hummer, location casting director for *The River* (1984), starring Mel Gibson, needed two different sets of extras for that film. One group consisted of farmers, who were to assemble at an auction of a farm that had to be sold. Many of the farm extras in the scene had been through such an auction themselves and responded with great sadness and even tears, and their sincerity showed on the screen. A second set of extras was needed to play a group of drifters hired by the film's villain to break down the levee protecting the riverside farms from flooding. For the drifters, Hummer assembled a group of rough-looking unemployed men who appeared desperate enough to take any kind of a job.

In the casting of extras, each face must be right, matching our preconceived notions of what a farmer looks like, what a truck driver looks like, or what a drifter looks like. Each extra should fit the type but look different from every other individual in the group. An impression is thus created of a representative sampling of the particular group (Figure 10.18).

FIGURE 10.18 **Extras**   In *The Majestic,* director Frank Darabont selected a whole town full of distinctive-looking extras to back up his central actors, Jim Carrey, Martin Landau, Laurie Holden, and David Ogden Stiers.

Extras are not always cast only on the basis of appearance, because their part may require a special skill. Even in the brief moment they are on-screen, they must do their assigned tasks with naturalness, a lack of self-consciousness, and a competence that shows. Bob Fosse demanded absolute realism in his films. If a scene called for waiters to serve drinks, instead of actors he used real waiters because they knew the proper way to put a glass down on a table. For early scenes in *Up in the Air,* a George Clooney drama about firing workers, veteran casting director Mindy Marin helped director Jason Reitman locate, and interview on camera, vulnerable men and women who had recently lost their jobs in real life.

Movies are actually a series of brief moments woven into a whole by the editing process. Great movies are therefore movies that achieve as many great moments as possible, and those great moments in many cases are created not by the stars but by the supporting players or the extras. If we are so dazzled by the performance of the stars that we fail to be fully conscious of the rich moments provided by the supporting actors, bit players, and extras, we miss an important part of the film experience. In Zeffirelli's *The Taming of the Shrew,* for example, the screen is packed with fascinating faces, from the major supporting roles to the briefest appearance by an extra. In a well-cast movie there are no weak links. Each member of the cast contributes significantly to the film, whether he or she is on the screen for five seconds, five minutes, or two hours.

ACTORS AS CREATIVE CONTRIBUTORS

Alfred Hitchcock supposedly felt that actors should be treated like cattle, and he came to production with a complete, detailed plan for every shot. Other directors, like Elia Kazan, came to view actors as collaborators in the development of a film.

FIGURE 10.19 **Crediting the Actor**   Director Elia Kazan credits Marlon Brando for directing himself in this memorable scene (with Rod Steiger) from *On the Waterfront*.

This attitude is best illustrated in Kazan's retelling of the events leading to the famous "I coulda been a contender" scene in *On the Waterfront* (Figure 10.19):

> [T]he extraordinary element in that scene and in the whole picture was Brando, and what was extraordinary about his performance, I feel, is the contrast of the tough-guy front and the extreme delicacy and gentle cast of his behavior. What other actor, when his brother draws a pistol to force him to do something shameful, would put his hand on the gun and push it away with the gentleness of a caress? Who else could read "Oh, Charlie!" in a tone of reproach that is so loving and so melancholy and suggests that terrific depth of pain? I didn't direct that; Marlon showed me, as he often did, how the scene should be performed. I could never have told him how to do that scene as well as he did it.[26]

The modern trend has been more and more toward allowing actors a significant role in determining the nature of their characters and giving them a great deal of input into the total creative process. After directing Susan Sarandon in *The Tempest*, director Paul Mazursky paid tribute to her value as a collaborator: "In working on *Tempest*, Susan helped make the character more dimensional than the one I wrote. She had a lot of good criticisms, and I did some rewriting because of her input. . . . Susan would often say to me, 'There's something wrong here; I really think this is a cliché.' She was usually right." Sarandon says that she enjoys a lively give-and-take with her directors, preferring to act in films where "whatever comes into your head you can express. I don't think I've ever worked on a film where I haven't also worked on rewriting the script—except maybe *The Front Page*. Billy Wilder has a very set idea of a film, and everything has to be done to the letter, to the comma."[27]

Dustin Hoffman, who is credited by director Mike Nichols with making several significant contributions to his character in *The Graduate*, believes that the relationship between the actor and the director should be "a real partnership, not the classically imagined situation where a supposedly 'solid, objective' director simply 'handles' a 'neurotic, subjective' actor." As Hoffman explains it, "I think that some directors are closed minded about what an actor can contribute. . . . An actor is as capable of considering 'the whole' as the director, and often does. Sure we care about our own parts, but we have a responsibility to the entire film also, and I don't think many of us ignore that responsibility."[28]

Hoffman's problems with director Sydney Pollack on *Tootsie* have been well documented. In his struggle with Pollack over who had final control over *Tootsie*, Hoffman, who conceived the idea for the film and wanted to produce it, finally worked out a bargain with the director, giving Pollack the ultimate power of **final cut** (final edited version). But Hoffman maintained script and cast approval as well as the right to go into the cutting room, watch the film being edited, and disagree and show alternatives before the final cut was made.

Actress Emma Thompson (who won an Academy Award for her acting in *Howards End*) wrote the Oscar-winning screenplay for the film adaptation of *Sense and Sensibility*, but this fact did not make her major performance in the Ang Lee–directed movie any easier, apparently. In the production diary that she published along with her screenplay, Thompson gives her reader an excellent sense of the day-to-day pressures with which a working actor (even one who happens to be a star) must cope. Near the end of the shoot, when she is called upon to do a demanding emotional scene, Thompson records her intimate observations about the whole process:

> Interesting and difficult scene this—getting the level of Elinor's [her character's] explosion just right. The level of control. I rely entirely on Ang—I can't quite get outside it. Pleased so far and hope I can hit it again this p.m. Barely able to eat, stomach knotted. We shoot largely out of sequence, of course—so I've already done the loss of control in the last scene, which I tried to make as involuntary as possible. A case of the diaphragm taking over. I remembered going to the bank shortly after my father died to try and sort through his papers. I was feeling perfectly calm and sat in the office talking to the manager when suddenly my diaphragm lurched into action and I was unable to do anything but sob helplessly. . . . It's never happened before or since and was as though the emotion was quite disconnected from actual thought. That was what I wanted to duplicate for the scene when Elinor finds out Edward [the man she loves] isn't married [as she had thought. . . . In the event I play it several different ways so that during the editing Ang has plenty of choices. He won't know what the right note is until he sees it in context. This is the real bugger with film—sometimes you cannot tell where to pitch an emotion and the only safe course is to offer up as many alternatives as possible.[29]

Perhaps the most extreme example of an actor's influence on the overall direction of a film is that of Jon Voight's creative input in *Coming Home*. After two days of shooting, director Hal Ashby, recognizing the impact of Voight's interpretation of his character, threw out the first script. From that point on, the script was written as they shot. Ashby described the process: "I would talk with the actors the night before. . . . And all was guided by Jon's character—I threw out a screenplay because of where he was. That man received incredible amounts of resistance—down to everybody, including Jane Fonda, wanting him to play it more macho."

And all of this creative input came from the actor for whom Ashby had to fight United Artists to cast. When told by Ashby that he wanted Voight in the cast, producer Mike Medavoy simply said, "No way. Absolutely. The man has no sex appeal." He then proceeded with "a whole big line of reasons not to cast Jon Voight in the role."[30] Voight won an Academy Award for the part.

SUBJECTIVE RESPONSES TO ACTORS

Our response to actors is very subjective and personal, and often our views are diametrically opposed to those of our friends or our favorite critics. Critics themselves disagree violently in their personal response to acting performances. Meryl Streep, an actor to whom people respond in various ways, summarized this problem herself: "Once a year I come out in a film and go around and listen to people or read people who tell me what they think of me. It's a revelation. I have too many mannerisms . . . or not enough mannerisms . . . to become a real movie star. Someone says I don't put enough of my own character into my roles."[31]

Those who think she has too many mannerisms apparently see them as acting gimmicks, techniques that make the viewer aware she is acting. Others accept the mannerisms (her nervous tics or twitches) as perfectly natural for the character and accept her as the perfect embodiment of the personality of the character she is playing. Whether Streep's acting style works or not may be a matter of casting. Her mannerisms seemed to fit perfectly in *Still of the Night*, where the audience suspected her all along of being a murderer. The nervous mannerisms made us suspect that the *character* she played was acting as she tried to deceive Roy Scheider (playing a psychiatrist). But *Time* critic Richard Schickel objected to her technique in *Silkwood*: "She is an actress of calculated effects, which work well when she is playing self-consciously intelligent women. But interpreting a character who . . . shows her contempt for authority by flashing a bare breast at its representative, she seems at once forced and pulled back."[32]

Although some actors seem to create a wide range of responses, most stars project some essential image, some profound quality of their personality that comes through on the screen in every role they play (Figure 10.20). These are basic qualities that cannot be changed, and intelligent casting will rarely ask this kind of star to move outside his or her essential being. Director Sidney Lumet made this point in discussing the special essence of Montgomery Clift (Figure 10.21):

> One of the things that was so extraordinary about Monty Clift as an actor—and he was certainly one of the great ones—was that he had a quality that had nothing to do with his talent as an actor. He had a vulnerability, an openness, an almost masochistic receptivity to pain that was terrifying. . . . When you cast Monty, you would have been foolish to put him in something where that quality wasn't what you were going for.[33]

FIGURE 10.20 **What Stars Project** Most movie stars continually project essential qualities of their personalities on the screen. This axiom seems to apply even in films that may toy with altering those celebrated traits. Case in point: Denzel Washington in *American Gangster*.

FIGURE 10.21 **Special Qualities** Montgomery Clift, shown here in John Huston's *The Misfits* (with Marilyn Monroe), projected an unusual sense of vulnerability and "an almost masochistic receptivity to pain that was terrifying."

ANALYZING ACTING

1. Which actors did you feel were correctly cast in their parts? Which actors were not cast wisely? Why?
2. How well were the physical characteristics, facial features, and voice qualities of the actors suited to the characters they were attempting to portray?
3. If a performance was unconvincing, was it unconvincing because the actor was miscast, or did he or she simply deliver an incompetent performance?
   a. If faulty casting seems to be the problem, what actor would you choose for the part if you were directing the film?

b. If the actor proved incompetent in the part, what were the primary reasons for his or her failure?

4. What kind of acting is required of the actors in the starring roles—action acting or dramatic acting? Are the actors well suited to the type of acting demanded by the roles they play? If not, why not? Where are their weaknesses or limitations most evident? If they are well suited, in what scenes is their special type of acting skill most apparent?

5. Drawing on your knowledge of their past performances, classify the actors in the major roles as impersonators, interpreters, or personalities.

6. Consider the following questions with respect to each of the starring actors:
   a. Does the actor seem to depend more on the charm of his or her own personality, or does he or she attempt to become the character?
   b. Is the actor consistently believable in the portrayal of the character, or does he or she occasionally fall out of character?
   c. If the actor seems unnatural in the part, is it because he or she tends to be overdramatic or wooden and mechanical? Is this unnaturalness more apparent in the way the actor delivers the lines or in the actor's physical actions?

7. In which specific scenes is the acting especially effective or ineffective? Why?

8. In which scenes are the actors' facial expressions used in reaction shots? What reaction shots are particularly effective?

9. How strong is the cast of supporting actors, and what does each contribute to the film? How does each help bring out different aspects of the star's personality? Do the supporting players create memorable moments or steal the show in spots? If so, where in the film do such moments occur?

10. What contributions do the small parts and extras make to the film? Are the faces and bodies well chosen to fit our preconceived notions of what they should look like? Are their "working tasks," if any, performed with confidence and naturalness?

WATCHING FOR ACTING

1. Watch the "Scar Competition" scene from *Jaws* [1:26:03 to 1:32:53]. What do the following factors contribute to the power of this sequence: character interaction, voice qualities, reaction shots, camerawork, and lighting?

2. Watch the "Group Captain Mandrake Tries to Call the White House" sequence from *Dr. Strangelove* [1:08:48 to 1:12:32]. Identify specific factors in the performances of Peter Sellers and Keenan Wynn that contribute to the effectiveness and believability of this scene.

3. Watch the "Ma Joad Burns the Souvenirs" sequence from *The Grapes of Wrath* [0:29:14 to 0:31:08]. Carefully note each item Ma Joad examines; then watch her reaction and describe what her face reveals about her feelings connected with that item. Turn the sound off and watch the sequence again. Is the sequence more powerful with or without the music? Why? What role does the lighting play in this sequence?

An adaptation of a novella by Jerzy Kosinski (who wrote the screenplay), the darkly satiric drama *Being There* (1979) was the undervalued American director Hal Ashby's last significant work. And it also contains the final substantive movie performance by a superb actor, Peter Sellers (of *Pink Panther* and *Dr. Strangelove* fame).

Scrutinize the 27-minute sequence that commences this film. Begin by following the character Chance's awakening with the credits and stop only after he has left the safe seclusion of his urban (Washington, D.C.) refuge (Chapters 1–6 of the DVD version). In other words, watch the film from its introduction of softly played classical music until just past its use of the majestic (and loud) strains of Richard Strauss's "Also Sprach Zarathustra," music familiar to viewers of *2001: A Space Odyssey* as the apt theme for entering any "brave new world."

Between these musical cues, look for on-screen evidence that a master actor is at work. Contemporary reviewers of the film alternately praised Sellers for the nuances of his portrayal of the "special person" Chance and condemned him for giving what they called a "one-note performance." As an individual viewer, what value do you find in Sellers's acting in this "mini-movie"?

In interviews, Sellers spoke of modeling his character's voice on memories of having heard the speaking tones of comedian Stan Laurel (of the Laurel and Hardy film comedy team). Does this observation taint the performance for you, or heighten it?

Jim Jarmusch is surely the most *independent* film writer-director actually working in American film today. Although he has created such fascinating, critically-acclaimed, low-budget features as *Stranger Than Paradise*, *Down by Law*, *Night on Earth*, *Ghost Dog*, *Dead Man*, and *Broken Flowers*, he has steadfastly refused to accept domestic studio funding, and he continues to own completely the rights to all his films. Sporadically, during a more than seventeen-year period when he was producing his full-length works, he also made *Coffee and Cigarettes* (2004), which might, in some ways, be considered an extended "home movie," starring a host of his famous friends and colleagues, including Bill Murray, Roberto Benigni, Steve Buscemi, Alfred Molina, Steve Coogan, Meg and Jack White, and Iggy Pop. The results of this experimentation in black and white are eleven brief dialogues that, by most accounts, are wildly uneven in

their accomplishments. But one sequence that constitutes a sparkling demonstration of the nuanced art of acting presents Cate Blanchett in two roles, "the actress herself" and her "cousin Shelley," who are clearly very dissimilar individuals and appear, through a polished bit of camera trickery, simultaneously on screen throughout the mini-movie's 11-minute running time.

Check out the double dose of Blanchett on the *Coffee and Cigarettes* DVD. First, observe how smoothly the whole unified piece works. Then, examine more closely the skillful manner in which this talented actress differentiates between her own amusing version of her famous-actress self (perhaps uneasy with fame and wealth) and her poor-relation, slightly-flaky, passive-aggressive, aspiring "industrial-rock" singer cousin. Consider, of course, the contrasts in clothing, hair color and style, and makeup that Jarmusch manipulates. But look at and listen to, even more carefully, the delightful choices that Cate Blanchett has made in conveying sensibility and thought via body posture, stance, and movement, and also her control of voice timbre, diction, and accent. The actress's "natural" calculation here may be just as impressive, if not so sustained, as in her Oscar-winning channeling of "Katharine Hepburn" in Martin Scorsese's *The Aviator*.

DVD FILMMAKING EXTRAS

The Graduate (Special Edition):
  The extensive interview "One on One with Dustin Hoffman" on this DVD presents, from a unique angle, the art of casting and acting in classic film comedy.

Carrie (Special Edition):
  Here, a forty-five-minute documentary, "Acting Carrie," provides reflections of both a personal and professional nature from stars Sissy Spacek, Amy Irving, Betty Buckley, and others (but not John Travolta), including director Brian De Palma (who also presents on the disc a lengthy documentary called "Visualizing Carrie").

Shadow of the Vampire:
  Interviews with actor Willem Dafoe and director E. Elias Merhige reveal the secrets of bringing both Max Schreck and his faux Dracula, Count Orlock, back to life.

Unfaithful:

"The Charlie Rose Show" hosted director Adrian Lyne and actors Richard Gere and Diane Lane in a discussion of this film's dramatic effects, and that program is included on this DVD. The disc also contains a telling conversation with veteran film editor Anne V. Coats, who has worked to present the performances of many actors in the best possible light, including those by Peter O'Toole in *Lawrence of Arabia*, Anthony Hopkins and John Hurt in *The Elephant Man*, and Julia Roberts in *Erin Brockovich*.

Dr. Strangelove:

During the early 1960s, when Stanley Kubrick made this film, studios often provided split-screen interviews (one side of the frame photographed, the other blanked out) with the stars of their pictures. Local television stations could then insert their own questioners, who worked from the original script. It is fascinating to see both George C. Scott and Peter Sellers play that game here. But the greatest incentive to watch this footage is to observe—and hear—Sellers's brilliant demonstration of numerous British accents, one after another, without even taking a deep breath.

Love and Basketball:

This DVD reproduces audition tapes of scenes from the script by actors Omar Epps and Sanaa Lathan. Viewers are able to compare the acting, early and late, by toggling between these tests and the corresponding finished scenes in director Gina Prince-Blythewood's film.

Being John Malkovich (Special Edition):

Most of the extras on this DVD version of Spike Jonze's picture are tongue-in-cheek (or tongue-*out*-of-cheek, in the case of the director's brief, in-car interview feature, which seems to open seriously enough, but ends with his having to exit the vehicle rather swiftly, head first . . .). Nevertheless, like the film itself, "An Intimate Portrait of the Art of Puppeteering" may begin to make an eloquent case for accepting marionettes as authentic actors. (Perhaps Alfred Hitchcock would have approved the notion, with no strings attached.)

Star Wars, Episode II: Attack of the Clones:

An "all-new, full-length documentary," "From Puppets to Pixels," is a major part of the feature package on this DVD. In it, George Lucas and his filmmakers reveal the intricate process through which some of his series characters have evolved from Muppets to multi-dimensional "created actors." Beyond a digital Yoda, of course, stands a superiorly digitized Gollum (in *Lord of the Rings: The Two Towers*) amid talk of a Best Supporting Actor nomination—and in *The Hulk* (2003), director Ang Lee insisted upon "directing" his green CGI creature as if it were indeed a human actor.

Garbo: The Signature Collection:

This boxed set of nine DVDs, which include all of Greta Garbo's major sound films (e.g., *Anna Christie, Ninotchka, Anna Karenina*) and many of her silents, also presents *Garbo*, the original Turner Classic Movies documentary, narrated by Julie Christie, that offers "analysis and reminiscences" by friends and colleagues who knew her best.

The Chaplin Collection, Volumes I and II:
   A treasure trove of film acting, both in its silent and talking forms, Warner Brothers' two boxed sets give us the very best of the little tramp and beyond—in the very best sharp, remastered form. Also in the second package, and especially noteworthy, is a disc containing the entertaining and superbly helpful documentary produced, written, and directed by the critic Richard Schickel called "Charlie: The Life and Art of Charles Chaplin."

FILMS FOR STUDY

Acting

Adam's Rib (1949)
The African Queen (1951)
Another Year (2010)
Becket (1964)
Brokeback Mountain (2005)
Capote (2005)
Carlos (2010)
Crash (2004)
Crazy Heart (2009)
Driving Miss Daisy (1989)
Eat Pray Love (2010)
The Elephant Man (1980)
Fargo (1996)
Get Low (2009)
The Grapes of Wrath (1940)
The Great Santini (1979)
Inglourious Basterds (2009)
The Kids Are All Right (2010)
The King's Speech (2010)
La Strada (1954)
La Vie en Rose (2007)
The Messenger (2009)
Midnight Cowboy (1969)
Million Dollar Baby (2004)
Modern Times (1936)
My Left Foot (1989)
On the Waterfront (1954)
The Pianist (2002)
The Piano (1993)
Precious (2009)
The Queen (2006)
Raging Bull (1980)
Rain Man (1988)
The Reader (2008)
RED (2010)
Schindler's List (1993)
Sense and Sensibility (1995)
The Social Network (2010)
A Streetcar Named Desire (1951)
Taxi Driver (1976)
There Will Be Blood (2007)
The Trip to Bountiful (1985)
Winter's Bone (2010)

Silent Film Acting

The Birth of a Nation (1915)
Broken Blossoms (1919)
City Lights (1931)
The General (1926)
The Gold Rush (1925)
The Great Train Robbery (1903)
Greed (1924)
Intolerance (1916)
The Last Laugh (1924—Germany)
Modern Times (1936)
Napoleon (1927—France)
Nosferatu (1922—Germany)
Potemkin (1925—Russia)
Safety Last (1923)
Sherlock, Jr. (1924)
Sunrise (1927)
The Temptress (1926)

Shutter Island

Actually, everything a director puts up on the screen is revelatory. Don't you really know all about John Ford from his films? Or Hitchcock, or Howard Hawks? If I reveal a character on the screen, I am necessarily also revealing myself. . . . I think I have an idea of what my work is about, but I'm not interested in articulating it in words.

—SIDNEY LUMET, DIRECTOR

In his book of interviews, *Who the Devil Made It*, Peter Bogdanovich, accomplished filmmaker (*The Last Picture Show*, *What's Up, Doc?*, *Paper Moon*, *Mask*) and writer about films and their creators, tries at the outset to define the role of the movie director:

> In 1915, when President Wilson was asked for his reaction to [film pioneer D. W.] Griffith's new picture—*The Birth of a Nation* was the first film ever shown at the White House—the president is recorded as having said: "It is like writing history with lightning." This was a particularly apt description for more than one reason: lightning not only has enormous powers, it is accidental. When I once repeated to [Orson] Welles Mr. [John] Ford's comment about "most of the good things in pictures" happening "by accident," Orson leapt on it right away. "Yes!" he said. "You could almost say that a director is a man who *presides* over accidents."[1]

Welles's "almost" is very important here, because he was well aware that every director needs as many good helpers as he or she can possibly manage in taking full advantage of these "accidents." Director Sidney Lumet, in *Making Movies*, provides an illustration of this wisdom:

> On my second picture, *Stage Struck*, a scene between Henry Fonda and Christopher Plummer took place in Central Park. . . . During lunch, snow started to fall. When we came back, the park was already covered in white. The snow was so beautiful, I wanted to redo the whole scene. Franz Planner, the cameraman, said it was impossible because we'd be out of light by four o'clock. I quickly restaged the scene, giving Plummer a new entrance so that I could see the snow-covered park; then I placed them on a bench, shot a master and two close-ups. The lens was wide open by the last take, but we got it all. Because the actors were prepared, because the crew knew what it was doing, we just swung with the weather and wound up with a better scene. Preparation allows the "lucky accident" that we're always hoping for to happen.[2]

A motion picture, then, is always a cooperative effort, a joint creative interaction of many artists and technicians working on diverse elements, all of which contribute to the finished film. Because of the technical and physical complexity of filmmaking and the large number of people involved, it might seem misleading to talk of any single individual's style. The director, however, generally serves as the unifying force and makes the majority of the creative decisions, so it is perhaps proper to equate the film's style with the director's style.

The actual amount of control that directors have varies widely. At one extreme is the director who functions primarily as a hireling of a big studio. The studio buys a story or an idea, hires a scriptwriter to translate it into film language, and then assigns the script to a director who more or less mechanically supervises the shooting of the film. At the other extreme is the concept of the director as *auteur*, or author, of the film. An ***auteur*** is a complete filmmaker. He or she conceives the idea for the story, writes the script or the screenplay, and then carefully supervises every step in the filmmaking process, from selecting the cast and finding a suitable setting down to editing the final cut. The Swedish director Ingmar Bergman and the American director Orson Welles are viewed by many as the ultimate *auteurs*. Among current directors, Quentin Tarantino and Christopher Nolan (*Inception*) might have the qualifications (Figure 11.1).

FIGURE 11.1 A Contemporary American *Auteur*? Filmmaker Quentin Tarantino has been a multiple-threat operator in late twentieth- and early twenty-first-century American film. Celebrated for beginning his public movie life as an amazingly knowledgeable video store clerk, he has produced a relatively small body of feature-film work so far (including *Reservoir Dogs, Pulp Fiction, Jackie Brown,* and *Inglourious Basterds*), but his movies have brilliantly showcased him as writer, actor, director, producer, and even career guru (notably for John Travolta in that popular actor's later career). In this production still, the director is rehearsing his actors for a scene in *Kill Bill* (a long film that was ultimately released in two parts, *Volumes I* and *II*).

Most directors fall into the gray area between those two extremes, for the degree of studio involvement or control and the director's dependence on other creative personalities can vary considerably. But regardless of the actual degree of control, the director has the greatest opportunity to impart a personal artistic vision, philosophy, technique, and attitude into the film as a whole, thereby dictating or determining its style. In analyzing or evaluating a director's style, therefore, we assume that the director has exercised aesthetic control over at least the majority of complex elements that make up a finished film (Figure 11.2).

A meaningful assessment of any director's style requires the careful study of at least three of his or her films, concentrating on those special qualities of the work

FIGURE 11.2 **The Price of Perfection Without Words**   In this scene from *City Lights* (1931) (left), a blind flower girl believes the tramp to be a tycoon, sells him a flower for his last coin, and keeps the change. Director/actor Charlie Chaplin had a problem figuring out why the blind girl would assume the tramp was a rich man. He finally solved it by having the tramp wander through heavy traffic and then walk onto the sidewalk through the back doors of a limousine parked at the curb. The blind girl, hearing the heavy door close, assumed that the "tycoon" was getting out of an expensive car. To achieve the exact effect he wanted, Chaplin shot 342 takes of this scene. In contrast to Chaplin, Buster Keaton, another great silent comedy creator, seemed to have minimal interest in receiving both acting and directing credits. Although his name appears as director on such great works as *The General* (1927) (right photo) and *Sherlock, Jr.* (1924), many films that he essentially directed (including *Steamboat Bill, Jr.*, and *The Cameraman*, both 1928) were actually attributed to others.

that set the individual apart from all other directors. The study of six or more films may be necessary to characterize the style of directors who go through a long evolutionary period of stylistic experimentation before they arrive at anything consistent enough to be called a style.

THE CONCEPT OF STYLE

A director's style is the manner in which the director's personality is expressed through the language of the medium. A director's style is reflected in almost every decision the director makes. Every element or combination of elements may reveal a unique creative personality that shapes, molds, and filters the film through intellect, sensibility, and imagination. If we assume that all directors strive to communicate clearly with the audience, then we can further assume that directors want to manipulate our responses to correspond with their own, so that we can share that vision. Thus, almost everything directors do in making a film is a part of their style, because in almost every decision they are in some subtle way interpreting or commenting on the action, revealing their own attitudes, and injecting their own personality indelibly into the film.

Before examining the separate elements that reveal style in film, it is worthwhile to make some observations about the film as a whole. In this general analysis, we might consider whether the film is

intellectual and rational	*or*	emotional and sensual
calm and quiet	*or*	fast-paced and exciting
polished and smooth	*or*	rough and crude-cut
cool and objective	*or*	warm and subjective
ordinary and trite	*or*	fresh and original
tightly structured, direct, and concise	*or*	loosely structured and rambling
truthful and realistic	*or*	romantic and idealized
simple and straightforward	*or*	complex and indirect
grave, serious, tragic, and heavy	*or*	light, comical, and humorous
restrained and understated	*or*	exaggerated
optimistic and hopeful	*or*	bitter and cynical
logical and orderly	*or*	irrational and chaotic

An accurate assessment of these values is a good first step toward an analysis of the director's style. A complete analysis must examine his or her treatment of subject matter, cinematography, editing, and other individual film elements.

SUBJECT MATTER

Perhaps no other element reveals more about a director's style than the choice of subject matter. For a director who is truly an *auteur*—a person who conceives the idea for a film and then writes the script or supervises the writing to conform to his or her own vision—the subject is an essential aspect of style. Directors who are not *auteurs* but are free to choose the stories they want to film also express their style by their choice of subject matter. Even studio assignments may reveal a director's style if they call for the director to make a film that is similar to films that he or she has already made.

An examination of subject matter might begin with a search for common themes running through all the films under study. One director may be concerned primarily with social problems, another with men's and women's relationship to God, and yet another with the struggle between good and evil. Directors' choices of subject matter may be related to their tendency to create similar emotional effects or moods in everything they do. Alfred Hitchcock, for example, is clearly identified with the terror/suspense film, in which the mood becomes a kind of theme (Figure 11.3). Some directors specialize in a genre such as the western, historical pageant, or comedy. Others focus upon adapting novels or plays to film.

A director's personal background may be a significant influence on the kind of stories he or she is drawn to. For example, Martin Scorsese, who grew up in New York City, often uses his old neighborhood and his old haunts as his setting, and seems to focus on types of characters he has known. Scorsese is a very personal

FIGURE 11.3 **Master of Suspense**   Because he supposedly felt that actors should be treated like cattle and came to production with a detailed plan for every shot, Alfred Hitchcock gained a reputation as an *auteur* director. Hitchcock, however, did not write the screenplays for the major American films he directed—although he worked closely with his writers. Traditionally, he made cameo appearances in his films, including these four: *North by Northwest*, *Strangers on a Train*, *Notorious*, and *Family Plot* (clockwise, from top right).

filmmaker. Steven Spielberg (Figure 11.4), in contrast, was a child of the suburbs and is more inclined toward fantasy bigger-than-life stories and characters. Spielberg describes the different subjects that appeal to him and Scorsese: "I could never make *Raging Bull*. I don't think Marty could have made, let's say, *Close Encounters*, in the same way.... Marty likes primal life, he likes the primal scream.... The primal scream scares the stuff out of me...."[3]

That both directors are capable of tackling new subject matter, however, is clearly evidenced by some of their later achievements: Spielberg's brutally realistic docudrama on Jewish persecution during World War II, *Schindler's List*, and Scorsese's richly textured study of the manners and mores of upper-crust New York society in the 1870s, *The Age of Innocence*—not to mention his exploration of the mystical traditions and tragic history of Tibet in *Kundun*.

FIGURE 11.4 **Tackling New Subjects** Steven Spielberg, known for his fantasy films, took a dramatic turn in choice of subject matter with *Schindler's List,* and, later, he continued his journey into realism by directing *Saving Private Ryan*, starring Tom Hanks (shown here). Between these two films, he directed Morgan Freeman and Anthony Hopkins in *Amistad*, about the consequences of a slave ship revolt. In 2005, Spielberg examined politics and morality in *Munich*.

The types of conflicts that directors choose to deal with constitute an important thematic thread. Some directors lean toward a serious examination of subtle philosophical problems concerning the complexities of human nature, the universe, or God. Others favor simple stories of ordinary people facing the ordinary problems of life. Still others prefer to treat physical conflict such as occurs in action/adventure films.

The subjects that a director chooses may also show some consistency with respect to the concepts of time and space. Some directors prefer a story in which the action takes place in a very short time period—a week or less. Others prefer historical panoramas spanning a century or more. Spatial concepts may be equally diverse. Some directors specialize in epic films, with casts of thousands and a broad, sweeping landscape as a canvas. Others restrict themselves to a limited physical setting and keep the number of actors in the cast to a bare minimum. Screenwriters like to know who is going to direct the script they are writing, so they can tailor the script to fit that particular director's strengths and limitations. As William Goldman tells it, "If you were writing an Alfred Hitchcock picture, you knew you didn't want to give him scope. He couldn't shoot scope. And if you have David Lean, you don't give David Lean a scene in a room. You give David Lean scope and he can *shoot* it. . . . Directors *do* different things well."[4]

In some cases, study of a director's typical subject matter may reveal a unified worldview, a consistent philosophical statement on the nature of man and the universe. Even the use of **irony**—the juxtaposition of opposites—can take on philosophical implications reflecting the director's worldview if he or she uses it enough (see the section on irony in Chapter 3). Most directors, however, aren't consciously striving to express or develop a unified worldview, possibly because doing so would stifle their creativity. But that doesn't mean that philosophical patterns don't emerge, as Sydney Pollack (*Tootsie, Out of Africa*) explains:

> As I've gotten older and done more films, it's something I read more and more often about my own work. I would constantly read articles . . . that would say, for instance, all my films are "circular." And I kept saying, what the hell is "circular"? Then I started looking at my films, and, by God, they are circular. But what does that mean? I don't know what it means. . . . I'm fascinated to hear about this. But this is not something I set out consciously to do.
>
> When you direct a picture you may be concentrating on a particular task at hand, which taps all sorts of areas in your unconscious that you're not aware of. Those areas seep into the work itself. . . . Not in what they say, but in the actual handling of the actors—how do you place them, are they standing or seated, what's the lighting? Is it all in one shot and does the camera keep moving around them? Is it staccato and in cuts? Is the camera focusing only on eyes, or is it details of hands and skin? Now, in the doing of that, you take a kind of lie-detector test; you can't lie, something of who you are and what you believe in gets in there.[5]

CINEMATOGRAPHY

The cinematographer oversees the camerawork and plays a significant role in the conceptualizing and treatment of the visual elements. But how can we accurately assess the cinematographer's contribution to the director's style? We weren't present on the set, and we lack important inside information. We cannot really know how much of the visual style of *The Birth of a Nation* was the work of Billy Bitzer, how much imagery in *Citizen Kane* was conceived by Gregg Toland, or how much of *The Seventh Seal* resulted from the creative vision of Gunnar Fischer. Because directors usually choose the cinematographer they want, we can assume their selections are based on a compatibility of visual philosophies, and for simplicity's sake we usually attribute the film's visual style to the director (Figure 11.5).

In analyzing visual style, we must first consider the composition. Some directors use composition formally and dramatically; others prefer an informal or low-key effect. One director may favor a certain type of arrangement of people and objects in the frame; another may place special emphasis on one particular type of camera angle. Important differences may also be noted in "philosophies of camera." For example, some directors stress the **objective camera** (a camera that views the action as a remote spectator); others lean toward the **subjective camera** (a camera that views the scene from the visual or emotional point of view of a participant). Other marks of cinematic style include the consistent use of certain devices—such as unusual camera angles, slow or fast motion, colored or light-diffusing filters, or distorting lenses—to interpret the visual scene in some unique way.

FIGURE 11.5 **The Ultimate** *Auteurs* Swedish director Ingmar Bergman, shown here (top left) with his frequent cinematographer Sven Nykvist (in a checkered cap), is generally considered the ultimate *auteur* because his work over the years has projected a strong personal artistic vision. Orson Welles (in the top right photo, seen shooting *Citizen Kane* with his cameraman Gregg Toland, who is sitting at right) sometimes played this role in America. In contemporary filmmaking, the director who gives each of his films the distinctly proprietary label "A Spike Lee Joint," uses great originality and control in creating his works. At left, director/writer/producer/actor Lee appears with cinematographer Ernst Dickerson on the set of *Do the Right Thing*.

Lighting also expresses directorial style. Some directors prefer to work with low-key lighting, which creates stark contrasts between light and dark areas and leaves large portions of the set in shadow. Others favor high-key lighting, which is more even and contains many subtle shades of gray. Even the character of the lighting contributes greatly to the director's visual style, because a director may favor harsh, balanced, or diffused lighting throughout a series of films.

Likewise, treatment of color may be an element of cinematic style. Some directors use sharp, clear images dominated by bright, highly contrasting hues. Some favor soft, muted, pastel shades and dim or even blurred tones.

Camera movement reveals a director's style, as well. The possibilities range from favoring the static camera, which moves as little as possible, to favoring the fixed camera, which creates a sense of movement through panning and tilting. Another choice is the "poetic" mobile camera, whose slow, liquid, almost floating movements are achieved by mounting the camera on a dolly or boom crane. And although one director may favor the freedom and spontaneity of the jerky hand-held camera, another may make great use of the zoom lens to simulate movement into and out of the frame. The type of camera movement that directors favor is an important stylistic element, for it affects a film's sense of pace and rhythm and greatly affects the film's overall impression.

Some directors are especially concerned with achieving three-dimensionality in their images, and the techniques they use to achieve this effect become an integral part of their visual style.

EDITING

Editing is an important stylistic element because it affects the overall rhythm or pace of the film. The most obvious element of editorial style is the length of the average shot in the film. Generally the longer the time between editorial cuts, the slower is the pace of the film.

Editorial cuts that make time/place transitions may take on a unique rhythmic character. One director may favor a soft, fluid transition, such as a slow dissolve, where another would simply cut immediately from one sequence to the next, relying on the soundtrack or the visual context to make the transition clear. David Lynch (*The Straight Story*, *Mulholland Dr.*) says that he seeks a subtle balance between slow and fast pacing: "[A] certain slowness contrasted with something fast is very important. It's like music. If music was all just fast it would be a bummer. But symphonies and stuff are built on slow and fast and high and low, and it thrills your soul. And film is the same way."[6]

When editorial juxtapositions are used creatively, the director's style may be seen in the relationships between shots. Directors may stress an intellectual relationship between two shots by using ironic or metaphorical juxtapositions, or they may emphasize visual continuity by cutting to similar forms, colors, or textures. They might choose to emphasize aural relationships by linking two shots solely through the soundtrack or the musical score.

Other special tricks of editing, such as the use of parallel cutting, fragmented flash cutting, and dialogue overlaps, are indicators of style, too. Editing may also be characterized by whether it calls attention to itself. One director may lean toward editing that is clever, self-conscious, and tricky, whereas another may favor editing that is smooth, natural, and unobtrusive. Montages and the nature of the images used also help to characterize editing style.

SETTING AND SET DESIGN

Closely related to the choice of subject matter is the choice of setting and the degree to which it is emphasized. The visual emphasis placed on the setting may be an important aspect of the director's style. One director may favor settings that are stark, barren, or drab; another may choose settings of great natural beauty. Some may use setting to help us understand character or as a powerful tool to build atmosphere or mood; others may simply allow setting to slide by as a backdrop to the action, giving it no particular emphasis at all.

By choosing to photograph certain details in the setting, the director may stress either the sordid and the brutal or the ideal and the romantic. This type of emphasis may be significant, for it may indicate an overall worldview. Other factors of setting that may reflect the director's style are which social and economic classes the director focuses on, whether the settings are rural or urban, and whether the director favors contemporary, historical past, or futuristic time periods. Also, when elaborate or unusual sets have been constructed especially for a film, the director's taste is often apparent in the set design.

SOUND AND SCORE

Directors make use of the soundtrack and the musical score in unique and individual ways. Whereas one may simply match natural sounds to the corresponding action, another may consider sound almost as important as the image and use off-screen sound imaginatively to create a sense of total environment. Yet another director may use sound in an impressionistic or even symbolic manner; still another might stress the rhythmic and even musical properties of natural sounds and use them instead of a musical score.

With respect to screen dialogue, some directors want every word to be clearly and distinctly heard, and they record with this aim in mind. Others allow—even encourage—overlapping lines and frequent interruptions because of the realism these effects produce.

Loudness or softness of the soundtrack as a whole may also reflect something of a director's style. One director may employ silence as a sound effect, whereas another may feel a need to fill every second with some kind of sound. Similarly, some may use a minimum of dialogue, whereas others fill the soundtrack with dialogue and depend on it to carry the major burdens of the film's communication.

Directors also may vary greatly in their utilization of the musical score. One director may be completely dependent on music to create and sustain mood; another may use it sparingly. One may use music to communicate on several levels of meaning, whereas another may use music only when it reinforces the rhythms of the action. One director may desire the music to be understated or even completely inconspicuous, so we are not even aware of the score; another may employ strong, emotional music that occasionally overpowers the visual elements. Some favor music scored expressly for the film; others employ a variety of familiar music as it fits their purpose. Instrumentation and size of orchestra are also elements of style. Some directors prefer a full symphony sound; others find a few instruments or even a single instrument more effective. For *Match Point*, Woody Allen made the idiosyncratic (but highly effective) choice of antique recordings of opera arias. More and more, younger directors are using the work of soloists and groups from the contemporary popular music scene to help create their movies' appeal. Sam Mendes, for example, in *Jarhead*, set during 1993, utilizes Public Enemy, T. Rex, and Social Distortion (among others)—in addition to a unique orchestral score composed by Hollywood favorite Thomas Newman.

CASTING AND ACTING PERFORMANCES

Most directors have a hand in selecting the actors they work with, and it must be taken for granted that they can have a strong influence on individual acting performances. In the choice of actors, one director may take the safe, sure way by casting established stars in roles very similar to roles they have played before. Another may prefer to try relatively unknown actors who do not already have an established image. Another may like to cast an established star in a role entirely different from anything he or she has played before. Some directors never work with the same actor twice; others employ the same stable of actors in almost every film they make. One such artist is the British director Mike Leigh (*Secrets and Lies, Vera Drake, Another Year*), famous for the unusual rehearsal time and improvisational power he allows his actors (Figure 11.6). Working frequently with the same actors can greatly increase a director's efficiency. Knowing the strengths and weaknesses of the cast and having already established rapport with them, the director can concentrate on getting high-level performances. The downside of such familiarity is the danger that the director and cast will slip into comfortable patterns and repeat themselves in films that seem too much alike.

In their choice of actors, directors may also reveal an emphasis on certain qualities. A director can have a remarkable feel for faces and choose stars and even bit players who have faces with extremely strong visual character—that is, faces that may not be beautiful or handsome but are strikingly powerful on the screen. Or a director may prefer to work with only the "beautiful people." One director may seem to stress the actors' voice qualities, and another may consider the total body or the physical presence of the actor more important.

The director may have a tremendous influence on the acting style of the cast, although the extent of this influence may be difficult to determine even in a study of several films. Almost every aspect of an actor's performance can be influenced by the director—the subtlety of the facial expressions, the quality of the voice and physical gestures, and the psychological depth of the interpretation of the role. Thus, an actor who has a tendency to overplay for one director may show more subtlety and restraint with another. Whether a director has the ability to influence the acting style of each actor under his or her direction is, of course, impossible to detect, but in some cases the director's influence may be obvious. When asked about his technique for rehearsing actors, Orson Welles replied, "There *are* fine directors who are so much themselves that the actors have to toe the line and follow them. But I've always thought . . . that the job of the director is slightly overrated, overinflated, and I think the director must think of himself as the servant of the actors and the story—even when he wrote the story."[7]

FIGURE 11.6 **Repeated Directions**   Some directors (such as Mike Leigh) choose to hire certain distinctive-looking and -acting performers more than once, thus contributing to a kind of filmmaking repertory company of their own. Frequently, directors cast family and friends who just happen to be actors. Noah Baumbach, for example, has used Jennifer Jason Leigh, his wife, in both *Margot at the Wedding* (shown here) and *Greenberg*.

SCREENPLAYS AND NARRATIVE STRUCTURE

The way a director chooses to tell the story—the narrative structure—is also an important element of style. A director may choose to build a simple, straightforward, chronological sequence of events, as in *Shane* or *High Noon*, or a complex elliptical structure, jumping back and forth in time, as in *Pulp Fiction* or *Citizen Kane*. A director may choose to tell a story objectively, putting the camera and the viewer in the vantage point of a sideline observer, bringing the action just close enough so that we get all the necessary information without identifying with any single character. Or a director may tell the story from the viewpoint of a single character and manipulate us so that we essentially experience the story as that character perceives it. Although the camera does not limit itself to subjective shots, we emotionally and intellectually identify with the **point-of-view character** and see the story through his or her eyes. A director may structure the film so that we get multiple viewpoints, seeing the same action repeated as it is perceived from the different viewpoints of several characters. Along the way, there may be side trips into the characters' minds, into fantasies or memories as in *Midnight Cowboy, The World According to Garp, Annie Hall, Out of Sight* (1998), *Proof, Broken Embraces, The Secret in Their Eyes,* and *Flipped.*

Sometimes there may be some confusion about whether what we are seeing is reality or illusion. The dividing line between those two may be clear or blurred. Time may be compressed in montages or clever transitions that jump huge segments of time. Changing time frames may be made clear with newsreel inserts, TV news segments, or popular music on radio, phonograph, or tape or CD players.

Unusual techniques, like the witnesses in *Reds*, may be inserted into the narrative to provide both background information and varying viewpoints. Voice-over narration may be provided from the point-of-view character to set up a frame at beginning or end and to fill in gaps in the filmed narrative. Or voice-over narration may be employed not just to help structure the film but to provide style and humor (as in *Forrest Gump*) or the sense of an author telling the story (as in *American Splendor*).

Beginnings may be slow and leisurely; the director may prefer to establish characters and exposition before conflict develops. Or he or she may prefer exciting, dynamic *in medias res* beginnings, where conflict is already developing when the film opens. Some directors may prefer endings in which the tying up of all loose ends provides a sense of completeness. Others may prefer endings without a clear-cut resolution—endings that leave questions unanswered and give us something to puzzle about long after the film is over. Some directors prefer upbeat endings—that is, endings on a heroic note, with strong, uplifting music. Some prefer downbeat endings that offer little or no hope. There are spectacular endings, quiet endings, happy endings, and sad endings. Some directors may use trick endings, withholding information from the audience until the end and devising strange and unusual plot twists to produce endings for which we're not prepared.

Some directors create a tight structure so that every single action and every word of dialogue advance the plot. Others prefer a rambling, loosely structured plot with side trips that may be interesting but actually have little or nothing to do with the stream of the action. Some structures let the audience in on the secrets but keep the characters guessing, creating a sense of dramatic irony. Other structures withhold information from the audience and create suspense with mystery. Repeated patterns of character are often used. The entire film may end with the resolution of one problem and establish the fact that the character has taken on another similar problem at the end, so that we get a sense that the character has not really learned anything from the experience but will continue going about his or her crazy business (as in *Breaking Away* or *The Informant!*).

Directors also differ in the way they handle films with multiple narrative levels. Complex plots, with several lines of action occurring simultaneously at different locations, can be broken into fragments jumping quickly back and forth from one developing story to another (Figure 11.7). Or each stream of action can be developed rather completely before switching to another stream of narrative.

One director may prefer a lazy, slow-paced, gradual unfolding of character or information, focusing on each single detail. Another director may prefer compressed, machine-gun dialogue and images to get exposition out of the way and introduce characters quickly so that he or she can use more time later to focus on the most dramatic scenes.

What actually carries the narrative forward may also vary greatly from one director to the next. Some may provide dialogue for the most important bits of story and action, and others may prefer to tell the story in strictly visual terms with a bare minimum of dialogue. Some narrative structures use traditional formulas for beginnings and endings, emphasizing set patterns like the hero arriving at the beginning and leaving at the end. Others use a structure in which the characters of the story are already present in the beginning, and at the end the camera leaves them to continue their lives. We leave and they stay, but we leave with a strong sense that their story goes on, their lives continue.

FIGURE 11.7 **Focused Fragments** Director Robert Altman, supremely celebrated for his improvisational work with actors, is also remarkable for the large canvases on which he works. Often (as in *Nashville, Short Cuts, The Player, Gosford Park,* and *A Prairie Home Companion,* top), he deals with multiple characters and storylines, ultimately creating coherence out of apparent fragmentation. A younger director who emulates Altman is Paul Thomas Anderson (*Boogie Nights, Magnolia*). Anderson often follows several different narrative strands, as in *There Will Be Blood* (with Paul Franklin Dano and Daniel Day-Lewis, bottom).

The sense of what makes a story and how to tell it, of course, is often determined by the screenwriter, but it should be remembered that many directors simply view the screenplay as a rough outline for a movie and impose their own feel for narrative structure on it, expressing themselves creatively in their fashioning of the film's overall shape and form.

For decades in the Hollywood system of making movies the greatest power typically resided with the producers, who called all the shots, at least in a financial sense. Near the middle of the twentieth century, as the studio system was broken down by antimonopoly legislation and the popularity of television, among other influences, the seat of power shifted: Directors came to have more clout, initiating and sustaining projects. Only late in the twentieth century did screenwriters truly begin to be recognized, through sometimes spectacular remuneration, for their contributions (see Flashback: "The Writer's Place in Hollywood" in Chapter 13).

FIGURE 11.8 **Respected Interpreter**   Sidney Lumet, shown here directing Joanne Woodward in *The Fugitive Kind*, is widely admired not only for the quality of his diverse films but also for his ability to write about the movie industry, as in his popular book *Making Movies*.

Frequently, now, writers boldly challenge how directors handle their scripts. But in discussing screenwriters' power, director Sidney Lumet (Figure 11.8) appears to seek a certain balance: "Movie-making works very much like an orchestra: the addition of various harmonies can change, enlarge, and clarify the nature of the theme. In that sense, a director is 'writing' when he makes a picture. . . . Sometimes the writer includes directions in the script. . . . I may follow them literally or find a completely different way of expressing the same intention."[8] As we observed in Chapter 3, the struggle between director and writer is essentially the very basic conflict between kinds of language—literary versus cinematic.

But Lumet also emphasizes the film director's necessary talent for seeing the big picture. In observing director Ang Lee's work on her film *Sense and Sensibility*, screenwriter-actor Emma Thompson says that "he's very interesting on the flow of energy in a film. Always thinks of everything in its widest context." And later, in keeping a daily chronicle of her thoughts, actions, and emotions while making the film, she notes,

> We seem to feel our way into the shots. Ang's style of leadership is somehow to draw us all to him silently and wait for things to happen. He has the shape of shots in his head always and will stand for silent minutes on end thinking through the flow of the scenes to see if what we're doing will fit his vision. I find it very inspiring but it's quite different to being told what to do. More collaborative.[9]

EVOLVING STYLES AND FLEXIBILITY

Some directors do not arrive at a static mature style but continue to evolve and experiment throughout their careers. Several prominent directors are examples of constant experimentation and artistic growth. Robert Altman is perhaps one of the most experimental. A certain freedom of form and an emphasis on texture permeate everything he does, but the films Altman has directed have little in common in subject matter, worldview, or even visual style: *M*A*S*H*; *Buffalo Bill and the Indians*; *Nashville*; *3 Women*; *A Wedding*; *McCabe & Mrs. Miller*; *Popeye*; *Come Back to the Five and Dime, Jimmy Dean, Jimmy Dean*; *Vincent & Theo*; *The Player*; *Short Cuts*; *Ready to Wear*; *Cookie's Fortune*; *Gosford Park*; *The Company*; and *A Prairie Home Companion*.

Woody Allen has also experimented with a wide variety of styles. Although his most successful films have focused on the familiar Allen persona (*Take the Money and Run, Bananas, Sleeper,* and *Annie Hall*), experimentation and artistic growth are evident in such works as *Interiors, Manhattan, Stardust Memories, Zelig, Broadway Danny Rose, The Purple Rose of Cairo, Hannah and Her Sisters, Radio Days, Crimes and Misdemeanors, Husbands and Wives, Manhattan Murder Mystery, Bullets Over Broadway, Mighty Aphrodite, Everyone Says I Love You, Deconstructing Harry, Celebrity, Sweet and Lowdown, Small Time Crooks, Melinda and Melinda, Match Point, Scoop, Cassandra's Dream, Vicky Cristina Barcelona, Whatever Works,* and *You Will Meet a Tall Dark Stranger.*

Francis Ford Coppola, Mike Nichols, Alan Parker, Martin Scorsese, and Stanley Kubrick are also experimental directors who do films with entirely different kinds of subject matter and narrative structure (Figure 11.9). As the careers of such innovators progress, the films that they direct may become more formal or less formal, more serious or less serious. A filmmaker who directs a comedic farce after

FIGURE 11.9 Coppola, Allen, and Scorsese—Three *Auteurs* for the Price of One   An excellent opportunity to study directing style is provided by *New York Stories*, a feature-length anthology of three comedies: *Life With Zoe* (directed by Francis Ford Coppola, left), *Oedipus Wrecks* (Woody Allen, center), and *Life Lessons* (Martin Scorsese, right).

FIGURE 11.10 **Cultural Perceptiveness**
Among directors whose first language was not
English, these three have shown extraordinary
perception in making films about American and
British cultures: Ang Lee (*Sense and Sensibil-
ity, The Ice Storm, Brokeback Mountain, Taking
Woodstock*), from Taiwan (top left); John Woo
(*Broken Arrow, Face/Off, Windtalkers*), from
China (top right); and Milos Forman (*Ragtime,
Taking Off, One Flew Over the Cuckoo's Nest,
Hair, The People vs. Larry Flynt, Man on the
Moon, Amadeus*) from Czechoslovakia (bottom).

having directed a serious drama has not taken a stylistic step backward. Growth
results from taking on a new kind of challenge, tackling an entirely new genre, or
perhaps even bringing new styles to bear on a familiar genre. Or a director may
simply break out of genre films altogether.

Innovative directors are often Hollywood outsiders (Figure 11.10) who maintain a high degree of independence, perhaps because they also write and produce.
Or they are filmmakers who have achieved such financial success that they can
afford a gamble or two and put their own money into their experiments. Such
experiments, however, often are not well received by the public. Audiences were
so enamored of the familiar Woody Allen persona that they were unable to accept
the Bergmanesque *Interiors,* for which Allen served as director only and attempted
to make a serious and profound art movie. Audiences did accept the serious art of
Manhattan, mainly because it featured the familiar Allen persona and its humor
did not take it too far from the popular *Annie Hall.* It is perhaps much easier for a
director like Alan Parker (*Midnight Express, Pink Floyd—The Wall*) to avoid the trap
of audience expectations, because all of the films he has directed have been radically
different kinds of stories with very different styles.

Directors must guard against typecasting as carefully as actors do—for practically the same reasons: (1) the expectations of movie-goers who feel betrayed if a director does not continue to deliver the same kind of popular fare that they associate with his or her name; and (2) conservative thinking by studios, production companies, and financial backers that are unwilling to gamble huge amounts of money on a director who wants to stretch his or her creative wings (Figure 11.11). Getting financing for a director to do the tried-and-true for which he or she has a proven track record is much easier than finding investors willing to risk money on a more speculative project. One wonders not only whether even Alfred Hitchcock could have succeeded with a film like *Interiors*, or with any other film that did not contain the suspense element that audiences grew to expect from him in film after film after film, but also whether Hitchcock would have been allowed to direct it.

SPECIAL EDITION: THE DIRECTOR'S CUT

A studio or releasing company may be persuaded to re-release a film in a special director's edition if the film does extremely well at the box office or if the director has considerable clout because of the reception accorded his or her entire body of work. Some directors are frustrated when their film is first released because the studio insisted that they shorten the work to about two hours to conform to standard theater showing schedules. The re-released film, or **director's cut**, includes footage that the director felt should never have been dropped. Director's cuts of David Lean's *Lawrence of Arabia*, Francis Ford Coppola's *Apocalypse Now*, Sergio Leone's *Once Upon a Time in America*, Oliver Stone's *JFK*, James Cameron's *The Abyss* and *Avatar*, and Paul Haggis's *Crash* (2005), for example, have been released. One of the most drastically changed films was Ridley Scott's *Blade Runner*, re-released with some additional footage (including a dream of a unicorn) and a new soundtrack but without the voice-over narration that accompanied the original version.

A most unusual "director's cut" was released in 1998 for *Touch of Evil*, a *film noir* (see Chapter 14 for a definition) first seen in 1959. The film's director (and one of its stars), Orson Welles, lost creative control of the work after shooting had ceased, so Universal Studios formulated its own final cut. But more than ten years after Welles's death, the accomplished film editor Walter Murch (*The Godfather I–III*, *The Conversation*, *Apocalypse Now*, *The English Patient*, *The Talented Mr. Ripley*, *Cold Mountain*, *Jarhead*) became aware of a fifty-eight-page memorandum that Welles had written to promote his own plans for re-editing the film—a scheme that had never come to fruition. Ultimately, and ironically, Universal itself financed Murch's new version of the film to fit Welles's blueprint. Among the most radical changes that Murch made involved excising the now-famous music Universal had commissioned Henry Mancini to write for the beginning title sequence. Like Welles, Murch believed that the celebrated, spectacularly sustained one-shot that opened the film should not be diluted with an overlay of either titles or musical score. Thus, he used, as Welles had instructed, only the ambient music and other sounds that would have occurred naturally in the scene. Seamlessly, the camera winds its complex way through extreme close-ups and multiple long shots down the night streets of a Mexican border town. (For more on this extraordinary story, consult

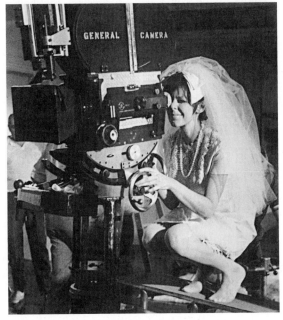

FIGURE 11.11 Stretching Her Creative Wings
Of all filmmaking categories, feature directing, the almost-exclusive domain of men for many decades, was perhaps the hardest for women to enter. These three women, though, were American pioneers: Dorothy Arzner (top left), who directed her first film in 1927 and later became the first female member of the Directors Guild of America; Ida Lupino (top right), who moved beyond acting into directing and producing in the early 1950s with such hits as *The Hitch-Hiker* (1953); and Elaine May (bottom), who forged a path for women directors in comedy and satire with *The Heartbreak Kid* (1972). Now, worldwide, more and more films are being made by directors who happen to be women. Among the most accomplished are Allison Anders, Jane Anderson, Asia Argento, Gilliam Armstrong, Kathryn Bigelow, Jane Campion, Niki Caro, Lisa Cholodenko, Joyce Chopra, Martha Coolidge, Julie Dash, Claire Denis, Nora Ephron, Jodie Foster, Marleen Goris, Debra Granik, Lee Grant, Mary Harron, Amy Heckerling, Agnieszka Holland, Nicole Holofcener, Miranda July, Diane Keaton, Diane Kurys, Alison Maclean, Penny Marshall, Nancy Meyers, Ruba Nadda, Mira Nair, Claire Peploe, Sarah Polley, Sally Potter, Gina Prince-Blythewood, Leni Riefenstahl, Patricia Rozema, Nancy Savoca, Susan Seidelman, Adrienne Shelly, Joan Micklin Silver, Penelope Spheeris, Barbra Streisand, Julie Taymor, Betty Thomas, Liv Ullmann, Margarethe von Trotta, Agnes Varda, Claudia Weill, and Lina Wertmuller.

Michael Ondaatje's book *The Conversations: Walter Murch and the Art of Editing Film* [Knopf, 2002]).

Steven Spielberg's rationale for his "Special Edition" of *Close Encounters of the Third Kind* and his description of the changes provide some interesting insights into the process:

> . . . I always felt the second act was the weakest area of my movie, and I tried very, very hard to fix the second act after the first sneak preview—but I simply didn't have the time. . . . [I]t was a work-in-progress that I literally had to abandon. And, despite the phenomenal success of the film, I had no satisfaction, as a filmmaker; that was not the movie I had set out to make. So when the film was a big hit, I went back to Columbia and said, "Now . . . I need another million dollars to shoot some added footage." Those added scenes were in the original script, by the way, not just scenes I concocted for the Special Edition, but they were scenes that became expendable when the budget became inordinate.[10]

Spielberg contradicts himself in two separate interviews on the addition of the scenes inside the mother ship. In 1982, he told Judith Crist that those scenes were something he himself was curious about so he had the set built. In a 1990 interview with Gene Siskel, he claimed that the studio would not have given him another million dollars without some kind of "real hook to be able to justify re-releasing the film." Whatever the reason for including those scenes, Spielberg never thought they worked and he cut them when he released a *special* special edition, the "30th Anniversary Ultimate Edition."

Regardless of one's reaction to Steven Spielberg's indecision, we obviously must consider it in the context of the enormous financial burdens of modern film-making. It seems as if every person in Los Angeles is writing a screenplay, and every successful actor and screenwriter has ambitions to direct. Few are hired, however. In the title of his book about Hollywood, journalist Billy Frolick satirizes this phenomenon: *What I Really Want to Do Is DIRECT.* Frolick's subtitle is *Seven Film School Graduates Go to Hollywood,* and he emphasizes in his commentary the serendipity, the accidental nature, of not only directing, but of getting to direct a film. As part of his conclusion, he writes:

> In a 1994 *New Yorker* interview, [the influential film critic] Pauline Kael was asked what kind of person it takes to become a movie director.
>
> "Let's be brutal," Kael answered. "It takes a person who can raise the money to make a movie."
>
> Kael's response *was* brutal—brutally accurate. However, funding features no longer means raising millions of dollars. . . . [A]cclaimed movies costing well under $100,000 have heralded a golden age of guerrilla narrative and documentary filmmaking. This generation's credo may well be, "Forget the car for graduation, Mom and Dad—finance my directorial debut."
>
> Sadly, though, as instant auteurs emerge regularly from the independent scene, opportunities at the studio level continue to shrink.[11]

A PORTFOLIO OF FOUR DIRECTORS

The pictures that follow represent films by four different directors: Stanley Kubrick, Steven Spielberg, Federico Fellini, and Alfred Hitchcock. Although it is very difficult (perhaps impossible) to capture a director's visual style in a limited number of frames from the films themselves, the pictures reproduced here contain strong stylistic elements. Study the following figures—Figure 11.12 (Kubrick), Figure 11.13 (Spielberg), Figure 11.14 (Fellini), and Figure 11.15 (Hitchcock)—and consider these questions about each director.

1. What does each set of pictures reveal about the director's visual style as reflected by such elements as composition and lighting, philosophy of camera or point of view, use of setting, methods of achieving three-dimensionality, and choice of actors?

2. The pictures represent four films by each director. Study the frames *from each film,* and see what you can deduce about the nature of the film.

    a. What do the pictures reveal about the general subject matter of the film or the kind of cinematic theme being treated?

    b. Characterize as clearly as possible the mood or emotional quality suggested by the still from each film.

    c. If you are familiar with other films by the same director (consult the lists at the end of this chapter), how do these thematic concerns and emotional qualities relate to those other films?

3. Considering all the frames from each director, indicate whether each director is

    a. intellectual and rational *or* emotional and sensual

    b. naturalistic and realistic *or* romantic, idealized, and surreal

    c. simple, obvious, and straightforward *or* complex, subtle, and indirect

    d. heavy, serious, and tragic *or* light, comical, and humorous

4. Which directors represent *extremes* of each of the descriptive sets listed in question 3?

5. The films of which director seem most formal and structured in composition? The films of which director seem most informal and natural in composition?

6. Which director seems to be trying to involve us emotionally in the action or dramatic situation portrayed in the frames? How does he attempt to achieve this effect? Which director's viewpoint seems most objective and detached, and why do the pictures have that effect?

7. Which director relies most on lighting for special effects, and what effects does he achieve?

8. Which director places the most emphasis on setting to create special effects or moods?

9. What general observations, based on your answers to all the preceding questions, can you make about each director's style?

FIGURE 11.12 **Stanley Kubrick**

a. *A Clockwork Orange*

b. *Full Metal Jacket*

c. *The Shining*

d. *Dr. Strangelove*

FIGURE 11.13 **Steven Spielberg**

a. *Minority Report*

b. *Close Encounters of the Third Kind*

c. *The Terminal*

d. *The Color Purple*

FIGURE 11.14 **Federico Fellini**

a. *8½*

b. *La Dolce Vita*

c. *Juliet of the Spirits*

d. *Amarcord*

FIGURE 11.15 **Alfred Hitchcock**

a. *North by Northwest*

b. *Psycho*

c. *Rear Window*

d. *Vertigo*

1. After viewing several films by a single director, what kinds of general observations can you make about his or her style? Which of the adjectives listed below describe his or her style?
   a. intellectual and rational *or* emotional and sensual
   b. calm and quiet *or* fast-paced and exciting

    c. polished and smooth *or* rough and crude-cut

    d. cool and objective *or* warm and subjective

    e. ordinary and trite *or* fresh and original

    f. tightly structured, direct, and concise *or* loosely structured and rambling

    g. truthful and realistic *or* romantic and idealized

    h. simple and straightforward *or* complex and indirect

    i. grave, serious, tragic, and heavy *or* light, comical, and humorous

    j. restrained and understated *or* exaggerated

    k. optimistic and hopeful *or* bitter and cynical

    l. logical and orderly *or* irrational and chaotic

2. What common thematic threads are reflected in the director's choice of subject matter? How is this thematic similarity revealed in the nature of the conflicts the director deals with?

3. In the films you have seen, what consistencies do you find in the director's treatment of space and time?

4. Is a consistent philosophical view of the nature of man and the universe found in all the films studied? If so, describe the director's worldview.

5. How is the director's style revealed by composition and lighting, philosophy of camera, camera movement, and methods of achieving three-dimensionality?

6. How does the director use special visual techniques (such as unusual camera angles, fast motion, slow motion, and distorting lenses) to interpret or comment on the action, and how do these techniques reflect overall style?

7. How is the director's style reflected in the different aspects of the editing in the films, such as the rhythm and pacing of editorial cuts, the nature of transitions, montages, and other creative juxtapositions? How does the style of editing relate to other elements of the director's visual style, such as the philosophy of camera or how the point of view is emphasized?

8. How consistent is the director in using and emphasizing setting? What kind of details of the natural setting does the director emphasize, and how do these details relate to his or her overall style? Is there any similarity in the director's approach to entirely different kinds of settings? How do the sets constructed especially for the film reflect the director's taste?

9. In what ways are the director's use of sound effects, dialogue, and music unique? How are these elements of style related to the image?

10. What consistencies can be seen in the director's choice of actors and in the performances they give under his or her direction? How does the choice of actors and acting styles fit in with the style in other areas?

11. What consistencies do you find in the director's narrative structure?

12. If the director seems to be constantly evolving instead of settling into a fixed style, what directions or tendencies do you see in that evolution? What stylistic elements can you find in all his or her films?

Frank Capra's 1934 film *It Happened One Night*, often called the original screwball comedy, was the first movie to win all five of the major Academy Awards: Best

Picture, Best Actress (Claudette Colbert), Best Actor (Clark Gable), Best Screenplay (Robert Riskin), and Best Director. Like Capra's later sleeper, *It's a Wonderful Life* (1946), this film was not particularly well received by the reviewers when it was released, but it obviously built its audience. And perhaps its popular appeal can be identified in part by examining this director's cinematic style.

Practice what you have learned about analyzing the elements of a director's style by watching Chapter 18 ("Hitchhiker's Guide") of the DVD version of *It Happened One Night*. Clark Gable plays an opportunistic journalist who needs a hot story; coincidentally, he meets Claudette Colbert, a runaway heiress who could provide him one. But, of course, they fall in love—after a sufficient number of scenes in which they drive each other half mad. In this famous "self-contained" sequence, may they simply be viewed as Man and Woman in eternal conflict? Can Capra's own attitudes about gender be found in this entertaining contest of ingenuity? What do Capra's choices involving such topics as camera placement, shot types, focal distances, lighting, and sound effects tell us about his style as a director?

The anthology film *Paris, Je T'Aime* presents a splendid opportunity to experience, enjoy, and (in its two-disc DVD afterlife) examine both the work and the working methods of not one, but 18 different accomplished directors.

Each of the filmmakers chose, or was assigned, a separate area of the city of Paris on which to focus. Although the overall quality of the finished five-minute films is somewhat uneven, all of them are worthy of a film student's study. And disc two in this set provides an intriguing eight- to ten-minute documentary about each director's making of his or her film.

For this exercise, watch (at least) the following five mini-movies. Then select one to examine in light of your reading of "Chapter 11: The Director's Style." Use the summary list of questions offered above to guide you.

CHAPTER 5: "Tuileries" (directed by Joel and Ethan Coen)

CHAPTER 16: "Pere-LaChaise" (directed by Wes Craven)

CHAPTER 10: "Tour Eiffel" (directed by Sylvain Chomet)

CHAPTER 17: "Fauborg-St. Denis" (directed by Tom Twykwer)

CHAPTER 19: "14e Arrondisement" (directed by Alexander Payne)

On the Waterfront (Special Edition):
"A Conversation with Elia Kazan" stresses the importance of this acclaimed director's collaboration with actor Marlon Brando, writer Budd Schulberg, and producer Sam Spiegel. Kazan relates how the latter two honed the screenplay together and served as what he terms "Persistence" (Schulberg) and "Insistence" (Spiegel) on the project.

"The Making of *The Portrait of a Lady*" inexplicably never appeared on the DVD of director Jane Campion's adaptation of the Henry James novel. But the fifty-five-minute documentary can be found as a feature on one whole side of the disc *Short Cinema Journal I: 2 (Dreams)* (also reissued as simply *Short 2*). There, it is described as "an intimate study of an auteur at the height of her powers. . . . Directed by Peter Long and Kate Ellis, this glimpse into the creative process prevails as a work of art in its own right." Along with Campion at work, we see Nicole Kidman, John Malkovich, Barbara Hershey, and Richard Grant, and the production scenes that involve the director's use of the veteran star Shelley Winters are riveting and heartrending.

Unforgiven (Two-Disc Special Edition):
Numerous substantial filmmaking features enrich this set. On disc two, find the lengthy career profile *Eastwood on Eastwood*, created by *Time* reviewer and film historian/producer Richard Schickel.

Pulp Fiction (Collector's Edition) and *Pollock (Special Edition):*
The director of each of these films (Quentin Tarantino and Ed Harris, respectively) appears in a substantial interview from PBS's *The Charlie Rose Show.*

Memento:
Elvis Mitchell, a reviewer for the *New York Times* and a host on IFC (Independent Film Channel), discusses this enigmatic film with its director, Christopher Nolan.

The Ghost Writer
This DVD contains a timely interview with director Roman Polanski.

The Others (Dimension Collector's Series):
A valuable feature portrait of Alejandro Amenábar on disc two of this set is especially telling in its scenes that present the director working with the film's key child actors.

Eat Drink Man Woman and *Brokeback Mountain:*
This first DVD captures an intriguing early interview with director Ang Lee; the second, called "Directing from the Heart: Ang Lee," focuses on his later work.

Amélie:
The two-disc set features two separate Q&A segments with the film's co-writer and director as well as "An Intimate Chat with Director Jean-Pierre Jeunet."

Lumiere & Company: Forty Intriguing Films from the World's Leading Directors:
This DVD takes full advantage of what is called "high concept" in Hollywood. Forty world-class film directors—including Spike Lee, Wim Wenders, Zhang Yimou, John Boorman, Peter Greenaway, Liv Ullmann, Lasse Hallstrom, James Ivory, Costa Gavras, and Arthur Penn—were invited to use a restored 100-year-old silent camera to make a single one-minute film each. A century before, the famous Lumière Brothers had utilized this same instrument to create their first motion pictures. The running time of the disc is eighty-eight minutes, so each director also gets approximately one minute of interview time about his or her original movie, in many cases while the shooting is taking place. A highlight of the program is David Lynch's mysterious, intriguing distillation of what may seem to be his whole body of film work, including his later cinematic puzzles *Mulholland Dr.* and *Inland Empire.*

Landmarks of Early Film:
Films that the Lumière Brothers made between 1895 and 1897 are also featured on this compilation of early motion pictues. In addition, the disc includes such famous shorts as Thomas Edison's momentary documentary "The Kiss," Méliès's brief fantasy "A Trip to the Moon" (1902), and Edwin Porter's ten-minute, hand-tinted western "The Great Train Robbery" (1903).

Unknown Chaplin: The Master at Work:
In three separate, hour-long programs ("My Happiest Years," "The Great Director," and "Hidden Treasures"), celebrated writer and producer Kevin Brownlow presents a wealth of new images by and information about one of America's greatest directors, the Brit Charles Chaplin. The second part is especially noteworthy for including, via newly unearthed home movie footage, the only extant film of Chaplin directing while in his Little Tramp costume, during the production of *City Lights.* A special feature on this DVD (released in 2005) finds Brownlow meticulously recounting the steps of his amazing archival discoveries (with the late historian David Gill). The actor James Mason laconically narrates the 1983 documentary.

George Stevens: A Filmmaker's Journey:
Director George Stevens's wide interests and multiple talents were suggested in the variety within the titles of some of his most famous works: *Alice Adams* (a domestic romance), *Swing Time* (an Astaire and Rogers musical), *Gunga Din* (an action-adventure tale), *Shane* (a western), *Giant* (a star-driven epic). Through interviews with scores of famous actors who worked with the director, this fine documentary, "produced, written, directed, and narrated by" his son, George Stevens, Jr., honors both the film professional and the man.

Me & Orson Welles:
Noteworthy for its docu-fictional take on one aspect of Orson Welles's multifaceted professional life, this charming and accomplished film by director Richard Linklater stars Zac Efron and Claire Danes—and, in a credibly entertaining impersonation of Welles, newcomer Christian McKay. Linklater is interviewed in the disc's special features.

Ingmar Bergman

Smiles of a Summer Night (1955)
Wild Strawberries (1957)
The Seventh Seal (1957)
Through a Glass Darkly (1961)
Persona (1966)
Cries and Whispers (1972)
Scenes from a Marriage (1973)
The Magic Flute (1975)
Autumn Sonata (1978)
Fanny and Alexander (1982)
Saraband (2003)

Jane Campion

Sweetie (1989)
An Angel at My Table (1990)
The Piano (1993)
The Portrait of a Lady (1996)
Holy Smoke (1999)
In the Cut (2003)
Bright Star (2009)

Frank Capra

It Happened One Night (1934)
Mr. Deeds Goes to Town (1936)
Lost Horizon (1937)
Mr. Smith Goes to Washington (1939)
Meet John Doe (1941)
It's a Wonderful Life (1946)
State of the Union (1948)

Joel and Ethan Coen

Blood Simple (1984)
Raising Arizona (1987)
Miller's Crossing (1990)
Barton Fink (1991)
The Hudsucker Proxy (1994)
Fargo (1996)
The Big Lebowski (1998)
O Brother, Where Art Thou? (2000)
The Man Who Wasn't There (2001)
Intolerable Cruelty (2003)
The Ladykillers (2004)
No Country For Old Men (2007)
Burn After Reading (2008)
A Serious Man (2009)
True Grit (2010)

Francis Ford Coppola

The Rain People (1969)
The Godfather (1972)
The Conversation (1974)
The Godfather Part II (1974)
Apocalypse Now (1979)
Rumble Fish (1983)
Tucker (1988)
The Godfather Part III (1990)
Bram Stoker's Dracula (1992)
The Rainmaker (1997)
Youth Without Youth (2007)
Tetro (2009)

Federico Fellini

I Vitelloni (1953)
La Strada (1954)
La Dolce Vita (1960)
8½ (1963)
Juliet of the Spirits (1965)
Fellini Satyricon (1969)
Amarcord (1973)
City of Women (1980)
And the Ship Sails On (1983)
Ginger and Fred (1986)

Alfred Hitchcock

Rebecca (1940)
Spellbound (1945)
Notorious (1946)
Rope (1948)
Strangers on a Train (1951)
Rear Window (1954)
The Trouble With Harry (1955)
Vertigo (1958)
North by Northwest (1959)
Psycho (1960)
The Birds (1963)
Marnie (1964)
Torn Curtain (1966)
Topaz (1969)
Frenzy (1972)
Family Plot (1976)

Agnieszka Holland

Europa Europa (1990)
Olivier Olivier (1992)
The Secret Garden (1993)
Total Eclipse (1995)
Washington Square (1997)
Copying Beethoven (2006)

Stanley Kubrick

Paths of Glory (1957)
Lolita (1962)
Dr. Strangelove (1964)
2001: A Space Odyssey (1968)
A Clockwork Orange (1971)
Barry Lyndon (1975)
The Shining (1980)
Full Metal Jacket (1987)
Eyes Wide Shut (1999)

Akira Kurosawa

Rashomon (1950)
The Seven Samurai (1954)
Throne of Blood (1957)
Yojimbo (1961)
Kagemusha (1980)
Ran (1985)
Akira Kurosawa's Dreams (1990)
Rhapsody in August (1991)

Spike Lee

She's Gotta Have It (1986)
Do the Right Thing (1989)
Mo' Better Blues (1990)
Malcolm X (1992)
Clockers (1995)
Get on the Bus (1996)
He Got Game (1998)
Summer of Sam (1999)
Bamboozled (2000)
25th Hour (2002)
She Hate Me (2004)
Inside Man (2006)

Louis Malle

Murmur of the Heart (1971)
Lacombe, Lucien (1974)
Pretty Baby (1978)
Atlantic City (1980)
My Dinner With Andre (1981)
Alamo Bay (1985)
Au Revoir Les Enfants (1987)
May Fools (1990)
Damage (1992)
Vanya on 42nd Street (1994)

Mira Nair

Salaam Bombay! (1988)
Mississippi Masala (1991)
The Perez Family (1995)
Kama Sutra (1996)
Monsoon Wedding (2001)
Vanity Fair (2004)
The Namesake (2006)
Amelia (2009)

Christopher Nolan

Following (1998)
Memento (2000)
Insomnia (2002)
Batman Begins (2005)
The Prestige (2006)
The Dark Knight (2008)
Inception (2010)

John Sayles

Return of the Secaucus Seven (1979)
Lianna (1983)
The Brother From Another Planet (1984)
Matewan (1987)
Eight Men Out (1988)
The Secret of Roan Inish (1994)
Lone Star (1996)
Men With Guns (1997)
Limbo (1999)
Sunshine State (2002)
Casa de los Babys (2003)
Silver City (2004)
Honeydripper (2007)

Martin Scorsese

Mean Streets (1973)
Taxi Driver (1976)
Raging Bull (1980)
The King of Comedy (1982)
The Last Temptation of Christ (1988)
GoodFellas (1990)
The Age of Innocence (1993)
Casino (1995)
Kundun (1997)
Gangs of New York (2002)
The Aviator (2004)
The Departed (2006)
Shine a Light (2008)
Shutter Island (2010)

Steven Spielberg

The Sugarland Express (1974)
Jaws (1975)
Close Encounters of the Third Kind (1977)
Raiders of the Lost Ark (1981)
E.T. The Extra-Terrestrial (1982)
The Color Purple (1985)
Empire of the Sun (1987)
Jurassic Park (1993)
Schindler's List (1993)
Amistad (1997)
Saving Private Ryan (1998)
A.I. Artificial Intelligence (2001)
Minority Report (2002)
Catch Me If You Can (2002)
The Terminal (2004)
War of the Worlds (2005)
Munich (2005)
Indiana Jones and the Kingdom of the Crystal Skull (2008)

Zhang Yimou

Red Sorghum (1987)
Ju Dou (1990)
Raise the Red Lantern (1991)
The Story of Qiu Ju (1992)
To Live (1994)
Shanghai Triad (1995)
Happy Times (2000)
Hero (2002)
House of Flying Daggers (2004)
Curse of the Golden Flower (2006)
A Woman, a Gun and a Noodle Shop (2010)

A Serious Man

[O]f all the duties required of the professional critic, perhaps the least important—certainly the least enduring—is the delivery of a verdict. I am always sorry to hear that readers were personally offended, even scandalized, that my opinion of a film diverged from theirs. I wish I could convince them that I am merely stating an argument, as everyone does over dinner, or in a crowded bar, after going to see a film, and that their freedom to disagree is part of the fun. The primary task of the critic . . . is the recreation of texture—not telling moviegoers what they should see, which is entirely their prerogative, but filing a sensory report on the kind of experience into which they will be wading, or plunging, should they decide to risk a ticket.

—ANTHONY LANE, FILM CRITIC, *THE NEW YORKER*

In the previous chapters, we broke the film down into its separate parts. Now we attempt to put the separate parts together, to relate them to one another, and to consider their contribution to the film as a whole.

THE BASIC APPROACH: WATCHING, ANALYZING, AND EVALUATING THE FILM

When we enter the theater to watch the film, we need to keep certain things in mind. We cannot freeze the film for analysis—only in its continuous flowing form is it truly a motion picture. Therefore, we must concentrate most of our attention on responding sensitively to what is happening on the screen—the simultaneous interplay of image, sound, and motion. Yet at the same time, in the back of our minds, we must be storing up impressions of another sort, asking ourselves How? Why? and How effective is it? about everything we see and hear. We must make an effort to become immersed in the reality of the film, while at the same time maintaining some degree of objectivity and critical detachment.

If we can see the film twice, our analysis will be a much easier task. The complexity of the medium makes it difficult to consider all the elements of a film in a single viewing; too many things happen on too many levels to allow for a complete analysis. Therefore, we should try to see the film twice whenever possible. In the first viewing, we can concern ourselves primarily with plot elements, the total emotional effect, and the central idea or theme. Ideally, after the first viewing, we will have some time to reflect on and clarify the film's purpose and theme. Then, in the second viewing, because we are no longer caught up in the suspense of what happens, we can focus our full attention on the hows and whys of the filmmaker's art. The more practice we have in the double-viewing technique, the easier it will become for us to combine the functions of both viewings into one.

It is sometimes possible in film classes to view the entire film and then screen selected segments that illustrate the function and interrelationship of the different elements to the film as a whole. Then the film can be viewed again in its entirety so that the parts can be seen in the continuous stream of the whole. Use of a DVD player makes the process even simpler. This practice can be very helpful in developing the habits and skills needed for film analysis. Double-viewing not only helps with our analysis but, in the case of exceptional films, also increases our appreciation. For example, critic Dwight Macdonald wrote, in regard to Fellini's *8½*, "The second time I saw *8½*, two weeks after the first, I took more notes than I had the first time, so many beauties and subtleties and puzzles I had overlooked."[1]

Regardless of which option we have, single-viewing, double-viewing, or breaking the film into segments, we can use basically the same procedure in approaching the film for analysis.

Theme

The first step in analysis should be to get a fairly clear idea of the film's **theme**—its unifying central concern. Is the element that unifies the work its plot, a single unique character, the creation of an emotional mood or effect, or the creation of a

FIGURE 12.1 **Interpreting Themes**   The task of articulating a central theme is relatively easy with some films. With others, such as Robert Altman's complex "western," *McCabe & Mrs. Miller* (starring Julie Christie and Warren Beatty, top), and Jason Reitman's *Up in the Air* starring (George Clooney and Vera Farmiga, bottom), accurately identifying the filmmakers' central concerns may be more challenging.

certain style or texture? Or is the film designed to convey an idea or make a statement? Once we have identified the central concern, we can move on to a clearer and more specific statement of theme. What we really want to ask is this: *What is the director's purpose or primary aim in making the film? What is the true subject of the film; and what kind of statement, if any, does the film make about that subject?* (Figure 12.1.)

The Relationship of the Parts to the Whole

Once we have tentatively identified the film's theme and have stated the theme as concisely and precisely as possible, we should move on to see how well our decisions stand up under a complete analysis of all film elements. After we have tried to answer all the applicable and relevant questions relating to each separate element, we are prepared to relate each element to the whole. The basic question is this: *How do all the separate elements of the film relate to and contribute to the theme, central purpose, or total effect?* Answering this question involves at least some consideration of all the elements in the film, although the contribution of some is much greater than the contribution of others. Every element should be considered at this point: story, dramatic structure, symbolism, characterization, conflict, setting, title, irony, cinematography, editing, film type, frame shape and size, sound effects, dialogue, the musical score, the acting, and the film's overall style.

If we can see clear and logical relationships between each element and the theme or purpose, then we may assume that our decision about the film's theme is valid. If we cannot see these clear relationships, we may need to reassess our initial understanding of the theme and modify it to fit the patterns and interrelationships we see among the individual film elements.

Once our analysis at this level is complete and we have satisfied ourselves that we understand the film as a unified work of art, ordered and structured around a central purpose of some kind, we are almost ready to move on to an evaluation process.

The Film's "Level of Ambition"

Before beginning an objective evaluation, we must consider the film's level of ambition. It is grossly unfair to judge a film that seeks only to entertain as though it were intended as the ultimate in serious cinematic art. Thus we must adjust our expectations to what the film aims to do. Renata Adler describes the need for this adjustment: "[T]he reviewer tries to put himself in a . . . sympathetic frame of mind . . . , but once the ingredients are fairly named, the reader knows and is freed to his taste. I think it is absolutely essential in a review to establish the level of ambition that a film is at, to match it, if possible with the level of your own, and then to adjust your tone of voice."[2] This is not to say that we should give up our own standards or ground rules. But we should try to judge the film in terms of what the director appears to be trying to do and the level at which he or she is trying to communicate, before we apply our own yardsticks of evaluation. Therefore, before we make any kind of objective evaluation, we must consider this question: *What is the film's level of ambition?* (See Figure 12.2.)

Objective Evaluation of the Film

Once we have clearly established the theme and the level of ambition and have seen how the elements function together to contribute to the theme, we are ready to begin our objective evaluation. The overall question to consider is simply this: *Given the film's level of ambition, how well does the film succeed in what it tries to do?* After considering this question, we must review our earlier assessment of the

FIGURE 12.2 From Real to Reel Movie watchers must attempt to gauge the level of a film's ambitions. For example, one should be aware that the makers of *Bonnie and Clyde* were at least as interested in depicting the legend of the criminals as in presenting them with full historical accuracy. Thus, they deliberately glamorized the images of Bonnie Parker and Clyde Barrow (Faye Dunaway and Warren Beatty, left). The real Bonnie and Clyde appear here in a vintage photograph at the right.

effectiveness of all individual film elements to determine the effect each element has on our answer. Once we have done this, we can proceed to the next question: *Why does the film succeed or fail?*

In attempting to answer this question, we should be as specific as possible, determining not only Why? but Where? We should look into individual elements for strengths and weaknesses, deciding which parts or elements contribute the most to the film's success or failure: *Which elements or parts make the strongest contribution to the theme and why? Which elements or parts fail to function effectively? Why do they fail?* We must be careful to weigh each strength and weakness in terms of its overall effect on the film, avoiding petty nitpicking such as concentrating on slight technical flaws.

Because we are making an objective evaluation, we should be prepared to defend each decision with a logical argument based on or supportable by our analysis as a whole. We must explain *why* something works well or *why* a given scene fails to achieve its potential. Every part of this evaluation should be as logical and rational as possible, and we should be able to defend each judgment with a just argument based on a viable framework of critical standards.

Subjective Evaluation of the Film

Up to this point, we have been using a systematic and reasonable critical method. But we have done so with the full awareness that we cannot reduce art to reason or make it as simple as $2 + 2 = 4$. Our reaction to films is much more complex than this, for we are human beings, not computers, and we know that much of art is intuitive, emotional, and personal. Thus, our reaction to it will include strong feelings, prejudices, and biases. It will be colored by our life experiences, by our moral and social conditioning, by our degree of sophistication, by our age, by the time and place in which we live, and by every unique aspect of our personality.

Having completed our objective analysis and evaluation, we are ready to allow ourselves the luxury of leaving the rationally ordered framework to describe the nature and intensity of our own response to the film: *What is our personal reaction to the film? What are our personal reasons for liking or disliking it?*

OTHER APPROACHES TO ANALYSIS, EVALUATION, AND DISCUSSION

Once we have completed our personal and subjective evaluation, we may want to approach the film from several rather specialized angles or critical perspectives. These exercises in criticism might be especially meaningful as guidelines for classroom discussion. Each approach has its own focus, bias, perspective, and intentions, and each looks for something a little different in the film.

The Film as Technical Achievement

If we have sufficient understanding of the film medium and the techniques of filmmaking, we may want to focus on the technical devices that the filmmaker uses and the importance of these techniques to the film's overall impact. In evaluating the film in this manner, we are more concerned with *how* the director communicates than with *what* he or she communicates or *why*. By these standards, the most nearly perfect film is the one that best utilizes the potential of the medium. Films such as *Citizen Kane* and *2001: A Space Odyssey* both rate very high in this respect. Here are some questions that we should consider with this kind of focus in mind:

- How well does the film utilize the full potential of the medium?
- What inventive techniques are employed, and how impressive are the effects they create?
- Judged as a whole, is the film technically superior or inferior?
- Technically speaking, what are the film's strongest points and what are its weakest?

The Film as Showcase for the Actor: The Personality Cult

If our primary interest is in actors, acting performances, and screen personalities, we may want to focus on the performances of the major actors in the film, especially the established stars or film personalities. Taking this approach, we assume that the leading actor has the most important effect on the quality of the film, that he or she carries the film because of his or her acting skill or personality. Judged through this framework, the best film is one in which the basic personality, acting style, or personal idiosyncrasies of the leading actor in the cast are best projected. In this approach, then, we look on the film as a showcase for the actor's talent and think of it as a Meryl Streep, Jack Nicholson, Humphrey Bogart, Katharine Hepburn, Tom Hanks, Reese Witherspoon, or Tom Cruise movie. To give this approach validity, we must be familiar with a number of other films starring the same actor so that we can evaluate the performance in comparison with the roles played by the actor in the past. To evaluate a film through this approach, we might consider these questions:

- How well are the actor's special personality traits or acting skills suited to his or her character and to the action of the film?
- Does this role seem tailored to fit the actor's personality and skills, or does the actor bend his or her personality to fit the role?
- How powerful is the actor's performance in this film compared with his or her performance in other starring roles?
- What similarities or significant differences do you see in the character the actor plays in this film and the characters he or she played in other films?
- Compared with past performances, how difficult and demanding is this particular role for the actor?

The Film as Product of a Single Creative Mind: The *Auteur* Approach

In this approach we focus on the style, technique, and philosophy of the film's dominant creative personality—the director, the *auteur*, the complete filmmaker whose genius, style, and creative personality are reflected in every aspect of the film. Because all truly great directors impose their personalities on every aspect of their films, the film in this approach is viewed not as an objective work of art but as a reflection of the artistic vision or style of the person who made it. A good movie, according to *auteur* theory, is one whose every element bears the director's trademark—the story, the casting, the cinematography, the lighting, the music, the sound effects, the editing, and so on (Figure 12.3). And the film itself must be judged not alone but as part of the director's whole canon. In using this approach to evaluate a film, we should consider these questions:

- Judging from this film and other films by the same director, how would you describe the directorial style?
- How does each element of this film reflect the director's artistic vision, style, and overall philosophy of film or even his or her philosophy of life itself?
- What similarities does this film have to other films by the same director? How is it significantly different?

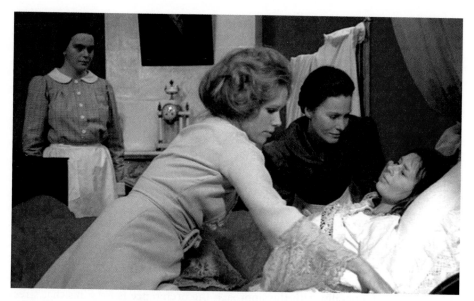

FIGURE 12.3 **The *Auteur* Approach**   For many admiring students of film, Ingmar Bergman's *Cries and Whispers* (starring Liv Ullmann, Harriet Andersson, Ingrid Thulin, and Kari Sylwan) is a disturbing but celebratory demonstration of a strong director's artistry and power.

- Where in the film do we get the strongest impressions of the director's personality, of his or her unique creativity shaping the material?
- What is the special quality of this film as compared with other works in the director's canon? As compared with those other films, how well does this film reflect the philosophy, personality, and artistic vision of the person who made it?
- Does this film suggest growth in some new direction away from the other films? If so, describe the new direction.

The Film as Moral, Philosophical, or Social Statement

In this approach, often called the *humanistic approach*, we focus attention on the statement the film makes, because the best films are built around a statement that teaches us something. In this kind of evaluation, we must determine whether the acting and the characters have significance or meaning beyond the context of the film itself—moral, philosophical, or social significance that helps us gain a clearer understanding of some aspect of life, human nature, or the human condition. We judge the film as an expression of an idea that has intellectual, moral, social, or cultural importance and the ability to influence our lives for the better. Acting, cinematography, lighting, editing, sound, and so on are all judged in terms of how effectively they contribute to the communication of the film's message, and the overall value of the film depends on the significance of its theme. We might consider these questions when using the humanistic approach to evaluate a film:

- What statement does the film make, and how significant is the truth we learn from it?
- How effectively do the different film elements communicate the film's message?
- How does the film attempt to influence our lives for the better? What beliefs and actions does it attempt to change?
- Is the message stated by the film universal, or is it restricted to our own time and place?
- How relevant is the theme to our own experience?

The Film as Emotional or Sensual Experience

In this approach, which is the opposite of the more intellectual humanistic approach, we judge a film by the reality and intensity of its impact on the viewer. The stronger the emotional or sensual experience provided by the film, the better the film is. Generally, with this approach the preference is for films that stress fast-paced action, excitement, and adventure. Because a strong physical or visceral response is desired, a film is judged favorably if it is simply hard hitting and direct, like a punch in the jaw.

Those who favor this approach show an anti-intellectual bias. They want no message in their films, no significance beyond the immediate experience. They prefer pure action, romance, excitement, and the simple, direct, unpretentious telling of a story. If the experience provided by the film is extremely realistic, vivid, and intense, the film is considered good (Figure 12.4). In evaluating a film by these standards, we might consider these questions:

- How powerful or intense is the film as an emotional or sensual experience?
- Where in the film are we completely wrapped up and involved in its reality? Where is the film weakest in emotional and sensual intensity?
- What role does each of the film elements play in creating a hard-hitting emotional and sensual response?

The Film as Repeated Form: The Genre Approach

A **genre film** is a film based on subjects, themes, or styles that have become familiar because they have been used often. Audiences who watch genre films (discussed in detail in Chapter 14)—westerns are one example—know what sorts of characters, settings, plots, and so on to expect. In the genre approach, we judge a film according to how it fits into a body of films having essentially the same setting, characters, conflict, resolution, and/or values. We begin our analysis and evaluation by determining in what ways the film conforms to the standards of the genre it represents, as well as how it deviates from them.

Because we probably have seen a great many films of this genre before viewing the film under present study, we have clear expectations. As we watch the film, we will be disappointed if our expectations are not fulfilled. At the same time, we

FIGURE 12.4 **The Emotional or Sensual Approach** Lasse Hallström's *Chocolat* clearly invites a viewer to take comfort and delight in the emotional appeal of Juliette Binoche and Lena Olin's own enjoyment of their sweet life as candy purveyors/magicians.

should look for variations and innovations that make this film different from others in the genre, for we will be disappointed if the film offers no variety or innovation. A good genre film not only fulfills our expectations by following the traditional patterns and providing satisfying resolutions, but provides enough variations to satisfy our demand for novelty. Because genre films are made for a truly mass audience and reinforce the values and myths sacred to that audience, we might also consider how well any American genre film reflects and reinforces basic American beliefs. We might consider these questions in evaluating a genre film:

- What are the basic requirements for this particular genre, and how well does this film fit them?
- Does the film work in such a way that all our expectations for films of this type are fulfilled (Figure 12.5)?
- What variations and innovations are present in the film? Are these variations fresh enough to satisfy our need for novelty? What variations make the film stand out from other films of the same genre?
- What basic regional or national beliefs, values, and myths are reflected and reinforced by the film? Are these beliefs, myths, and values outdated, or are they still relevant?

The Film as Political Statement

Film may reflect a variety of political stances. For example, one perspective that has been significant might be called Marxist. For some analysts the work of Karl Marx has become an important filter through which to view cinema. Marxist criticism is based on the premise that film—as well as literature and other forms of artistic expression—is a passive product of the economic aspects of a culture and that all

FIGURE 12.5 **The Genre Approach** Even an elementary knowledge of the 1940s *film noir* genre (see Chapter 14) will facilitate a movie-goer's appreciation of Lawrence Kasdan's *Body Heat*. The 1981 homage stars Kathleen Turner as a deliciously evil, manipulatory temptress and William Hurt as her gullible lover.

movies are ultimately statements about the struggle for power between economic classes. The Marxist approach may include consideration of racial issues, because minority groups are often forced into lower socioeconomic classes by the dominant racial and economic group. To evaluate a film from the Marxist perspective, we might consider these questions:

- What is the socioeconomic level of the main character? Do statements in the script indicate the answer, or do the film's costumes and setting imply the answer?
- How do members of the various social classes interact?
- Is any sort of pattern evident in the types of actors cast in supporting and bit parts? For example, is there a relationship between the race and class of the characters and where they fall on the good guy/bad guy scale?
- Are ambition and the acquisition of wealth and material goods (climbing the social ladder) important to the characters? Does the film present ambition positively or negatively? What factors are important in determining success or failure?
- Does the film seem to celebrate a traditional value system, or does it question the mainstream view?

The Film as Gender or Racial Statement

To focus, in any manner, on gender or race in films is to view them through another kind of political filter. In fact, one might argue that virtually any controversial group (especially minority group) may be at the thematic center of the political approach to movies. Critical reactions—both popular and professional—to modern films have demonstrated the possibilities. Quentin Tarantino's use and treatment

FIGURE 12.6 **The Gender Approach**   Early in Neil Jordan's *The Crying Game*, Stephen Rea's character (right) hears from his prisoner (Forest Whitaker) about the latter's sweetheart. Much later, when Rea manages to meet this beloved person, the movie begins to pose some intriguing questions about gender.

of African Americans in *Jackie Brown* (not to mention *Pulp Fiction*), for instance, has raised the ire of Spike Lee. Evangelical Christians have questioned some of the central characterizations in Robert Duvall's *The Apostle*. The elderly, and others, have wondered about the iconic value of Hume Cronyn's aged character in *Marvin's Room*. *Shallow Hal*, some observers have maintained, risked offending the obese. Long before political correctness, critics noted that Natalie Wood was not Hispanic and asked why she dared pretend to be so in *West Side Story*. *Rain Man*, *Forrest Gump*, *Sling Blade*, and *I Am Sam* have all elicited charges of possible exploitation of blessedly "different" people. And evolving gay, lesbian, queer, bisexual, and transgender criticism has scrutinized such films as *The Object of My Affection*, *The Opposite of Sex*, *Flawless*, *Transamerica*, and *I Love You, Phillip Morris* for their political gender statements (or lack thereof) (Figure 12.6).

Similarly, and perhaps more broadly, the feminist approach rests on the assumption that art not only reflects but influences the attitudes of a culture. Feminist film critics attempt to show audiences how traditional cinematic language and symbolism reflect a masculine ideology. They encourage proportionate representation of women in film and urge that female characters not be relegated to traditional, stereotyped roles. Feminist analysis also considers the gender of directors and screenwriters and how it affects the presentation of the material.

To evaluate a film from the gender perspective, we might consider these questions:

- Are the main characters male or female? Was the decision about their gender made by the filmmakers based on the requirements of the story, or do the role assignments reflect gender-based stereotypes?
- How are women or gays portrayed in the film? Are they passive, victimized, or ornamental, or are they active, assertive, and important to the development of the story?
- Who made the film? Do you think the gender of the filmmakers influenced their treatment and presentation of the story?

- Did the film seem to advocate any specific political ideas about the rights and equality of women or gays (workplace discrimination, harassment, abortion or adoption rights, and so on)? Were these issues central to the story, or did their inclusion seem halfhearted?

The Film as Insight to the Mind: The Psychoanalytical Approach

Freudian Criticism   Advocates for the interpretation of film from a Freudian perspective believe that a movie is an expression of the filmmaker's psyche and that a film's meaning lies beneath the obvious images on the screen. Knowing how the unconscious mind of a neurotic disguises secret thoughts in dream stories or bizarre actions, Freudian critics believe that directors (and screenwriters) rely heavily on symbols and purposely cloak or mystify events and ideas in images that require interpretation for true understanding. They tend to view a film as a kind of fantasy, dream, or daydream, and they use psychoanalysis to provide insights into the mind of the *auteur* who produced it. Recently, there has been a shift away from the analysis of the film's creator and toward the analysis of the film's audience—on the way the film appeals to *our* neuroses by tapping into *our* unconscious, repressed wishes, fantasies, and dreams. When examining the film from a Freudian perspective, one might consider these questions:

- What particular qualities of the film suggest that its true meaning lies beneath the surface and requires psychological analysis to unravel? Where in the film does the director seem to cloak and mystify events and ideas? (Figure 12.7.)
- Do you find any of the basic concepts usually associated with Freud suggested or symbolized in this film: the Oedipus complex, the ego, the id, the superego, the libido, unconscious desires, or sexual repression? What insights do they provide into the director's psyche?
- What other symbols do you find in the film, and what is your interpretation of them? What do they reveal about the director's psyche?
- Which of the symbols discussed in the previous two questions strike responsive chords in you personally? Do you think your responses to these symbols and images are unique to your personality, or are they universal audience responses? If your responses were unique, what kinds of insights or self-discovery resulted from them?

Jungian Criticism   The Jungian critic begins with some important basic assumptions. The first of these is that all human beings share a deep psychological bond, a collective unconscious, a kind of shadowy imprinting of universal images, patterns, and life experiences known as archetypes. These archetypes exist beneath the surface and are discernible only in fragments that surface as archetypal images, or shadows. One goal of the Jungian critic is to get a sense of the underlying archetypes suggested by the surface images evident in a film's characters, plot, and iconography. Carl Jung also believed that all stories and legends are variations or aspects of a central myth, a monomyth, that undergirds all archetypal images and suggests their relationship to an archetype. This all-encompassing myth is the quest, in which the hero struggles to become an independent, self-reliant being. To accomplish

FIGURE 12.7 **The Psychoanalytical Approach**   Writer-director Todd Haynes's decision to cast six radically different actors to portray Bob Dylan in *I'm Not There* virtually demands that the viewer supply a psychoanalytical reading of the film. Shown here are Richard Gere, Heath Ledger, Christian Bale, Marcus Carl Franklin, Cate Blanchett, and Ben Whishaw.

this, the hero must free himself from the Great Mother (apparently an image for any kind of entangling or debilitating dependency). When he becomes independent and self-sufficient, he is rewarded by union with his feminine ideal, the anima. Therefore, another goal of the Jungian critic is to analyze the film's characters and their actions in relationship to the monomyth. The following questions might be considered by the Jungian approach:

- Do any of the characters seem familiar beyond ordinary stereotyping? Do they possess universal qualities to such a degree that they might be the surface shadows of archetypes? What aspects or qualities of the characters seem strikingly familiar or universal? What archetypes might these qualities suggest?
- Examine the possible relationships of the story's characters, conflicts, and resolutions to the quest monomyth. Do we have a male hero struggling for freedom from some kind of dependency? Is there a character or concept in the film that could be related to the Great Mother image? Does the hero become a separate, self-sufficient being? Does the resolution of the film's story include the hero's union with his ideal feminine other?
- What other films can you think of which reflect the general universal patterns of the quest monomyth? In what important ways do the universal patterns in these films differ from those in the film under analysis?
- Back off mentally from the specific characters, conflicts, actions, and images of the film, and try to view them as abstractions: broad, general patterns and concepts. Does generalizing and abstracting story elements in this way make the film's images seem more clearly archetypal?

The Eclectic Approach

To analyze every film from the narrow critical framework drawn from one or another of the approaches discussed so far would severely hamper our evaluation. To be fair, we must consider the director's intentions and choose an approach that complements them. Consider the result, for example, of applying the humanistic approach to a James Bond film or an Alfred Hitchcock film.

Vincent Canby's *New York Times* review of Hitchcock's *Frenzy* demonstrates the difficulty of judging a Hitchcock film from a humanistic frame of reference:

> Alfred Hitchcock is enough to make one despair. After 50 years of directing films, he's still not perfect. He refuses to be serious, at least in any easily recognizable way that might win him the Jean Hersholt Award, or even an Oscar for directorial excellence. Take, for example, his new film, "Frenzy," a suspense melodrama about a homicidal maniac, known as the Necktie Killer, who is terrorizing London, and the wrong man who is chased, arrested and convicted for the crimes. What does it tell us about the Human Condition, Love, the Third World, God, Structural Politics, Environmental Violence, Justice, Conscience, Aspects of Underdevelopment, Discrimination, Radical Stupor, Religious Ecstasy or Conservative Commitment? Practically nothing.
>
> It is immensely entertaining, yet it's possible to direct at "Frenzy" the same charges that have been directed at some of his best films in the past, meaning that it's "not significant," that "what it has to say about people and human nature is superficial and glib," that it "does nothing but give out a good time," that it's "wonderful while you're in the theater and impossible to remember 24 hours later."[3]

FIGURE 12.8 **The Eclectic Approach**   Often, the best critical approach to a film involves a synthesis of several possibilities. Arguably, Olivier Assayas's *Summer Hours* (starring Jérémie Renier and Juliette Binoche, right) could be interpreted using multiple approaches, including some of those highlighted in Figures 12.3 through 12.7.

Because Hitchcock is a strong personality and a strong director who imposes his own stylistic trademark on every film he makes, his films can be profitably discussed from the *auteur* viewpoint (although he did not write his major American films) and, perhaps more appropriately, can be analyzed as emotional or sensual experiences. Because he stresses the subordinate role of the actor to the film, the personality cult approach is worthless, and, as Vincent Canby's remarks indicate, the humanistic approach leads nowhere. The most valid approach is the one that best matches the director's stated and demonstrated interests.

But one approach to film evaluation seems more valid than any of the others described so far. The eclectic approach acknowledges that all approaches have some validity, and it selects the aspects of each approach that are appropriate and useful (Figure 12.8). In an eclectic evaluation, we might begin by asking whether the film is good and then try to support our opinion with answers to several of these questions:

- How technically sound and sophisticated is the film, and how well does it utilize the full potential of the medium?
- How powerful is the star's performance?
- How well does the film reflect the philosophy, personality, and artistic vision of the director?
- How worthwhile or significant is the statement made by the film, and how powerfully is it made?
- How effective is the film as an emotional or sensual experience?
- How well does the film conform to the patterns of its genre, and what variations or innovations does it introduce into that format?

REREADING THE REVIEWS

We have seen the film, analyzed it, and interpreted it for ourselves. We have formed our own opinions about its worth and have noted our own personal and subjective reactions to it. Now we are ready to return to the reviews. At this point, we should read the review in an entirely different way from that in which we read it before seeing the film. Now we can read all parts of the review in depth, entering into a mental dialogue (perhaps even an argument) with the reviewer as we compare our mental notes and opinions on the film with the written review.

We may agree with the critic on many points and disagree completely on others. Reader and critic may analyze or interpret the film in the same way and yet reach opposite conclusions about its worth. In essence, what results here is a learning experience. Two separate minds—the reader's and the critic's—come together on the same work, seeking agreement perhaps but also relishing argument. Although we should be open-minded and try to see the critic's point of view and understand his or her analysis, interpretation, or evaluation, we must be independent enough not to be subservient.

EVALUATING THE REVIEWER

We might evaluate the reviewers we read, determining how well we think they have carried out their duties. The key function of the reviewer is to lead us toward a better understanding or a keener appreciation of specific films and of the medium in general. After rereading the review in depth, we might first ask ourselves how well the reviewer succeeds in carrying out this function. In other words: *Does the critic succeed in helping us understand more about the film than we could see for ourselves? Does he or she make the film medium itself seem exciting, so that we want to experience its art more deeply and intensely?*

After answering these basic questions, we can move on to a thorough evaluation of the review by considering these questions:

- In what parts of the review is the critic merely providing factual information, things that cannot possibly be argued with? How thorough is this information, and how clear an idea does it give of the nature of the film?
- In what parts of the review does the critic serve as an objective interpreter or guide by pointing out film elements that are worthy of special attention, by placing the film in context, or by describing the techniques employed? Does the critic try to analyze or interpret the film objectively?
- In what part of the review does the critic make relatively objective value judgments about the film's worth? How does the critic support judgments with critical ground rules? Does the critic make these critical ground rules clear? Does the critic provide a logical, convincing argument in support of the evaluation, or does he or she judge the film dogmatically?
- Where in the review does the critic reveal his or her subjectivity, prejudices, and biases? How much does the critic reveal about his or her own personality in this part of the review? How valuable are these subjective parts of the review in stimulating interest in the film or providing material for mental

dialogue or argument? What critical weaknesses, limitations, or narrow attitudes are reflected in this review? Does the critic bother to warn us about his or her prejudices?

- Which critical method or approach does the critic emphasize? Does he or she place emphasis on how the film was made (film as technical achievement), on who stars in the film (film as showcase for the actor), on who made the film (the *auteur* approach), on what the film says (the humanistic approach), on the reality and intensity of the experience of the film (the film as an emotional or sensual experience), or on how well the film conforms to or introduces variations on a more or less conventionalized form (the genre approach)? Does the critic focus on political or economic issues (the Marxist approach), or on issues of gender (the feminist approach), or on symbolic interpretation (the psychoanalytical approach)?
- Does the critic carefully consider the level of ambition of the film and then select an approach to adjust for this expectation? If not, how does this shortcoming affect the review?

So that we are not overly influenced by critics' opinions, we need to develop the discipline of independent thinking, which requires confidence in our skills of observation and analysis and some degree of faith in our own critical judgment. This discipline is extremely important as we develop the confidence to know what we like and the ability to explain why we like it.

Above all, we must develop enough confidence in our own taste, our own insight, our own perception, and our own sensitivity so that, although we may be influenced by critics' opinions or arguments, we are never intimidated by them. We must continually question and weigh every opinion the critics state, and we may question their intelligence, emotional balance, judgment, and even their humanity. For the fact is that, despite the critics' valuable services, criticism remains a secondary and subjective art. No work of criticism has ever provided the last word on film, and none should be accepted as such.

DEVELOPING PERSONAL CRITERIA

To achieve confidence in our critical abilities, it might be helpful to develop some personal criteria for film evaluation. The difficulty of this task is illustrated by the fact that few professional critics have a hard-and-fast set of rules by which they judge films. In the introduction to his collected reviews, *On Movies*, Dwight Macdonald discusses the difficulty of defining general principles:

> I know something about cinema after forty years, and being a congenital critic, I know what I like and why. But I can't explain the *why* except in terms of the specific work under consideration, on which I'm copious enough. The general theory, the larger view, the gestalt—these have always eluded me. Whether this gap in my critical armor be called an idiosyncrasy or, less charitably, a personal failing, it has always been most definitely there.
>
> But people, especially undergraduates hot for certainty, keep asking me what rules, principles or standard I judge movies by—a fair question to which I can never think of an answer. Years ago, some forgotten but evidently sharp stimulus spurred me to put

some guidelines down on paper. The result, hitherto unprinted for reasons which will become clear, was:

1. Are the characters consistent, and in fact, are there characters at all?
2. Is it true to life?
3. Is the photography cliché, or is it adapted to the particular film and therefore original?
4. Do the parts go together; do they add up to something; is there a rhythm established so that there is a form, shape, climax, building up tension and exploding it?
5. Is there a mind behind it; is there a feeling that a single intelligence has imposed its own view on the material?

The last two questions rough out some vague sort of meaning, and the third is sound, if truistic. But I can't account for the first two being here at all, let alone in the lead-off place. Many films I admire are not "true to life" unless that stretchable term is strained beyond normal usage: *Broken Blossoms, Children of Paradise, Zero de Conduite, Caligari, On Approval,* Eisenstein's *Ivan the Terrible.* And some have no "characters" at all, consistent or no: *Potemkin, Arsenal, October, Intolerance, Marienbad, Orpheus, Olympia.* The comedies of Keaton, Chaplin, Lubitsch, the Marx Brothers, and W. C. Fields occupy a middle ground. They have "consistent" characters all right, and they are also "true to life." But the consistency is always extreme and sometimes positively compulsive and obsessed (W. C., Groucho, Buster), and the truth is abstract. In short, they are so highly stylized (cf. "the Lubitsch touch") that they are constantly floating up from *terra firma* into the empyrean of art, right before my astonished and delighted eyes. . . .

Getting back to general principles, I can think offhand (the only way I seem able to think about general principles) of two ways to judge the quality of a movie. They are rules of thumb, but they work—for me anyway:

A. Did it change the way you look at things?
B. Did you find more (or less) in it the second, third, *N*th time?

(Also, how did it stand up over the years, after one or more "periods" of cinematic history?)

Both rules are *post facto* and so, while they may be helpful to critics and audiences, they aren't of the slightest use to those who make movies. This is as it should be.[4]

Although Macdonald has little faith in *rigid* principles or guidelines, guidelines of some sort seem necessary for a foundation from which to watch, analyze, interpret, and evaluate films. The basic problem with ground rules, however, is that they tend to be inflexible and fail to expand or contract to fit the work being evaluated. What is needed is a general but flexible set of guidelines or critical principles that apply to most films but provide for exceptions. A groundbreaking film that conforms to none of the basic guidelines, even though it is a great film, may come along. Flexible critical guidelines, which see absolute consistency of approach as neither necessary nor desirable, will let us evaluate such a film. Because we are constantly experiencing new types of films, our guidelines must be constantly changing and growing to meet our needs.

In developing personal criteria for film evaluation, we (like Macdonald) might begin by trying to formulate a series of questions to ask about each movie that we see. Or we might simply try to list the qualities we think are essential to any good movie. Whichever course we choose, the task is not easy, but just making the effort should add to our understanding of why some movies are better than others. Even if we do come up with a set of guidelines that we consider adequate, we should resist the temptation to carve them into stone. The cinema is a dynamic, evolving art form, always capable of providing us with new films that won't fit the old rules. And it is equally important that we keep our minds and eyes open for discovering new things in old films.

Perhaps most important of all, we must keep our hearts open to films of all sorts so that we can continue to respond to movies emotionally, intuitively, and subjectively. Watching films is an art, not a science. The analytical approach should complement or deepen our emotional and intuitive responses, not replace or destroy them. Used properly, the analytical approach will add rich, new levels of awareness to our normal emotional and intuitive responses and help us become more proficient in the art of watching films.

ANALYZING THE WHOLE FILM

On the Basic Approach: Watching, Analyzing, and Evaluating the Film

1. What seems to be the director's purpose or primary aim in making the film?
2. What is the true subject of the film, and what kind of statement, if any, does the film make about that subject?
3. How do all the separate elements of the film relate to and contribute to the theme, central purpose, or total effect?
4. What is the film's level of ambition?
5. Given the film's level of ambition, how well does the film succeed in what it tries to do? Why does it succeed or fail?
6. Which elements or parts make the strongest contribution to the theme and why? Which elements or parts fail to function effectively? Why do they fail?
7. What were your *personal* reactions to the film? What are your *personal* reasons for liking or disliking it?

On Evaluating the Reviewer

1. Of what film reviewers in the popular press (newspapers and magazines, local and beyond) are you aware? Do you read their work regularly? If not, choose one critic whose writing is available to you and read carefully at least five of his or her reviews. Can you discern a pattern of central expectations upon which this reviewer's observations are based? Attempt to record them succinctly.
2. Choose two of the nationally known film critics listed below. Then, make a comparative study of their work by locating, through research, each reviewer's opinions of three of your favorite movies. Use the questions on pages 362–363 to guide your evaluations. Some influential film reviewers: Anthony Lane or David Denby (*The New Yorker*), A. O. Scott, Stephen Holden, or Manohla Dargis (*The New York Times*), Stanley Kauffmann (*The New Republic*), Roger Ebert (*Chicago Sun-Times*), Richard Schickel or Richard Corliss (*Time*), Kenneth Turan (*Los Angeles Times*), Joseph Morgenstern (*The Wall Street Journal*),

Peter Travers (*Rolling Stone*), David Edelstein (*New York*), and Owen Gleiberman or Lisa Schwarzbaum (*Entertainment Weekly*).*

On Developing Personal Criteria

1. Try to construct a set of five to ten questions that you think you should answer when judging the merits of a film, or list five to ten qualities that you think are essential to a good movie.

2. If you fall short on the preceding question or lack confidence in the validity of the qualities you've listed as essential, try another approach: List your ten all-time favorite films. Then answer these questions about your list, and see what your answers reveal about your personal criteria for film evaluation:

   a. Consider each film on your list carefully, and decide what three or four elements you liked best about it. Then decide which of these played the most important role in making you like or respect the film.

   b. How many of the films on your list share the qualities that most appeal to you? Which films seem to be most similar in the characteristics you like best?

   c. Do the qualities you pick show an emphasis on any single critical approach, or are your tastes eclectic? To decide this, answer the following:

      (1) How many of the films on your list do you respect primarily for their technique?

      (2) Do several of the films on your list feature the same actor?

      (3) How many of your favorite films are made by the same director?

      (4) Which of the films on your list make a significant statement of some kind?

      (5) Which of the films have a powerful, intense, and very real emotional or sensual effect?

      (6) Which of the films on your list could be classified as genre films, and how many of them belong to the same genre?

      (7) Which films deal with basic conflicts between the "haves" and "have nots"?

      (8) Which films show women (and members of minority groups) breaking out of traditional, stereotypical roles?

      (9) Which of the films on your list rely heavily on complex symbols that require interpretation?

   d. What do your answers to questions (1) through (9) reveal about your personal preferences? Do your tastes seem restricted?

   e. How does your list of favorite films measure up against your first attempt to establish personal criteria for evaluation? How can your standards be changed, perhaps added to, in order to better match your list of film favorites?

*For reviewers published exclusively on the Internet (such as James Bernardinelli), consult www.imbd.com (click on "External Reviews" on the individual film's home page) or www.rottentomatoes.com.

A blurb on the DVD packaging for *Short Cinema Journal/I: 2 (Dreams)* describes one of the films it contains, Chris Marker's *La Jetée* ("The Pier"), as "universally acclaimed . . . a bona fide masterpiece of world cinema."

Test this proclamation by attempting to examine very carefully all elements of the twenty-eight-minute science fiction film: its plot, themes, visual design, photography, editing, hues, sound effects, music, acting, and "director's style."

(Note: Marker himself supposedly produced two versions of this film's soundtrack, one in French, the other in English; this disc provides an English narration. *La Jetée* was the inspiration for director Terry Gilliam's 1995 feature *Twelve Monkeys*, starring Bruce Willis and Brad Pitt.)

(This DVD was originally part of a video periodical three-disc series. The works were later reissued under the rubric *Short* and expanded to include a total of at least eleven available discs. The subtitle of each issue suggests its central theme: 1: Invention; 3: Authority; 4: Seduction; 5: Diversity; 6: Insanity; 7: Utopia; 8: Vision, 9: Trust; 10: Chaos; and 11: Ecstasy.)

Nine Lives, an emotionally moving 2005 film by writer-director Rodrigo Garcia, may be viewed either as one loosely integrated, but thoughtfully arranged, work of film narrative or as simply a compilation of individual short works. All of its nine sections are formally noteworthy, though, because each is photographed in "real time," i.e., in one smooth (yet technically intricate) 11- to 14-minute take or "long shot," using a Steadicam and digital video. In each of the nine, a woman's name serves as a title—and as a guide to its central focus: "Sandra" (Elpidia Carrillo), "Diana" (Robin Wright Penn), "Holly" (Lisa Gay Hamilton), "Sonia" (Holly Hunter), "Samantha" (Amanda Seyfried), "Lorna" (Amy Brenneman), "Ruth" (Sissy Spacek), "Camille" (Kathy Baker), and "Maggie" (Glenn Close).

Although any one of these mini-movies might well serve as a worthy "text" for an examination of all of its literary and cinematic elements, "Maggie" is perhaps the one best suited for this exercise. The whole film's first eight separate sections each connect to at least one other because it contains a "repeated" character. This final story, however, presents two entirely new characters, a mother (Close) and her young daughter (Dakota Fanning), on a visit to a cemetery.

Obtain a DVD copy of *Nine Lives* and watch Chapters 26–28 (:10). Consider carefully how Rodrigo Garcia and his creative team have unified the many elements of this film. Note especially the slow revelation of its "plot" and characters. Also consider the symbolic *cinematic* effects and possibilities represented by each of these elements: the setting and its ambient sounds; the grey cat ("King of the Hill"); the dialogue, such as the daughter's line "I need to pee" and the mother's "We go on. . . . Everyone here went on . . . with their baggage"; action and objects (climbing a tree, playing a hand-clap game, "serving" a bunch of grapes); camera movement (including a 360-degree pan); and a musical cue for solo piano.

Now, return to the opening seven questions above (p. 365) and use them to study this work even more completely.

DVD FILMMAKING EXTRAS

Citizen Kane:
This DVD, like the earlier laserdisc version, encompasses a wide variety of approaches for film study. The auxiliary platter in the two-disc set provides the documentary "The Battle Over Citizen Kane," which puts the movie into social, historical, and political contexts. The main disc gives us a newly remastered picture and sound, and, among other elements, two feature-length audio commentaries: one by film critic Roger Ebert and the other by director/Welles biographer Peter Bogdanovich. (As Marc Saltzman points out in *DVD Confidential*, the set also contains several "Easter eggs," including an interview with actor Ruth Warrick, who plays Kane's first wife, and a dialogue between Ebert and editor/[later] director Robert Wise.)

Dark City:
So far, Roger Ebert has chosen to record DVD commentaries for very few movies. Before he bestowed this honor upon *Citizen Kane*, his enormous admiration for Alex Proyas' film *Dark City* led him to lend his voice to support it—even though, as he has indicated, he had never even met or talked with the director. In this commentary, film students can find a wide-ranging affirmation of the overall quality and unity of the movie's components.

Pulp Fiction (Collector's Edition):
Here, a student interested in comparing the stated judgments of several writers about the same film can find multiple "Reviews and Articles Analyzing the Film" on disc, with two of them also printed on the brochure provided. Reviewers include Janet Maslin (*New York Times*), Richard Corliss (*Time*), Roger Ebert (*Chicago Sun-Times*), Anthony Lane (*The New Yorker*), J. Hoberman (*Village Voice*), Owen Gleiberman (*Entertainment Weekly*), Elizabeth Pincus

(*L.A. Weekly*), Julie Burchill (*London Times*), and Alexander Walker (*Evening Standard*). Also, a special edition of the television review program *Siskel and Ebert & the Movies* called "Pulp Faction: The Tarantino Generation" is made available in its entirety.

The Stunt Man (Limited Edition):
The full story of the development, making, "selling," and delayed distribution of this seldom-seen comedy/drama/action thriller is told by director Richard Rush, who acts as on-screen host throughout the two-DVD set. On disc two, Rush presents a 114-minute documentary that he wrote and directed; it includes interviews with principal actors Peter O'Toole, Steve Railsback, and Barbara Hershey.

The Namesake:
Included on this DVD is "The Anatomy of *The Namesake*: A Class at Columbia University's Graduate Film School," a fascinating seminar conducted by producer-director Mira Nair.

FILMS FOR STUDY

Angels and Insects (1995)
Animal Kingdom (2010)
Another Year (2010)
Barney's Version (2010)
Black Swan (2010)
Body Heat (1981)
Bonnie and Clyde (1967)
Brokeback Mountain (2005)
Citizen Kane (1941)
Crash (2004)
The Crying Game (1992)
The Deer Hunter (1978)
The Devil Wears Prada (2006)
Diary of a Mad Black Woman (2005)

8½ (1963)
The Fighter (2010)
Gangs of New York (2002)
Girlfight (2000)
The Ice Storm (1997)
Inception (2010)
Inside Job (2010)
Julie and Julia (2009)
The Kids Are All Right (2010)
The King's Speech (2010)
Little Miss Sunshine (2006)
Lovely and Amazing (2001)
McCabe & Mrs. Miller (1971)
Never Let Me Go (2010)

127 Hours (2010)
Ordinary People (1980)
Persona (1966)
A Scanner Darkly (2006)
Secretariat (2010)
The Secret in Their Eyes (2009)
Secrets & Lies (1996)
A Serious Man (2009)
The Social Network (2010)
2001: A Space Odyssey (1968)
Toy Story 3 (2010)
True Grit (2010)
United 93 (2006)
Winter's Bone (2010)

ADAPTATIONS

The Girl With the Dragon Tattoo

The Maltese Falcon was produced three times before I did it, never with very much success, so I decided on a radical procedure: to follow the book rather than depart from it. This was practically an unheard of thing to do with any picture taken from a novel, and marks the beginning of a great epoch in picture making.

—JOHN HUSTON, DIRECTOR

An **adaptation** is a film based on another work. A significant percentage of Hollywood films are adaptations, and in fact publishers routinely send advance copies of their books to agents in the hopes of landing a lucrative film deal. Although the original work is typically a novel, short story, play, or biography, adaptations have been made from television series (*Miami Vice*), computer games (*Tomb Raider*), graphic novels (*A History of Violence*), children's books (*Shrek*), and magazine articles (*The Fast and the Furious*). Adaptations range from the close or faithful adaptation, in which the filmmaker translates nearly every character and scene from page to screen, to the loose adaptation, in which many elements from the original work have been dropped and many new elements added. By comparing a film adaptation and its source, we can learn a great deal about what is unique to each medium while experiencing different interpretations of the story.

THE PROBLEMS OF ADAPTATION

When we see a film adaptation of a favorite book or show, we may expect the film to duplicate the experience we had when we read or saw the original work. That is, of course, impossible. In a sense, we have the same reaction to many film adaptations that we might have toward a friend whom we haven't seen for a long time and who has changed greatly over the intervening years. Mentally prepared to meet an old friend, we meet a stranger and take the changes as a personal affront, as though the friend has no right to undergo them without our knowledge or permission. The changes involved in taking a work to the screen are as inevitable as the changes brought by age. To know what we can reasonably expect from films based on other works requires insight into all kinds of changes that adaptation will bring, as well as an understanding of the differences in the media involved.

Change in Medium

The medium in which a story is told has a definite effect on the story itself. Each medium has its strengths and limitations, and any adaptation from one medium to another must take these factors into account and adjust the subject matter accordingly. For example, a novel may be of any length and can develop elaborate plots with many characters; a film's scope is limited by its screen time. Fans of the Tolkien saga *The Lord of the Rings: The Return of the King* must accept that even a three-hour-and-twenty-minute film has to leave out large chunks of the lengthy novel. The audience's point of view when watching a play is limited by the position of the seats and stage, but watching a film we can view an interior room one minute and an aerial view of the city the next. Audiences in the Broadway production of *Chicago* experienced the thrill of watching a live performance; film audiences can enjoy the musical's fast-paced rhythms and star close-ups. If we are to judge a film adaptation fairly, we should recognize that although a novel, a play, or a film can tell the same story, each medium is a work of art in its own right, with its own distinctive techniques and conventions. Just as an oil painting has a different effect than a statue depicting the same subject, a film adaptation has a different effect than its literary source.

FIGURE 13.1 **Objection Sustained** Sometimes problems arise that are totally beyond the screenwriter or director's control. Fifties novelist J. D. Salinger became a fascinating fictional character in W. P. Kinsella's fantasy novel, *Shoeless Joe*. Salinger, however, objected to his name being used for the character, so when the film version (*Field of Dreams*) came out, the character had become a black novelist/civil rights fighter from the sixties played by James Earl Jones, shown here with Kevin Costner.

Change in Creative Artists

In our analysis we certainly must consider the influence that any change in creative talents has on a work of art. No two creative minds are alike, and when the reins are passed from one creative hand to another, the end product changes. Some kind of creative shift occurs in almost any kind of adaptation. As filmgoers, we must develop an equally tolerant attitude toward all film adaptations and freely grant the new creative talents some artistic license (Figure 13.1).

Of course, there are limits to which artistic license can justifiably be carried. If a work is changed so much that it is almost unrecognizable, it should probably not bear the same title as the original—as was the case for John Irving's novel *A Prayer for Owen Meany*, whose title was changed to *Simon Birch* for the film adaptation. It has been said, perhaps with justification, that Hollywood frequently distorts the meaning of a novel so thoroughly that nothing is left but the title. Two brief examples may illustrate the validity of that statement.

John Ford, when asked about his indebtedness to the novel in making *The Informer*, supposedly replied, "I never read the book." In a similar vein, playwright Edward Albee was once asked whether he was pleased with the screen adaptation of *Who's Afraid of Virginia Woolf?* He replied ironically that, although it omitted some things he felt were important, he was rather pleased with the adaptation, especially in light of the fact that a friend had called him to pass on the rumor that the filmmakers were seeking someone to cast in the role of George and Martha's nonexistent son. (Screenwriter Ernest Lehman's first draft included a real son who had committed

FIGURE 13.2 Literature Meets Cinema Although conventional wisdom dictates that successful writers most often seem to resent what Hollywood does to their literary works, exceptions do occur. John Irving proudly won an Academy Award for adapting his own novel *The Cider House Rules* for the screen. He is shown here in the small role of "the disapproving stationmaster" (with Tobey Maguire in the foreground). *My Movie Business* is the memoir he wrote about his experiences—both rewarding and frustrating—in the film world.

suicide, but director Mike Nichols would not accept that radical change.) Many screenwriters, however, aim to remain true to the original work, and on occasion the original writer may even be hired to write the adaptation (Figure 13.2).

Cinematic Potential of the Original Work

Renata Adler has observed, "Not every written thing aspires to be a movie." And, indeed, some works are more adaptable to the film medium than others. Much of the humor in the film *Adaptation* comes from the screenwriter character's frustration at not being able to find "the story" in the book he has been hired to adapt. The style in which a work is written also affects its adaptability to film. The many adapters of Henry James's short stories and novels, perhaps drawn to his work by its complex characters, moral dilemmas, and visual possibilities, have had to contend with a prose style that is abstract, analytical, and some say, convoluted. Consider this opening sentence from James's *The Golden Bowl*: "The Prince had always liked his London, when it had come to him; he was one of the modern Romans who find by the Thames a more convincing image of the truth of the ancient state than they had left by the Tiber."[1]

In contrast, the concrete, simple prose style of Ernest Hemingway, as in the beginning of "The Battler," is clearly more cinematic: "Nick stood up. He was all right. He looked up the track at the lights of the caboose going out of sight around the curve. There was water on both sides of the track, then tamarack swamp."[2]

Although the problems of adapting a play to the screen are not generally as great as those presented by James, playwrights also have styles that affect the ease with which their plays can be adapted to film. Tennessee Williams, for example, uses specific and sensual verbal imagery, and his plays contain speeches—such as the one describing Sebastian's death in *Suddenly, Last Summer*—that lend themselves to visual flashbacks.

ADAPTATIONS OF PROSE FICTION

The general elements just discussed influence our reactions to film adaptations of any type of work. A more complete understanding requires a deeper examination of the specific challenges posed by each medium. To better understand what is involved in translating a work of prose fiction into film, we will look at certain characteristics of novels, novellas (short novels), and short stories.

Literary Versus Cinematic Points of View

In literature, point of view refers to the vantage point from which the author presents the action of the story. In film, the term "point of view" is generally used in connection with a type of shot taken from the place where the character's eyes would be, but it can also apply to how the entire film's story is told. A filmmaker who attempts to translate a novel into film must decide how to adapt the novel's point of view. It is useful, then, to be familiar with the main types of **literary point of view.**

1. **First-Person Point of View.** A character who has participated in or observed the action of the story gives us an eyewitness or firsthand account of what happened and his or her responses to it (Figure 13.3). A series of first-person narrators tell the story of Russell Banks's novel *The Sweet Hereafter;* here school bus driver Dolores Driscoll begins to describe the accident that killed many of her town's children: "A dog—it was a dog I saw for certain. Or thought I saw. It was snowing, pretty hard by then, and you can see things in the snow that aren't there, or aren't exactly there, but you also can't see some things that are there. . . ."[3]

   Most first-person narrators use "I," although some writers have experimented with "you," as in Jay McInerney's *Bright Lights, Big City:* "You are not the kind of guy who would be at a place like this at this time of the morning. But you are, and you cannot say that the terrain is entirely unfamiliar, although the details are fuzzy. You are at a nightclub talking to a girl with a shaved head."[4]

2. **Third-Person Narrator Point of View.** A narrator who is not a character or participant in the story's events tells the tale. The narrator can be "omniscient," or all-seeing, all-knowing, and capable of reading the thoughts of all the characters, as in this excerpt about ghosts from Toni Morrison's *Beloved:* "The grandmother, Baby Suggs, was dead, and the sons, Howard and Buglar, had run away by the time they were thirteen years old—as soon as merely looking into a mirror shattered it . . . ; as soon as two tiny hand prints appeared in the cake. . . ."[5]

   A third-person narration can also be "limited," that is, it can focus on the thoughts and emotions of a single character within the story. This character's

FIGURE 13.3 Two Strong "Voices": First-Person vs. Third-Person Point of View In Alice Sebold's best-selling novel *The Lovely Bones*, the vibrant main character, Susie, speaks directly to the reader. When Peter Jackson created his controversial film adaptation of the novel, he retained this essential point of view, periodically allowing the young actress Saorise Ronan to talk aloud to the audience. By contrast, novelist Daniel Woodrell, in *Winter's Bone*, chose to present his strong young female protagonist, Ree Dolly, via third-person point of view. In her film version, director Debra Granik followed through in true cinematic fashion by capturing the extraordinary performance of Jennifer Lawrence without using voice-over.

thoughts are extremely important, for they become the central manner through which we view the action. The narration of Virginia Woolf's novel *Orlando*, for example, follows the main character's life from his adolescence in Elizabethan England, through his transformation into a woman, to the year 1928. Throughout this fictional biography, the narrator may guess at other characters' motivations, but Orlando's actions are authoritatively explained to us: "Orlando had inclined herself naturally to the Elizabethan spirit, to the Restoration spirit, to the spirit of the eighteenth century. . . . But the spirit of the nineteenth century was antipathetic to her in the extreme. . . ."[6]

3. **Stream of Consciousness or Interior Monologue.** Woolf and other writers of her generation also pioneered the "stream of consciousness" or "interior monologue," which is a combination of third-person and first-person narrative, although the participant in the action is not consciously narrating the story. What we get instead is a unique kind of inner view, as though a microphone and a movie camera in the fictional character's mind were recording for us every thought, image, and impression that passes through the character's brain, without the conscious acts of organization, selectivity, or narration, as in these lines from William Faulkner's *The Sound and the Fury*:

> *Stay mad. My shirt was getting wet and my hair. Across the roof hearing the roof loud now I could see Natalie going through the garden among the rain. Get wet I hope you catch pneumonia go on home Cowface. I jumped hard as I could into the hog-wallow the mud yellowed up to my waist stinking I kept on plunging until I fell down and rolled over in it.* "Hear them in swimming, sister? I wouldn't mind doing that myself." *If I had time. When I have time. I could hear my watch. Mud was warmer than the rain it smelled awful.*[7]

THE WRITER'S PLACE IN HOLLYWOOD

Indispensable and (like editors) invisible, writers have historically had a complicated relationship with other segments of the film industry. Lacking the glamour and box-office appeal of the starring actors and the power of producers, writers frequently portray themselves in films as marginalized and victimized by producers and directors who use their talents but quickly drop them once their services are no longer needed.

The screenwriter's tenuous position in Hollywood can even affect an actor playing the role of a screenwriter. In the late 1970s, actor Allen Goorwitz apparently suffered just such an identity crisis. He was already well known under his stage name, Allen Garfield, for feature roles in such films as Francis Ford Coppola's *The Conversation* (1974). Yet he suddenly began using his birth name professionally just before he began work on *The Stunt Man* (1980), in which he played a screenwriter. His name change seems somehow apt, considering that, just as Peter O'Toole portrayed a stereotypically manipulative, god-like film director (Eli Cross), Goorwitz's Sam was clearly meant to represent the archetypal Hollywood author—an "insecure" human being who complains loudly that "Everybody wants to take things away from me!"

Among all the iconic variations of screenwriters in films themselves, none is more searing than the figure of the hack screenwriter (played by William Holden) at the center of Billy Wilder and Charles Brackett's classic *Sunset Boulevard* (1950). Here, with operatic gestures, Gloria Swanson's faded, mad silent movie star, Norma Desmond, consumes this writer in the same fashion in which the hungry industry itself has earlier devoured her.

Filmic representations of the screenwriter's experience in Hollywood draw heavily on reality.

D. W. Griffith, the essential and controversial "father of American film," worked in silent movies after a very brief and unsuccessful career as a playwright. His acquired dramatic writing skills served him well in helping to create the first extended film narratives, and he wrote or co-scripted most of his celebrated works, including *Birth of a Nation* (1915) and *Intolerance* (1916). However, the prototypical urge to direct soon seized him, and he managed quickly to rise above the curse of being a "mere" writer in Hollywood. With Charlie Chaplin, Mary Pickford, and Douglas Fairbanks, Griffith in 1919 established United Artists, an independent production and distribution company that ultimately helped lead to the powerful studio filmmaking system of the 1930s, '40s, and '50s. There, generally, producers ruled the magic realms, and scriptwriters, who sometimes were manipulated to compete unknowingly against each other, filled the dungeons of the creative hierarchy.

1915
D. W. Griffith plays multiple roles in the making of his films, both writing and directing *Birth of a Nation*.

1930s
The studio filmmaking system becomes more hierarchical. With some exceptions in the decades to follow, writers remain marginalized.

1940s
Screenwriters such as Preston Sturges (*Sullivan's Travels*, 1941) and John Huston (*The Maltese Falcon*, 1941) shift their attention to the more lucrative pursuit of directing.

1950
Leading actor William Holden portrays a hapless screenwriter in *Sunset Boulevard*.

1964
Holden plays another stereotypical (but happier) writer of movies in *Paris, When It Sizzles*.

Near the height of the studio system's power, the novelist Raymond Chandler published a critical essay in the *Atlantic Monthly* (November 1945) in which he recounted his own adventures in the screenwriting trade, expressing hurt feelings about his treatment. Although he attempted to see the big picture, his analysis of the talented writer's fate in Hollywood is bleak: "The challenge of screenwriting," he wrote, "is to say much in little and then take half of that little out. . . ." But given the studio's power, Chandler observed that "an art of the screenplay" does not exist, "for it is the essence of this system that it seeks to exploit a talent without permitting it the right to be a talent."

During the four- or five-decade reign of the studio system, various novelists and (especially) playwrights were, in fact, recognized for their scriptwriting contributions. Among those who won Academy Awards for either original or adapted screenplays were the "outside" artists Sidney Howard (*Gone With the Wind*, 1939), Robert E. Sherwood (*The Best Years of Our Lives*, 1946), and Budd Schulberg (*On the Waterfront*, 1954). But even the most famous American novelists who served tours of duty in Hollywood, William Faulkner and F. Scott Fitzgerald, obtained little recognition for their work.

Screenwriters often struggled to step into other roles that would give them more recognition for their work and more power and control over the scripts they wrote. During the 1940s, a few talented screenwriters such as Preston Sturges (*Sullivan's Travels*, 1941) and John Huston (*The Maltese Falcon*, 1941), managed to become successful directors. Later, Francis Ford Coppola (*The Godfather* saga) and Lawrence Kasdan (*The Big Chill*, 1983) accomplished similar feats. But in the 1960s, 1970s, and 1980s, writing Oscars went to more "outside" workers, including John Osborne (*Tom Jones*, 1963), Robert Bolt (*Doctor Zhivago*, 1965; *A Man for All Seasons*, 1966), Ruth Prawer Jhabvala (*A Room With a View*, 1986), and Alfred Uhry (*Driving Miss Daisy*, 1989).

By the 1970s, when the monopoly of the studio system began to give way to independents, some directors finally took on major power in Hollywood. However, the most notable screenwriters did not win such huge paychecks until 1990. In the last paragraph of his "Writers in Hollywood" essay, Raymond Chandler may have anticipated this move: "For the very nicest thing Hollywood can possibly think of to say to a writer is that he is too good to be only a writer."

Screenwriters-turned-directors are rare, but role-shifting became more common in the mid-1990s. Actors were already central to the picture-making system and unintimidated by the specters of early Orson Welles (*Citizen Kane*, 1941) and Woody Allen (*Annie Hall*, 1977). They emerged as winners in the writing sweepstakes—for example, Emma Thompson (*Sense and Sensibility*, 1995) and Ben Affleck and Matt Damon (*Good Will Hunting*, 1997) won screenwriting Oscars. At the end of the 1990s, Tom Stoppard (*Shakespeare in Love*, 1998) and John Irving (*The Cider House Rules*, 1999) brought acclaim back to playwrights and novelists.

Charlie Kaufman (*Being John Malkovich*, 1999) provided a screenwriter's gravest examination of the profession's identity crisis in *Adaptation* (2002). Ostensibly based on a nonfiction book by Susan Orlean, this wildly creative movie (starring Nicolas Cage, shown in the photo on the previous page) seems, in fact, to profess the true madness of its writer. His feelings of inadequacy are tattooed on every frame. The clever device—both literary and cinematic—that Kaufman conjures up to objectify his position is an immensely commercially successful scriptwriting twin, Donald Kaufman. By contrast, Charlie, an insecure schlub, can get no respect from anyone in Hollywood. Ultimately, Charlie and his fictional brother Donald were both nominated for Oscars; neither won. And, of course, the real-life writer Kaufman finally *had* to make his directing debut, with *Synecdoche, NY* in 2008.

Sources: Chandler: *Later Novels & Other Writings;* David Thomson's *New Biographical Dictionary of Film;* Ira Konigsberg's *Complete Film Dictionary.*

1990
Maverick Joe Eszterhas receives $3 million for *Basic Instinct*—the highest amount paid for a screenplay to date.

1992
The satire of Robert Altman's *The Player* (written by novelist Michael Tolkin) toys with ideas of revenge for the screenwriter.

2007
Screenwriter Daniel J. Snyder creates *Dreams on Spec*, a revealing feature-length documentary that examines the working lives of three aspiring screenwriters; Snyder also interviews several successful filmmakers, including actress and celebrated "script doctor" Carrie Fisher.

1960s AND '70s
Influential screenwriters such as Robert Benton and David Newman (*Bonnie and Clyde*, 1967) and Robert Towne (*Chinatown*, 1974) flourish creatively.

1991
Filmmakers Joel and Ethan Coen excoriate movie scribes with dark wit in *Barton Fink*.

1999
Writer M. Night Shyamalan directs *The Sixth Sense*, and later is paid $5 million each for *Unbreakable* and *Signs* scripts.

4. **Dramatic** or **Objective Point of View.** We are not conscious of a narrator, for the author does not comment on the action but simply describes the scene, telling us what happens and what the characters say, so we get a feeling of being there, observing the scene as we would in a play. This is also known as the *concealed*, or *effaced, narrator point of view.* Here it is seen in the opening paragraphs of "The Killers," by Ernest Hemingway:

> The door of Henry's lunchroom opened and two men came in. They sat down at the counter.
> "What's yours?" George asked them.
> "I don't know," one of the men said. "What do you want to eat, Al?"
> "I don't know," said Al. "I don't know what I want to eat."
> Outside it was getting dark. The street light came on outside the window. The two men at the counter read the menu. From the other end of the counter Nick Adams watched them.[8]

The dramatic or objective point of view is the only literary viewpoint that can be directly translated into cinema. Few if any novels, however, are written from the strict dramatic point of view, because it requires so much of the reader's concentration.

Third-Person Point of View: Challenges

Omniscient, third-person limited, and stream of consciousness points of view all stress the thoughts, concepts, or reflections of a character—elements that are difficult to depict cinematically. These points of view have no natural cinematic equivalents. George Bluestone discusses this problem in *Novels into Film:*

> The rendition of mental states—memory, dream, imagination—cannot be as adequately represented by film as by language. . . . The film, by arranging external signs for our visual perception, or by presenting us with dialogue, can lead us to *infer* thought. But it cannot show us thought directly. It can show us characters thinking, feeling, and speaking, but it cannot show us their thoughts and feelings. A film is not thought; it is perceived.[9]

The usual solution to such problems is to ignore the novel's point of view, ignore the prose passages stressing thought or reflection, and simply duplicate the most dramatic scenes. However, the prose passages and the point of view often constitute much of the novel's essence. This means that filmmakers cannot always capture a novel's essence cinematically. They can attempt to suggest thoughts, emotions, and moods through cinematic elements—through the actors' expressions and gestures, through the *mise-en-scène*, through music, and through dialogue. These make for a different, but not necessarily diminished, experience than the story or novel.

First-Person Point of View: Challenges

The first-person point of view has no true cinematic equivalent. The completely consistent use of the **subjective camera** (a camera that records everything from the point of view of a participant in the action) does not work effectively in film. Even if it did, the cinematic subjective point of view is not really equivalent to the literary first-person viewpoint. The subjective camera lets us feel that we are involved in the action, seeing it through a participant's eyes. But the literary first-person point of view does not equate reader with participant. Instead, the narrator and the reader are two separate entities. The reader listens while the first-person narrator tells the story.

In novels with a first-person point of view, such as Mark Twain's *Huckleberry Finn* and J. D. Salinger's *The Catcher in the Rye*, the reader has an intimate relationship with the narrator, who tells the story as a participant in the action. The writer speaks directly to the reader and forms emotional ties with him or her. The reader feels that he or she knows the narrator, that they are intimate friends. This bond between narrator and reader is much closer than any tie that a remote, unseen director—who shows the story through pictures—might strive to create with a viewer. The intimacy of the warm, comfortable relationship between a first-person narrator and reader can rarely be achieved in film, even with the help of voice-over narration.

Furthermore, the unique personality of the narrator is often extremely important in the first-person novel. Much of this personality, however, may be impossible to show in action or dialogue, for it is the aspect of personality revealed by the way the narrator tells a story, not the way the narrator looks, acts, or speaks in dialogue, that comes across in the novel. This quality, which would certainly be missing from the film, might be called the *narrator's essence*, a quality of personality that gives a certain flair or flavor to the narrative style and that, though essential to the tone of the book, cannot really be translated into film.

Consider, for example, the verbal flow of Holden Caulfield's first-person narration from *The Catcher in the Rye:*

> Where I want to start telling is the day I left Pencey Prep. Pencey Prep is this school that's in Agerstown, Pennsylvania. You probably heard of it. You've probably seen the ads, anyway. They advertise in about a thousand magazines, always showing some hotshot guy on a horse jumping over a fence. Like as if all you ever did at Pencey was play polo all the time.[10]

It is virtually impossible to imagine a film version of *The Catcher in the Rye* without a great deal of voice-over narration running throughout the film. Although such approaches have been tried in film (in adaptations of Nick Hornby's *High Fidelity* and Henry Miller's *Tropic of Cancer,* for example), for the most part filmmakers avoid the extensive use of this device because it interferes with the illusion of naturalism (Figure 13.4).

One fairly successful attempt in which the flavor of the first-person narrator is suggested by the voice-over narration is *To Kill a Mockingbird.* The voice-over, however, is used with restraint, so that the feeling of unnaturalness that often results when someone tells us a story while we are watching it unfold is avoided. And the personality of the narrator here is not as distinctive as Holden Caulfield's in *The Catcher in the Rye* or that of Miller's narrator in *Tropic of Cancer,* so the burden of style and tone does not rest so much on the narrator's verbal essence. Especially in films that come from original scripts rather than novels, voice-over narration is best used *only* as a method for conveying style and the tone of personality (as in the case of *Taxi Driver, Days of Heaven,* and *The Opposite of Sex;* see Chapter 8).

FIGURE 13.4 Sustained "Fourth Wall"-Breaking Voice-Over In Stephen Frears's *High Fidelity,* the protagonist, a record store proprietor played by John Cusack, spends much of his time bursting through what, in theatre, is called the "fourth wall." Frequently, throughout the movie, he looks straight into the camera and speaks directly to the audience—sometimes, even, while he is simultaneously carrying on a conversation with another of the narrative's characters.

The Problem of Length and Depth

Because of the rather severe limitations imposed on the length of a film and on the amount of material it can successfully treat, a film is forced to suggest pictorially a great many things that a novel can explore in more depth. Novelist/screenwriter William Goldman sums up the problem this way: "When people say, 'Is it like the book?' the answer is, 'There has never in the history of the world been a movie that's really been like the book.' . . . All you can ever be in an adaptation is faithful in spirit."[11] At best, the film version can capture a small fraction of the novel's depth. It is doubtful that it can ever capture much of what lies beneath the surface. The filmmaker, nevertheless, must attempt to suggest the hidden material. The filmmaker's task is eased a bit if he or she can assume that viewers have read the novel. But we still must accept the fact that some dimensions of the novel are inaccessible to film.

A long novel creates an interesting dilemma: Should the filmmaker be satisfied with doing only part of the novel, dramatizing a single action that can be thoroughly treated within cinematic limits? Or should the filmmaker attempt to capture a sense of the whole novel by hitting the high points and leaving the gaps unfilled? If the latter strategy is attempted, complex time and character relationships may wind up being implied rather than clearly stated. Usually the filmmaker must limit not only the depth to which a character can be explored but also the actual number of characters treated. This limitation may give rise to the creation of composite characters, embodying the plot functions of two or more characters

FIGURE 13.5 *All the King's Men* (1949)—Change of Focus   Because Robert Penn Warren's powerful novel centers on a first-person narrator addicted to philosophical reflection, Robert Rossen's film version shifts its focus to the man of action, politician Willie Stark (Broderick Crawford).

from the novel in one film character. Furthermore, in adapting a long novel to film, complex and important subplots might have to be eliminated. Generally, then, the shorter the novel, the better are the chances for effective adaptation to the screen. Many short stories have been translated into film with little or no expansion. (To many readers/viewers, John Huston's adaptation of James Joyce's "The Dead" seems exemplary. Even with short stories, though, the sense of loss in film adaptation can be great, as the short story–to–film video series *The American Short Story* repeatedly demonstrates.) Occasionally, a very popular but superficial novel will become the source for a much more substantial film, such as Clint Eastwood's *The Bridges of Madison County*.

Philosophical Reflections

Often, the most striking passages in a novel are those in which we sense an inner movement of the author's mind toward some truth of life and are aware that our own mind is being stretched by his or her contemplation and reflection. Such passages do not stress external action but rather lead to an internal questioning of the meaning and significance of events, taking the reader on a kind of cerebral excursion into a gray world where the camera cannot go (Figure 13.5). The following passage from Robert Penn Warren's novel *All the King's Men*, for example, could not be effectively treated in film:

> There is nothing more alone than being in a car at night in the rain. I was in the car. And I was glad of it. Between one point on the map and another point on the map, there was the being alone in the car in the rain. They say you are not you except in terms of relation to other people. If there weren't any other people there wouldn't be any you, and not being you or anything, you can really lie back and get some rest. It is a vacation from being you. There is only the flow of the motor under your foot spinning that frail thread of sound out of its metal gut like a spider, that filament, that nexus, which isn't really there, between the you which you have just left in one place and the you which you will be when you get to the other place.[12]

Because *All the King's Men* is full of such passages, this one could not be singled out for treatment in voice-over narration. It is also highly improbable that the dramatic scene described here (the narrator, Jack Burden, driving alone in the rain at night) could suggest his thoughts even to a viewer who had read the novel.

When a visual image in a novel is more closely related to a philosophical passage and serves as a trigger to a reflection, there is a greater probability that the filmmaker will be able to suggest the significance of the image to those who have read the novel, but even this is by no means certain. The first of the following two passages from *All the King's Men* gives us a rather clear visual image and could be effectively treated on film. The second is primarily the narrator's reflection on the significance of the visual image and could at best be only suggested in a film:

> In a settlement named Don Jon, New Mexico, I talked to a man propped against the shady side of the filling station. . . . He was an old fellow, seventy-five if a day. . . . The only thing remarkable about him was the fact that while you looked into the sun-brittled leather of the face, which seemed as stiff and devitalized as the hide on a mummy's jaw, you would suddenly see a twitch in the left cheek, up toward the pale-blue eye. . . . It was remarkable, in that face, the twitch which lived that little life all its own. I squatted by his side, where he sat on a bundle of rags from which the handle of a tin skillet protruded, and listened to him talk. But the words were not alive. What was alive was the twitch, of which he was no longer aware. . . .
>
> We rode across Texas to Shreveport, Louisiana, where he left me to try for north Arkansas. I did not ask him if he had learned the truth in California. His face had learned it anyway, and wore the final wisdom under the left eye. The face knew that the twitch was the live thing. Was all. . . . Did the man's face know about the twitch, and how it was all? Ah, I decided, that is the mystery. That is the secret knowledge. . . . [I]n the mystic vision, you feel clean and free. You are at one with the Great Twitch.[13]

Summarizing a Character's Past

In the novel, when a character first appears, the novelist often provides us with a quick thumbnail sketch of his or her past, as illustrated by the summary of the origins and history of Billy, the deaf-mute boy from Larry McMurtry's novel *The Last Picture Show:*

> Billy's real father was an old railroad man who had worked in Thalia for a short time just before the war: his mother was a deaf and dumb girl who had no people except an aunt. The old man cornered the girl in the balcony of the picture show one night and

FIGURE 13.6 **Film Character Without a Past** Billy, the deaf-mute boy in *The Last Picture Show* (played by Sam Bottoms as a "mystery" child in Peter Bogdanovich's movie adaptation), is given an extensive history in Larry McMurtry's source novel.

begat Billy. The sheriff saw to it that the old man married the girl, but she died when Billy was born and he was raised by the family of Mexicans who helped the old man keep the railroad track repaired. . . .

From then on, Sam the Lion took care of him. Billy learned to sweep, and he kept all three of Sam's places swept out: in return he got his keep and also, every single night, he got to watch the picture show. He always sat in the balcony, his broom at his side: for years he saw every show that came to Thalia and so far as anyone knew, he liked them all. He was never known to leave while the screen was lit.[14]

McMurtry summarizes a character's whole background in two brief paragraphs. In the film version, no background on Billy is provided whatsoever (Figure 13.6). Such information could not be worked into the film's dialogue without bringing in an outsider, some character who didn't know Billy, to ask about his past. But having characters spend a great deal of time talking about the backgrounds of other characters does not make for good cinema—it becomes too static, too talky. The only alternative is to dramatize such paragraphs visually. But this type of material not only lacks the importance to justify such treatment but would have to be forced into the main plot structure in a very unnatural manner. The kind of background information that the novelist gives in the passages above is simply not suited to a natural cinematic style, and the background of many film characters therefore remains a mystery. Because novels can and do provide this kind of information, they possess a depth in characterization that films usually lack.

The Challenge of Summarizing Events

Film is capable of making clear transitions from one time period to another and suggesting the passage of time, but it is not as effective as literature in filling in the events between the two periods. In *All the King's Men*, Robert Penn Warren summarizes seventeen years of a woman's life in two of the novel's 602 pages; this summary could make an entire film by itself if treated in detail. As you read part of Warren's summary, consider the challenge it would present to a filmmaker who needed to present this information in a few moments only:

> As for the way Anne Stanton went meanwhile, the story is short. After two years at the refined female college in Virginia, she came home. . . . Anne spent a year going to parties in the city, and got engaged. But nothing came of it. After awhile there was another engagement, but something happened again. By this time Governor Stanton was nearly an invalid. . . . Anne quit going to parties. . . . She stayed at home with her father, giving him his medicine, patting his pillow, assisting the nurse, reading to him . . . , holding his hand in the summer twilights or in the winter evenings . . . . It took him seven years to die. After the governor had died . . . Anne Stanton lived in the house fronting the sea. . . . Anne moved to the city. . . . By this time she was pushing thirty.
>
> She lived alone in a small apartment in the city. Occasionally she had lunch with some woman who had been a friend of her girlhood but who now inhabited another world. . . . She became engaged for a third time. . . . But she did not marry him. More and more, as the years passed, she devoted herself to sporadic reading . . . and to work without pay for a settlement house and an orphanage. She kept her looks very well and continued, in a rather severe way, to pay attention to her dress. . . . Occasionally in a conversation she seemed to lose track and fall into self-absorption, to start up over-whelmed by embarrassment and unspoken remorse. . . . She was pushing thirty-five. But she could still be good company.[15]

Literary Past Tense Versus Cinematic Present Tense

Regardless of the point of view, most novels are written in the past tense, giving the reader a definite sense that the events happened in the past and are now being remembered and recounted. For the novelist there is a distinct advantage to using the past tense. It gives a clear impression that the novelist has had time to think about the events, measure their importance, reflect on their meaning, and understand their relationship to one another.

In contrast, even though a film may be set in the past or take us into the past by way of flashback, a film unfolds before our eyes, creating a strong sense of present time, of a here-and-now experience. The events in a film are not things that once happened and are now being remembered and recalled—they are happening right now as we watch. Various techniques have been employed to overcome this limitation. Special filters have been used to create a sense of a past time, as with the Rembrandt effect in *The Taming of the Shrew*, the hazy and rather faded memory images from *Summer of '42*, or the sepia-tone snapshot stills in *Butch Cassidy and the Sundance Kid* and *Bonnie and Clyde*. In *Little Big Man*, voice-over narration is used to capture the past tense, the sense of experience remembered: the main character recalls significant events of his long life (Figure 13.7). *Lord of War* begins and ends with Nicolas Cage, as an international arms dealer, speaking directly to the camera while he contemplates his career and his life.

Another important distinction is the amount of time a reader spends in experiencing a novel versus the amount of time a viewer spends in watching a film. If the novel is long, readers may linger in its world for days or even weeks. They can control the pace and stretch the experience out as much as they like; they can even

FIGURE 13.7 **Cinematic Past Tense** In *Little Big Man*, Dustin Hoffman was made up to look 121 years old to portray Jack Crabb, the sole survivor of Custer's Last Stand. As the film begins, the old man is being interviewed by a historian. As Crabb recounts his adventures, the film flashes back to scenes from his youth like this one, in which Faye Dunaway is bathing the young Crabb.

reread passages that interest them. And readers can take time out from the reading process, stopping or freezing the novel's flow to reflect on the writer's ideas at a certain point. In film, however, the pace is predetermined. The visual flow, the sparkling stream of images moves on. Beautiful images, significant truths, strong lines of dialogue cannot be replayed. Thus, the very quickness with which a film sweeps by—its quality of cinematic restlessness—distinguishes it from the novel. (Of course, segments of a film can be replayed on a DVD player, and even individual frames may now be frozen for examination, but breaking the visual flow significantly alters the viewing experience.)

Other Factors Influencing Adaptations of Fiction

Commercial considerations play a role in determining whether and how a novel is made into a film. A best-seller with a built-in audience makes an attractive project for film producers. It will also influence the filmmaker's approach to the adaptation—if filmmakers know that much of their audience will be coming to the film as loyal fans of the book, they are likely to aim for a close adaptation. Creative tampering with the plot will be kept to a minimum, and the most important characters will be left unchanged and carefully cast. In the best adaptations, no matter how well known the source, the director will attempt to capture the overall emotional spirit or tone of the literary work. If creative and selective choices reflect a true understanding and appreciation of the novel or short story, the filmmaker can remind viewers who have read the book of the rich emotional and philosophical material beneath the surface and make them feel its presence. Outstanding films, such as *The English Patient*, *The World According to Garp*, and *The Sweet Hereafter*

FIGURE 13.8 **See the Book, Read the Movie** The film *The Sweet Hereafter* independently manages to capture the essential spirit of Russell Banks's emotionally charged novel—even though screenwriter/director Atom Egoyan jettisoned the immensely "cinematic" ending of the literary work and added a very "literary" device to the movie. In this scene, a central character, babysitter Nicole Burnell (Sarah Polley), reads Robert Browning's "The Pied Piper of Hamelin" as a bedtime story to her charges.

(Figure 13.8), may even be able to suggest to those who haven't read the book the meaning that lies beneath the surface.

Some filmmakers seem to assume that very few filmgoers will know the novel. These filmmakers disregard the basic spirit of the novel in adapting it to film, thus destroying the film completely for those familiar with the book. In such cases, the film must be judged as a completely distinct work of art. This type of film, a very loose adaptation, actually may be better suited to the medium than is the close adaptation. Ironically, a loose adaptation may seem a better film to those who are not familiar with the novel than to those who have read and loved it. Thus, a viewer who read the book before seeing the film may have a distinct advantage when the film depends on the viewer's knowledge of the book. But when the filmmaker so deviates from the essence of the novel as to create an entirely different work, reading the novel before seeing the film is a real disadvantage for the viewer. Already familiar with the novel, the filmgoer will not be able to judge the film as a film without preconceived notions.

It is sometimes advantageous, then, to see the film before reading the book. The film may aid our visual imagination, and we may later read the novel with relatively clear-cut ideas of how the characters look and sound. And certainly if the film is less successful in its own language than its novel source, then such a choice may be wise. For instance, one should probably experience Clint Eastwood's movie version of John Berendt's tremendously accomplished and best-selling nonfiction "novel" *Midnight in the Garden of Good and Evil before* reading the immensely popular book. On the other hand, seeing a film first may restrict much of our imaginative participation in reading the book; our brains lock in the screen's particular images of the book's characters forever.

ADAPTATIONS OF PLAYS

The similarity between the film adaptation of a play and the play itself is likely to be greater than the similarity between the film adaptation of a novel and the novel itself. The problems of length and point of view are minimized. The actual running time for a play (not including time between acts or scenes) is seldom longer than three hours. Although some cutting for the film version generally occurs and some selectivity and change may be apparent to viewers who saw the play on the stage, these changes are usually not drastic.

Differences in point of view result from the fact that theatergoers are bound to a single point of view because they must stay in their seats and watch the stage. In contrast, the film version, like a novel, can spirit viewers back and forth from one of the four cinematic viewpoints (see pages 105–111) to another so that they see the action from a variety of physical positions. Through the use of close-ups, the filmmaker can give us a sense of physical and emotional closeness and of being involved in the action. Elia Kazan discovered the power of the close-up during his transition from stage to film directing: "[T]he camera is not only a recording device but a penetrating instrument. It looks *into* a face, not *at* a face. Can this kind of effect be achieved on stage? Not nearly! A camera can even be a microscope. Linger, enlarge, analyze, study. . . . The close-up underlines the emotional content. There is no technique on stage to match it. . . ."[16] A kind of closeness can sometimes be achieved in the small or intimate theatre, but the point of view and the physical distance between theatergoer and actors remain essentially the same throughout the play.

In both media the director is able to comment on or interpret the action for the audience, but the film director probably has more options and techniques available for expressing subjective and interpretive views. Stage directors must rely primarily on lighting for these effects; screen directors have at their command additional techniques such as fast motion, slow motion, distorting lenses, changes from sharp to soft focus, and music. Some carry-over exists between the two media, however, for sometimes stage productions simulate certain cinematic effects. For example, a flashing strobe light on actors in motion gives the effect of the fast, jerky motion of the early silent comedies and is used by stage directors to create this effect.

Structural Divisions

Unlike films, plays have clear-cut structural divisions—acts or scenes—that influence the positioning of peaks of dramatic power and intensity. The end of an act may build to a roaring emotional peak, setting up a strong dramatic echo to carry over into the next act. Film has **sequences,** which roughly correspond to acts in plays, but one continuous sequence flows smoothly into the next. Sometimes there are similarities even here, however, for the **freeze frame** gives a sequence a sense of ending much as the conclusion of an act might do. The cinematic device also approximates the effect of the **tableau,** a technique in which actors onstage held dramatic postures for a few seconds before the curtain fell in order to etch the scene deeply in the audience's memory.

FIGURE 13.9 "Opening Up" a Famous Play The 2002 movie *The Importance of Being Earnest* (starring Reese Witherspoon and Rupert Everett) insisted upon taking its characters and action outside the confined sets of Oscar Wilde's best comic drama. Director Oliver Parker's version of "nature" is pretty to see, but it may manage to help distract many viewers from the playwright's brilliant dialogue and tone.

Such structural divisions may in some cases work well in both media, but sometimes the end of a stage act builds up to a pitch that is too high for a cinema sequence, where its power would seem unnatural or out of place. Perceptive critics spot such problems. Renata Adler described them in her review of *The Lion in Winter*: "The film is far too faithful to the play. It divides neatly into acts, has a long sag in the middle, is weakest in its climaxes."[17] Neil Simon, who adapts his own plays for the screen, describes the difference this way:

> The curtain doesn't come down; and there are no particular breaks—but it does have a rhythm of its own. You set up the problem, which is the first act; the second act is the complication of the problem; and the third act is the working out of the problem. So it has to have a certain harmony to it, like a piece of music; but I don't have to look for a curtain line in a screenplay as I would with a play.[18]

Sense of Space

The change most certain to occur in a film adaptation of a play is the breaking out of the tight confining physical bonds and limitations imposed by the stage setting. Some kind of movement in space is almost essential to film, and to keep the image moving, the filmmaker usually expands the concepts of visual space involved (Figure 13.9). He or she may find some excuse to get the action moved outdoors for a while at least or may decide to introduce as much camera movement and as many editorial cuts between different viewpoints as possible to keep the image alive.

In *The Sound of Music* screenwriter Ernest Lehman found himself with a special problem. The "Do, Re, Mi" song had been performed on the stage in its entirety in the living-room set and ran a total of 11½ minutes. Knowing that a sequence of this length confined in a room would create a claustrophobic effect, Lehman wrote it as a montage sequence, cutting to various locations with the children in different costumes as the song progressed. The impression thus created was that the sequence covered a period of weeks. This solution also made it more convincing that Maria had established a better relationship with the children. Some of the children had obviously grown to like her during the montage. An additional bonus was that director Robert Wise was able to use some of the beautiful scenery around Salzburg.

In the film version of *Who's Afraid of Virginia Woolf?* Mike Nichols moved the camera about constantly, dollying it down hallways and around corners for cinematic effect. He also extended space by adding the scene in the roadhouse, which required a wild car ride to get there and back (in the play, this scene was confined to the living-room set). The film of *Long Day's Journey Into Night* did not go to such extremes, but it employed camera movement and editing to keep the image alive in what was a very confining set—down to the final set-up. Sidney Lumet observes that, in the playwright's work,

> [t]he characters are on a downward spiral of epic, tragic proportions. To me, *Long Day's Journey* defies definition. One of the nicest things that ever happened to me happened on that picture: the last shot. The last shot of the movie is of Katharine Hepburn, Ralph Richardson, Jason Robards, and Dean Stockwell sitting around a table. Each is lost in his or her own addictive fantasy, the men from booze, Mary Tyrone from morphine. A distant lighthouse sweeps its beam across the room every forty-five seconds. The camera pulls back slowly, and the walls of the room gradually disappear. Soon the characters are sitting in a black limbo, getting tinier and tinier as the light sweeps across them. Fade out. After he saw the movie, Jason told me that he had read a letter of Eugene O'Neill's in which he describes his image of his family "sitting in blackness, around the table-top of the world." I hadn't read that letter. My heart leapt with happiness. That's what happens when you let the material tell you what it's about. But the material had better be great.[19]

Such changes may alter a play's total effect significantly. Narrowly confined, restricted movement in a play may serve a powerful dramatic end. By keeping the physical action and movement static, by narrowing the physical boundaries in which the characters operate and bottling up the dramatic scene, the director is often able to intensify the conflict. Dramatic tension created by psychological conflicts and developed through verbal means often seems more potentially explosive when its physical setting is narrow and confined (Figure 13.10). In the stage version of *Virginia Woolf* the guests, Nick and Honey, are virtual prisoners in the home of George and Martha. The narrow confines of the set stress their trapped feeling. Although the trip to the roadhouse in the film version adds a cinematic quality, it also relaxes the tension of confinement to some degree.

Film is simply better and more naturally suited to action and movement, the kind provided by physical conflicts on an epic scale. The restless need for motion built into the film medium makes it difficult to cope with static, confined dramatic tension. Film builds its tension best through rhythmic physical action and especially by physical movement toward resolution. Film is also better equipped to portray physical conflict than the stage. Camera angles, sound effects, and the ability to draw the viewer into close emotional involvement make a fistfight on film much more real than it could ever appear onstage.

FIGURE 13.10 **Characters on a Powder Keg** The tightly confined set of *Who's Afraid of Virginia Woolf?* makes the psychological conflicts especially explosive.

Film Language Versus Stage Language

Film dialogue differs from stage dialogue. Generally, film dialogue is simpler than that used on the stage. Language that is too refined, too elaborate, and too poetic is generally out of place and unnatural in film. Poetic dialogue is usually better suited to the stage. If film is to speak poetically, it must do so not with words but with its primary element—the image. Director Nicholas Ray observed, "In the theatre, words are eighty to eighty-five percent of the importance of what is happening to you for your comprehension. In film, words are about twenty percent. . . . For the words are only a little bit of embroidery, a little bit of lacework."[20] Because the visual image carries so much more weight in film than on the stage, much that might require dialogue on the stage is shown pictorially in film. Filmmakers generally prefer to advance the action by showing what happens rather than by having someone—a character or narrator—tell what happens.

Filmmakers who have attempted to bring Shakespeare to the screen have had to contend with works that are defined by their highly verbal and poetic texts. Director Baz Luhrmann chose to foreground the jarring differences between poetic language and cinematic imagery in his surreal *Romeo + Juliet*. Director Franco Zeffirelli offered a naturalistic version of the tragedy, capturing the spirit of Shakespeare's love story without using the entire text (Figure 13.11). Actor/director Kenneth Branagh appears intent upon settling for no less than the integration of the fully cinematic and the literary in his *Henry V, Much Ado About Nothing, Hamlet* (unabridged), and *Love's Labour's Lost*.

Stage Conventions Versus Cinema Conventions

Certain conventions that are perfectly acceptable on the stage cannot always be reproduced cinematically. Among these is the Shakespearean soliloquy. In Sir Laurence Olivier's adaptation of *Hamlet*, for example, the "Frailty, thy name is woman" soliloquy is filmed in the following manner: Through some parts of the speech, Hamlet's face is pictured in tight close-up without lip movement while

FIGURE 13.11 Cinematic Shakespeare Olivia Hussey as Juliet and Leonard Whiting as Romeo appear in a scene from Franco Zeffirelli's "traditionally edited" version of *Romeo and Juliet* (left). Kenneth Branagh (shown with Derek Jacobi and Julie Christie) insisted that his film of *Hamlet* (1996) use *all* of the play's dialogue.

Olivier's voice speaks the lines on the soundtrack as an interior monologue. At times, Hamlet's lips move, perhaps to show the intensity of his thought. Whatever the intention, the Shakespearean soliloquy, with its ornate, poetic language and structure, does not translate effectively as a cinematic interior monologue, and it seems equally artificial if done as it would be on the stage. Theatergoers accept, even expect, such artificiality. Generally, however, viewers of movies have been programmed to think of film as a more realistic medium.

There is also the problem of whether to leave space for laughter in the screen version of a comedy. On the stage, the actors can simply wait for laughter to subside before resuming. But Neil Simon believes that laughter is too unpredictable to leave space for it in the screenplay; he says, however, that "if you think something is a really big funny moment, it's always safe to cover it with something visual and not come in with another line right on top of it."[21]

Surrealistic and expressionistic stage sets also cause difficulties in translation to film. To some degree, they can be represented or suggested through the use of special camera techniques, such as unusual camera angles and distorting lenses, or the use of special digital effects. But for the most part we expect the physical setting and background in film to be realistic. For example, today we would probably reject as noncinematic the kind of distorted, expressionistic set used in *The Cabinet of Dr. Caligari*, made in 1919. If *Caligari* were remade, it would probably achieve its strange effects solely through the use of special filters and distorting lenses (Figure 13.12). Again, whereas the stage audience expects the stage set or some part of it to suggest or represent reality without being real, the modern film audience is conditioned to expect real settings and will accept no substitute. This observation is equally true of other aspects of stagecraft as they are translated into film. For example, when Peter Shaffer's *Equus*, a play about a disturbed stable boy who mutilates the eyes of horses, was produced on the stage, it utilized actors dressed in stylized wire armatures to represent its horses. But in Sidney Lumet's film version, real horses were thought necessary, and the effect of the violence shifted radically from mainly symbolic to horrifically realistic (Figure 13.13).

FIGURE 13.12 **Expressionistic Distortion** Robert Wiene's film *The Cabinet of Dr. Caligari* (1919) utilized a surrealistic set more suited for theatre than for cinema.

FIGURE 13.13 **Real Horses** In the film *Equus*, a stable boy (Peter Firth) is accused of blinding the horses in his care. Here, the animals are very real; in the original stage production on which the film is based, the horses were stylized and representational, formed of wire frames upon actors' bodies, and their effect on the audience was radically different.

Other Changes

Other types of change can be expected in an adaptation of a play. Even if the original stage actors of a successful play are available, the screen version may not feature them, either because some of the stage actors will not be convincing in front of the camera or because a bigger name is needed as a box-office attraction. Thus, Audrey Hepburn was hired to play Eliza Doolittle in the film *My Fair Lady*, rather than the less-celebrated Julie Andrews (who, ironically, earned an Oscar within the year for her title role in *Mary Poppins*). Kathy Bates, when she was known mainly as an excellent stage actor, lost a central role in *'Night, Mother* to Sissy Spacek for the same reason and, later, a role in *Frankie and Johnny* to Michelle Pfeiffer for slightly different ones. At the time of Pfeiffer's casting, much was made in the press about the cruel employment contrast between the brilliant but "stout" brunette stage actress and the miscast slender blonde movie star. Of course, Bates soon settled that score with an Oscar of her own for film acting in *Misery*.

FIGURE 13.14 **Poetic Justice** In Maxwell Anderson's play *The Bad Seed,* seemingly sweet but evil little Rhoda (Patty McCormack), shown here charming her mother (Nancy Kelly), survived; in Mervyn Leroy's 1956 film version, censors commanded that she must die. The final fate of each young protagonist in Juan Antonio Bayona's *The Orphanage* (2007) (Roger Princep) and Jaume Collet-Serra's *Orphan* (2009) (Isabelle Fuhrman) is foreordained by more complex forces within their narratives.

In the past, the big-city theatre audience was assumed to be more sophisticated than the nationwide movie audience, and changes to the play were made with this difference in mind. An effort was usually made to simplify the play in the film version, and harsh language was censored to some degree. Endings were even changed to conform to the expectations of the mass audience. The stage version of *The Bad Seed* (1956), for example, ends chillingly with little Rhoda, the beautiful but evil child-murderer who has killed at least three people, alive and well, still charming her naive and unsuspecting father. In the ending of the film version, Rhoda is struck by lightning; in this way the demands of the mass audience for poetic justice are satisfied (Figure 13.14). Such changes, of course, are less frequent since the Motion Picture Rating System went into effect in the late 1960s. A modern version of *The Bad Seed* would probably keep Rhoda alive for a possible sequel.

FROM FACT TO FILM: REALITY TO MYTH

Controversies about the factual or fictional nature of some films showcase another problem for the filmgoer, a problem similar in some ways to those presented by adaptations of novels or plays. Whether Jerry Lee Lewis really torched a piano, as portrayed in *Great Balls of Fire,* is not an earthshaking question. But when events

FIGURE 13.15 Perfectly True?   In *A Perfect Storm* (starring Mark Wahlberg and George Clooney), director Wolfgang Petersen and screenwriter Bill Wittliff transformed Sebastian Junger's speculative account of what happened on the *Andrea Gail* fishing boat into a Hollywood story. In the book, the boat's demise is caused by forces outside the crew's control, but in the movie, the men's actions lead to disaster.

of recent history of a magnitude sufficient to be memorable to many people are twisted and distorted or ignored by filmmakers, the issue of factual accuracy versus creative license raises some genuine concern (Figure 13.15).

The mixture of fictional materials with a factual background has always brought some confusion to filmgoers. As we noted in Chapter 11, President Woodrow Wilson was so impressed with D. W. Griffith's *The Birth of a Nation* that he called it "history writ with lightning." Although Griffith's story focused on the Civil War and its aftermath in the South during Reconstruction, he based his film on a sentimental and highly racist novel, *The Clansman*, and did not even attempt to pass it off as factual. Yet some of the devices he used to establish the setting for certain scenes gave the film an aura of authenticity. For example, a still frame sets up a tableau of the South Carolina state legislature in session with the following detailed caption:

> The negro party in control of the State House of Representatives, Columbia, South Carolina. 101 blacks against 23 whites.—An historical facsimile of the actual photographed scene.

Alan Parker's *Mississippi Burning* takes its title from the official FBI file on the case that it portrays. *Time* critic Richard Corliss described the problem raised by Parker's approach to the subject: "*Mississippi Burning* is a fiction based on fact; it invents characters and bends the real-life plot. . . . May a movie libel the historical past? And has *Mississippi Burning* done so? Artistic liberty vs. social responsibility: the stakes are high."[22]

Similar charges of excessive cinematic license have been made against the adaptation of Sylvia Nasar's biography of John Forbes Nash, Jr., *A Beautiful Mind*. The filmmakers, director Ron Howard and screenwriter Akiva Goldsman, leave out significant aspects of Nash's life that do not fit with their theme of the triumph of the human spirit or that paint a less than sympathetic portrait of their hero. Writing for salon.com, critic Charles Taylor explains his objection to this kind of adaptation, insisting that the popular film is "a typical example of Hollywood's chickening out on chancy material, softening the edges of a story and characters, and shoehorning things into a tidy inspirational package. . . . It's John Nash's life, being turned into an Oscar machine and an easy way to jerk tears."[23]

> When Robert Redford directed *Quiz Show*, he was "accused of hedging the truth to improve the story of the movie and boost box office receipts": "From invented dialogue to fabricated court transactions, 'Quiz Show' often takes broad dramatic license. Because the film uses the names of real people (some still living) and has been positioned by its makers as a righteous statement on ethics and morality, the 'Quiz Show' deviations raise provocative questions about Hollywood's conscience—or its lack of one."[24]

The real problem with films like *Mississippi Burning, A Beautiful Mind,* and *Quiz Show* is that the viewers have no way of knowing how the factual material has been handled or distorted. The confusion can be cleared up with the simple addition of a disclaimer. If films can protect themselves by declaring that the events and characters depicted are completely fictitious, they should perhaps be required to inform viewers of how fact and fiction are blended. A disclaimer shown before both episodes of the ABC miniseries *Small Sacrifices* (starring Farrah Fawcett) provides a clear solution to the problem (the story was based on the true story of a mother convicted of shooting her three children): "The following dramatization is based on the book *Small Sacrifices* by Ann Rule. It contains composite changes, name changes and the resequencing of events. Some dramatic license has been taken in the resequencing of events." Another approach is the disclaimer appearing before the opening credits for *Walking Tall* (1973): "A motion picture suggested by certain events in the life of Buford Pusser, Sheriff of McNary County, Tennessee . . . a living legend."

Even though the parallels between *Citizen Kane* and the life of William Randolph Hearst are obvious, *Kane* keeps enough distance from the Hearst story to qualify as a fictionalized biography: The names are changed; the mistress is an opera singer, not an actress; and so on. The RKO legal department, however, was concerned enough to insert the following disclaimer at the film's beginning: "This is not the story of any man be he living or dead. This is the story of the power and strength which impels the lives of many great men seen through the eyes of little men."

When Orson Welles learned of the statement, he was furious about its content (possibly because he had not written it) and replaced it with his own version: "*Citizen Kane* is an examination of the personal character of a public man, a portrait according to the testimony of the intimates of his life. These, and Kane himself, are wholly fictitious." Later the disclaimer was dropped.

Hoffa, which plays fast and loose with the disappearance of Jimmy Hoffa because nobody really knows what ultimately happened to the former Teamster boss, includes an almost illegible disclaimer at the end of the credits. However, the holes in the factual record were important to Jack Nicholson in his performance: "It's not a biography, it's a portrait, and there is a difference. Because no one really knows what happened to Hoffa, it gives you license to do a lot of guessing with other things too. I had a certain amount of license in my job as an actor to have an inside interpretation of the guy."[25] It may be a bit more difficult to take liberties

FIGURE 13.16 **Historical Accuracy** With the exception of some too-modern exploding cannonballs, *Glory* has been praised as one of the most historically accurate Civil War films. Denzel Washington, pictured here, won an Academy Award as best supporting actor in that film. Likewise, *Saving Private Ryan*, starring Tom Hanks and Matt Damon, was considered to be meticulous in its depiction of the visual details of World War II.

with the accepted facts about a personality with Mount Rushmore status, as the Merchant-Ivory team found with their release of *Jefferson in Paris*.

Oliver Stone's *JFK* has seemed to many to be the most arrogant of the fact-to-film efforts, largely because of the docudrama techniques used (newsreel footage, excerpts from the famous Zapruder film showing the assassination of the president, and familiar real names of those involved in later investigations), a clear antigovernment bias, a far-fetched conspiracy theory, and the lack of any kind of disclaimer. (Later, Stone's *Nixon* and *W.* created, similar controversies.) *Executive Action*, a 1973 conspiracy film focusing on the many inconsistencies in the official explanation of the events in Dallas, used a beginning-of-the-film disclaimer that would have made *JFK* more acceptable: "Although much of this film is fiction, much of it is also based on documented historical fact. Did the conspiracy we described actually exist? We do not know. We merely suggest that it could have existed." Otherwise, however, *JFK* is much superior in its filmmaking to *Executive Action*, which is rated in Leonard Maltin's indispensable *Movie & Video Guide* as a "BOMB."[26]

We should approach any fact-based film with care, therefore, and not assume that everything on film represents the truth. At the same time, however, we can take advantage of the opportunities film presents to imagine the past and experience it through the filmmaker's vision (Figure 13.16).

Sometimes, even fiction films must follow these necessities. Although director Stephen Daldry's *The Hours* is definitely not a nonfiction work, one of its three main characters (women from different times and environments during the twentieth century) attempts to recapture a factual person: Virginia Woolf, the celebrated English novelist and critic. Indeed, the most minute historical details of Woolf's suicide in 1941 are reproduced in both this film and in the Pulitzer Prize–winning novel from which it was adapted by the playwright David Hare. Michael Cunningham, the novel's author, took great literary care to honor the historical truth of Virginia Woolf's death. But he also sought to bring the texture of her thematic truth to the fictional characters he was inspired to create by her extraordinary life and work.

For most novelists, one witty contemporary American author once observed, the ideal relationship with filmmakers would involve a book's being "optioned" but never getting produced. In this scenario, of course, the novelist would receive considerable remuneration but would not have to endure the stereotypical pain of seeing his or her child displayed—cosmetically and even genetically altered—at the local multiplex. Upon watching the film version of his novel, though, Michael Cunningham was almost apologetic in his enthusiastic embrace of the finished work. In an essay written for *The New York Times* when the film went into wide release in 2003, Cunningham announced, "I find myself in an enviable if slightly embarrassing position as one of the only living American novelists happy about his experience in Hollywood." But he reached this conclusion only after examining the film with the vivid awareness of how it was couched in a language very different from that of his novel. When Cunningham had visited the set of the film, he had observed the work of Nicole Kidman (as Woolf), Julianne Moore, and Meryl Streep, and, as he tells us, he

> understood that what you lose in turning fiction into film—the ability to enter your characters' minds, and to scan their pasts for keys to their futures—can be compensated for by actors. You lose interiority. You gain Ms. Streep's ability to separate an egg with a furious precision that communicates more about [her character's] history and present state of mind than several pages of prose might do. You gain Ms. Moore's face when she looks at her son with an agonizing mix of adoration and terror, knowing she will harm him no matter what she does.
>
> Actors, too, if they're this good, can introduce details you can't convey on paper, if only because by writing them down you'd render them too obvious. Actors have the incidental at their disposal. Ms. Streep's [character] is stunningly complex, in part because she creates a whole person out of movements, expressions and inflections. . . . If there's a way to do things like that on paper, I haven't found it. . . . It's no wonder we love the movies as much as we do.[27]

Finally, any true twenty-first-century literature *and* movie lover would like to think it was no accident that, in the same issue of the *Times* containing this paean by Michael Cunningham, a similar essay by novelist Louis Begley appeared. In contrast to *The Hours*, a rather "faithful" film adaptation, *About Schmidt*, starring Jack Nicholson, radically transformed its source material. In this case, the filmmakers even transfigured the protagonist from a "fancy New York lawyer" to an Omaha actuary. Nevertheless, while noting the changes, Begley called his reaction to the film "atypically benevolent," observing that "for all the . . . changes in the plot and milieu, my most important themes were treated with great intelligence and sensitivity. . . . I was able to hear them rather like melodies transposed into a different key."[28]

ANALYZING ADAPTATIONS

On Adaptations of Novels

After reading the novel, but before seeing the film, consider these questions concerning the novel.

1. How well is the novel suited for adaptation to the screen? What natural cinematic possibilities does it have?

2. Judged as a whole, does the novel come closer to stressing a sensuous and emotional rendering of experience (as in the Hemingway excerpts) or an intellectual analysis of experience (as in the James excerpt)?

3. How essential is the author's verbal style to the spirit or essence of the novel? Could this verbal style be effectively translated into a pictorial style?

4. What is the novel's point of view? What will necessarily be lost by translating the story into film?

5. If the novel is written from the first-person point of view (as told by a participant in the action), how much of the spirit of the novel is expressed through the narrator's unique narrative style—that is, the particular flair or flavor built into his or her *way of telling* the story rather than the story itself? Could this verbal style be suggested through a minimum of voice-over narration on the soundtrack, so that the device would not seem unnatural? Is the feeling of a warm, intimate relationship between reader and narrator established by the novel, as though the story is being told by a very close friend? How could this feeling be captured by the film?

6. Is the novel's length suited to a close adaptation, or must the novel be drastically cut to fit the usual film format? Which choice would seem most logical for the filmmaker in adapting the novel:

   a. Should he or she try to capture a sense of the novel's wholeness by hitting the high points without trying to fill in all the gaps? What high points do you think must be dramatized?

   b. Should the filmmaker limit himself or herself to a thorough dramatization of just part of the novel? What part of the novel could be thoroughly dramatized to make a complete film? What part of the story or what subplots should be left out of the film version?

7. How much of the novel's essence depends on the rendition of mental states: memories, dreams, or philosophical reflections? How effectively can the film version be expected to express or at least suggest these things?

8. How much detail does the author provide on the origins and history of the characters? How much of this material can be conveyed cinematically?

9. What is the total time period covered by the novel? Can the time period covered be adequately compressed into a normal-length film?

After seeing the film version, reconsider your answers to the questions listed above, and also answer the following.

10. Is the film version a close or a loose adaptation of the novel? If it is a loose adaptation, is the departure from the novel due to the problems caused by changing from one medium to another or by the change in creative personnel?

11. Does the film version successfully capture the spirit or essence of the novel? If not, why does it fail?

12. What are the major differences between the novel and the film, and how can you explain the reasons for these differences?

13. Does the film version successfully suggest meanings that lie beneath the surface and remind you of their presence in the novel? In which scenes is this accomplished?

14. Did reading the novel enhance the experience of seeing the film, or did it take away from it? Why?

15. How well do the actors in the film fit your preconceived notions of the characters in the novel? Which actors exactly fit your mental image of the characters? How do the actors who don't seem properly cast vary from your mental image? Can you justify, from the director's point of view, the casting of these actors who don't seem to fit the characters in the novel?

On Adaptations of Plays

1. How does the film version differ from the play in its concept of physical space? How does this difference affect the overall spirit or tone of the film version?
2. How cinematic is the film version? How does it use special camera and editing techniques to keep the visual flow of images in motion and to avoid the static quality of a filmed stage play?
3. What events that are only described in dialogue during the play does the filmmaker show happening? How effective are these added scenes?
4. Are the play's structural divisions (into acts and scenes) still apparent in the film, or does the film successfully blend these divided parts into a unified cinematic whole?
5. What stage conventions employed in the play are not translatable into cinematic equivalents? What difficulties and changes does this bring about?
6. How does the acting style of the film differ from that of the play? What factors account for these differences?
7. What basic differences can be observed in the dialogue in the two versions? Are individual speeches generally longer in the play or in the film? In which version is the poetic quality of the language more apparent?
8. What other important changes have been made in the film version? Can you justify these in terms of change in medium, change in creative personnel, or differences in moral attitudes and sophistication of the intended audience?

From Fact to Film

1. How does the film story differ from the true story or historical event on which it is based?
2. Can these changes be justified for dramatic purposes?
3. Do the changes significantly distort the essence of the story and the characters involved? How?
4. Was any disclaimer provided to warn viewers that the film was not completely factual? Was there any reason for viewers to believe they were watching a completely factual story?

MINI-MOVIE EXERCISE

Obtain a copy of Ernest Hemingway's early story "Hills Like White Elephants." It should be easy to locate in either its original publication source—the author's short fiction collection *Men Without Women*—or in anthologies of the author's work.

After reading the exceedingly brief story several times, find and watch a DVD version of the made-for-HBO film, directed by Tony Richardson (*Tom*

Jones), that was based upon it. (The movie is part of a grouping of three short films called *Women & Men: Stories of Seduction*; it stars James Woods and Melanie Griffith.)

The screenwriters on this project were the married team of Joan Didion and John Gregory Dunne, who are well known, separately and together, for both fiction and nonfiction. Note carefully how Didion and Dunne have adapted Hemingway's celebrated story from the page to the screen. Identify and catalog their cinematic deductions from and additions to the narrative—no matter how small they may seem. Finally, attempt to gauge the effects, both positive and negative, that this literary/cinematic math appears to create in us as readers/watchers of this metamorphosis.

DVD FILMMAKING EXTRAS

The Sweet Hereafter:
For students of the prose fiction-to-film adaptation process, this DVD is extraordinarily valuable. Not only do both director Atom Egoyan and novelist Russell Banks participate in full audio commentary, but they also appear together in a video discussion of the book and movie. And a considerable portion of the included Charlie Rose interview with Egoyan focuses upon the director's model-breaking experiences in adapting the script himself—and upon the creative trust and certification he received from Banks. In addition, this disc provides the full text (with illustrations) of the Robert Browning poem "The Pied Piper of Hamelin" that Egoyan grafted into the script.

Minority Report:
On disc two in this two-disc set, Steven Spielberg presents a substantial documentary called "*Minority Report* from Story to Screen," which is divided into the sections "The Story/The Debate" and "The Players." Screenwriter Jon Cohen comments upon his decisions and experiences in adapting the Phillip K. Dick story to motion picture form.

Secret Window:
In a nineteen-minute feature called "From Book to Film," screenwriter/director David Koepp discusses his experiences in adapting one of the stories in Stephen King's collection *Four Past Midnight* for film.

The War of the Worlds (2005): Two-Disc Limited Edition:
Three descendants of novelist H. G. Wells speak with Steven Spielberg about the author's probable reactions to how this director and his screenwriters (Josh Friedman and David Koepp) have handled the famous science fiction work.

Spielberg seems fascinated that Wells "was a scientist who allowed himself to have an imagination."

The Constant Gardener:

A special featurette, "John Le Carré: From Page to the Screen," provides not only interviews with director Fernando Meirelles and producer Simon Channing-Williams, but also a statement from the novelist, who examines his expectations for Hollywood's treatment of his work. Le Carré announces, "The job of the movie . . . is to take the minimum intention of the novel and illustrate it with the maximum of freedom in movie language, in movie drama. There's hardly a line left, there's hardly a scene intact in the movie that comes from my novel. Yet, I don't know of a better translation from novel to film."

Memento:

The most "useful" part of this disc for adaptation study is its full-text inclusion of the original short story "Memento Mori" by Jonathan Nolan, the director/screenwriter's brother. From this narrative Christopher Nolan created his shooting script.

The Lord of the Rings: The Fellowship of the Ring (Special Extended DVD Edition):

Four discs compose this immensely elaborate version of the film and the history of its making. See especially the third one, labeled "The Appendices: Part One: From Book to Vision," which provides sections marked "J. R. R. Tolkien, Creator of Middle-Earth," "From Book to Script," and "Storyboard and PreViz: Making Words into Images."

Sleuth (1972):

"A Sleuthian Journey with Anthony Shaffer" provides a twenty-three-minute feature that examines the process by which a playwright transforms his own successful stage work to fit the screen.

FILMS FOR STUDY

(The author of the original work is noted after the film date. See also the Web site for *The Art of Watching Films* for an extensive list of more adaptation films for study.)

Novels and Stories Into Films

Atonement (2007); Ian McEwan

Cold Mountain (2003); Charles Frazier

The Door in the Floor (2004); *A Widow for One Year*, John Irving

The Fantastic Mr. Fox (2009); children's book, Roald Dahl

The Girl With the Dragon Tattoo (2009); Stieg Larsson

Harry Potter and the Deathly Hallows, Parts I and II (2010, 2011); J. K. Rowling

House of Sand and Fog (2003); Andre Dubus III

The Human Stain (2003); Philip Roth

In the Cut (2003); Susanna Moore

The Kite Runner (2007); Khaled Hosseini

The Lovely Bones (2009); Alice Sebold

Million Dollar Baby
(2004); F. X. Toole
Mystic River (2003);
Dennis Lehane
The Namesake (2006);
Jhumpa Lahiri
*No Country for Old
Men* (2007); Cormac
McCarthy
The Notebook (2004);
Nicholas Sparks
The Phantom of the Opera
(2004); Gaston Leroux
Precious (2009); *Push*,
Sapphire
Secret Window (2004);
"Secret Window, Secret
Garden," Stephen King
Sin City (2005); graphic
novel, Frank Miller
Spider-Man 2 (2004);
graphic novels, Stan Lee
That Evening Sun (2009);
"I Hate to See That
Evening Sun Go
Down," William Gay
There Will Be Blood
(2007); *Oil!*, Upton
Sinclair
True Grit (1969 and
2010); Charles Portis
Vanity Fair (2004);
William Makepeace
Thackeray
A Very Long Engagement
(2004); Sébastien
Japrisot

War of the Worlds (2005);
H. G. Wells
*Where the Wild Things
Are* (2009); children's
book, Maurice Sendak

Plays Into Films

Closer (2004); Patrick
Marber
Doubt (2008); John
Patrick Shanley
Finding Neverland (2004);
*The Man Who Was
Peter Pan*, Alan Knee
Off the Map (2003); Joan
Ackermann
The Merchant of Venice
(2004); William
Shakespeare
Stage Beauty (2004);
*Compleat Female Stage
Beauty*, Jeffrey Hatcher
Sweeney Todd (2007);
book for Stephen
Sondheim musical,
Hugh Wheeler
The Woodsman (2004);
Steven Fechter

Fact-Based Films

American Splendor (2003);
graphic novel, Harvey
Pekar
Capote (2005); Gerald
Clark
*The Diving Bell and
the Butterfly* (2007);

Jean-Dominique
Bauby
An Education (2009);
Lynn Barber
Flags of Our Fathers (2006);
William Broyles, Jr. and
Ron Powers
Gods and Monsters
(1998); novel, *Father
of Frankenstein*,
Christopher Bram
*I Love You, Phillip
Morris* (2009); Steve
McVicker
Into the Wild (2007); Jon
Krakauer
Marley and Me (2008);
John Grogan
*Midnight in the Garden of
Good and Evil* (1997);
John Berendt
Persepolis (2007); graphic
novels, Marjane
Satrapi
The Social Network
(2010); *The Accidental
Billionaires*, Ben
Mezrich
Syriana (2005); *See No
Evil*, Robert Baer
*The Wild Parrots of
Telegraph Hill* (2003);
Mark Bittner

GENRE FILMS, REMAKES, *and* SEQUELS

14

The Dark Knight

Hollywood does not simply lend its voice to the public's desires, nor does it simply manipulate the audience. On the contrary, most genres go through a period of accommodation during which the public's desires are fitted to Hollywood's priorities (and vice versa). Because the public doesn't want to know that it is being manipulated, the successful . . . "fit" is almost always one that disguises Hollywood's potential for manipulation while playing up its capacity for entertainment. Whenever a lasting fit is obtained . . . it is because a common ground has been found, a region where the audience's ritual values coincide with Hollywood's ideological ones.

—RICK ALTMAN, CRITIC

GENRE FILMS

The term **genre film** has very often been used to describe film stories that have been repeated again and again with only slight variations, following the same basic pattern and including the same basic ingredients. Setting, characters, plot (conflict and resolution), images, cinematic techniques, and conventions are considered practically interchangeable from one film to another in the same genre—much as the parts for Henry Ford's Model T were interchangeable from one car to another.

This narrow definition of *genre* focuses exclusively upon the formula film, but the term is also used broadly to refer to films dealing with a common subject matter or style. For example, Rex Reed said in his review of *Patton* and *M*A*S*H* that those films "raise the artistic level of the war-movie genre."[1] As the critic Stephen Schiff wrote in *Film Comment* in 1982,

> There was a time when the development of genre was relatively predictable. When moviegoing was an American habit, genre films begat genre films. . . . For a fine director like Howard Hawks . . . , directing a genre film was probably like being a blues musician who could wring sublimity out of three chords and a standard 4/4 groove. . . . It was a tiny arena, and a real artist could load a great deal into it.[2]

Schiff continued, "People went to a genre movie because of its movieness, because they knew it would make them feel happy or sad or just plain entertained in a way that only a certain kind of movie could."[3] And, in noting how movie-making was changing radically in the past few years, he bemoaned the loss of "simple pleasures." Schiff concluded that "directors of the Auteur Age no longer worked *within* the old genres, they worked *on* them."[4] By 1994, in providing the "Preface" for a collection of reviews of genre films, Schiff observed a kind of resurgence of some genres, with the westerns *Dances With Wolves* (1990) and *Unforgiven* (1992) having won best picture Oscars, for example. And he seemed mildly puzzled by the "recombinant genres" phenomenon (the "most boggling of all, perhaps [being] . . . the Teenage Mutant Ninja Turtle films: chopsocky-cartoon-animal-monster-boys'-book-sci-fi-beauty-and-the-beast-buddy fantasies").[5] More recently, writers have remarked upon the difficulty of defining *genre*—in part because of this overlap present in many less exotic films.

Close observers of the form have long called for much more inclusive definitions. Two decades ago, for example, the theorist Rick Altman, in a groundbreaking and much anthologized essay, "A Semantic/Syntactic Approach to Film Genre," tried to mediate various conceptions of genre study by showing how two basic types *must* be synthesized. Altman insisted upon our using this method as an "ability to account for the numerous films that innovate by combining the syntax of one genre with the semantics of another."[6] More recently, Steve Neale, in *Genre and Hollywood*, has concluded that "genre . . . has been used in different ways in different fields, and . . . many of its uses have been governed by the history of the term within these fields—and by the cultural factors at play within them—rather than by logic or conceptual consistency." He insists that we must "rethink" genres "as ubiquitous, multifaceted phenomena rather than as one-dimensional entities to be found only within the realms of Hollywood cinema or of commercial popular culture."[7]

So we are now led to see that there is "less of a difference between genre films and other forms of cinema at least in terms of the basic processes of communication and reading. All communicative forms, including all films, are underpinned by systems . . . against which they acquire their significance and meaning."[8]

It is not difficult to understand how genre films came into being or why they have enjoyed such success. Because of the expense of film production, the studios wanted to create films that would draw a large audience, so that they could realize a substantial profit. The reaction of the mass audience flocking to westerns, gangster movies, *film noir*, war stories, horror pictures, science fiction or fantasy films, screwball romantic comedies, and musicals, for instance, let the studios know what people wanted (and expected), and the studios responded to the great success of these films by repeating the genres, remaking successful pictures, and producing sequels.

As the success of genre films inspired frequent repetition of the basic types, their popularity presented the studios and the directors assigned to direct them with an interesting challenge. So that the public would not become bored, they were forced to introduce variations and refinements while keeping enough of the essence intact to please audiences.

In *Film Genre 2000: New Critical Essays*, editor Wheeler Winston Dixon emphasizes the importance of our continuing to respect and study genre films:

> With genre filmmaking . . . constituting the bulk of film production . . . more than ever [we must try] to understand precisely how contemporary genre cinema shapes and mirrors our collective dreams and desires. . . . [O]ne thing is certain: genre cinema will continue to be the dominant force in American cinema, if only because it is a tried and tested commodity that can reliably be called upon to entertain and satisfy.[9]

Values

The popularity of genre films has always been at least partly due to their ability to reinforce basic American beliefs, values, and myths. The Motion Picture Production Code, which was enforced from the early 1930s until around 1960, encouraged all American films to reflect and reinforce middle-class American institutions, values, and morality. The sincerity of most genre films during this period, however, seems to indicate that, generally, the studio heads and directors probably shared those values. In any case, the audience obviously took great pleasure in seeing their values threatened and then triumphant, for the triumph reinforced people's belief in the strength and validity of their values and made them feel secure in Truth, Justice, and the American Way. Early genre films usually fulfilled their expectations with easy, complete, and totally satisfying resolutions.

The Strengths of Genre Films

For the director, there were certain advantages to working within a given genre. Because the characters, the plot, and the conventions were already established, they provided the director with a kind of cinematic shorthand that greatly simplified the task of storytelling. The best directors, however, did not simply copy the conventions and string together a predictable pattern of stock situations and images. Accepting the limitations and formal requirements of the genre as a challenge, directors such as John Ford provided creative variations, refinements, and complexities that imprinted each film they directed with a rich and distinctive personal style.

The genre film simplifies film watching as well as filmmaking. In a western, because of the conventions of appearance, dress, manners, and typecasting, we recognize the hero, sidekick, villain, female lead, and so on, on sight and assume they will not violate our expectations of their conventional roles. Our familiarity with the genre makes watching not only easier but in some ways more enjoyable. Because we know and are familiar with all the conventions, we gain pleasure from recognizing each character, each image, each familiar situation. The fact that the conventions are established and repeated intensifies another kind of pleasure. Settled into a comfortable genre, with our basic expectations satisfied, we become more keenly aware of and responsive to the creative variations, refinements, and complexities that make the film seem fresh and original, and by exceeding our expectations, each innovation becomes an exciting surprise.

Basic Genre Conventions—And Their Variations

Although each genre has its own conventions, it is perhaps easier to recognize a genre film than it is to delineate clearly all its ritual elements. The basic elements may seem simple when viewed from the distance of memory, but observation reveals that the variations are almost infinite. The five rudimentary conventions of a genre are setting, characters, conflict, resolution, and values reaffirmed.

Genre films were viable over a fairly long period of time and offered directors enough flexibility to create many interesting innovations on the standard elements. But changes in social values, the advent of television, and a changing movie audience made some of the conventions much too limiting. Thus, movies like *Shane* and *High Noon* introduced complex new elements, and the western began to break away from the traditional formula. And the gangster film evolved from *Little Caesar* to *Bonnie and Clyde* to *The Godfather* to *Kill Bill* to *The Departed* to *The American* (2010) in its transformation.

Two elements are probably more important than any of the others in keeping the basic forms viable: the personal code of the hero and the values reaffirmed at the end of the film. When the hero's code is significantly altered and the basic social values are no longer reaffirmed, the essence vanishes. The early western and the gangster film depend on good triumphing over evil, on law and order conquering chaos, on civilization overcoming savagery, and on justice prevailing. When these concepts are brought into question, when shades of gray replace clear distinctions between black and white, when the complexities of reality replace the simplicity of myth, the core is destroyed. In like manner, if the western hero becomes an antihero and is cruel, petty, and overly vengeful, our expectations for the hero are not satisfied—or they become satiric (Figure 14.1).

However, if these changes reflect changes within the society and its value system, and new heroic codes are established, new rituals may rise from the ashes of the old, and they will be repeated as long as the new values and heroic codes prevail. But they will ultimately constitute very different genres.

The following discussion attempts to crystallize the basic elements of westerns, gangster movies, *film noir,* war stories, horror pictures, sci-fi and fantasy films,

FIGURE 14.1 Genre-Based Satire Much of the humor in modern parodies of film genres is based on our familiarity with basic plots, conventions, and characters. Films like *Blazing Saddles* (westerns) (top right), *Knocked Up* (romances) (top left), *Hot Tub Time Machine* (sci-fi) (bottom left), and *MacGruber* (suspenseful adventure) (bottom right) first build on our habitual expectations for their genres and then violate them. Because each of these films incorporates the essential elements of dozens of films, they can be helpful in studying the genres they satirize.

screwball romantic comedies, and musicals—and to suggest how these genres have changed in recent decades.

The Western The action in the traditional western takes place in the American West or Southwest, west of the Mississippi River, usually at the edge of the frontier, where civilization encroaches on the free, untamed land beyond. The time span is usually between 1865 and 1900.

The original western hero is a rugged individualist, a natural man of the frontier, often a mysterious loner. Somewhat aloof and very much his own man, he acts in accordance with his personal code, not in response to community pressures or for personal gain. His personal code emphasizes human dignity, courage, justice, fair play, equality (the rights of the underdog), and respect for women. Intelligent and resourceful, he is also kind, honest, firm, and consistent in his dealings with others, never devious, cruel, or petty. Even-tempered and peaceable by nature, he does not seek violent solutions but responds with violent action when the situation demands it. Extraordinarily quick *and* accurate with pistol or rifle, he is also adept

FIGURE 14.2 The Western Hero One of the most durable of American heroic types is the western or cowboy hero. He represented essentially the same code and values in hundreds of films over a span of four decades. Bob Steele, a typical western hero of the 1940s, is pictured here, wearing his customary white hat (left). Contrast this heroic type with that played by Kevin Costner (shown here with Graham Greene) in *Dances With Wolves* (right).

at horsemanship and barroom brawling and is quietly confident of his own abilities. He can act as a capable leader or alone, as the situation requires. As a loner, he stands apart from the community but believes in and fights to preserve its values. His lack of community ties (he usually has no job, no ranch or possessions, no wife or family) gives him the freedom and flexibility for full-time heroics. As a lawman or cavalry officer, however, his independence diminishes. Peace makes him restless. With order restored, he moves on to discover another troubled community (Figure 14.2).

Traditionally, two categories of villain seem to prevail. The first includes outlaws (the uncivilized elements of the untamed frontier) who bully, threaten, and generally terrorize the respectable elements of the frontier community, trying to take what they want by force: rustling cattle, robbing banks or stages, or attacking stagecoaches, wagon trains, forts, or ranches. Stereotypically, Native Americans often fall into this first category. Real motives for their hostility are seldom developed. They are viewed not as individuals but en masse as innately savage and cruel. Sometimes they are led by crazed chieftains seeking vengeance for past crimes against their tribe, or they are manipulated by renegade whites to facilitate their own evil purposes.

Villains in the second category work under the guise of respectability: crooked bankers, saloon owners, and sheriffs, or wealthy ranchers, all motivated by greed for wealth or lust for power. Slick, devious, and underhanded in their methods, they may hire or manipulate "savages" and outlaws to obtain their goals (Figure 14.3).

FIGURE 14.3 **The Western Villain** One typical western villain operates under the guise of respectability. His dress is impeccable (maybe *too* impeccable). But if there's any doubt, check the mustache and the steely-eyed glare. Sometimes in modern westerns, though, as with Gene Hackman's sheriff in *Unforgiven*, great ambiguity resides in such characters.

Villains not killed in the gunfights are frightened off or imprisoned. With the society in decent, just, and capable hands, the hero is free to move on. Justice prevails, civilization conquers savagery, and good triumphs over evil. Law and order are restored or established, and progress toward a better life on the frontier may resume.

The conventions of the early western are so familiar that they need little description. There is a clear and simple definition of character types by conventions of costume and grooming. The hero typically wears a white or light-colored hat, the villain a black hat. Heroes are clean-cut and clean-shaven. Mustaches are reserved for villains. Sidekicks and villains may have beards, but sidekicks' beards are gray and rustic, and villains' beards are black and impeccably groomed.

In addition to conventions of appearance, there are conventions of action. Most westerns have one or more of the following: a climactic shootout between the hero and villain in the town's only street or among the rocks of a canyon, a prolonged chase on horseback (usually accompanied by shooting), a knockdown drag-out barroom brawl (with a scared bartender periodically ducking behind the bar), and a cavalry-to-the-rescue scene.

Although a love interest may develop between hero and heroine, and the attraction may be apparent, it never reaches fruition and the hero moves on at the end. To create tension and direct attention to the love interest, the heroine often misunderstands the hero's motives or his actions until the final climax, when he regains her trust and respect before good-byes are said.

At least one convention is structural. Many westerns begin with the hero riding into view from the left side of the screen and end with him riding off in the opposite direction, usually into a fading sunset.

The most recent well-known examples of the western genre have turned many of these conventions on their heads. Kevin Costner's *Dances With Wolves*, for

FIGURE 14.4 The Gangster Hero   Both Paul Muni (left), in 1932, and Al Pacino (right), in 1983, played the protagonist of *Scarface*, each fitting practically every definition of the gangster hero formula. But during the sixty years between the original and remake, the story's language changed radically.

instance, has softened the edges of the traditional hero, making him more sensitive to both Woman and "Indian." And the "true" villains are drawn more ambiguously. Writer Chuck Berg, in a essay entitled "Fade-Out in the West," has noted a general weakening in this genre's impact, and he says that "in spite of Costner's good intentions, the film's rose-colored revisionism, the erasure of the genocidal forces let loose by Manifest Destiny, rings false."[10] Characterizing Clint Eastwood's *Unforgiven* as "a critique of his own western persona" and "dark," Berg observes that here "Eastwood has not come to praise the western, but to deconstruct and deglamorize its myths." He insists that the actor/director's "mannerist endgame puts the mirror up to his career as a western icon" and declares, finally, that "the western as a means of transmitting epic and unifying tales of the American experience has passed."[11]

The Gangster Film   The classic gangster film usually takes place in the concrete jungle, among the endless streets and crowded buildings of a decaying older part of the modern city. Much of the action occurs at night, and rain is often used to add atmosphere. In the rural-bandit gangster film, the action takes place in a rural setting with small depressed towns, roadhouses, and filling stations.

The gangster hero is a brutal, aggressive, lone-wolf type. He is cocky and ambitious, the self-made man who fought his way up from nothing and graduated from the school of hard knocks (Figure 14.4).

Women, generally, are sexual ornaments, symbols of the hero's status. They are cheap, mindless, and greedy, fascinated by the hero's cruelty and power. Sometimes a decent, intelligent woman associates with the hero early in the film but soon discovers his true nature and abandons him. The gangster's mother and sister are civilized and social women with traditional values; the mother is respected, the sister protected.

On the most abstract level, the basic conflict is the anarchy of the gangsters versus the social order. Because the police represent the social order, the conflict also involves cops versus robbers. There is usually a conflict of robbers versus robbers, with the struggle involving leadership of the gang or a territorial-rights gang war against a rival mob. An internal conflict within the hero is also probable, with his latent good or social instincts struggling for expression against his essentially cruel and selfish nature.

The classic gangster "hero" achieves success temporarily but eventually meets his deserved end. Although he may be given a chance for reform and redemption, the criminal side of his nature is too strong to be denied. He often dies in the gutter, in a cowardly, weak manner. His dignity and strength are gone—everything we admired about him is destroyed. The other gang members are either killed or jailed, and the social order is restored.

Justice prevails, good conquers evil, or evil destroys itself. Crime does not pay, and the weeds of crime bear bitter fruit. Civilized values of human decency, honesty, and respect for law and order are reaffirmed.

Machine guns, pistols, and bombs are standard weapons. Machine guns are often carried in violin cases. At least one chase scene, with passengers in each car exchanging gunfire, seems required. Whiskey and cigars are necessary props for every interior scene. Speakeasies and posh nightclubs are common sites for conducting business. Montage sequences are frequently used for violent action. They feature fast editing, compression of time, and explosive sound effects (machine-gun fire or bombings).

Unlike westerns, gangster films have remained popular and potent. One observer of the genre, Ron Wilson, suggests that part of this hardiness may be attributed to the modern way in which "gangster films appear to us on an aesthetic level, because their characters are driven by success within the *business* of crime itself." Further, he notes, "The 'classic' gangster-film narrative typically revolved around the rise and fall of the gangster hero, . . . [who] was often portrayed as an almost Shakespearean tragic figure, whose inevitable downfall was documented in near-Aristotelian terms." By contrast, according to Wilson, films such as the Coen brothers' *Miller's Crossing*, Martin Scorsese's *Casino*, and Mike Newell's *Donnie Brasco* "often look . . . at the lower echelons of the corporate ladder, at small-time hoods who also are striving for success but on a smaller perspective."[12]

Director Sam Mendes's *The Road to Perdition*, a gangster-film adaptation of a popular graphic novel, seemingly attempts to combine these two types of gangster protagonists. On the one hand, the older, "aristocratic" character played by Paul Newman epitomizes the classic gangster hero; on the other, his protégé, portrayed by Tom Hanks, represents the newer type—one imbued with the modern moral ambiguity of a business/family man. But at least some of the film's critical and commercial acclaim may be attributable to the bizarre combination of old-movie and new-film "recklessness" embodied by actor Jude Law. His wicked character Maguire is fleshed out in bold strokes of cold, maniacal violence accompanied with a very contemporary-appearing, psychic kind of impunity (Figure 14.5).

Film Noir Although the *film noir* genre flourished in America in the 1940s and 1950s and then seemed to die out, the form has continued in the hearty *noir* resonances of many movies in more recent decades. Foster Hirsch, one of the

FIGURE 14.5 **Amoral Criminals?** According to *New York Times* critic A. O. Scott, director Jean-Luc Godard's film *Breathless* (*à bout de souffle*) (1960), starring Jean Seberg and Jean-Paul Belmondo as lovers on the lam, is "saturated with [genre] references and echoes and attitudes." Obsessed with the art of the cinema, this prime part of the French New Wave looked both backward and forward in the movies that influenced it and those later works (including *Bonnie and Clyde*) that it inspired.

genre's earliest and most ardent admirers, has attempted a comprehensive definition of the type:

> *Film noir* is a descriptive term for the American crime film. . . . From stylized versions of the city at night to documentary-like reports of the city at mid-day, from the investigations of the wry, cynical sleuth to the "innocent" man momentarily and fatally tempted by luxury, to the desperate flailing of the confirmed and inveterate criminal, the genre covers a heterogeneous terrain. In range of theme and in visual style, it is both varied and complex, and in level of achievement it is consistently high. *Film noir* is one of the most challenging cycles in the history of American films.[13]

Eddie Muller, another observer, defines it more poetically: "*Film noirs* were distress flares launched onto America's movie screens by artists working the night shift at the Dream Factory."[14]

Lovers of *film noir* have embraced the resurgence of its popularity in the neo-*noir* movies of the '60s, '70s, '80s, '90s, and into the twenty-first century (see "Films for Study" at the end of the chapter), but they appear unable to agree about their relative merits. For example, some fans of Lawrence Kasdan's impressive debut

FIGURE 14.6 **Femmes Fatales** Frequently in classic *film noir* of the 1940s, women proved extremely dangerous to the gullible men who desired them. Jane Greer, in Jacques Tourneur's *Out of the Past*, attempted to outtalk and manipulate Robert Mitchum (left). In the neo-*noir* films of the 1970s, '80s, '90s, and after, women characters (such as Connie Nielsen's Renata in Harold Ramis's *The Ice Harvest*, right) could remain just as coldly calculated as their earlier sisters.

film, *Body Heat* (1981), claimed that it surpassed its models—such classics of the genre as Billy Wilder's *Double Indemnity* (1944) and Jacques Tourneur's *Out of the Past* (1947) (Figure 14.6). Since the mid-1970s, critics have maintained that Roman Polanski and Robert Towne's *Chinatown* opened new territory for the genre.[15] But others claimed that these newer films were merely perverse, pale copies. In 1997 this same kind of disagreement arose about the value of Curtis Hanson's *L.A. Confidential*. Although a majority of the critics praised the Oscar-winning film, James Naremore, in his *More Than Night: Film Noir in Its Contexts*, calls it "a big-budget, highly publicized, and critically overrated feature that begins in darkly satiric fashion and then segues into crowd-pleasing melodrama."[16]

The noted American director and screenwriter Paul Schrader has observed that "for a long time film noir, with its emphasis on corruption and despair, was considered an aberration of the American character. The western, with its moral primitivism, and the gangster film, with its Horatio Alger values, were considered more American than the film noir."[17] Meanwhile, the movie that Schrader called "film noir's epitaph," Orson Welles's *Touch of Evil* (1958), starring Charlton Heston, Janet Leigh, and Welles himself, was triumphantly re-released in 1998 in a re-edited version based on a long memo that the director wrote after his studio refused him final cut.[18] *Film noir*, then, is one genre that refuses to die.

War Films Dying and refusing to die are staples of another resurgent genre, the war movie. Many filmmakers—including Richard Rush in *The Stunt Man* and, most famously, perhaps, François Truffaut—have observed that it is probably impossible to make a genuine antiwar film. For the medium, with its glittering, large-screen images, is ever glorifying its subject. But, during an era when both Steven Spielberg's

FIGURE 14.7 The Appeal of War Because the film medium inherently glorifies its subject matter, viewers must constantly scrutinize their motives for watching all war pictures, regardless of how different they may appear in their similar narratives. Compare Roland Emmerich's eighteenth-century American military epic *The Patriot* (2000) (right) with Paul Haggis's *In the Valley of Elah* (2007) (left). Does each condemn battle or subtly celebrate it?

Saving Private Ryan and Terrence Malick's *The Thin Red Line* (the former a closely observed account of the D-Day Invasion of Normandy, the latter a long lyric poem based on the James Jones novel set on Guadalcanal) were released within a six-month period, directors obviously continued to fight the good fight, cinematically. Although Spielberg's somber effort was rewarded with both box-office and critical acclaim, more cynical critics insisted that "*Saving Private Ryan* isn't . . . any different from most other Hollywood war movies,"[19] including, one must assume, both gung ho military films and earnest portrayals such as *The Patriot* and, conceivably, international classics such as Jean Renoir's *Grand Illusion* (Figure 14.7). War may still be hell, but movie war is, still and always, profitable for the cinematic troops. In consuming war films, then, we must be eternally aware of the complexity of our reasons for watching. And at the 2010 Academy Awards, the Iraqi War film *The Hurt Locker* won six Oscars, including Best Picture, Director (Kathryn Bigelow), Editing, and Writing (Mark Boal).

Horror Films "The presiding irony of horror," Anthony Lane writes in *The New Yorker*,

> . . . is that while no genre offers more imaginative license, few of the directors—or, indeed, the novelists—who turn to it have more than a thimbleful of imagination in the first place. (They have a sweet tooth for the fantastic and the glutinous, which is hardly the same thing.) When visionaries and obsessives deign to frighten us, on the other hand, the results can be spectacular: look at Murnau's "Nosferatu," Dreyer's "Vampyr," or Karloff's "Frankenstein" pictures (which redefined horror as a species of warped romance).[20]

Lane's dissatisfaction with the genre, however, does not appear to stem from the frequent charge that such "romantic" horror films as John Carpenter's *Halloween* turned viewers away from classic movies like *Frankenstein* and *The Wolf Man* and opened the floodgates for teen-aged terror in so-called slasher horror films. In fact, Lane believes "Carpenter's achievement was to suggest that there was nothing exotic about horror; that it is more inbred than outlandish; and that it was best considered as the evil twin of what one might call the lyrical conservatism of American movies"[21] (Figure 14.8).

FIGURE 14.8 **Scared Unconscious** The horror film genre relishes the psychological tension generated through such memorable characters as those played by Adrien Brody and Sarah Polley in *Splice* (left) and Natalie Portman in Darren Aronofsky's lyrical *Black Swan* (right). Other attempts to recapture this scariness include *The Ring* (with Naomi Watts) and *The Ring Two*—the first a remake of a Japanese movie hit (*Ringu*), the second a sequel to the American version.

And far beyond the domain of mere slasher flicks are the mid-career films of director Wes Craven (for example, *The People Under the Stairs, Scream, Scream 2,* and *Scream 3*), who adds what is, for some viewers, a delightfully self-conscious wit to the mayhem. However, consciousness, self or otherwise, is not truly part of the classic horror genre formula.

Science Fiction and Fantasy Films Cultural critic Bruce Kawin has analyzed the way that "particular genre forms appeal psychologically to their audiences." He "defines the audience's experience with horror and science fiction in terms of myths and dreams" and observes that "one goes to the horror film in order to have a nightmare . . . a dream whose undercurrent of anxiety both presents and masks the desire to fulfill and be punished for certain conventionally unacceptable impulses." Kawin distinguishes between science fiction films and horror films by maintaining that these "appeal to different mental activities: 'Science fiction appeals to consciousness, horror to the unconscious.'"[22]

J. P. Telotte, in *Replications: A Robotic History of the Science Fiction Film*, adds, "Certainly, the contemporary science fiction film invites us to catalogue our culture's major anxieties" (including race, gender, and sexuality, as evident in such films as *Blade Runner* and *Aliens*). But Telotte also concludes that "the genre has obviously staked out as its special territory the latest possibilities of artifice . . . through the very latest of technological developments of the cinema. . . . And yet artifice finally seems to be less its end than its method, like our films, simply a most effective way we have developed for gauging the human."[23] Perhaps, then, we should not be amazed to find in such radically different science fiction films as Alex Proyas's expensive, luxurious *Dark City* and Darren Aronofsky's cheaply made and stark-looking *Pi* multiple visual and thematic patterns of the spiral, signifying the chain of human life (Figure 14.9).

Traditional wisdom suggests that the fantasy genre may be the hardest to define—the one whose boundaries are most difficult to survey. Certainly, what is fantastical appears to permeate several realms, including those of horror and sci-fi.

FIGURE 14.9 Sci-Fi Consciousness   Steven Spielberg's *Close Encounters of the Third Kind* (1977) seemed remarkable in part because of its friendly aliens. Other science fiction films before and since—including Robert Wise's *The Day the Earth Stood Still* (1951, with Michael Rennie) (top left), Spielberg's *E. T. The Extra-Terrestrial* (1982, featuring Henry Thomas) (top right), and Robert Zemeckis's *Contact* (1997)—have also posited benevolent beings from other realms. In *Solaris* (2002), Steven Soderbergh's remake of a 1972 Russian film by Andrei Tarkovsky, characters played by George Clooney and Natascha McElhone (at left in the bottom photo, with Viola Davis and Jeremy Davies) leave the viewer asking intriguing questions about alien intentions. And in 2005 Spielberg created scary metallic monster aliens in *War of the Worlds*.

As *New York Times* reviewer A. O. Scott has written, "Fantasy literature . . . depends on patterns, motifs and archetypes. It is therefore hardly surprising that the most visible modern variants of the ancient genres of saga, romance and quest narrative are so richly crosspollinated." Their key characters, "following a convention so deep it seems to be encoded in the human story-telling genre," are "orphans, summoned out of obscurity to undertake a journey into the heart of evil that will also be a voyage of self-discovery." In observing how Hollywood, "perhaps more than ever before," has currently become "an empire of fantasy," Scott focuses upon Frodo Baggins, Luke Skywalker (Figure 14.10), Harry Potter, and Peter Parker (Figure 14.11), movie protagonists whose celluloid universes have created billions of dollars in box-office revenues. For Scott, one way to explain the enduring popularity of fantasy films involves examining their essential nature: "Unlike virtually everything else in the irony-saturated, ready-to-recycle cosmos of postmodern pop culture, [fantasy] stories don't seem to date." And their "appeal is perennial because it fulfills the widespread and ever-renewing desire for a restoration of innocence."[24]

FIGURE 14.10 **Fantasy Voyages of Self Discovery** Among the most intensely vivid figures in recent fantasy films is Gollum (acted and voiced by Andy Serkis, left), one of the CGI marvels in the second and third parts of *The Lord of the Rings*. He combines the haunted whine of classic horror actor Peter Lorre and the tormented schizoid temperament of Norman Bates. Very strangely, poor Gollum repulses us and makes us faintly sympathetic to equal degrees. In *Star Wars Episode II: Attack of the Clones*, Padme (the former Queen of Naboo, played by Natalie Portman) and Anakin Skywalker (Hayden Christensen) appear, by comparison, almost to inhabit a fantasy world of comfortable familiarity (below).

Upon the release of the second installment of Peter Jackson's film trilogy of J. R. R. Tolkien's *The Lord of the Rings*, Lev Grossman, writing in *Time*, also sought to fathom the world's, and especially America's, contemporary voracious appetite for all narratives fantastic (movies, books, and, especially, games)—as opposed to those strictly sci-fi:

> [W]e are seeing what might be called the enchanting of America. A darker, more pessimistic attitude toward technology and the future has taken hold, and the evidence is our new preoccupation with fantasy, a nostalgic, sentimental, magical vision of a medieval age. The future just isn't what it used to be—and the past seems to be gaining on us.

Grossman discovers darker motivations, though. He suggests that "sometimes fantasies tell us less about who we are than who we wish we were." Like A. O. Scott, he expresses reservations about the genre's obsession with Caucasian male protagonists, wondering aloud whether we should "worry about all these strapping men poking each other with sharpened phallic symbols." Grossman agrees with Scott

FIGURE 14.11 **Graphic Combat** In this action scene from *Spider-Man 2*, our hero (Tobey Maguire as Peter Parker) risks being squeezed to death by his nemesis Dr. Octopus, or Doc Ock (Alfred Molina).

about our seeming desire to recapture a lost innocence—up to a point: "The clarity and simplicity of Middle-earth are comforting, but there's also something worryingly childish, even infantile, about it. Things are too simple there . . . either good or evil, with no messy gray area in between." However, his exposition turns circular, finally . . . or, once again, spiral-shaped, perhaps. He asks, "Are we running away from reality when we indulge in fantasy? Or are we escaping reality just to find it again and wrestle with it in disguise? Not everything is as simple as it looks" in reel fantasy or in real life.[25] The astounding popular (and critical) success of—for example—Christopher Nolan's resurgent Batman movies (including *The Dark Knight*) perhaps reinforces this truth.

Screwball Comedies The iconic spirals of sci-fi and fantasy films can have more than one frame of reference, of course. The image is a staple, too, in the classic romantic comedies of the 1930s and 1940s called screwball. According to Ed Sikov, one of the most authoritative and wittiest writers about the genre, "Screwball comedies play with a funny contradiction: they tantalize us with sumptuous romantic ideals even while they horrify us with the farce lurking underneath."[26] The exact nature of this "horror" may differ greatly between early classic "couple" comedies such as *Nothing Sacred* and *It Happened One Night*, on the one hand, and modern romantic farces such as *My Best Friend's Wedding*, *There's Something About Mary*, and (in the genre's most extreme mix of conservatism and outrageousness) the films of Judd Apatow (including *The 40-Year-old Virgin*, *Knocked Up*, and *Funny People*) and movies by his acolytes (*Superbad*; *Forgetting Sarah Marshall*; *I Love You, Man*; *The Hangover*; and *Due Date*, for example) on the other. But these films contain an underlying sameness (and universality) that is, finally, humanly comforting (as well as hilarious) (Figure 14.12).

FIGURE 14.12 **Wacky Couples**   Romantic screwball comedies originated in the 1930s with such now-classic hilarious duos as Katharine Hepburn and Cary Grant (in Howard Hawks's *Bringing Up Baby*, 1938) (right). Although the genre's comedy has either evolved or disintegrated (depending upon one's perspective) into the raucous ribaldry of the Farrelly Brothers' *There's Something About Mary* (1998, with Cameron Diaz and Ben Stiller) (left), and what is sometimes called "The Judd Apatow Factory" (*The 40-year-old Virgin*), the form has still retained its "old-fashioned" romantic focus.

Film Musicals   The film historian and theorist Rick Altman has called the American film musical "the most complex art form ever devised."[27] Another critic, Jane Feuer, points out that

> twenty-five years ago most film buffs would have scoffed at the idea that serious books could be written about John Wayne bang-bang Westerns and Rock Hudson kiss-kiss weepies. It was only when Hollywood genre films began to be seen from the perspective of their ideological and cultural meanings (rather than as star vehicles or "pure entertainment") that Westerns, melodramas and *films noirs* became accessible to critical inquiry. Yet the genre most of us think of as quintessentially Hollywood was the only one not fertilized by the new interest in film as ideology. Westerns might now be seen as a conflict between chaos and civilization, but Fred Astaire remains ineffable.[28]

But Feuer insists that "the musical is Hollywood writ large" and, like Altman, believes that it is worthy of our attention.

For his analysis, Altman classifies film musicals into three categories: the fairy-tale musical, the show musical, and the folk musical. The first type includes such titles as *Top Hat*, *The Wizard of Oz*, Disney's *Cinderella*, *An American in Paris*, *Hair*, and *Annie*. Illustrations of the show musical type begin with cinema's first talkie, *The Jazz Singer* (1927), encompass what many call the epitome of the form, *Singin' in the Rain*, and extend to the dark visions of Bob Fosse's *Cabaret* and *All That Jazz*. The third type, the folk musical, includes *Rose-Marie*, *Meet Me in St. Louis*, *Show Boat*, *Oklahoma!*, *Porgy and Bess*, *West Side Story*, *Woodstock*, *Nashville*, and *Yentl*.[29]

In this new century, some observers have expressed great hopes for a revival of musical films. So far, Lars von Trier's *Dancer in the Dark* (2000), Baz Luhrmann's *Moulin Rouge!* (2001), Rob Marshall's *Chicago* (2002) and *Nine* (2009), and Chris Columbus's *Rent* (2005) have tried to nourish that dream (Figure 14.13).

FIGURE 14.13 Film Musical Types—Sugar-Coated or Bitter Many viewers believe that the traditional film musical genre reached its apex in *Singin' in the Rain* (1952, starring Gene Kelly), whose comedy and romance sweetly and joyfully recaptured the silent movie days of the late 1920s, when movie sound was just beginning to make a noise in Hollywood. During recent decades the genre has mainly been dormant, moribund, or considerably transformed in its conventions. Two remarkable examples of later musical film experimentation, though, are Bob Fosse's brilliantly cynical *Cabaret* (1972, starring Liza Minnelli) and Herbert Ross and Dennis Potter's riveting, flawed, bleak *Pennies From Heaven* (1981, with Steve Martin)—both set in the early 1930s. Recently, independently produced, high-profile musicals have been beckoning to Hollywood again. At left, Oscar-winner Catherine Zeta-Jones cracks open the cynically exuberant *Chicago* by singing and dancing "All That Jazz." On the right, the cast of *Rent* parties hard in the face of individual and communal problems.

REMAKES AND SEQUELS

Remakes and sequels are nothing new in the motion picture industry, as this rather startling picture caption from Kevin Brownlow's *Hollywood: The Pioneers* tells us:

> Violence was discouraged by the Hays Office, but this scene had strong precedents. Fannie Ward had been branded in *The Cheat* (1915), Pola Negri in the 1922 remake, Barbara Castleton in *The Branding Iron* (1920) and now Aileen Pringle in the remake of that, *Body and Soul*.[30]

Although remakes and sequels occur throughout film history, there have been periods of peak production. The industry's most recent obsession with redoing the tried and true began during the early 1970s and has intensified since. Although it may seem strange for Hollywood to rely on remakes and sequels in a period when the number of feature films being released each year is declining drastically, there is solid support for this kind of filmmaking.

The primary reason for Hollywood's reliance on remakes and sequels has to do with increases in the cost of producing motion pictures. As movies become more expensive to make, the gamble becomes much greater. Running a movie studio may be compared to running an aircraft factory that continually builds new models with new configurations, with untested control and power systems, and with $10 million to $200 million invested in each plane. When finished, each plane taxis to the runway, develops tremendous speed, and tries to get off the ground. There is no turning back. If it flies, it flies; but if it crashes, most of the investment is lost. Aircraft executives operating such a business would be very careful with the planes they designed, and the equivalent of a great many remakes and sequels would be turned out.

Of course the aircraft industry doesn't really operate this way. New models are tested for long periods, with very little risk. Miniatures can be tested in a wind tunnel and then flown before the full-size prototype takes to the air. Some reliable constants also provide security: The laws of physics and aerodynamics do not change; they are constant and predictable.

In the motion picture industry, there is no way to test miniature versions of a film in a wind tunnel. A film's success (its ability to fly) is based not on predictable constants like the laws of physics and aerodynamics but on the unpredictable and whimsical laws of human likes and dislikes. Remakes and sequels bring at least a degree of predictability to the marketplace.

Most remakes and sequels are based on movies that, if they are not film classics, have proved by their continuing popularity that they really don't need to be remade at all and usually don't beg for a sequel. Therefore, the studios that remake films are guaranteeing themselves a strange combination of success and failure. Just out of curiosity, the mass audience will go to see remakes of movies they know and love. The urge to make a critical judgment about the remake of any well-known film is almost irresistible—it is probably one of the few laws of human behavior that the studios can predict and trust. The better the original and the more popular it is, the greater is the number of people who can be counted on to see the remake or sequel. Thus, remakes and sequels guarantee a financial return. They also, however, guarantee a kind of failure, for the better the original, the higher are the expectations of the audience for the remake or sequel, which almost always fails to meet those expectations. (A natural human law governs audience response to remakes and sequels: The higher expectations are, the greater the disappointment.) Although there are rare exceptions, remakes and sequels generally lack the freshness and creative dynamics of the original, so the disappointment is usually justified.

Taking for granted that the prime motivation for producing remakes and sequels is profit and the improved odds of betting on a proven winner, we should also admit that there are valid reasons for producing remakes and sequels, and there is a creative challenge involved. Directors of remakes have been clear about that point: They want to make creative changes in new versions—they never attempt to make a photocopy. These creative changes take different forms and are justified in different ways. Startling exceptions to this observation have occurred. For example, director Gus Van Sant (*Drugstore Cowboy, My Own Private Idaho, To Die For, Good Will Hunting, Elephant, Last Days* [2005], *Paranoid Park, Milk*), created a poorly received remake of Alfred Hitchcock's *Psycho*. He first made the announcement that he would utilize the same script and shooting schedule as the 1960 film. Then he insisted that the characters would be adjusted slightly to fit the film's modern audience. Finally, he shot in color and pronounced his movie "an anti-remake film," adding, "I don't have much faith in Hollywood's ability to do remakes. There's a remake curse." Still, after making his movie, he indicated that he'd "be interested in redoing 'Psycho' again."[31] Austrian director Michael Haneke created two versions of his cruel work *Funny Games*—first in 1997 and then a "replicant" remake in 2008.

Remakes

Paul Schrader, director for the 1982 remake of *Cat People* (1942), looks on most remakes with contempt: "The whole remake trend is an indication of cowardice, obviously. . . . With the cost of movies being such, everybody's trying to protect their jobs. For an executive to redo *Animal House* or *Jaws* is clearly a much safer decision."[32]

A reasonably long period of time usually elapses between different versions of the same film, so one of the most frequently used justifications for remaking a film is to update it. Filmmakers have their own ways of explaining what their goal is in updating a film. In their view, they are usually improving the original work by giving it a more contemporary quality or providing a new sensibility for modern audiences. A movie can be updated in a variety of ways:

- **Important changes in style—updating to reflect social change, cinematic styles, lifestyles, or popular tastes:** *Heaven Can Wait* (1978)—a remake of *Here Comes Mr. Jordan* (1941); *A Star Is Born* (1954/1976)—new music, new lifestyle, a whole new ambience for an old story; *The Wizard of Oz/ The Wiz* (1939/1978)—modern music and a black cast, a filmed version of a Broadway show; *The Getaway* (1972/1994)—new star couple; *The Karate Kid* (1984/2010).
- **Changes in film technology—updating to take advantage of new potential in the art form:** *Stagecoach* (1939/1966)—color, wide screen, stereophonic sound; *Ben-Hur* (1926/1959)—color, wide screen, stereophonic sound (1926 version was silent); *King Kong* (1933/1976/2005)— color, wide screen, stereophonic sound, sophisticated animation techniques; *The Thing* (1951/1982)—color, wide screen, stereophonic sound, special effects; *A Guy Named Joe/Always* (1943/1989)—color, wide screen, stereophonic sound; *Dracula/Bram Stoker's Dracula* (1931/1992)—color, wide screen, stereophonic sound, special effects (Figure 14.14); *Frankenstein/Mary Shelley's Frankenstein* (1931/1994)—color, wide screen, stereophonic sound; *Clash of the Titans* (1981/2010); *Piranha/Piranha 3-D* (1978/2010); *Creature From the Black Lagoon* (1954/2011).
- **Changes in censorship:** *The Postman Always Rings Twice* (1946/1981)—explicit treatment of steamy passions; *The Blue Lagoon* (1949/1980)—emphasis on sexual awakening of young couple; *Cape Fear* (1962/1991); *Alfie* (1966/2004).
- **New paranoias:** *Invasion of the Body Snatchers* (1956/1978)—from subconscious fears of communist takeover in the original to fears of "pod people" takeover in the first remake; also remade in 1994 and 2007.
- **The musical version:** A type of remake that usually provides a greater challenge and greater creative freedom for the filmmaker is the translation of the film into a musical version, where words and music must be integrated into the dramatic framework of the original. Examples: *Oliver Twist* (1948) to

FIGURE 14.14 Popular Subjects Some cultural obsessions have always attracted filmmakers. The human vampire legend, for example, has inspired many movies since German director F. W. Murnau's 1922 film version of the Dracula story, *Nosferatu*. Pictured here are Bela Lugosi in Tod Browning's 1931 *Dracula* (left), and Robert Pattinson and Kristen Stewart in Chris Weitz's *The Twilight Saga: New Moon* (right) (followed by 2010's *Eclipse*). Director Clint Eastwood continues to address the universal human (and cinematic) question "What happens after we die?" in *Hereafter* (starring Matt Damon, Cécile De France, Bryce Dallas Howard, and, shown here holding a funeral urn, Frankie McLaren).

Oliver! (1968); *A Star Is Born* (1937 drama to 1954 musical); *The Philadelphia Story* (1940) to *High Society* (1956); *Lost Horizon* (1937 drama to 1973 musical); *Anna and the King of Siam* (1946 drama) to *The King and I* (1956 musical); and *Pygmalion* (1938 drama) to *My Fair Lady* (1964 musical).

- **Change in format—the TV version:** Television movies have gotten into the remake business, with the following contributions: *Of Mice and Men, The Diary of Anne Frank, All Quiet on the Western Front, From Here to Eternity, In Cold Blood, The Shining, Rear Window,* and *David and Lisa.*
- **Remakes of international films:** The creative challenge of transplanting a film from one culture/language/geography to another has produced some interesting results. *The Seven Samurai* (Japan, 1954) became *The Magnificent Seven* (USA, 1960). *Smiles of a Summer Night* (Sweden, 1955) became first a Broadway show and later the film *A Little Night Music* (USA, 1978). *Breathless* (France, 1959) was remade in the United States in 1983, changing the setting from Paris to Los Angeles and reversing the nationalities of the principal characters. *The Return of Martin Guerre* (France, 1982) became *Sommersby* (USA, France, 1993). *The Vanishing* (France, Netherlands, 1988) was remade in the United States in 1993 (by its original director). *Insomnia* (2002) substituted American stars for Norwegian actors; *La Femme Infidele* (France, 1969) became *Unfaithful* (USA, 2002); *Mostly Martha* (Germany, 2001) transformed into *No Reservations* (USA, 2007); and *The Dinner Game* (France, 1998) lost some of its caustic flavor as *Dinner for Schmucks* (USA, 2010).

Influential producers seldom appear completely willing merely to accept successful foreign language films for wide distribution in America. Rather, they somehow must always remake them, in English. Thus, Edouard Molinaro's *La Cage aux Folles* had to move from France to America and become *The Birdcage*, directed by Mike Nichols and starring Robin Williams. Jean-Pierre Melville's *Bob Le Flambeur* was obligated to transform into Neil Jordan's *The Good Thief*, starring Nick Nolte. And *Abre Los Ojos* (*Open Your Eyes*) was fated to metamorphose into *Vanilla Sky*. At least this last-named movie kept its original leading lady, Penélope Cruz; and its director, Aleajandro Amenábar, in the process of turning the reins over to Cameron Crowe, acquired *Vanilla Sky*'s leading man, Tom Cruise, as his producer for a new project (in English, of course): *The Others*. Most recently, the three Swedish-language films adapted from Stieg Larsson's *Millennium Trilogy* (beginning with *The Girl With the Dragon Tattoo*) were being remade in the United States.

Finally, the critic Leo Braudy has noted that

> the remake resides at the intersection of the genetic and the generic codes. In even the most debased version, it is a meditation on the continuing historical relevance (economic, cultural, psychological) of a particular narrative. A remake is thus always concerned with what its makers and (they hope) its audiences consider to be unfinished cultural business.[33]

Sequels

People love sequels—they wait for them, read about them, and usually see them more than once. But in a town where executives make a habit of looking over their shoulders, selling something already regarded as a sure hit creates a tremendous burden. Movies are not necessarily better the second time around.[34]

—BETSY SHARKEY, ENTERTAINMENT WRITER

Remakes generally allow the original to age for a while (sometimes long enough for a whole new generation or two to come along who may not know the original) (Figure 14.15). Sequels have the best chance of success when they follow the original quickly, so that they can capitalize on the original's success. Audiences attend sequels for the same reason they go to remakes. If they enjoyed the original, they go seeking more of the same, and they are curious to see how well the sequel stands up to the original. The motivation for shooting sequels is similar to that for shooting remakes—profit. But the thinking is a little different. With the remake it's a case of "They liked it once; let's make it again." With the sequel, it's a matter of "We've got a good thing going; let's get all the mileage out of it we can." Occasionally, "prequels" (works whose action occurs *before* the original film's) attempt to create this same type of success (Figure 14.16).

There are relatively few good reasons for making a sequel other than to realize the profit potential. Nevertheless, there are some very natural sequels— made simply because there was more story to tell—and these sequels can match the original in quality if the story is continued. First-class sequels, for example, have been made

FIGURE 14.15 **Re-Fade to Black** Producers usually wait at least several years before remaking popular movies. Sometimes, however, neither length of interval nor relative success seems to affect these decisions. One unusual case in point: the farce *Death at a Funeral*. Although the director Frank Oz released his British production of that film in 2007 with minor critical and commercial attention, Neil LaBute created another version in 2010, this time using predominantly African American actors (including producer Chris Rock). LaBute did carry over two key elements from the original film: the scriptwriter Dean Craig, and a key actor, Peter Dinklage. Pictured here is Dinklage in similar scenes from the two movies—first with actress Jane Asher (left), and then with her counterpart, actress Loretta Devine. Guess which version collected the most box-office money.

FIGURE 14.16 **Hopeful Prequels** Successful films (particularly those in which central characters die) sometimes inspire attempts to account for time and events set before their action. Called "prequels," such movies rarely manage to capture the invention or energy that made their originals work. For example, the makers of the excellent *Gettysburg* (1993), with the considerable aid of Ted Turner's enthusiasm and funding, released *Gods and Generals* (starring Robert Duvall as General Robert E. Lee) in 2003. Their efforts produced poor box office and utterly dismal reviews, but continuing devotion from many Civil War buffs (including those who value its accurate attention to historic details, excepting those who accuse it of purveying a distasteful pro-Confederate bias).

FIGURE 14.17 Natural Genre Extensions In 2003, the great commercial success of the character-driven adventure *Pirates of the Caribbean: The Curse of the Black Pearl*, starring Johnny Depp and Keira Knightley, virtually guaranteed that sequels would be produced. Indeed, with director Gore Verbinski continuing to pilot two vessels at once, *Pirates of the Caribbean: Dead Man's Chest* created even bigger box-office numbers in 2006, and *Pirates of the Caribbean: At World's End* (shown here) followed in 2007. Still more sequels have raised their flags on the horizon. . . .

of *The Godfather* (*The Godfather Part II*) and in the *Harry Potter*, *The Lord of the Rings*, and *Pirates of the Caribbean* series (Figure 14.17). Most sequels, however, do not have the natural relationship to their original that these do.

Because sequels don't try to tell the same story but can build on characters already established in the original, they give the filmmakers much more room for creative freedom than remakes do. As long as they pick up some characters from the original, maintain a certain degree of consistency in the treatment of those characters, and retain something of the style of the original, sequels can take off in almost any direction they want to go. A good example of flexibility in sequels can be seen in the sequels to James Whale's original *Frankenstein* (1931). It was followed by *Bride of Frankenstein* (1935), in which Whale introduced odd baroque elements and black humor, and by a kind of combo-sequel, *Frankenstein Meets the Wolf Man* (1943). The parody/sequel *Young Frankenstein* (1974) combines elements of both of the original Frankenstein films and succeeds largely because it lovingly recaptures the style of the original (Figure 14.18).

Much more important than the potential within the original story for a sequel is the audience's response to the original characters. If it becomes clear that a large film audience is fascinated with the cast of the original and would love to see those actors together again, we can be reasonably sure that a sequel will soon be in the making. On any film where the profit potential looks good enough to inspire a sequel, studio contracts will obligate actors to do the sequel. The continuity provided by keeping the actors of the original in the sequel is tremendously important to box-office appeal. Roy Scheider, Lorraine Gary, and Murray Hamilton, for

FIGURE 14.18 Parody/Sequel One of the most successful film parodies ever is Mel Brooks's *Young Frankenstein*, starring Peter Boyle, Gene Wilder, and Teri Garr. Through striking black-and-white cinematography and attention to details of setting and atmosphere, the film captures the style so well that it pays homage, as a kind of sequel, to the original.

example, served as important links between *Jaws* and *Jaws 2*; Ben Stiller, Robert De Niro, and Blythe Danner were essential for the move from *Meet the Parents* (2000) to *Meet the Fockers* (2004) to *Little Fockers* (2010).

But *Jaws 2* also provides an example of how important the behind-the-camera people are to making a successful sequel. When the writers, directors, and editors who participated in the original do not participate in the sequel, the film can suffer considerably, often losing the spirit, style, and impact of the original. Therefore, the most successful sequels (or series of sequels) result when the whole winning team (actors, director, writers, editor, producers, and so on) stays pretty much intact throughout (Figure 14.19). The phenomenal success of the *Rocky* series was probably due to the continuing participation of most of the original *Rocky* team.

Similar in some ways to the *Rocky* and *Superman* sequels, but very different from the ordinary exploitation-of-a-smash-hit sequel, is the character series. The character series can be developed from a series of novels featuring the same character or characters (Tarzan, James Bond, and Sherlock Holmes), or it can be developed around a character or combination of characters appearing in a single film. If a character or combination of characters has tremendous audience appeal, a series of films may be structured around the character or characters—for example, Nick and Nora Charles (William Powell and Myrna Loy, *The Thin Man* series), Abbott and Costello, Crosby and Hope (the "Road" series), Peter Sellers as Inspector Clouseau (the "Pink Panther" series, Figure 14.20), and Percy Kilbride and Marjorie Main as Pa and Ma Kettle. *Raiders of the Lost Ark*, *Indiana Jones and the Temple of Doom*, *Indiana Jones and the Last Crusade*, and *Indiana Jones and the Kingdom*

FIGURE 14.19 **Continuity in the Sequel**   For the sequels to *Back to the Future*, the producers signed director Robert Zemeckis and actors Michael J. Fox, Christopher Lloyd (shown here), and Lea Thompson. To carry the continuity one step further and increase cost-efficiency, they filmed *II* and *III* at the same time, as, later, did Peter Jackson in his *The Lord of the Rings* trilogy and the Wachowski brothers in *The Matrix Reloaded* and *The Matrix Revolutions*.

FIGURE 14.20 **The Long-Running Character Series**   Chief Inspector Jacques Clouseau, the character played by Peter Sellers in the *Pink Panther* series, enjoyed a long and prosperous life, even after the great comic actor's death. When Sellers died after completing five Pink Panther films, director Blake Edwards put together a sixth, *The Trail of the Pink Panther*, made up of outtakes (unused footage) from the earlier films woven into a new story featuring some of the series actors. Arnold Schwarzenegger, seen here with Edward Furlong in *Terminator 2: Judgment Day*, continued his action-adventure journey in *Terminator 3: The Rise of the Machines* (but bypassed *Terminator Salvation*).

of the Crystal Skull show that American audiences are still responsive to character series (Figure 14.21). The 1989–1997 *Batman* series (*Batman, Batman Returns, Batman Forever,* and *Batman & Robin*) seemingly changed focus from the hero to fascinating villains, even to the point of trading actors playing the caped crusader (George Clooney for Val Kilmer for Michael Keaton) in midstream. Recently,

FIGURE 14.21 New Character The addition of Indiana's son (Shia LaBeouf) to the cast of *Indiana Jones and the Kingdom of the Crystal Skull* provided a delightful interplay between the characters that became the highlight of the whole film. Many viewers hope that synergy will continue in any additional sequel.

Batman Begins placed Christian Bale back at the vigilante hero's starting point, and the new series gained extraordinary momentum with *its* sequel, *The Dark Knight.* At least for reviewers, though, a similar success with the original film *Iron Man* could not repeat its freshness in the follow-up effort of its production team—except for Robert Downey, Jr.'s strong performance as the title hero.

In a character series, continuation of the actors from one film to the next is essential, but so is good writing built around consistency of character. The overall style of the series should be consistent so that the expectations of the audience are satisfied, guaranteeing their return to the next film in the series. The need of the audience for the predictable, for seeing familiar faces in familiar kinds of film story formats extends beyond the satisfaction provided by weekly situation comedies and dramatic series on television.

In rare cases, a series of films are designed as parts of a preconceived larger whole. Although each film can stand on its own as a unified work, each is linked by characters, setting, and events to a larger whole. George Lucas's *Star Wars* (1977), *The Empire Strikes Back* (1980), and *Return of the Jedi* (1983) were designed as a trilogy, and now *The Phantom Menace* (1999), *Attack of the Clones* (2002), and *Revenge of the Sith* (2005) create another trilogy, set in an earlier time. Although the profit motive might also be involved in such plans, the writing and dramatic power should be superior to the "Hey! That one made money! Let's whip out another and another!" kind of afterthought, which often seems to impel Hollywood sequels (as in the case of much in the *Planet of the Apes* series—before the 2001 Tim Burton remake).

Critic Wheeler Dixon observes that current "remakes of genre classics seek to obscure their humble, or perhaps more accurately, populist origins with a panoply of expensive sets . . . , all to justify the price of an increasingly expensive admission ticket." He continues:

> What is happening here is a return to the past, but with a new series of values imposed on source material that was once upon a time more in tune with average audience/consumer expectations. Thus, the new versions of these films are triumphs of style over substance. . . . The day of the modestly budgeted genre film is a memory. . . .[35]

He extends his argument further, suggesting that recent "American genre cinema . . . seems, in many respects, more formulaic than ever, even if it is presented with a fine sheen thanks to digital special effects." Still, he admits, "there is nevertheless a core of meaning embedded in even the most desultory entertainments. . . ." Many critics may well disagree with what they might term Dixon's still "limited" definition of genre, but few, surely, would deny his conclusion that "for better or worse, American genre cinema dominates the globe."

ANALYZING GENRE FILMS, REMAKES, AND SEQUELS

On Genre Films

1. Study three films by the same director in one genre, along with at least two films in the same genre by different directors. Are three different directorial styles apparent, or are the styles indistinguishable? Consider the three films by the same director in chronological order. Does the director incorporate personal stylistic trademarks into each of the films? What are those trademarks, and what makes them stand out?

2. What innovations or refinements on the genre does the director introduce as he or she moves from one film to another? Are these innovations and refinements superficial and cosmetic, or are they significant enough to stretch the genre, creating a strain or tension against the outer boundaries of its form? Does the director seem to learn something new with each film and build on that in the next? Do we see changes in the director's personal vision or worldview from one film to another? How are those changes reflected? (For example, does the director seem to grow more serious or less serious, more pessimistic or more optimistic?)

3. Compare and contrast the styles of two directors working within the same genre. Examine at least two films by each director, and decide how their styles create important differences within the same genre. (For example, how is a Frank Capra screwball comedy different from a Preston Sturges screwball comedy?)

On Remakes

1. Was the remake really necessary? Why is the older version outdated? Why do modern audiences need the story retold? What aspects of the original film are inaccessible to modern audiences? Are these inaccessible aspects so important as to make the film incomprehensible to contemporary filmgoers or are they relatively insignificant?

2. What important changes were made in the remake? Why were they made? Which changes are improvements over the original and which are only changes for the sake of novelty?
3. Which is the better film? Does the remake have the freshness and the creative dynamic of the original? Were you disappointed in the remake? Why or why not?
4. How is the remake like the original? Is an effort made through casting, cinematic style, and so on to capture the spirit and flavor of the original? Do these efforts succeed?
5. What advantages does the remake have over the original in terms of freedom from censorship and new technology in the medium? How does it make use of these advantages?
6. If the remake involves a foreign original, how does a change of setting, language, or cultural values affect the remake?

On Sequels

1. Does the sequel grow naturally out of the original? In other words, was there enough story left over from the original to make a natural sequel?
2. How many important members of the original cast and of the behind-the-scenes team were involved in the sequel? If some characters had to be recast, how did that change affect the quality of the sequel?
3. Does the sequel build on the original in such a way that it seems incomplete unless you've seen the original, or is it complete enough to stand on its own as a separate, unified work?
4. Does the sequel capture the flavor and spirit of the original in story and visual style? Is it equal in quality to the original in every aspect? Where does it surpass the original and where is it weaker?
5. If the sequel becomes a character series, what are the qualities of the characters that make them wear well? Why do we want to see them again and again? Are the writers able to keep their characters consistent in film after film? How consistent are the other stylistic elements from one film to another?

MINI-MOVIE EXERCISE

Director Tim Burton has built his colorful career upon the creation of remakes, sequels, and genre films. His techno-savvy *Planet of the Apes* (2001) attempts to re-imagine the 1968 original. His dark *Batman Returns* (1992) was the first sequel to his own more arresting *Batman* (1989). His other genre films—including the giddy horror picture *Beetlejuice* (1988), the lyrically romantic oddity *Edward Scissorhands*

(1990), the all-star sci-fi spoof *Mars Attacks!* (1996), and his bloody film adaptation of Stephen Sondheim's stage musical *Sweeney Todd* (2007)—also either emanate from cartoon sources or seem to possess a comic book sensibility. And they usually function simultaneously as loving homage and bold satire: They operate both as replicative remembrances of cinema past and chic, visually witty parodies.

Burton's first live-action film, a short called *Frankenweenie* (1984), was a sure foreshadowing of his later works. This "children's film" (which the Disney studio financed but never gave a general theatrical release) captures all that is best in its model, the 1931 horror film *Frankenstein.* But it establishes, too, a wickedly amusing tone that proffers a sly wink to watchers of all ages. The movie's basic narrative is not original, but its canine-monster transference is at least very clever. For true newness in plot and image, one need only focus upon a film whose story, characters, and design Burton "merely" thought up, and whose screen arrival he produced—*The Nightmare Before Christmas*, directed by Henry Selick (see the "Animated SF/X Films" section of Chapter 5).

However, locate a copy of the DVD *The Nightmare Before Christmas (Special Edition)* and you will find there, among other extra features, two early Burton films. "Vincent," his first work, is a very brief animated act of admiration for Vincent Price and his screen world, narrated by Price himself. "Frankenweenie" appears in its thirty-six-minute "director's cut" and stars Shelley Duvall, Daniel Stern, and Barret Oliver. Watch the latter. Pay special attention to those elements of Burton's burgeoning artistry that help him to walk that fine line between embracing and poking fun at the genres in which he is working: the camera angles, the lighting placement, the choice of black-and-white film, the editing style, the musical scoring.

DVD FILMMAKING EXTRAS

American Cinema: One Hundred Years of Filmmaking:
Over nine hours of movie history, documentary, and criticism make up this invaluable two-disc set (first shown on PBS). Among its narrators are directors Spike Lee, George Lucas, Martin Scorsese, Steven Spielberg, Oliver Stone, and Quentin Tarantino, and actors Julia Roberts and Harrison Ford. Its substantive episodes scrutinize, along with many other topics, four specific film genres: the western, the combat film, *film noir*, and the romantic (including "screwball") comedy.

The Godfather DVD [Five-Disc] *Collection:*
This DVD set is, quite simply, an offer you can't (of course) refuse: the mother, aunt, and stepsister of all latter-day gangster films, in pristine, wide-screen form—plus three hours' worth of filmmaking extra features.

Carnival of Souls (1962) *(Criterion Collection):*
Despite how expensive this special two-disc set may initially seem, movie lovers who cherish cheaply made B-movie horror will embrace its wealth of special features. Included are two versions of the celebrated black-and-white flick, a documentary covering the 1989 reunion of cast and crew, and multiple examinations of its eerie Saltair resort setting in Salt Lake City.

Jaws (Anniversary Collector's Edition):
This DVD's "Spotlight on Location" feature demonstrates that trying to walk on water might have been easier than trying to shoot a suspense movie on water . . . *and* appease a most uncooperative title actor.

Joyride (Special Edition):
Alfred Hitchcock often asserted that precise timing through editing could make or break a thriller. One might begin to test this theory by studying the relative effectiveness of four alternative endings to John Dahl's genre movie. They are made available on a twenty-nine-minute "extras" section of the DVD.

Crouching Tiger, Hidden Dragon:
The making of Ang Lee's intensely "original" genre film is recorded in a Bravo channel special on the DVD: "Unleashing the Dragon."

The Lord of the Rings: The Fellowship of the Ring (Special Extended DVD Edition):
Choose the disc marked "The Appendices: Part Two: From Vision to Reality." Select "Filming . . ." from the menu. Learn the true meaning of "genre-fealty" by listening to the conversational tattoos of "The Fellowship of the Cast."

The Wizard of Oz:
If merely watching the extensive documentary hosted by Angela Lansbury on this classic fantasy-genre disc does not convince one of its worth, then discovering the very special "outtake musical numbers" included undoubtedly will.

Cabaret (Special Edition):
Two documentaries on this DVD provide details about the creation of director/choreographer Bob Fosse's influential musical film set in 1931 Berlin: "*Cabaret:* A Legend in the Making" (1979) and "The Recreation of an Era" (1972).

(NOTE: See also the DVD Filmmaking Extras section for Chapter 9: The Musical Score.)

Twelve Monkeys (Collector's Edition):
This "science fiction thriller" remake is actually a feature film "inspired by" *La Jetée,* the classic short work by Chris Marker (see Mini-Movie Exercise I for Chapter 12: Analysis of the Whole Film). The DVD includes a full-length (1:27) "making of" film, "The Hamster Factor and Other Tales of *Twelve Monkeys,*" which sometimes uses Monty Pythonesque animation to make its points.

FILMS FOR STUDY

Westerns—and Antiwesterns

The Assassination of Jesse James by the Coward Robert Ford (2007)
Fort Apache (1948)
Heaven's Gate (1980)
High Noon (1952)
Little Big Man (1970)
The Long Riders (1980)
McCabe & Mrs. Miller (1971)
My Darling Clementine (1946)
Once Upon a Time in the West (1968)
Open Range (2003)
Red River (1948)

Ride the High Country (1962)
Rio Bravo (1959)
The Searchers (1956)
Shane (1953)
She Wore a Yellow Ribbon (1949)
Stagecoach (1939)
3:10 to Yuma (1957; remade in 2007)
Tumbleweeds (1925)
The Wild Bunch (1969)

Gangster Films

The Asphalt Jungle (1950)
The Big Heat (1953)
Bugsy (1991)
The Departed (2006)
The Godfather (1972; sequels: *Part II*, 1974, and *Part III*, 1990)
GoodFellas (1990)
Kill Bill, Vol. I (2003), and *Vol. II* (2004)
Kiss of Death (1947)
Little Caesar (1931)
The Maltese Falcon (1941)
Mean Streets (1973)
Miller's Crossing (1990)
Natural Born Killers (1994)
Prizzi's Honor (1985)
Public Enemies (2009)
The Public Enemy (1931)
Reservoir Dogs (1992)
The Town (2010)
The Untouchables (1987)
The Usual Suspects (1995)
White Heat (1949)

Film Noir and Neo-Noir

The Big Sleep (1946)
Blood Simple (1984)
Body Heat (1981)
Chinatown (1974)
Detour (1945; remade in 1992)
Devil in a Blue Dress (1995)

D.O.A. (1950; remade in 1988)
Double Indemnity (1944)
Gilda (1946)
The Grifters (1990)
The Killers (1946)
A Kiss Before Dying (1956; remade in 1991)
Kiss Me Deadly (1955)
L.A. Confidential (1997)
The Lady From Shanghai (1947)
The Last Seduction (1994)
Laura (1944)
Memento (2000)
Murder, My Sweet (1944)
The Naked Kiss (1964)
Night and the City (1950)
One False Move (1992)
Pickup on South Street (1953)
The Postman Always Rings Twice (1946; remade in 1981)
Sin City (2005)
Sunset Boulevard (1950)
To Have and Have Not (1944)
Touch of Evil (1958; re-edited from Orson Welles's notes in 1998)

War Films

All Quiet on the Western Front (1930)
Apocalypse Now (1979)
Battleground (1949)
Black Hawk Down (2001)
The Bridge on the River Kwai (1957)
Das Boot (1981—German)
The Dirty Dozen (1967)
The Eagle Has Landed (1976)
Grand Illusion (1937—French)
The Hurt Locker (2008)

Letters From Iwo Jima (2006)
*M*A*S*H* (1970)
Paths of Glory (1957)
Patton (1970)
Platoon (1986)
Stalag 17 (1953)
They Were Expendable (1945)
The Thin Red Line (1998; remake of 1964 film)

Horror Films

Alien (1979)
The Birds (1963)
Black Swan (2010)
The Blair Witch Project (1999)
The Cabinet of Dr. Caligari (1920—German)
Carrie (1976)
Cat People (1942)
Dr. Jekyll and Mr. Hyde (1931; remade in 1941)
Eraserhead (1976)
The Exorcist (1973)
The Fly (1958; remade in 1986)
Frankenstein (1931; sequels include *Bride of Frankenstein*, 1935)
Freaks (1932)
Friday the 13th (1980)
Halloween (1978)
The Innocents (1961)
The Lair of the White Worm (1988)
The Mummy (1932)
A Nightmare on Elm Street (1984)
Night of the Living Dead (1968)
The Omen (1976)
The Others (2001)
Psycho (1960)
Saw (2004; sequels)
Shadow of the Vampire (2000)

Shutter Island (2010)
The Shining (1980)
The Silence of the Lambs (1991)
Splice (2009)
Suspiria (1977—Italian)

Science Fiction and Fantasy Films

A.I. Artificial Intelligence (2001)
Alphaville (1965—French)
Blade Runner (1982)
Brazil (1985)
The Brother From Another Planet (1984)
Close Encounters of the Third Kind (1977)
The Day the Earth Stood Still (1951)
Dune (1984)
eXistenZ (1999)
Fahrenheit 451 (1966)
The Fifth Element (1997)
The Incredible Shrinking Man (1957)
Invasion of the Body Snatchers (1956)
The Invisible Man (1933)
Island of Lost Souls (1932)
The Man Who Fell to Earth (1976)
The Matrix (1999)
Metropolis (1927)
Minority Report (2002)
Moon (2009)
Pi (1998)
Planet of the Apes (1968)
Seconds (1966)
Soylent Green (1973)
Star Trek—The Motion Picture (1979; followed by several sequels)
The Terminator (1984; sequels: *2*, 1991; *3*, 2003)
Them! (1954)

The Thing (1951; remade in 1982)
THX 1138 (1971)
A Trip to the Moon (1902, Mèliés short)
2001: A Space Odyssey (1968)
X-Men (2000, plus sequels in 2003 and 2006)

Romantic Screwball Comedies

Adam's Rib (1949)
The Awful Truth (1937)
Ball of Fire (1941)
Bringing Up Baby (1938; remade in 1972 as *What's Up, Doc?*)
Easy Living (1937)
The 40-Year-Old Virgin (2005)
His Girl Friday (1940)
Holiday (1938)
It Happened One Night (1934)
The Lady Eve (1941)
Mr. Deeds Goes to Town (1936; remake: *Mr. Deeds*, 2002)
My Best Friend's Wedding (1997)
My Big Fat Greek Wedding (2002)
My Man Godfrey (1936)
Nothing Sacred (1937)
The Palm Beach Story (1942)
The Philadelphia Story (1940; remade as *High Society*, 1956)
The Thin Man (1934; plus a series of sequels)
Tin Cup (1996)
Topper (1937; sequels)

Twentieth Century (1934)
Unfaithfully Yours (1948; remade in 1984)

Musicals

Across the Universe (2007)
All That Jazz (1979)
An American in Paris (1951)
Cabaret (1972)
Chicago (2002)
De-Lovely (2004)
Dreamgirls (2006)
Fame (1980)
Fiddler on the Roof (1971)
Footloose (1984)
42nd Street (1933)
Funny Girl (1968)
Gold Diggers of 1933 (1933; also 1935 and 1937)
Grease (1978)
Guys and Dolls (1955)
Hair (1979)
A Hard Day's Night (1964)
Jailhouse Rock (1957)
The Jazz Singer (1927)
The King and I (1956)
Mary Poppins (1964)
Meet Me in St. Louis (1944)
Moulin Rouge! (2001)
My Fair Lady (1964)
Nashville (1975)
New York, New York (1977)
Nine (2009)
Oklahoma! (1955)
Oliver! (1968)
One Hundred Men and a Girl (1937)
Pennies From Heaven (1981)
Road to Singapore (1940; first in a series)
The Rocky Horror Picture Show (1975)
Rose-Marie (1936)
The Sound of Music (1965)

Top Hat (1935)
Topsy-Turvy (1999)
The Umbrellas of Cherbourg (1964—French)
West Side Story (1961)
The Wizard of Oz (1939)
Yentl (1983)

Remakes

Ben-Hur (1925/1959)
Down and Out in Beverly Hills (1986/Boudu Saved From Drowning, 1932—French)
Clueless (1995/Emma, 1996)
Death Takes a Holiday (1934/Meet Joe Black, 1998)
Father of the Bride (1950; sequel: Father's Little Dividend, 1951/1991; sequel: Father of the Bride Part II, 1995)
The Getaway (1972/1993)
Godzilla (1954—Japanese/ 1998—plus many mutations)
Great Expectations (1934/ 1946/1974/1998)
A Guy Named Joe (1943/Always, 1989)
Here Comes Mr. Jordan (1941/Heaven Can Wait, 1978/Down to Earth, 2001)
King Kong (1933/1976/2005)
The Ladykillers (1955— British/2004)
Les Liaisons Dangereuses (1959—French/ Dangerous Liaisons, 1988/Valmont, 1989/ Cruel Intentions, 1999)

Lord of the Flies (1963/1990)
Love Affair (1939/An Affair to Remember, 1957/Love Affair, 1994)
The Man Who Knew Too Much (1934—British/ 1956, both directed by Alfred Hitchcock)
A Midsummer Night's Dream (1935/1968/1999)
The Nutty Professor (1963/1996; sequel: II: The Klumps, 2000)
Ocean's Eleven (1960/2001; sequels: Twelve, 2004, and Thirteen, 2007)
Of Mice and Men (1939/1992)
Purple Noon (1960— French/Italian/The Talented Mr. Ripley, 1999)
The Return of Martin Guerre (1982—French/ Sommersby, 1993)
The Seven Samurai (1954—Japanese/The Magnificent Seven, 1960)
The Shop Around the Corner (1940/In the Good Old Summertime, 1949/You've Got Mail, 1998)
The Taming of the Shrew (1929/1967/10 Things I Hate About You, 1999)
The Thomas Crown Affair (1968/1999)
To Be or Not To Be (1942/1983)

The Vanishing (1988— French-Dutch/1993— both directed by George Sluizer)
Wings of Desire (1987— West German–French; sequel: Faraway, So Close!, 1993/City of Angels, 1998)

Sequels

Babe (1995—Australian/ Babe: Pig in the City, 1998—Australian)
Barbershop (2002; 2, 2004)
The Decline of the American Empire (1986—Canadian/The Barbarian Invasions, 2003)
Die Hard (1988/Die Hard 2, 1990/Die Hard With a Vengeance, 1995)
Jean de Florette (1986— French; Manon of the Spring, 1986)
The Last Picture Show (1971/Texasville, 1990)
My Father's Glory (1990— French; sequel: My Mother's Castle, 1990)
Smiles of a Summer Night (1955—Swedish/ inspired A Little Night Music, 1978, and A Midsummer Night's Sex Comedy, 1982)

FILM *and* SOCIETY

The Lives of Others

A movie is a kind of séance, or a drug, where we are offered the chance to partake in the lifelike. No, it's not life: we will never meet Joan Crawford or Clark Gable. Yet we are with them. It is surreptitious; it is illicit, if you like, in the sense of being unearned or undeserved. It is vicarious, it is fantastic, and this may be very dangerous. But it is heady beyond belief or compare. And it changed the world. Not even heroin or the supernatural ever went so far.

—DAVID THOMSON, FILM HISTORIAN AND CRITIC

Most Americans have grown up with movies, both in the theater and on television. We're so familiar with genre films, remakes, and sequels that we experience them as easily as drawing a breath. They are part of our natural environment. But sometimes we are not very comfortable with foreign language, silent, and documentary films, because they seem to be products of other cultures, other lifestyles, other sensibilities, or other generations. The "strangeness" of these kinds of films can pose formidable challenges to appreciation and understanding. In addition, in our culture we often have difficulty dealing with feature films whose main significance may involve our focusing on social problems or whose apparent aim is to stretch the boundaries of our culture's standards regarding censorship issues. However, if we make a conscious effort to overcome these obstacles, we will be amply rewarded by the worlds of experience awaiting in movies that help us to define ourselves and our society.

FILM FOREIGNNESS

As we have seen in Chapter 8, the language problem is one obstacle for Americans in understanding and appreciating international films. Another factor that influences our responses is editing rhythm. The editing rhythms of international films differ from those of American films. Whether these filmic differences reflect the different pace of life in other countries would certainly make an interesting study. But, whatever the cause, there are differences. Traditionally, Italian films, for example, average about fifteen seconds per running shot, whereas American films average about five seconds per shot. This difference makes Italian films seem strange to American viewers, and there is danger that American viewers will be bored by the film without knowing why. In addition, a typical (sometimes stereotypical) observation about differences is that American films tend to be plot based whereas European films are usually character based.

The musical scores to many international films, especially Italian and French films, have often seemed dated, like American music of an earlier era. Swedish and Danish films, particularly, use little or no music, a fact that also takes getting used to. In some cases, the music may be present to trigger responses that are particular to that culture, to which we simply have not been conditioned to respond.

Other important cultural differences may limit or distract our response. A story about a Russian attempt to use *The Grapes of Wrath* as a propaganda tool against the United States in the late 1940s indicates that cultural differences have a profound effect on how a film is received. Russian officials viewing *The Grapes of Wrath* had seen in it an example of the exploitation of migrant workers by the capitalistic ranch owners. The officials started showing the film to Russians in order to demonstrate how terrible life in America was and to convince them of the evils of capitalism. The idea backfired when the peasants responded not with contempt for the capitalists but with envy for the Joads, who owned a truck and had the freedom to travel across the country.

Similarly, American audiences might miss some of the nuances of a French film like Jean Renoir's classic *Grand Illusion* or of an Italian film like Lina Wertmuller's *Swept Away . . .* (Figure 15.1), a film narrative operating on several different levels. On a very basic level, *Swept Away . . .* is an allegory about the never-ending battle between the sexes. The principal characters, a deckhand (Giancarlo Giannini) and a yacht owner's wife (Mariangela Melato), are ship-wrecked on an island. The couple are opposites in a variety of ways. He is dark haired and dark skinned; she is fair

FIGURE 15.1 **Cultural Differences**   An American audience might have difficulty understanding the symbolic importance of class distinctions in a French film like Jean Renoir's *Grand Illusion* (left, with Marcel Dalio and Jean Gabin) or an Italian film such as Lina Wertmuller's *Swept Away . . .* (1975) (right, with Mariangelo Melato and Giancarlo Giannini).

skinned and blonde. He is a southern Italian and lower class; she is a northern Italian and upper class. Politically, she is a capitalist; he is a social democrat. As the male/female battle is waged, a very Italian class and political struggle is also being waged, with levels of meaning beyond the understanding of the average American viewer. Although we can catch the broad outlines of these symbolic levels, the fine nuances and subtleties are lost to us. This is not to say that we cannot enjoy the film, but we must face the fact that we are not really seeing quite the same film that a native Italian would see. The battle of the sexes and the love story it evolves into are universal and clearly understood. The north/south conflict and the political/class struggle are less familiar to an American, in the same way that an Italian would lack an intimate understanding of our basic myths of North/South differences, political parties, black/white social problems, our particular American concept of social status, or American democracy. (Perhaps ironically, the critically pummeled 2002 English remake of *Swept Away . . .*, directed by Guy Ritchie and starring Madonna and the son of the original film's male star, somehow managed to be both tone-deaf and intensely confusing on multiple cultural and gender levels.)

Sometimes, Europeans appreciate certain aspects of American films that Americans cannot see. For example, French critics were initially much more lavish in their praise of *Bonnie and Clyde* than were American critics. A foreign director's cinematic style may have greater power and fascination because of its strangeness to viewers who are not moved in the same way by the home-grown styles they have become accustomed to. Surely this concept begins to explain the immense popularity in America of such exotic and powerful talent as the Spanish director Pedro Almodóvar (*Women on the Verge of a Nervous Breakdown, All About My Mother, Talk to Her, Volver, Broken Embraces*).

Foreign films offer us the opportunity to experience customs, moral attitudes, and codes of behavior very different from our own. Mira Nair's *Monsoon Wedding*, for example, offers American audiences a glimpse of Indian wedding rituals, class differences, and beliefs about romantic love, arranged marriage, and the importance of family, while also showing the influence of Western culture in contemporary Indian life. The bride-to-be's cousin in *Monsoon Wedding,* for example, dresses and wears her hair in a looser style than the other women, suggesting her rebellion against traditional sex roles in Indian society. Although foreign films may demand more of us as audiences, they can also take us beyond an American view of the world.

"Strange" Silents

A category of films that may seem as foreign to Americans as works of another country is the silent film. Part of the "silent" film's "strangeness" arises because its name is something of a misnomer. In fact, these films were intended to be shown with a musical accompaniment. Sometimes a complete score was distributed along with the film and played by a large orchestra, as was the case with *The Birth of a Nation* (1915). Usually, a single piano or organ player simply improvised as the film was shown. Such music filled a definite vacuum, and the silent film without it has a ghostly kind of incompleteness. Many of the silent film's best moments lose their impact for modern viewers when their rhythmic qualities and emotional moods are not underscored musically as was intended.

Accustomed to the levels of communication conveyed by the sound film, and conditioned to half-watch everything by the ever-present television, we may have lost our ability to concentrate on purely visual elements, as in a silent film. If we are to fully appreciate the silent film, we must master a new set of watching skills and become more sensitive to the essentially nonverbal language of the earlier form. Because silent films are the product of another age, they must be judged, at least to some extent, as reflections of the society and culture of that day. Although these films adequately expressed the sensibility of their own times, some of the best ones have survived until our own era because of their universal themes.

In the past, modern viewers seldom have had the opportunity to see silent films as they were intended to be seen; instead, we have watched copies that are dead, decayed, and corrupted, with much of their original brightness and impact lost forever. But now the DVD is helping to rescue our cinematic past by preserving these films for current and future generations.

If we carefully study silent films, we can learn to appreciate the effectiveness of narrative told clearly and quickly through purely pictorial means (or with a minimum of subtitles). The absence of dialogue can actually make us more sensitive to the film's visual rhythmic qualities. And, as we have noted earlier (see the Chapter 10 "Flashback" feature on the history of silent-film acting), in rising above the formidable barrier of language differences, silent film has a unique ability to speak a universal language.

DOES AMERICAN FILM SHAPE OR REFLECT SOCIAL AND CULTURAL VALUES?

No art form exists in a vacuum. The more popular an art is, and the wider its appeal to all segments of the population, the more closely it is tied to the social values, mores, and institutions of its audience. As both an extremely popular medium and an industry involving great financial risk and profit potential, the American film naturally must be responsive to social and economic pressures. Therefore, a

FIGURE 15.2 **The Changing Face of Censorship**
Producer/director Howard Hughes filmed *The Outlaw* in 1941 and released it in 1943. The Motion Picture Association of America later withdrew its seal of approval and local community pressure caused many theaters to cancel its showing. Although the Doc Holliday/Billy the Kid story featured starlet Jane Russell showing more cleavage and passion than the code allowed, the film would receive a ho-hum PG rating if released today.

complete understanding of many American films requires an analysis of the social and economic pressures that have affected the final products seen on the screen.

So film is not an independent entity but an integrated part of the social fabric, for its very survival depends on maintaining and continuing its popularity. To achieve real popularity, a movie must, first, be believable. Its action must take place in an environment that has credibility, and its story must reflect the common truths of the society in which it is made, or at least mirror people's hopes, dreams, fears, and inner needs. When real life does not fulfill these needs, people are primed to respond sympathetically to an artistic expression of them in film.

Film does not create *new* truths for society. It cannot reshape a society that is not ready for change. But this fact does not mean that film is not a powerful instrument of social change. The motion picture's power as a social force comes from its ability to pick up, amplify, and spread to society as a whole currents that already exist among segments of the population. Film also speeds popular acceptance of social change. The dramatically powerful presentation of new ways of thinking and behaving on screens twenty feet high in thousands of movie theaters across the country gives those new ways a significant seal of approval.

It is because of film's potential for legitimizing new standards of behavior—and for inspiring imitation of that behavior, especially by young members of its audience—that most systems of censorship or control have originated. In fact, the way systems of censorship develop usually follows a pattern that goes something like this. A traumatic event disrupts the stability of the social structure (some past examples: World War I, the Depression, World War II, the Vietnam War, the women's movement, the sexual revolution, the drug revolution, the civil rights movement, "9/11/01"). This event causes a significant shift in moral values and codes of behavior within certain segments of the population. Such changes create pressure for the entertainment media to reflect the truth of the new attitudes and standards of behavior. But a conservative element within the society vigorously resists the changes and demands that films be controlled or censored to prevent the spread of the shocking behavior and ensure that movies reflect the truths of society as the conservative element believes they *should be*. Most censorship within the film industry reflects an uneasy compromise between advocates of change and supporters of the status quo (Figure 15.2).

THE MOTION PICTURE PRODUCTION CODE, 1930–1960

In the decades following World War I, Hollywood films began reflecting a change in moral standards. Sex, seduction, divorce, drinking, and drug use—new symbols of the sophisticated life—all became standard film fare. In 1922 public outrage against this change led a frightened film industry to organize the Motion Picture Producers and Distributors of America, Inc. They hired Postmaster General Will B. Hays to front the organization, which became known as the Hays Office. Hays and his staff first reacted to state and local censorship by codifying the most frequent objections to film content and advising member companies on what to avoid. By 1930, the organization (now known as the MPAA—Motion Picture Association of America) had published an official Motion Picture Production Code and set up a Production Code Administration to enforce its rulings.

Members of the MPAA agreed not to release or distribute a film without a certificate of approval. In addition, they were required to submit copies of all scripts under production, and each completed film had to be submitted for viewing by the Production Code board before it was sent to the laboratory for printing. A $25,000 penalty for producing, distributing, or exhibiting any film without the seal encouraged member companies to comply with the agreement. Through voluntary compliance, this industry-imposed regulation served to control the moral standards of the American film for the next three decades.

Although the code had strong ties with the Catholic Church, its practical rules did not reflect any single theology. Translated into simplest terms, the code and its rules were designed to require motion pictures to reflect, respect, and promote the institutions and moral values of the American middle class.

Excerpts of the code are reprinted in the box beginning on page 443. Evident throughout the document is a belief in the powerful influence that movies can exert on the moral standards of an audience. Most of the code deals with the dangers of film as a corrupting influence, but film is also shown to have tremendous potential for good:

> If motion pictures consistently *hold up for admiration high types of characters* and present stories that will affect lives for the better, they can become the most powerful natural forces for the improvement of mankind.

The writers of the code believed that if the motion picture's creative energies were correctly channeled (through conformity to the code), film would become a supermedium—fighting for truth, justice, and the American way.

That film is a mass medium available to children as well as adults was a major concern. In fact, the code can best be understood by relating it to the industry's concern with the "twelve-year-old mind." It was this young, highly impressionable age group—in the process of forming its values and its moral sense and picking its role models—that the code was determined to protect.

It may be difficult for modern film students to take the code seriously. However, an in-depth study of any complex realistic or naturalistic novel of the period and the film based on that novel will illustrate the effect of the code on such adaptations. The profound influence of the code on the American film product can also be seen by studying a relatively small number of American films produced between 1934 and 1966.

Excerpts From the Motion Picture Production Code*

Reasons Supporting Preamble of Code

1. Theatrical motion pictures . . . are primarily to be regarded as ENTERTAINMENT. . . .

   The MORAL IMPORTANCE of entertainment is something which has been universally recognized. It enters intimately into the lives of men and women and affects them closely; it occupies their minds and affections during leisure hours; and ultimately touches the whole of their lives. A man may be judged by his standard of entertainment as easily as by the standard of his work. . . .

   > *Correct entertainment raises* the whole standard of a nation. *Wrong entertainment lowers* the whole living conditions and moral ideals of a race.

   > *Note,* for example, the healthy reactions to healthful sports, like baseball, golf; the unhealthy reactions to sports like cockfighting, bullfighting, bear baiting, etc.

   > *Note,* too, the effect on ancient nations of gladiatorial combats, the obscene plays of Roman times, etc.

2. Motion pictures are very important as ART.

   Though a new art, possibly a combination art, it has the same object as the other arts, the presentation of human thought, emotion, and experience, in terms of an appeal to the soul through the senses. Here, as in entertainment,

   Art *enters intimately* into the lives of human beings.

   Art can be *morally good,* lifting men to higher levels. This has been done through good music, great painting, authentic fiction, poetry, drama. . . .

   It has often been argued that art in itself is unmoral, neither good nor bad. This is perhaps true of the THING which is music, painting, poetry, etc. But the thing is the PRODUCT of some person's mind, and the intention of that mind was either good or bad. . . . Besides, the thing has its EFFECT upon those who come into contact with it. . . . In the case of the motion pictures, this effect may be particularly emphasized because no art has so quick and so widespread an appeal to the masses. . . .

3. The motion picture . . . has special MORAL OBLIGATIONS.

   A. Most arts appeal to the mature. This art appeals at once to *every class.* . . .

*Editor's Note: To simplify the reader's task, some parts of the code have been re-ordered so that all materials relating to a given topic appear together. As originally presented, the code consisted of two parts. The first part began with the section "Preamble," which was followed, in sequence, by the sections "General Principles" and "Particular Applications." The second part consisted of "Reasons Supporting" or "Reasons Underlying" each of the "Particular Applications." Here, the sections have been rearranged so that the supports or reasons appear beneath the particular application to which each pertains.

B. By reason of the mobility of a film and the ease of picture distribution . . . this art *reaches places* unpenetrated by other forms of art.

C. Because of these two facts, it is difficult to produce films intended for only certain classes of people. . . . Films, unlike books and music, can with difficulty be confined to certain selected groups.

D. The latitude given to film material cannot . . . be as wide as the latitude given to *book material.* . . .

    a. A book describes; a film vividly presents. One presents on a cold page; the other by apparently living people.

    b. A book reaches the mind through words merely; a film reaches the eyes and ears through the reproduction of actual events.

    c. The reaction of a reader to a book depends largely on the keenness of the reader's imagination; the reaction to a film depends on the vividness of presentation. . . .

E. Everything possible in a *play* is not possible in a film:

    a. Because of the *larger audience of the film,* and its consequential mixed character. Psychologically, the larger the audience, the lower the moral mass resistance to suggestion.

    b. Because through light, enlargement of character, presentation, scenic emphasis, etc., the screen story is *brought closer* to the audience. . . .

    c. The enthusiasm for . . . *actors* and *actresses,* developed beyond anything of the sort in history, makes the audience largely sympathetic toward the characters they portray and the stories in which they figure. Hence the audience is more ready to confuse actor and actress and the characters they portray. . . .

Particular Applications: Crimes Against the Law

The technique of murder must be presented in a way that will not inspire imitation. . . .

Revenge in modern times shall not be justified. . . .

Methods of crime should not be explicitly presented. . . .

The illegal drug traffic must not be portrayed in such a way as to stimulate curiosity concerning the use of, or traffic in, such drugs; nor shall scenes be approved which show the use of illegal drugs, or their effects. . . .

The use of liquor . . . when not required by the plot . . . will not be shown. . . .

There must be no display, at any time, of machine guns, submachine guns, or other weapons generally classified as illegal weapons in the hands of gangsters . . . and there are to be no off-stage sounds of the repercussions of these guns. There must be no new, unique or trick methods shown for concealing guns. . . .

Pictures dealing with criminal activities, in which minors participate, or to which minors are related, shall not be approved if they incite demoralizing imitation. . . .

Particular Applications: Sex, Costume, and Dance

Sex

The sanctity of the institution of marriage and the home shall be upheld. Pictures shall not infer that low forms of sex relationship are the accepted or common thing. . . . Out of regard for the sanctity of marriage and the home, the *triangle*, that is, the love of a third party for one already married, needs careful handling. The treatment should not throw sympathy against marriage as an institution. . . . Excessive and lustful kissing, lustful embraces, suggestive postures and gestures are not to be shown . . . passion should be treated in such a manner as not to stimulate the lower and baser emotions. . . . Many scenes cannot be presented without arousing dangerous emotions on the part of the immature, the young or the *criminal classes*. . . .

Costume

The fact that the nude or semi-nude body may be *beautiful* does not make its use in the films moral. For, in addition to its beauty, the effect of the nude or semi-nude body on the normal individual must be taken into consideration.

Nudity or semi-nudity used simply to put a "*punch*" into a picture comes under the head of immoral actions. . . . Nudity can never be permitted as being *necessary for the plot*. . . .

Transparent or *translucent materials* and silhouettes are frequently more suggestive than actual exposure. . . .

Dance

Dancing in general is recognized as an *art* and as a *beautiful* form of expressing human emotions. . . . But dances which suggest or represent sexual actions, whether performed solo or with two or more; dances intended to excite the emotional reaction of an audience; dances with movement of the breasts, excessive body movement while the feet are stationary, violate decency and are wrong.

Particular Applications . . . Profanity

No approval by the Production Code Administration shall be given to the use of words and phrases . . . including, but not limited to, the following: Alley cat (applied to a woman); bat (applied to a woman); broad (applied to a woman); Bronx cheer (the sound); chippie; cocotte; God, Lord, Jesus, Christ (unless used reverently); cripes; fanny; fairy (in a vulgar sense); finger (the); fire, cries of; Gawd; goose (in a vulgar sense); "hold your hat" or "hats"; hot (applied to a woman); "in your hat"; louse, lousy; Madam (relating to prostitution); nance; nerts; nuts (except when meaning crazy); pansy; razzberry (the sound); slut (applied to a woman); S.O.B.; son-of-a; tart; toilet gags; tom cat (applied to a man); traveling salesman and farmer's daughter jokes; whore; damn, hell (excepting when the use of said last two words shall be essential and required for portrayal, in proper historical context, of any scene or dialogue based upon historical fact or folklore, or for the presentation in proper literary context of a Biblical, or other religious quotation, or a quotation from a literary work provided that no such use shall be permitted which is intrinsically objectionable or offends good taste). . . .

One of the clearest examples of the Motion Picture Production Code's effect on the medium is the case of *On the Waterfront* (1954), which would have been quite a different movie if the Code had not forced its director, Elia Kazan, to alter the ending. As actor Rod Steiger tells it:

> I remember a magazine review of *On the Waterfront* that called Brando's fight at the end of the picture a March to Calvary and analyzed the entire film in terms of how Kazan had been influenced by the life of Christ. Actually, the scene didn't appear in the original ending of the picture. It was to have concluded with a shot of the dead boy floating down the river. But the Hays Office had called up and said, "Wait a minute. We have a rule: crime cannot triumph in films." Okay, they had a point. A lot of young people were going to see the picture. So in the middle of making the film, Kazan had to improvise a new ending. March to Calvary? We were just trying to get out of a hole.[1]

In his spinoff novel *Waterfront*, published a year after the film was released, screenwriter Budd Schulberg returned to his original ending, which gave the story what one critic called the "substance impossible in a movie." In the novel, after testifying against Johnny Friendly at the Crime Commission Hearings, Terry Malloy (played in the film by Marlon Brando) sees Friendly on a street corner and attacks him verbally. But there is no terrible beating at the hands of Friendly's men by the dockside tool shed, no courageous, painful walk by Terry leading the men up to the loading dock. Friendly simply gives his henchmen "the slightest nods" because "Johnny had already passed down the execution order. 'He's got to go.'" Here is how the novel ends:

> Three weeks later the remains of a human being were found in a barrel of lime that had been tossed on one of the multi-acre junk heaps in the Jersey swamps. The coroner's report after the inquest attributed death to twenty-seven stab wounds, apparently inflicted with an icepick. No next of kin came forward. The lime-mutilated corpse was never identified. But the boys along River Street, pro mob and anti, knew they had seen the last of a pretty tough kid.[2]

The power of the Production Code Administration diminished slowly from 1952, when Otto Preminger released *The Moon Is Blue* without a seal of approval (but *with* box-office success), until 1966, when Jack Valenti was named president of the Motion Picture Association of America. At that time, machinery for developing a new method of control was set into motion, resulting in the MPAA Rating System of 1968.

CENSORSHIP IN TRANSITION, 1948–1968

The Production Code Administration controlled the American film product with an iron hand until 1948, when an important Supreme Court antitrust decision (*U.S.* v. *Paramount Pictures*) ruled that the major production companies could no longer own large theater chains. As a result, thousands of theaters across the country were no longer obligated to show any film, regardless of its quality, just because the parent company had produced it, and the major studios lost control of a large captive audience. The Supreme Court decision also opened the door for independently produced movies to be distributed without a code seal.

As early as 1949, Samuel Goldwyn recognized that the industry would have a monumental fight on its hands "to keep people patronizing our theaters in preference to sitting at home and watching a program of entertainment" on television.[3] By 1954, movie attendance had dropped to half of what it had been in 1946. When this decline in attendance continued in spite of the industry's technical innovations such as Cinemascope, Cinerama, 3-D, and stereophonic sound, filmmakers recognized that they would have to handle more mature subjects than were being treated on television if they hoped to lure audiences back into the theaters.

Changes were made in the code to allow more flexibility. In 1956, the code was amended to allow themes of miscegenation, prostitution, and narcotics. In 1961 discreet treatments of homosexuality and other "sexual deviations" were permitted.

In the 1950s and early 1960s, a number of powerful foreign films shown in large cities were having an important influence on American audiences. Strong, provocative films like *The Seventh Seal*, *The Virgin Spring*, *The Lovers*, *La Dolce Vita*, and *Hiroshima, Mon Amour* made code-approved American products seem bland, antiseptic, and dull by comparison. American filmmakers were inspired to take some chances and push for more artistic freedom (Figure 15.3).

FIGURE 15.3 **Provocative Foreign Films**   The code-bound American films of the 1950s and early 1960s seemed bland and antiseptic when compared to powerful imports like *La Dolce Vita* (1960—Italy).

FIGURE 15.4 **American Breakthrough**   Rod Steiger gave a touching performance as a middle-aged man haunted by memories of his experiences in a Nazi concentration camp in *The Pawnbroker* (1965). The film was granted an MPAA seal of approval despite two nude scenes, both crucial to understanding the story.

By the mid-1960s the industry had begun to accept the idea that not all movies should be made for one mass audience. *Lolita* (1962) was given a seal despite its theme of a middle-aged man's obsessive love for an adolescent. *The Pawnbroker* (1965) was approved despite two nude scenes (Figure 15.4). *Who's Afraid of Virginia Woolf?* (1966) won a seal despite clear violations in theme and language, and *Alfie* (1966) was cleared despite its frank treatment of sex and abortion. With the approval of the last two films, the Production Code Administration made a significant move toward the present rating system. Warner Brothers agreed to restrict attendance to *Who's Afraid of Virginia Woolf?* to adults eighteen and older, and Paramount agreed to advertise *Alfie* as "recommended for mature audiences."

In 1966, the code was simplified, and the Code Administration divided approved films into two categories. The first category included films that presented no problems for the mass audience. The second category was labeled "Suggested for Mature Audiences." The label was advisory only; there were no enforced restrictions.

Two important court decisions in April 1968 forced the industry to provide a clearer system of classification. In *Ginsburg* v. *New York* the court ruled that material protected by the Constitution for adults could still be considered obscene for

FIGURE 15.5 **A Profoundly Significant G Rating**   A common misconception about the MPAA Rating System is that G always signifies a children's film. It often does, but an occasional "profoundly significant film" like *The Straight Story*, a moving drama starring Richard Farnsworth and Sissy Spacek, fits the "General Audiences" classification. Of course, in this case, the film's director, David Lynch, is notorious otherwise for barely being able to obtain an R rating for his pictures (including *Mulholland Dr.*).

minors. In *Interstate* v. *Dallas* the court invalidated a city classification ordinance because its standards of classification were vague, but the court indicated that more tightly drawn standards of classification could be constitutional. To prevent state and local classification boards from springing up in response to this ruling, the film industry hurriedly tightened its own classification system and announced the MPAA Movie Rating System to the public six months after the *Dallas* decision. That rating system, with slight modifications, remains in effect today.

THE MPAA RATING SYSTEM

The new rating system was announced to the public on October 7, 1968, and went into effect on November 1. Like the Motion Picture Production Code, which it was designed to replace, the MPAA Rating System is a form of self-regulation put into operation to guard against government, state, and local control. By 1966 it was clear that American society had outgrown the moral standards that governed the 1930 code, and honest, realistic films could no longer be produced in conformance with its prohibitions. The new system was conceived as a system of classification rather than as censorship, and each film rated by the Rating System board was (and still is) classified in terms of its suitability for children (Figure 15.5). The board does not prohibit or ban the production or distribution of any motion picture. Its responsibility is limited to the classification of films, to labeling each film clearly so that theater managers can control the audience for each picture in accordance with its classification.

Since November 1968, practically every motion picture exhibited in the United States has carried a rating. Slight modifications have been made in the wording and symbols to clarify misunderstood points, but the rating system in use today is

Motion Picture Association of America Voluntary Movie Rating System

G	GENERAL AUDIENCES	All ages admitted.
PG	PARENTAL GUIDANCE SUGGESTED	Some material may not be suitable for children.
PG-13	PARENTS STRONGLY CAUTIONED	Some material may be inappropriate for children under 13.
R	RESTRICTED	Under 17 requires accompanying parent or adult guardian.
NC-17	NO ONE 17 AND UNDER ADMITTED	

essentially the same one introduced in 1968. As it now stands, the MPAA Rating System classifies films in the manner described in the box shown above.

Perhaps the simplest explanation of the first MPAA Rating System (and a fairly accurate one) was found in an old joke: "In a G- or PG-rated movie, the guy in the white hat gets the girl. In an R-rated movie, the guy in the black hat gets the girl. In an X-rated movie everybody gets the girl." The joke accurately reflects the stigma attached to the X rating, which became synonymous with pornography. TV stations and newspapers would not advertise X-rated films; most theaters wouldn't show them. In the fall of 1990, the MPAA moved to counteract that image by changing the X designation to NC-17 (no one 17 and under admitted). The change was brought about by industry pressure to give serious "adults only" films such as *Henry & June* a fair chance in the marketplace, but few NC-17 films are released, for this same stigma remains, essentially. Some producers and directors choose, instead, to use the designation NR ("Not Rated"). In recent years, for example, such sexually explicit works as *Intimacy* (starring the Shakepearean actor Mark Rylance), *Fat Girl*, *The Brown Bunny*, and *Shortbus* have taken this path.

A brochure published when the rating system was introduced in 1968 included a list of eleven Standards for Production, but that list provides no help whatsoever in determining how films are actually classified. The biggest problem was the confusion the system caused parents of children sixteen or younger. Most of the confusion was spawned by the PG category, those films that anybody could see with "parental guidance suggested." Although television had certainly made the modern child a more sophisticated viewer than his or her pretelevision counterpart, there is a great difference between the maturity of an eight-year-old and that of a sixteen-year-old. Many parents were not sure what to expect in a PG movie and whether to allow their eight-year-old or twelve-year-old to go alone on a Saturday afternoon to see one.

An attempt to solve this problem was first made in 1972, when the industry added this caution to its PG rating: "Some material may not be suitable for children." Although some pressure was applied to encourage the MPAA to follow

FIGURE 15.6 **Too Intense for Young Children** Steven Spielberg's *Indiana Jones and the Temple of Doom* and Joe Dante's *Gremlins* drew so much criticism for the intensity of their violence that the industry instituted a new PG-13 rating for such films.

the example of the European systems, which distinguish between children (up to twelve) and teenagers (thirteen to sixteen), there was no move to do so until the summer of 1984.

When *Indiana Jones and the Temple of Doom* and *Gremlins* came out in June 1984, there was an immediate negative reaction from critics and parents alike to the amount and intensity of violence portrayed in both films. A new rating called PG-13 (to cover the gray area between the PG and the R ratings) was instituted on July 1, 1984. Its purpose is to warn parents to use extra caution in allowing young children to attend such films (Figure 15.6).

Because theater owners do not want to enforce a second restrictive rating, PG-13 puts the burden of control squarely on parents, a philosophy very much in tune with the MPAA's stated policies since 1968. Despite the confusion over the PG rating, nationwide surveys prior to 1980 indicated that the public was reasonably well satisfied with the MPAA rating system—three out of five parents approved of it. And the PG-13 rating seems to be eliminating the gray area between the PG and R ratings. However, some critics of the system believe otherwise. When *Austin Powers in Goldmember* was released in July 2002, *Time* magazine reviewer Richard Corliss published an essay that protested the stupidity and vulgarity with which the MPAA had awarded the film a PG-13 rating. Using both conviction and vivid facetiousness, Corliss wrote, "Crude humor and violence used to earn films R ratings. These days, to get an R, you need to show something really outrageous, like a naked woman." And he concluded that "the easy, sleazy PG-13 rating makes truly adult movies an endangered species. If even our most powerful filmmakers are afraid to make an R-rated film, how will American movies ever mature? And what will the preteens raised on *Austin Powers* have to watch—or want to watch—when they grow up?"[4]

Behind the scenes, the power that the board exercises over the film industry still constitutes a form of censorship, for the board continues to interfere with the creative process. The rating that a film is given exercises a tremendous influence on a film's potential for commercial success. An R rating reduces the potential audience for a film by 20 percent, and an NC-17 rating eliminates 50 percent of the potential audience. To guard against the automatic elimination of potential audience, studio contracts with producers and directors specify that an NC-17 rating must be avoided or that a film must be granted a G or PG rating before it shall "be deemed to have been delivered."[5] Such contracts obligate the producer to make whatever changes are necessary to obtain a desirable rating. If the producer cannot secure an acceptable rating, the studio has two options. It can refuse to accept delivery of the picture (and presumably refuse to pay the producer or director for his or her efforts), or it may accept the film and exercise the right to make "such changes, alterations, or deletions . . . as may be necessary or desirable"[6] for achieving an acceptable rating. Thus the producer and director lose creative control if they do not secure the specified rating *before* the film is delivered to the studio.

To prevent the loss of creative control at this late stage of production, producers and directors often submit scripts to the MPAA Code and Rating Administration for approval ahead of time, so that rating problems can be solved before shooting begins. The Code and Rating Administration, in advising what changes have to be made, enters into the filmmaking process itself by editing both scripts and finished films. Although the pressures causing this censorship are economic rather than social, they are nevertheless very real and constitute a form of censorship not totally unlike that of the 1930 Motion Picture Production Code.

A filmmaker who has not secured a satisfactory rating does have the option of appealing the Code and Rating Administration's decision. The MPAA Code and Rating Appeals Board meets in New York; it is separate from the Code and Rating Administration. When a film's rating is appealed, the appeals board screens the film; then before voting, it hears arguments from both the company challenging the rating and the Code and Rating Administration. Ratings are rarely reversed. During the first three years of the MPAA Rating System, only ten of thirty-one appeals were successful. Between 1974 and 1980, around 2,500 films were rated, and only seven appeals were successful.

Perhaps the most successful appeal yet heard by the board involved David Lean's *Ryan's Daughter*, an MGM film. When the film received an R rating, the studio threatened to pull out of the MPAA and claimed that an R rating would so limit the audience for this then-expensive ($10 million) film that the studio's very life was at stake. Under this considerable pressure from a great and historic motion picture institution, the board changed its rating of *Ryan's Daughter* to a PG so they would not have the demise of a major studio on their conscience. Paramount was in serious financial trouble also when it made a similar appeal for *Paint Your Wagon*, but the board twice refused its appeal for a G rating. In 2006, however, the French war film *Joyeux Noël* was given an R rating, but that was unaccountably changed to a PG-13 after critics Roger Ebert and Richard Roeper complained about the R rating on their syndicated movie review television program.

The ratings for other important films have been changed. *Midnight Cowboy*, rated X when it came out in 1969, was re-rated to an R with only the omission of several seconds of violence—but not before it had won three major Academy Awards (Best Picture, Best Director, and Best Adapted Screenplay). Likewise, *A Clockwork Orange*, initially rated X, became an R after a few seconds of violent action were cut (but for many years the film could not legally be exhibited in England). *Saturday*

FIGURE 15.7 Uh Oh, Kenny May Die of Embarrassment! Some viewers and reviewers labeled the popular, animated, R-rated 1999 feature *South Park: Bigger, Longer & Uncut* vile, vile, vile. Probably nothing could have made its creators, the movie mavericks Trey Parker and Matt Stone, any happier, happier, happier. Nearly ten years later, Ari Folman directed *Waltz With Bashir,* an intensely gruesome animated war film that incorporates a deliberately "pornographic" sequence.

Night Fever, originally shown as an R, was edited to remove objectionable language and redistributed as a PG to take advantage of its appeal to the "under-seventeen" crowd. *Last Tango in Paris,* released in theaters as an X, has been cut and re-released for cable television as an R but without the impact of the original.

Later, Steven Spielberg's appeal to change the R rating on *Poltergeist* to a PG was granted, and *Lone Wolf McQuade,* which received an R rating for violence, received a PG from the board after actor Chuck Norris appealed that the violence in *McQuade* "was of a stylized nature similar to that in John Wayne westerns." Brian De Palma fought long and hard and cut some violent scenes to prevent his *Scarface* from getting an X rating. And De Palma waged a similar struggle with the ratings board to receive a PG-13, rather than an R, rating for *Snake Eyes,* starring Nicolas Cage, because he was contractually obligated to deliver a film with the lower rating to Paramount Studios. When the board rejected *South Park*'s original subtitle as too risqué, the film's creators attained a kind of revenge by getting a possibly racier one naively approved: *Bigger, Longer & Uncut* (Figure 15.7).

In its effort to adjust to changing parental attitudes in our society, the rating board has indicated in recent years that it has become harder on violence and softer on nudity and sensuality. In the words of Richard D. Heffner, former chairman of the Classification and Rating Administration: "A moment of nudity that automatically drew an R years back may be PG-rated today, while violence is often rated R now that was not restricted before. It's a result of what we perceive to be changing parental attitudes toward these subjects."[7] But Kirby Dick's crafty 2006 documentary film about the MPAA ratings board, *This Film Is Not Yet Rated,* emphatically suggests otherwise.

As long as the rating board remains responsive to shifts in parental attitudes, it will continue to function as the effective instrument of industry control it was designed to be. However, some filmmakers and studios have learned to take full advantage of the constantly changing makeup of the board. Independent director and writer Neil LaBute, whose R-rated first film *In the Company of Men* created much controversy among viewers and critics, received an NC-17 rating for his second feature, *Your Friends & Neighbors*. Most unhappy with this label, LaBute says, he and his financial backers just "waited out that group, and a new one came through and we got an R. The new system is to go early and wait out the tenure of that group and try again."[8] Others, such as director Tom Hooper, with his 2010 crowd- and critic-pleasing *The King's Speech*, are less able to play this game and must simply accept the MPAA Rating Board's decision (Figure 15.8).

CENSORSHIP AND FILMS ON TELEVISION

Censorship has caused problems for many feature films shown on television. In the past, objectionable segments were simply cut out so they would not be seen by the television audience. Some experiments have been made with shooting two versions of the same film: one for the theater market, which can restrict its audience through the movie rating code, and a precensored version for the television market, which cannot restrict its audience. The television version of a film may differ radically from the theater version in its treatment of sexual material, nudity, coarseness of language, and violence. Plot changes may be so extensive that the two versions have little in common.

Today such extreme changes are not common, but when a feature film with definite network potential is in production, "cover shots" are often filmed to substitute for shots that are sexually explicit or contain strong language. In this way, a mild version of the film can be created for network TV. The original R-rated version of *Saturday Night Fever* that was re-edited in 1979 and given a PG rating was not only rerun in theaters but also shown on TV.

When the networks feel that parents should exercise special care in allowing young children to watch certain films, special warnings are provided concerning language or mature subject matter, along with one of the television ratings symbols, such as "TVMA." But as a general rule, no film appears on network television until it is edited to at least a PG level (Figure 15.9). The real problem occurs when network greed overcomes good sense and an R-rated movie that does not lend itself to PG editing is scheduled. By the time *Serpico* had been edited to eliminate coarse language, the raw thrust of the movie was gone, and the plot was almost incoherent. The ribald *Animal House* was totally fragmented by the necessary butchering, which left eleven minutes of its running time on the cutting-room floor (Figure 15.10). However, more recently, heated competition from controversial popular shows on premium cable channels (such as HBO's *Oz*, *Six Feet Under*, *The Sopranos*, and *Hung*, and Showtime's *Queer as Folk*, *Weeds*, and *Dexter*) has begun to force major changes in network standards for series and feature films alike.

BEYOND THE CODE AND RATING SYSTEM

The motion picture industry has attempted to enforce codes and ratings to offset demands for some form of censorship, but certain segments of society do not always agree that the codes and ratings fulfill their intent. Films that touch on religious matters often seem to generate the most impassioned criticism by the viewing

FIGURE 15.8 **From PG-13 to R—A Few Choice Words**   Although the award-winning, humane, and witty British drama *The King's Speech* should be superb family entertainment, the MPAA awarded it an R-rating, denying its director's request for a PG-13 label. Why? Because, in one scene, a speech therapist (Geoffrey Rush, right) attempts to help a character who stutters (Colin Firth as George VI, on the floor with Helena Bonham-Carter as his wife) by urging him to shout repression-releasing four-letter words. The editor of the *Quarterly Review of Film* has declared this crucial moment "the heart of the movie" and he insists that it "is not gratuitous or for shock value."

FIGURE 15.9 **From G to Network—One Choice Word**   In *True Grit* (1969), just before taking the reins in his teeth for his headlong charge toward Lucky Ned Pepper (Robert Duvall) and his gang, Rooster Cogburn (John Wayne) yells a challenge containing an unkind reference to the villainous Pepper's mother. An early 1970s showing on NBC bleeped the epithet—a 1995 showing on TNT left it in. (Contrast the 2010 PG-13–rated Coen Brothers' adaptation of Charles Portis's popular novel.)

FIGURE 15.10 **Censoring Sex and Ribald Humor**   The eleven minutes cut from *Animal House* for its initial network TV showing practically destroyed the film's ribald humor and left its plot almost incoherent.

FIGURE 15.11 Unofficial Censorship

Martin Scorsese's *The Last Temptation of Christ* (1988) (with Willem Dafoe as Jesus, left) offended fundamentalist religious groups across the country because it portrayed a very human Jesus struggling with temptation. Nicholas Ray's *King of Kings* (1961) (starring Jeffrey Hunter, top right) had presented a more traditional picture of Jesus, and no feathers were ruffled. In 2004, Mel Gibson's *The Passion of the Christ* (with Jim Caviezel, bottom right) actually used traditional Christian organizations as a major component of its marketing network—even though the ultraviolent film carried an R rating.

audience. Religious leaders and their supporters have at times managed to impose an unofficial censorship through their condemnation of a particular film. An example of this type of censorship is the 1988 reaction to Martin Scorsese's *The Last Temptation of Christ* (Figure 15.11).

The movie, which presents a less-than-perfect Christ, enraged Christian fundamentalists, who protested and boycotted theaters that planned to show the film. As a result of those protests, many theaters pulled the film from their schedules. Several states in the Bible Belt had no commercial showings of the movie. In their violent antipathy to the film, many protesters charged the Jewish leadership of Universal Pictures with plotting an attack on Christianity and called for a boycott of all Universal productions. The release of the film to video retailers across the country was done quietly without the advertising hoopla that usually surrounds new releases. Although many retailers purchased the videocassette version for subsequent rental and resale, they kept it under the counter in an attempt to forestall public outcry in their communities.

The Scorsese film, rated R, did not receive any formal or codified form of censorship, but its reception is an example of the unofficial censorship that operates in the United States. An unwritten code applies to films that offend the moral sensibilities of the population or at least segments of the population. In many areas, community leaders and theater owners often agree not to show NC-17–rated films or other controversial motion pictures, to avoid protests or more official types of censorship.

Protests have occurred, though. And Charles Lyons, in an essay titled "The Paradox of Protest," has written that both freedom from censorship and "rules" are necessary for a balanced "cultural climate":

> Debates over film censorship from 1980 to 1992 reflected a culture in conflict over sex, race, family values, and homosexuality. They also demonstrated that political struggles were being fought in a cultural arena. Similar conflicts within society and art have existed throughout history. . . . Among the groups that have protested against movies—antipornography feminists, Asian Americans, and gays and lesbians on the left, and religious groups on the right—the only ones to achieve censorship . . . were associated with the new Christian right.

Lyons later observes, however,

> After Asian Americans and homosexual groups protested against *Year of the Dragon* and *Basic Instinct*, respectively, these constituencies found Hollywood more willing to listen to them. . . . While groups may wave placards and chant against any movie they choose, it is evident that protests can produce unanticipated effects. Some protests, such as those from the religious right, result in recognizable acts of censorship; others, such as those from left groups, create an environment that legitimizes suppression and encourages self-censorship.[9]

CHANGING FORMULAS FOR THE TREATMENT OF SEX, VIOLENCE, AND LANGUAGE

Contrary to popular belief, the motion picture did not invent violence, sex, or even rough language. Fiction and drama were making use of such materials long before the first movie was shot. Each art form, with or without a formal code of censorship, has its own standards of what's acceptable and what's not at any given time. Standards of acceptability reflect what might be called the fashion of the day. They give rise to formulas for realism, which are determined much as the proper length for hemlines is determined—by what everyone else is doing. Thus, to a degree, violence, sex, and rough language appear in movies not just for their shock value but because their appearance is fashionable. If it were not, we would be offended by what we see and would stop going to movies altogether.

Formulas for realism do change. When a breakthrough film becomes a popular success, it sets new fashions and imitators begin to treat it as a standard. Consider, for example, how the formula for realism has evolved in the treatment of death by gunshot. In *Birth of a Nation*, men shot during the Civil War battles typically threw their arms skyward and fell sideways to the ground. By the 1940s, a cowboy shot in a grade B western clutched one hand to his chest (usually where cowboys were wounded) and crumpled forward. In the 1950s, *Shane* established a new style when the impact of the bullet from villain Jack Palance's gun knocked his victim ten feet backward into a mud puddle. In the 1960s, *Bonnie and Clyde* introduced the slow-motion dance of death, with bullets exploding holes through clothing. When a sensational new effect is introduced in a milestone film like *Bonnie and Clyde* or *Natural Born Killers*, audiences feel cheated if the same sense of heightened reality is not achieved in the films they see after it.

FIGURE 15.12 Subjective Damnation Sometimes subject matter alone (pedophilia, for instance), not mainly treatment, damns a film to censorship—either active or passive—or faint praise. Two exemplary cases: Todd Solondz's *Happiness* (starring Dylan Baker as a father/psychiatrist/child abuser) and Adrian Lyne's film version of Vladimir Nabokov's novel *Lolita*, starring Jeremy Irons as Humbert Humbert and Dominique Swain as the young object of his obsession (pictured here, with Melanie Griffith as her mother).

Similar changes can be traced in the way sexual intimacy is suggested, from *Tarzan, the Ape Man* (1932) to *Last Tango in Paris* (1973) to *Brokeback Mountain* (2005); and in the way rough language is treated, from *Gone With the Wind* (1939) to *Scarface* (1983) to *Due Date* (2010). Still, there are clearly limits to modern American culture's apparent permissiveness regarding cinema. Todd Solondz's controversial *Happiness* (1998), which includes a father who is a child molester, and his later *Palindromes* (2005), were released without an MPAA rating, as Solondz had anticipated. (In 2010, when Solondz released a strange sequel to *Happiness*—called *Life During War*, with a completely different cast playing the characters—he was awarded an R rating, however.) And Adrian Lyne's $50 million 1997 remake of Stanley Kubrick's *Lolita* never obtained general theatrical release in the United States—settling instead, ironically, for screenings on cable television's Showtime, which has suggested in advertisements for itself that only Showtime has the fearlessness to be both gritty and good in American movie entertainment (Figure 15.12).

Multiple controversies involving censorship issues in cinema continue to brew, of course. For example, one independent filmmaker, Doug Atchison (2006's *Akeelah and the Bee*, rated PG), writing in *MovieMaker* magazine about his own experiences and, especially, those of producer Eric Watson in making Darren Aronofsky's *Requiem for a Dream*, charges that the MPAA practices a kind of monetary and perceived-power bias. At the end of his article, Atchison insists that "the real problem lies with the secretive, inconsistent and confusing manner in which the MPAA Rating Board assesses motion pictures." And he quotes Watson, who questions why

FIGURE 15.13 **Looking for Light** Not censorable sexuality, but consuming themes of postapocalyptic bleakness and violence (including suicide and cannibalism) may overwhelm viewers of almost any age in John Hillcoat's film adaptation of Cormac McCarthy's novel *The Road,* produced by the Weinstein Brothers' Dimension Films and rated R. Shown at left, in despair, but searching for hope, are father (Viggo Mortensen) and his son (Kodi Smit-McPhee). In director Campbell Scott's PG-13–rated, independently produced *Off the Map* (based on Joan Ackermann's play), a precocious young woman (Valentina de Angelis, right) accidentally discovers a much lighter illumination in a watercolor scroll on wallpaper painted for her by an IRS agent-turned-artist.

"'morally bankrupt studio films will continue to be released unscathed due to their financial and political muscle, while independent films dealing with powerful moral themes are going to be scapegoated'"[10] (Figure 15.13).

During 2003, a major film censorship argument flourished between a group of eight Hollywood studios and various private entrepreneurs over whether anyone has the legal rights to alter, repackage, and sell videocassettes and DVDs that have been "sanitized" for a ready-made (often religion-based) audience. Like similar confrontations that occurred during the 1980s about companies' freedom to "colorize" films originally shot in black and white, this battle ultimately seemed to lose momentum rather than reveal a victor, although organizations such as CleanFlicks and Trilogy Studios have aggressively promoted their own special edits of films. In addition, they have marketed such software as "MovieMask" and "ClearPlay" that allows viewers, they suggest, to avoid sex, violence, and all the other "sinful" pleasure *and* unpleasantness that reel life may possibly ape from real life.[11] But in early July 2006, a U.S. district court judge in Colorado ruled that such companies must immediately stop their commercial "sanitizing" activities. For parents who desperately seek guidance in locating films they deem suitable for viewing by their children, one alternative solution may be found in the attempts at "objective" descriptions on such Web sites as screenit.com (which is now subscriber-driven).

However, the most basic challenge of movie censorship issues may still appear to reside not in questions of public morality or even legality, but in the realm of individual taste, aesthetic or otherwise. One example: critical reaction to the immensely controversial filmmaker Larry Clark's (*Kids*) unrated, violent, and sexually explicit movie *Bully,* starring the young actors Nick Stahl, Bijou Phillips, Rachel Miner, and Brad Renfro. In considering the film's achievement, Roger Ebert awarded it his highest rating, four stars, and called the work "a masterpiece on its own terms, a frightening indictment of a society that offers absolutely nothing to some of its children—and an indictment of the children, who lack the imagination and courage to try to escape."[12] In radical contradiction to this judgment, Lou Lumenick, in the *New York Post*, pronounced *Bully* "a truly repulsive piece of trash that says far more about the absence of values from contemporary filmmaking than the waywardness of teens." He then added, "I'm no prude, but it almost made me wish the old Legion of Decency [a Catholic censorship board that was created in 1934 and operated for just over thirty years] were still around to give Mr. Clark a thrashing."[13]

SOCIAL PROBLEM FILMS AND DOCUMENTARY FILMMAKING

A category of special interest to the serious student encompasses social problem films, which are difficult to evaluate, for their aging can occur very rapidly. A film can become not only dated but completely irrelevant within society in just a few years. This happens when the problem attacked by the film is eliminated or corrected. In a sense the social problem film can enjoy a long life only by failing in its purpose, for its impact is generally lost as soon as the problem portrayed no longer exists. This is especially true of a film that treats a narrow, topical, and very contemporary problem. The more general the problem, the more widespread its effects; and the more resistant it is to reform, the longer is the life span of the social problem film directed against it. As long as the social problem exists, the film has relevance. Thus, a film such as *The Snake Pit* (1948), starring Olivia de Havilland, will retain much of its impact as long as our society continues to stigmatize mental illness and its treatment. And, in the face of continued drug and alcohol abuse within our culture, Otto Preminger's *The Man With the Golden Arm* (1955) and Billy Wilder's *The Lost Weekend* (1945), though dated, continue to disturb and shock us despite more recent and graphic takes on the problems, including *Traffic* (2000), *Trainspotting* (1996) (Figure 15.14), and *Leaving Las Vegas* (1995).

Once in a while, if a social problem film is artistically done, it becomes more than a mere vehicle to encourage social reform, and it may outlive the problem it attacks. Strong, memorable characters and a good story give social problem films durability even after the specific problem dealt with no longer has relevance. In its specific references, of course, John Ford's magnificent adaptation of John Steinbeck's *The Grapes of Wrath* (1940) is a perfect example of such a film. Other recent films to which the "social problem" label might be applied, such as *Smoke Signals* (Figure 15.15), an examination of contemporary Native American life, and *The Fast Runner (Atanarjuat)* (Figure 15.16), a representation of the Inuit culture, often appear to be more purely descriptive than argumentative about difficulties in their subjects' worlds.

As we observed earlier in this chapter, formulas for realism do change in American society. This fact must surely begin to account for much of the intense interest that movie-goers have shown, belatedly, in the past few years, in tasting the formerly exotic fruits of documentary filmmaking. As standards of privacy have shifted, audiences in many areas of our culture have become more and more fascinated with the "realistic" manner in which this voyeuristic form can closely examine individual lives both famous and "ordinary." And, of course, by the broadest possible definition, virtually all documentary films are inherently "social problem" works.

FIGURE 15.14 **Energetic Ennui** In Danny Boyle's social problem film *Trainspotting*, Ewan McGregor and his mates dive with dirty vigor into the drug-infested underground of Edinburgh, Scotland.

FIGURE 15.15 **Historic Native American Cinema** *Smoke Signals*, a dramatic comedy written by poet and fiction writer Sherman Alexie and directed by Chris Eyre, became, in 1998, the first feature film created exclusively by Native American artists. Pictured here are Evan Adams and Adam Beach.

Erik Barnouw, in *Documentary: A History of the Non-Fiction Film*, maintains that "true documentarists have a passion for what they *find* in images and sounds—which always seems to them more meaningful than anything they can invent."[14] Barnouw defines the roles of the documentarist as those of prophet, explorer, chronicler, painter, and catalyst (among others), suggesting that the method by which such an

FIGURE 15.16 **Inuit Adventure**   Director Zacharias Kunuk's unique *The Fast Runner* (*Atanarjuat*) is a film about Inuit culture that is not quite documentary and yet clearly much more than fiction.

artist decides to utilize these discovered "images and sounds" varies enormously. Although there are, in fact, many possibilities for the treatment of documentary evidence, two techniques exemplify the opposite ends of the spectrum: Either the filmmaker can present a clearly articulated thesis about the documentary's subjects, or the filmmaker can assiduously avoid all such insistence.

The first type, the thesis documentarist, is perhaps most graphically illustrated by the creator of propaganda. For instance, Leni Riefenstahl, the official filmmaker for Adolf Hitler, made movies on a grand scale, including *Triumph of the Will* (1935), documenting Hitler's rallies in Nuremberg in 1934, and *Olympia* (1936), recording at great length and in magnificent style the 1936 Berlin Olympics. At least in their original versions, these films attempted to leave no doubt in the viewer's mind about the worthiness of the Third Reich.

Although much critical controversy exists about the true effects of such propaganda, the intentions of these two films are self-evident. Nevertheless, Riefenstahl herself, although sometimes admitting a certain naïveté, steadfastly maintained that her interests were purely artistic, not political. Interestingly, she most vociferously asserts her innocence in a film—Ray Muller's *The Wonderful, Horrible Life of Leni Riefenstahl* (1993)—that is, in turn, an example of a thesis documentary.

Other excellent models of this type: Michael Moore's films, including his first, *Roger & Me* (1989), which examines the relationship between General Motors and its former workers in Flint, Michigan; and Barbara Kopple's Oscar-winning *Harlan County, U.S.A.* (1977), which portrays the seemingly eternal union struggles of mine workers in eastern Kentucky. Although Kopple's later *American Dream* (1989), also an Academy Award winner, seems by comparison more complicated in its narrative point of view than *Harlan County, U.S.A.*, it nevertheless demonstrates obviously the pain and losses of all parties involved in a Hormel meat-packing company strike

FIGURE 15.17 A Documentary Mix
The eccentric appeal of the underground cartoonist R. Crumb and his strange family is perfectly captured in the documentary film *Crumb* (1994), even though viewers are left to draw their own conclusions about the filmmakers' intentions.

in Minnesota. Roger Ebert writes that, in *American Dream*, "the people . . . are so real they make most movie characters look like inhabitants of the funny page."[15]

The antithetical type of documentary tries very hard to avoid judging its subject, attempting instead simply to describe it. Among its best examples—at least outside the confines of experimental films like *Koyaanisqatsi* (1983)—are the works of Frederick Wiseman. In such documentaries as *Public Housing* (1997), about the Ida B. Wells development in Chicago, and *Titicut Follies* (1967), about the inmates of a mental hospital in Massachusetts, this prolific documentarist has used the **direct cinema** method of shooting, giving his viewers an objective view and understanding of worlds that they are rarely permitted to enter. Erik Barnouw has noted, however, that

> one of the problems hanging over observer-documentarists was the extent to which the presence of the camera influenced events before it. Some practitioners— [Stephen] Leacock, [Louis] Malle—worried about this. Others—[Arthur] Mayles, Wiseman— tended to minimize it. Some filmmakers, notably Jean Rouch, held still another view. Rouch maintained that the presence of the camera made people act in ways truer to their nature than might otherwise be the case.[16]

Michael Apted's remarkable series of films about the developing lives of British children—*7 Plus 7, 21, 28, 35 Up, 42 Up, 49 Up*—seems to demonstrate the truth of Rouch's theory, especially in Apted's later interviews. There, he uses a **cinéma vérité** technique, which is supposedly "objective unstaged, non-dramatized, non-narrative."[17] Sometimes, though, his very presence seems to incite action from his subjects, rather than merely to observe and record it.

Most documentary filmmakers use a mixture of these extreme approaches. One of the best-received documentaries, Terry Zwigoff's *Crumb* (1994), seems, given the manner of its editing, "thesis positive" in its sympathetic approach to famous cartoonist R. Crumb and his eccentric family (Figure 15.17). Yet, finally, the viewer is freely left to make his or her own judgments.

FLASHBACK

FILMING LIFE: A HISTORY OF THE DOCUMENTARY

Even the earliest films were inspired by the "documentary urge" of their creators, who wished, quite simply, to document life. But documentary films, as a genre, have traditionally been the most underfinanced, underpublicized, underreviewed, and underattended of all movies widely available for viewing.

The increased availability of media outlets has nevertheless made it easier to access and watch documentary films. The critically acclaimed *Hoop Dreams* (1994), directed by Steve James, for example, has been seen by millions of enthusiastic viewers regardless of whether they are fans of high school basketball.

Still, documentary films remain an orphan genre in the eyes of the general public, in part, because the audience perceives them to be less enjoyable than fiction films. Likewise, in the annual Academy Awards competition, filmmakers themselves further minimize the documentary's significance with sometimes careless and irresponsible nominations. Furthermore, the watcher of documentary films also naturally comes to the screen with a different set of expectations than does the casual viewer of fictional movie narratives. In that sense, more is demanded of the documentary form at the same time that its art is generally ignored. Despite this, when it is at its best, a documentary film can not only gather, articulate, and preserve "reality" but also be superbly entertaining.

The term *documentary* may itself be misleading, for it belies the complexity that potentially resides in the form. Since it was coined by the English filmmaker John Grierson in the 1930s to describe a type of film that focused on social realities, the word has broadened its connotations to include an emphasis on its aesthetic aspects. The most celebrated early practitioner of the art, Robert Flaherty, in such films as *Nanook*

of the North (1922) and *Moana* (1925) (about Eskimo and Polynesian life, respectively), examined alien cultures from a sociological perspective. But Flaherty came to understand that moving pictures, even documentary ones, do not merely record objective reality. Like nonfiction literature, nonfiction film inevitably presents the subjective vision of

1921
Manhatta documents a day in the life of New York City.

1922
The popularity of *Nanook of the North* signals the rise of the feature-length documentaries during the late silent era.

1926
John Grierson, a trailblazing documentarian himself, coins the term "documentary" while defending *Moana*, Robert Flaherty's follow-up to *Nanook of the North*.

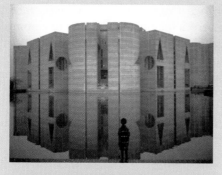

its maker as well. Grierson, too, finally admitted clearly the genre's need to break free of the boundaries of didacticism, and the need to teach a lesson, observing, "At one level the [documentary's] vision may be journalistic; at another it may rise to poetry and drama. At another level, again, its artistic quality may lie in the mere lucidity of its exposition."

Documentary makers have often reinterpreted the affairs of our times, and they extend the traditional expeditions into distinctly modern social debates. Louie Psihoyos's Oscar-winning, suspenseful *The Cove* (2009), for example, takes us to the waters off Taijii, Japan, and exposes shocking animal and environmental abuse by the tourist industry's largest supplier of dolphins. David and Albert Maysles's *Grey Gardens* (1976) (see bottom photo on the previous page) patiently examines the fascinating, complex lives of Edith Bouvier Beale and her adult daughter, "Little Edie," refugees from East Hampton aristocracy, living in a decaying-mansion squalor. Laurent Cantet's *The Class* (2008) blurs the line between fiction and documentary, adapting novelist François Bégaudeau's written account of his experience teaching an ethnically diverse group of high school students in one of the roughest neighborhoods in Paris. Frederick Wiseman's classic but highly controversial *Titicut Follies* shows us the world inside an institution for the mentally ill. And Nathaniel Kahn's *My Architect* (2003) (top left photo above) takes us on a magnificent film journey on which an illegitimate son tries to recapture the personal and professional essence of his world-famous father, Louis I. Kahn. Tina Mascara and Guido Santi blend old home movies, journal entries, and new interviews to create *Chris and Don: A Love Story* (2007), a documentary about the enduring familial and artistic partnership between writer Christopher Isherwood and artist Don Bachardy (top right photo). While fictional film narratives may explore similar terrain (environmental catastrophe in *2012;* the mentally ill in *One Flew Over the Cuckoo's Nest,* for example), the experience of hearing real people tell their stories is extraordinarily compelling.

Source: Bluem, A. William. *Documentary in American Television: Form, Function, Method.* New York: Hastings House, 1965.

1950s
Lighter cameras and better sound equipment make documenting life on film easier. Documentary filmmakers worldwide experiment with more spontaneous styles than ever before.

1942
Memphis Belle and *The Battle of Midway* document World War II for audiences at home and blur the line between documentary and propaganda.

2008
Filmmaker Agnès Varda pushes the limits of the documentary concept with *The Beaches of Agnès,* an autobiographical film in which Varda "reinvents" herself through the cinematic gaze of photos, old film clips and home movies, interviews, and mirrors.

No documentarist, however, surpasses Errol Morris in his insistence upon injecting this venerable genre with a very modernist ambiguity. Beginning with *Gates of Heaven*, which Roger Ebert calls "one of the greatest films ever made,"[18] and working rather slowly through several other carefully constructed nonfiction feature films, Morris has established himself as the most visible artist documentarist. Watching *Gates of Heaven*, we are certain of its enormous good humor, but we are less sure about what attitudes we are to construct from it. *The Thin Blue Line* (1988) is famous for having been the catalyst that freed a man wrongly convicted of murder, but in its artful reconstructions of the crime and its utilization of an eerie Philip Glass score, among other techniques, the film's intentions are otherwise ultimately unclear.

"Constructed" documentaries such as *The Thin Blue Line* have always been useful for the information they present about the past. Two other works that admirably illustrate the type are *When We Were Kings* (1996) and *Theremin* (1993). The former examines the heavyweight title fight between Muhammad Ali and George Foreman in Zaire, twenty-one years after its original photography; the latter celebrates the inventor of electronic music. *Theremin*, like Morris's *The Thin Blue Line*, also solves a mystery: It finally explains, after decades of uncertainty, the disappearance of its title character, Professor Leon Theremin.

Two other films by Errol Morris contain more mixtures of his characteristic earnestness and humor: *A Brief History of Time* (1992) scrutinizes theoretical physicist Stephen Hawking; and *Fast, Cheap & Out of Control* (1997) is an intense meditation upon the subtly interconnected lives of a lion trainer, a topiary artist, a rodent scientist, and a robot designer. In these works, and in *Vernon, Texas* (1981), *Dr. Death* (1999), *The Fog of War* (2003), and *Standard Operating Procedure* (2008), Morris continues to extend his general desire to make the documentary form as complex and fascinating as the fiction feature film.

One method documentary filmmakers have frequently utilized to add complexity and fascination to their work is to star in their own movies. Sometimes, a double narrative occurs through their examining stories within stories. In a review of Kevin MacDonald and Mark Cousins's *Imagining Reality: The Faber Book of the Documentary*, Ian Christie observes that "Al Pacino's recent Shakespearean documentary, *Looking for Richard*, belongs to a distinctive vein of cinematic non-fiction, in which the filmmaker appears on-screen and becomes, in effect, the protagonist of a drama—which is the making of the film we are watching."[19]

Christie also mentions other excellent models for this type, including Moore's *Roger & Me* and Orson Welles's *F for Fake* (1974), and, at least in spirit, he might well have added *Hearts of Darkness: A Filmmaker's Apocalypse* (1991) and *Marlene* (1984), even though these two films' show business subjects did not actually direct the works. *Hearts of Darkness*, directed by Fax Bahr and George Hickenlooper (with the valuable assistance of Eleanor Coppola, who had shot documentary footage of her husband in the Philippines), records Francis Ford Coppola's struggle in making *Apocalypse Now*. *Marlene* is actor Maximilian Schell's attempt to let us see (in the sense of "understand") as well as hear the aging Marlene Dietrich, who refused to be photographed for it and would only allow audiotaped interviews. Both films were enriched and also made more problematically complicated by the direct (in

FIGURE 15.18 **Three Sides to Every Story** In the documentary film *The Kid Stays in the Picture*, legendary producer Robert Evans (*Chinatown, Rosemary's Baby, Love Story, The Godfather*), shown here with director Roman Polanski, narrates the story of his career with this caveat: "There are three sides to every story: My side, your side, and the truth."

Dietrich's case) or subtle (in Coppola's) manipulation of the filmmakers by their subjects.*

In 1998 Barbara Kopple, a director best known for documenting labor disputes in America (*Harlan County, U.S.A.*), shifted to show business and released *Wild Man Blues*, an energetic *cinéma vérité* account of clarinet player Woody Allen's tour of European concerts with his Dixieland jazz band, his sister, and his soon-to-be-wife, whom he introduces facetiously at one point as "the notorious Soon-Yi Previn." Although Allen specifies clearly that he intends the film's audience to be primarily interested in his music, he repeatedly undercuts this stance by providing spontaneous one-liners, which Kopple and her crew eagerly record. In the documentary's final, splendid scene, which takes place back in New York in the apartment of Allen's aged parents, the comedian/musician/filmmaker, through calculated quips, also helps Kopple create a hilarious, incendiary ending for her film.

It is noteworthy that most of the accomplished documentaries mentioned above are also *about* filmmakers and the art of cinematic illusion (Figure 15.18). And it should not surprise us that many directors of fiction films have dreamed of creating documentary works. For example, Nicca Ray, the daughter of Nicholas Ray, who directed *Rebel Without a Cause*, starring James Dean, tells us that her father's fondest hope, late in his life, was to complete a documentary.[20] Other directors who

---

*A magnificent precedent for *Hearts of Darkness* exists in Les Blank's documentary *Burden of Dreams* (1982), which chronicles the director Werner Herzog's obsession with making the film *Fitzcarraldo*, itself an examination of obsessive behavior.

do not seize the opportunity to work in the form in its ill-financed state—who, instead, continue to make fiction films—nevertheless find ways to play out their documentary urge.

Perhaps the most famous use of documentary elements in modern fiction film has involved James Cameron's techniques in his immensely popular *Titanic* (1997). In this film, the director's own documentary urge was so intense that he created new diving and photographic equipment—at extraordinary expense for his studio—to achieve textural (if not plot) authenticity by recording and presenting the eighty-five-year-old wreck of his subject.[21] *Titanic*, then, like so many other fiction films, pays the ultimate compliment to the documentary form: Cameron uses the real thing to inform his reel thing.

ANALYZING FILMS IN SOCIETY

On Censorship

1. Study three or more films with censorable subject matter made under the Motion Picture Production Code (prior to 1950), and answer these questions:
   a. Where in these films do you find obvious examples of code-caused suppression and restraint?
   b. How would these films be different if they were being made today? Which film (or films) could be significantly improved by being made today with a PG or R rating? How or why would they be improved?
   c. Do the films studied seem too mild mannered to have much impact, or do they effectively suggest such things as violence and sexuality in ways acceptable to the code?
   d. Do these films seem to go out of their way to promote traditional American values? Are American values or institutions questioned in any of these films? If so, how and where are such questions dramatized, and how are such problems resolved?

2. Examine three or more films with censorable subject matter made during the transitional period (1948–1968) and consider the questions above. What evidence do you find of the code's being stretched or disregarded? How do the films of the transitional period differ from those made before 1950?

3. Examine a film made under the Motion Picture Production Code and compare it with its remake produced under the MPAA Rating System. Possible choices include *Scarface*, 1932/1983; *The Postman Always Rings Twice*, 1946/1981; *Here Comes Mr. Jordan*, 1941, remade as *Heaven Can Wait*, 1978; *Godzilla*, 1954/1998; *The Thomas Crown Affair*, 1967/1999; and *Mr. Deeds Goes to Town*, 1936/*Mr. Deeds*, 2002. To what degree are these films different because of the difference in censorship restrictions? Where are the differences most obvious, and how is the overall effect of the film changed by the differences? Which of the two is the better film? Why?

4. Examine four films currently playing at your local theaters or on video (DVD or streaming): a film rated G, a film rated PG, a film rated PG-13, and a film rated R. What distinguishes a G film from a PG film, what separates a PG from a PG-13, and what differentiates a PG-13 from an R? Are these distinctions very clear?

5. Make an attempt to trace the evolution of the MPAA Rating System's classification decisions by comparing films rated PG and R at ten-year intervals. Use films released in 1976, 1986, 1996, and 2006. Can you discern any patterns of change affecting where the dividing line is drawn? If so, what do these patterns indicate?

6. Examine several films from each decade from the 1930s to the present, and try to describe the fashion of the age in terms of each decade's formulas for sexual intimacy, death scenes, and rough language. What other changing patterns or fashions are apparent in the films you viewed?

On Social Problem Films

1. Does the social problem attacked by the film have a universal and timeless quality, affecting all people in all time periods, or is it restricted to a relatively narrow time and place?

2. Is the film powerful enough in terms of a strong storyline, enduring characters, good acting, artistic cinematography, and so on, to outlive the social problem it is attacking? In other words, how much of the film's impact is caused by its relevance to a current problem and its timing in attacking the problem?

3. If the immediate social problems on which the film focuses were permanently corrected tomorrow, what relevance would the film have to the average viewer twenty years from now?

On Documentary Films

1. Has the documentary director apparently attempted to create a thesis type of film? If so, what clearly articulated statement does the film make? Do all elements of the filmmaking clearly support this thesis?

2. Has the direct cinema or the *cinéma vérité* technique of shooting been used? Has the presence of the documenting camera altered reality—or heightened it?

3. If the film obviously tries to avoid presenting a thesis, what methods has the director chosen to ensure "objectivity"? Has factual material been presented chronologically or thematically, without editing or artful rearrangement?

4. Does the documentary film reinforce the stereotypes about this form, or does it seem to suggest, through its example, that the genre can be as vital, entertaining, and complex as fiction films?

Like the American David Lynch, Mexican director Alfonso Cuarón is extremely versatile in his artistic tastes and talents. Although Lynch is most celebrated for his habitual wanderings into forbidden cinematic territories (*Eraserhead, Blue Velvet, Mulholland Dr.*), he was also

capable of surprising all his critics by directing a respected G-rated drama, *The Straight Story*. Cuarón first became famous in the United States for his delicate and artful 1995 remake of *The Little Princess*, also rated G, and he was chosen to direct the third installment of the *Harry Potter* movie series, *The Prisoner of Azkaban* (2004). But in 2002 his highly acclaimed coming-of-age film *Y Tu Mamá También* was released without an MPAA rating because of its explicit language and strong sexuality.

As *Y Tu Mamá También* appears on DVD (also unrated), its disc contains a short work directed by the feature film's writer, Carlos Cuarón, Alphonso's brother. This *La Ronde*–like (i.e., structurally circular) twelve-minute film is called *Me La Debes* ("You Owe Me One"). Like its full-length companion, it is a narrative at least nominally about the sensual side of life, and hence potentially controversial. However, the film is beautifully photographed, economically written and edited, very witty, and abundant in its earthy and laconic humor.

Seek out and watch *Me La Debes*. Considering what you have learned in this chapter about the standards apparently utilized by the MPAA system, attempt to assign an appropriate rating label to this mini-movie. Be prepared specifically to justify your choice.

A veritable seminar in the art of silent-film music appears in special sections of these first three DVDs:

The Harold Lloyd Comedy Collection
 The four discs in this boxed set admirably cover the career of silent-film's "third comic genius." Volume two, disc two, contains a substantial featurette called "Scoring for Comedy: Movie Music in the Silent Era." In it, Carl Davis, the esteemed composer for restored silent films, and one of his younger colleagues, Robert Israel (who created scores for twenty of the Lloyd movies in this collection), offer cogent observations, general and specific, about their work.

Greta Garbo: The Signature Collection
 For several years, Turner Classic Movies has conducted an annual "Young Film Composers Competition." The contest for 2004, in which one artist won the

right to create a soundtrack for Garbo's seldom-seen silent *The Temptress*, is wonderfully documented in the feature "Settling the Score."

Sunrise

On this DVD presentation of one of silent-film drama's greatest triumphs, a viewer/listener can examine director F. W. Murnau's work in two musical settings: one with the original "movietone" score in mono, the other with a modern stereophonic recording by the Olympic Chamber Orchestra.

Dressed to Kill (Special Edition):

Brian De Palma's controversial violent and erotic thriller serves to demonstrate, through two featurettes on this DVD, the differences between "Unrated," "R-Rated," and "TV Rated" edits. One section simply presents scene-specific illustrations. The other, called "Slashing *Dressed to Kill*," gives the viewer a fascinating and revealing set of interviews, including observations by director De Palma; actors Angie Dickinson, Nancy Allen, and Keith Gordon; editor Jerry Greenburg; and producer George Litto.

Storytelling:

The DVD of this controversial drama by Todd Solondz (who had earlier become celebrated as a rule-breaking director with *Welcome to the Dollhouse* and *Happiness*) offers the film not only in its R-rated theatrical-release form, but in an unrated version as well.

The Fast and the Furious (Collector's Edition):

In a brief but "exclusive" featurette here, director Rob Cohen talks to the viewer directly on-camera as he and editor Peter Honess calculate what individual frames of film must be cut to obtain a desired PG-13 rating. At one point, Cohen explains that "we've mitigated the intensity of violence on [one] sequence" because the ruling by the MPAA is "very important to this film commercially"—i.e., so that it will be permitted, officially, to reach its young target audience.

Kissing Jessica Stein:

Many reviewers of this film, which is a comedic examination of various gender issues, identified it as a notable "date movie." Originally, it had a different ending—one that seemingly attempted to treat the politics of "sexual preferences" more straightforwardly than does its final version. Compare that alternative conclusion (to be found in the "Deleted Scenes" section of this DVD) with the "finished" equivalent.

Bamboozled:

Director Spike Lee baffled many of his most fervent fans with this incendiary 2000 "joint" (his term for a Lee picture) about the history of racism as observed in American popular culture. On the DVD of his film, he has included a "Making of . . ." documentary that obviously is meant, at least in part, to answer some of his critics.

Hedwig and the Angry Inch:

Undoubtedly, some "accidental" viewers of this film by writer/director/star John Cameron Mitchell will feel alienated from and seek to "censor" the musical drama and its bizarre, almost-transgendered protagonist. Perhaps they should watch the eighty-five-minute feature on this disc called "Whether You Like It or Not: The Story of Hedwig." In it, one of the filmmakers asserts the universality of the movie's title character, insisting that all of us should note, "I have everything *in common* with Hedwig." Even more convincing for the skeptical may be the fond interview segments with the creator's parents, U.S. Army Major General John Mitchell and Mrs. Mitchell.

All About My Mother:
In "An Intimate Conversation with Pedro Almodóvar," the Spanish Oscar-winner, a controversial and popular *auteur,* speaks on-camera with Columbia University film professor Annette Insdorf about the origins and development of this film and others.

A History of Violence (New Line Platinum Series):
David Cronenberg has often filled his films (such as *The Fly* [1986] and *Crash* [1996], not to be confused with Paul Haggis's 2005 Oscar-winner with the same title) with grotesque violence. Yet in his 2005 drama *A History of Violence,* whose title appears straightforwardly to announce this characteristic subject, Cronenberg chose to delete an expensively made dream scene that showcased the movie's most "grotesque" element. On this DVD, he also gives the viewer a brief but telling glimpse into the process necessary for both creating an "international version" and satisfying the MPAA for American audiences.

FILMS FOR STUDY

Foreign Language Films

(See p. 247 for a list of International Films.)

Censorship

Alfie (1966—Britain)
Bamboozled (2000)
Basic Instinct (1992)
Bonnie and Clyde (1967)
Breaking the Waves (1996—Denmark)
The Brown Bunny (2003)
Bully (2001)
City of God (2002)
A Clockwork Orange (1971)
8 Mile (2002)
Eyes Wide Shut (1999)
Fat Girl (2001—France/Italy)

Femme Fatale (2002)
Gremlins (1984)
Happiness (1998)
Henry & June (1990)
A History of Violence (2005)
Howl (2010)
Indiana Jones and the Temple of Doom (1984)
Intimacy (2001)
La Dolce Vita (1960—Italy)
Last Tango in Paris (1972—France/Italy)
The Last Temptation of Christ (1988)
L.I.E. (2001)
Lolita (1962—Britain; 1997)
Midnight Cowboy (1969)
The Moon Is Blue (1953)

National Lampoon's Animal House (1978)
Natural Born Killers (1994)
On the Waterfront (1954)
The Outlaw (1943)
The Pawnbroker (1964)
Requiem for a Dream (2000)
Saturday Night Fever (1977)
Scarface (1932, 1983)
Serpico (1973)
Shortbus (2006)
South Park: Bigger, Longer & Uncut (1999)
Spanking the Monkey (1994)
Storytelling (2001)
Team America: World Police (2004)

The Virgin Spring
(1960—Sweden)
Where the Truth Lies
(2005—Canada)
*Who's Afraid of Virginia
Woolf?* (1966)
Year of the Dragon (1985)
Your Friends & Neighbors
(1998)

Silent Films

*(See p. 308 for a list of
silent films.)*

Social Problem Films

Dead Man Walking (1995)
Do the Right Thing (1989)
Falling Down (1993)
Far from Heaven (2002)
For Colored Girls (2010)
The Grapes of Wrath
(1940)
*Guess Who's Coming to
Dinner* (1967)
The Ice Storm (1997)
In the Company of Men
(1997)
In the Heat of the Night
(1967)
Invictus (2009)
Kids (1995)
Leaving Las Vegas (1995)
The Lost Weekend (1945)
Manny & Lo (1996)
Margaret's Museum
(1995—Canada)
Natural Born Killers (1994)
Norma Rae (1979)
North Country (2005)
Philadelphia (1993)
Sling Blade (1996)
The Snake Pit (1948)
The Social Network (2010)
Traffic (2000)

Trainspotting (1996—
Britain)
Wild in the Streets (1968)

Documentary Films

The Beaches of Agnès
(2008)
*The Beales of Grey
Gardens* (2006)
Bowling for Columbine
(2002)
Burden of Dreams (1982)
Capitalism: A Love Story
(2009)
Capturing the Friedmans
(2003)
Catfish (2010)
*Chris and Don: A Love
Story* (2007)
The Cove (2009)
Crazy Love (2007)
Crumb (1994)
Dogtown and Z-Boys
(2001)
*Enron: The Smartest Guys
in the Room* (2005)
Every Little Step (2008)
*Exit Through the Gift
Shop* (2010)
Fahrenheit 9/11 (2004)
*Fast, Cheap & Out of
Control* (1997)
The Fog of War (2003)
49 Up (2005)
Gates of Heaven (1978)
The Gleaners & I (2002—
France)
*Gonzo: The Life and
Work of Dr. Hunter
S. Thompson* (2008)
Grey Gardens (1975)
Grizzly Man (2005)
Harlan County, U.S.A.
(1976)

Hoop Dreams (1994)
*Joan Rivers: A Piece of
Work* (2010)
An Inconvenient Truth
(2006)
Inside Job (2010)
*The Kid Stays in the
Picture* (2002)
The Line King (1996)
Looking for Richard (1996)
Marlene (1984—
Germany)
Mr. Death (1999)
Murderball (2005)
My Architect (2003)
My Best Fiend (1999—
Germany)
Olympia (1936—
Germany)
Roger & Me (1989)
*Roman Polanski: Wanted
and Desired* (2008)
Shoah (1985)
Sicko (2007)
*Standard Operating
Procedure* (2008)
Shine a Light (2008)
The Thin Blue Line (1988)
This Film Is Not Yet Rated
(2006)
Titicut Follies (1967)
Triumph of the Will
(1935—Germany)
Trouble the Water (2008)
Trumbo (2007)
Waiting for "Superman"
(2010)
When We Were Kings
(1996)
Wild Man Blues (1997)
*The Wild Parrots of
Telegraph Hill* (2005)
Woodstock (1970)
Young@Heart (2007)

notes

Chapter 1

1. A. O. Scott, "The Lasting Picture Show," *The New York Times* (November 3, 2002), sec. 6, p. 41.
2. Ernest Lindgren, *The Art of the Film* (New York: Macmillan, 1963), pp. 204–205.
3. Aldous Huxley, *Brave New World* (New York: Harper, 1946), p. 23.
4. Richard Dreyfuss, quoted in Judith Crist, *Take 22: Moviemakers on Moviemaking*, new expanded ed. (New York: Continuum, 1991), p. 413.
5. David Cronenberg, "Last Rant," *IFCRant* (November/December 2002), p. 32.
6. Eugene Hernandez, Erin Torneo, "Back & Forth," *IFCRant* (November/December 2002), p. 5.
7. Peter M. Nichols, "From Directors, a Word, or Two," *The New York Times* (September 6, 2002), *www.nytimes.com/2002/09/06/movies/06VIDA.html*. For further consideration, see also Charles Taylor, "Will the DVD Save Movies?" *Salon.com* (November 14, 2002), *www.salon.com/ent/movies/feature/2002/11/14/dvd_era/index.html*.

Chapter 2

1. Sidney Lumet, *Making Movies* (New York: Knopf, 1995), p. 10.

Chapter 3

1. Cesare Zavattini, "Some Ideas on the Cinema," *Sight and Sound* (October 1953), p. 64.
2. Neil Simon, quoted in John Brady, *The Craft of the Screenwriter* (New York: Simon & Schuster, 1981), p. 318.
3. Ernest Lehman, quoted in Brady, pp. 203–204.
4. Danny De Vito, quoted in Robert Seidenberg, "Funny as Hell," *American Film* (September 1989), p. 47.
5. Griffin Dunne, quoted in Anna McDonnell, "Happily Ever After," *American Film* (January–February 1987), p. 44.
6. Robert Penn Warren, "Why Do We Read Fiction?" in *An Approach to Literature*, edited by Cleanth Brooks et al. (New York: Appleton-Century-Crofts, 1964), p. 866.
7. Frank Capra, quoted in *Directing the Film: Film Directors on Their Art*, edited by Eric Sherman (Los Angeles: Acrobat Books, 1976), pp. 308–309.

8. Paul Schrader, quoted in Brady, pp. 298–299.
9. Robert Towne, quoted in Brady, p. 394.
10. Tennessee Williams, *Suddenly, Last Summer*. Copyright © 1958 by Tennessee Williams. All rights reserved. All quotations reprinted by permission of New Directions Publishing Corporation.
11. Ernest Lehman, quoted in Brady, pp. 199–200.

Chapter 4

1. John Ford, quoted in *Film Makers Speak: Voices of Film Experience*, edited by Jay Leyda (New York: DaCapo Press, 1984), p. 145.
2. Peter Bogdanovich, quoted ibid., p. 40.
3. Nestor Almendros, *A Man With a Camera*, translated by Rachel Phillips Belash (Boston: Faber and Faber, 1984), p. 15.
4. Ibid., pp. 12–13.
5. Bart Mills, "The Brave New World of Production Design," *American Film* (January–February 1982), p. 40.
6. Paul Sylbert, quoted in Vincent LoBrutto, *By Design: Interviews With Production Designers* (Westport, CT: Praeger, 1992), p. 85.
7. Patrizia Von Brandenstein, quoted ibid., p. 186.
8. Paul Sylbert, quoted ibid., p. 82.
9. John Box, quoted in *Film Makers Speak*, p. 45.
10. Charles Rosher, quoted ibid., p. 404.
11. Tennessee Williams, *Suddenly, Last Summer*. Copyright © 1958 by Tennessee Williams. All rights reserved. Reprinted by permission of New Directions Publishing Corporation.
12. Chuck Rosen, quoted in Linda Gross, "On Golden River," *Los Angeles Times Calendar* (November 13, 1983), p. 22.
13. Kristi Zea, quoted in LoBrutto, p. 248.
14. Robert Boyle, quoted ibid., p. 16.
15. Mills, p. 45.
16. Edith Head, quoted in *Film Makers on Film Making: The American Film Institute Seminars on Motion Pictures and Television*, vol. 2, edited by Joseph McBride (Los Angeles: J. P. Tarcher), p. 166.
17. Edith Head, quoted ibid., p. 167.
18. Edith Head, quoted ibid., p. 169.

19. Mary Astor, quoted in *Film Makers Speak*, p. 17.
20. Todd Rainsberger, *James Wong Howe: Cinematographer* (New York: A. S. Barnes, 1981), p. 75.
21. "Zsigmond," *American Film* (September 1982), p. 55.
22. "Almendros," *American Film* (December 1981), p. 19.

Chapter 5

1. Vilmos Zsigmond, "Dialogue on Film," *American Film* (June 1979), p. 41.
2. Alfred Hitchcock, quoted in Richard Dyer MacCann, ed., *Film: A Montage of Theories* (New York: Dutton, 1966), p. 57. From "Direction" by Alfred Hitchcock, in *Footnotes to the Film*, edited by Charles Davy; reprinted by permission of Peter Davies Ltd., publishers.
3. Alfred Hitchcock, quoted in *Directing the Film: Film Directors on Their Art*, edited by Eric Sherman (Los Angeles: Acrobat Books, 1976), pp. 254–255.
4. Nestor Almendros, *Man With a Camera*, translated by Rachel Phillips Belash (Boston: Faber and Faber, 1984), p. 14.
5. Quoted from program brochure obtained by the author.
6. Alan Dwan, quoted in *Directing the Film*, p. 108.
7. Frank Brady, *Citizen Welles: A Biography of Orson Welles* (New York: Doubleday, 1989), p. 257.
8. Lily Tomlin, as told to Jane Wagner, "Memoirs of an Usherette," *The Movies* (July 1983), pp. 41–42.
9. The American Film Institute, *Visions of Light: The Art of Cinematography*, written and directed by Todd McCarthy, 1993.
10. Peter Biskind, quoted in "Jungle Fever," *Premiere* (July 1993), p. 67.
11. David Ansen, quoted in David Ehrenstein, "One From the Art," *Film Comment* (January–February 1993), p. 30.
12. Anne Bancroft, quoted in "AFI's 100 Years . . . 100 Movies," *CBS Television* (June 16, 1998).
13. Richard Edlund, quoted in Vision Films/Smithsonian Video (DVD), *The Art of Illusion: One Hundred Years of Hollywood Special Effects*, 1990, rev. 1995.
14. *Baseline's Encyclopedia of Film*, "Animation," Microsoft Cinemania 97 (CD-ROM).
15. Nick Park, quoted in Kevin Macdonald, "A Lot Can Happen in a Second," *Projections 5: Filmmakers on Filmmaking*, edited by John Boorman and Walter Donahue (London: Faber and Faber, 1996), p. 91.
16. Jeffrey Katzenberg, quoted in "No Dancing Teapots in 'Prince of Egypt,'" *New York Times* (December 14, 1998), *www.nytimes.com/yr/mo/day/news/arts/prince-egypt-katzenberg/html*.
17. Richard Corliss, "Can a Prince Be a Movie King?" *Time* (December 14, 1998), p. 92.
18. Roger Ebert, *www.suntimes.com/output/ebert1/18prin.html*.

Chapter 6

1. V. I. Pudovkin, *Film Technique and Film Acting* (New York: Grove Press, 1976), p. 24.
2. Alfred Hitchcock, quoted in Richard Dyer MacCann, ed., *Film: A Montage of Theories* (New York: Dutton, 1966), p. 56.
3. Evan Lottman, quoted in Vincent LoBrutto, *Selected Takes: Film Editors on Film Editing* (Westport, CT: Praeger, 1991), p. 144.
4. Tom Rolf, quoted ibid., p. 90.
5. Ralph Winters, quoted ibid., p. 44.
6. Richard Marks, quoted ibid., pp. 181–182.
7. Alfred Hitchcock, quoted in *Directing the Film: Film Directors and Their Art*, edited by Eric Sherman (Los Angeles: Acrobat Books, 1976), p. 107.
8. Elia Kazan, *A Life* (New York: Doubleday, 1989), p. 380.
9. Ephraim Katz, *The Film Encyclopedia*, 3rd ed., revised by Fred Klein and Ronald Dean Nolan (New York: HarperPerennial, 1998), p. 718.
10. Sergei Eisenstein, *The Film Sense*, translated by Jay Leyda (New York: Harcourt, Brace and World, 1947), pp. 30–31.
11. Katz, p. 956.

Chapter 7

1. Lewis Jacobs, "The Mobility of Color," in *The Movies as Medium*, ed. Lewis Jacobs (New York: Farrar, Straus, and Giroux, 1970), p. 196.
2. Weldon Blake, *Creative Color: A Practical Guide for Oil Painters* (New York: Watson-Guptill, 1972), p. 14.
3. Robert Boyle, quoted in Vincent LoBrutto, *By Design: Interviews With Film Production Designers* (Westport, CT: Praeger, 1992), p. 7.
4. Mark Rydell, quoted in Judith Crist, *Take 22: Moviemakers on Moviemaking*, new expanded ed. (New York: Continuum, 1991), p. 180.
5. Jonathan Baumbach, "From A to Antonioni," in *Great Film Directors: A Critical Anthology*, edited by Leo Braudy and Morris Dickstein (New York: Oxford University Press, 1978), p. 29.
6. Gerald Mast, *A Short History of the Movies* (Indianapolis: Bobbs-Merrill, 1981), p. 295.
7. Paul Schrader, quoted in John Brady, *The Craft of the Screenwriter* (New York: Simon & Schuster, 1981), p. 302.
8. Michael Pye and Lynda Myles, *The Movie Brats: How the Film Generation Took Over Hollywood* (New York: Holt, Rinehart and Winston, 1979), p. 213.
9. Richard Corliss, "Extra! Dick Tracy Is Tops," *Time*, June 18, 1990, p. 76.
10. John Huston, *John Huston: An Open Book* (New York: Knopf, 1980), p. 211.
11. Laszlo Kovacs, "Dialogue on Film," *American Film* (June 1979), p. 43.
12. John Schlesinger, "Dialogue on Film," *American Film* (November 1987), p. 15.
13. "Almendros," *American Film* (December 1981), p. 19.
14. Editors of the Eastman Kodak Company, *More Joy of Photography*, rev. ed. (Reading, MA: Addison-Wesley, 1988), p. 50.
15. Martin Scorsese, quoted in Mary Pat Kelly, *Martin Scorsese: A Journey* (New York: Thunder's Mouth Press, 1991), p. 125.

16. Robert Edmond Jones, "The Problem of Color," in *The Emergence of Film Art*, 2nd ed., edited by Lewis Jacobs (New York: Norton, 1970), pp. 207–208.
17. Martin Scorsese, quoted in "State of the Art," *Dateline NBC* (June 28, 1998).

Chapter 8

1. Leonard Bernstein, *The Joy of Music* (New York: Simon & Schuster, 1959), p. 66.
2. Frank Warner, quoted in Vincent LoBrutto, *Sound-on-Film: Interviews with Creators of Film Sound* (Westport, CT: Praeger, 1994), p. 36.
3. Ray Sawhill, "Pumping Up the Volume: Movie Sound Has Been Getting Better—and Louder," *Newsweek* (July 6, 1998), p. 66.
4. Skip Lievsay, quoted in LoBrutto, *Sound-on-Film*, p. 264.
5. Steven Spielberg, quoted in Judith Crist, *Take 22: Moviemakers on Moviemaking*, new expanded ed. (New York: Continuum, 1991), p. 369.
6. Mark Mangini, quoted in LoBrutto, *Sound-on-Film*, p. 279.
7. Skip Lievsay, quoted ibid., p. 264.
8. Roger Ebert, "The Opposite of Sex," *Chicago Sun-Times* (June 19, 1998), *http://www.suntimes.com/ebert/.*
9. Renata Adler, *A Year in the Dark* (New York: Berkley Medallion Books, 1971), pp. 158–159.

Chapter 9

1. Muir Mathieson, quoted in Roger Manvell and John Huntley, *The Technique of Film Music* (London: Focal Press, 1957), p. 210.
2. Quincy Jones, quoted in Fred Baker with Ross Firestone, "Quincy Jones—On the Composer," in *Movie People: At Work in the Business of Film* (New York: Lancer Books, 1973), p. 191.
3. Jerry Goldsmith, quoted in *Filmmakers on Filmmaking: The American Film Institute Seminars on Motion Pictures and Television*, vol. 2, ed. Joseph McBride (Los Angeles: J. P. Tarcher, 1983), pp. 136–137.
4. Frank Brady, *Citizen Welles: A Biography of Orson Welles* (New York: Doubleday, 1989), pp. 264–265.
5. Jonathan Demme, quoted in Roger Catlin (*Hartford Courant*), "The Perfect Soundtrack Is Music to a Director's Ears," *The* [Fort Wayne] *Journal Gazette* (April 11, 1998), p. 2D.
6. "Peter Weir, Reflecting on the Score for *The Truman Show*," *The Truman Show*, soundtrack compact disc notes, Milan Entertainment Inc., 1998.
7. Brady, p. 264.
8. John Badham, quoted in Judith Crist, *Take 22: Moviemakers on Moviemaking*, new expanded ed. (New York: Continuum, 1991), pp. 420–421.
9. Jerry Bruckheimer, quoted in Ray Sawhill, "Pumping Up the Volume," *Newsweek* (July 6, 1998), p. 66.
10. Martin Scorsese, quoted in "About Elmer Bernstein," *The Age of Innocence*, soundtrack compact disc notes, Epic Soundtrax, 1993.

11. Terry Atkinson, "Scoring With Synthesizers," *American Film* (September 1982), p. 70.
12. Ibid., p. 68.
13. David Shire, quoted in Tony Thomas, *Music for the Movies*, 2nd ed. (Los Angeles: Silman-James Press, 1997), pp. 309–310, 311–312. Tony Thomas has also created (as writer and coproducer) the indispensable American Movie Classics documentary *The Hollywood Soundtrack Story* (1995). Hosted by composer Randy Newman, the film discusses and illustrates the careers of many noteworthy film composers, including the following: Elmer Bernstein (*The Ten Commandments, The Magnificent Seven*), Danny Elfman (*Batman, Edward Scissorhands, Men in Black*), Jerry Goldsmith (*Patton, Air Force One*), Bernard Hermann (*Citizen Kane, Psycho*), Maurice Jarre (*Lawrence of Arabia, Doctor Zhivago*), Erich Wolfgang Korngold (*The Adventures of Robin Hood*), Henry Mancini (*The Pink Panther, Breakfast at Tiffany's*), Alan Menken (*The Little Mermaid, Beauty and the Beast*), Alex North (*A Streetcar Named Desire, Who's Afraid of Virginia Woolf?*), Basil Poledouris (*Conan the Barbarian*), Rachel Portman (*Benny & Joon, Emma*), David Raksin (*Laura*), Leonard Rosenman (*East of Eden*), Miklos Rozsa (*The Last Weekend, Spellbound*), Marc Shaiman (*City Slickers, Sleepless in Seattle*), Max Steiner (*King Kong, Gone With the Wind, The Treasure of the Sierra Madre*), Dimitri Tiomkin (*High Noon*), Franz Waxman (*Sunset Boulevard, A Place in the Sun*), and John Williams (*Star Wars, E.T. The Extra-Terrestrial, Schindler's List*).

   Another very helpful and enjoyable video source about film music is the documentary/performance work *John Barry: Moviola*, which was first broadcast on the PBS series *Great Performances* in 1993 (Big Shot Films). Barry, the prolific composer of many of the James Bond film scores, is perhaps best known for the lyrical works in the films *Born Free, Midnight Cowboy, Somewhere in Time, Body Heat, Out of Africa, Dances With Wolves,* and *Chaplin.* In the documentary sections of this film, the extraordinary relationships between Barry and his movies' directors are examined through interviews with Kevin Costner, Sir Richard Attenborough, and Sydney Pollack.
14. Randy Newman, quoted in "Movie Music: Coupla White Guys Sitting Around Talking," *Premiere* (June 1989), p. 139.
15. Sidney Lumet, *Making Movies* (New York: Knopf, 1995), pp. 176, 178.
16. David Morgan, *Knowing the Score* (New York: HarperEntertainment, 2000), p. xii.

Chapter 10

1. George R. Kernodle, *An Invitation to the Theatre* (New York: Harcourt, Brace and World, 1967), p. 259.
2. Alfred Hitchcock, quoted in Richard Dyer MacCann, ed., *Film: A Montage of Theories* (New York: Dutton, 1966), p. 57.
3. Rydell, "Dialogue on Film," p. 23.
4. Michael Caine, quoted in Judith Crist, *Take 22: Moviemakers on Moviemaking*, new expanded ed. (New York: Continuum, 1991), p. 446.

5. Edward James Olmos, quoted in Linda Seger and Edward Jay Whetmore, *From Script to Screen: The Collaborative Art of Filmmaking* (New York: Henry Holt, 1994), p. 161.

6. Cliff Robertson, quoted in Crist, pp. 106–107.

7. Joanne Woodward, quoted ibid., p. 60.

8. Michael Caine, *Acting in Film: An Actor's Take on Movie Making*, revised expanded ed. (New York: Applause Theatre Books, 1997), pp. 88–89.

9. Elia Kazan, *A Life* (New York: Doubleday, 1989), p. 530.

10. Henry Fonda, as told to Howard Teichman, *Fonda: My Life* (New York: New American Library, 1981), p. 104.

11. Robert Shaw, quoted in "Ask Them Yourself," *Family Weekly* (June 11, 1972).

12. Julian Fast, *Body Language* (New York: M. Evans, 1970), p. 185.

13. Jack Kroll, "Robert De Niro," in *The National Society of Film Critics on the Movie Star*, edited by Elisabeth Weiss (New York: Viking Press, 1981), p. 198.

14. Béla Balázs, *Theory of the Film: Character and Growth of a New Art*, translated by Edith Bone (New York: Dover, 1970), p. 168.

15. Michael Caine, quoted in Crist, p. 445.

16. V. I. Pudovkin, *Film Technique and Film Acting*, memorial edition, translated and edited by Ivor Montagu (New York: Grove Press, 1958), p. 168.

17. Sergio Leone, quoted in David Morrison, "Leonesque," *American Film* (September 1989), p. 31.

18. Edward A. Wright and Lenthiel H. Downs, *A Primer for Playgoers* (Englewood Cliffs, NJ: Prentice-Hall, 1969), pp. 217–220.

19. Steven Spielberg, quoted in Crist, p. 371.

20. Sidney Lumet, *Making Movies* (New York: Knopf, 1995), p. 67.

21. Steven Spielberg, quoted in Crist, p. 377.

22. Billy Wilder, quoted in Tom Wood, *The Bright Side of Billy Wilder, Primarily* (New York: Doubleday, 1970), p. 140.

23. Gary Busey, quoted in Thomas Wiener, "Carny: Bozo Meets Girl," *American Film* (March 1980), p. 28.

24. Paul Newman, quoted in Crist, p. 64.

25. Gene Hackman, quoted in Robert Ward, "I'm Not a Movie Star; I'm an Actor!" *American Film* (March 1983), p. 42.

26. Kazan, p. 525.

27. Paul Mazursky, quoted in Stephen Farber, "Who Is She This Time?" *American Film* (May 1983), pp. 32–33.

28. Dustin Hoffman, quoted in "Dialogue on Film," *American Film* (April 1983), p. 27.

29. Emma Thompson, *The "Sense and Sensibility" Screenplay & Diaries: Bringing Jane Austen's Novel to Film* (New York: Newmarket Press, 1995), pp. 266–267.

30. Hal Ashby, quoted in "Dialogue on Film," *American Film* (May 1980), p. 55.

31. Meryl Streep, quoted in Richard Schickel, "A Tissue of Implications," *Time* (December 19, 1983), p. 73.

32. Schickel.

33. Sidney Lumet, quoted in Fred Baker with Ross Firestone, "Sidney Lumet—On the Director," in *Movie People: At Work in the Business of Film* (New York: Lancer Books, 1973), p. 58.

Chapter 11

1. Peter Bogdanovich, *Who the Devil Made It* (New York: Knopf, 1997), pp. 40–41.

2. Sidney Lumet, *Making Movies* (New York: Knopf, 1995), pp. 26–27.

3. Steven Spielberg, quoted in Roger Ebert and Gene Siskel, *The Future of the Movies: Interviews with Martin Scorsese, Steven Spielberg, and George Lucas* (Kansas City: Andrews and McMeel, 1991), p. 71.

4. William Goldman, quoted in John Brady, *The Craft of the Screenwriter* (New York: Simon & Schuster, 1981), p. 168.

5. Sydney Pollack, quoted in Judith Crist, *Take 22: Moviemakers on Moviemaking*, new expanded ed. (New York: Continuum, 1991), pp. 213–214.

6. David Lynch, quoted in *Reel Conversations: Candid Interviews With Film's Foremost Directors and Critics*, edited by George Hickenlooper (New York: Carol Publishing Group, 1991), p. 103.

7. Orson Welles and Peter Bogdanovich, *This Is Orson Welles* (New York: HarperCollins, 1992), pp. 314–315.

8. Lumet, pp. 46–47.

9. Emma Thompson, *The "Sense and Sensibility" Screenplay & Diaries* (New York: Newmarket Press, 1995), pp. 236, 240.

10. Steven Spielberg, quoted in Crist, p. 362.

11. Billy Frolick, *What I Really Want to Do Is DIRECT: Seven Film School Graduates Go to Hollywood* (New York: Dutton, 1996), p. 347.

Chapter 12

1. Dwight Macdonald, *On Movies* (New York: Berkley Medallion Books, 1971), p. 15. Reprinted by permission of Dwight Macdonald. Copyright © 1969 by Dwight Macdonald.

2. Renata Adler, *A Year in the Dark* (New York: Berkley Medallion Books, 1971), p. 330.

3. Vincent Canby, "Hitchcock: The Agony Is Exquisite," *New York Times* (July 2, 1972). © 1972 The New York Times. Reprinted by permission.

4. Macdonald, pp. 9–12. Reprinted by permission of Dwight Macdonald. Copyright © 1969 by Dwight Macdonald.

Chapter 13

1. Henry James, *The Golden Bowl* (New York: Scribner, 1904; Penguin, 1966), p. 1.

2. Reprinted from "The Battler" by Ernest Hemingway with the permission of Charles Scribner's Sons.

3. Russell Banks, *The Sweet Hereafter* (New York: HarperCollins, 1991), p. 1.

4. Jay McInerney, *Bright Lights, Big City* (New York: Random House/Vintage, 1987), p. 1.

5. Toni Morrison, *Beloved* (New York: Knopf, 1987), p. 1.
6. Virginia Woolf, *Orlando* (New York: Harcourt Brace Jovanovich, n.d.; originally published in 1928), p. 244.
7. Reprinted by permission of Random House, Inc., from William Faulkner, *The Sound and the Fury*. Copyright 1929 by William Faulkner. Copyright renewed 1956 by William Faulkner.
8. Reprinted from "The Killers" by Ernest Hemingway with the permission of Charles Scribner's Sons.
9. George Bluestone, *Novels Into Film* (Berkeley: University of California Press, 1957), pp. 47–48.
10. J. D. Salinger, *The Catcher in the Rye* (New York: Bantam Books, 1951), p. 2.
11. William Goldman, quoted in John Brady, *The Craft of the Screenwriter* (New York: Simon & Schuster, 1981), p. 163.
12. Excerpted from *All the King's Men*, copyright 1946, 1974 by Robert Penn Warren. Reprinted by permission of Harcourt Brace Jovanovich, Inc. Excerpt appears on pp. 128–129 of the Bantam Books (1974) edition.
13. Excerpted from *All the King's Men*, copyright 1946, 1974 by Robert Penn Warren. Reprinted by permission of Harcourt Brace Jovanovich, Inc. Excerpt appears on pp. 313–314 of the Bantam Books (1974) edition.
14. Excerpted from *The Last Picture Show* by Larry McMurtry (New York: Dell, 1966), pp. 8–9.
15. Excerpted from *All the King's Men*, copyright 1946, 1974 by Robert Penn Warren. Reprinted by permission of Harcourt Brace Jovanovich, Inc. Excerpt appears on pp. 308–309 of the Bantam Books (1974) edition.
16. Elia Kazan, *A Life* (New York: Doubleday, 1989), p. 381.
17. Renata Adler, *A Year in the Dark* (New York: Berkley Medallion Books, 1971), p. 302.
18. Neil Simon, quoted in Brady, p. 342.
19. Sidney Lumet, *Making Movies* (New York: Knopf, 1995), pp. 15–16.
20. Nicholas Ray, quoted in *Directing the Film: Film Directors on Their Art*, edited by Eric Sherman (Los Angeles: Acrobat Books, 1976), p. 279.
21. Neil Simon, quoted in Brady, p. 341.
22. Richard Corliss, "Fire This Time," *Time* (January 9, 1989), pp. 57–58.
23. Charles Taylor, "A Beautiful Mind," *Salon.com* (December 21, 2001), *www.salon.com/ent/movies/review/2001/12/21/beautiful_mind*.
24. John Horn (Associated Press), "Redford Fudges Facts to Make Story Spicier," *The [Fort Wayne] Journal-Gazette* (October 7, 1994), p. 1D.
25. Jack Nicholson, quoted in Linda Seger and Edward Jay Whetmore, *From Script to Screen: The Collaborative Art of Filmmaking* (New York: Henry Holt, 1994), p. 159.
26. Leonard Maltin, *Movie & Video Guide* (New York: Signet, 2003), p. 424.
27. Michael Cunningham, "For 'The Hours,' an Elation Mixed With Doubt," *The New York Times* (January 19, 2003), *www.nytimes.com/2003/01/19/movies/19CUNN.html*.
28. Begley, Louis, "'About Schmidt' Was Changed, But Not Its Core," *The New York Times* (January 19, 2003), *www.nytimes.com/2003/01/19/movies/19BEGL.html*.

Chapter 14

1. "Rex Reed at the Movies: From Blood and Guts to Guts and Blood," *Holiday Magazine*, vol. 47, no. 4 (April 1970), p. 24. Permission to reprint granted by Travel Magazine, Inc., Floral Park, New York 11001.
2. Stephen Schiff, quoted in "Preface" of Richard Jameson, ed., *They Went Thataway: Redefining Film Genres* (San Francisco: Mercury House, 1994), p. xiv.
3. Ibid., pp. xviii–xix.
4. Ibid., p. xv.
5. Ibid., p. 6.
6. Rick Altman, *Film/Genre* (London: British Film Institute, 1999), p. 221.
7. Steve Neale, *Genre and Hollywood* (London: Routledge, 2000), p. 28.
8. Tom Ryall, "Genre and Hollywood," in John Hill and Pamela Church Gibson, eds., *The Oxford Guide to Film Studies* (New York: Oxford University Press, 1998), p. 337.
9. Wheeler Winston Dixon, in Wheeler Winston Dixon, ed., *Film Genre 2000: New Critical Essays* (Albany: State University of New York Press, 2000), p. 11.
10. Chuck Berg, in Dixon, p. 217.
11. Berg, pp. 217, 224.
12. Ron Wilson, in Dixon, pp. 151, 152.
13. Foster Hirsch, *Film Noir: The Dark Side of the Screen* (New York: Da Capo Press, 1981), p. 21.
14. Eddie Muller, *Dark City: The Lost World of Film Noir* (New York: St. Martin's, 1998), p. 10.
15. See, for example, Jim Shephard's "'Chinatown': Jolting Noir With a Shot of Nihilism," in *The New York Times* (February 7, 1998), *www.nytimes.com/yr/mo/day/artsleisure/chinatown.film.html*.
16. James Naremore, *More Than Night: Film Noir in Its Contexts* (Berkeley: University of California Press, 1998), p. 275.
17. Paul Schrader, "Notes on Film Noir," in Barry Keith Grant, ed., *Film Genre Reader II* (Austin: University of Texas Press, 1995), p. 225.
18. Schrader is quoted in Jonathan Rosenbaum's "*Touch of Evil* Retouched," *Premiere* (September 1998), p. 81.
19. See Louis Menard, "Jerry Don't Surf," *The New York Review of Books* (September 24, 1998), p. 7.
20. Anthony Lane, *The New Yorker* (August 10, 1998), p. 78.
21. Ibid.
22. Bruce Kawin, quoted in Leo Braudy and Marshall Cohen, eds., *Film Theory and Criticism*, 5th ed. (New York: Oxford University Press, 1999), p. 610.
23. J. P. Telotte, *Replications: A Robotic History of the Science Fiction Film* (Urbana: University of Illinois Press, 1995), p. 195.
24. A. O. Scott, "A Hunger for Fantasy, an Empire to Feed It," *The New York Times* (June 16, 2002), *www.nytimes.com/2002/06/16/movies/16SCOT.html*.

25. Lev Grossman, "Feeding on Fantasy," *Time* (December 2, 2002), p. 91.

26. Ed Sikov, *Screwball: Hollywood's Madcap Romantic Comedies* (New York: Crown, 1989), p. 32.

27. Rick Altman, *The American Film Musical* (Bloomington: Indiana University Press, 1987), p. ix.

28. Jane Feuer, *The Hollywood Musical*, 2nd ed. (New York: Macmillan, 1993), p. ix.

29. Altman, pp. 371–378.

30. Kevin Brownlow, *Hollywood: The Pioneers* (London: Collins, 1979), p. 129.

31. Quoted in David Ansen, "'Psycho' Analysis," *Newsweek* (December 7, 1998), pp. 70–71.

32. Quoted in Stephen Rebello, "Cat People: Paul Schrader Changes His Spots," *American Film* (April 1982), pp. 40–43.

33. Leo Braudy, quoted in "Afterword" in Andrew Horton and Stuart Y. McDougal, eds., *Play It Again, Sam: Retakes on Remakes* (Berkeley: University of California Press, 1998), p. 331.

34. Betsy Sharkey, "The Return of the Summer Sequels," *American Film* (June 1989), p. 4.

35. Dixon, p. 7.

Chapter 15

1. Fred Baker with Ross Firestone, "Rod Steiger—On the Actor," in *Movie People: At Work in the Business of Film* (New York: Lancer Books, 1973), p. 146.

2. Budd Schulberg, *Waterfront* (New York: Random House, 1955), pp. 307–309.

3. Charles Champlin, *The Movies Grow Up, 1940–1980* (Chicago: Swallow Press, 1981), p. 46.

4. Richard Corliss, "This Essay Is Rated PG-13," *Time* (July 29, 2002), p. 70.

5. Stephen Farber, *The Movie Rating Game* (Washington, DC: Public Affairs Press, 1972), p. 117.

6. Ibid.

7. "What G, PG, R, and X Really Mean," *TV Guide* (October 4, 1980), p. 44.

8. Neil LaBute, quoted in "Rebel Yells: Vanguard Roundtable," *Premiere* (October 1998), p. 90. For a fascinating, illustrative discussion of the composition of a typical ratings board group, see "I Know It When I See It," *60 Minutes*, CBS television (October 28, 1990).

9. Charles Lyons, in Francis G. Covares, ed., *Movie Censorship and American Culture* (Washington, DC: Smithsonian Institution Press, 1996), pp. 309–311.

10. Doug Atchison, "Separate and Unequal? How the MPAA Rates Independent Films," in John Landis, ed., *The Best American Movie Writing 2001* (New York: Thunder's Mouth Press, 2001), p. 69.

11. See Rick Lyman, "Hollywood Balks at High Tech Sanitizers," *The New York Times* (September 19, 2002), *www.nytimes.com/2002/09/19/movies/19CLEA.html*.

12. Roger Ebert, "Bully" (July 20, 2001), *www.suntimes.com/ebert/ebert_reviews/2001/07/072001.html*.

13. Lou Lumenick, "True Tale of Sex, Violence, Murder, and Horrible Filmmaking," *The New York Post* (July 13, 2001), *www.nypost.com/movies/29179.htm*.

14. Erik Barnouw, *Documentary: A History of the Non-Fiction Film*, 2nd rev. ed. (New York: Oxford University Press, 1993), p. 348.

15. Roger Ebert, *Roger Ebert's Video Companion, 1998 Edition* (Kansas City: Andrews and McMeel, 1997), p. 23.

16. Barnouw, pp. 251–253.

17. Ibid.

18. Ebert, p. 806.

19. Ian Christie, "Kings of Shadows," *Times Literary Supplement* (August 15, 1997), p. 19.

20. Nicca Ray, "A Rebel Because . . . ," *Icon* (December 1997), p. 109.

21. For a detailed account of the urgency of Cameron's photographic visit to the *Titanic*'s burial ground, see the early chapters of Paula Parisi's *"Titanic" and the Making of James Cameron* (New York: Newmarket Press, 1998).

glossary

action acting   The kind of acting seen in action/adventure films. It demands skill in facial reactions and body language, physical strength, and coordination but little subtlety or depth in communicating emotions or thoughts.

adaptation   A film based upon a literary work.

advancing colors   Colors that, when given high intensity and dark value, seem to advance toward the foreground and make objects seem larger and closer to the camera: red, orange, yellow, and lavender.

allegory   A story in which every object, event, and person has an immediately discernible abstract or metaphorical meaning.

ambient sounds   Off-screen sounds natural to any film scene's environment, such as telephones ringing in a busy office building or birds chirping in a forest.

analogous harmony   The effect created by colors adjacent to each other on the integrated color wheel, such as red, red-orange, and orange. Such combinations result in a soft image with little harsh contrast.

aspect ratio   The shape of projected screen images. Basically, two types exist: **standard** (whose width is 1.33 times larger than its height; often called "academy ratio") and **wide screen** (whose width ranges from 1.66 to 2.55 times its height).

atmospheric color   Color that is influenced by the various colors and light sources in a color-rich environment.

auteur   Literally, the "author" of the film. *Auteur* film criticism holds that certain directors provide the controlling vision for their films, conceiving the idea for the story, writing the script, producing, directing, and closely supervising most other steps in the filmmaking process.

blue-screen process   A special visual effects film technique by which actors who are photographed in front of a blue (or green) screen can later be inserted into various movie environments; a kind of **matte shot.**

caricature   The exaggeration or distortion of one or more personality traits; a technique common in cartooning.

Cinemascope.   *See* **wide screen.**

cinematic point of view.   *See* **point of view, cinematic.**

cinéma vérité   "The term means 'camera truth' in French and applies to . . . documentary films which strive for immediacy, spontaneity, and authenticity through the use of portable and unobtrusive equipment and the avoidance of any preconceived narrative line or concepts concerning the material. . . . A distinctive technique . . . is the filmmaker questioning and probing those interviewed" (Ira Konigsberg, *The Complete Film Dictionary*, 2nd ed. [New York: Penguin, 1997], p. 57). *See also* **direct cinema.**

climax   The point at which the **complication** reaches its maximum tension and the forces in opposition confront each other at a peak of physical or emotional action.

close-up   A close shot of a person or object; a close-up of a person generally focuses on the face only.

color   A purely human perception of a radiant energy creating a visual quality distinct from light and shade.

colorization   The computerized coloring of older black-and-white films for use on television and for sale and rental in video form.

color palette   A limited number of specific colors used or emphasized throughout a film to subtly communicate various aspects of character and story.

color wheel   A standard reference device that artists use to clarify the relationships that exist between primary and secondary hues.

commentators   *See* **interpreters.**

complementary harmony   The effect created by colors directly opposite each other on the integrated color wheel. Such colors react most vividly with each other, as in the case of red and green.

complication   The section of a story in which a conflict begins and grows in clarity, intensity, and importance.

computer-generated images (CGI)   Visual images that are created exclusively by computer commands rather than by standard live photography or **stop-motion animation.** This method has been widely used in many types of films, but only during the 1990s did entirely CGI features such as *Toy Story* and *A Bug's Life* appear.

cool colors   Colors that seem to convey or suggest a cool temperature: blues, greens, and beiges.

cross cutting   *See* **parallel cutting.**

dailies   Unedited footage of a day's shooting that the director evaluates for possible inclusion in the final version of a film.

day-for-night   Filming technique sometimes used by makers of silent movies. Because film stock was too slow for night shooting, daylight footage was overexposed to simulate night scenes.

dead screen   A frame in which there is little or no dramatically or aesthetically interesting visual information. *See also* **live screen.**

dead track   The complete absence of sound on the soundtrack.

deep focus   Special lenses allow the camera to focus simultaneously and with equal clarity on objects anywhere from two feet to several hundred feet away.

dénouement   A brief period of calm following the **climax,** in which a state of relative equilibrium returns.

desaturated color   A color of lowered intensity or value. A color is desaturated by being made lighter or darker than its normal value.

developing or dynamic characters   Characters who are deeply affected by the action of the plot and who undergo some important change in personality, attitude, or outlook on life as a result of the action of the film. *See also* **static characters.**

digital sound   Vastly improved quality sound reproduction in movie theaters that utilizes processes (such as Dolby and DTS) that convert standard optical sound to binary digital information.

direct cinema   "A type of documentary that developed in America during the 1960s and was given this name by filmmaker Albert Maysles to suggest its direct, immediate, and authentic approach to the subject matter. A planned narrative and approach are avoided. . . . Events seem recorded exactly as they happened without rehearsal and with minimal editing. People are allowed to speak without guidance or interruption. . . . The zoom lens focuses directly on subjects, waiting for them to expose themselves. . . . Direct Cinema and *cinéma vérité,* which developed in France at the same time and employs many of the same techniques and . . . equipment, have been confused . . . , but *cinéma vérité* is quite distinct, with the filmmaker's voice intruding into the film, interviewing and probing the subject with questions in order to elicit the truth and create the dramatic exposure and situation" (Konigsberg, p. 96).

director's cut   A special version of a motion picture that differs from its theatrical-release form. It most often appears on videocassette, laserdisc, or DVD under the personal supervision of its director, whose right of final edit may originally have been superseded by the film's producers or studio.

director's interpretive point of view   *See* **point of view, cinematic.**

dissolve   The gradual merging of the end of one shot with the beginning of the next, produced by superimposing a fade-out onto a fade-in of equal length or by imposing one scene over another.

Dolby-Surround Sound   A multitrack stereophonic system for theaters that employs an encoding process to achieve a 360-degree sound field—thus creating the effect of more speakers than are actually present.

dramatic acting   Acting that requires emotional and psychological depth, usually involving sustained, intense dialogue without physical action.

dramatic point of view   *See* **point of view, literary.**

editing patterns   *See* **inside/out editing; outside/in editing.**

ensemble acting   A performance by a group of actors whose roles are of equal importance.

establishing shot   A beginning shot of a new scene that shows an overall view of the new setting and the relative position of the actors in that setting.

exposition   The part of a story that introduces the characters, shows some of their interrelationships, and places them within a believable time and place.

expressionism   A dramatic or cinematic technique that attempts to present the inner reality of a character. In film, there is usually a distortion or exaggeration of normal perception to let the audience know that it is experiencing a character's innermost feelings.

external conflict   A personal and individual struggle between the central character and another character or between the central character and some nonhuman force such as fate, society, or nature.

extrinsic metaphor   *See* **metaphor, visual.**

eye-line shot   A shot that shows us what a character is seeing.

fade-out/fade-in   A transitional device in which the last image of one scene fades to black as the first image of the next scene is gradually illuminated.

fast motion   The frantic, herky-jerky movement that results when a scene is filmed at less-than-normal speed (24 frames per second) and then projected at normal speed.

film noir   "A term coined by French critics to describe a type of film that is characterized by its dark, somber tone and cynical, pessimistic mood. Literally meaning 'dark (or "black") film,' the term . . . was coined to describe those Hollywood films of the '40s and early '50s which portrayed the dark and gloomy underworld of crime and corruption. . . . The *film noir* characteristically abounds with night scenes, both interior and exterior, with sets that suggest dingy realism, and with lighting that emphasizes deep shadows and accents the mood of fatalism" (Ephraim Katz, *The Film Encyclopedia*, 3rd ed. [New York: HarperPerennial, 1998], p. 456). **Neo-*film noir*** refers to any film made after the mid-1960s that attempts to replicate many of these characteristics.

final cut   A film in its finished form. A guarantee of final cut assures the filmmaker or producer that the film will not be tampered with after he or she approves it.

first-person point of view   *See* **point of view, literary.**

fish-eye lens   A special type of extreme wide-angle lens that bends both horizontal and vertical planes and distorts depth relationships.

fixed frame movement   The camera remains in a fixed position, pointing at a single spot, as one might look at something with a frozen stare. The director creates variety in the shot by moving the subject within the frame. *See also* ***mise-en-scène.***

flashback   A filmed sequence that goes back in time to provide expository material—either when it is most dramatically appropriate and powerful or when it most effectively illuminates the theme. *See also* **flash-forward.**

flash cuts   Fragmented bursts of images used to compress action.

flash-forward   A filmed sequence that moves forward in time—the visual scene jumps from the present into the future.

flat characters   Two-dimensional, predictable characters who lack the complexity and unique qualities associated with psychological depth. *See also* **round characters.**

flip frame   A transitional device in which the entire frame seems to flip over to reveal a new scene—an effect very similar to turning a page.

foils   Contrasting characters whose behavior, attitudes, opinions, lifestyle, physical appearance, and so on are opposites and thus serve clearly to define their personalities.

Foley artist   A film sound technician who is responsible for adding **visible sounds** (such as walking, fighting, or falling) to enhance a soundtrack after the primary production has been completed.

forced perspective   A production design technique that physically distorts certain aspects of the set and diminishes the size of objects and people in the background to create the illusion of greater foreground-to-background distance.

form cut   A transition accomplished by framing objects or images of similar contour in two successive shots, so that the first image flows smoothly into the second.

freeze frame   An effect, achieved in the laboratory after the film is shot, whereby a frame is reprinted so many times on the film strip that when the film is shown, the motion seems to stop as though frozen. *See also* **thawed frame.**

generalized score   A musical score that attempts to capture the overall emotional atmosphere of a sequence and the film as a whole, usually by using rhythmic and emotive variations on only a few recurring motifs or themes. Also called **implicit score.**

genre film   A motion picture (such as a western, a gangster film, a musical, or a *film noir*) that plays on the expectation of the audience regarding familiar plot structures, characters, setting, and so on. More broadly, the terms *genre* and *subgenre* are used to refer to various film types.

glancing rhythms The built-in sense of excitement or boredom created by fast or slow editing. Slow editing simulates the glancing rhythms of a tranquil observer; quick cutting simulates the glancing rhythms of a highly excited observer.

glass shot A cinematic technique that involves photographing live action through a scene painted on glass. In such celebrated films as *Gone With the Wind* and *Ben-Hur*, **glass shots** have been used to integrate characters and stories into landscapes that would have been either impossible or too costly to construct in three-dimensional form. Increasingly, **CGI** techniques are being used to enhance or replace glass shots in contemporary filmmaking.

high-angle shot A shot made with the camera above eye level, thereby dwarfing the subject and diminishing its importance. *See also* **low-angle shot.**

high-key lighting Lighting that results in more light areas than shadows; subjects are seen in middle grays and highlights, with little contrast. *See also* **low-key lighting.**

hue A synonym for color.

impersonators Actors who have the talent to leave their real identity and personality behind and assume the personality and characteristics of a character with whom they may have little in common.

implicit score *See* **generalized score.**

indirect-subjective point of view *See* **point of view, cinematic.**

in medias res A Latin phrase meaning "in the middle of things" that refers to a method of beginning a story with an exciting incident that, chronologically, occurs after the complication has developed.

inside/out editing A dynamic editing pattern in which the editor takes us suddenly from a line of action that we understand to a close-up of a detail in a new setting. Because this detail is not shown in the context of a setting, we don't know where we are or what is happening. Then, in a series of related shots, the editor backs us off from the close-up to reveal the detail in relationship to its surroundings.

internal conflict A psychological conflict within the central character. The primary struggle is between different aspects of a single personality.

interpreters Actors who play characters that closely resemble themselves in personality and physical appearance and who interpret these parts dramatically without wholly losing their own identity. Also called *commentators.*

intrinsic metaphor *See* **metaphor, visual.**

invisible sound Sound emanating from a source *not* on the screen. *See also* **visible sound.**

irony A literary, dramatic, and cinematic technique involving the juxtaposition or linking of opposites.

jump cut The elimination of a strip of insignificant or unnecessary action from a continuous shot. The term also refers to a disconcerting joining of two shots that do not match in action and continuity.

letterboxing The use of black bands at the top and bottom of the frame when **wide-screen** films are shown on a **standard**-ratio video surface.

leitmotif The repetition of a single phrase or idea by a character until it becomes almost a trademark for that character. In music, the repetition of a single musical theme to announce the reappearance of a certain character.

literary point of view *See* **point of view, literary.**

live screen A frame packed with dramatically or aesthetically interesting visual information, usually with some form of motion incorporated into the composition. *See also* **dead screen.**

local color Color seen in isolation from other colors in a totally white environment illuminated by a perfectly white light.

long shot A shot, taken from some distance, that usually shows the subject as well as its surroundings.

long take A continuous film shot that lasts for several minutes. Some directors (following the famous sustained opening movement in Orson Welles's *Touch of Evil*) have made a kind of game of creating such shots in their films. Notable examples include Martin Scorsese in *GoodFellas* (and other films), Paul Thomas Anderson in *Boogie Nights*, Brian De Palma in *The Bonfire of the Vanities*, and Robert Altman in *The Player* (in an opening scene that both parodies and competes with Welles's work in *Touch of Evil*).

look of outward regard An objective shot that shows a character looking off-screen and thereby cues us to wonder what the character is looking at.

low-angle shot A shot made with the camera below eye level, thereby exaggerating the size and importance of the subject. *See also* **high-angle shot.**

low-key lighting   Lighting that puts most of the set in shadow and uses just a few highlights to define the subject. *See also* **high-key lighting.**

matte shot   Any special visual effects technique that uses some type of visual mask to allow more than one image to be photographed on a single film frame.

metaphor, visual   A brief comparison that helps us understand or perceive one image better because of its similarity to another image, usually achieved through the editorial juxtaposition of two images in two successive shots. Two types of visual metaphors are commonly used in films:

   extrinsic   A metaphor that has no place within the context of the scene itself but is imposed artificially into the scene by the director.

   intrinsic   A metaphor found within the natural context of the scene itself.

Mickey Mousing   The exact, calculated dovetailing of music and action that precisely matches the rhythm of the music with the natural rhythms of the objects moving on the screen.

microcosm   Meaning "the world in little," a special type of isolated, self-contained setting in which the human activity is actually representative of human behavior or the human condition in the world as a whole.

mise-en-scène   "A French term meaning 'putting into the scene' that was originally used to describe the staging of a theater director, the way he or she arranged all the visual components on the stage. The term has become fashionable in film criticism and has taken on new meanings and connotations from its filmic context. *Mise-en-scène*, in discussions of film, refers to the composition of the individual frame—the relation of objects, people, and masses; the interplay of light and dark; the pattern of color; the camera's position and angle of view—as well as the movement within the frame" (Konigsberg, p. 240). "Andre Bazin, and subsequently other theoreticians and critics, have used [the term] to describe a style of film directing basically distinct from that known as montage. Whereas montage derives its meaning from the relationship between one frame to the next through editing, *mise-en-scène* emphasizes the content of the individual frame. Its proponents see montage as disruptive to the psychological unity of man with his environment and cite such films as Orson Welles's *Citizen Kane* with its **deep-focus** compositions . . . as examples to support their argument. The schism between *mise-en-scène* and

montage is deeper in theory than in practice; most filmmakers employ both in directing their films" (Katz, p. 956). *See also* **montage.**

monochromatic harmony   The effect created by variations in the value and intensity of a single color.

montage   A series of images and sounds that derive their meaning from complex internal relationships to form a kind of visual poem in miniature. "The term . . . as it is generally understood today is associated with the work and theory of [Russian filmmaker] Sergei Eisenstein, in which it came to represent the rhetorical arrangement of shots in juxtaposition so that the clash between two adjoining images suggests a third, independent entity and creates a whole new meaning. Eisenstein's ideas of montage were inspired by the editing techniques of [pioneer American filmmaker] D. W. Griffith" (Katz, p. 965). *See also* **mise-en-scène.**

motifs   Images, patterns, or ideas that are repeated throughout the film and are variations or aspects of the film's theme.

muted color   *See* **desaturated color.**

name typing   The use of names possessing appropriate qualities of sound, meaning, or connotation to help describe a character.

objective camera   A camera that views the action as a remote spectator. *See also* **point of view, cinematic, objective.**

objective point of view   *See* **point of view, cinematic.**

omniscient-narrator point of view   *See* **point of view, literary.**

opticals   Effects created in the lab during the printing of the film. The primary image is superimposed on another image, and the two are composited onto one strip of film by an optical printer. Modern optical printers are guided by computer, affording precise matching of a tremendous number of different images.

outside/in editing   The traditional editing pattern in which the editor begins with an establishing shot of the new setting—to help the audience get its bearings—and then follows with shots that gradually take us farther into the setting. Only after we are completely familiar with our surroundings does the editor focus our attention on details.

painterly effects   The effects created by filmmakers who are consciously trying to imitate certain looks achieved by painters.

Panavision   *See* **wide screen.**

panning   Moving the camera's line of sight in a horizontal plane to the right and left.

panning and scanning   A technique used to transfer films shot in **wide screen** to a format that will fill a traditional television screen. The lateral movement of the reproducing camera that allows this process to occur also generally ruins the original composition and pacing created by directors and cinematographers.

parallel cuts   Shots that quickly alternate back and forth between two actions taking place at separate locations, creating the impression that the two actions are occurring simultaneously and will possibly converge. (Also called **cross cutting** and intercutting.)

period piece   A film that takes place not in the present but in some earlier period of history.

personality actors   Actors whose primary talent is to be themselves. Although personality actors generally possess some dynamic and magnetic mass appeal, they are incapable of assuming any variety in the roles they play, for they cannot project sincerity and naturalness when they attempt to move outside their own basic personality.

Peter-and-the-Wolfing   Musical scoring in which certain musical instruments represent and signal the presence of certain characters.

point of view, cinematic   Essentially, there are four points of view that may be employed in a film:

>   **director's interpretive**   Using the special techniques of the medium, the director manipulates us so that we see the action or the character in the way the director interprets them.

>   **indirect-subjective**   A viewpoint that brings us close to the action and increases our involvement. It provides us with the feeling and sense of immediacy of participating in the action without showing the action through a participant's eyes.

>   **objective**   The viewpoint of a sideline observer, which suggests an emotional distance between camera and subject. The camera seems simply to be recording, as straightforwardly as possible, the characters and the actions of the story.

>   **subjective**   The viewpoint of a character participating in the action. *See also* **point of view, literary.**

point of view, literary   There are five viewpoints employed in literature:

>   **dramatic or objective**   A viewpoint wherein we are not conscious of a narrator, for the author does not comment on the action but simply describes the scene, telling us what happens and what the characters say, so we get a feeling of being there, observing the scene as we would in a play.

>   **first person**   An eyewitness gives a firsthand account of what happened as well as his or her response to it.

>   **omniscient narrator, third person**   An all-seeing, all-knowing narrator, capable of reading the thoughts of all the characters and capable of being in several places at once if need be, tells the story.

>   **stream of consciousness or interior monologue**   A third-person narrative that seems to incorporate the first-person form, although the participant in the action is not consciously telling the story. It is a unique inner view, as though a microphone and movie camera in the character's mind were recording every thought, image, and impression that passes through, without the conscious acts of organization, selectivity, or narration.

>   **third-person selective or limited**   The narrator is omniscient except for the fact that his or her powers of mind reading are limited to or at least focused on a single character, who becomes the central figure through whom we view the action.

point-of-view character   A film character with whom we emotionally or intellectually identify and through whom we experience the film. **Voice-over narration,** editing, and camera position may be employed for this effect.

rack focus   Changing the focus setting on the camera during a continuous shot so that audience attention is directed deeper and deeper into the frame as viewers follow the plane of clearest focus. The technique can also be reversed so that the plane of clearest focus moves closer and closer to the camera.

reaction shot   A shot that shows a character reacting rather than acting. The reaction shot is usually a closeup of the emotional reaction registered on the face of the person most affected by the dialogue or action.

receding colors   Colors that seem to recede into the background, making objects appear smaller and more distant from the camera: green, pale blue, and beige.

Rembrandt effect   The use of a subtle, light-diffusing filter to soften focus slightly and subdue the colors so that the whole film has the quality of a Rembrandt painting.

rough-grain film stock   Film stock that produces a rough, grainy-textured image with harsh contrasts between blacks and whites and almost no subtle differences in contrast. *See also* **smooth-grain film stock.**

round characters Unique, individualistic characters who have some degree of complexity and ambiguity and who cannot easily be categorized. Also called *three-dimensional characters*. *See also* **flat characters.**

rushes *See* **dailies.**

saturated color A strong, unadulterated, pure color. A saturated red cannot be made any redder.

scene A series of shots joined so that they communicate a unified action taking place at one time and place.

sequence A series of scenes joined in such a way that they constitute a significant part of a film's dramatic structure, like an act in a play.

setting The time and place in which the film's story takes place, including all of the complex factors that come packaged with a given time and place: climate, terrain, population density, social structures and economic factors, customs, moral attitudes, and codes of behavior.

shade Any color darker than its normal value. Maroon is a shade of red.

shot A strip of film produced by a single continuous running of the camera. After the editing and printing processes, a shot becomes the segment of film between cuts or optical transitions.

Skycam A small, computerized, remote-controlled camera that flies on wires at speeds of up to twenty miles per hour and can go practically anywhere that cables can be strung.

slow motion The effect of slowed action created by exposing frames in the camera at greater-than-normal speed and then projecting that footage at normal speed (24 frames per second).

smooth-grain film stock Film stock capable of reproducing an image that is extremely smooth or slick, registering a wide range of subtle differences between light and dark, and creating fine tones, artistic shadows, and contrasts. *See also* **rough-grain film stock.**

soft focus A slight blurring of focus for effect.

sound link A bridge between scenes or sequences created through the use of similar or identical sounds in both.

standard screen A screen whose width is 1.33 times its height.

star system An approach to filmmaking that capitalizes on the mass appeal of certain actors to increase the likelihood that a film will be a financial success.

static characters Characters who remain essentially the same throughout the film, either because the action does not have an important effect on their lives or because they are insensitive to the meaning of the action. *See also* **developing or dynamic characters.**

Steadicam A portable, one-person camera with a built-in gyroscope that prevents any sudden jerkiness and provides a smooth, rock-steady image.

stereotypes Characters who fit into preconceived patterns of behavior common to or representative of a large number of people (at least a large number of fictional people), allowing the director to economize greatly in treating them.

stills Photographs in which the image itself does not move. A sense of movement is imparted to the images by the camera zooming in or out or simply moving over their surface.

stock characters Minor characters whose actions are completely predictable or typical of their job or profession.

stop-motion animation A variation on drawn-animation techniques that uses puppets or other three-dimensional objects. To give the appearance of life on film when projected at the normal 24-frames-per-second speed, subjects are moved minimally between shots as they are being photographed.

stream of consciousness *See* **point of view, literary.**

subjective camera A camera that views the scene from the visual or emotional point of view of a participant in the action. *See also* **point of view, cinematic, subjective.**

subjective point of view *See* **point of view, cinematic.**

subtitling The method of providing visible words at the bottom of frames to translate the dialogue of films from one language into another. *See also* **voice dubbing.**

surrealism A dramatic or cinematic technique that uses fantastic imagery in an attempt to portray the workings of the subconscious. Surrealistic images have an oddly dreamlike or unreal quality.

symbol A literal element (such as an object, name, or gesture) in art, literature, and film that also stands for an abstract idea. This representation is established by triggering previously associated areas in the mind of the perceiver.

tableau A technique, used in melodrama, in which actors held dramatic postures for a few seconds before the curtain fell in order to etch the scene in the audience's memory.

take Variations of the same shot. In the cutting room, the editor assembles the film from the best take of each shot.

telephoto lens A lens that, like a telescope, draws objects closer but also diminishes the illusion of depth.

thawed frame An effect opposite to that of a **freeze frame**—the scene begins with a frozen image that thaws and comes to life.

theme The central concern around which a literary work or film is structured, its unifying focus. In film, theme can be broken down into five categories: plot, emotional effect or mood, character, style or texture, and ideas.

third-person limited point of view *See* **point of view, literary.**

three-dimensional characters *See* **round characters.**

tilting Moving the camera's line of sight in a vertical plane, up and down.

time-lapse photography An extreme form of fast motion in which a single frame is exposed at regular intervals (from a second to an hour or even longer) and then projected at normal speed (24 frames per second), thus compressing an action that usually takes hours or weeks into a few seconds on the screen.

tint Any color lighter than its normal value. Pink is a tint of red.

tinting The chemical coloring of film stock before the image is printed on it. When printed, the white portions of the image retain the color of the tint, resulting in an image composed of two colors—black and the color of the tint.

toning Adding dyes to the film emulsion so that the lines and tones of the image itself are colored.

traveling music Music that is employed almost as a formula to give the impression of various means of transportation.

triad harmony The effect created by the use of three colors equidistant from each other on the color wheel, such as the primary colors: red, yellow, and blue.

typecasting The tendency of major studios and some directors to lock certain actors into a narrow range of almost identical roles.

value The proportion of light or dark present in a given color.

visible sound Sound that would naturally and realistically emanate from the images on the screen. *See also* **invisible sound.**

voice dubbing The replacement of the dialogue soundtrack in a foreign language with an English-language soundtrack. Voices in English are recorded to correspond to the mouth and lip movements of the foreign actors. *See also* **subtitling.**

voice-over narration A voice off-screen that conveys necessary background information or fills in gaps for continuity.

warm colors Colors that seem to convey or suggest a warm temperature: red, orange, yellow, and lavender.

wide-angle lens A lens that takes in a broad area and increases the illusion of depth but sometimes distorts the edges of the image.

wide screen Known by many trade names such as Cinemascope, Panavision, and Vistavision, a screen whose width varies from 1.66 to 1.85 to 2.35 to 2.55 times its height (as compared with the standard 1.33 times).

wipe A transitional device in which a new image is separated from the previous image by means of a horizontal, vertical, or diagonal line that moves across the screen to wipe the old image away.

zoom lens A complex series of lenses that keep the image constantly in focus and, by magnifying the subject, give the camera the apparent power to vary movement toward or away from the subject without requiring any movement of the camera.

index

Page numbers in *italics* indicate photos or illustrations. Entries in **bold** are defined terms.

Evans, Robert, *467*

Everett, Rupert, 46, *388*

Everybody's All-American, 295

"Everybody's Talking at Me," 261

Everyone Says I Love You, 325

Excalibur, 130, 134

Executive Action, 395

exposition, 44, 45

expressionism, 202–203

external action, characterization through, 51–52

external conflict, 48

extreme close-ups, 113, *114*

extrinsic metaphors, 64–65

eye-line shot, 108

Eyes Wide Shut, 288

Eyre, Chris, *461*

Eyre, Richard, 296–297, *298*

F

F Is for Fake, 466

Face/Off, 326

facial expressions in acting, 279, *279*, 282–283, *282*

fade-out/fade-in, 160

"Fade-Out in the West," 410

Fahrenheit 451, 72, 271

Fairbanks, Douglas, 376

fairy–tale musical, 419

"Fall of the House of Usher, The," 84–85

Family Plot, 65, *314*

Fanning, Dakota, *279*, 295, 368

Fantasia, 143

Fantastic Mr. Fox, *100–101*, 145

Fantastic Voyage, 136

fantasy films, 416–418

fantasy worlds, visual design of, 90

Far from Heaven, *194*, 195, 264

Fargo, 50, *50*, 295

Farmer Takes a Wife, The, 276

Farmiga, Vera, *348*

Farnsworth, Richard, *449*

Farrelly brothers, *419*

Farrow, Mia, 289

Fast and the Furious, The, 371

Fast, Cheap, and Out of Control, 466

Fast, Julian, 278

fast motion, 132, 179

Fast Runner (Atanarjuat), The, 460, *462*

Fatal Attraction, 46, 67

Fat Girl, 450

"Fauborg-St. Denis," 341

Faulkner, William, 55, 375

Fawcett, Farah, 395

Fellini, Federico, 270, *335–336*

Fellowes, Julian, 73

feminist film analysis, 357

Fernandez, Wilhelmina Wiggins, 269

fiction, adaptation of to film, 374

analyzing, 397–399

literary past tense versus cinematic present tense, 384–385

literary versus cinematic points of view, 374–375, 378–379

other factors, 385–386

philosophical reflections, 381–382

problem of length and depth, 380–381

summarizing a character's past, 382–383

summarizing events, 383–384

Fiddler on the Roof, 152

Field of Dreams, 372

Field, Sally, 263

Fields, W. C., *240*, 364

Fiennes, Joseph, *209*

Fiennes, Ralph, 150, 170, *207*, 293, *294*

Fifth Element, The, 85

Fight Club, 27

Fillon, Nathan, *123*

film

as actor's showcase (personality cult), 351–352

auteur approach to, 352–353, *353*

as emotional or sensual experience, 354, *355*

foreignness of, 440

as gender statement, 356–357, *357*

as political statement, 355–356

shaping or reflecting social and cultural values, 440–441

as technical achievement, 351

uniqueness of, 3–4

film analysis

analyzing your responses to a film, 16

basic approach to, 347, 365–366

challenges of, 5–6

developing personal criteria, 363–365, 366

eclectic approach, 360–361, *361*

feminist, 357

humanistic approach to, 353–354

level of ambition, 349

literary analysis and, 34

objective analysis, 349–350

psychoanalytic approach to, 358–360, *359*

relationship of parts to the whole, 348–349

subjective evaluation, 350

theme, 347–348

value of, 6–8

of whole film, 365–366

Film Comment, 404

Film Encyclopedia, The, 172, 184

Film Genre 2000: New Critical Essays, 405

film musicals, 419, *420*

film noir, 200, 206, 327, *356*, 411–413

films

colorizing, 459

MPAA rating, 14

preparing to see, 14–16

receptive viewing of, 8–10

"sanitizing," 459

about social problems, 460

Web sites dedicated to, 15–16

film stock, 79

film-viewing environment, 10–13

final cut, 301

Final Cut, The, 157, 159

Fincher, David, 27, *81*, 134

Find Me Guilty, 267

Finding Nemo, 141, *146*, *147*

Finding Neverland, 296

first-person point of view, 374, *375*, 378–379

Firth, Colin, *237*, *455*

Firth, Peter, *392*

Fischer, Gunnar, 316

Fisher, Carrie, 377

fish-eye lens, 132

Fisk, Jack, 88

F.I.S.T., 208

Fitzcarraldo, 290–291, 467

(500) Days of Summer, 31

fixed-frame movement, 116–120

Flaherty, Robert, 464

flash cuts, 171

flashbacks, 36, 44–45, 227

flash-forward, 45

flat characters, 57–58

Fleisher, Max, 142

Fleming, Victor, 276

Fletcher, Louise, 48

flip frame, 160

Flipped, 321

Fly, The, 13, 136, 472

flying-vehicle effects, 134–135, *135*

focus

sharpness of, 112, *113*

theme and, 30

Fog of War, The, 466

"Foggy Mountain Breakdown," 260

foils, 53–54, 295

Foley artist, 220

folk musical, 419

Following, 151

Fonda, Henry, 56, 133, *185*, 276–277, 285, 310

Fonda, Jane, 179–180, 302

Fonda, Peter, 172

forced perspective, 82

Ford, Harrison, 88, *89*, 432

Ford, John, 310

black–and–white film used by, 75

editing, 184, *185–186*

on filming adaptations, 372

as genre film director, 406

Grapes of Wrath, 28, 98, 184, *185–186*, 230

The Informer, 372

as social problem film director, 460

use of lighting, 98

use of sound, 230

use of star system, 285

Ford, Tom, 102, *237*

foreground framing, 12, 113, *115*, *123*, *124*

foreign language films, dubbing versus subtitles in, 241–245, 438

foreshadowing, 40, 255–256

Forgetting Sarah Marshall, 418

Forman, Milos, 81, *326*

metaphors
    extrinsic, 64–65
    intrinsic, 65
    visual, 64, *65*
Metropolis, 81, 134
Meyers, Nancy, *328*
Miami Vice, 371
Michael Clayton, *57*
Mickey Mousing, 252–253
microcosm, setting as, 86–87
Midnight Cowboy, 25, 209, 261, 274, 293, 321, 452
Midnight Express, 265, 291, 326
Midnight in the Garden of Good and Evil, 386
Midsummer Night's Dream, A, 277
Midway, 223
Mighty Aphrodite, 325
Mighty Joe Young, 145
Milk, 21, 159, 421
Miller, Frank, *214*
Miller, George, 133, 146
Miller, Henry, 379
Miller, Joshua, *211*
Miller's Crossing, 411
Million Dollar Baby, 25, 284
Miner, Rachel, *459*
miniaturization, 134, *135*
Minnelli, Liza, *83*, *420*
Minority Report, *333*, 400
Mirren, Helen, *57*
mis-en-scène, 159, 184
Misery, 392
Misfits, The, *303*
Mishima, 133
Mississippi Burning, 394, 395
Mitchell, Elvis, 342
Mitchell, Thomas, 295
Mitchum, Robert, *126*, *128*, *413*
Miyazaki, Hayao, 141, *144*, 153
Moana, 464
mobile camera, 119
"Modest Proposal, A," 68
Molina, Alfred, 305, *418*
Molinaro, Edward, 424
Monroe, Marilyn, *303*
Monsoon Wedding, 439–440
Monster, 246, 290
Monsters, Inc., 146
montage, 159, 183–184, 187
Montgomery, Robert, 108
mood, focus on, 18, *19*
Moon Is Blue, The, 446
Moore, Dudley, 287
Moore, Julianne, 297–298, 397
Moore, Mary Tyler, 287, 290
Moore, Michael, 462, 466
moral implications, 22, *23*
moral or philosophical riddle, focus on, 26, *27*
More Than Night: Film Noir in Its Contexts, 413
Morgan, David, 267
Morgenstern, Joseph, 365

Moriarty, Michael, 180
Moroder, Giorgio, 265
Morris, Errol, 466
Morrison, Toni, 374
Mortensen, Viggo, *459*
Mostly Martha, 423
motifs, 28
motion control, 134
Motion Picture Association of America (MPAA), 14, *441*
Motion Picture Producers and Distributors of America, Inc., 442
Motion Picture Production Code, 405, 442–446, 452
Moulin Rouge (1952), 207–208
Moulin Rouge! (2001), 81, 189, 419
movement, 113, *114*, 116
    dead screen and live screen, 120
    editing and, 120
    fixed-frame movement, 116–120
    mobile camera, 119
    panning and tilting, 116
    zoom lens, 117–119
Movie & Video Guide, 396
"MovieMask," *459*
MPAA Rating System, 14, 446, 449–454, 468
Mr. and Mrs. Smith, 294
Mr. Deeds, 468
Mr. Deeds Goes to Town, 468
Mr. Smith Goes to Washington, 36, 48, 130, 184, 187, 222, 295
Mrs. Dalloway, 172
Much Ado About Nothing, 390
Mulan, 143
Mulholland Dr., 198, 318, 343, *449*, 470
Mullally, Megan, 54
Muller, Eddie, *412*
Muller, Ray, 462
Mulligan, Carey, 25
Mulroney, Dermot, 46
Multiplicity, 134
Muni, Paul, *410*
Munich, 241, *315*
Munson, Ona, *197*
Murch, Walter, 327, 329
Murder on the Orient Express, 267
Murdoch, Iris, 298
Murnau, F. W., 82, 281, *423*, 471
Murphy, Eddie, 101
Murray, Bill, 305
musical score
    adding levels of meaning to visual image, 256–257, 267
    analyzing, 267–268
    balancing, 265–267
    as base for choreographed action, 262–264, *262*
    characterization through, 257–259, 267
    covering possible weaknesses in film, 264, 268
    director's style of, 319–320
    in foreign films, 438

    foreshadowing or building dramatic tension, 255–256, 267
    general functions of, 251–253, 267
    generalized, 253
    heightening dramatic effect of dialogue, 253
    importance of, 250–251
    as interior monologue, 261–262
    Mickey Mousing, 252–253
    movies without, *266*
    musical sounds as part of, 261
    providing transitions, 260–261
    sense of time and place provided by, 254–255, 267
    symbolic use of, 62–63
    synthesizer scoring, 265
    telling an inner story, 253–254, *254*, 267
    traveling music, 260, 268
    triggering conditioned responses, 259–260, 268
    used for characterization, 52
    watching, 268–269
musicals, film, 419, *420*
My Architect, 245, *254*, 465
My Best Fiend, 291
My Best Friend's Wedding, 46, 418
My Big Fat Greek Wedding, 60, 98
My Fair Lady, 392, 423
My Movie Business, *373*
My One and Only, 26
My Own Private Idaho, 159, 421
My Winnipeg, 212

N

Nadda, Ruba, *328*
Nair, Mira, *115*, 195, *328*, 369, 439–440
Namesake, The, *115*, 369
name typing, 54–55, *56*
Nanook of the North, 464
Napoleon, 119, 194–195, 281
Napoleon Dynamite, 98
Naqoyqatsi, 132, 271
Naremore, James, 413
narrative structure, director's style of, 321–324
Nasar, Sylvia, 394
Nash, John Forbes, Jr., 394–395
Nashville, 233, 259, *259*, *323*, 325, 419
Natural, The, 208, 266
Natural Born Killers, 457
Navigator, The: A Medieval Odyssey, 199–200
NC-17 rating, 450, 452, 454
Neal, Patricia, 95
Neale, Steve, 404
Near Dark, 210, *211*
Neeson, Liam, *213*
Nelson, Tim Blake, *263*
Nelson, Willie, 268
Network, 267
Newell, Mike, 411
Newman, David, 377

credits

Text

Chapter 2 p. 17, from *Making Movies* by Sydney Lumet, copyright © 1995 by Sydney Lumet. Used by permission of Alfred A. Knopf, a division of Random House, Inc.; **Chapter 3** pp. 43, 44, 54, 57, 65, reprinted with permission of Simon & Schuster, Inc., from *The Craft of the Screenwriter* by John Brady. Copyright © 1981 by John Brady; p. 49, from *Directing the Film: Film Directors on Their Art*, edited by Eric Sherman. Acrobat Books, 1976. Used by permission of Eric Sherman; p. 63, by Tennessee Williams, from *Suddenly Last Summer*, copyright ©1958 by The University of the South. Reprinted by permission of New Directions Publishing Corp.; **Chapter 4** pp. 81, 82, 89, 90, *By Design: Interviews with Production Designers*, Vincent LoBrutto. © 1992. Reproduced with permission of ABC-CLIO, LLC, Santa Barbara, CA; p. 86, by Tennessee Williams, from *Suddenly Last Summer*, copyright ©1958 by The University of the South. Reprinted by permission of New Directions Publishing Corp.; **Chapter 5** pp. 109, 121, from *Directing the Film: Film Directors on Their Art*, edited by Eric Sherman. Acrobat Books, 1976. Used by permission of Eric Sherman; p. 148, Review of "The Prince of Egypt" by Roger Ebert. © 1998 Chicago Sun-Times; **Chapter 6** pp. 156, 157, 170, *Selected Takes: Film Editors on Film Editing*, Vincent LoBrutto. © 1991. Reproduced with permission of ABC-CLIO, Santa Barbara, CA; p. 171, from *Directing the Film: Film Directors on Their Art*, edited by Eric Sherman. Acrobat Books, 1976. Used by permission of Eric Sherman; **Chapter 7** p. 197, *By Design: Interviews with Production Designers*, Vincent LoBrutto. © 1992. Reproduced with permission of ABC-CLIO, LLC, Santa Barbara, CA; p. 199, from Judith Crist, *Take 22: Moviemakers on Moviemaking*, Continuum, 1991. Reprinted with permission from the author; p. 204, reprinted with permission of Simon & Schuster, Inc., from *The Craft of the Screenwriter* by John Brady. Copyright © 1981 by John Brady; **Chapter 8** pp. 220, 226, 234, *Sound-on-Film: Interviews with Creators of Film Sound*, Vincent LoBrutto. © 1994. Reproduced with permission of ABC-CLIO, Santa Barbara, CA; **Chapter 9** p. 262, from Judith Crist, *Take 22: Moviemakers on Moviemaking*, Continuum, 1991. Reprinted with permission from the author; p. 267, from *Making Movies* by Sydney Lumet, copyright © 1995 by Sydney Lumet. Used by permission of Alfred A. Knopf, a division of Random House, Inc.; **Chapter 10** pp. 275, 276, 282, 293, from Judith Crist, *Take 22: Moviemakers on Moviemaking*, Continuum, 1991. Reprinted with permission from the author; p. 286, from *Making Movies* by Sydney Lumet, copyright © 1995 by Sydney Lumet. Used by permission of Alfred A. Knopf, a division of Random House, Inc.; p. 301, reprinted from *Sense & Sensibility: The Screenplay & Diaries, Bringing Jane Austen's Novel to Film*, by Emma Thompson. Copyright © 1995 by Emma Thompson. All rights reserved. Reprinted by permission of Newmarket Press, 18 E. 48th Street, New York, NY 10017. www.newmarketpress.com; **Chapter 11** pp. 310, 323, from *Making Movies* by Sydney Lumet, copyright © 1995 by Sydney Lumet. Used by permission of Alfred A. Knopf, a division of Random House, Inc.; p. 315, reprinted with permission of Simon & Schuster, Inc., from *The Craft of the Screenwriter* by John Brady. Copyright © 1981 by John Brady; p. 316, from Judith Crist, *Take 22: Moviemakers on Moviemaking*, Continuum, 1991. Reprinted with permission from the author; p. 324, reprinted from *Sense & Sensibility: The Screenplay & Diaries, Bringing Jane Austen's Novel to Film*, by Emma Thompson. Copyright © 1995 by Emma Thompson. All rights reserved. Reprinted by permission of Newmarket Press, 18 E. 48th Street, New York, NY 10017. www.newmarketpress.com; **Chapter 12** pp. 347, 363, 364, from Dwight MacDonald, *On Movies*, Berkeley, Medallion Books, 1971, p. 15. Copyright © 1969 by Dwight McDonald. Reprinted by permission of the author; p. 360, from *The New York Times*, © July 2, 1972 The New York Times. All rights reserved. Used by permission and protected by the Copyright Laws of the United States. The printing, copying, redistribution, or retransmission of the Material without express written permission is prohibited; **Chapter 13** pp. 380, 388, 391, reprinted with permission of Simon & Schuster, Inc., from *The Craft of the Screenwriter* by John Brady. Copyright © 1981 by John Brady. pp. 382, 384, excerpts from *All the King's Men*, © 1946 and renewed 1974 by Robert Penn Warren, reprinted by permission of Houghton Mifflin Harcourt Publishing Company; p. 389, from *Making Movies* by Sydney Lumet, copyright © 1995 by Sydney Lumet. Used by permission of Alfred A. Knopf, a division of Random House, Inc.; p. 390, from *Directing the Film: Film Directors on*

Photo Credits